LISP

Objects, and Symbolic Programming

Robert R. Kessler
University of Utah

With the Assistance of Amy R. Petajan

SCOTT, FORESMAN/LITTLE, BROWN COLLEGE DIVISION
Scott, Foresman and Company
Glenview, Illinois Boston London

To Julie,

for your patience and understanding

Library of Congress Cataloging-in-Publication Data
Kessler, Robert R.
LISP, objects, and symbolic programming / Robert R. Kessler with the assistance of Amy R. Petajan.
p. cm.
Bibliography: p.
Includes Index.
ISBN (invalid) 0-673-39773-1
1. LISP (Computer program language) I. Petajan, Amy R.
II. Title.
QA76.73.L23K47 1988
005.13'3–dc19 87-32312
CIP

1 2 3 4 5 6 7 8 9 10 – RRC – 93 92 91 90 89 88 87

Printed in the United States of America

PREFACE

THIS TEXTBOOK IS for students who have had some exposure to programming. However, it doesn't presume prior LISP experience. This book was derived from the course notes developed for a number of different audiences. Several one-quarter courses at the University of Utah used the notes. The students were mainly upper-division computer science undergraduate and graduate students. There also was an intensive, one-week version of the course taught for industrial companies. Those students were experienced computing professionals with no background in LISP. Although one week is too short to cover this material completely, it provides an adequate foundation of terms and concepts for independent study.

The textbook is structured around case studies of general symbolic computing and artificial intelligence (AI). This textbook is not an in-depth study of AI but provides examples of some algorithms and techniques from that field of computer science. Although you may not be directly involved in AI, the ideas will help you in writing applications in LISP. The chapters before a case study discuss the techniques and features of LISP necessary to solve the case study. Chapter examples are often taken from the case study itself. The chapter discussing the case study doesn't introduce any new LISP programming constructs but demonstrates techniques for developing and interfacing LISP software. It also shows the steps to solve the problem defined by the case study. The discussion of good LISP programming practice is important in each case study chapter.

LISP is a highly interactive language, so you need a running system to learn it. You should spend time directly interacting with a LISP system. Try the various examples to make sure you fully understand the concepts. Determine answers for the exercises and try them out on a running LISP. If you don't understand something, sit down and write some experimental code fragments. Close interaction with a LISP system is the best way to become a good LISP programmer. *All* of the example programs have been run on an existing Common LISP system, specifically Hewlett-Packard Common LISP running on a HP 9000 Model 350 AI workstation. They should all run on any Common LISP.

In the years that I have taught this class to both students in academia and industry, I have observed an interesting phenomenon. Students in academia with a traditional computer science background are comfortable with "black boxes." For example, they think of compilers as software that makes their programs run faster, or "and" gates as performing a particular hardware operation. They are not concerned with the internals of the compiler or with the transistors that make up an "and" gate. Those students should cover the chapters in sequential order. Students with industrial experience, especially those with backgrounds in assembly language, like to see the internals of everything. For those students, the first few sections of Chapter 13 should be covered early. These sections discuss the internal representation of list structures and help you visualize the method in the various LISP functions. Appendix B provides answers to selected exercises. An asterisk before the exercise number in the text indicates that the answer is included in the appendix. The complete set of answers can be found in the solutions manual.

Students with some prior knowledge of LISP might want to skip to Chapter 4, the algebra system case study. An instructor might want to leave the case studies for independent study. However, the salient programming style features should be discussed in class. An instructor might also want to cover the debugging sections of Chapter 10 early on, to help the students as they develop their LISP programs. Chapter 14 covers various LISP programming style rules and should be consulted often during the reading of the text.

A number of people have helped to make this book possible. First and foremost is Tom Casson, executive editor at Scott Foresman/Little, Brown College Division. He convinced me that the book needed to be written and has continually helped push it to its conclusion. Although Amy Petajan only recently became involved in the project, she has helped to improve the presentation immensely. Many members of the Utah Portable AI Support Systems project have reviewed parts of the manuscript. Specifically, Harold Carr, Jed Krohnfeldt, Stan Shebs and Lane Stevens have helped review the technical aspects of the text. Stan has been especially helpful in all phases of the text, including writing the code for the compiler in Chapter 18. Eric Muehle helped to develop many exercises and provided their solutions. Tony Hearn of the Rand Corporation helped with aspects of the Algebra package. Wayne Anderson of the Los Alamos National Laboratory, Martin Griss and Mike Lemon of Hewlett-Packard Research Labs, and Mark Ring of the University of Texas at Austin provided valuable comments to early drafts. Loretta Looser helped in proofreading many of the chapters. The students in CS 546, Autumn 1986, at the University of Utah provided many editing suggestions and answers to some exercises. Thanks to Gerald Maguire, Jr., of Columbia University and John C. Peterson of the University of Arizona for their feedback on early drafts used in their classes. The reviewers of the book, Jeffrey Bonar, Peter Buneman, Douglas Dankel III, Stan Kwasny, Michael Lebowitz, James Meehan, and Margaret P. Mize are gratefully acknowledged. I appreciate the book title suggestions, both serious and humorous, from Wayne Anderson, Mark Bradakis, Al Davis, Martin Griss, Tony Hearn, Micke Hucka, Mike Lemon, Gary Lindstrom, Kwan-Liu Ma, Chip Maguire, Julian Padget, John W. Peterson, Mohammad Pourheidari, Shane Robison, and Leigh Stoller. I also would like to thank Professor Donald Knuth for TEX and Leslie Lamport for LATEX; they have constructed a great document formatting system. I also would like to thank Nelson Beebe of the University of Utah for his help with some of the trickier LATEX commands. I appreciate Hewlett-Packard for donating the many AI workstations, one of which was used to process this book and also as a LISP engine to execute all of the code. Finally, I would like to thank my wife, Julie, for putting up with the long evenings and weekends of writing "the book" during the past two years.

CONTENTS

1 INTRODUCTION TO LISP

JOHN MCCARTHY [27] developed the LISP programming language in the late 1950s. It is the second oldest high-level programming language still in use (FORTRAN is the oldest). LISP is gaining popularity because people are interested in application areas, such as artificial intelligence (AI), requiring the power of LISP. Hardware and software capable of running LISP efficiently is more available as well. As described by Alan Kay [21], programming languages have evolved in distinct generations. LISP has evolved with them. It has been a high-level (FORTRAN, ALGOL), very high-level (SIMULA, PROLOG), and ultra high-level language (VISICALC, EURISKO). This feature has allowed a thirty-year-old language to remain viable.

Due to LISP's long history, many prominent AI programs have been developed in LISP. You can see the history and pragmatics of these implementations by studying the language. You should also study PROLOG [11], another AI language, since it has important features. PROLOG is useful when the control representation is not explicit in the problem, like in data base applications and natural language parsing. LISP makes the control information explicit. This is more natural to programmers familiar with imperative programming languages. There are intensive research efforts to merge the two languages because of significant overlap between them.

Rapid prototyping and program development is a benefit of LISP. Some of the features that allow this are:

- The programmer doesn't need to deal explicitly with pointers, because LISP lets you define and manage flexible, hierarchical data structures;
- The development of systems programs (compilers, editors, etc.) is easy, because LISP programs are represented as LISP data;
- The programmer can manipulate symbolic expressions as well as numeric expressions.
- LISP uses run-time type checking, so the programmer doesn't need to worry about type declarations at compile-time.
- LISP lets you express programs as collections of many small functions, leading to more maintainable software;

- You can develop software in a highly interactive environment; and
- The programmer can strongly customize his or her programming environment to improve software development time.

The following sections describe each of these features in detail. Case studies illustrate them in the rest of the text.

1.1 Data Structures

LISP is an acronym for LISt Processing. The *list* is a flexible, hierarchical data structure that represents arbitrarily long collections of items (for example, numbers and other lists). A list is like those that we use in our everyday lives (lists of things to do, grocery lists, etc.). They grow and shrink as we add and remove items from them. As long as there is enough paper and ink, the lists can be arbitrarily long. Lists can be hierarchical since they can contain other lists (for example, a grocery list referencing all the ingredients in banana bread).

The LISP system has a dynamic storage manager that frees the programmer from worrying about sizes of data structures. In other programming languages, a programmer might allocate a fixed-length vector for a set of values and characteristics of an object. Adding a new value and characteristic is then a problem. The programmer would have to increase the size of the vector for the new characteristic. If a list representation is used, a LISP programmer simply adds the new information to the original list with no other changes necessary. Lists can grow and shrink as necessary, and it's up to the dynamic storage manager to make storage available. Programming languages like Pascal permit this type of structure, but the management of the memory is left to the programmer.

1.2 LISP Programs as LISP Data

LISP programs are collections of user-defined functions. LISP represents them in the same way that it represents data; lists are used to contain both programs and data. This adds a consistency not present in any other language.

Functions that manipulate lists don't distinguish between lists that are functions and those that are data. With this consistency between programs and data, the programmer can edit a function definition from within LISP. For example, suppose that a function has been defined with a variable named `FOOBAR`. Suppose one of the variable references within the function uses the name `FOBAR` (a typographical error). A LISP substitution function could redefine this function, replacing the instance of `FOBAR` with `FOOBAR`.

It is also easy to write system programs (like compilers, editors, and the LISP system itself) in LISP. So there is little distinction between a LISP application programmer and systems programmer. This has helped LISP systems to evolve, since there is no need for extended communication between the two.

1.3 Symbolic Expressions

A programmer can develop software in LISP that manipulates symbolic expressions, which are collections of words and numbers. Suppose that we wished to describe a clown. For this example, we choose the following subset of characteristics:

Characteristic	Value
shoe size	27
nose	red
expression	frown
name	Freddy

The format of the preceding table shows the relationships between each characteristic and value. The grouping of parentheses in LISP indicates the same relationships:

```
((shoe-size 27) (nose red) (expression frown) (name Freddy))
```

To describe Freddy in a traditional programming language, you might map each characteristic to a numeric value. Thus, the nose color might be a 1 to represent blue, a 2 to represent yellow, a 3 to represent red, and a 4 to represent green. In LISP, you use the natural representation of the word (the *symbol* `red`) for the color of the clown's nose. This technique can also define rules for mixing primary colors. Using a numeric representation, you would have to say something like "if the first color is a 1 and the second is a 2, then the result is a 4." In LISP, you could say "if the first color is `blue` and the second color is `yellow`, then the result is `green`." Since programmers can manipulate these symbols, they don't have to map an abstract notion of color into a numeric representation.

1.4 Variable Declarations

LISP does not require a type declaration for each variable. LISP variables are actually typeless – the values have types instead. A variable's value may at different times be a number, string, list, or any other LISP data type. A LISP function determines its types of arguments during execution and may dynamically coerce one type into another according to the operation. For example, to add an integer and a real number, LISP converts the integer into a real, performs the addition, and returns the sum as a real. Writing generic functions is easy with this dynamic determination and propagation of arbitrary types. You don't need type-specific functions for each combination of argument types. In a strongly typed language like Pascal, if the same function can accept either an integer or a real argument, two separate functions must be written. In LISP, you write generic functions to dynamically determine and coerce data types as necessary.

A lack of variable declarations does have its disadvantages. Type mismatch errors occur at run-time instead of compile-time, forcing the programmer to do extra debugging. Also, run-time type checking adds computational overhead resulting in slower running programs. Optional type declarations and the development of smarter compilers have alleviated this problem. When the programmer requires more efficiency, he or she may add type declarations to LISP variables. These declarations specify that a variable's value will always be a particular type. The compiler then performs some of the checking at compile-time and generates more efficient code. Recent compilers perform some compile-time type analysis by inferring the types by their usage. This technique generates more efficient code without any additional programmer-supplied declarations. Rapid program development is easier when you can transition no declarations and fully declared LISP code. In the early prototyping stages, the programmer can effectively ignore the data types and concentrate on coding a particular algorithm. Explicit declarations (or inferred ones) can be added for faster program execution as the program moves from experimental to production quality.

1.5 Program Development

LISP is amenable to top-down, bottom-up, or other program development styles. Developing code in any of these styles is easier in LISP than in other languages. This development is an evolutionary process. The programming environment is conducive to experimentation and permits "on the fly" program development. Bottom-up development proceeds naturally from a general idea of the program and data structures. Each part is incrementally developed and tested, eventually resulting in a completed program. Top-down development works like in other languages. The LISP programmer uses the same *Edit*, *Compile*, *Link and Load*, *Execute*, and *Debug* cycle. The main difference is in LISP's dynamic error system, which intercepts calls to undefined functions. When the error occurs, the programmer supplies a return value and then continues execution. This eliminates the need for explicit stub functions and can shorten development time.

Bottom-up development begins with writing many very small functions (functions are rarely longer than one screen). Small functions isolate the processing into small manageable modules. The overhead of function calls is typically very small with LISP, and so this style costs little extra. Highly modular code is easier to maintain. Each module contains small conceptual parts of the program. Isolated changes to a module are less likely to affect the rest of the program. This leads to fewer mistakes and higher quality code. The programmer combines these functions in a larger task. This is a "Tinkertoy™" approach to software construction – a number of parts are collected together to build a wall, then those are collected to form the house, and so on. This technique makes programs easier to debug and maintain.

The management of LISP software also fits this "Tinkertoy" style. Collecting many related small functions together into files adds modularity. Then one or more top-level, driver functions can be added for a complete system. As the programs evolve, more modules can be created and added to the system.

1.6 LISP Interpreter

Most programming languages are dependent upon a compiler for program development. However, a few programming languages, like BASIC, APL and LISP, use an *Interpreter* to improve the development cycle. The entire development cycle then occurs directly within the environment. A programmer can interactively modify, examine, and debug a program with the interpreter. LISP's mechanism for this accepts LISP expressions and performs operations based on those commands.* This is like an operating system that accepts commands, performs operations based upon those commands, and displays any results. Some of the commands define functions, edit function definitions, access variables, perform calculations, and compile functions. Most LISP implementations even permit you to perform operating system commands (for example, deleting files, sending electronic mail, etc.).

The interactive interpreter is referred to as the *Read/Eval/Print Loop* and performs the following operation:

1. `Read` – Read a command;
2. `Eval` – Perform the operation specified by the command;
3. `Print` – Print any results;
4. Go to Step 1.

Each of these steps is based on a family of mechanisms available to the LISP programmer. Subsequent chapters will discuss each of them.

When the `read` process is interacting directly with a user, it normally prints a prompt (like `LISP>`) to show that it's waiting for input. The exact nature of this interaction is implementation dependent. Therefore, we'll adopt the style used in the Common LISP manual [40] of no prompt for the input expressions and a right arrow "⇒" indicating the result. The semicolon is the comment character in LISP, so all characters to the end of the line are ignored after it.

*The term *interpreter* has a technical meaning within LISP that is not the same as that used in other languages. It actually means the function `eval` and its associated routines which are described later.

Comments provide additional documentation for the human reader.* A sample interaction using this style follows:

```
; This is a comment line -- it is ignored.
; The following adds 345 to 1234.
(+ 345 1234)
 ⇒ 1579

; The next expression multiplies 12 and 19.
(* 12 19)
 ⇒ 228
```

Significant programs are developed frequently in LISP with this type of interpreted environment. Some programs are developed more quickly in LISP than in any other programming language. Programmers can quickly find and eliminate program bugs using various interactive debugging tools. These tools vary in complexity from printouts of a function call's dynamic environment, to tracing various function executions, and on to LISP language level steppers which step through the execution of LISP expressions.

You can also combine compiled and interpreted code – an important feature. Code can be compiled for greater efficiency and then used in the development of more code. If a compiled function has a bug, it can be redefined as an interpreted function and debugged. This permits a smooth transition between code under development and production code.

1.7 Extending LISP

The *Read/Eval/Print Loop* helps provide a dynamic programming environment. The LISP programmer can also customize the system to meet immediate or recurring needs. The programmer can actually redefine system functions and change the programming syntax. This makes LISP ideal for producing embedded languages. Some embedded languages (for example, RLISP [19]) are surface languages that provide a Pascal-like syntax that translates into LISP. Other embedded languages are designed for specific applications. For example, suppose that a new language has been designed for describing three-dimensional graphic images. Implementing the language within LISP is easy with either a LISP-based translator writing tool (STACC [38, Section 7.4]), or by enhancing the LISP system to read and translate the new language. The programmer can modify the input processes and syntax tables of LISP to translate the new

*Comments are rarely used when interacting directly with LISP. This is primarily due to the one-on-one interaction between the LISP system and the user. For example, when interacting with an operating system you seldom write a comment when you are about to delete a file. However, comments within command files are often used.

language. The *list* is a natural representation for the intermediate form of the translated program. It can then be manipulated for further translation or direct execution.

A common folk saying (with some truth to it) is that no one really writes code in LISP. LISP programmers adapt their environment to their particular style and method and then program in an extended LISP. This is one reason that LISP has evolved so gracefully. Much like "Darwinian natural selection" it has adapted to its environment and survived.

1.8 LISP Dialects

During the twenty-five year history of LISP, many different dialects have evolved. They vary from small, fast, highly portable implementations on stock hardware (Portable Standard LISP [17]) to sophisticated, fancy systems on micro-coded LISP engines (ZetaLisp [45] and InterLISP [43]) and everything in between. This variety of LISP systems made it difficult to exchange software between LISP users, and it hampered joint research efforts. A committee was formed to solve the problem and specify a dialect of LISP that could become a standard LISP language. The committee consisted of about thirty leading members of the LISP community from both academia and industry. The result of that work is the Common LISP dialect. The committee was successful, as Common LISP has now become the de facto standard. It is available or under production for many computing systems. Therefore, Common LISP is the dialect used in this text. Instances where Common LISP differs from other dialects in interesting ways will be noted.

1.9 Summary

LISP is used for work in a wide range of areas. They vary from traditional LISP-based applications like artificial intelligence and computer algebra systems to applications previously written in languages like C or Pascal (for example, VLSI design tools, computer graphics and computer-aided geometric design). As more programmers see how efficiently they can develop and maintain systems with the LISP environment, we will see LISP enter new application areas. Also, the use of LISP will flourish as LISP compilers evolve and programmers are better able to write delivery systems (stand-alone applications that don't require the full LISP environment).

All the features described remove tedium from programming. The programmer can concentrate on the solution of the particular problem without having to express the solution in some arcane representation totally unrelated to the problem. LISP is quite different from other programming languages. Once you are an experienced LISP programmer, it's hard to return to any other language.

1.10 Notations

Throughout the rest of the text, new LISP constructs are introduced by placing their syntax within a box, as follows:

(defun *symbol* (*symbol**) *S-expression**)

In this notation, a word shown in fixed-width, bold font indicates a LISP symbol (as the symbol **defun**). Those appearing in italics refer to an object of that particular designation (that is, *symbol* indicates that a symbol must be placed in that position). The raised asterisk following an object indicates that there may be zero or more occurrences of the preceding object. In this example, the construct may have zero or more symbols within the parentheses after **defun** and some *symbol*.

LISP interaction is continuously illustrated in the text. The fixed-width, "typewriter" font indicates *Read/Eval/Print Loop* interactions. Comments in each example provide more detailed information about the evaluation of a particular LISP expression. The result of each expression evaluation is indented a few spaces and follows a right arrow.

2

BASIC LISP

WE BEGIN BY PRESENTING the number data type, some mathematical operations, and LISP's prefix notation. We then discuss other primitive data types and their manipulation. Of particular interest is the *list* data type, which is an ordered collection of arbitrary items. We then discuss function definition and comment placement in LISP programs.

2.1 Numbers

The *number* data type includes integer, floating point, and fractional (rational) numbers. The notation for each number type is consistent with other programming languages. LISP integers can be arbitrarily large (that is, they contain as many digits as necessary). This can be useful for high precision when manipulating very large numbers. In languages without this feature, the programmer would use less precise floating point numbers.

The `Read/Eval/Print` Loop repeatedly reads LISPRead/Eval/Print Loop expressions, evaluates them, and prints their results. In LISP, every expression returns a value, so there is something to print for each expression evaluation. A number is a simple LISP expression that evaluates to itself. Notice the semicolon as the comment character in the following examples. A semicolon indicates that all of the remaining characters on the line should be ignored.

```
;; When we supply a simple integer, the integer is echoed
;; back as the result of the evaluation.
5
 ⇒ 5

;; The convention is that the printing portion of the
;; Read/Eval/Print Loop prints the result on a line by
;; itself.

-123 ; A negative number (notice this comment is on the same
```

```
        ; line and the next).
  ⇒ -123
```

In the next example, we present three numbers on the same line. Each is evaluated and printed on a separate line, but none are evaluated before there is a carriage return. Some LISP systems begin evaluation as soon as a well-formed expression is complete. In systems of this type, the result of evaluating the first expression would appear as soon as the space is typed.

```
77.344 8. +0.998
 ⇒ 77.344
 ⇒ 8
 ⇒ 0.998

;; The following is a 50-digit number.
12345678901234567890123456789012345678901234567890
 ⇒ 12345678901234567890123456789012345678901234567890
```

EXERCISES

***2.1** What criterion must LISP expressions satisfy?

2.2 Name a data type that evaluates to itself.

2.2 Mathematical Operations

Most programming languages use a mixture of infix notation (where the operator is between the operands, for example, `x+y*z`) and prefix notation (where the operator precedes all of its operands, for example, `write(x,y,z)`) to specify operations. LISP consistently uses prefix notation and requires parentheses around the elements of an expression. In other programming languages, parentheses are not required, since precedence rules determine how to process an expression. LISP requires parentheses to avoid ambiguity, since there are effectively no precedence rules. Following the left parenthesis of an expression is the operator. The operator is then followed by all the operands. Parenthesized expressions can be nested if the operator still directly follows the left parenthesis.

Every LISP expression, from simple arithmetic expressions to function definitions, returns a value. Some programming languages distinguish procedures and functions, where only the latter can return a value. These languages also distinguish statements and expressions – only expressions can be part of a computation. This is not the case with LISP, since every LISP expression returns a value.

The following table illustrates some of the most common mathematical operators defined in Common LISP. The Args column specifies the number of arguments that may be supplied to the operator, where n indicates that the operator will accept an arbitrary number of arguments.

Operators	Args	Description
`+ - * /`	n	Add, Subtract, Multiply, and Divide.
`1+ 1-`	1	Sum or Difference of argument and 1
`max min`	n	Maximum and Minimum.
`gcd`	n	Greatest Common Divisor.
`exp`	1	e raised to the argument power.
`expt`	2	Raise first argument to the second argument power.
`log`	1	Logarithm.
`sqrt`	1	Square root.
`abs`	1	Absolute value.
`sin cos tan`	1	Sine, Cosine, and Tangent.
`asin acos atan`	1	Arc Sine, Arc Cosine, Arc Tangent.
`truncate`	1 *or* 2	Truncation, or Division with truncation.
`round`	1 *or* 2	Rounding, or Division with rounding.
`rem`	2	Remainder.
`random`	1	Returns random number between 0 and argument.

These operators follow a left parenthesis with the operands following the operator. For example, to add the numbers 123 and 4567 together, we would write the following:

```
(+ 123 4567)
⇒ 4690
```

If we wanted to multiply them together we would use the * operator.

```
(* 123 4567)
⇒ 561741
```

The computation of the sum of the squares of 12 and 13 would be expressed as follows:

```
(+ (expt 12 2) (expt 13 2))
⇒ 313
```

Notice that the syntax for the operations `1+` and `1-` are a little strange, but they compute the sum or difference of the argument and 1.

```
;; Sum of argument and 1.
(+ 3 1)
⇒ 4
```

```
;; The same using the shorter operator.
(1+ 3)
⇒ 4

;; Or difference.
(1- 4)
⇒ 3
```

In most other languages, adding extra parentheses doesn't change the meaning of the program. However, in LISP, proper placement of parentheses is very important. They may not be arbitrarily placed within expressions. Extra parentheses added to an expression make it invalid as illustrated by the following:

```
;; ALL OF THESE ARE INVALID.
(+ ((expt 12 2) (expt 13 2)))
(+ (expt (12) (2)) (expt 13 (2)))
(+ (expt (12) (2)) ((expt 13 2)))
```

In LISP, many operators allow an arbitrary number of arguments. So, one could express seven factorial (the product of the integers from 1 to 7) as either nested multiplications or as a single multiplication with seven arguments.

```
;; Two operand calls to * to compute seven factorial.
(* 1 (* 2 (* 3 (* 4 (* 5 (* 6 7))))))
⇒ 5040

;; Multiple argument version that also computes seven
;; factorial.
(* 1 2 3 4 5 6 7)
⇒ 5040
```

In the first example, the innermost expression is evaluated first and the values are propagated outward. In the second example, the processing is from left to right, by evaluating the operation on the first two operands, then performing the operation on the value returned and the third operand and so on (for example, `(* (* 1 2) 3 4 5 6 7)`, `(* (* (* 1 2) 3) 4 5 6 7)`, etc.). This isn't significant for commutative operators like `+`, `*`, and `max` but is important for non-commutative operators like `-` and `/`. The following example demonstrates the order of evaluation for a non-commutative operator:

```
;; A three operand division.
(/ 24 4 2)
⇒ 3
```

This is equivalent to the normal precedence, left-to-right interpretation of the infix form: `(24 / 4 / 2)`, written with two operand division operators as `((24 / 4) / 2)` and not `(24 / (4 / 2))`.

```
(/ (/ 24 4) 2)   ; Correct left to right ordering.
```

```
 ⇒ 3

(/ 24 (/ 4 2))   ; Incorrect right to left ordering.
 ⇒ 12
```

Division within Common LISP differs from most other dialects because when the result is not evenly divisible, a fraction is produced (the other dialects usually round or truncate the division). These fractions are simplified and printed as rational numbers with a /. Rational division guarantees no loss of accuracy when computing large expressions with a mixture of multiplication and division.

```
(/ 100 10)
 ⇒ 10

(/ 100 15)
 ⇒ 20/3

(* (/ 100 15) 3)
 ⇒ 20
```

Round or **truncate** produce a rounded or truncated result when the operands are not evenly divisible and you don't want a rational result.*

```
(round 20 3)
 ⇒ 7
 ⇒ -1

(truncate 20 3)
 ⇒ 6
 ⇒ 2

(round 20 4)
 ⇒ 5
 ⇒ 0
```

These examples demonstrate that many operators can take more than just two operands. Common LISP also lets you pass one argument to some of those functions which normally take two values. For example, when / is passed only one argument it computes the reciprocal of the argument (as if the first operand had been a one). When - is passed only one argument, it performs unary minus. The following illustrates the effect of one argument versions of some of these operators:

*Common LISP differs from most other LISPs in that expressions can return multiple values. Access to extra return values must be accomplished using one of the multiple value functions (see [40, Chapter 7]), otherwise the extra values are ignored. In Common LISP, **round** and **truncate** return two values, the integer result and the remainder. When multiple values are printed, each one appears on a separate line (as in this example).

```
;; Division with one argument.
(/ 5)
⇒ 1/5

(/ 5.0)
⇒ 0.2

;; This is unary minus.
(- 4)
⇒ -4

;; Unary plus, simply returns the argument.
(+ 99)
⇒ 99

;; Unary multiplication also returns the argument.
(* 7)
⇒ 7
```

We have seen that every expression returns a value, and some may even return multiple values. These features make LISP consistent and therefore easier to understand and use.

EXERCISE

2.3 Evaluate each of these expressions without the aid of a running LISP system. Once you have determined the answers, submit each expression to a running LISP system and verify your results.

```
(+ 1 2 3 -4)
(* (- 100 50) (+ 25 25))
(+ (max 12 2 15 3) (min 12 2 15 3))
(truncate 44 9)
(round 44 9)
```

2.3 Symbols

In the preceding examples, all of the operands were constant numbers. Expressions with variable operands need to assign a value to a variable. A LISP *symbol* is associated with a value, either through assignment using `setf` or a process called *binding* described in the next chapter. There are two main differences between LISP symbols and variables of other programming languages:

1. The type of a particular value is associated with the value and not the symbol. During a computation, a particular symbol can be a number part of the time and some other value the rest of the time. This is a result of LISP's dynamic typing. Languages like Pascal use static typing where the

type is associated with the symbols. They require declaration of a type for every variable.

2. A symbol is a first-class data object and is manipulated independent of its value. First-class means that a symbol has the same features as any other data object, within the semantics of the operation.

Dynamic typing allows more rapid program development since the programmer doesn't need to worry about the types of variables and can concentrate on solving the particular problem. The ability to do "symbolic computation" is a distinguishing feature of LISP and is one reason why LISP is the primary programming language in artificial intelligence research.

Anything in Common LISP that is not a number or a special character (these are ( ) " # ‘ , ; ’ |) is defined as a symbol. This allows significant flexibility in creating symbols. Programmers develop conventions for symbol names. They often use multi-word symbols, separating words with hyphens. This text follows that convention for symbol names.

The assignment expression in Common LISP is `setf`. `Setf` takes two arguments: the first is the symbol that will take on the value, and the second is the expression whose evaluation determines the value.*

(`setf` *symbol value*)

```
;; A simple setf expression.
(setf clown-shoe-size 7)
⇒ 7
```

Every expression returns a value. A `setf` expression returns the value of the second argument.

The original assignment expression in previous LISP dialects was `setq`, which has the same syntax as `setf`. Partly for compatibility with previous LISP dialects, Common LISP provides both definitions. However, we will see later that `setf` is actually more powerful and has many more uses than `setq`.

(`setq` *symbol value*)

```
;; The same assignment expression using setq.
(setq clown-shoe-size 7)
⇒ 7
```

Once a symbol has a value, it can be used in an expression where it will

*See section 1.10 for a description of notations used in the syntax boxes.

represent its current value. If you use the symbol alone, the Read/Eval/Print Loop will evaluate it and print its current value.

```
clown-shoe-size
 ⇒ 7

(setf larger-shoe-size (+ clown-shoe-size 3))
 ⇒ 10

(max larger-shoe-size clown-shoe-size)
 ⇒ 10

(min larger-shoe-size clown-shoe-size)
 ⇒ 7
```

In the previous examples, the symbols are like variables in other programming languages. Any time a symbol is found, it is evaluated, and the value is used in the computation. If we want to manipulate the symbol itself, we need to suppress this evaluation. The quote operator performs this suppression and returns the symbol.

(quote *symbol*)

```
(quote freddy-the-clown)
 ⇒ FREDDY-THE-CLOWN
```

In practice, symbols are quoted frequently. The shorthand notation equivalent to quote is the " ' " character. The only difference is that the parentheses are not permitted.

'*symbol*

```
'freddy-the-clown ; Show that ' is equivalent to quote.
 ⇒ FREDDY-THE-CLOWN
```

In both these examples, the symbol freddy-the-clown was converted into uppercase characters. The default of Common LISP is to convert all symbols into uppercase independent of the actual case. Symbols can be used in expressions just like numbers (although attempts to perform arithmetic operations on a symbol will result in errors).

Multiple quotes before a symbol helps to demonstrate that ' actually translates into quote. It also shows that you can quote expressions other than symbols.

```
'freddy-the-clown
 ⇒ FREDDY-THE-CLOWN
```

```
''freddy-the-clown
 ⇒ (QUOTE FREDDY-THE-CLOWN)

'''freddy-the-clown
 ⇒ (QUOTE (QUOTE FREDDY-THE-CLOWN))
```

There is another assignment statement, **set**, which is different than both **setf** and **setq** because it evaluates its first argument. This allows you to control which variable is given a value by the evaluation of an expression.

(set *expression value*)

```
larger-shoe-size
 ⇒ 10

(set 'larger-shoe-size 15)
 ⇒ 15

larger-shoe-size
 ⇒ 15
```

EXERCISE

2.4 Evaluate each of these expressions without the aid of a running LISP system. Once you have determined the answers, submit each expression to a LISP system and verify your results.

```
(setf degree-of-poly-1 4)
(setf degree-of-poly-2 (1- degree-of-poly-1))
(setf smallest-degree
      (min degree-of-poly-1 degree-of-poly-2))
'smallest-degree
smallest-degree
(+ smallest-degree degree-of-poly-1 degree-of-poly-2)
```

2.4 Lists

The list is a fundamental data type of the LISP language. A list is defined as a left parenthesis "(", followed by zero or more atoms or lists, and a right parenthesis ")". An atom is any data object that is not a list.* Atoms that we

*Atom originated with early LISP systems and represented objects that couldn't be subdivided like numbers. Strings and arrays were not part of the original LISP systems but are now data types in modern LISPs. They can be subdivided but are classified as atoms.

have seen are numbers and symbols. Atoms and lists are collectively known as Symbolic Expressions, abbreviated as S-expressions or simply S-exprs.

A list is an interesting data structure for several reasons:

- Lists may be arbitrarily long, so they are ideal when you don't want to predefine the size of a data structure. In other programming languages, a vector typically collects a number of items together. However, the vector must be preallocated to a fixed size and an error occurs if the number of items exceeds this size. This wastes storage space if the number of items is less than the preallocated size.
- Random access to individual items in a list is slower than access to items in a vector. Instead of a simple index computation, it requires memory accesses and the tracing of pointers. This slower access must be traded against the previous length advantage of lists. However, performing a calculation on an entire list is no more expensive than performing the same operation on a vector.
- A list differs from a set in that a list can contain multiple instances of the same element, and the elements are in a strict order (much like a vector).

The expressions evaluated in the previous examples are also lists since they fit the definition above. This is another area of consistency within LISP; there is no difference between the lists for storage of data and the lists for program expressions. In fact, one can write LISP programs to manipulate other LISP programs as if they were data. This is the case for many LISP compilers and interpreters.

```
;; Although the following is an S-expression, it is
;; also a 3-element list.
(+ 3 4)
 ⇒ 7

;; The quoted version of the same 3-element list.
'(+ 3 4)
 ⇒ (+ 3 4)
```

The last example includes a quoted list that contains an embedded expression (for example, `(+ 3 4)`). The result contains the original expression (for example, `(+ 3 4)`) rather then the evaluated expression.

There may be *zero or more* elements in a list. A list with zero elements is known as the empty list or `nil`. The empty list `()` evaluates to itself, as numbers do.

```
;; The empty list assigned to a symbol.
(setf empty-polynomial nil)
 ⇒ NIL

empty-polynomial
 ⇒ NIL
```

```
;; () is equivalent to nil.
()
 ⇒ NIL

nil
 ⇒ NIL
```

EXERCISE

***2.5** Without performing any evaluation, which of the following are lists:

```
(setf degree-of-poly-2 (- degree-of-poly-2 1))
smallest-degree
nil
(+ (+ (+ 1 2) 3) (+ 4 5))
```

2.5 List Construction

There are four main techniques for creating and adding elements to lists:

1. `Quote` returns a list without any evaluation of its list operand.
2. `List` takes an arbitrary number of arguments and constructs a list from those arguments' evaluations. The list will be the same length as the number of arguments.
3. `Append` concatenates its argument lists into a single list. Note: `append` takes an arbitrary number of arguments.
4. `Cons` adds its first argument to the list that is the second argument.

`Quote` operates upon a list argument like it operates on symbols (actually it operates on any S-expression). `Quote` constructs static lists. Static lists should not change over the lifetime of the list. Since a quoted list is static, LISP is free to optimize its construction which limits the operations you may perform to the list. Quoted lists are primarily useful for retrieving information.

(quote *S-expression*)

'*S-expression*

```
;; A list using '
'(this is a list of 7 elements)
 ⇒ (THIS IS A LIST OF 7 ELEMENTS)
```

```
;; A list with embedded lists.
'((3 X 2) (2 X 1) (-4 X 0))
 ⇒ ((3 X 2) (2 X 1) (-4 X 0))
```

The `list` operator constructs dynamic lists and takes an arbitrary number of arguments.

(list *S-expression**)

```
;; Construct a polynomial term for 2*x in prefix notation,
;; where the 2 is the result of a computation.
(setf single-term (list '* (- 6 4) 'X))
 ⇒ (* 2 X)
```

Now construct a 4-element prefix list of the polynomial: $3x^3 + 2x + 4$ using the value of `single-term`.

```
;; Construct the polynomial.
(list '+ '(* 3 (** X 3)) single-term 4)
 ⇒ (+ (* 3 (** X 3)) (* 2 X) 4)
```

When `list` takes a `nil` argument, the corresponding element of the list is `nil`.

```
;; List with a nil argument.
(list '+ nil 4)
 ⇒ (+ NIL 4)
```

The **append** function takes an arbitrary number of list arguments and concatenates them into a single new list.* The length of the concatenated list is the sum of the argument lists' lengths.

(append *S-expression**)

```
;; Build a prefix representation for a polynomial 8*x+7.
;; First construct the leading term using different
;; variations with append.
(setf leading-term (append '(*) '(8 X)))
 ⇒ (* 8 X)

(setf leading-term (append '(*) '(8) '(X)))
 ⇒ (* 8 X)
```

*There is a subtle issue on how **append** handles the last argument, which is described in detail in Chapter 13.

```
(setf leading-term (append '(* 8) '(X)))
 ⇒ (* 8 X)

;; Each of the previous calls to append produced the same
;; result.
(setf two-terms (append (list leading-term) '(7)))
 ⇒ ((* 8 X) 7)

;; Add 9*x**2 term and the leading + operator.
(append '(+) '((* 9 (** X 2))) two-terms)
 ⇒ (+ (* 9 (** X 2)) (* 8 X) 7)
```

When append is given only one argument, it returns the argument.

```
(append '(+ X 7))
 ⇒ (+ X 7)
```

When an argument is nil, then the nil is effectively ignored.

```
(append () '(+ X 7))
 ⇒ (+ X 7)

(append '(+ X 7) ())
 ⇒ (+ X 7)
```

The following shows the differences between list and append when given the same list. They also behave differently with a nil argument, which is left for the exercises.

```
(list '(* X 2) '(* Y 2))
 ⇒ ((* X 2) (* Y 2))

(append '(* X 2) '(* Y 2))
 ⇒ (* X 2 * Y 2)
```

The cons function adds the first argument to the front of the second argument, which should be a list. This constructs a new list.

(cons *S-expression S-expression*)

```
;; Create a prefix form of a first degree polynomial
;; without a leading + operator.
(setf partial-1st-degree '((* 6 X) 7))
 ⇒ ((* 6 X) 7)

;; Construct a new list with the + operator included.
(cons '+ partial-1st-degree)
 ⇒ (+ (* 6 X) 7)
```

```
;; Notice that partial-1st-degree was not changed.
partial-1st-degree
 ⇒ ((* 6 X) 7)

;; Construct a second degree polynomial, using two calls to
;; cons.
(cons '+ (cons '(* 5 (** X 2)) partial-1st-degree))
 ⇒ (+ (* 5 (** X 2)) (* 6 X) 7)
```

When the second argument is `nil`, `cons` creates a list of the first argument. This is the same as passing one argument to `list`.

```
(cons 'x ())
 ⇒ (X)

(list 'x)
 ⇒ (X)
```

`Cons` is actually the primitive list construction function and `list` could be built from a number of calls to `cons`. Likewise, `append` could be defined with `cons` as the primitive operation.

```
;; Show that list is just a set of calls to cons.
(list 'a 'b 'c)
 ⇒ (A B C)

(cons 'a (cons 'b (cons 'c ())))
 ⇒ (A B C)

;; The same for append.
(append '(a b) '(c))
 ⇒ (A B C)

(cons 'a (cons 'b '(c)))
 ⇒ (A B C)
```

Notice that implementing `append` with `cons` requires breaking the first argument into its constituent parts.

EXERCISES

2.6 Evaluate each of these expressions without the aid of a running LISP system. Once you have determined the answers, submit each expression to a LISP system and verify your results.

```
(quote (red green blue))
(append (list (cons 1 (list 1))) (quote ((2 4) (3 9))))
(cons (append (list 1) '(red)) (list (list 2 'green)
                                     '(3 blue)))
```

***2.7** What is the difference between a `nil` argument to `list` and a `nil` argument to `append`?

***2.8** What is the difference between the values returned by evaluating the following two expressions?

```
(cons 'red '(green blue))
(append '(red) '(green blue))
```

2.6 List Manipulation

`Length` and `reverse` are functions that manipulate entire lists. Both take a single list argument and operate only on the top-level elements of this list. Embedded lists are considered a single element, so their substructure is ignored. The `length` function returns the number of top-level elements in the argument.

(length *list*)

```
(length '(1 2 3 4))
 ⇒ 4

(setf misc '(1 2 (3 (ignore-this part) ignore-me-too)))
 ⇒ (1 2 (3 (IGNORE-THIS PART) IGNORE-ME-TOO))

(length misc)
 ⇒ 3
```

`Reverse` constructs a new list with the top-level elements in reverse order. `Reverse` is useful when you want to construct a list backward and then reverse it when finished. Notice that, in the second call to `reverse` below, the sublists are not reversed.

(reverse *list*)

```
(reverse '(1 2 3 4))
 ⇒ (4 3 2 1)

misc
 ⇒ (1 2 (3 (IGNORE-THIS PART) IGNORE-ME-TOO))

(reverse misc)
 ⇒ ((3 (IGNORE-THIS PART) IGNORE-ME-TOO) 2 1)

misc ; Misc hasn't been changed.
 ⇒ (1 2 (3 (IGNORE-THIS PART) IGNORE-ME-TOO))
```

EXERCISES

2.9 Evaluate each of these expressions without the aid of a running LISP system. Once you have determined the answers, submit each expression to a LISP system and verify your results.

```
(length '((((heavily nested list)))))
(reverse (reverse '(+ (* 3 x) 55)))
(reverse (list '+ (reverse '(* 3 x)) 55))
```

***2.10** What is the difference between the values returned by evaluating the following two expressions?

```
(length (append () (list 'red) '(green blue)))
(length (reverse (list 'red 'green 'blue)))
```

2.7 List Access

Another interesting problem is determining the specific elements of a list. For example, what are the first, second, and third elements of the following list:

```
'(((+ b x) c) d e)
 ⇒ (((+ B X) C) D E)
```

In this case, the first element is `((+ B X) C)`, the second is `D`, and the third is `E`.

In the following example, what does the list look like after the first element is removed?

```
'((+ a b) (+ b c))
 ⇒ ((+ A B) (+ B C))
```

After removing the first element `(+ A B)`, we have left `((+ B C))`. Notice that we don't have the three-element list `(+ B C)`, but a list with one element which is the three-element list. The following figure shows why removing the first element results in the doubly nested list.

```
      First Element
   ┌──────────────┐
(  │   (+ A B)    │ (+ B C) )

      Result:

(                   (+ B C) )
```

The primary functions that gain access to parts of a list are `car` and `cdr`.*

*`Cdr` is pronounced "Could-er".

Car returns the first element of a list, while `cdr` returns the list with all but the first element. When `cdr` is given a list with only one element, it will return `nil`. Note that these functions gain access to the particular part of the list, but do *not* change the list.

```
(car S-expression)
```

```
(cdr S-expression)
```

```
;; The car function returns the first element of a list.
(car '(+ X 1))
 ⇒ +

(setf weird-list '((123 polynomial) 88 foobar))
 ⇒ ((123 POLYNOMIAL) 88 FOOBAR)

(car weird-list)
 ⇒ (123 POLYNOMIAL)

;; Evaluating the original symbol verifies that the original
;; list has not changed.
weird-list
 ⇒ ((123 POLYNOMIAL) 88 FOOBAR)
```

`Car` and `cdr` are functions and can be arbitrarily nested like the mathematical functions. Therefore, to extract the `123` from `weird-list`, the `car` and then another `car` are evaluated.

```
(car (car weird-list))
 ⇒ 123

(cdr '(+ X 2))
 ⇒ (X 2)

(cdr weird-list)
 ⇒ (88 FOOBAR)

(cdr (car weird-list))
 ⇒ (POLYNOMIAL)

(cdr (cdr weird-list))
 ⇒ (FOOBAR)

(cdr (cdr (cdr weird-list)))
 ⇒ NIL
```

Access to the "nth" element of a list can be accomplished with the appropriate nesting of a single `car` and "$n - 1$" `cdr`'s.

```
;; Access the second element of the list.
(setf short-poly '(+ X 2))
 ⇒ (+ X 2)

(car (cdr short-poly))
 ⇒ X

;; The third element is the nesting of a car and two calls to
;; cdr.
(car (cdr (cdr short-poly)))
 ⇒ 2
```

Common LISP specifies that the `car` and `cdr` functions must operate on a `list`, including the empty list `nil`. The `car` and `cdr` of `nil` is `nil`.* Finally, it is an error to give `car` and `cdr` a non-`list` argument.

```
(car nil)
 ⇒ NIL

;; Why is the next expression not an error?
(cdr (cdr (cdr '(zero-degree-term))))
 ⇒ NIL

;; Because the first cdr returns a nil, and the rest
;; of the cdr's also return nil.
(car 'zero-degree-term)

Error: ZERO-DEGREE-TERM is not a list
```

You normally write a lot of code to manipulate lists in LISP. Functions composed of up to four levels of `car`'s and `cdr`'s help with this task. They are constructed with "a"s (for `car`) and "d"s (for `cdr`) between "c" and "r." Instead of typing `(car (cdr x))` to gain access to the second element, you can use `(cadr x)`. Notice the a's and d's in `cadr` directly correspond to the "outside-in" ordering of the calls to `car` and `cdr`. That is, the leftmost "a" or "d" corresponds to the outer `car` or `cdr` and proceeds to the right and inside.

```
;; Manipulate a second degree polynomial in prefix
;; notation: 3*X**2+4*X+6.
(setf 2nd-degree-poly '(+ (* 3 (** X 2)) (* 4 X) 6))
 ⇒ (+ (* 3 (** X 2)) (* 4 X) 6)

;; Extract the second element from the list, which
;; is the second degree term.
```

*The primary reason for the feature is that you can gain access to the nth element of a list without actually checking that the list is at least n long.

```
(car (cdr 2nd-degree-poly))
 ⇒ (* 3 (** X 2))

;; Try the combined form.
(cadr 2nd-degree-poly)
 ⇒ (* 3 (** X 2))

;; The third element, which is the first degree term.
(caddr 2nd-degree-poly)
 ⇒ (* 4 X)

;; The fourth element, which is the constant term.
(cadddr 2nd-degree-poly)
 ⇒ 6

;; The second cdr.
(cddr 2nd-degree-poly)
 ⇒ ((* 4 X) 6)

;; The polynomial is only of order 2, so it has four
;; elements (three terms and the plus sign).  Therefore, if
;; we look at the fifth element, we should get nil.
(car (cddddr 2nd-degree-poly))
 ⇒ NIL
```

Although you can combine up to four `car`s and `cdr`s, you shouldn't use them arbitrarily. For example, `(cadadr x)` is legal and means the second element of the second element of `x`. This can be very confusing to the reader; `(cadr (cadr x))` is better. Another strange combination is `(cddaar x)`, which is the rest after the second element of the first element of the first element. The following combinations are acceptable, and all others should be avoided.

`caar`	First element of the first element
`cadr`	Second element
`cdar`	Rest of the first element
`cddr`	Rest after the second element
`caddr`	Third element
`cdddr`	Rest after the third element
`cadddr`	Fourth element
`cddddr`	Rest after the fourth element

Recall that `cons` constructs a list whose first argument is the front of the list and whose second argument is the rest of the list. The arguments to a `cons` are actually the `car` and `cdr` of a new list.

```
partial-1st-degree
 ⇒ ((* 6 X) 7)
```

```
(setf complete-1st-degree (cons '+ partial-1st-degree))
 ⇒ (+ (* 6 X) 7)

(car complete-1st-degree)
 ⇒ +

(cdr complete-1st-degree)
 ⇒ ((* 6 X) 7)
```

There is also a function that gains access to the "nth" element of the list, called the `nth` function. Its first argument is the element to retrieve from the list given as the second argument (numbered from 0, therefore the `car` is 0, `cadr` is 1, etc.).

(`nth` *integer S-expression*)

```
(nth 0 '(+ (* 3 (** X 2)) (* 4 X) 6))
 ⇒ +

(nth 2 '(+ (* 3 (** X 2)) (* 4 X) 6))
 ⇒ (* 4 X)
```

Another interesting function is `assoc`. Like `car` and `cdr`, `assoc` gains access to parts of lists. However, the lists that `assoc` operate on are special lists called *association lists* (also known as a-lists). An association list associates keys with values. You create the a-list as a list of lists. The `car` of each sublist is the key and the `cdr` is the associated value. `Assoc` takes two arguments, the first is the key for the search and the second argument is an a-list. It sequentially scans the a-list, comparing the `car` of each sublist against the key. It returns the entire sublist when a match is found. If there are multiple matches, it returns the first one found. If there's no match, then `nil` is returned.

(`assoc` *S-expression a-list*)

The first argument to `assoc` is any S-expression. An association list is like a little data base. The keys become the field names and the values are the field values.

```
;; This creates an initial data base of information for a
;; clown.
(setf clown '((nose red) (expression frown) (name Freddy))
 ⇒ ((NOSE RED) (EXPRESSION FROWN) (NAME FREDDY))

;; Locate the name of the clown in the data base.  Since
;; we want only the name, it is extracted as the cadr.
(cadr (assoc 'name clown))
```

```
⇒ FREDDY

;; This data base is very flexible, since we can add new
;; fields and values at any time.  First check that shoe-size
;; doesn't exist in the a-list.
(cadr (assoc 'shoe-size clown))
⇒ NIL

;; Now add shoe-size.
(setf clown (cons '(shoe-size 27) clown))
⇒ ((SHOE-SIZE 27) (NOSE RED) (EXPRESSION FROWN)
⇒  (NAME FREDDY))

;; Now accessing the new information reveals the clown's
;; shoe size.
(cadr (assoc 'shoe-size clown))
⇒ 27
```

An association list is good for representing sparse polynomials (ones with very few terms, but at least one large exponent). The key is the exponent and the value is the coefficient. So an association list for a polynomial would have the same number of elements as non-zero terms. The number of elements in a regular list representation would be the size of the largest exponent plus 1. The polynomial $3x^{12} + 5x^6 + 9$ would be represented as follows:

```
;; This is the regular list representation.
(setf poly-regular-list '(3 0 0 0 0 0 5 0 0 0 0 0 9))
⇒ (3 0 0 0 0 0 5 0 0 0 0 0 9)

;; Create an association list representation of the
;; polynomial.
(setf poly-alist '((12 3) (6 5) (0 9)))
⇒ ((12 3) (6 5) (0 9))
```

Now `assoc` can find the exponent and associated coefficient. When the exponent is not present, a `nil` is returned.

```
(assoc 6 poly-alist)
⇒ (6 5)

(assoc 1 poly-alist)
⇒ NIL
```

In these examples, we only need the coefficient and not the entire association. Therefore, we take the `cadr` of the `assoc` result. This will work even if `assoc` doesn't find the exponent, since the `cadr` of `nil` is `nil`.

```
(cadr (assoc 0 poly-alist))
⇒ 9
```

```
(cadr (assoc 1 poly-alist))
 ⇒ NIL
```

EXERCISES

***2.11** What value for x in (nth *x somelist*) retrieves the same result as the call (cadddr *somelist*)?

2.12 Suppose that you have the following code. What is the result of evaluating each of the assoc expressions?

```
(setf colors (list '(red 0) '(blue 5) '(green 9)))
(assoc 'blue colors)
(setf colors (cons '(blue 7) colors))
(assoc 'blue colors)
(setf colors (append colors (list '(blue 9))))
(assoc 'blue colors)
```

2.8 Simple User-Defined Functions

The functions that LISP provides take a few arguments, perform some operation, and return a value. User-defined functions group function calls to perform some task. The Common LISP operator for defining functions is defun and its syntax is:

(defun *symbol* (*symbol**) *S-expression**)

The first argument is the name of the function being defined. The second is the list of arguments to the function (which may be empty). The third and succeeding arguments are the S-expressions that make up the body of the function.* When the function is invoked, each S-expression is evaluated and the value of the last S-expression is returned as the result of the function. Functions can group complicated expressions into a single function.

Suppose we represent the second degree polynomial $3x^2 + 4x - 9$ as the list (-9 4 3). In other words, we represent polynomials as a list of coefficients ordered from left to right with increasing degree of the representative term. Now suppose we want to evaluate a polynomial by substituting a constant value for the polynomial variable. This makes the polynomial computable, resulting in a value. For the internal polynomial $(a \quad b \quad c)$ and the value v the result of the evaluation is $a + bv + cv^2$. We can write the computation of the polynomial as the following expressions:

*A function may be defined without any body expressions (which is very peculiar). When this type of empty function is invoked, it will always return nil.

```
;; A polynomial as a list of coefficients.
(setf polynomial '(-9 4 3))
 ⇒ (-9 4 3)

;; The variable v is arbitrarily set to 3.
(setf v 3)
 ⇒ 3

;; Thus, the value of the polynomial with v set to 3 is:
(+ (car polynomial)
   (* (cadr polynomial) v)
   (* (caddr polynomial) (expt v 2)))
 ⇒ 30
```

If you want to compute the value of any polynomial with any value for v, you would have to type the expression many times. This is a perfect case for a user-defined function. We can define `evaluate-2nd-degree-polynomial` which takes two arguments – the polynomial coefficients and the value of the variable – and computes the result.

```
;;; Evaluate the second-degree polynomial in the first
;;; argument with respect to the second argument.

(defun evaluate-2nd-degree-polynomial (poly value)
  (+ (car poly)
     (* (cadr poly) value)
     (* (caddr poly) (expt value 2))))
 ⇒ EVALUATE-2ND-DEGREE-POLYNOMIAL
```

Notice in this example that the value returned by the `defun` is the name of the function. We can now invoke this function, just like the system functions that we have seen in earlier examples.

```
;; This example results in just returning the constant term.
(evaluate-2nd-degree-polynomial '(5 0 0) 15)
 ⇒ 5

;; The next example results in the sum of the coefficients
;; because the variable is set to 1.
(evaluate-2nd-degree-polynomial '(2 3 4) 1)
 ⇒ 9

;; This performs a full evaluation of each term with the
;; variable set to 3.
(evaluate-2nd-degree-polynomial '(-9 4 3) 3)
 ⇒ 30
```

Addition or subtraction of two second-degree polynomials is easy. The resulting second-degree polynomial is simply the sum or difference of the corresponding coefficients.

```
;;; Add two second-degree polynomials.

(defun add-second-degree-polynomial (poly1 poly2)
  (list (+ (car poly1) (car poly2))
        (+ (cadr poly1) (cadr poly2))
        (+ (caddr poly1) (caddr poly2))))
 ⇒ ADD-SECOND-DEGREE-POLYNOMIAL

;;; Subtract two second-degree polynomials.

(defun subtract-second-degree-polynomial (poly1 poly2)
  (list (- (car poly1) (car poly2))
        (- (cadr poly1) (cadr poly2))
        (- (caddr poly1) (caddr poly2))))
 ⇒ SUBTRACT-SECOND-DEGREE-POLYNOMIAL

;; Test these functions on some examples.
(add-second-degree-polynomial '(3 0 3) '(-4 3 5))
 ⇒ (-1 3 8)

(subtract-second-degree-polynomial '(4 3 2) '(1 1 1))
 ⇒ (3 2 1)
```

Although these functions are relatively simple, they show the utility of dividing the computations into small functions. Instead of embedding long expressions within a computation, you can encapsulate the information into a function and then invoke the function within the computation. If meaningful names are chosen for the functions, this programming style can clarify computations.

EXERCISES

***2.13** Write a function that takes three arguments, a key, a value, and an association list and adds the new key and value to the list.

```
(add-alist 'yellow 7 '((red 4)))
 ⇒ ((YELLOW 7) (RED 4))
```

***2.14** Write a function that multiplies two first-degree polynomials and produces a second-degree polynomial. The function should use a two-element list of coefficients for the representation of the polynomial.

```
(multiply-first-degree-polynomial '(2 3) '(1 3))
 ⇒ (2 9 9)
```

2.9 Comments

The semicolon is Common LISP's comment character. When the LISP reader finds a semicolon, it ignores the rest of the line. Many programming languages also provide a comment convention that allows comments to be bracketed by a pair of diphthongs [like the (* and *) used in Pascal]. This allows comments to cross multiple lines. Common LISP provides this facility with proper nesting of the #| and |# diphthongs. Just as for parenthetical nesting of expressions, these symbols must be properly balanced. This style comments out large blocks of text or program that can also contain comments.

```
; Here we have typed in a comment character and a comment.
; Notice that no output is produced, since read is waiting
; for an expression to evaluate.  We may also ;; have ;
; multiple
  ;;;; semicolons on each line, which
  ; are ; simply ; ignored.
#| A block comment may span many lines
searching for the trailing symbol which follows and is the
end of the comment. |# ;; We now start the semicolon-based
                      ;; comment convention.
#| Notice that block comments must be properly nested:
#| entering level two |# and back to level one of the
nesting.  |#
#| Comment out the following function.
(defun frobble (something)
  (+ (car something) (cadr something)))
|#
```

Common LISP does not demand a particular comment convention. However, certain conventions have been adopted and are the basis for program analyzing tools. For example, if a particular comment style indicates the comment description of a function, a program can extract the description from the source code and produce a document describing the code.

Throughout this chapter, the commenting style that we have adopted is two semicolons to designate the description of an S-expression and one semicolon when commenting a partial S-expression. Three semicolons to indicate the beginning of a function is also good style. Some programmers also use four semicolons to indicate major parts of a program. You should consider adopting this particular commenting convention. The following table summarizes this comment convention.

;;;;	Subheading – Indicating major breaks within a program
;;;	Function – Description of following function
;;	S-expression – Comments describing individual S-expr
;	Partial – Comments on partial elements of an S-expr

EXERCISE

2.15 What is the result of evaluating the following expressions?

```
;;; WARNING! VERY POOR STYLE
(defun mystery (polynomial)
  #| (+ (caddr polynomial)
       (cadr |# (cadr polynomial)); ))
(mystery '(+ (* 3 x) 4))
```

2.10 Summary

You use the `Read/Eval/Print` loop to interact with a LISP system. Numbers in LISP are similar to numbers in other programming languages, although the presence of arbitrary precision integers gives LISP an advantage over those languages. LISP uses a single consistent prefix style for writing expressions. It is also consistent in that everything is a value returning expression. Using symbols as variables and manipulating them directly are unique features of LISP. The list data type is fundamental to LISP and can construct arbitrary collections of items. Various primitives construct, manipulate, and gain access to lists. The user can define functions using the `defun` construct and should write programs as a collection of many small functions rather than a few large ones.

Either the semicolon or the `#|`,`|#` diphthongs define a comment. The commenting style that you use is largely personal preference, although some LISP systems provide tools that can aid in both writing comments and analyzing source code based on a comment style convention.

Chapter Exercises

***1.** If the roots of the second-degree polynomial (represented as ax^2+bx+c) are available, they can be determined using the quadratic equation: $(-b \pm \sqrt{b^2 - 4ac})/2a$. Write a function `Quadratic` that takes 3 arguments (`A`, `B` and `C`) and performs the computation described by the quadratic equation using only the + part of the equation. You may assume that $b^2 - 4ac$ will never be less than zero. Also, recall that the square root function is `sqrt` and that `-` may take zero or more arguments.

```
(quadratic 1 1 -6)
⇒ 2.0
```

***2.** Write a function `Extract` that given a second-degree polynomial and an exponent, will extract the associated coefficient. We have already seen a LISP primitive function that will perform exactly this operation.

```
(extract '(-6 1 2) 0)
 ⇒ -6

(extract '(-6 1 2) 1)
 ⇒ 1

(extract '(-6 1 2) 2)
 ⇒ 2
```

***3.** Write a function `One-Root` that computes a root of a second degree polynomial. `One-Root` takes one argument, which is the internal representation of a second order polynomial. It must call the previous two functions to perform the computation.

```
(one-root '(-6 1 1))
 ⇒ 2
```

Function Summary

The following summarizes the functions and topics covered in this chapter.

- Number data type
- Arithmetic operations
- Symbols
- `(setf` *symbol expression*`)`
- `(setq` *symbol expression*`)`
- `(quote` *S-expression*`)`
- `'`*S-expression*
- `(set` *expression expression*`)`
- `(list` *S-expression**`)`
- `(append` *S-expression**`)`
- `(cons` *S-expression S-expression*`)`
- `(length` *list*`)`
- `(reverse` *list*`)`
- `(car` *S-expression*`)`
- `(cdr` *S-expression*`)`
- `(nth` *integer S-expression*`)`
- `(assoc` *S-expression a-list*`)`
- `(defun` *symbol* `(`*symbol**`)` *S-expression**`)`
- Comments using ; and pairs of `#|`, `|#`

3 CONDITIONALS, LOCALS, AND RECURSION

IN THIS CHAPTER, we learn more about LISP functionality. First, we discuss the basic predicate functions. The conditional operator `cond` is then covered, followed by the logical operators. We then look at recursion as a control mechanism for LISP. We go on to describe the `let` and `let*` expressions that introduce local variables to a LISP function. Finally, we introduce global variables and discuss a different mechanism for calling functions.

3.1 Basic Predicates

A predicate tests an S-expression and returns a true or false result. In LISP, a false result is designated by `nil` and a true result is anything else – anything that is not `nil`. This can include LISP's truth symbol `T`, numbers, symbols, or non-empty lists. Some functions return boolean values, `nil` or `T`, while others return `nil` or some value other than `T`. This is like the distinction between the questions "Is someone in the room?" and "Who is in the room?" The first elicits a boolean answer, `nil` or `T` ("yes" or "no"), and the other elicits `nil` ("nobody") or a list ("Bob, Carol, Ted, and Alice").

The `atom` predicate tests to see if its single argument is atomic. Anything that is not a list is an atom. The `listp` predicate tests to see if its argument is a list. Both of these predicates return either `T` or `nil`.

(atom *S-expression*)

(listp *S-expression*)

```
;; Use atom on a number, symbol and list.
(atom 100)
⇒ T
```

```
(atom 'first-order)
⇒ T

;; Atom test on a list.
(atom '(* 3 X))
⇒ NIL

(setf first-order '(+ (* 3 X) 4))
⇒ (+ (* 3 X) 4)

(atom first-order)
⇒ NIL

(listp 'first-order)
⇒ NIL

(listp first-order)
⇒ T

(listp (cdr first-order))
⇒ T
```

`Nil` is the only data object within Common LISP that is both an atom and a list (`nil` is equivalent to the empty list `()`). Be aware with these predicates that the argument can be `nil`.

```
(atom nil)
⇒ T

(atom ())
⇒ T

(listp nil)
⇒ T

(listp ())
⇒ T
```

Common LISP has predicates that test whether a single argument is of a particular type. The convention for naming these functions is to concatenate the name of the type with a "p", indicating predicate. Thus, the function named `listp` tests to see if an argument is a list. Since the "p" indicates a question like a question mark, you pronounce these predicates with a rising inflection on the "p".

The `numberp` predicate tests if its argument is a number. It is true for both integers and floating point numbers.

(numberp *S-expression*)

```
;; Assign to leading-coefficient the value 7.
(setf leading-coefficient 7)
 ⇒ 7

(numberp leading-coefficient)
 ⇒ T

(numberp 1.233)
 ⇒ T

(numberp 'leading-coefficient)
 ⇒ NIL
```

`Symbolp` tests if its argument is a symbol. Notice that the `atom` function tests for a non-list argument, while `symbolp` tests for a non-list argument that is a symbol.

(symbolp *S-expression*)

```
(symbolp 'first-order)
 ⇒ T

first-order
 ⇒ (+ (* 3 X) 4)

;; Check the "symbolness" of the value of first-order.
(symbolp first-order)
 ⇒ NIL

;; Compare atom and symbol.
(atom 'first-order)
 ⇒ T

(atom 23)
 ⇒ T

(symbolp 23)
 ⇒ NIL
```

The `null` predicate tests if its argument is `nil`.

(null *S-expression*)

```
(null ())
 ⇒ T

(null nil)
```

```
    ⇒ T

(null 'a)
    ⇒ NIL

(null '(+ (* 3 X) 6))
    ⇒ NIL

(null (cdr '(x)))
    ⇒ T
```

The `equal` predicate determines if its two arguments are structurally identical. That is, it returns `T` if the arguments are of the same type (for example, both integers, both symbols, etc.) and have the same value – they're equal. It returns `nil` if they have different types. If they are lists and the corresponding elements of the lists are equal, then they are equal.*

(`equal` *S-expression S-expression*)

We will create two polynomials in prefix notation to illustrate the comparison of lists with `equal`.

```
;; Create two polynomials to manipulate.
(setf poly-1 '(+ (* 3 x) 4))
    ⇒ (+ (* 3 X) 4)

(setf poly-2 '(- (* 3 x) 4))
    ⇒ (- (* 3 X) 4)
```

The following two `equal` expressions compare symbols, which are always atoms. If the arguments are different symbols, the result is `nil`, while same symbols result in `T`.

```
(equal 'poly-1 'poly-1)
    ⇒ T

(equal 'poly-1 'poly-2)
    ⇒ NIL
```

The next comparison is of the value of a symbol against a symbol. In this case, the value of the symbol is a list. This results in `nil` because they are not the same type.

```
(equal 'poly-1 poly-1)
    ⇒ NIL
```

*Notice the recursive definition here. If an element of a list is itself a list, then the corresponding element must also be a list, and these lists must also be equal

This next comparison is between an explicit 4 and one extracted from `poly-1`.

```
(equal (caddr poly-1) 4)
 ⇒ T
```

This last one compares the same extracted 4 against a floating point 4. It fails because an integer and a floating point number are different types.

```
(equal (caddr poly-1) 4.0)
 ⇒ NIL
```

The following calls to `equal` compare lists in various forms.

```
(equal poly-1 poly-1)
 ⇒ T

(equal poly-1 poly-2)
 ⇒ NIL

(equal (cdr poly-1) (cdr poly-2))
 ⇒ T

(equal poly-1 '(+ * 3 x 4))
 ⇒ NIL
```

The previous example resulted in `nil` because the second element of `poly-1` is a list and the second element of the second argument is the symbol *.

```
(equal poly-1 '(+ (* 3 x) 4))
 ⇒ T
```

The comparison operator = determines if its arguments are numerically equal. It should be used in numeric comparisons, while `equal` is used in most other instances. The other standard arithmetic comparison operators are predicates that operate only upon numeric arguments. The Common LISP versions of these operators permit an arbitrary number of arguments. When there are more than two arguments, each pair of arguments is compared. For example, in the expression `(> a b c)`, the result is `T` if the following relations are true:

`A>B` *and* `A>C` *and* `B>C`

However, due to the transitivity of `>`, only two comparisons are needed:

`A>B` *and* `B>C`

The only comparison operator that doesn't exhibit transitivity is `/=` (not equal). It must compare all operands. The ability to have more than two arguments is useful for checking if a number is within a certain range.

Operator	Args	Description
=	n	Numeric equal
/=	n	Not equal
>	n	Greater than
>=	n	Greater than or equal
<	n	Less than
<=	n	Less than or equal

Two-argument versions of each of the comparison operators are first demonstrated.

```
(= 3 3.0) ; Works for floats and integers
⇒ T

(/= 3 4)
⇒ T

(> 4 2)
⇒ T

(< 4 2)
⇒ NIL

(>= 3 3.0)
⇒ T

(<= 0.0 4)
⇒ T
```

Now, a few multi-argument versions are illustrated.

```
;; With equal, each argument must be equal to the others.
(= 3 3.0 3 3.0)
⇒ T

(setf first-coefficient 3)
⇒ 3

(setf second-coefficient 4)
⇒ 4

;; When using not equal, all of the arguments must be
;; different.
(/= first-coefficient second-coefficient 3.0)
⇒ NIL

;; Is first-coefficient in the range from 0 to 9?
(<= 0 first-coefficient 9)
⇒ T
```

Another interesting predicate is `member`, which is used to test for membership. It takes two arguments and determines if the first argument is a member of the list passed as the second argument. `Member` is an example of a predicate function that returns something other than `T` to designate truth. When it finds a match, it returns the rest of the list, with the matched element as the `car` of the list. This allows you to use `member` as a simple predicate, or as a more powerful function to find the beginning of a list that matches an argument.

(member *argument list*)

```
;; Test the member function.
(member 'x '(** x 2))
⇒ (X 2)

(member 'y '(** x 2))
⇒ NIL
```

EXERCISES

***3.1** Write a function `atom-and-list` that tests if its argument is both an atom and a list. You may not use any logical or conditional operators.

```
(atom-and-list 'first-coefficient)
⇒ NIL
```

3.2 What is the result of evaluating each of the following expressions?

```
(setf polynomial-1 '(+ (* 2 x) 3))
(setf polynomial-2 '(+ (* 3 x) 2))
(equal (cadr (cadr polynomial-1))
  (caddr polynomial-2))
(> (caddr polynomial-1) (cadr (cadr polynomial-2)))
(= (cadr (cadr polynomial-1)) (caddr polynomial-2)
   (cadr (cadr polynomial-2)))
(equal (append '(* 2 x) '(3)) (list '(* 2 x) '(3)))
(<= 1 (caddr polynomial-2) (caddr polynomial-1))
(equal (member 'red '(red blue green)) t)
(equal (member 'green '(red blue green)) '(green))
```

3.2 Conditional Expression

Conditional expressions in LISP, as in other programming languages, introduce a branch in the sequential processing of a program. The primary conditional expression in LISP is `cond`. `Cond` takes an arbitrary number of clauses. Each clause is a list whose `car` is a test expression and whose `cdr` is a list of S-expressions that are evaluated if the test expression is true. The syntax is:

`(cond (`*test-expression S-expression*`*)*)`

The test expressions are evaluated in order until one is found that is non-`nil`, then the corresponding S-expressions are evaluated. The result of the `cond` expression is the evaluation of the last associated S-expression. If no associated S-expressions are given, the result of the `cond` is the evaluation of the test expression. If all test expressions evaluate to `nil`, the result of the entire `cond` expression is `nil`. When a test expression evaluates to non-`nil`, `cond` ignores any subsequent clauses. So if more than one clause is non-`nil`, those after the first are ignored.

An important test expression is `T`, whose value is always non-`nil`. `T` as the test expression guarantees that the associated S-expressions will be evaluated when the preceding test expressions evaluate to `nil`. In `cond`, `T` functions like an *else* or *otherwise* case. If a clause has a `T` test expression, then any following clauses aren't evaluated. This clause therefore should be last in a `cond` expression. The following function uses a simple conditional form similar to *if-then-else* of other programming languages. The purpose of the function is to construct a list of the argument if it is not already a list.

```
;;; Listify the argument if not already a list.

(defun listify (argument)
  (cond ((listp argument) argument)
        (t (list argument))))
 ⇒ LISTIFY

;;; Test the function on two examples.
(listify 44)
 ⇒ (44)

(listify '(* 3))
 ⇒ (* 3)
```

In many of the examples, we have been manipulating polynomials in a prefix notation. A polynomial term may assume many forms to represent the coefficient, the variable, and the exponent. We will require that a term always include the variable and exponent with the coefficient optional (when the coefficient is a one, it is not needed). The term cx^e will be represented as `(*` c `(**` x e`))` for $c \neq 1$ and `(**` x e`)` for $c = 1$. The exponent e must be a positive integer.

Now that we have the representation, we can write a function to extract the coefficient from a term. If a term is simply a number, then it is the coefficient. If it is a symbol, then the coefficient is a 1. Finally, if the `car` of the term is a $*$ then the `cadr` is the coefficient. Otherwise the coefficient is a 1. The function coefficient-from-term performs the extraction. The function doesn't need to check that the term is a list, since we assume that the term matches one of our representations, which are both lists.

```
;;; A function to extract a coefficient from a term:
;;; Term Given                          Resulting Coefficient
;;; coefficient                           coefficient
;;; x                                     1
;;; (* coefficient (** x exponent))       coefficient
;;; (** x exponent)                       1

(defun coefficient-from-term (term)
  (cond ((numberp term) term)
        ((symbolp term) 1)
        ;; If not a number and not a symbol, then it
        ;; must be a list, so we can check for the *.
        ((equal (car term) '*) (cadr term))
        ((equal (car term) '**) 1)))
⇒ COEFFICIENT-FROM-TERM

;; Test the function on some terms.
(coefficient-from-term '(* 4 (** x 2)))
⇒ 4

(coefficient-from-term 'x)
⇒ 1

(coefficient-from-term 5)
⇒ 5
```

This function also illustrates proper indentation of expressions. Since the LISP language has very little syntax, proper indentation is important.* Until now our expressions were only a few lines long and therefore indentation was not necessary. However, in this example proper nesting helps you understand the function. It should be clear from the code what each cond clause does, and the structure of the function. Each clause should be indented the same number of spaces as the preceding clause.

It is a matter of personal taste whether to place the first clause on the same line as the cond or indented a few spaces on the next line. Also, some programmers place the test expression on a separate line from the corresponding S-expressions, instead of grouping them all on one line. In some cases, the test expression's length forces the remaining S-expressions to be placed on separate lines. Notice how the same function is hard to understand when we write it without indentation.

*For the human reader, the LISP reader ignores the superfluous white space.

```
;;; IMPROPERLY INDENTED FUNCTION.

(defun bad-style-coefficient-from-term (term)(cond (
 (numberp term) term)((symbolp
 term) 1)((equal (car
 term) '*) (cadr term))((equal (car term) '**) 1)))
```

One problem with this version of `coefficient-from-term` is that if the term doesn't match any of the conditions, the result of the `cond` and, therefore, the result of `coefficient-from-term` would be `nil`. When the result of a `cond` expression is meaningful to a computation, then the default `nil` return value should *not* be used. It would be more appropriate to include `(t nil)` as the final clause. This alerts the human reader that the value of this expression is significant.

However, in this case, the final `(t nil)` clause is unnecessary, since we are assuming that the terms must match the given criteria; all four clauses encompass all possible term conditions. Thus, the final test is redundant and could be replaced by a clause with a true test.

```
;;; A function to extract a coefficient from a term that is
;;; either:
;;; Term Given                          Resulting Coefficient
;;; coefficient                           coefficient
;;; x                                     1
;;; (* coefficient (** x exponent))       coefficient
;;; (** x exponent)                       1

(defun coefficient-from-term (term)
  (cond ((numberp term) term)
        ((symbolp term) 1)
        ;; If not a number and not a symbol, then it
        ;; must be a list, so we can check for the *.
        ((equal (car term) '*) (cadr term))
        (t 1)))
 ⇒ COEFFICIENT-FROM-TERM
```

Common LISP also defines `if` as a restricted version of `cond`. `If` is similar to `if` conditional expression in other programming languages. When you use `if`, you may specify a *test* expression, a *then* expression, and an optional *else* expression. The general syntax is:

(if *test-expression then-expression optional-else-expression*)

The main restriction is that the *then* and *else* expressions must be single expressions. Obviously, `if` has an equivalent `cond` form. The first example in this section demonstrated a simple `cond` expression in `listify`. That function could be written as:

```
;;; Listify the argument if not already a list.

(defun listify (argument)
  (if (listp argument) argument (list argument)))
 ⇒ LISTIFY
```

As you can see from this example, `if` and `cond` are similar. `Cond` permits multiple clauses, which can be accomplished using nested `if` expressions. The only other difference is `if`'s limitation of a single expression in the "then" and "else" expressions. `Progn` eliminates this restriction. It permits multiple S-expressions to be grouped as one. Each S-expression is sequentially evaluated and the result is the value of the last S-expression. An *implicit* `progn` is a term that means the same grouping capability without the explicit inclusion of the `progn` symbol. `Cond` can be said to have an implicit `progn` following the test expression in a clause. We have also seen another instance of an implicit `progn` in the expressions in a `defun`.

(progn *S-expression**)

The following example illustrates the use of `progn` by setting two variables depending upon the status of a third variable.

```
;; Random-term has a term.
(setf random-term '(* 3 (* x 4)))
 ⇒ (* 3 (* X 4))

;; Set the variables to the appropriate values.
(if (listp random-term)
    (if (equal (car random-term) '*)
      (progn (setf coefficient (cadr random-term))
             (setf variable-part (caddr random-term)))
      (progn (setf coefficient 1)
             (setf variable-part random-term))))
 ⇒ (* X 4)
```

The result of the `if` is the result of setting `variable-part`, thus, `variable-part` should have `(* X 4)` as its value.

```
coefficient
 ⇒ 3

variable-part
 ⇒ (* X 4)
```

Since the same function is accomplished with either `cond` or `if`, which to choose is a matter of style. The rule of thumb is to use `if` on single tests with simple "then" and "else" expressions and `cond` otherwise. `Cond` is better for maintaining code, since you can easily add a new clause by inserting it into the appropriate place. Adding a new clause to an `if` expression requires rewriting the expression.

EXERCISES

3.3 What expression is equivalent to the following?

```
(cond (t (car polynomial)))
```

***3.4** Rewrite `coefficient-from-term` to use nested `if` expressions instead of a single `cond` clause. Leave out the `symbolp` test in this first version.

***3.5** Modify the `if` version of `coefficient-from-term` of the previous exercise by adding the `symbolp` test back into the function. Notice the difficulty of this change.

***3.6** Modify the `quadratic` function used in the previous chapter so it verifies that $b^2 - 4ac$ is positive before taking the square root. To make this task easier, write a function to compute $b^2 - 4ac$ and then call it as is appropriate. If the result is negative, return `'error`. Don't worry if you have to call the function that computes $b^2 - 4ac$ more than once.

```
(quadratic 5 5 5)
⇒ ERROR
```

3.3 Logical Operators

The primary LISP logical operators are `and`, `or`, and `not`. The `not` operator is synonymous with the `null` operator, but is more natural in logical expressions. The proper style is to use `null` when examining lists and `not` when performing logical operations.

(not *S-expression*)

```
(not ())
⇒ T

(not nil)
⇒ T

(not 'first-order)
⇒ NIL
```

```
(not '(+ (* 3 X) 4))
⇒ NIL

(not (atom 'first-order))
⇒ NIL

(not (listp 'first-order))
⇒ T
```

Both **and** and **or** take an arbitrary number of arguments. **And** evaluates each argument in order, until one evaluates to `nil` or all arguments have been evaluated to non-`nil`, in which case it returns the value of the last argument. When an argument evaluates to `nil`, no more arguments are evaluated and a `nil` is returned. `Or` works similarly searching for a non-`nil` value. The early termination feature is very useful when writing LISP code and makes the **and** and **or** expressions a type of control structure.

(**and** *S-expression**)

(**or** *S-expression**)

In the degenerate cases, **and** returns `T`, while **or** returns `nil`.

```
(and)
⇒ T

(or)
⇒ NIL
```

If **and** doesn't find a null argument, it returns the value of the last argument. `Or` also returns the value of the last argument if all preceding arguments are `nil`. Thus, if either operation is given a single argument, then the result will be the value of that argument.

```
(setf polynomial '(+ (* 3 x) 5))
⇒ (+ (* 3 X) 5)

(and polynomial)
⇒ (+ (* 3 X) 5)

(or polynomial)
⇒ (+ (* 3 X) 5)

(and t)
⇒ T

(or T)
```

```
⇒ T

(and nil)
⇒ NIL

(or nil)
⇒ NIL
```

The result of an `and` will always be the evaluation of the last argument when all of the preceding arguments are non-`nil`. `And` can be used to perform a test and, based on the test result, return some value. This is exactly what happens with a clause of a `cond` expression with only one expression following the test. When the test succeeds, the result of the `cond` is the result of the next expression. Likewise, `or` can be used to perform a series of tests, searching for the first one that is non-`nil` and returning that value. This is the same mechanism that `cond` uses for finding a clause with a valid test. Thus, it is possible to convert between the use of logical operators and `cond`. Using these guidelines, you could rewrite `Coefficient-from-term` as follows:

```
;;; A function to extract a coefficient from a term as
;;; defined earlier.

(defun coefficient-from-term (term)
  (or (and (numberp term) term)
      (and (symbolp term) 1)
      (and (equal (car term) '*)
           (cadr term))
      1))
⇒ COEFFICIENT-FROM-TERM

;; Test the function on two terms.
(coefficient-from-term '(* 4 (** x 2)))
⇒ 4

(coefficient-from-term '(** x 2))
⇒ 1
```

Converting between logicals and `cond` can be difficult. The previously defined `listify` function illustrates this point. This is the definition of `listify` using a conditional operator:

```
;;; Turn the argument into a list, if not already a list.

(defun listify (argument)
  (if (listp argument) argument (list argument)))
⇒ LISTIFY
```

When the argument is `nil`, the result is still `nil`, since `nil` is a list.

```
(listify nil)
 ⇒ NIL
```

Now suppose that you change `listify` to use logical operators as with the function `coefficient-from-term`. This results in the following definition:

```
;;; Turn the argument into a list, if not already a list.

(defun listify (argument)
  (or (and (listp argument) argument)
      (list argument)))
 ⇒ LISTIFY

(listify nil)
 ⇒ (NIL)
```

When this new version receives `nil`, it returns a list of `nil`. This is because the `and` expression returns `nil` and the `or` then returns the result of the next expression. So, you should be careful using these constructs. You should use `and` for small simple problems and `cond` for complicated ones.

Suppose we want to write a function that takes a polynomial and returns the square of the leading coefficient. A polynomial can be either a single term or a `+` followed by any number of terms. `Square-leading-coefficient` must call the `coefficient-from-term` function on the `cadr` of the polynomial if there is a `+` operator. Otherwise, it must call the function on the polynomial itself. In this case, we will check that the polynomial is a list before testing for the `+` operator. This ensures correct handling of non-list arguments – a good programming practice.

```
;;; Square the leading coefficient of the argument
;;; polynomial, which may be either a list of terms with a
;;; leading + operator or a single term.

(defun square-leading-coefficient (polynomial)
  (expt (coefficient-from-term
          (or (and (listp polynomial)
                   (equal (car polynomial) '+)
                   (cadr polynomial))
              polynomial))
        2))
 ⇒ SQUARE-LEADING-COEFFICIENT

(square-leading-coefficient '(+ (** X 1) (* 4 (** X 0))))
 ⇒ 1

(square-leading-coefficient '(* 4 (** X 2)))
 ⇒ 16
```

```
(square-leading-coefficient '(+ (* 3 X) 4))
 ⇒ 9

(square-leading-coefficient '(+ X 4))
 ⇒ 1

(square-leading-coefficient 5)
 ⇒ 25
```

This realization of `square-leading-coefficient` might not be what you expected. A first attempt might have called `coefficient-from-term` on both the second element of the polynomial and on the polynomial itself. Also, the call to `expt` (exponentiate) might have been placed around each invocation of `coefficient-from-term`. The method shown here is better since there's only one instance of each function call. This improves maintainability, because if the function call were changed, it would only be changed in one place. It also uses the fact that all LISP expressions return a value. This style works because we can guarantee that both parts of the `or` expression will always return a meaningful term.

The next exercise instructs you to define your own version of a function that already exists in the LISP system. It tells you to call your new function something other than the original version. In LISP, you can replace the definition of any function, even a system one, by defining a function with the same name. If you define it incorrectly, other functions that you write could fail because they rely on a bad function definition. Other programming languages have reserved words that restrict redefinition. LISP has no such restrictions, so be careful when choosing names for functions.

EXERCISES

3.7 Define `my-numberp` which performs the same function as `numberp` without an explicit call to `numberp`.

```
(my-numberp 34.4)
 ⇒ T

(mynumberp 'mynumberp)
 ⇒ NIL
```

***3.8** Write a function which, given a polynomial in prefix notation, will find the constant term. You may assume that the polynomial will be at most second degree.

```
(const-term '(+ (* 3 X) 4))
 ⇒ 4

(const-term 'X)
 ⇒ 0
```

3.9 What is the result of evaluating the following expressions?

```
(setf coefficient (coefficient-from-term '(* 4 x)))
(and nil (setf coefficient (coefficient-from-term 44)))
coefficient
(or (setf coefficient (coefficient-from-term '(** x 3)))
    (setf coefficient (coefficient-from-term 'x)))
coefficient
```

***3.10** What is the `cond` equivalent of `(or a b c)`?

***3.11** Further enhance `quadratic` defined in previous exercises so it checks to see if the three arguments are all numbers. If they are not numbers, then return `'error`.

```
(quadratic 3 'x 5)
 ⇒ ERROR
```

3.4 Recursion

Dividing a problem into small, manageable subproblems usually allows you to approach a solution more rapidly. So far, we have used the subdivision technique, calling different functions to solve each of the exercises. Recursion is another subdivision technique where the function directly or indirectly calls itself to solve the parts of the problem. A direct recursive call is where the recursive function calls itself within its own code body. An indirect recursive call means the function calls some other function that then (directly or indirectly) calls the first function. Every recursive function must contain some code to *terminate* the recursion, otherwise a call to the function would recurse infinitely. There is no special syntax for calling a function recursively; you simply mention the name of the function as the operator of an expression in the function.

Many recursive functions have a similar format. Generally, there is a `cond` expression that first checks for the terminating condition(s). That is followed by one or more clauses that test some particular condition and then perform a recursive call. This standard recursive style can be illustrated in the following template:

```
;;; Template of the standard recursive style.
(defun some-function (arguments)
  (cond (terminating-test some-value)
        (optional-test-condition (some-function changed-arguments))
        (t (some-function different-changed-arguments))))
```

Writing a `factorial` function is a good exercise in recursion. Factorial is defined in mathematical notation as:

$$n! = \begin{cases} 1 & \text{if } n = 0; \\ n(n-1)! & \text{otherwise.} \end{cases}$$

```
;;; The following function computes the factorial of its
```

```
;;; argument.

(defun factorial (n)
  (if (= n 0)
    1
    (* n (factorial (1- n)))))
⇒ FACTORIAL
```

Factorial matches the template without any of the optional tests.

```
(factorial 0)
⇒ 1

(factorial 4)
⇒ 24

;; To verify that (factorial 4) is equivalent to the
;; corresponding multiplication, we can simply type in the
;; expression directly.
(* 4 3 2 1 1)
⇒ 24
```

Each recursive call to factorial adds factors to an expression to compute the factorial. The following illustrates the process of building and then collapsing the expression.

```
(factorial 4)  →  (* 4 (factorial 3))
               →  (* 4 (* 3 (factorial 2)))
               →  (* 4 (* 3 (* 2 (factorial 1))))
               →  (* 4 (* 3 (* 2 (* 1 (factorial 0)))))
               →  (* 4 (* 3 (* 2 (* 1 1))))
               →  (* 4 (* 3 (* 2 1)))
               →  (* 4 (* 3 2))
               →  (* 4 6)
               →  24
```

There is a potential problem with this definition for factorial. Suppose that it is given an argument value that is less than zero. If this occurs, the function will loop indefinitely. Therefore, the function should be written to do something reasonable in this case. An easy solution changes the test to check for less than or equal to zero and return a one in those cases when the argument is negative.

```
;;; The following function computes the factorial of its
;;; argument.

(defun factorial (n)
  (if (<= n 0)
```

```
    1
    (* n (factorial (1- n)))))
 ⇒ FACTORIAL

(factorial -4)
 ⇒ 1
```

Recursive functions are excellent for processing lists. They are ideal for determining some collective value from all the elements of the argument list (like the minimum value of the elements or the presence of a particular symbol in the list). The Common LISP function `length` fits well into this category. Its purpose is to count the number of top-level elements in the list. The solution matches the template and looks just like `factorial`. The first step is to determine the termination condition. In this case, the function stops when there are no more elements left in the argument list. Otherwise, it adds one to the length of the rest of the list. `My-length` performs this operation.

```
;;; Our version of length, which recursively counts the
;;; number of elements in the argument list.

(defun my-length (some-list)
  (if (null some-list)
    0
    (1+ (my-length (cdr some-list)))))
 ⇒ MY-LENGTH

;; Now a couple of tests.
(my-length '(this list has 5 elements))
 ⇒ 5

(my-length ())
 ⇒ 0
```

Recursive functions also work well for constructing a new list from a modified argument list. Just as in the `my-length` example, the terminating test is usually a `null` test. However, the return value is usually specified to be `nil`. If the list is non-empty, then the function constructs a new list from a modified `car` and a recursive call on the `cdr`. The only decision is how to construct the new list. Using our standard recursive template, we would have the following function:

```
;;; Perform some operation to each element of the list
;;; argument.

(defun some-function (list-argument)
  (cond ((null list-argument) nil)
        (t (some-construction-operation
```

```
                (some-operation (car list-argument))
                (some-function (cdr list-argument)))))
```

When `some-function` receives a null list, the result is `nil`. If the function receives a list with only one element `X`, then the recursive call on the `cdr` will result in `nil` and the result of the function will be:

```
(some-construction-operation (some-operation X) nil)
```

The result that we want is a single element list. The construction function that takes two arguments, an S-expression, and `nil` and produces a list of the S-expression is the `cons` function. `Append` will not work because the result of `some-operation` may not be a list. `List` will is not appropriate because it creates a two-element list. Therefore, we can let `some-construction-operation` be `cons`. If we try the function on a list of two elements `(X Y)`, then the result of the function will be equivalent to:

```
(cons (some-operation X)
      (cons (some-operation Y)
            nil))
```

Using `cons` in this case will construct exactly the list that we need. The call to `cons` with the modified `Y` argument will create a one-element list, and the outer call will add the modified `X` to the front. We can now use this style to write a function that takes one argument, which is a list of numbers, and constructs a list with one added to each element of the list.

```
;;; Adds 1 to all elements of the list argument.

(defun add-1-to-list (list-of-numbers)
  (cond ((null list-of-numbers) nil)
        (t (cons (1+ (car list-of-numbers))
                 (add-1-to-list (cdr list-of-numbers))))))
 ⇒ ADD-1-TO-LIST

(add-1-to-list '(1 2 3 4))
 ⇒ (2 3 4 5)
```

This version of `add-1-to-list` works fine for flat lists (those with no nested sublists), but causes an error if the list has any nesting (the error will occur when the code tries to add one to a list, which is impossible). To allow nested lists, it must make a recursive call on both the `car` and `cdr` of the list. Thus, whenever a list is found as an element, it is treated like a top-level list. We also have to add a new test to check for a number and perform the addition.

```
;;; Modified add-1-to-list that permits a nested list of
;;; numbers and adds 1 to each element.
```

```
(defun add-1-to-list (list-of-numbers)
  (cond ((null list-of-numbers) nil)
        ((numberp list-of-numbers) (1+ list-of-numbers))
        (t (cons (add-1-to-list (car list-of-numbers))
                 (add-1-to-list (cdr list-of-numbers))))))
⇒ ADD-1-TO-LIST

(add-1-to-list '(1 2 3 4))
⇒ (2 3 4 5)

(add-1-to-list '((2 3 (4 5) 6) 7 (8)))
⇒ ((3 4 (5 6) 7) 8 (9))
```

The only problem with this function is that if the list contains non-numeric values, then an error will occur. For example:

```
;; Demonstrate that add-1-to-list will fail if the list has
;; some non-numeric elements.
(add-1-to-list '((3 4 (x y) 3)))

!!!!! Error: The argument X is not a valid list.
  Condition signaled in: CAR.
```

A reasonable solution makes sure that the argument is a list, prior to performing the recursion. If it is not a list, then the function can return some error indicator (like the symbol ERROR).

```
;;; Add-1-to-list that checks for non-numeric elements.

(defun add-1-to-list (list-of-numbers)
  (cond ((null list-of-numbers) nil)
        ((numberp list-of-numbers) (1+ list-of-numbers))
        ((listp list-of-numbers)
         (cons (add-1-to-list (car list-of-numbers))
               (add-1-to-list (cdr list-of-numbers))))
        (t 'error)))
⇒ ADD-1-TO-LIST

(add-1-to-list '((2 3 (4 5) 6) 7 (8)))
⇒ ((3 4 (5 6) 7) 8 (9))

(add-1-to-list '((3 4 (x y) 3)))
⇒ ((4 5 (ERROR ERROR) 4))
```

Cons constructs lists by adding elements to the front. Recursion counteracts this process and results in creating the list from right to left. For example, suppose we want to create an ascending list of integers within a range of values:

```
;;; Ascending list of integers inclusive of the start and
;;; exclusive of the end.

(defun integer-list (start end)
  (cond ((>= start end) nil)
        (t (cons start
                 (integer-list (1+ start) end)))))
⇒ INTEGER-LIST

(integer-list 2 4)
⇒ (2 3)
```

The following figure demonstrates this recursive process. Each call elicits a `cons` whose second value will be computed by another recursive call. Eventually a `nil` is returned and the outstanding `cons` operations are performed. Nothing is actually constructed until the recursion terminates.

```
(integer-list 2 4)→(cons 2 (integer-list 3 4))
                  →(cons 2 (cons 3 (integer-list 4 )))
                  →(cons 2 (cons 3 NIL))
                  →(cons 2 (3))
                  →(2 3)
```

EXERCISES

***3.12** Some of the functions we have used can be written using recursion. Write a recursive function for `assoc` and `reverse`. Call them `my-assoc` and `my-reverse`.

***3.13** Write `super-reverse`, which reverses nested sublists as well as the top-level elements.

```
(super-reverse '(a b (c (d (((f g)) e)))))
⇒ ((((E ((G F))) D) C) B A)
```

3.14 Write the function `flatten` that takes a single-list argument and creates a new list with all of the structure removed. For example, `(flatten '(a b (c d (e f) g) h))` results in `(a b c d e f g h)`.

3.15 Write a function `make-same-list` that takes two arguments, an integer n and a value, and creates a list with the value replicated n times.

```
(make-same-list 4 'a)
⇒ (A A A A)
```

***3.16** Write `my-nth` that performs the same function as `nth`.

3.17 Modify `add-1-to-list` so it ignores non-numbers by leaving them alone.

```
(add-1-to-list '((3 4 (x y) 3)))
⇒ ((4 5 (X Y) 4))
```

3.5 Local Variables

Often while writing the definition of a function, you want to use the result of a computation in more than one place. For example, suppose you want to compute the square root of an expression that may be positive or negative. When the expression is negative, you want to return the symbol `negative` otherwise you just want to compute the root. The following code performs that operation:

```
;;; Compute the square root of the difference of the squares
;;; of the arguments.  Return the symbol negative if the
;;; difference is less than zero.

(defun strange-square-root (a b)
  (if (< (- (* a a) (* b b)) 0)
    'negative
    (sqrt (- (* a a) (* b b)))))
⇒ STRANGE-SQUARE-ROOT
```

As you can see from this example, one solution is to simply perform the computation more than once. Although this is usually semantically correct, it can add a computational burden by performing the same operation many times. It can also be semantically incorrect if the computation has some side effects (for example, if it reads or writes to the terminal or increments a variable). The solution is to save the result of the computation in some kind of variable. The variable should have the characteristics that it is temporary and is only defined in the context of the function being defined. The former constraint is important so that when the function requiring the variable no longer needs its services, the variable disappears. The latter constraint is also important to avoid a conflict when two different functions define the same temporary variable. Variables that fit these two constraints are called local variables.

Common LISP defines the `let` and `let*` expressions to introduce local variables. They can also specify initial values for the locals. Local variables exist only while the function is active and are not visible from other functions. Both expressions have identical syntax, but they differ in the technique used to provide the locals with their initial values. The process of providing a variable with a value is called *binding*. The syntax of `let` and `let*` is like the `defun` expression. Since `let` and `let*` are LISP expressions, they can be placed anywhere in any other LISP expression (or used alone). But, they are usually the top-level expression within a function (as with most programming languages' variable declarations).

(let (*local**) *S-expression**)

(let* (*local**) *S-expression**)

Let and let* return the value of the last S-expression, their S-expressions are an implicit progn. A *local* can either be a single symbol or a two-element list whose first element is a symbol and second is an initial value S-expression (this *initializes* the first element to the second-element value). When the *local* is just a symbol, that symbol is given an initial value of nil.

local ← *symbol*

local ← (*symbol S-expression*)

```
;; Simple top-level let, just to demonstrate values.
;; A and c will have initial values of nil, while b is set to
;; 99.
(let (a
      (b 99)
      c)
  (list a b c))
 ⇒ (NIL 99 NIL)
```

Notice in this syntax that the local variables are contained in a list following the let symbol. Many beginning students don't notice this part of the syntax and incorrectly define the symbols without the list.

```
;;; INCORRECT USE OF LET.
(let a
  (b 99)
  c
  (list a b c))

!!!!! Error: Improper LET syntax:
      (LET A (B 99) C (LIST A B C))
```

The use of let makes the definition of strange-square-root more reasonable as follows:

```
;;; Compute the square root of the difference of the squares
;;; of the arguments.  Return the symbol negative if the
;;; difference is less than zero.
```

```
(defun strange-square-root (a b)
  (let ((difference-of-squares (- (* a a) (* b b))))
    (cond ((< difference-of-squares 0) 'negative)
          (t (sqrt difference-of-squares)))))
⇒ STRANGE-SQUARE-ROOT
```

The difference between `let` and `let*` is the way that the initial S-expression is bound to the local variable. `Let*` performs sequential binding, while `let` performs parallel binding. In sequential binding, the first initial value S-expression is evaluated and bound to the first variable. Then the next S-expression is evaluated and bound to the next variable and so on. This means that any S-expression following a previous variable binding can use the value of that variable in its calculation. With parallel binding, all of the initial S-expressions are first evaluated and then bound to the local variables in parallel. So, an initial value S-expression can't use any previous variable values because they won't have their value until after the computation. Under most circumstances, you don't need access to the local variables within the initial value S-expression and so `let` is used. Whenever access to the locals is required, then `let*` should be used.

You can bind local variables, whose initial values depend upon other locals, by properly nesting `let`.

```
;; Example of dependent local variable initialization.
(let ((a 55))
  (let ((b (* a 2)))
    (let ((c (+ a b)))
      (list a b c))))
⇒ (55 110 165)
```

However, using `let*` makes this a much cleaner implementation.

```
;; Let* version of the previous code.
(let* ((a 55)
       (b (* a 2))
       (c (+ a b)))
  (list a b c))
⇒ (55 110 165)
```

You might wonder why you would ever use `let` instead of `let*`. `Let` is important for gaining access to variables defined outside of the `let` S-expression. The best way to see the differences is with an example. Suppose you have a function that draws a point on a screen. The function takes two arguments, the `x` and `y` coordinates of each point. Also suppose these points are transformed into a new `x` and `y` by some operation that takes the values of the original `x` and `y`. This mutually recursive nature makes the use of `let*` incorrect:

```
;; Draw point on the screen, mapping the coordinates into
;; screen coordinates.
```

```
(defun draw-point (x y)
  (let ((x (map-to-screen-x x y))
        (y (map-to-screen-y y x)))
    ... Code to use x and y ...
    ))
```

In this case, if a `let*` had been used, then the call to `map-to-screen-y` would get the new value for `x` instead of the argument value.

In the last chapter, we discussed an internal representation of a polynomial which was a three-element list of coefficients. This internal representation is useful for the various algebraic operations. But, the resulting list of coefficients must be converted back into a form that the user can recognize. This can be done with a function that takes one argument, the list of coefficients, and produces a polynomial in prefix notation. Since the prefix notation is for external communication to the user, the function will be called `internal-to-external`. The following example shows the expected results from invoking the function:

```
;; Function doesn't exist, this just shows what should
;; happen.
(internal-to-external '(4 5 0 6))
 ⇒ (+ (* 4 (** X 0)) (* 5 (** X 1)) (* 6 (** X 3)))
```

The challenging part of this task is to design the function so it doesn't convert a term that has a zero coefficient. To solve this problem, we will write an auxiliary function that recursively constructs the list of converted terms, but doesn't include terms with a zero coefficient. The convention for naming an auxiliary function uses the same name as the main function with an `-aux` appended to the name. In this case, our main function is `internal-to-external`, so the auxiliary function is called `internal-to-external-aux`. Generating each term requires both the coefficient and the exponent. The exponent is implicit in the position of the coefficient within the list. As the list is scanned, the exponent increases by one starting at zero. The easiest way to maintain this exponent value is to pass it as a parameter to the function. It will be initialized to zero and incremented in each recursive call.

```
;;; Convert the list of coefficients into a list of prefix
;;; terms. It ignores zero coefficients and uses a simple
;;; representation of a term as (* coefficient (** x
;;; exponent)). The first argument is a list of coefficients
;;; and the second is the current exponent value (initially a
;;; zero).

(defun internal-to-external-aux (coefficients
                                 current-exponent)
  (cond ((null coefficients) nil)
        ((= (car coefficients) 0)
```

```
          (internal-to-external-aux (cdr coefficients)
                                    (1+ current-exponent)))
         (t (cons
              (list '*
                     (car coefficients)
                     (list '** 'x current-exponent))
              (internal-to-external-aux
               (cdr coefficients)
               (1+ current-exponent))))))
⇒ INTERNAL-TO-EXTERNAL-AUX

(internal-to-external-aux '(4 5 6) 0)
⇒ ((* 4 (** X 0)) (* 5 (** X 1)) (* 6 (** X 2)))

(internal-to-external-aux '(4 0 0) 0)
⇒ ((* 4 (** X 0)))
```

This auxiliary function returns a list of the prefix version of the terms. `Internal-to-external` must call this function and then decide if a `+` should be added to the front of the list. If there are two or more terms, then the `+` should be inserted, otherwise the `car` of the list should be returned (as a single term). This is an example of when a local variable should be used. The local variable saves the value returned from `internal-to-external-aux` with the code then deciding which option to use.

```
;;; Map from the internal list of coefficients to the
;;; external prefix notation.

(defun internal-to-external (internal-form)
  (let ((list-of-terms
          (internal-to-external-aux internal-form 0)))
    (if (= (length list-of-terms) 1)
      (car list-of-terms)
      (cons '+ list-of-terms))))
⇒ INTERNAL-TO-EXTERNAL

(internal-to-external '(4 5 6))
⇒ (+ (* 4 (** X 0)) (* 5 (** X 1)) (* 6 (** X 2)))

(internal-to-external '(0 0 3))
⇒ (* 3 (** X 2))
```

This version works just fine, except for the case when all of the coefficients are zero. Can you determine what will happen when `internal-to-external` is called with `'(0)`?

```
(internal-to-external '(0))
⇒ (+)
```

This result is because the `cond` checks for a list with only one term. The result from the `internal-to-external-aux` is the empty list. One solution is to check for an empty list and then return zero. A `null` test can do this, but to illustrate the need for `let*`, we will test for a length of zero. Instead of calling `length` twice, `internal-to-external` computes the length and saves it in a local variable. The first version doesn't use `let*`, but illustrates that nesting of `let` expressions is equivalent. The second version shows that `let*` makes a more readable (human-readable) function.

```
;;; Map from the internal list of coefficients to the
;;; external prefix notation.

(defun internal-to-external (internal-form)
  (let ((list-of-terms
          (internal-to-external-aux internal-form 0)))
    (let ((number-of-terms
            (length list-of-terms)))
      (cond ((= number-of-terms 0) 0)
            ((= number-of-terms 1) (car list-of-terms))
            (t (cons '+ list-of-terms))))))
⇒ INTERNAL-TO-EXTERNAL
```

This requires the nesting of the `lets`, since `number-of-terms` must be computed with `list-of-terms` properly bound.

```
;;; Map from the internal list of coefficients to the
;;; external prefix notation.

(defun internal-to-external (internal-form)
  (let* ((list-of-terms
           (internal-to-external-aux internal-form 0))
         (number-of-terms
           (length list-of-terms)))
    (cond ((= number-of-terms 0) 0)
          ((= number-of-terms 1) (car list-of-terms))
          (t (cons '+ list-of-terms)))))
⇒ INTERNAL-TO-EXTERNAL

(internal-to-external '(4 5 6))
⇒ (+ (* 4 (** X 0)) (* 5 (** X 1)) (* 6 (** X 2)))

(internal-to-external '(0))
⇒ 0
```

EXERCISES

3.18 Rewrite `internal-to-external` to use a `null` test instead of comparing the length of the generated list against zero.

***3.19** Write a function which given two points, will compute the slope of the line between them. A point is represented as a two-element list of X and Y position. For the two points (x_1, y_1) and (x_2, y_2), the slope is defined to be

$$\frac{(y_2 - y_1)}{(x_2 - x_1)}$$

If the result of $(x_2 - x_1)$ is zero then return `'infinity`.

```
(slope '(0 0) '(1 4))
⇒ 4

(slope '(3 5) '(3 8))
⇒ INFINITY
```

***3.20** Write `collinearp` that determines if the third argument point is on a line defined by the first two argument points. A point is on a line if the slope between it and one of the other points is the same as the slope of the original line.

```
(collinearp '(0 0) '(2 2) '(4 4))
⇒ T
```

***3.21** Write a function that determines if a point given as the third argument is on a line *between* the two points given as the first argument.

```
(between '(0 0) '(4 4) '(2 2))
⇒ T

(between '(0 0) '(2 2) '(4 4))
⇒ NIL
```

3.6 Global Variables

A global variable is defined at the top level. It can be mentioned in a function without explicit declaration as a function argument or a local variable (this is further discussed in Chapter 6). It is a good idea to limit your use of global variables. When writing functions in the LISP environment, everything is accessible: functions, globals, and so on. Programs that affect the environment by defining many globals may interact poorly with other programs.* For example, suppose you write a set of functions that uses the global `balance` to maintain your bank account balance. Also, suppose that you are using a graphics package written by a friend to display your account information in a nice form. Suppose that

*The package system [40, Chapter 11] helps to alleviate these problems, but you should still limit the number of globals.

the package also uses the global `balance`, except it uses it to determine if the objects on the screen are aesthetically balanced between the left and right sides. Then the programs will conflict in their use of the common variable. However, there are cases when you must save information between function calls, so you should be careful to not use the variables defined by others.

A `setf` to a variable at the top level effectively allocates a global variable. A function may access this variable and update its contents. These changes are then visible to all functions accessing the variable. Gratuitous creation of global variables within a function is a bad habit because of the same interaction problem. Also, if their creation is buried deep within a function, it is not obvious that a global is being allocated and used.

The correct style is to use `defvar` to allocate all global variables. `Defvar` takes two arguments; the first is the symbol name of the global variable and the second is an initial value S-expression. Calls to `defvar` should only occur at the top level and should be placed at the top of a program file. This makes it clear to the human reader which globals are used in the program.

(`defvar` *symbol S-expression*)

A useful convention is to surround all global symbols with asterisks (or some similar notation). This makes no difference in how the programs operate, but it makes the global symbols more noticeable.

```
;; Declare a global state variable containing the maximum
;; degree of the polynomials.
(defvar *maximum-polynomial-degree* 2)
 ⇒ *MAXIMUM-POLYNOMIAL-DEGREE*
```

You must be careful when trying to redefine a `defvar`-declared variable. You can't just change the initial value and reevaluate `defvar`. The change will not take effect. You must use `setf` to force a change.

```
;; Check the value of *maximum-polynomial-degree*.
*maximum-polynomial-degree*
 ⇒ 2

;; Now we try to change it with defvar.
(defvar *maximum-polynomial-degree* 3)
 ⇒ *MAXIMUM-POLYNOMIAL-DEGREE*

;; Check the value of *maximum-polynomial-degree* again.
*maximum-polynomial-degree*
 ⇒ 2

(setf *maximum-polynomial-degree* 3)
 ⇒ 3
```

```
*maximum-polynomial-degree*
⇒ 3
```

You should be careful with this – it can happen unexpectedly.

EXERCISE

***3.22** Define a global variable that contains the name of the variable used in the polynomial (previously we have used `X`). Modify `internal-to-external-aux` to use this global variable instead of the hard-coded `'x`. This permits operations upon polynomials that have a variable other than `X`.

3.7 Calling Functions

Suppose you want to pass a function name as an argument to another function. Then, depending upon some value, the program selects which function to call. The function that you write is `perform-operation`, which takes three arguments. The first is the operation and the second two are the operands. Assume the operations that you select between are addition and subtraction. In this simple example, the arguments are the symbols naming the function.

```
;;; Perform the requested binary operation (+ or -) on the
;;; two operands.

(defun perform-operation (operator operand1 operand2)
  (cond ((equal operator '+) (+ operand1 operand2))
        ((equal operator '-) (- operand1 operand2))))
⇒ PERFORM-OPERATION

;; Now for a couple of tests.
(perform-operation '+ 5 6)
⇒ 11

(perform-operation '- 32 66)
⇒ -34
```

Since `perform-operation` doesn't know about any other operations, the use of a * operator returns `nil`.

```
(perform-operation '* 3 4)
⇒ NIL
```

The problem with this solution is that the function must be changed every time a new operator is added. The reason that this is difficult is because of the way S-expressions are evaluated. When an S-expression is found, the first element determines which function to invoke. The rest of the elements are evaluated and passed to the designated function. The first element is not evaluated and must be the exact name of the function. This is fine, except for cases like `perform-operation` where you want to dynamically select the function to invoke. In those cases, we pass the function as an argument and use the regular evaluation strategy. Then, function names can be passed as arguments to functions and bound into list structures. This distinguishes between imperative programming languages like C and Pascal and applicative languages like LISP. Common LISP provides the `apply` function to perform this task.

(`apply` *S-expression S-expression* List-S-expression*)

The first *S-expression* must evaluate to the name of a function. This is followed by zero or more *S-expressions*, which are the initial arguments, and then a list of the remaining arguments. The final list is mandatory, but may be empty. Our first example uses these expressions to call functions where the function-name is simply a quoted symbol. Although each of these perform the same operation, they show the different ways to specify the "applied" arguments.

```
;; Call the + operator four different ways.
(+ 1 2 3 4)
⇒ 10

(apply '+ (list 1 2 3 4))
⇒ 10

(apply '+ 1 2 (list 3 4))
⇒ 10

(apply '+ 1 2 3 4 '())
⇒ 10
```

The function `perform-operation` can be enhanced by using `apply`, which removes the restriction on the set of operations that it may perform.

```
;;; Perform the requested operation (anything that is a legal
;;; binary operation) on the two operands.

(defun perform-operation (operator operand1 operand2)
  (apply operator operand1 operand2 '()))
⇒ PERFORM-OPERATION

(perform-operation '+ 5 6)
⇒ 11

(perform-operation '- 32 66)
⇒ -34

;; This new version is more powerful, since it will work with
```

```
;; any binary operator.
(perform-operation '* 3 7)
 ⇒ 21

(perform-operation 'list 'x 3)
 ⇒ (X 3)
```

As you can see, `apply` allows one to write generic functions that don't need to be modified for new operations.

EXERCISES

***3.23** Write a function `my-map` that takes a predicate and a list as arguments and creates a list of the predicate applied to every member of the input list.

```
(my-map 'numberp '(1 a b 2 3))
 ⇒ (T NIL NIL T T)
```

3.24 Suppose we are from another planet and wish to use numeric operators that are our names instead of English names. Define the function `gzorp` which takes our function name as the first argument and the two operands as the second and third arguments. `Gzorp` should convert our name into a LISP function name and `apply` the resulting function to the two arguments. Perform the following translation: `greeble` into `+`, `ngreeble` into `-` and `prozg` into `*`. Evaluate the following expressions:

```
(gzorp 'prozg 34 -4)
(gzorp 'ngreeble 22 -22)
```

3.8 Summary

There are a number of predicates available to the LISP programmer, which return `nil` to represent false, and any other value to represent true. Many predicates return `T` or `nil`, while others return some LISP object or `nil`. The `cond` and `if` expressions are used to add branching to LISP programs. The logical operators `and` and `or` can also be control structures. With just this limited set of LISP functionality, we are ready to write a substantial program. Recursive functions allow the programmer to break the problem into smaller parts and then solve the parts. `Let` and `let*` introduce local variables and respectively use parallel and sequential binding of initial values to the local variables. `Defvar` introduces global variables. It should only be used when the value of a variable must be maintained across a wide range of function calls. Finally, `apply` can be used to call a function determined dynamically.

Chapter Exercises

***1.** Change the `quadratic` function so it computes both the `+` and `-` parts of the equation and returns both roots as a list. Use a local variable to save the result of the discriminant $\sqrt{b^2 - 4ac}$.

```
(quadratic 1 1 -6)
⇒ (2.0 -3.0)
```

***2.** Write a function `roots`, which given a second-degree polynomial, returns a two-element list of the first-degree polynomial roots.

```
;; x**2+x-6=(x+3)*(x-2).
(roots '(-6 1 1))
⇒ ((3 1) (-2 1))
```

Function Summary

The following lists the functions and topics covered in this chapter.

- `(atom` *S-expression*`)`
- `(listp` *S-expression*`)`
- `(numberp` *S-expression*`)`
- `(symbolp` *S-expression*`)`
- `(null` *S-expression*`)`
- `(equal` *S-expression S-expression*`)`
- `(=` *S-expression S-expression*`)`
- `(/=` *S-expression S-expression*`)`
- `(>` *S-expression S-expression*`)`
- `(>=` *S-expression S-expression*`)`
- `(<` *S-expression S-expression*`)`
- `(<=` *S-expression S-expression*`)`
- `(member` *argument list*`)`
- `(cond (`*test-expression S-expression**`)*)`
- `(if` *test-expression then-expression optional-else-expression*`)`
- `(progn` *S-expression**`)`
- `(not` *S-expression*`)`
- `(and` *S-expression**`)`
- `(or` *S-expression**`)`
- Recursive functions and the standard recursive style
- `(let (`*local**`)` *S-expression**`)`
- `(let* (`*local**`)` *S-expression**`)`
- `(defvar` *symbol S-expression*`)`
- `(apply` *S-expression S-expression* List-S-expression*`)`

4 CASE STUDY: SIMPLE ALGEBRA SYSTEM

THE CASE STUDY in this chapter investigates a simple computer algebra system. Various computer algebra systems have evolved over the last twenty years, including Reduce [19], Macsyma [26], muMath [36], and others. These systems primarily perform algebraic operations like simplification, differentiation, integration, factoring, and so on. The simple algebra system presented here performs a few operations on univariate polynomials. A univariate polynomial is an algebraic formula in one variable

$$c_i x^i + c_{i-1} x^{i-1} + \ldots + c_0 x^0$$

where each c_i represents the constant integer coefficient and x is the variable. Each element consisting of a coefficient, variable, and exponent is called a term.

4.1 Goals of the Algebra System

Most algebra systems are interactive. A user typically defines algebraic equations in an infix notation. The user specifies manipulations like differentiation and results are printed. Although it may appear that the system operates directly upon the infix form, in reality the system converts the equation to a manageable, internal representation. Once the operations have been performed, the computed result is then translated back into infix notation. So, an important consideration in designing an algebra system is choosing an appropriate internal representation. It must facilitate the particular manipulations to be performed (in this case, we will perform polynomial addition, subtraction, and differentiation) as well as convert between it and the external representation. In order to make our simple algebra system as realistic as possible, we will perform similar translations (although we will make simplifying assumptions because a complete infix to internal form parser is beyond the scope of this book). Our algebra system will perform the following operations:

1. Convert an external representation of an algebraic equation into an internal representation.

2. Perform the requested operation on the internal representation.
3. Convert the resulting equation back into the external infix notation.

4.2 Design of the Internal Form

The first step in designing the algebra system is to determine an internal representation. Our polynomials can have an arbitrary degree* and will consist of a sum of terms. Since the exact number of terms is arbitrary and lists can be arbitrarily long, a list of terms is a natural representation. The polynomials that we will process are univariate (that is, there is only one variable), so it is unnecessary to include the variable with each term. Finally, depending on the types of polynomials, it may or may not be advantageous to include the exponent with each term. If the polynomials are very sparse (that is, if there are very few terms, and some terms have a large exponent), then it could be more efficient to include the exponent. For example, the polynomial

$$3x^9 - 4$$

could be represented as a list of two-element lists, each containing a coefficient and exponent:

```
((3 9) (-4 0))
```

The same list without an explicit exponent would be represented as:

```
(3 0 0 0 0 0 0 0 0 -4)
```

In this case study we assume that the polynomials are relatively dense and so only the coefficient is necessary. A zero will be used to represent a missing term, because the term $0x^i$ evaluates to zero. The other design decision is an appropriate ordering for the list of coefficients. If the left to right ordering is from the highest exponent to the constant term, then extracting an arbitrary coefficient is difficult. One has to extract the terms from the right side going backward. The polynomial

$$3x^3 + 2x + 5$$

would be represented as:

```
(3  0  2  5)
```

So, the first-degree coefficient is second from the right. Another representation reverses the coefficient list, going from the constant term to the coefficient with the highest exponent. This representation permits the `nth` function to extract a

*The degree of a polynomial is defined to be the value of the largest exponent, so our polynomials can have terms with arbitrarily large exponents.

coefficient given its exponent. So, the previous polynomial would be represented as:

```
(5 2 0 3)
```

Also, for simple arithmetic operations on polynomials of different degrees, the coefficients of terms with the same exponent are in the same list position. In the other representation, the first term could be a coefficient of any term. This makes arithmetic operations simpler to define. Therefore, we will adopt the lowest to highest representation.

Now that we've decided on an internal representation, we can write the routines to convert between the external and internal representations. Normally, you would write a parser to translate from the mathematical infix notation into the internal representation. This would require lexical analysis and a reasonably sophisticated parser, which is beyond the scope of these first few chapters. We will assume that a parser has already translated the expression into a prefix "LISP-like" format. This is either a single term in prefix notation, or a list of terms with a leading "+" operator. We will also assume that the polynomial has been normalized – there are no terms with the same exponent. The ** symbol represents exponentiation and the standard +, -, *, and / symbols represent addition, subtraction, multiplication, and division, respectively. The following illustrates some polynomial expressions, their corresponding prefix representations, and their internal form:

Polynomial		Prefix Format		Internal Format
55	→	`55`	→	`(55)`
$-34x$	→	`(* -34 x)`	→	`(0 -34)`
x^2	→	`(** x 2)`	→	`(0 0 1)`
$3x^2+8$	→	`(+ (* 3 (** x 2)) 8)`	→	`(8 0 3)`

EXERCISE

***4.1** One way to make the parsing problem a little simpler is to ignore lexical analysis. This could be done with an infix notation within a list of tokens. Write a set of functions to convert the "infix list" notation into the prefix notation, which could then call the **external-to-internal** function defined in the next section. You may assume that the polynomial has already been normalized.

```
(infix-to-prefix '(55))
 ⇒ 55

(infix-to-prefix '(-34 * x))
 ⇒ (* -34 X)

(infix-to-prefix '(x ** 2))
 ⇒ (** X 2)
```

```
(infix-to-prefix '(3 * x ** 2 + 7 * x + 8))
 ⇒ (+ (* 3 (** X 2)) (* 7 X) 8)
```

4.3 External to Internal Conversion

Now that we have an internal and an external representation, we can write functions to convert between the two. First, we determine the cases of the input polynomial – either a single term or a list of terms with a leading `+` operator. So that we can handle every case as a list, we begin by making the single terms into one-item lists. For multiple terms, we remove the leading `+` operator, creating a list of the terms.

The next step is to generate the ordered set of coefficients. The terms in the input polynomial don't have to be in any particular order. So, we have at least two options for processing the polynomial:

1. Explicitly sort the terms from lowest to highest exponent value, then extract the coefficients and build the list; or
2. First, scan the polynomial to determine its degree and assign that to "n." Next, search for the zero-exponent term, the one-exponent term, and so forth up to the "nth" exponent, and construct the list of coefficients from these. If a term is missing, a zero appears in its position in the list of coefficients. (You could also scan from "n" down to zero, and then reverse the list.) This is essentially a selection sort.

The first option has the disadvantage that a sort function must be written. This could vary in complexity from a simple bubble sort to any of the more sophisticated sorting algorithms.* The second option has the advantage of sorting and extracting simultaneously. But this is computationally expensive because of the number of times that the polynomial must be scanned (in the worst case, if the polynomial is already sorted from highest to lowest, it requires approximately n^2 comparisons). This is as inefficient as a bubble sort, except that a separate sorted structure isn't created and then scanned for the coefficients. So, we will choose the second option.

The conversion requires the following functions:

1. Given a term, extract the coefficient (`coefficient-of-term`);
2. Given a term, extract the exponent (`exponent-of-term`);
3. Scan a polynomial searching for the coefficient of the term that has a matching exponent value (`find-coefficient-of-matching-term`);
4. Scan a polynomial and determine its degree (`degree-of-polynomial`).

The first two functions need to recognize the possible formats of a term:

*Common LISP provides a `sort` function, but its discussion is beyond the scope of these early chapters.

Term	Coefficient	Exponent
55	55	0
x	1	1
(* 34 x)	34	1
(** x 3)	1	3
(* 33 (** x 2))	33	2

The `coefficient-of-term` function doesn't need to distinguish between the third and fifth cases because the coefficient is the second element of the argument in both cases. But, the `exponent-of-term` function must distinguish all five different forms because the position of the exponent differs in each case. Neither function has to do any error checking since we assume a consistent internal representation. Also, we don't need `listp` checks after testing for a `number` and a `symbol` since there are no other possible forms for the term except lists. The code for the first two functions follows:

```
;;; Retrieve the coefficient from the argument term.  This
;;; function tests each possible term format and retrieves
;;; the coefficient as appropriate.

(defun coefficient-of-term (term)
  (cond ((numberp term) term)
        ((symbolp term) 1)
        ((equal (car term) '*)
         (cadr term))
        (t 1)))
⇒ COEFFICIENT-OF-TERM

;; Test the function on a few values
(coefficient-of-term 55)
⇒ 55

(coefficient-of-term 'x)
⇒ 1

(coefficient-of-term '(* 3 x))
⇒ 3

(coefficient-of-term '(** x 3))
⇒ 1

(coefficient-of-term '(* 3 (** x 2)))
⇒ 3

;;; Retrieve the exponent from the argument term.

(defun exponent-of-term (term)
```

```
  (cond ((numberp term) 0)
        ((symbolp term) 1)
        ((equal (car term) '**)
         (caddr term))
        ((and (listp term) (listp (caddr term)))
         (caddr (caddr term)))
        (t 1)))
⇒ EXPONENT-OF-TERM

;; Test the function on a few values
(exponent-of-term 55)
⇒ 0

(exponent-of-term 'x)
⇒ 1

(exponent-of-term '(* 3 x))
⇒ 1

(exponent-of-term '(** x 3))
⇒ 3

(exponent-of-term '(* 3 (** x 2)))
⇒ 2
```

The third function is `find-coefficient-of-matching-term`. Given an exponent, if a term with that exponent is found, its coefficient is returned. If not, the function returns a zero.

This is a typical recursive function. It first tests for the terminating condition (there are terms left in the list), and returns zero. Then it checks the first element of the list to see if the exponent matches the first argument, `matching-exponent`. If successful, it returns the coefficient of the first element of the list. Otherwise it calls itself on the remainder of the list. The code for the third function follows.

```
;;; Recursively scan the list of terms searching for a
;;; matching exponent.  If one is found then return the
;;; coefficient, otherwise return 0.

(defun find-coefficient-of-matching-term (matching-exponent
                                          list-of-terms)
  (cond ((null list-of-terms) 0)
        ((= (exponent-of-term (car list-of-terms))
            matching-exponent)
         (coefficient-of-term (car list-of-terms)))
        (t (find-coefficient-of-matching-term
            matching-exponent (cdr list-of-terms)))))
```

```
⇒ FIND-COEFFICIENT-OF-MATCHING-TERM

;; Test the function on a few values
(find-coefficient-of-matching-term 4
 '((** x 4) (* 3 (** x 3)) (* 2 x) 1))
⇒ 1

(find-coefficient-of-matching-term 3
 '((** x 4) (* 3 (** x 3)) (* 2 x) 1))
⇒ 3

(find-coefficient-of-matching-term 2
 '((** x 4) (* 3 (** x 3)) (* 2 x) 1))
⇒ 0

(find-coefficient-of-matching-term 1
 '((** x 4) (* 3 (** x 3)) (* 2 x) 1))
⇒ 2

(find-coefficient-of-matching-term 0
 '((** x 4) (* 3 (** x 3)) (* 2 x) 1))
⇒ 1
```

The fourth auxiliary function is `degree-of-polynomial`. This function can also be recursive. We find which is greater – the exponent of the current term or the highest exponent already encountered. When we finish the last term, we have the degree of the polynomial. This function differs from the `find-coefficient-of-matching-term` function because the terminating condition is not when the list is exhausted, but when only one term is left. This can be determined by a null `cdr` on the list. When the last term is found, we can use it as the current maximum value. If we were to terminate with an empty list, we would have to choose the smallest possible exponent value (which is zero for our polynomials). The code for the fourth function follows.

```
;;; Determine the degree of the list of terms, which is
;;; defined to be the value of the largest exponent.

(defun degree-of-polynomial (list-of-terms)
  (if (null (cdr list-of-terms))
    (exponent-of-term (car list-of-terms))
    (max (exponent-of-term (car list-of-terms))
         (degree-of-polynomial (cdr list-of-terms)))))
 ⇒ DEGREE-OF-POLYNOMIAL

;; Test the degree-of-polynomial on a few lists of terms.
(degree-of-polynomial '(55 (* 3 x) (** x 4)))
 ⇒ 4
```

```
(degree-of-polynomial '(55))
 ⇒ 0

(degree-of-polynomial '((* 3 (** x 2)) 4))
 ⇒ 2
```

Last, we must create the driver function to perform the external to internal conversion. This first transforms the polynomial into a list of terms and computes the polynomial's degree. The function then calls the `build-internal-form` function; this recursively extracts each coefficient to build the new internal representation.

The most efficient way to construct lists is to `cons` a new member of the list onto the front of the list. `Append`ing an element on the end of the list is inefficient because each invocation of `append` will scan the list to find its end.

We have the following two options for constructing the list of coefficients:

1. Pass two arguments into `build-internal-form`: the starting exponent (which will always be zero) and the ending exponent (the degree of the polynomial).
2. Construct the list from largest to smallest, then reverse the list when finished.

The first solution is slightly better even though it requires an extra argument to the function; the list is constructed once and doesn't need to be reversed. The code for the driver function follows.

```
;;; Convert an external polynomial into an internal list of
;;; coefficients.

(defun external-to-internal (polynomial)
  (let ((list-of-terms
         (if (and (listp polynomial)
                  (equal (car polynomial) '+))
             (cdr polynomial)
             (list polynomial))))
    (build-internal-form
     list-of-terms
     0
     (degree-of-polynomial list-of-terms))))
 ⇒ EXTERNAL-TO-INTERNAL

;;; Recursively construct the list of coefficients from the
;;; list of terms argument.  The coefficient corresponding to
;;; the exponent argument is cons'd onto the coefficient
;;; list.

(defun build-internal-form (list-of-terms start-exponent
```

```
                                               end-exponent)
  (if (> start-exponent end-exponent)
    nil
    (cons
     (find-coefficient-of-matching-term start-exponent
                                        list-of-terms)
     (build-internal-form list-of-terms
                          (1+ start-exponent)
                          end-exponent))))
⇒ BUILD-INTERNAL-FORM

;; Now we may test the conversion process.
(external-to-internal '(* 4 (** x 2)))
⇒ (0 0 4)

(external-to-internal '(+ 3 (* 4 x)))
⇒ (3 4)

(external-to-internal '(+ (** x 5) (* 3 (** x 3)) 4))
⇒ (4 0 0 3 0 1)
```

EXERCISES

4.2 Combine `coefficient-of-term` and `exponent-of-term` into a single function that returns a list of the coefficient and exponent of a term.

```
(coefficient-and-exponent-of-term '(* 3 (** X 2)))
⇒ (3 2)
```

***4.3** Define the `build-internal-form` function using both schemes mentioned in the text and then time their execution to see which is the fastest. The Common LISP function `time` can be used to time the execution of an S-expression (see Chapter 17 or [40, Chapter 25] for more details).

4.4 Combine `infix-to-prefix` defined in the exercises in the last section with the `external-to-internal` function. The goal is to translate directly from the infix to the internal notation.

4.5 One of the problems with `infix-to-internal` is that `infix-to-prefix` places the `+` onto the prefix list and `external-to-internal` removes it. Define a better way of performing this operation without the unnecessary work.

4.4 Internal to External Conversion

Converting from internal to external representation is easier than from external to internal. The internal representation is simpler and more regular. This regularity leads to fewer special cases. You can write a function `convert-term` that takes an exponent and coefficient and returns a term. For the full external representation, collect the terms into a list and add a + to the front (if there aren't at least two terms, the single term is returned). The interesting implementation question is how to construct the external representation when terms don't have a zero coefficient. One way is to `append` the results of the calls to `convert-term` together. `Append` is effectively ignored if its first argument is `nil`. So, `convert-term` could return `nil` when the coefficient is zero and a list including the single term otherwise. For example:

```
;; Demonstrate append without the extra list nesting.
(append '(* 3 x) '(* 4 (** x 2)))
⇒ (* 3 X * 4 (** X 2))

;; Add the extra nesting level to produce the proper result.
(append '((* 3 x)) '((* 4 (** x 2))))
⇒ ((* 3 X) (* 4 (** X 2)))
```

The code for `Convert-term` follows. Since we are processing univariate polynomials, the function assumes that the variable is `X`.*

```
;;; Convert the exponent and coefficient into an external
;;; representation term.  When the coefficient is zero,
;;; nil is returned, otherwise a list of the term is
;;; returned, suitable for appending into the list of terms.

(defun convert-term (coefficient exponent)
  (cond ((= coefficient 0) nil)
        ((= exponent 0) (list coefficient))
        ((and (= coefficient 1) (= exponent 1)) '(x))
        ((= coefficient 1)
         (list (list '** 'x exponent)))
        (t (list
            (list '*
                  coefficient
                  (if (= exponent 1) 'x
                      (list '** 'x exponent)))))))
⇒ CONVERT-TERM
```

The `build-list-of-terms` function takes a list of coefficients and generates a list in external representation for each term. Since the function calls `convert-term` with the current exponent, it recursively increments the expo-

*This is a possible problem with our internal representation – we have not included the variable anywhere in the list. One solution would be to add the variable as the first element of the internal list. The functions could be modified to ignore the first element, while manipulating the equations (although they should be enhanced to forbid an operation on two polynomials with different variables).

nent starting from zero. You can either write an auxiliary function, or call `build-list-of-terms` with an extra argument that is initially a zero. We choose the latter since it saves writing another function. `Build-list-of-terms` appends the result of `convert-term` to the list under construction, using the standard recursive style.

```
;;; Convert the list of coefficients into a list of external
;;; representation terms.  The calling function must pass the
;;; exponent of the first coefficient as the second argument
;;; (should always be a zero).

(defun build-list-of-terms (list-of-coefficients
                            exponent)
  (if (null list-of-coefficients)
    nil
    (append
     (convert-term (car list-of-coefficients) exponent)
     (build-list-of-terms (cdr list-of-coefficients)
                          (1+ exponent)))))
⇒ BUILD-LIST-OF-TERMS

(build-list-of-terms '(0 0 2) 0)
⇒ ((* 2 (** X 2)))

(build-list-of-terms '(3 2 1) 0)
⇒ (3 (* 2 X) (** X 2))
```

As you can see, the list of terms is in the same order as the list of coefficients. This is not the usual ordering and so the list should be reversed. This could be performed in the `internal-to-external` function. All that remains for this function is to determine the number of terms and add the appropriate `+` operator.

```
;;; Convert an internal form of a polynomial as a list of
;;; coefficients into the external prefix notation.

(defun internal-to-external (list-of-coefficients)
  (let ((list-of-terms
         (reverse
          (build-list-of-terms list-of-coefficients 0))))
    (if (= (length list-of-terms) 1)
      (car list-of-terms)
      (cons '+ list-of-terms))))
⇒ INTERNAL-TO-EXTERNAL

(internal-to-external '(0 0 2))
⇒ (* 2 (** X 2))
```

```
(internal-to-external '(3 2 1))
 ⇒ (+ (** X 2) (* 2 X) 3)
```

EXERCISES

***4.6** Can you think of a way to write `build-list-of-terms` that returns the list in the proper order that is as efficient as these versions? Note, attempting to reverse the list of coefficients or using `nth` to extract each coefficient is too inefficient.

4.7 In the function `internal-to-external` we must take the `length` to determine if the `+` should be added to the list of terms. As an alternative, write a function to test if its list argument is longer than one element. The function should not use `length` and may be placed in `internal-to-external` to replace the call on `length`.

4.8 An alternative is to change `build-list-of-terms` to compute the number of terms during the building process and use that value in `internal-to-external`. Change these functions to operate in this manner.

4.5 Polynomial Arithmetic

We are now ready for some polynomial arithmetic – operations such as addition, subtraction, and differentiation. These operations have surprisingly little in common. Addition and subtraction are related, since they operate on each pair of coefficients of the same degree. Differentiation is a unary operation that operates on single terms and collects the results together. These differences force us to write a separate function for each.

The first functions add and subtract the list of coefficients. We assume that the top-level function `manipulate` has already converted to the internal format. So, these functions need only add or subtract the corresponding element. We recursively scan the two coefficient lists and perform the operation on current coefficients in the lists. But what if the polynomials have different degrees, so one of the lists of coefficients is shorter than the other? You could pad the shorter list with zeros on the right side. This is unnecessary, since in a recursive implementation we could simply recognize an empty argument and supply the operation with a zero. The following code implements polynomial addition this way. Pay careful attention to the `if` expression within the `+` expression. If either argument is the empty list, a zero is used. If not, the `car` of the argument is used. This functional style eliminates local variables for extracting the coefficients.

```
;;; Add the two argument lists (possibly of different
;;; lengths) of polynomial coefficients.
;;; CAN BE IMPROVED - SEE NEXT FUNCTION.

(defun poly-add (poly-1 poly-2)
```

```
  (cond ((and (null poly-1) (null poly-2)) nil)
        (t (cons (+ (if (null poly-1) 0 (car poly-1))
                    (if (null poly-2) 0 (car poly-2)))
                 (poly-add (cdr poly-1) (cdr poly-2))))))
⇒ POLY-ADD

(poly-add '(0 1 7) '(3 0 4 5 5))
⇒ (3 1 11 5 5)
```

With this solution, the number of recursive calls is equal to the larger degree of the two polynomials. The last few operations are wasted adding zero to the coefficient. A better solution adds or subtracts the coefficients up to the length of the shortest list (the one with the smaller degree) and then appends the remaining coefficients to the result. For example:

```
    (0 1 7)
+   (3 0 4 5 5)
---------------
    (0 1 7)
+   (3 0 4)         append (5 5)
---------------
    (3 1 11)        append (5 5)
=   (3 1 11 5 5)
```

This way the number of recursive calls is equal to the smaller degree of the two polynomials. We can modify poly-add to check either polynomial for its end and if so return the other one. The call to cons properly adds the new sum to the front of the lists.

```
;;; Add two univariate polynomials that may be of different
;;; degree.

(defun poly-add (poly-1 poly-2)
  (cond ((and (null poly-1) (null poly-2))
         nil)
        ((null poly-1)
         poly-2)
        ((null poly-2)
         poly-1)
        (t (cons (+ (car poly-1) (car poly-2))
                 (poly-add (cdr poly-1) (cdr poly-2))))))
⇒ POLY-ADD

(poly-add '(0 1 2) '(5 4 3 2 1))
⇒ (5 5 5 2 1)

(poly-add '(5 4 3 2 1) '(0 1 2))
⇒ (5 5 5 2 1)
```

Notice the problem when you add two polynomials that are signed inverses.

```
(poly-add '(5 4 3) '(-5 -4 -3))
⇒ (0 0 0)
```

This is obviously not a simplified form. The exercises at the end of this section help to solve this problem.

Using `poly-add` as a guide, polynomial subtraction is easy. But the most recent solution to `poly-add` breaks down when subtracting two polynomials when the second has higher degree. The following illustrates the error:

```
     (0 1 7)
  -  (3 0 4 5 5)
  ----------------
     (0 1 7)
  -  (3 0 4)        append (5 5)
  ----------------
     (-3 1 3)       append (5 5)
  =  (-3 1 3 5 5)   <<< ERROR should be (-3 1 3 -5 -5)
```

When the second polynomial has higher degree, then each remaining coefficient must be inverted. Or you could change the sign on each element in the second polynomial and add the two polynomials. A better solution inverts the sign of the remaining coefficients before appending them to the coefficient list. `Poly-subtract` can be written with `invert-sign`, which changes the sign of all coefficients in a list. We then just change the operator in the `t` clause of the `cond` from addition to subtraction.

```
;;; Subtract two univariate polynomials that may be of
;;; different degree.

(defun poly-subtract (poly-1 poly-2)
  (cond ((and (null poly-1) (null poly-2))
         nil)
        ((null poly-1)
         (invert-sign poly-2))
        ((null poly-2)
         poly-1)
        (t (cons (- (car poly-1) (car poly-2))
                 (poly-subtract (cdr poly-1)
                                (cdr poly-2))))))
⇒ POLY-SUBTRACT
```

`Invert-sign` is a simple recursive function that constructs a new list with the sign of each element changed. Invoking unary minus on the element does change the sign.

```
;;; Invert the sign of the argument polynomial.
```

```
(defun invert-sign (polynomial)
  (if (null polynomial)
    nil
    (cons (- (car polynomial))
          (invert-sign (cdr polynomial)))))
⇒ INVERT-SIGN

(invert-sign '(1 2 -3))
⇒ (-1 -2 3)

(poly-subtract '(0 1 7) '(3 0 4 5 5))
⇒ (-3 1 3 -5 -5)

(poly-subtract '(3 0 4 5 5) '(0 1 7))
⇒ (3 -1 -3 5 5)
```

Differentiation of a univariate polynomial is relatively easy. The derivative of a sum of terms is the sum of the derivatives of each term. The derivative of a term cx^e with respect to x is ecx^{e-1}, where c is the coefficient and e is the exponent. The derivative of a constant is zero. This means that the degree of a polynomial is reduced by one when taking its derivative. Reducing the degree by one is trivial given the representation that we have chosen – we simply take the `cdr` of the list of coefficients.

`Poly-derivative` takes one argument, which is the polynomial, to differentiate. Since taking a derivative requires both the coefficient and the exponent, we need some way to provide the exponent. The exponent of the first element is zero, the next is one, and so on – the code must increment a value each time. To simulate an iteration construct we can pass an additional argument to the function that is incremented in each recursive call. So, implementation of `poly-derivative` requires an auxiliary function that takes an additional argument, the exponent. Using good programming style, the auxiliary function is called `poly-derivative-aux`. This function also must ignore the coefficient of the constant term. Thus, `poly-derivative-aux` is called with the `cdr` of the argument polynomial, along with an exponent value of one.

```
;;; Top level derivative function of a polynomial represented
;;; as a list of coefficients.

(defun poly-derivative (polynomial)
  (poly-derivative-aux (cdr polynomial) 1))
⇒ POLY-DERIVATIVE
```

`Poly-derivative-aux` uses the standard recursive format, calculating the derivative of the first coefficient in the polynomial. It then recurses with the rest of the list and the next exponent.

```
;;; Auxiliary derivative function that actually takes the
```

```
;;; derivative.  The first argument is the polynomial (with
;;; the constant coefficient removed) and the second is the
;;; exponent of the car of the polynomial. (THIS HAS A BUG)

(defun poly-derivative-aux (polynomial exponent)
  (if (null polynomial)
    nil
    (cons (* (car polynomial) exponent)
          (poly-derivative-aux (cdr polynomial)
                               (1+ exponent)))))
 ⇒ POLY-DERIVATIVE-AUX

(poly-derivative '(1 2 3))
 ⇒ (2 6)

(poly-derivative '(0 0 4))
 ⇒ (0 8)
```

These functions will not correctly process a polynomial that has only a single constant term. The result should be zero, but the result will be `nil`.

```
(poly-derivative '(5)) ; ERROR - result should be zero.
 ⇒ NIL
```

Therefore, the `poly-derivative` function must check to see if the argument polynomial is of degree zero. A simple check verifies that the length of the polynomial is one (or the `cdr` is `nil`). Checking that the `cdr` is `nil` is more efficient, since `length` scans the complete list.

```
;;; Modified poly-derivative, which checks for zero degree
;;; polynomial and returns a zero polynomial if found.
;;; Top level derivative function of a polynomial represented
;;; as a list of coefficients.

(defun poly-derivative (polynomial)
  (if (null (cdr polynomial))
    '(0)
    (poly-derivative-aux (cdr polynomial) 1)))
 ⇒ POLY-DERIVATIVE

(poly-derivative '(5))
 ⇒ (0)
```

The check for a zero degree polynomial is not exactly correct. It will not handle a polynomial that is disguised as a polynomial of a degree greater than zero, with trailing zero coefficients (perhaps the result of a polynomial addition or subtraction). The first two exercises of this section solve this potential problem. Also note that trailing zero coefficients won't affect any other part of the system.

When the final result is translated back to the external representation, any term with a zero coefficient is ignored.

Now that we've written the polynomial arithmetic functions, we can write the `manipulate` function to call each one. We assume that the function is given a single argument, which is a prefix expression whose `car` is the arithmetic operator (`+` for `poly-add`, `-` for `poly-subtract` and `df` for `poly-derivative`). The rest of the expression is the external prefix notation of the arguments. For example, sample calls to `manipulate` are:

```
(manipulate '(+ (+ (* 3 x) 4) (+ (** x 2) (* -4 x) 5)))
(manipulate '(df (+ (* 4 (** x 3)) (* -4 x) 6)))
```

`Manipulate` determines how many operands the function requires, converts them to the internal form, calls the appropriate arithmetic function, and converts the result back to external notation. We assume that only those operators defined above will be "manipulated."

```
;;; Perform the requested manipulation of the argument
;;; polynomials converting between the external and internal
;;; representation.

(defun manipulate (operation-and-polynomials)
  (let ((operand-1
          (external-to-internal
           (cadr operation-and-polynomials)))
         (operand-2
          (if (not (equal (car operation-and-polynomials)
                          'df))
            (external-to-internal
             (caddr operation-and-polynomials))
            nil)))
    (internal-to-external
     (cond ((equal (car operation-and-polynomials) '+)
            (poly-add operand-1 operand-2))
           ((equal (car operation-and-polynomials) '-)
            (poly-subtract operand-1 operand-2))
           (t (poly-derivative operand-1))))))
⇒ MANIPULATE

(manipulate '(+ (+ (* 3 x) 4) (+ (** x 2) (* -4 x) 5)))
⇒ (+ (** X 2) (* -1 X) 9)

(manipulate '(df (+ (* 4 (** x 3)) (* -4 x) 6)))
⇒ (+ (* 12 (** X 2)) -4)
```

This solution doesn't take advantage of *data abstraction*. Data abstraction is a powerful programming technique. It abstracts the representation of the data by hiding its access in small utility functions. Instead of directly calling operations like `car`, `cadr`, and `nth`, you use a function whose name describes the data element you wish to access. Hiding the structure can isolate the access code, letting you change the underlying representation without changing the invoking code. For example, in `manipulate`, the operation is the `car` of the argument. A function `operator` can simply take the `car` of its argument. `Operator` is then used to retrieve the operator. This allows you to change the invocation of `manipulate` without changing its code body – it isolates the changes to `operator`. For example, suppose you want to include the symbol for the variable used in the polynomial. This symbol now resides in the first position of the expressions instead of the operator, so `manipulate` is called as follows:

```
(manipulate '(x + (+ (* 3 x) 4) (+ (** x 2) (* -4 x) 5)))
(manipulate '(x df (+ (* 4 (** x 3)) (* -4 x) 6)))
```

`Operator` can be changed to access the `cadr` of the first element instead of the `car`. The third exercise of this section discusses changes to `manipulate` to utilize data abstraction.

EXERCISES

***4.9** Write a function that determines if the argument polynomial is of degree zero. It must verify that there is either no terms following the leading coefficient or if there are any terms, they are all zero. Incorporate your function into `poly-derivative`.

```
(zero-degreep '(55 0 0))
⇒ T
```

***4.10** Generalize `poly-add` and `poly-subtract` so they do not produce polynomials with any trailing zeros.

***4.11** Change `manipulate` to use data abstraction. Write three functions – `operator`, `first-operand`, and `second-operand`. Each takes one argument, which is the external representation of the polynomial and returns the appropriate operator or operand. You should make `second-operand` return `nil` when the operator is unary. Finally, modify the `manipulate` function to call these functions.

4.12 Change `manipulate` to call an auxiliary function that converts a list of external polynomials into a list of internal polynomials. Then, modify `manipulate` so it calls each arithmetic function and passes the arguments by extracting the appropriate operand from the list instead of binding each one to a local variable.

4.6 Data-Driven Programming

The `manipulate` function takes a very "hard-coded" approach to invoking each polynomial arithmetic function. "Hard-coded" means that the selection of which function to invoke and the actual invocation is coded into the control structures of the function. If we add a new unary operator, we have to change the `cond` expression whose result binds a value to `second-operand`. We would also have to add another case to the `cond` expression in the body. A new binary operator would only add another case to the same `cond` within the body. In either case, we must change `manipulate` in some way to accommodate the new operator.

In `Manipulate`, the selection of the function is determined by the operator in the argument *data*. Suppose we instead had a data structure that provided this mapping. `Manipulate` could then be modified to scan the structure, search for the operator that matches the argument data, and then invoke the associated function on the appropriate arguments (the number of arguments could also be encoded into the data structure). If the data structure were defined outside of the scope of `manipulate` then adding, removing, or changing the arithmetic operators would only modify the data structure without changing `manipulate` itself. Using the data to drive the flow of control is called data-driven programming. This results in highly modular code. Each new feature (in this case a new polynomial arithmetic operator) involves only the functions that perform the operation and the addition of a new mapping to the data structure.

One possible mapping data structure is an association list using `assoc` for the lookup. Once we have the function symbol, we can use `apply` to invoke the function. `Apply` takes a list of arguments, and so `manipulate` should convert the list of external polynomials into a list of internal polynomials. We will assume that the proper number of polynomial arguments will be supplied for each operation. We first define `list-external-to-internal` which accepts a list of polynomials in external notation and returns a list in internal form.

```
;;; Convert a list of external polynomials into a list of
;;; internal polynomials.

(defun list-external-to-internal (polynomials)
  (if (null polynomials)
    nil
    (cons (external-to-internal (car polynomials))
          (list-external-to-internal (cdr polynomials)))))
⇒ LIST-EXTERNAL-TO-INTERNAL
```

The association list that maps the operation into its associated function is introduced using `defvar`. We will initially assign it the `+` and `df` operators. After testing, we will add `-` to demonstrate the data-driven approach.

```
;; *Operators* is the polynomial operators used by
;; manipulate.
(defvar *operators*
  (list '(+ poly-add) '(df poly-derivative)))
⇒ *OPERATORS*
```

Finally, we define a new version of `manipulate` that uses the data-driven style of calling the appropriate polynomial arithmetic function. Not only is this easier to enhance, it is also much shorter.

```
;;; Perform the requested manipulation of the argument
;;; polynomials converting between the external and internal
;;; representation.

(defun manipulate (operation-and-polynomials)
  (internal-to-external
   (apply (cadr (assoc (car operation-and-polynomials)
                       *operators*))
          (list-external-to-internal
           (cdr operation-and-polynomials)))))
⇒ MANIPULATE

(manipulate '(+ (+ (* 3 x) 4) (+ (** x 2) (* -4 x) 5)))
⇒ (+ (** X 2) (* -1 X) 9)

(manipulate '(df (+ (* 4 (** x 3)) (* -4 x) 6)))
⇒ (+ (* 12 (** X 2)) -4)
```

Now we will add polynomial subtraction to the `*operators*` list and verify that we need not change `manipulate`.

```
;; Add (- poly-subtract) to the list of valid operators.
(setf *operators* (cons '(- poly-subtract) *operators*))
⇒ ((- POLY-SUBTRACT) (+ POLY-ADD) (DF POLY-DERIVATIVE))

(manipulate '(- (+ (* 3 x) 4) (+ (** x 2) (* -4 x) 5)))
⇒ (+ (* -1 (** X 2)) (* 7 X) -1)
```

EXERCISES

4.13 Define three functions – `add-operator`, `remove-operator`, and `change-operator` that add, remove, and change an operator and function name from the list stored in `*operators*`.

***4.14** Write `poly-multiply` that will multiply two polynomials. It may be advantageous to develop a simplified version that multiplies two first-degree polynomials and produces a polynomial of second degree. Add `poly-multiply` and the corresponding `*` operator to `*operators*`. The product of two polynomials (sum of terms) is defined as the sum of the products of each term from the first polynomial and each term from the second. The product of two terms ax^i and bx^j is defined to be the product of the coefficients and the sum of the exponents: abx^{i+j}. For example:

$$(ax^2 + bx + c)(dx + e) = (adx^3 + bdx^2 + cdx) + (aex^2 + bex + ce)$$

which can be simplified to

$$adx^3 + (bd + ae)x^2 + (cd + be)x + ce$$

The following illustrates the multiplication process using the internal representation (notice the left padding of zeros):

```
      (1 2 3)
*     (3 4 5)
  ----------------
      (3 6 9)
      (0 4 8 12)
+     (0 0 5 10 15)
  ----------------
      (3 10 22 22 15)
```

4.7 Summary

The development of a simple algebra system capable of performing addition, subtraction, and differentiation has been presented. The LISP style of dividing the task into many small manageable parts, each with an associated function, is quite appropriate and permits rapid development of LISP software. The interactive nature of LISP permits incremental testing and rapid development. The data-driven programming paradigm has been demonstrated as allowing the modification and enhancement of existing code without changing many functions. This style aids in the maintenance of existing software.

Chapter Exercises

***1.** Write `poly-integral` that returns the result of integrating the argument polynomial. The following defines polynomial integration:

$$\int ax^n + bx^{n-1} + ... + k \Rightarrow \frac{a}{n+1}x^{n+1} + \frac{b}{n}x^n + ...kx + C$$

C is an arbitrary constant, but for our purposes, it will be zero. Add the function `poly-integral` and the operator `int` to the list of available operations.

```
(poly-integral '(3 4 9))
⇒ (0 3 2 3)
```

***2.** Write a function to perform synthetic division upon two polynomials. Assume that the polynomials are evenly divisible. Synthetic division is performed essentially the same way "grade school" division of integers is performed. The following illustrates the process, dividing the polynomial $6x^2 - 11x - 10$ by $3x + 2$.

$$3x + 2 \,\overline{\big)\, 6x^2 - 11x - 10}$$

$$\begin{array}{r|l} & \quad\quad 2x \\ \hline 3x+2 & 6x^2 - 11x - 10 \\ & 6x^2 + 4x \\ \hline \end{array}$$

$$\begin{array}{r|l} & \quad\quad 2x \\ \hline 3x+2 & 6x^2 - 11x - 10 \\ & 6x^2 + 4x \\ \hline & \quad\; - 15x - 10 \end{array}$$

$$\begin{array}{r|l} & \quad\quad 2x - 5 \\ \hline 3x+2 & 6x^2 - 11x - 10 \\ & 6x^2 + 4x \\ \hline & \quad\; - 15x - 10 \\ & \quad\; - 15x - 10 \\ \hline & \quad\quad\quad\quad\; 0 \end{array}$$

The key to the division process is that the coefficient of each resulting term is chosen so that it exactly cancels the leading term of the dividend.

```
(poly-division '(-10 -11 6) '(2 3))
⇒ (-5 2)
```

3. Modify the previous function to process non-evenly divisible polynomials. This implies that a remainder will also have to be returned. Thus, the result will have to be a two-element list of answer and remainder. This model doesn't quite fit with the scheme used in **manipulate**, since such a list couldn't be readily converted back into an external representation. Modify **manipulate** so the resulting remainder is included as part of the constant term. For example:

$$\frac{2x^2 + 4x + 4}{x + 1} = 2x + 2 \textit{ Remainder } 2$$

```
(manipulate '(/ (+ (* 2 (** X 2)) (* 4 X) 4)
                (+ (* 2 X) 2)))
⇒ (+ X (1 R 2))
```

5 OBJECTS

THIS CHAPTER INTRODUCES the topic of object-oriented programming. Currently, there is no standard object system defined for Common LISP, although the Common LISP Object System (CLOS) is currently being specified. However, since some objects system is needed here, a pedagogical one will be used (the generic Common LISP code for the system is in Appendix A). Most of the object systems are similar, and so if you know one you essentially know the others. Our objects system is syntactically similar to Common Objects developed at the Hewlett-Packard Research Labs [39].

In this and the next four chapters, we develop an expert system programming shell. An expert system is a program that demonstrates some level of human expertise. An expert system shell is a program that helps build an expert system. Expert systems are typically composed of facts, rules, and an inference engine. The facts are the static knowledge. The rules are *if/then* specifications. The inference engine combines facts and rules to derive new facts. Objects are a natural structure for the knowledge base. In this chapter, we develop a genealogical knowledge base using objects.

5.1 Objects

Objects are similar in concept to programming language data types. A data type defines the techniques for representing and manipulating one kind of data. For example, the floating point data type might specify double-precision notation for numbers. It also specifies the set of operations applicable to these numbers (for example, addition, subtraction, multiplication, division, and others). Thus, a data type can be thought of as a template for representing a data value, along with the operations to manipulate the data. An instance of the data type can actually be manipulated. For example, `3.14159` is an instance of a floating point number data type.

Objects are essentially user-defined data types. Objects combine the concepts of data and functions into a single entity as would a data type. The template description is often called a *class*, as in Smalltalk [16] and CommonLoops [6], or a *flavor*, as on the LISP machines [45]. In this objects system we call it a *type*. An instance of a type is called an object. The operations defined for each type are called *methods*. They manipulate objects and are the only link to the internal state of an object. The internal state of an object is a set of data values. Each value in the set is named for easy access. These name-value relationships are known as *slots*. The value of a slot may be any valid datum, including an object. An association list functions similarly and can demonstrate a very simple object system.

Suppose that we want to create a clown type. A clown has a name, a shoe size, and an expression. All clowns have these characteristics but with possibly different values. You can write a function that simply takes values for each of the characteristics and returns an association list that is the clown object.

```
;;; Create a clown object from the characteristics, name,
;;; shoe-size, and expression.

(defun make-clown-object (name shoe-size expression)
  (list (list 'name name)
        (list 'shoe-size shoe-size)
        (list 'expression expression)))
 ⇒ MAKE-CLOWN-OBJECT
```

This function can now be used to create any clown.

```
(setf freddy (make-clown-object 'freddy 27 'frowning))
 ⇒ ((NAME FREDDY) (SHOE-SIZE 27) (EXPRESSION FROWNING))

(setf barney (make-clown-object 'barney 4 'smiling))
 ⇒ ((NAME BARNEY) (SHOE-SIZE 4) (EXPRESSION SMILING))
```

These expressions define two clowns `freddy` and `barney` with different characteristics. We can now write a function (called a method in object terminology), which takes a clown object and returns the mood of a clown. It takes one argument, which is the object to determine the mood. It should return a three-element list containing the name of the clown, the symbol `is`, and the `expression` in that order.

```
;;; Return the mood of a clown.

(defun mood (clown)
  (list (cadr (assoc 'name clown))
        'is
        (cadr (assoc 'expression clown))))
 ⇒ MOOD

(mood freddy)
```

```
 ⇒ (FREDDY IS FROWNING)

(mood barney)
 ⇒ (BARNEY IS SMILING)
```

Another method you can write tickles the clown. When you tickle a clown, he or she starts to smile, thus changing his or her expression.

```
;;; Tickle a clown and change the expression slot to be
;;; smiling.

(defun tickle (clown)
  (cons '(expression smiling) clown))
 ⇒ TICKLE

(setf freddy (tickle freddy))
 ⇒ ((EXPRESSION SMILING) (NAME FREDDY) (SHOE-SIZE 27)
 ⇒  (EXPRESSION FROWNING))

(mood freddy)
 ⇒ (FREDDY IS SMILING)
```

As a final example, we can write a method to determine which of two clowns has bigger feet. The method compares the two values and returns the name of the clown with the largest feet.

```
;;; Compare the shoe-sizes of two clowns and return the name
;;; of the one with the biggest feet.

(defun biggest-feet (clown1 clown2)
  (if (> (cadr (assoc 'shoe-size clown1))
         (cadr (assoc 'shoe-size clown2)))
    (cadr (assoc 'name clown1))
    (cadr (assoc 'name clown2))))
 ⇒ BIGGEST-FEET

(biggest-feet freddy barney)
 ⇒ FREDDY
```

The access to the slots of an object is limited to method invocation. This is an important feature. The methods that access an object, rather than its internal state, determine the characteristics of an object. This is the characteristic important for data abstraction. It allows the internal state to be modified without affecting external programs that reference the object. As long as the interface to the methods remains unchanged, external programs don't require changes. Programs written with objects are easier to maintain because changes can be isolated. Figure 5.1 illustrates how external programs can't penetrate the barrier to access objects, while methods can.

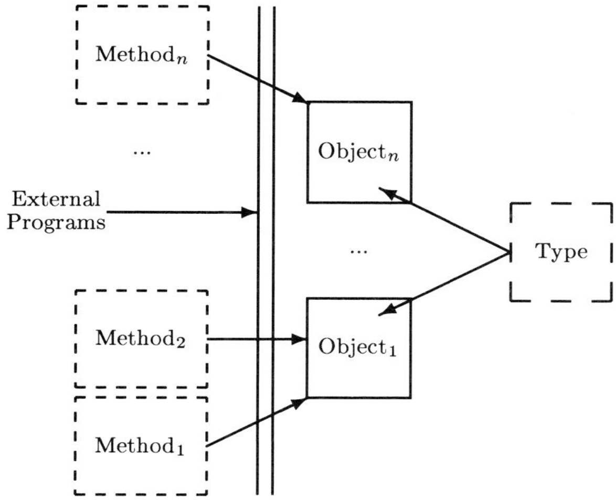

Figure 5.1 A Type, Object, and Methods

EXERCISES

5.1 Using our association list definition of an object, define two methods to retrieve the `name` and `shoe-size` slots of a clown.

***5.2** Write a method to give a clown a new set of shoes. Don't bother to change the `shoe-size` slot if the new shoe size is the same as the old shoe size.

***5.3** The problem with the association list representation for an object is that any time a change is made to the internal state, the modified association list must be returned and reassigned to the variable representing the object. Suggest an alternative that would eliminate this problem.

5.2 A Simple Object System

We will implement a genealogical knowledge base that determines genealogical relationships between people. Initially only the name, mother, father, and sex of each person will be supplied. The system then determines the relationships. For example, it should determine who are brothers, if David is Jimmy's uncle, and so on. A single object type, `person`, defines the characteristics of each person. The `person` type should include slots for each of the initialized values and each of the pertinent relationships. The `define-type` function defines a new type. The syntax is:

```
(define-type Type-Name slot*)
```

where *slot* is defined as

slot ←(`:var` *slot-name option**) | *type-option*

A type definition includes a name and the specification of the slots. Each slot specification follows the keyword `:var` and is then placed within parentheses. A keyword is a symbol beginning with a colon – it is treated specially by the LISP system. A keyword indicates, in this case, that what follows is the slot name and specification. The *option* isn't necessary, but can enhance the definition of a slot. One important slot option is (`:init` *expression*), which specifies an initial value for the slot. When the object is created, the initial value is computed and assigned to the slot. When an `:init` option is not specified the slot's initial value is `nil`.

Each person has the four slots mentioned previously. We must also add some other slots for determining relationships. For our purposes, two additional slots are parent and sibling. These will be initialized to the symbol `?` to indicate that the relationship is unknown. You want to distinguish between not knowing the contents of a slot and knowing that a slot contains nothing. For example, if someone has no brothers or sisters, then the sibling slot contains `nil` to indicate none, while an unknown sibling is indicated with ?. Proper programming practice places the unknown value in a global symbol so the programs can use abstraction when testing for an unknown slot.

```
;; *unknown* is used to indicate that a slot has an unknown
;; value.
(defvar *unknown* '?)
 ⇒ *UNKNOWN*
```

Using this information, we can define our first type, `person`.

```
;;; Define the person type.

(define-type person
  (:var name)
  (:var mother)
  (:var father)
  (:var sex)
  (:var parent (:init *unknown*))
  (:var sibling (:init *unknown*))
  )
 ⇒ PERSON
```

In this example, `name`, `mother`, `father`, `sex`, `parent`, and `sibling` are all slots, which, when provided with values, specificially describe a particular person object.

A type is only a template for an object's characteristics. The function `make-instance` actually creates an object instance. It takes the name of the type and returns an object instance. *Initialization* specifications are optional and allow the specification of initial values to the slots.

(make-instance *type-name initialization**)

Using this function, we can create some person objects.

```
(setf bob (make-instance 'person))
 ⇒ #<Object PERSON>

(setf jimmy (make-instance 'person))
 ⇒ #<Object PERSON>
```

Notice the printed representation of an object. It tells you the type of the object, but not which object instance.

None of the slots in the above person objects have associated values (except for those that have been initialized), and there are no methods to gain access to the slots. In this case, you can only manipulate the entire object.

```
;; Create a list of all of the person objects defined so far.
(setf all-people (list bob jimmy))
 ⇒ (#<Object PERSON> #<Object PERSON>)

;; Access the first person.
(car all-people)
 ⇒ #<Object PERSON>
```

This doesn't tell you whether the `car` of the list is `bob` or `jimmy`. We must write some methods that allow access to the slots in an object.

EXERCISES

***5.4** Define a type for a cat and another for a dog. Make sure that you include enough slots to distinguish between the two.

***5.5** Since a slot may contain anything, how could you construct an object which has a slot containing another object?

5.6 Using `define-type`, define the clown type as specified in the previous section.

5.3 Method Definition

In the clown example, we created methods by writing LISP functions. True method definition is a little more involved. A method is defined with the expression `define-method`. Its syntax is like `defun`, except the first argument is a two-element list. The first element is the type that is the basis for the method, and the second element is the name of the method. The second argument to `define-method` is the list of arguments (which may be empty). Following the argument list are the S-expressions that make up the body of the method.

> `(define-method (`*type-name method-name*`) (`*argument**`)` *S-expression**`)`

A method performs some operation on an object. The operation might return some information or change the internal state of an object. So, in a method we need to gain access to the slots of an object. In this object system, any slot may be reached by mentioning the slot name like a variable. Essentially, all of the slots of an object are implicitly defined in the body of the method. `Setf` stores a value in a slot.

> `(setf` *slot-name value*`)`

The following are two simple methods that set and examine the `father` slot of a `person` object.

```
;;; Method to set the father slot of a person.

(define-method (person set-father) (new-value)
  (setf father new-value))
 ⇒ SET-FATHER

;;; Return the value of the father slot of a person.

(define-method (person father) ()
  father)
 ⇒ FATHER
```

Calling a method is like calling a function. The name of the method comes first. Next is the object to which the method is applied. The remaining arguments are the method parameters.

> `(`*method-name object S-expression**`)`

```
;; Set the father of bob to be the symbol jim.
```

```
(set-father bob 'jim)
⇒ JIM
```

This is a little cumbersome since you must remember the name of the method which stores a value into the slot, along with the name of the method which retrieves a value. Common LISP cleans this up with `defsetf`. Recall that `setf` is used for assignment. `Defsetf` is an extension of `setf` which include new forms of assignment.

(`defsetf` *accessor-symbol function-symbol*)

This defines the following `setf` form:

(`setf` (*accessor-symbol destination*) *value*)

Accessor-symbol tells `setf` which *function-symbol* to call. In this case, we are setting the `father` slot, so a reasonable choice for *accessor-symbol* is `father`. The *function-symbol* is the previously defined function, `set-father`. Thus, the expression:

```
(setf (father bob) 'jim)
```

invokes `set-father`, passing it `bob` and the symbol `jim`. This assigns `jim` to the `father` slot of `bob`.

```
;; Define a setf form for set-father.
(defsetf father set-father)
⇒ FATHER

;; Now test it on Jimmy.
(setf (father jimmy) 'jim)
⇒ JIM
```

The next step invokes the accessor methods to verify the assignments.

```
;; Invoke the accessor methods.
(father bob)
⇒ JIM

(father jimmy)
⇒ JIM
```

Let's see what happens when we try to gain access to the father slot of the first element of the `all-people` list.

```
;; Find out the father of the first person in the all-people
;; list.
(father (car all-people))
⇒ JIM
```

It returned Bob's father as defined in the call to `set-father`. This illustrates a very important feature of objects. Even though an object may be passed from variable to variable, it always maintains its internal state. Therefore, the first element of `all-people` and the object stored in the variable `bob` are the same object; changing the internal state of one changes the internal state of the other.

```
;; Make the fred symbol access the jimmy object.
(setf fred jimmy)
 ⇒ #<Object PERSON>

;; Verify that the object maintains the state and not the
;; symbol.
(father fred)
 ⇒ JIM
```

This example illustrates that objects maintain their state when manipulated as entire entities. Invoking a method is the only way to effect a change.

Writing these simple methods is somewhat time consuming, so the object system lets you automatically generate these methods. When defining a type you may define which slots may be retrieved (`:gettable`), assigned (`:settable`), or initialized when an instance is created (`:initable`). These methods are generated automatically by placing the appropriate slot option (`:gettable`, `:settable`, or `:initable`) within the slot specification. For a `:gettable` slot `foo`, the system generates the `foo` method and with a `:settable` slot `foo`, the system permits `setf` access to the slot as follows:

```
(setf (foo object) value)
```

These symbols with a leading : indicate key words and don't need to be quoted. When a person object is created, its name, mother, father, and sex slots' values will be specified. Therefore, these must be `:initable`. These slots cannot be changed and therefore are not `:settable`. The remaining slots, `parent` and `sibling`, cannot be `:initable`, but must be `:settable`. All slots must be `:gettable`.

```
;;; Define the person type to automatically create the
;;; various methods.
(define-type person
  (:var name :gettable :initable)
  (:var mother :gettable :initable)
  (:var father :gettable :initable)
  (:var sex :gettable :initable)
  (:var parent (:init *unknown*) :gettable :settable)
  (:var sibling (:init *unknown*) :gettable :settable)
  )
 ⇒ PERSON
```

When all slots are either `:gettable`, `:settable`, or `:initable` then a type option can be used. The type option specifies that all slots have a particular characteristic, in this case, `:all-gettable`, `:all-settable`, or `:all-initable`. Type options are placed at the same nesting level as the slot specification. They may be placed in any order – they don't have to follow the slot definitions. The `person` type could be created as follows:

```
;;; Define the person type to automatically create the
;;; various methods.

(define-type person
  (:var name :initable)
  (:var mother :initable)
  (:var father :initable)
  (:var sex :initable)
  (:var parent (:init *unknown*) :settable)
  (:var sibling (:init *unknown*) :settable)
  :all-gettable
  )
 ⇒ PERSON
```

`:Initable` lets you specify initial values to `make-instance` for any of the `:initable` slots. Initial values are provided by listing the instance variable name (using the `:` keyword form) and value as alternating arguments to the call on `make-instance`. If a slot is `:initable` and has an initial value from the type definition, then an initial value in the `make-instance` call overrides the type definition.

```
;; Create bob with more information in the object.
(setf bob (make-instance 'person
                  :name 'bob :mother 'joanne :father 'jim
                  :sex 'male))
 ⇒ #<Object PERSON>

(setf jimmy (make-instance 'person
                  :name 'jimmy :mother 'joanne :father 'jim
                  :sex 'male))
 ⇒ #<Object PERSON>
```

With the new methods already defined, we can gain access to `bob` as follows:

```
;; Access and update some of the bob slots.
(father bob)
 ⇒ JIM

;; Verify that parent is unknown.
(parent bob)
```

```
 ⇒ ?

;; Change the parent slot to include Jim.
(setf (parent bob) 'jim)
 ⇒ JIM

;; Verify that parent now contains Jim.
(parent bob)
 ⇒ JIM
```

More complicated methods may require an additional argument that is another object. For example, suppose you want to write a method that determines if two persons have the same father and mother. The comparison is simple, but you might wonder how to gain access to the second object. Access to the slots of the first object is simple – you just mention the name. Access to the slots of the second object requires the same syntax as method invocation. Whatever argument name that is chosen for the second object is passed to the method so the information can be retrieved. Thus, if `other-person` is the name of the second object, `(father other-person)` is used to retrieve the value in the father slot.

```
;;; Compare two persons and determine if they have the same
;;; father and mother.

(define-method (person compare-parents) (other-person)
  (and (equal father (father other-person))
       (equal mother (mother other-person))))
 ⇒ COMPARE-PARENTS

(compare-parents bob jimmy)
 ⇒ T
```

As you use the object system, you will eventually need to be able to examine an object more closely. If you happen to have an object and wish to know the values of its slots, you would have to invoke the appropriate methods. An easier way is to use the `describe` function for this debugging. `Describe` takes an object as an argument and prints all of the slots and the current values.

(describe *object*)

```
(describe bob)
 ⇒  SIBLING: ?
 ⇒  PARENT: ?
 ⇒  SEX: MALE
 ⇒  FATHER: JIM
 ⇒  MOTHER: JOANNE
 ⇒  NAME: BOB
```

```
⇒ NIL
```

Another useful debugging tool is the :printable slot option. When a slot is designated as :printable, then that slot and current value is printed whenever the object is printed. There is also a corresponding :all-printable to designate that all slots should be printed. This tool helps you to distinguish the various objects in a system. For example, we redefine **person** to have the **name** slot printable.

```
(define-type person
  (:var name :initable :printable)
  (:var mother :initable)
  (:var father :initable)
  (:var sex :initable)
  (:var parent (:init *unknown*) :settable)
  (:var sibling (:init *unknown*) :settable)
  :all-gettable
  )
⇒ PERSON
```

Notice what happens when we create a couple of instances.

```
;; Create bob with more information in the object.
(setf bob (make-instance 'person
                   :name 'bob :mother 'joanne :father 'jim
                   :sex 'male))
⇒ #<Object PERSON NAME=BOB>

(setf jimmy (make-instance 'person
                   :name 'jimmy :mother 'joanne :father 'jim
                   :sex 'male))
⇒ #<Object PERSON NAME=JIMMY>
```

EXERCISES

***5.7** What is the difference between the method defined with the option :gettable, the option :all-gettable, and defined with a method that simply returns the value of the slot?

***5.8** Make sure that the type definition for dogs in the exercises in the previous section includes a slot for tricks. Define the following three methods on dogs:

1. **Train**, takes one argument, which is the name of the trick that you just trained the dog to do. It should add the trick to the slot of all of the dogs tricks. It shouldn't bother to add the trick if the dog already knows how to do the trick.
2. **Trickp**, takes one argument, which is the name of a trick. It is a predicate to tell if the dog knows how to do the trick.
3. **Showtime**, takes no arguments. This method returns an arbitrary list of all of

the tricks that the dog knows how to do. One way to perform this task is to randomly index into the list of tricks and return a list of the remaining elements at the front and the initial elements on the end.

5.9 Define each of the clown methods illustrated earlier with `define-method`. Those methods include `mood`, `tickle`, and `biggest-feet`. Define both `freddy` and `barney` and verify that your methods produce the same answers as the functions. Invoke `describe` on your objects.

5.4 Advanced Methods

The information hiding capability is an important feature of objects. It means that the characteristics of a particular object lie in its external behavior – its response to method invocation. This feature permits changes to the internal representation of an object without affecting any programs that manipulate the objects, as long as the methods are changed as well. Software is easier to maintain if you can localize changes to a type definition and its associated methods.

Suppose we realize that maintaining a separate parent slot is a waste of resources. The parent of a person is always the person's mother and father (assuming parent means biological parent). So, invocation of the `parent` method should return the list of mother and father and not the parent's slot value. The first step is to redefine `person` to exclude the `parent` slot.

```
;;; Person without an explicit parent slot.

(define-type person
  (:var name :initable)
  (:var mother :initable)
  (:var father :initable)
  (:var sex :initable)
  (:var sibling (:init *unknown*) :settable)
  :all-gettable
  )
 ⇒ PERSON
```

When a type is redefined, all the associated instances must be redefined. This is because the redefinition changes the slots, invalidating the old slot definitions. Any methods defined for the type must also be redefined for the same reason.

```
(setf bob (make-instance 'person
                         :name 'bob :mother 'joanne :father 'jim
                         :sex 'male))
 ⇒ #<Object PERSON>
```

The parent method can now be defined to return a list of the values of the mother and father slots.

```
;;; A modified parent method, that doesn't use the parent
;;; slot.

(define-method (person parent) ()
  (list mother father))
 ⇒ PARENT

;; Now invoke the parent method.
(parent bob)
 ⇒ (JOANNE JIM)
```

Notice how effectively changes are localized – any functions that needed access to the parent slot don't require changes.

In this genealogical example, relationships between people can be bidirectional. For example, if Bob has a sibling Patty, then Patty also has a sibling Bob. It would be useful to maintain this linkage between objects. We can write a new set-sibling method that defines this relationship. So, when Bob is stored into the sibling slot of Patty, the method also stores Patty into Bob's sibling slot. The best way to accomplish the second store is to invoke the newly defined set-sibling method. It is easy enough to just write the definition of this method as follows:

```
;;; Set the sibling slot of the object to be the argument.
;;; Then set the sibling slot of the argument to be the name
;;; of the object.
;;; BUGGY VERSION

(define-method (person set-sibling) (new-sibling)
  (setf sibling new-sibling)
  (set-sibling new-sibling name)
  new-sibling)
 ⇒ SET-SIBLING
```

The problem with this method is that it will loop indefinitely setting the sibling slots to the values already stored there. If the slot already has the correct value, you shouldn't change it or the sibling.

```
;;; Set the sibling slot of the object to be the argument.
;;; Then set the sibling slot of the argument to be the name
;;; of the object.
;;; STILL A BUGGY VERSION

(define-method (person set-sibling) (new-sibling)
  (cond ((not (equal sibling new-sibling))
```

```
          (setf sibling new-sibling)
          (set-sibling new-sibling name)))
   new-sibling)
 ⇒ SET-SIBLING
```

Calling this method with bob should now work.

```
(set-sibling bob 'patty)

!!!!! Error: PATTY is not a known object,
      invoked with method SET-SIBLING
```

The problem is that the recursive call to set-sibling gets the symbol patty and not the patty object. The patty object doesn't even currently exist after the new definition of the person data type. One solution is to invoke set-sibling passing it the object instead of the symbol. This is acceptable, but it affects the slot access – sibling would return the object and not the name. Another solution is to get the object from a symbol. In the previous examples, we have assigned the person instance to the name of the object. Thus, the symbol bob actually contains the object itself. Typing bob to LISP causes the symbol to be read, evaluated, and the result printed.

```
;;; Get the value of bob.
bob
 ⇒ #<Object PERSON>
```

But, if we have only the symbol bob, we can still get at the value of the symbol via the symbol-value function. It takes one argument, which must be a symbol and returns the value of that symbol.

(symbol-value *symbol*)

```
;; Quote returns the symbol.
'bob
 ⇒ BOB

(symbol-value 'bob)
 ⇒ #<Object PERSON>
```

Notice in the following that using symbol-value is like indirection in assembly language programming.

```
;; Jims-brother is set to the symbol bob.
(setf jims-brother 'bob)
 ⇒ BOB

;; Check the value of jims-brother.
```

```
jims-brother
 ⇒ BOB

;; Do the indirection.
(symbol-value jims-brother)
 ⇒ #<Object PERSON>

;; Verify that this object is actually bob, by using the name
;; method.
(name (symbol-value jims-brother))
 ⇒ BOB
```

With symbol-value we can write a method that updates the sibling's slot.

```
;;; Set the sibling slot of the object to be the argument.
;;; Then set the sibling slot of the argument to be the name
;;; of the object.
;;; YET ANOTHER BUGGY VERSION

(define-method (person set-sibling) (new-sibling)
  (cond ((not (equal sibling new-sibling))
         (setf sibling new-sibling)
         (set-sibling (symbol-value new-sibling) name)))
  new-sibling)
 ⇒ SET-SIBLING

;; Remake bob with an empty sibling slot.
(setf bob (make-instance 'person
                 :name 'bob :mother 'joanne :father 'jim
                 :sex 'male))
 ⇒ #<Object PERSON>

;; Set the sibling slot.
(set-sibling bob 'patty)

!!!!! Error: The symbol PATTY has no value.
  Condition signaled in: SYMBOL-VALUE.
```

The problem here is that we forgot to assign the patty instance to patty. So, we need to enhance the definition of set-sibling to check that the symbol has a value. This can be accomplished with the LISP predicate boundp. It takes a symbol and determines if it currently has a value; in LISP terminology, having a value means that it is *bound*.

(boundp *symbol*)

```
(boundp 'bob)
 ⇒ T

(boundp 'patty)
 ⇒ NIL
```

We also need the predicate `objectp` to check to see if the argument is actually an object.

(objectp *S-expression*)

```
(objectp bob)
 ⇒ T

;; Check patty.
(objectp patty)

!!!!! Error: The symbol PATTY has no value.
  Condition signaled in: SYMBOL-VALUE.
```

The last check indicates that we must test for `boundp` before checking to see if the value is actually an object.

Notice, that when the sibling is not bound, or not an object, then we simply return an error symbol without setting anything. This guarantees that our knowledge base remains consistent.

```
;;; When assigning a value to the sibling slot of a person,
;;; the sibling object must have its sibling updated.  Name
;;; is the name slot within the person object.  If the
;;; sibling isn't a valid object, then we return the symbol
;;; error-sibling-not-an-object.

(define-method (person set-sibling) (new-sibling)
  (cond ((not (equal sibling new-sibling))
         (cond ((and (boundp new-sibling)
                     (objectp (symbol-value new-sibling)))
                (setf sibling new-sibling)
                (set-sibling (symbol-value new-sibling) name)
                ;; Return the name of the new-sibling
                new-sibling)
               (t 'error-sibling-not-an-object)))))
 ⇒ SET-SIBLING

;; Remake bob with an empty sibling slot.
(setf bob (make-instance 'person
```

```
                  :name 'bob :mother 'joanne :father 'jim
                  :sex 'male))
⇒ #<Object PERSON>

;; Create Patty with all of the information present.
(setf patty (make-instance 'person
                  :name 'patty :mother 'joanne :father 'jim
                  :sex 'female))
⇒ #<Object PERSON>

;; Test the new method.
(sibling patty)
⇒ ?

(sibling bob)
⇒ ?

(set-sibling bob 'patty)
⇒ PATTY

(sibling patty)
⇒ BOB

(sibling bob)
⇒ PATTY
```

Finally, it may be useful to determine the type of a particular object. The function `object-type` takes an object and returns its type.

(`object-type` *S-expression*)

```
;; Determine the type of the bob object.
(object-type bob)
⇒ PERSON
```

EXERCISES

***5.10** The earlier definition of the **parent** method has the problem that if the father or mother slots do not have values, then a list is returned with embedded **nils**. Modify the method to check for these possibilities, and return a list with only one parent if defined or return **nil** when no parent is defined.

***5.11** Add two slots to the **person** type: **brother** and **sister**. Write the methods **set-brother** and **set-sister** that update the brother and sister slots in a manner similar to **set-sibling** above. Remember that if Bob's sister is Patty, then Patty's brother is Bob (so your method must use the **sex** slot in determining the correct action to take).

5.12 Enhance `set-sibling`, `set-brother` and `set-sister` to allow more than one relation, maintained as a list. Each `set-` method should add the relative to the list and update the link. Also write `remove-sibling`, `remove-brother`, and `remove-sister` to remove a relative from the list.

5.5 Accessing Self

Within the body of a method we can get at any of the instance variables defined for a particular type. Sometimes you need to invoke another method on the object manipulated in the method definition. This is done with the symbol `self`, which is bound within the method body to the current object. Any valid method can be called by invoking the method with `self`.

Suppose that we are interested in the genetics of the persons in the knowledge base and could somehow predict the traits of the offspring given the traits of the parents. These traits could include hair color, eye color, and blood type. First, we write a method for each trait to determine if that trait is dominant or recessive.

```
;;; The person type, now with fields of traits.

(define-type person
  (:var name :initable)
  (:var mother :initable)
  (:var father :initable)
  (:var sex :initable)
  (:var sibling (:init *unknown*) :settable)
  (:var hair-color :initable)
  (:var eye-color :initable)
  (:var blood-type :initable)
  :all-gettable
  )
 ⇒ PERSON

;;; Determine whether the hair-color is dominant or
;;; recessive.

(define-method (person gene-hair-color) ()
  (if (or (equal hair-color 'brown)
          (equal hair-color 'black))
     'dominant
     'recessive))
 ⇒ GENE-HAIR-COLOR
```

The member function makes writing this particular method much easier.

```
;;; Determine whether the hair-color is dominant or
;;; recessive.

(define-method (person gene-hair-color) ()
  (if (member hair-color '(brown black))
    'dominant
    'recessive))
 ⇒ GENE-HAIR-COLOR

;;; Similar method for eye-color.

(define-method (person gene-eye-color) ()
  (if (member eye-color '(brown blue))
    'dominant
    'recessive))
 ⇒ GENE-EYE-COLOR

;;; Finally a similar method for blood type.

(define-method (person gene-blood-type) ()
  (if (equal blood-type 'rh-positive)
    'dominant
    'recessive))
 ⇒ GENE-BLOOD-TYPE
```

With these methods as the base, we write a method that determines if there are more dominant than recessive genes. If so, the method can classify the person as dominant. The trick is to count the number of dominant and recessive genes. One way is with a set of nested calls to and and or. A majority occurs when two of the three are dominant. Notice that this method must invoke the previous three methods and use the symbol self to refer to the object that is being operated upon.

```
;;; Determine whether the person is dominant or recessive.
;;; Dominant occurs when there are more dominant genes than
;;; recessive.

(define-method (person gene-summary) ()
  (if (or (and (equal (gene-hair-color self) 'dominant)
               (equal (gene-eye-color self) 'dominant))
          (and (equal (gene-hair-color self) 'dominant)
               (equal (gene-blood-type self) 'dominant))
          (and (equal (gene-eye-color self) 'dominant)
               (equal (gene-blood-type self) 'dominant)))
```

```
        'dominant
        'recessive))
  ⇒ GENE-SUMMARY
```

This is a solution, but is an excessive amount of code. It would also be difficult to modify if another gene were included in the person type. A proper solution can be found if you reread the previous paragraph. Notice that it says: *The trick is to count the number of dominant and recessive genes.* The key to this sentence is that the method must *count* the number of dominant genes. So, we need a numeric operation instead of a symbolic one. LISP programmers, enamored with symbolic computation, sometimes lose perspective and use symbolic methods where numeric ones would be more appropriate. In this case, a method for counting the dominant and recessive genes would be more appropriate.

An interesting solution uses apply. Each of the gene- methods could return a numeric value, 0 to represent recessive and 1 to represent dominant. Then, adding up the results and comparing the sum against two would solve the gene-summary method. Apply can be used by calling + on the result of each of the gene- method. The first step is to redefine each of the gene- methods.

```
;; The values denoting recessive and dominate genes.
(defvar *recessive* 0)
 ⇒ *RECESSIVE*

(defvar *dominant* 1)
 ⇒ *DOMINANT*

;;; Determine whether the hair-color is dominant (1) or
;;; recessive (0).

(define-method (person gene-hair-color) ()
  (if (member hair-color '(brown black))
    *dominant*
    *recessive*))
 ⇒ GENE-HAIR-COLOR

;;; Similar method for eye-color.

(define-method (person gene-eye-color) ()
  (if (member eye-color '(brown blue))
    *dominant*
    *recessive*))
 ⇒ GENE-EYE-COLOR

;;; Finally a similar method for blood type.

(define-method (person gene-blood-type) ()
  (if (equal blood-type 'rh-positive)
```

```
    *dominant*
    *recessive*))
 ⇒ GENE-BLOOD-TYPE
```

Now, redefine gene-summary to use apply.

```
;;; Apply version of gene-summary method.

(define-method (person gene-summary) ()
  (if (>= (apply '+ (gene-hair-color self)
                    (gene-eye-color self)
                    (gene-blood-type self)
                    nil)
           2)
      'dominant
      'recessive))
 ⇒ GENE-SUMMARY

;; Create a bob instance and test the gene-summary.
(setf bob (make-instance 'person
                    :name 'bob :mother 'joanne :father 'jim
                    :sex 'male :hair-color 'brown
                    :eye-color 'blue :blood-type 'rh-positive))
 ⇒ #<Object PERSON>

(gene-summary bob)
 ⇒ DOMINANT
```

EXERCISES

***5.13** One problem with this solution is that adding another gene requires a modification to the **gene-summary** method. Change the **person** type, so that instead of defining each gene as an element of the type, there is only one slot, called **genes**. **Genes** contains an association list of the name of the gene and the recessive or dominant value. Write the method **gene-mapping** that accesses the **genes** slot and returns a list with a **0** or a **1** for each gene. Finally modify **gene-summary** so it invokes **gene-mapping** and determines if the majority of the genes are dominant.

5.14 Change the type again to include two lists, the dominant genes and the recessive genes. Write the **add-gene** method that takes a gene name and **recessive** or **dominant** and places it in the appropriate list. **Add-gene** should check to make sure that it doesn't exist in the other **dominant** or **recessive** list, remove it if it does, and then add it to the correct list (if not already present) there. Finally modify **gene-summary** to simply compare the lengths of the two lists to determine dominant or recessive.

5.6 Generic Functions

With object-oriented programming we can write generic functions that are independent of the particular object it manipulates. This provides an object-oriented approach to data-driven programming as introduced in Chapter 4. A function can get at an object through its methods and slots. Once defined, a function operates on any object that has the same set of methods and slots. As long as an object exhibits the same external characteristics, the generic function will succeed.

Suppose that the Voyager had discovered beings living on Saturn's moon Titan. Although these beings have characteristics similar to humans they are quite different. For instance, they are asexual. Thus, a Titanian doesn't have a brother or a sister, it just has a sibling. The definition of sibling is common between Earthlings and Titanians and, thus, could be manipulated using a generic function.

We want a function that updates the `siblings` slot for all siblings whenever an Earthling or Titanian is defined. Each parent could maintain a list of children. When a child is defined, the list is updated to include the new child, and then scanned to add the new child to the `siblings` slots of each child. First, we redefine `person` and define `Titanian`. Notice that in order to simplify adding entries into the `children` and `siblings` slots, they have been initialized to `nil`.

```
;;; The person type, now with siblings and children slots.

(define-type person
  (:var name :initable)
  (:var mother :initable)
  (:var father :initable)
  (:var sex :initable)
  (:var parent (:init *unknown*) :settable :initable)
  (:var siblings (:init nil) :settable)
  (:var children (:init nil) :settable)
  :all-gettable
  )
⇒ PERSON

;;; A Titanian has some similar characteristics.

(define-type Titanian
  (:var name :initable)
  (:var parent :initable :settable)
  (:var siblings (:init nil) :settable)
  (:var children (:init nil) :settable)
  (:var chemical-nutrient (:init 'gredzlit) :settable)
  (:var upper-brain-size (:init *unknown*) :settable)
```

```
  (:var lower-brain-size (:init *unknown*) :settable)
  :all-gettable
  )
⇒ TITANIAN
```

The generic function `update-sibling` takes one argument, which is the object having its sibling slot updated. The function cannot assume the number of parents (Earthlings have two, while Titanians have one) and so uses an auxiliary function that takes a list of parents as an argument. The function should also perform a little error checking to verify that the parent slot does have a meaningful value.

```
;;; Check to see if the parent slot is invalid and return the
;;; symbol error-no-parent-defined to so indicate.  Otherwise
;;; invoke update-sibling-aux with a list of parents
;;; (possibly containing only one element).

(defun update-sibling (object)
  (let ((parents (parent object)))
    (cond ((or (null parents) (equal parents *unknown*))
           'error-no-parent-defined)
          ((listp parents)
           (update-sibling-aux object parents))
          (t (update-sibling-aux object (list parents))))))
⇒ UPDATE-SIBLING
```

`Update-sibling-aux` does most of the work. It has to first get the parent object, extract the children slot, update the children slot to reflect the new child, and then update each child slot to reflect the new sibling. This function must also verify that the parent actually exists. If it doesn't exist, it can be ignored and the next parent processed. Alternately, we could try to create the parent object, however none of the useful information could be provided.

```
;;; Update the children and sibling for the child, the parent
;;; and all of the siblings.  When the parent is a real
;;; object, then update the parent's children list to include
;;; the new child, set the child's sibling list to be the
;;; list of parent's children and finally add the child to
;;; all of the siblings sibling list.

(defun update-sibling-aux (child parents)
  (cond ((null parents) nil)
        ((not (boundp (car parents)))
         (update-sibling-aux child (cdr parents)))
        ((let ((parent-object (symbol-value (car parents))))
           (cond ((objectp parent-object)
```

```
                    (let ((parents-children
                           (children parent-object)))
                      (setf (children parent-object)
                            (cons (name child)
                                  parents-children))
                      (setf (siblings child) parents-children)
                      (add-sibling (name child)
                                   parents-children))))
            (update-sibling-aux child (cdr parents))))))
 ⇒ UPDATE-SIBLING-AUX
```

`Add-sibling` works in a similar manner but doesn't need to verify that the object actually exists. The function can assume that the `children` slot will contain a value since `update-sibling` required the child to exist in the first place.

```
;;; Add the first argument sibling to the sibling slot of
;;; each member of the second argument.

(defun add-sibling (sibling sibling-list)
  (cond ((null sibling-list) nil)
        ((let ((sibling-object
                (symbol-value (car sibling-list))))
           (setf (siblings sibling-object)
                 (cons sibling (siblings sibling-object)))))
           (add-sibling sibling (cdr sibling-list)))))
 ⇒ ADD-SIBLING
```

Testing this particular code requires creating a large number of Earthlings and Titanians. We will just create the Titanians to demonstrate that the functions work properly.

```
(setf xxyxy (make-instance 'Titanian :name 'xxyxy
                           :parent 'xxy))
 ⇒ #<Object TITANIAN>

;; Now set the siblings properly.
(update-sibling xxyxy)
 ⇒ NIL

(siblings xxyxy)
 ⇒ NIL
```

Now we can create `xxy` and watch how the slots are supplied with values.

```
(setf xxy (make-instance 'Titanian :name 'xxy :parent 'x))
 ⇒ #<Object TITANIAN>
```

```
(children xxy)
 ⇒ NIL

(update-sibling xxyxy)
 ⇒ NIL

(siblings xxyxy)
 ⇒ NIL

(children xxy)
 ⇒ (XXYXY)

;; Finally add another sibling.
(setf xxyoo (make-instance 'Titanian :name 'xxyoo
                           :parent 'xxy))
 ⇒ #<Object TITANIAN>

(update-sibling xxyoo)
 ⇒ NIL

;; Verify that all of the appropriate slots now have values.
(siblings xxyxy)
 ⇒ (XXYOO)

(siblings xxyoo)
 ⇒ (XXYXY)

(children xxy)
 ⇒ (XXYOO XXYXY)
```

Now, verify that the same functions operate on humans.

```
;; One parent
(setf jim (make-instance 'person
                 :name 'jim :mother 'mary :father 'james
                 :sex 'male :parent '(mary james)))
 ⇒ #<Object PERSON>

(setf bob (make-instance 'person
                 :name 'bob :mother 'joanne :father 'jim
                 :sex 'male :parent '(joanne jim)))
 ⇒ #<Object PERSON>

(update-sibling bob)
 ⇒ NIL

(setf patty (make-instance 'person
                 :name 'patty :mother 'joanne :father 'jim
                 :sex 'female :parent '(joanne jim)))
 ⇒ #<Object PERSON>
```

```
(update-sibling patty)
 ⇒ NIL

(siblings bob)
 ⇒ (PATTY)

(siblings patty)
 ⇒ (BOB)
```

Notice in the definition of `person` and `Titanian` that there are a number of methods automatically created. Some of the names of those methods are the same, because the slots are the same. For example, the object system automatically creates a `children` method for `person` and the same `children` method for `Titanian`. Thus, if we invoke the `children` method on a Titanian and a person, you might think that one of them could get the wrong result, depending on which definition was done last.

```
(children xxy)
 ⇒ (XXYOO XXYXY)

(children jim)
 ⇒ (PATTY BOB)
```

The system retrieves the correct value in each case. The `children` method has to do a type discrimination on the argument before deciding which actual `children` method to invoke. It checks to see if the argument is a Titanian and if so calls the `children` method for Titanians. Otherwise, it checks to see if the argument is a `person` and invokes the appropriate `children` method for persons. This is an example of *polymorphism* – different methods may be defined for each type, but they have a common interface to the external world. Code then doesn't have to depend upon a particular type, as long as the semantics of the methods agree. We could redefine the `children` method to perform the task differently, but as long as it performs the same semantics the operation remains valid.

EXERCISES

5.15 It is commonly said that each year of a dog or cat's life is equivalent to seven human years. Write a generic function to compute the human age of a dog or a cat.

***5.16** Although the Titanians have many different characteristics, they do have a similar genetic structure to Earthlings. They don't happen to have hair and two of their three eyes are usually different colors, but they still have recessive and dominant genes. Add `dominant-genes` and `recessive-genes` to the Titanian type. Define `add-gene` and `gene-summary` as defined in the exercises at the end of the previous section as generic functions.

5.17 `Update-sibling` and the associated functions has a problem. When there are multiple parents, each with a list of children, it is quite possible that updating the sibling lists could create duplicate entries. Modify the code so that before adding a new sibling to the sibling list, it checks to see if the new sibling is already present.

5.7 Specialization

In many of the examples, the slots of different types have been duplicated between the types. For example, the `Titanian` and `person` types share the `name`, `parent`, `siblings`, and `children` slots. The `dog` and `cat` types used in the exercises also share some slots. When objects share common slots it is usually because they are somehow related. We need a generic type that includes the common slots, and then we need to create new types that automatically include all of the slots of the generic type, along with the specialized slots of the new type. This idea is called *specialization* and the implementation technique is *inheritance.* For example, all reproductive beings should have one or more parents, siblings, and children. Both persons and Titanians are reproductive beings, but also include other characteristics. They therefore specialize the definition of reproductive beings with more information. With specialization you don't need to specify all of the common slots and methods over and over again. Also, changes specific to the generic type can be done in one place.

An important characteristic of the specialization process is that the children types are "almost like" the parent types. This is not merely an additive process, where a child type is always specified to have more slots, methods, or both. The child type may override parent's slots and methods with new definitions. So, a child will always have at least as many slots and methods as the parent, although they may be semantically different.

You specify inheritance by using `:inherit-from` as a type option, followed by the name(s) of the parent(s).

(`:inherit-from` *parent-name**)

We can extract the common traits of Titanians and Earthlings into a new type, `reproductive-being`.

```
;;; Define a reproductive being.

(define-type reproductive-being
  (:var name :initable)
  (:var parent :initable)
  (:var siblings (:init nil))
  (:var children (:init nil))
  :all-gettable
  :all-settable
```

```
  )
 ⇒ REPRODUCTIVE-BEING
```

Now, to demonstrate that methods are inherited from the parent, we'll define `number-of-children` that returns a count of the number of children of this being. It returns the length of the list stored in the `children` slot.

```
;;; The number of children of a being.

(define-method (reproductive-being number-of-children) ()
  (length children))
 ⇒ NUMBER-OF-CHILDREN
```

`Person` and `Titanian` inherit all of the slots (and methods) defined in `reproductive-being`.

```
;;; A person is a kind of a reproductive-being.

(define-type person
  (:inherit-from reproductive-being)
  (:var mother :initable)
  (:var father :initable)
  (:var sex :initable)
  :all-gettable
  :all-settable
  )
 ⇒ PERSON

;;; Likewise, a Titanian is a kind of a reproductive-being.

(define-type Titanian
  (:inherit-from reproductive-being)
  (:var chemical-nutrient (:init 'gredzlit))
  (:var upper-brain-size (:init *unknown*))
  (:var lower-brain-size (:init *unknown*))
  :all-gettable
  :all-settable
  )
 ⇒ TITANIAN
```

The test defines a Titanian, adds values to the `children` slot and then invokes `number-of-children` to verify that it is inherited.

```
(setf xxyxy (make-instance 'Titanian :name 'xxyxy
                           :parent 'xxy))
 ⇒ #<Object TITANIAN>

(setf (children xxyxy) '(xxyxyzz xxyxyrr))
```

```
⇒ (XXYXYZZ XXYXYRR)

(number-of-children xxyxy)
⇒ 2
```

As you can see, slots and methods are inherited from the parent definition. Also, notice that invoking `describe` on a specialized object shows all of the slots, including the inherited ones.

```
(describe xxyxy)
⇒  LOWER-BRAIN-SIZE: ?
⇒  UPPER-BRAIN-SIZE: ?
⇒  CHEMICAL-NUTRIENT: GREDZLIT
⇒  CHILDREN: (XXYXYZZ XXYXYRR)
⇒  SIBLINGS: NIL
⇒  PARENT: XXY
⇒  NAME: XXYXY
⇒ NIL
```

You can also override the inheritance simply by defining a new version of a method or slot. Suppose that the number of children of Titanians is actually twice the number included in the list (the children divide into two separate Titanians soon after "ggidro" – which roughly translates into birth). A new `number-of-children` computes a value that is double the length of the list stored in the `children` slot.

```
;;; A Titanian number-of-children method, which returns twice
;;; what is done for other reproductive beings.

(define-method (Titanian number-of-children) ()
  (* 2 (length children)))
⇒ NUMBER-OF-CHILDREN

(number-of-children xxyxy)

!!!!! Error: The symbol CHILDREN has no value.
  Condition signaled in: SYMBOL-VALUE.
```

Slots defined in the parent are not directly accessible in the children methods. `Call-method` allows invocation of parent methods. The first argument to `call-method` is a list containing the parent type and the method name to be called. The remaining arguments are the arguments to the method.

(**call-method** (*type method*) *S-expression**)

```
;;; A Titanian number-of-children method, which returns twice
```

```
;;; what is done for other reproductive beings.

(define-method (Titanian number-of-children) ()
  (* 2 (length (call-method (reproductive-being children)))))
 ⇒ NUMBER-OF-CHILDREN

(number-of-children xxyxy)
 ⇒ 4
```

Call-Method allows you to invoke a parent method that has been overridden. In this example, the Titanian number-of-children produces a result which is twice the number of children of a reproductive being. Instead of explicitly computing the number of children, the method could have invoked the parent's version of number-of-children as follows:

```
;;; Compute the number of children of a Titanian.  The result
;;; is twice the number of children of a normal reproductive
;;; being.

(define-method (Titanian number-of-children) ()
  (* 2 (call-method (reproductive-being
                     number-of-children))))
 ⇒ NUMBER-OF-CHILDREN

(number-of-children xxyxy)
 ⇒ 4
```

This produces the same result, but provides data abstraction. The manipulation of the children slot is isolated in reproductive-being. So, if changes were made to the representation of the children slot, only one method needs changing.

EXERCISES

5.18 Clowns are people too, so change the definition of clown to inherit from person. Also change the mood method so it accesses the name slot of the parent, in this case, person.

***5.19** Cats and dogs are both pets. Define a pet type and then redefine the cat and dog types to inherit from pet. Some pertinent slots for pets might be: breed, name, age. Those for a cat could include favorite-cat-food or volume-of-purr, while a dog might have a list of tricks and favorite-dog-food. Add any slots that you think are appropriate.

***5.20** Write a method on person gets-pet-cat which is called when a person gets a new pet cat. The method takes as arguments the name, breed, and color of the cat. The method is supposed to create the cat object, store the argument values, and also

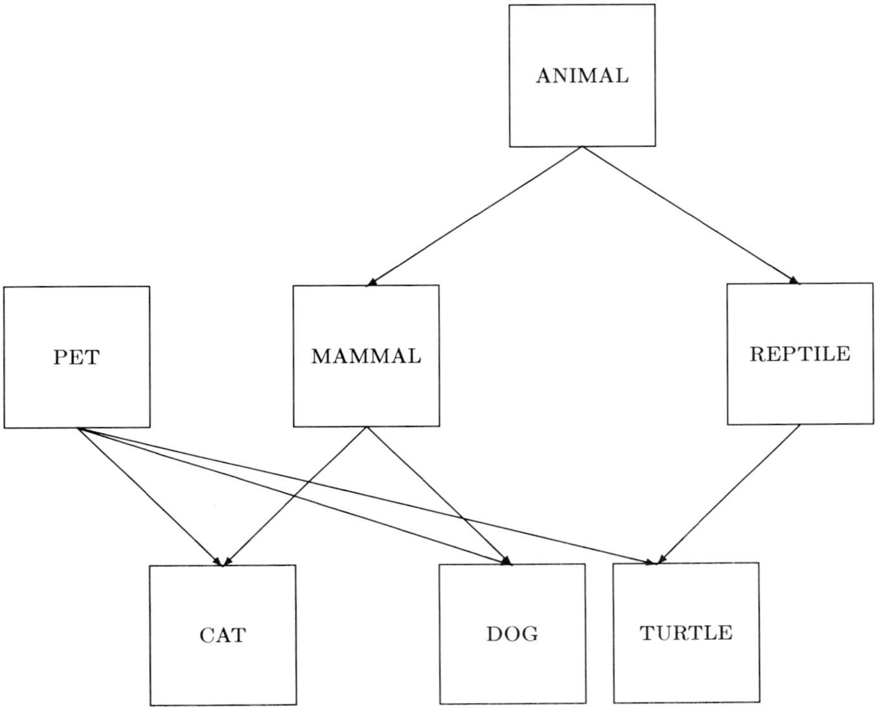

Figure 5.2 Example of Multiple Inheritance

store the person object itself in the owner slot of the cat object. `Gets-pet-cat` should return the cat object. Also, write a method `owners-name` on a pet, which returns the name of the owner.

5.8 Multiple Inheritance

Single inheritance is not always sufficient to represent the desired structure. A good example is the concept of a pet. Consider the types cat, dog, turtle, mammal, reptile, and animal. A cat and a dog can be a pet, but not all mammals are pets. Therefore, the pet type must be a parent of cat and dog. However, reptiles can also be pets, which means that pet cannot be placed in the single hierarchy. It must be placed outside as illustrated in Figure 5.2. This is the case where multiple inheritance is required.

Multiple inheritance can cause two problems:

1. When there are slots with the same names in different parents, what does the system do? It could create one slot in the child that has the same slot

name, but if the parents have different sets of initial values, which one does it choose? Another option creates a slot for each parent, but somehow gives them slightly different names (such as the concatenation of the parent name and the slot name). This problem is also related to the single inheritance anomaly where a parent and a child have slots with the same name.

2. When there are methods with the same name in different parents, how should the system handle the conflict? This is also related to method combination in which the programmer can invoke parent methods. You could either not directly inherit any conflicting methods, inherit the first one, or invoke all of the methods.

How these issues are handled depends on the particular object system. Our pedagogical system uses `call-method` to handle the conflicts. It permits all slots in all parent types to be accessible through the appropriate qualification in the `call-method` invocation. For example, if there were some kind of cross-breeding between Earthlings and Titanians, a child could inherit traits from both. In this case, it might inherit `shoe-size` from `person` and from `Titanian`. The access for the `person` and `Titanian` `shoe-size` slots would be `(call-method (person shoe-size))` and `(call-method (Titanian shoe-size))`, respectively. The child could also inherit methods from each parent in a like manner and must resort to using `call-method` to invoke the method in the appropriate parent.

Another potential area for the use of multiple inheritance is to define a person's job. Suppose that we create a new type, `job`, to include slots defining a person's employment. Also, suppose that we add an `occupation` slot to `person`. Finally, we can create the `employed-person` type, which inherits from `job` and `person`.

```
;;; A job is defined as an employer, salary, and occupation.

(define-type job
  (:var employer)
  (:var salary)
  (:var occupation)
  :all-initable
  :all-settable
  :all-gettable)
⇒ JOB

;;; A person is a kind of a reproductive-being, now with an
;;; occupation slot.

(define-type person
  (:inherit-from reproductive-being)
  (:var mother :initable)
  (:var father :initable)
```

```
  (:var sex :initable)
  (:var occupation :initable)
  :all-gettable
  :all-settable
  )
 ⇒ PERSON

;;; An employed person includes a job and a person.

(define-type employed-person
  (:inherit-from job person)
  (:var years-employed)
  :all-settable
  :all-gettable
  :all-initable)
 ⇒ EMPLOYED-PERSON
```

Access to the slots in the parents must be performed by writing a method that uses `call-method`. Suppose that the `occupation` slot in `person` specifies a person's original occupation, while the same slot within `job` specifies the current occupation. So, we can write some methods to get at and set these slots.

```
;;; Set a person's original occupation slot.

(define-method (employed-person set-original-occupation)
    (new-value)
  (call-method (person set-occupation) new-value))
 ⇒ SET-ORIGINAL-OCCUPATION

;;; Set a person's current occupation slot.

(define-method (employed-person set-current-occupation)
    (new-value)
  (call-method (job set-occupation) new-value))
 ⇒ SET-CURRENT-OCCUPATION

;;; Return both the current and original occupation slots.

(define-method (employed-person both-occupations) ()
  (list 'original (call-method (person occupation))
        'current (call-method (job occupation))))
 ⇒ BOTH-OCCUPATIONS

;; Now, create an instance.
(setf bob (make-instance 'employed-person
                 :years-employed 4))
 ⇒ #<Object EMPLOYED-PERSON>
```

```
;; Set some values in bob.
(set-original-occupation bob 'scientist)
 ⇒ SCIENTIST

(set-current-occupation bob 'manager)
 ⇒ MANAGER

;; Access the slots.
(both-occupations bob)
 ⇒ (ORIGINAL SCIENTIST CURRENT MANAGER)
```

Notice what happens if a shared, inherited method is invoked on the item. You can't guarantee which one is actually selected, so you shouldn't write code that uses this.

```
;; Try calling just occupation on the object.
(occupation bob)
 ⇒ SCIENTIST
```

Multiple inheritance can be used in another way with the concept from the flavors system called a *mixin* [45]. A mixin is a type and its associated methods which provide additional functionality to other types. This is just like adding chocolate chips to a cookie. The result is still a cookie, but it has some new characteristics. A mixin could be added to our system to deal with names. The name of a person, a pet, or whatever has similar characteristics. For example, a name may have a different translation in another language. So, a type definition for name might include the actual name slot and a method for determining the french name.

```
(define-type name
  (:var name)
  :all-initable
  :all-gettable
  :all-settable)
 ⇒ NAME

(define-method (name french-name) ()
  (or (cadr (assoc name '((john jean) (jack jacques))))
      name))
 ⇒ FRENCH-NAME
```

Now, define `person` to use the `name` mixin.

```
;;; Define a reproductive being.
(define-type reproductive-being
```

```
  (:var parent :initable)
  (:var siblings (:init nil))
  (:var children (:init nil))
  :all-gettable
  :all-settable
  )
 ⇒ REPRODUCTIVE-BEING

(define-type person
  (:inherit-from reproductive-being name)
  (:var mother :initable)
  (:var father :initable)
  (:var sex :initable)
  (:var occupation :initable)
  :all-gettable
  :all-settable
  )
 ⇒ PERSON

(setf john (make-instance 'person :name 'john :mother 'mary
                                  :father 'sam))
 ⇒ #<Object PERSON>

(french-name john)
 ⇒ JEAN
```

EXERCISES

5.21 Define an `occupation` method for `employed-person`, that returns the value of the `occupation` slot in `job`, instead of the one in `person`.

***5.22** Develop the types for the structure shown in Figure 5.2 for dog, cat, pet, and mammal.

5.9 Summary

Object-oriented programming lets you group items with similar characteristics. You can isolate functionality with objects, for easily maintained code. The assorted functions permit the definition of type structures, object instances, and methods for operating on the objects. Generic functions can operate on many different object types, as long as each type exhibits the same external characteristics as needed in the function. The object system is a means of describing a hierarchical structure of types including multiple inheritance which permits inheriting from more than one parent.

Chapter Exercises

***1.** Develop a set of objects describing a hardware maintenance configuration. The purpose of the set up is to define the various pieces of hardware, their maintenance schedules, whom to call when things break, characteristics of the hardware, etc.

All of the hardware will have the following fields:

- Date Installed
- Preventative Maintenance (PM) period
- Date of last PM
- Maintainer

Model the maintainers as objects with the following fields:

- Name of the maintainer
- Phone Number
- Office Address

***2.** Model individual hardware items grouped by types. For this problem, model a printer, workstation, and disk drive. Each should have different characteristics, like type, amount of memory, etc.

***3.** Define a `not-working` method for each type of hardware that tells the user what to do when the particular device is not working. `Not-working` should be invoked on a device, and it will output the information on the last preventive maintenance, along with the name, phone, and office number of the maintainer.

Function Summary

The following lists the functions and topics covered in this chapter.

- `(define-type` *Type-Name* `(`*Slot**`))`
- *slot* ←`(:var` *slot-name option**`)` | *type-option**
- `(make-instance` *type-name initialization**`)`
- `define-method (`*type-name method-name*`) (`*argument**`)` *S-expression**`)`
- `(`*method-name object S-expression**`)`
- `(defsetf` *accessor-symbol function-symbol*`)`
- `(describe` *object*`)`
- `(symbol-value` *symbol*`)`
- `(objectp` *S-expression*`)`
- `(boundp` *symbol*`)`
- `(object-type` *S-expression*`)`
- `(:inherit-from` *parent-name**`)`
- `(call-method (`*type method*`)` *S-expression**`)`

6 BINDING AND SCOPING

THIS CHAPTER BEGINS with a discussion of how LISP binds values to variables. It continues with the lexical and dynamic scoping rules of LISP. We implement the scoping as simple LISP functions to illustrate the concepts. Most of the examples in this chapter continue with the development of the data structures used in the expert system developed in Chapter 9.

6.1 Lambda Binding

Arguments to a LISP expression are always evaluated before the designated function is called. Then, the values of these arguments are assigned to the function's parameters before the body of the function is evaluated. In LISP, this is called *lambda* binding.* For example, `reverse-list` is a function that takes three arguments and constructs a list with the arguments reversed.

```
;;; Construct a list of the arguments in reverse order.

(defun reverse-list (arg-1 arg-2 arg-3)
  (list arg-3 arg-2 arg-1))
⇒ REVERSE-LIST

(setf sample-variable 15)
⇒ 15

(reverse-list 123 (+ sample-variable 3)
                  (* sample-variable 3))
⇒ (45 18 123)
```

Each argument in the function call is evaluated, returning the values `123`, `18`, and `45`. These are bound to the function parameters `arg-1`, `arg-2`, and `arg-3`,

*LISP has its early semantic roots in the theory of recursion equations, while some syntactic roots come from lambda calculus, which is where the name `lambda` originated [10,28].

respectively. The parameters are then manipulated in the function body producing `(45 18 123)`.

The scope of a variable is the area in which a binding holds. Binding means that a variable is set to some value, by an explicit assignment statement, function arguments, or local variables. An argument's binding overshadows any bindings to the same name outside of the argument's scope. But any previous binding is restored once outside the scope of the argument. So, if `arg-1`, `arg-2`, or `arg-3` has a value before calling `reverse-list`, then that value remains unchanged while the body of the function is evaluated. Suppose that we assign `arg-2` a value and then call `reverse-list`. Notice that after the function returns, `arg-2` still has the original value though it had the value `18` during the function execution. Effectively, a new `arg-2` is temporarily created to hold the value used in `reverse-list` and is then destroyed when `reverse-list` is finished.

```
(setf arg-2 'foobar)
 ⇒ FOOBAR

(reverse-list 123 (+ sample-variable 3)
                  (* sample-variable 3))
 ⇒ (45 18 123)

arg-2
 ⇒ FOOBAR
```

The goal of the expert system in the Chapter 9 is to determine genealogical relationships between various `person` objects given only the parentage and sex of each. The expert system must be able to determine characteristics like, "Is there another person with the same parents as this person?" So, when an object is created, it must be saved in some list for later retrieval. This list will be maintained in the global variable `*persons*`. Some functions must also use a list of the names of all person objects. Instead of forcing the maintenance of these lists to be done each time a `person` object is created, we can combine the functionality in one function `add-person`. `Add-person` takes `name`, `mother`, `father`, and `sex` as arguments and invokes `make-a-person` to create the person object and save the name in `*person-names*`. It then adds the object to the global list, and returns the newly created object.

```
;; Define the global variable used to maintain the list of
;; person objects.
(defvar *persons* nil)
 ⇒ *PERSONS*

;; Repeat the definition of person in this chapter, including
;; that for *unknown*.
(defvar *unknown* '?)
 ⇒ *UNKNOWN*
```

```
;; Define the person type.
(define-type person
  (:var name :initable)
  (:var mother :initable)
  (:var father :initable)
  (:var sex :initable)
  (:var parent (:init *unknown*) :settable)
  (:var siblings (:init nil) :settable)
  (:var children (:init nil) :settable)
  :all-gettable
  )
⇒ PERSON

;;; Add-person creates a person object, installs it in the
;;; *persons* list and returns the object.
(defun add-person (name mother father sex)
  (let ((new-person (make-a-person name mother father sex)))
    (setf *persons* (cons new-person *persons*))
    new-person))
⇒ ADD-PERSON

;; The names of all person objects.
(defvar *person-names* nil)
⇒ *PERSON-NAMES*

;;; Create a person instance.  This function also saves the
;;; name of the person in *person-names*.
(defun make-a-person (name mother father sex)
  (setf *person-names* (cons name *person-names*))
  (make-instance 'person :name name :mother mother
                 :father father :sex sex))
⇒ MAKE-A-PERSON
```

Within the scope of `add-person`, there are four parameters (`name`, `mother`, `father`, and `sex`) and one local variable (`new-person`). The variable `*persons*` is neither local nor a parameter and is called a *free* variable – it is free from any binding within the current function. `Add-person` is a top-level function (it is not nested within any other function definition), so the free variable `*persons*` references the global variable. The following example demonstrates bound and free variables within a function. First, we assign values to two of the variables bound within `add-person`. `Name` and `new-person` demonstrate that there is no difference between a bound local variable and a bound parameter. Also, `*persons*` is checked to verify that its value is `nil`.

```
;; Assign a value to name and new-person.
(setf name 'freddy)
```

```
 ⇒ FREDDY

(setf new-person '(some new person))
 ⇒ (SOME NEW PERSON)

*persons*
 ⇒ NIL
```

Now, we call add-person and check the value of each of the variables.

```
;; Create a bob instance and save in the list of objects.
(setf bob (add-person 'bob 'jim 'joanne 'male))
 ⇒ #<Object PERSON>

;; Now check the various variables.
(name bob)
 ⇒ BOB

*persons*
 ⇒ (#<Object PERSON>)

new-person
 ⇒ (SOME NEW PERSON)

name
 ⇒ FREDDY
```

This again demonstrates that no changes were made to the external definitions of bound variables, while modification of the free variable affects its external definition.

EXERCISES

6.1 Without the aid of a running LISP, what is the result of evaluating the following expressions? Once you have determined the answers, submit each expression to a running LISP system and verify your results:

```
(defun demo-binding (a b c)
  (let ((c b)
        (b c))
    (setf b 5)
    (let ((c 9))
      (setf c (+ 5 c)))
    (list a b c)))
(demo-binding 1 2 3)
```

***6.2** What is the result if the lets are replaced by let* in the previous exercise?

6.3 Once again, without the aid of a running LISP, what is the result of evaluating the following expressions? Once you have determined the answers, submit each expression to a running LISP system and verify your results:

```
(defun demo-binding-again (a b c)
  (let ((c (+ c b))
        (b (* c b)))
    (let ((c 9))
      (setf a (+ a b 5 c)))
    (list a b c)))
(demo-binding-again 1 2 3)
```

***6.4** Once again, what is the result if the `lets` are replaced by `let*` in the previous exercise?

6.2 Lexical Scoping

A binding environment is a mapping between variables and their current values. The system looks up the value of a variable in the appropriate environment. There may be many environments active and so the system must determine which one is appropriate. Function definition, `let` and `let*`, among others, create these environments. Thus, inside a `let` inside a function there is an environment for the function parameters, and another one for the local variables. Global variables are also defined in a similar global binding environment. So, there is an additional environment that can be scanned for a variable value. This process of searching for a variable in an environment is called scoping. All variables must be found in some environment. Those that are unbound are considered to reside in the global environment.

In `add-person`, there are three environments:

```
Line

 1   (defun add-person (name mother father sex)
 2     (let
 3       ((new-person
            (make-a-person name mother father sex)))
 4       (setf *persons* (cons new-person *persons*))
 5       new-person))
```

1. The global environment that defines `*persons*`;
2. The function definition that defines `name`, `mother`, `father`, and `sex`; and
3. The `let` environment defining `new-person`.

Contour diagrams help to illustrate the environments. The following three diagrams show the contours prior to the function call, before the call is made to `make-a-person`, and finally within the body of the `let` expression.

Prior to executing function

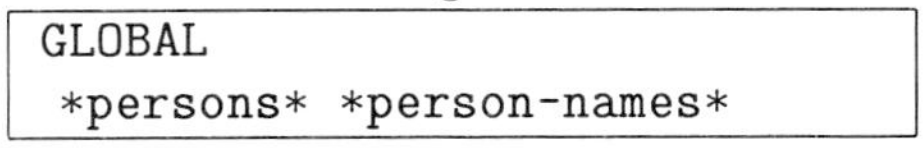

Prior to execution `let` at Line 2

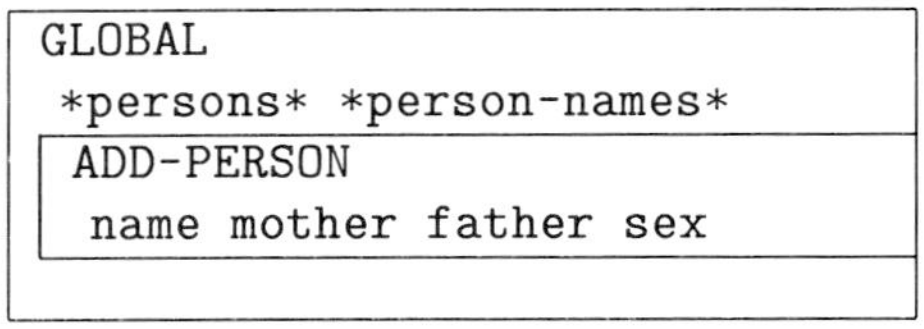

Prior to execution of `setf` at Line 4

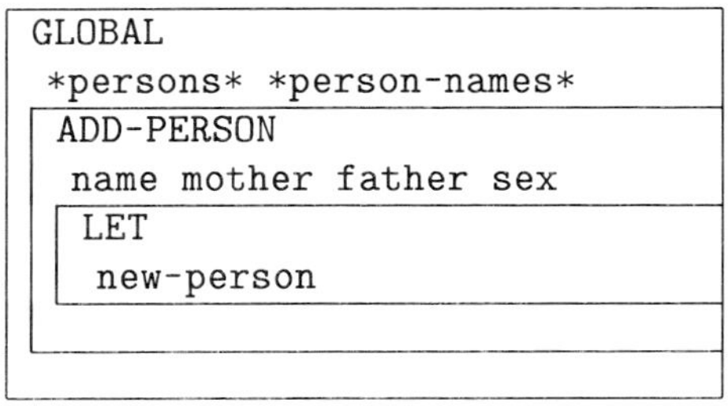

The contour within `make-a-person` is similar, except there is no `let` expression. The two sets of contours could be combined as follows:

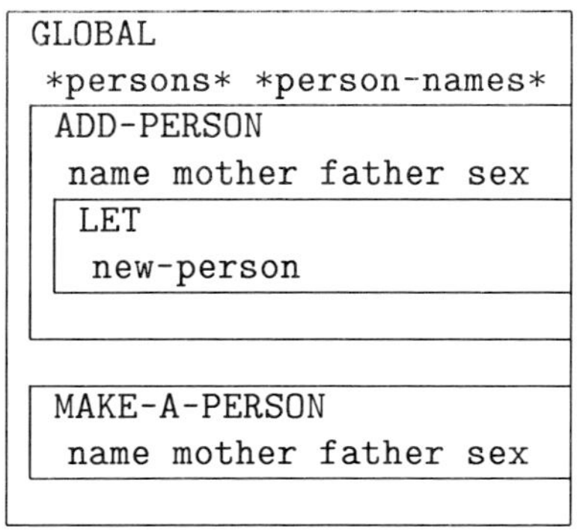

Lexical scoping uses the environments that exist when the expression referencing the variable is defined. This is the same technique that is used in languages like Pascal and FORTRAN. Dynamic scoping uses the environments in their dynamic execution order (dynamic scoping is demonstrated later). Some

LISP dialects are strictly lexical (Scheme [34], T [35], etc.) and others are strictly dynamic (PSL [17], Franz LISP [14], MACLISP [33], etc.). Common LISP provides both scoping methods, although lexical scoping is the default.

The last contour diagrams show the lexical scoping environment for both `add-person` and `make-a-person`. The current value for a variable is found by scanning each environment, from the current contour outward. So, when the system wants the current value for `name` within `add-person`, it checks first in the `let` environment. It's not present there, so it then successfully checks the `add-person` environment. When the same variable name is used in multiple environments, the system finds the variable that is closest to the expression being executed.

Note that the arguments to `make-a-person` are just the parameters defined in `add-person`. In other programming languages like Pascal, `make-a-person` would be defined within `add-person`. Then you wouldn't need to pass all of the arguments to the function, because the function could directly reference the parameters of `add-person`. `Flet` and `labels` accomplish this in Common LISP. The difference between these two expressions is similar to the differences between `let` and `let*`. `Flet`, like `let`, does not permit the locally defined functions to call any of the other functions defined within the `flet`. `Labels` allows the functions defined within the `labels` expression to call each other.

`(flet ((`*function-name*`(`*argument*`*)` *S-expression*`*)*)` *S-expression*`*)`

`(labels ((`*function-name*`(`*argument*`*)` *S-expression*`*)*)` *S-expression*`*)`

The following redefines `add-person` to use `flet`.

```
;;; Add-person creates a person object, installs it in the
;;; *persons* list, and returns the object.
(defun add-person (name mother father sex)
  (flet
   ((make-a-person ()
        (setf *person-names* (cons name *person-names*))
        (make-instance 'person :name name :mother mother
                       :father father :sex sex)))
   (let ((new-person (make-a-person)))
     (setf *persons* (cons new-person *persons*))
     new-person)))
⇒ ADD-PERSON
```

The contour diagram for this function definition is:

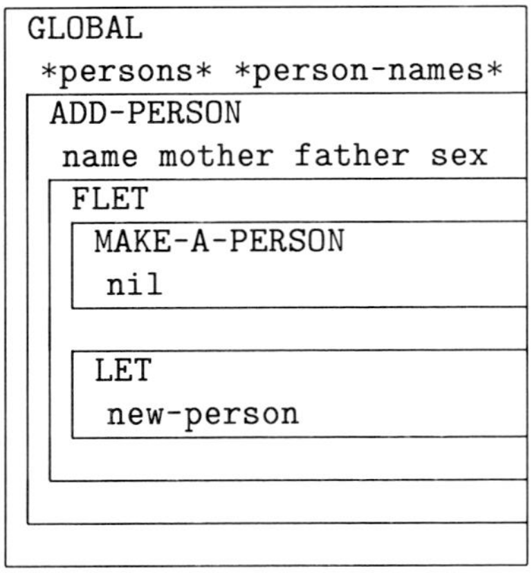

Thus, the `flet` creates an environment containing `make-a-person`, and its body is another `let` expression defining `new-person`. Within `make-a-person`, the four variables `name`, `mother`, `father`, and `sex` are all free variables. However, the variables are defined in `add-person`, so lexical scoping reaches those values. Also, `new-person` is not visible from `make-a-person` since it is defined in the body of the `flet`.

EXERCISES

***6.5** Draw a contour diagram for the same `demo-binding` function used in the previous section.

```
(defun demo-binding (a b c)
  (let ((c b)
        (b c))
    (setf b 5)
    (let ((c 9))
      (setf c (+ 5 c)))
    (list a b c)))
```

***6.6** Draw a contour diagram for the `demo-binding`, replacing the `let`s with `let*`s. Recall that a `let*` is equivalent to nested `let`s.

6.7 Suppose that we modify `demo-binding` to include a local function using `flet`, draw a contour diagram for this modified version.

```
(defun demo-binding-flet (a b c)
  (flet (local-function (c b)
           (setf b 5)
           (let ((c 9))
             (setf c (+ 5 c)))
           (list a b c))
    (local-function a b)))
```

6.3 Lexical Scoping Implementation

This section can be skipped on first reading. It simulates lexical scoping by implementation of LISP primitives.

We will implement primitives to explicitly create environments and manipulate their variables. Once the primitives are defined, the functions like `add-person` and `make-a-person` can be modified for this style of binding. You wouldn't actually use this style of programming, since the LISP system already provides the mechanism. However, explicit scoping through our own primitives will give you some insight into the scoping process.

Our first implementation decision is the environment representation. Recall that an environment is a mapping between a variable and its value. An appropriate data structure is the association list. It provides the required mapping mechanism and has supporting functions to manipulate the list. This choice has historical precedence – early versions of LISP actually used association lists as environments. Modern LISPs use many different techniques and the selection of an appropriate scheme is a popular research topic.

`Add-person` in the previous section had used three environments, the global environment, the one defined by the parameters to the function, and the one defined by the `let` statement. Representing each environment as an association list makes it easy to find a variable binding using `assoc`. However, we must link the environments together so that they can be scanned in the appropriate order. We want to scan from inside out, that is, scan the most nested environment first and the global environment last. The linking must capture the nesting illustrated in the contour diagrams. We can maintain the nesting as a list of environment association lists. When entering a new nesting level, we create a new environment and add it to the front of the list of environments. Upon exit, the most recently added environment is removed. Thus, `add-environment` is a call to `cons` and `remove-environment` calls `cdr`.

```
;;; Return a new environment with the environment argument
;;; added to the front.

(defun add-environment (environment environment-list)
  (cons environment environment-list))
 ⇒ ADD-ENVIRONMENT

;;; Remove the top environment from the list and return the
;;; new environment.

(defun remove-environment (environment-list)
  (cdr environment-list))
 ⇒ REMOVE-ENVIRONMENT
```

With this scheme a function could just scan the environment list, performing an assoc on each environment until the variable is found. However, changing the value of a variable is quite difficult. You either add a new binding to the front of the association list or reconstruct the list. If you add to the front of the list, you waste storage by increasing the size of the list every time you store a new value. For example, given the following association list:

```
(setf env '((name bob) (sex male) (mother joanne)
            (father jim)))
⇒ ((NAME BOB) (SEX MALE) (MOTHER JOANNE) (FATHER JIM))

(assoc 'mother env)
⇒ (MOTHER JOANNE)
```

Adding a new binding to the front will work just fine. Notice that if we add a variable that is the same as another, the old value is *shadowed* by the new value.

```
(setf env (cons '(mother mary) env))
⇒ ((MOTHER MARY) (NAME BOB) (SEX MALE) (MOTHER JOANNE)
⇒  (FATHER JIM))

(assoc 'mother env)
⇒ (MOTHER MARY)
```

However, the environment list will continue to grow. We could reconstruct the env list, removing the old value and adding in a new value. This is a lot of work and is also wasteful. We really want to replace the value stored in the environment list with a new value. Recall from the previous chapter that an object maintains a state. Thus, we could make an association list of variables and objects. For example:

```
(define-type variable
  (:var value :gettable :settable :initable))
⇒ VARIABLE

(setf env
  (list (list 'name (make-instance 'variable :value 'bob))
        (list 'sex (make-instance 'variable :value 'male))
        (list 'mother (make-instance 'variable
                                     :value 'joanne))
        (list 'father (make-instance 'variable
                                     :value 'jim))))
⇒ ((NAME #<Object VARIABLE>) (SEX #<Object VARIABLE>)
⇒  (MOTHER #<Object VARIABLE>) (FATHER #<Object VARIABLE>))

(value (cadr (assoc 'mother env)))
⇒ JOANNE

;; Now replace the value.
(setf (value (cadr (assoc 'mother env))) 'mary)
```

```
⇒ MARY

(value (cadr (assoc 'mother env)))
⇒ MARY
```

Using this scheme, `lookup` will retrieve the value from an environment list and `store` will change the value of a variable in an environment list. `Store` must do nearly everything that `lookup` does and, in addition, change the value. `Lookup` does the same scanning, but must return the value that is found. So, we should implement an auxiliary function that scans the list and then returns the `variable` object. `Lookup` then just returns the value, while `store` changes the value. So, `lookup-aux` scans each environment in the environment list searching for the variable. If it's not found, then it must search the global environment. The global environment is special because it is the same for all functions and therefore must be shared among the environments. For this reason, we will maintain it in a global variable `*global-environment*`. With lexical scoping, each top-level function starts with the global environment as the initial environment. So, the global environment must be visible from any function. This function doesn't perform any error checking, so if a variable isn't defined, `lookup-aux` returns `nil`.

```
;;; The global environment.
(defvar *global-environment* nil)
⇒ *GLOBAL-ENVIRONMENT*

;;; Look in each environment in the list for the argument
;;; variable. This auxiliary function returns either nil or
;;; the variable object.

(defun lookup-aux (variable environments)
  (cond ((null environments)
         (assoc variable *global-environment*))
        ((assoc variable (car environments)))
        (t (lookup-aux variable (cdr environments)))))
⇒ LOOKUP-AUX

;;; This is the main lookup routine.  It invokes lookup-aux
;;; to return the variable object (or nil) and then calls
;;; value on the object.

(defun lookup (variable environments)
  (let ((variable-object (lookup-aux variable environments)))
    (if variable-object
      (value (cadr variable-object))
      nil)))
⇒ LOOKUP
```

Store can also decide what to do if the variable doesn't exist in any environment. We will adopt the Common LISP convention that the value must be stored into the global environment.

```
;;; This routine changes the value of the binding to be the
;;; second argument. Care must be taken to make sure that a
;;; variable object has been returned by the call to
;;; lookup-aux.

(defun store (variable new-value environments)
  (let ((variable-object (lookup-aux variable environments)))
    (if variable-object
      (setf (value (cadr variable-object)) new-value)
      (setf *global-environment*
            (cons (list variable
                        (make-instance 'variable
                                       :value new-value))
                  *global-environment*)))))
⇒ STORE
```

These utililites are complete except for one more function, alistify, which turns a list of variable names and a list of the associated values into an association list. We can then change all functions that use the utilities to be called with only one argument, which is the list of arguments. They are then combined with the variable names using alistify. This makes it easy for each function to ignore the problems of passing too many or too few arguments. It will just ignore any extras and assign nil to any parameters that are not provided with a value.

```
;;; Turn the new list arguments into an association list,
;;; with the first list containing the keys.

(defun alistify (keys values)
  (cond ((null keys) nil)
        (t (cons (list (car keys)
                       (make-instance 'variable
                                      :value (car values)))
                 (alistify (cdr keys) (cdr values))))))
⇒ ALISTIFY

;; A quick test.
(alistify '(name father mother sex) '(bob jim joanne male))
⇒ ((NAME #<Object VARIABLE>) (FATHER #<Object VARIABLE>)
⇒  (MOTHER #<Object VARIABLE>) (SEX #<Object VARIABLE>))
```

Before using these utilities to demonstrate scoping, we test each operation.

```
;; Create an initial environment.
(setf env (add-environment (alistify '(foo bar) '(3 4)) nil))
 ⇒ (((FOO #<Object VARIABLE>) (BAR #<Object VARIABLE>)))

;; Add another one, with bar shadowing the previous version.
(setf env (add-environment (alistify '(bar mumble bletch)
                                     '(99 33 77)) env))
 ⇒ (((BAR #<Object VARIABLE>) (MUMBLE #<Object VARIABLE>)
 ⇒    (BLETCH #<Object VARIABLE>))
 ⇒  ((FOO #<Object VARIABLE>) (BAR #<Object VARIABLE>)))

;; Verify that it finds the latest value for bar.
(lookup 'bar env)
 ⇒ 99

;; Store a new value for bar into the top environment.
(store 'bar 100 env)
 ⇒ 100

;; Make sure that the store worked correctly.
(lookup 'bar env)
 ⇒ 100

;; Remove the top environment.
(setf env (remove-environment env))
 ⇒ (((FOO #<Object VARIABLE>) (BAR #<Object VARIABLE>)))

;; See if the first bar with a value of 4 is present.
(lookup 'bar env)
 ⇒ 4

;; Finally remove the last environment.
(setf env (remove-environment env))
 ⇒ NIL
```

To use this environment model in functions we need to change each expression that defines new variables into calls to `add-environment`. All variable accesses must be translated into a call to `lookup`. All assignments to a variable must be translated into a call to `store`. Finally, when exiting from each variable defining expression, the return value must be determined and the most recent environment removed. The following transformations should be used to convert regular LISP code:

```
Given: (defun name (parameters) body) ->
Result:(defun name (one-parameter)
         (let
           ((env (add-environment (alistify parameters
                                            one-parameter)
```

```
                                   ;; No initial environment
                                   nil)))
           body))
Given: (let locals body) ->
Result:(let (return-value)
            (setf env (add-environment
                           (alistify local-names local-values)
                           env))
            (setf return-value (progn body))
            (setf env (remove-environment))
            return-value)
Given: Variable access ->
Result:(lookup variable env)
Given: (setf variable expression) ->
Result:(store variable value env)
```

Using these templates, we can modify **add-person** to use our binding scheme.

```
;;; Add-person creates a person object, installs it in the
;;; *persons* list and returns the object.
(defun add-person (parameters)
  (let ((env (add-environment
               (alistify '(name father mother sex)
                          parameters)
               nil)))
    (let (return-value)
      (setf env
            (add-environment
             (alistify '(new-person)
                        (list
                         (make-a-person (lookup 'name env)
                                        (lookup 'mother env)
                                        (lookup 'father env)
                                        (lookup 'sex env))))
             env))
      (store '*persons*
             (cons (lookup 'new-person env)
                   (lookup '*persons* env))
             env)
      (setf return-value (lookup 'new-person env))
      (setf env (remove-environment env))
      return-value)))
⇒ ADD-PERSON
```

```
;; Define the global environment.
(setf *global-environment*
      (alistify '(name new-person *persons*)
                (list 'freddy '(some new person) nil)))
⇒ ((NAME #<Object VARIABLE>) (NEW-PERSON #<Object VARIABLE>)
⇒  (*PERSONS* #<Object VARIABLE>))

;; Now test to see if it works.
(add-person (list 'bob 'jim 'joanne 'male))
⇒ #<Object PERSON>

(lookup '*persons* (list *global-environment*))
⇒ (#<Object PERSON>)

;; Verify that it is the correct person.
(name (car (lookup '*persons* (list *global-environment*))))
⇒ BOB
```

EXERCISES

***6.8** Transform `make-a-person` into an equivalent function that uses the scoping utilities.

6.9 Without the aid of a running LISP, what is the result of evaluating the following expressions. Once you have determined the answers, submit each expression to a running LISP system and verify your results:

```
(setf for-fun 88)
(defun bar (for-fun)
  (setf for-fun (+ for-fun 12))
  (mumble)
  for-fun)
(defun mumble ()
  (setf for-fun (* for-fun 3)))
(bar 12)
for-fun
```

6.10 Transform the previous example into the equivalent code using the environment utilities.

6.4 Dynamic Scoping

Dynamic scoping uses the dynamic, execution-time environments, instead of the static, definition-time environments. So, the system looks up the value of a variable in the environments that are being maintained dynamically. If a function calls `foo`, which then calls `bar`, which then calls `mumble`, the dynamic environment includes all of the dynamic variables defined in each of the functions.

Unlike a dynamic variable, the location of a lexical variable can be determined when the function is compiled, so no run-time lookup is required. Dynamic variables must be found at run-time. Depending upon the implementation of the LISP, this could be an expensive operation.

Common LISP has dynamic scoping for partly historical reasons. The dialects that were the basis of Common LISP had dynamic scoping, thus, Common LISP has it. Dynamic scoping provides you with the same functionality as nested functions without using `flet` or `labels`. Older, dynamic-only dialects of LISP did not have `flet` or `labels`, and so dynamic scoping was the only way to provide that type of function. A function using dynamically scoped variables can be called from many other functions, instead of being hidden away in the definition of a parent function as with `flet` and `labels`.

If you want to use dynamic variables, you can't just define `make-a-person` with no arguments. This is because all of the now free variables will be lexically bound (as stated before, the default scoping is lexical) to the global variables. You must tell the system that the variables are dynamically scoped by adding a `special` declaration within the scope of access of the special variable.

`(declare (special` *symbol** `))`

All symbols mentioned in the declaration are special within the context of the declaration. The declaration must be placed after the parameter list in a function definition or after the local variables in `let` and `let*`. By convention, special variables should be defined with a leading and trailing asterisk. This same method is used to designate global variables defined with `defvar`. Globals declared with `defvar` are actually declared to be special variables. Common LISP doesn't truly have a global lexical variable. The result of assigning a value to a global variable not previously declared special is implementation dependent. Therefore, that practice should be avoided. Also, since `defvar` is global, you don't need to locally declare the variable special.

```
;;; Add-person creates a person object, installs it
;;; in the *persons* list, and returns the object.
(defun add-person (*name* *mother* *father* *sex*)
  (declare (special *name* *mother* *father* *sex*))
  (let ((new-person (make-a-person)))
    (setf *persons* (cons new-person *persons*))
    new-person))
⇒ ADD-PERSON

;;; Create a person instance.  This function also saves
;;; the name of the person in *person-names*.
(defun make-a-person ()
  (declare (special *name* *mother* *father* *sex*))
```

```
  (setf *person-names* (cons *name* *person-names*))
  (make-instance 'person :name *name* :mother *mother*
                 :father *father* :sex *sex*))
⇒ MAKE-A-PERSON
```

Since these functions use both lexical and dynamic variables, then both a lexical and a dynamic scope is created. Each lexical scope contains only the lexical variables, while the dynamic scope contains only those variables that are dynamic. Thus, we have to create two contours for these functions as follows. Notice that the global environment is part of the dynamic contour because the variables declared with `defvar` are actually dynamic variables.

Lexical

```
+------------------+
| ADD-PERSON       |
|  nil             |
| +----------------+
| | LET            |
| |  new-person    |
| +----------------+
|                  |
+------------------+

+------------------+
| MAKE-A-PERSON    |
|  nil             |
+------------------+
```

This is the dynamic contour when the execution is inside of `make-a-person`. This contour is very similar to the one created for the version of `add-person` that used the `flet`.

Dynamic

```
+-----------------------------------------+
| GLOBAL                                  |
|  *persons* *person-names*               |
| +---------------------------------------+
| | ADD-PERSON                            |
| |  *name* *mother* *father* *sex*       |
| | +-------------------------------------+
| | | MAKE-A-PERSON                       |
| | |  nil                                |
| | +-------------------------------------+
| |                                       |
| +---------------------------------------+
|                                         |
+-----------------------------------------+
```

Now a few tests to verify that it works like the lexical version.

```
;; Set *name* to something that shouldn't be used in the
;; functions.
(defvar *name* 'wrong-name)
 ⇒ *NAME*

;; Reset the list of persons.
```

```
(setf *persons* nil)
 ⇒ NIL

(add-person 'bob 'joanne 'jim 'male)
 ⇒ #<Object PERSON>

;; Verify that the fields were properly created.
(name (car *persons*))
 ⇒ BOB

*name*
 ⇒ WRONG-NAME
```

If the special variable binding hadn't worked properly, then the name would be the global value of `*name*`.

Dynamic scoping provides a nice way of temporarily rebinding the value of a variable. Upon exit from a function that dynamically rebinds a variable, the previous instantiation of the variable will be restored. So, you don't have to explicitly save and restore the variable. We have seen this in the last example of `add-person`. In that example, `*name*` was bound to `'wrong-name` at the top level. The function rebound it to `bob` which is what `make-a-person` saw for the value. Upon exit from `add-person`, the value was restored to its original `'wrong-name`.

EXERCISES

***6.11** What is the difference between free variables in a recursive and a non-recursive function?

6.12 Redefine `add-person` and `make-a-person` so that they still use dynamic scoping, but do not locally declare the special variables. (*Hint:* Consider using **`defvar`**.)

6.5 An Implementation of Dynamic Scoping

This section can be skipped on first reading. Like the section on lexical scoping, it demonstrates dynamic scoping using the same LISP primitives that simulate lexical scoping.

Implementing dynamic scoping with the environment utility functions requires a small change. Since the dynamic environment exists between procedures, the system must be able to save the state between function calls. So, we will use another utility variable to contain the list of dynamic environment variables. As each function is entered, any new dynamic variables are added to the dynamic environment list. Access to dynamic variables is through the dynamic environment list.

Another change is required because the global environment is a dynamic environment rather than a lexical environment. So, lookup and store shouldn't use the *global-environment*. The symbol *environments* can be initialized with the initial variables, *persons* and *person-names*. We will also assume that all special variables have been declared. This automatically adds them to the initial *environments*. So, we must first modify lookup and store to not use *global-environment*.

```
;;; Look in each environment in the list for the argument
;;; variable.  This auxiliary function returns either nil or
;;; the variable object.

(defun lookup-aux (variable environments)
  (cond ((null environments)
         nil)
        ((assoc variable (car environments)))
        (t (lookup-aux variable (cdr environments)))))
⇒ LOOKUP-AUX
```

Lookup doesn't directly use *global-environment* and so doesn't change. However, store must be modified as follows:

```
;;; This routine changes the value of the binding to be the
;;; second argument.  Care must be taken to make sure that a
;;; variable object has been returned by the call to
;;; lookup-aux.

(defun store (variable new-value environments)
  (let ((variable-object (lookup-aux variable environments)))
    (if variable-object
      (setf (value (cadr variable-object)) new-value)
      nil)))
⇒ STORE
```

This code implemented with the environment utilities follows. The only difference is that the environment list used for dynamic scoping is contained in a global variable.

```
;; The dynamic environment list.
(defvar *environments*
  (list (alistify '(*persons* *person-names*) '(nil nil))))
⇒ *ENVIRONMENTS*

;;; Add-person creates a person object, installs it in the
;;; *persons* list, and returns the object.

(defun add-person (parameters)
  (let ((env (add-environment nil nil))
```

```
        ;; No initial lexical environment.
        return-value)
    (setf *environments*
          (add-environment
           (alistify '(*name* *mother* *father* *sex*)
                     parameters)
           *environments*))
    (setf return-value
          (let (return-value)
            (setf env (add-environment
                       (alistify '(new-person)
                                 (list (make-a-person)))
                       env))
            (store '*persons*
                   (cons (lookup 'new-person env)
                         (lookup '*persons* *environments*))
                   *environments*)
            (setf return-value (lookup 'new-person env))
            (setf env (remove-environment env))
            return-value))
    (setf env (remove-environment env))
    (setf *environments* (remove-environment *environments*))
    return-value))
⇒ ADD-PERSON

;;; Create a person instance.  This function also saves the
;;; name of the person in *person-names*.

(defun make-a-person ()
  (let ((env (add-environment nil nil))
        return-value)
    (store '*person-names*
           (cons (lookup '*name* *environments*)
                 (lookup '*person-names* *environments*))
           *environments*)
    (setf return-value
          (make-instance 'person
                         :name (lookup '*name*
                                       *environments*)
                         :mother (lookup '*mother*
                                         *environments*)
                         :father (lookup '*father*
                                         *environments*)
                         :sex (lookup '*sex*
```

```
                                        *environments*)))
      (setf env (remove-environment env))
      return-value))
   ⇒ MAKE-A-PERSON

   (add-person (list 'bob 'joanne 'jim 'male))
   ⇒ #<Object PERSON>

   (name (car (lookup '*persons* *environments*)))
   ⇒ BOB
```

The disadvantage of using this style is that the "pseudo-nested" functions (like `make-a-person`) could be erroneously called from some other function, where the dynamic variables had not been properly assigned.

EXERCISES

***6.13** *Difficult* - Describe a way in which one function could tell if it is being called by the function which appropriately defined the dynamic variables.

6.14 As mentioned at the end of the previous section, special variables are nice because they can be bound to a new value in a function, and then they are automatically restored to their previous value upon exit from the function. Explain how this works in terms of the environment utility functions.

6.6 Summary

Lambda binding assigns arguments to the parameters of a function call. Scoping determines which variable is referenced by a free variable. Common LISP defines lexical scoping as the default scoping paradigm, but dynamic scoping can be achieved through variable declarations. Also, local variables and parameters shadow their external definitions.

Chapter Exercises

The goal of this set of exercises is to write a system that given a LISP function, will automatically translate it into calls on the environment utilities. You may assume that all variables are lexical. For example, your system will be able to do the following:

```
(translate '(defun foo (x) (+ x 3)))
⇒ (DEFUN FOO (PARAMETER)
⇒   (LET ((ENV (ADD-ENVIRONMENT
⇒                 (ALISTIFY (QUOTE (X)) PARAMETER) NIL)))
⇒     (+ (LOOKUP (QUOTE X) ENV) 3)))
```

```
(translate '(defun foo (a b) (let ((b 2) c)
                                  (setf b (+ a b c)))))
⇒ (DEFUN FOO (PARAMETER)
⇒  (LET ((ENV (ADD-ENVIRONMENT
⇒              (ALISTIFY (QUOTE (A B)) PARAMETER) NIL)))
⇒    (LET (RETURN-VALUE)
⇒      (SETF ENV
⇒             (ADD-ENVIRONMENT
⇒              (ALISTIFY (QUOTE (B C)) (QUOTE (2 NIL)))
⇒              ENV))
⇒      (SETF RETURN-VALUE
⇒             (PROGN
⇒               (STORE
⇒                (QUOTE B)
⇒                (+ (LOOKUP (QUOTE A) ENV)
⇒                   (LOOKUP (QUOTE B) ENV)
⇒                   (LOOKUP (QUOTE C) ENV))
⇒               ENV)))
⇒      (SETF ENV (REMOVE-ENVIRONMENT))
⇒      RETURN-VALUE)))
```

***1.** Your first choice in designing the system is whether to use procedural or declarative style. With procedural style, you implement the translation of the various S-expressions into new S-expressions with straight LISP code. With a declarative style, you could define a pattern-matching system which matches a pattern and produces a replacement transformation. We will use the procedural style, since a pattern matcher is implemented in Chapter 16. There are four different templates that we must define translators for. They are for `defun`, `let`, variable access, and variable store.

Write a function for each of these cases. Each function takes a single argument, which is the invoking S-expression, and it must then perform the translation. Remember that if there are subexpressions (like the body of the function) to be translated, they must call `translate` to define the translated body.

***2.** Write the function `translate`, which takes an S-expression and scans each part calling the appropriate translate function. Use proper data-driven style, and don't forget that the function should ignore the body of a quoted expression.

Function Summary

The following lists the functions and topics covered in this chapter.

- Lambda binding
- Lexical scoping

- Dynamic scoping
- `(flet ((`*function-name*`(`*argument**`)` *S-expression**`)*)` *S-expression**`)`
- `(labels ((`*function-name*`(`*argument**`)` *S-expression**`)*)` *S-expression**`)`
- `(declare (special` *symbol**`))`

7 ITERATION

THIS CHAPTER DISCUSSES the various iteration techniques provided in Common LISP. They vary in complexity from simple counting iterations to a fully general mechanism that subsumes all of the iteration clauses. These examples continue to develop the data structures used Chapter 9's expert system.

7.1 Simple Iteration

Common LISP provides a number of iteration constructs. The simplest is the `dotimes` definite iteration construct. Like the `do` in FORTRAN and the `for` in Pascal, this construct increments a variable from zero (inclusive) to a *count* (exclusive). It iterates *count* times over the S-expressions.

(dotimes (*symbol count return-S-expression*) *S-expression**)

You can specify a result expression that is evaluated after the last iteration. The `dotimes` expression then returns this result expression. The first element after `dotimes` is a list containing the iteration variable, the exclusive count value, and an optional result expression. If the result expression isn't provided, `dotimes` returns `nil`.

For example, we can write a function to compute the squares of all numbers between zero and an argument. The function returns a list containing two-element lists of the value and the square. We will present a recursive and an iterative version. As discussed in Chapter 3, a recursive function is one that calls itself. Recursive functions require no additional LISP expressions to perform their operation, while iterative versions must rely on iteration operators. In the following recursive version, we must have a variable that counts from zero up to the argument. One possibility is to pass the counter as another argument to the recursive function. We will use the `labels` construct to define the auxiliary function.

```
;;; Recursive computation of the squares of numbers up to the
;;; argument.
(defun compute-squares (number-of-squares)
  (labels ((compute-squares-aux (counter)
             (if (= counter number-of-squares)
               nil
               (cons (list counter (* counter counter))
                     (compute-squares-aux (1+ counter))))))
    (compute-squares-aux 0)))
⇒ COMPUTE-SQUARES

(compute-squares 4)
⇒ ((0 0) (1 1) (2 4) (3 9))
```

Now, the iterative version.

```
;;; Compute the argument number of squares starting with
;;; zero.
(defun compute-squares (number-of-squares)
  (let ((square-list nil))
    (dotimes (each-integer number-of-squares
                            (reverse square-list))
      (setf square-list
            (cons (list each-integer
                        (* each-integer each-integer))
                  square-list)))))
⇒ COMPUTE-SQUARES

(compute-squares 5)
⇒ ((0 0) (1 1) (2 4) (3 9) (4 16))
```

The `dolist` expression is similar to `dotimes`, except that it iterates over a list, instead of a numeric range of integers. The syntax is identical to `dotimes`, except that the count is replaced by the list to be iterated over.

(dolist (*symbol list return-S-expression*) *S-expression**)

We will use `dolist` to scan a list of `person` objects and determine the age of the oldest person.

```
(defvar *unknown* '?)
⇒ *UNKNOWN*

;; An enhanced person object with an age slot.
(define-type person
  (:var name :initable)
  (:var mother :initable)
```

```
  (:var father :initable)
  (:var sex :initable)
  (:var parent (:init *unknown*) :settable)
  (:var siblings (:init nil) :settable)
  (:var children (:init nil) :settable)
  (:var age :initable)
  :all-gettable
  )
 ⇒ PERSON

;;; What is the age of the oldest person in *persons*.
(defun oldest-person ()
  (let ((oldest (age (car *persons*))))
    (dolist (a-person (cdr *persons*) oldest)
      (setf oldest (max oldest (age a-person))))))
 ⇒ OLDEST-PERSON

;;; Modify add-person to include the initial age and remove
;;; the call to make-a-person.
(defun add-person (name mother father sex age)
  (let ((new-person
          (make-instance 'person :name name :mother mother
                                 :father father :sex sex
                                 :age age)))
    (setf *persons* (cons new-person *persons*))
    new-person))
 ⇒ ADD-PERSON

;; Reset the *persons* list.
(setf *persons* nil)
 ⇒ NIL

;; Add a few people to the knowledge base.
(add-person 'bob 'joanne 'jim 'male 33)
 ⇒ #<Object PERSON>

(add-person 'jim 'mary 'james 'male 62)
 ⇒ #<Object PERSON>

(add-person 'joanne 'margaret 'robert 'female 61)
 ⇒ #<Object PERSON>

;; Now find the oldest person in *persons*.
(oldest-person)
 ⇒ 62
```

Suppose that we are interested in *any* person over some age. This implies that the function may not need to look at the entire list. Since **dolist** iterates over the whole list, it's not appropriate for this problem. However, we can terminate the iteration early with the **return** expression.

```
(return S-expression)
```

When a **return** is evaluated in the middle of an iteration, the iteration immediately stops and returns the value of the S-expression argument. **Return** only terminates one level of the iteration (which is important in the case of nested iteration expressions). It returns a value only for the iteration expression and not the function or whatever else the expression is embedded in (which is different from other programming languages like C, where a return exits the entire function definition).

```
;;; Find a person in *persons* that is over the argument age.
(defun find-person-over-age (age-for-comparison)
  (dolist (each-person *persons*)
    (if (> (age each-person) age-for-comparison)
      (return each-person))))
⇒ FIND-PERSON-OVER-AGE

;; Check that it exits from the list early.
(setf someone-of-majority-age (find-person-over-age 20))
⇒ #<Object PERSON>

;; Grab the name and age of the person found.
(list (name someone-of-majority-age)
      (age someone-of-majority-age))
⇒ (JOANNE 61)

;; Everyone in *persons* is over the age of 20, so whoever is
;; first in the *persons* list, should be the same one that
;; the function found.
(list (name (car *persons*)) (age (car *persons*)))
⇒ (JOANNE 61)
```

EXERCISES

***7.1** Write the functions **oldest-person** and **find-person-over-age** recursively and observe the difference between them and the iterative versions.

7.2 The expression **dotimes** always starts counting from zero and always increments by one. Write a function **odd-numbers** that takes a starting value and an ending value and creates a list of the odd numbers between the two values. You must use **dotimes** to perform the operation.

```
(odd-numbers 5 9)
⇒ (5 7 9)
```

```
(odd-numbers 6 10)
 ⇒ (7 9)
```

7.3 Write a function that uses `dolist` to take a list of elements and produce a list of sequentially tagged elements.

```
(numeric-tags '(red blue green))
 ⇒ ((1 RED) (2 BLUE) (3 GREEN))
```

***7.4** Write a function that scans two lists and compares them to see if they have any different elements. When the function finds a difference, it returns a list of the two differing elements. If they are equal, the function should return `nil`. You must use an iteration construct. You may assume that the two lists are of equal length.

```
(first-difference '(1 2 a b) '(1 2 b a))
 ⇒ (A B)

(first-difference '(red blue green) '(red blue green))
 ⇒ NIL

(first-difference '(1 2 3 4) '(1 2 4 4))
 ⇒ (3 4)
```

7.2 Mapping Iteration

The *map* functions are similar to `dolist` in that they all perform iteration on lists. There are two main variants, the first designating what operation is performed to find the list elements. One of the two versions of this variant operate on successive elements and the other operates upon successive `cdr`s. The second variant specifies what is returned by the mapping function. One version operates on each element and returns a transformed list of the results. The other version simply returns the untransformed second argument. In this case, the function performs its operation as a side effect. This means that the function changes or "effects" something other than its arguments, "on the side." The following table indicates the functions and their operations.

		Operation	
		car	cdr
Transform	Yes	mapcar	maplist
List	No	mapc	mapl

The first argument to these functions is the name of the function to operate on each element, followed by the target lists. There must be at least one list argument. If there is more than one list, then the function is called with an element from each list until the end of the shortest list.

(`mapcar` *function-name list list**)

(mapc *function-name list list**)

(maplist *function-name list list**)

(mapl *function-name list list**)

For example, a simple application of mapcar creates a list of the names of all persons in *persons*.

```
;; Extract the names of all of the persons in *persons*.
(mapcar 'name *persons*)
 ⇒ (JOANNE JIM BOB)
```

We could also redefine alistify from the previous chapter, which takes two lists and merges them into an association list. The function mapcar is natural for this particular operation. It operates on each element of the list and can take multiple lists as arguments. Mapcar can call the list function to turn the two elements into a list. Finally, mapcar constructs a list from the results of each function call, giving us the desired result.

```
;;; Mapcar can be used to define alistify used in the
;;; previous chapter.

(defun mapcar-alistify (list-1 list-2)
  (mapcar 'list list-1 list-2))
 ⇒ MAPCAR-ALISTIFY

(mapcar-alistify '(name mother father sex)
                 (list 'bob 'joanne 'jim 'male))
 ⇒ ((NAME BOB) (MOTHER JOANNE) (FATHER JIM) (SEX MALE))
```

This version of alistify is slightly different from the previous version because of the way it handles short lists. If the list of variables is shorter than the list of values, you get a different result than if the list of values is shorter.

```
(alistify '(name mother father sex) (list 'bob 'joanne))
 ⇒ ((NAME BOB) (MOTHER JOANNE) (FATHER NIL) (SEX NIL))

(mapcar-alistify '(name mother father sex)
                 (list 'bob 'joanne))
 ⇒ ((NAME BOB) (MOTHER JOANNE))
```

Solving this problem is a part of the exercises.

The mapc function operates on each element of the list, but always returns the original list argument. So, it's used for side effect only. This next example generates a list of the names of each person in `*persons*`. The generated list is saved in the `*person-names*` global variable.

```
;; The variable in which the list of person names is saved.
(defvar *person-names* nil)
 ⇒ *PERSON-NAMES*

;;; Save all names of each person-object into *person-names*.

(defun determine-person-names (person-object)
  (setf *person-names*
        (cons (name person-object)
              *person-names*)))
 ⇒ DETERMINE-PERSON-NAMES

;; Get the names of all person objects into *person-names*.
(mapc 'determine-person-names *persons*)
 ⇒ (#<Object PERSON> #<Object PERSON> #<Object PERSON>)

*person-names*
 ⇒ (BOB JIM JOANNE)
```

`Maplist` operates on the entire list and successive `cdrs` of the list argument. The result of each function call is collected into a list and `maplist` then returns this list.

```
;; Maplist operates on each cdr (including the entire list
;; first).
(maplist 'reverse '(a b c d))
 ⇒ ((D C B A) (D C B) (D C) (D))

;; It accessed each cdr and then constructed a list of all of
;; the reversed cdrs.
;; The following simply reconstructs the list.
(maplist 'car '(a b c d))
 ⇒ (A B C D)
```

`Mapl` is just like `maplist`, except it doesn't return a transformed argument – it returns the second argument unchanged.

```
(defvar *transformed-list* nil)
 ⇒ *TRANSFORMED-LIST*

;;; Reverse the argument and save in the global.
(defun reverse-and-save (argument)
  (setf *transformed-list*
        (cons (reverse argument) *transformed-list*)))
```

```
 ⇒ REVERSE-AND-SAVE

;; Perform mapl on the same argument as the maplist.
(mapl 'reverse-and-save '(a b c d))
 ⇒ (A B C D)

*transformed-list*
 ⇒ ((D) (D C) (D C B) (D C B A))
```

These functions are good for operating on all elements of a list. They can discover things about lists as a whole, such as the largest and smallest numbers, how many occurrences of a specific symbol are present, or total of all of the numbers in a list. However, returning these *single values*, like the largest numbers, the sum of numbers, or some count is difficult. This is because all of the mapping expressions return some form of list. You must build code around the function to save and return these types of values.

As you can see, the *map* expressions are called with the same number of arguments as there are lists. Thus, if you wanted to provide some other information to the function, you can't do it by passing another argument. For example, when counting the number of occurrences of an argument symbol in a list, the *mapping* function must also have access to the argument symbol. The difficulty is that if the function is defined outside of the scope of the required variables, then dynamic variables must be used to pass information to the function. A better solution is to use the `flet` construct. With the function definition nested within the scope the variables, then access is easy. To illustrate this, we will implement `count-occurrences` which counts the number of occurrences of the first argument in the second argument list.

```
;;; Count the number of occurrences of the argument in a
;;; list, using mapc.

(defun count-occurrences (to-be-searched-for some-list)
  (let ((count-of-occurrences 0))
    (flet ((counter (list-element)
                    (if (equal list-element
                               to-be-searched-for)
                      (setf count-of-occurrences
                            (1+ count-of-occurrences)))))
      (mapc 'counter some-list)
      count-of-occurrences)))
 ⇒ COUNT-OCCURRENCES

;; Now a test.
(count-occurrences 'bob *person-names*)
!!!! Continuable error: Undefined function 'COUNTER' applied
       or called.
```

```
If continued: will reapply 'COUNTER' to the argument list
      (A).
  Condition signaled in: MAPC.
```

The error occurs because the system can't tell that the quoted `counter` is actually the same as the *function* `counter`. The problem is because of lexical scoping. The definition of `mapc` is outside of the scope of this function. When `mapc` is invoked the argument is a symbol which `mapc` must subsequently call. Within the lexical scope of `mapc`, the only visible `counter` would be a global one, not the local one inside of `count-occurrences`. The solution is to tell the LISP system that the first argument to `mapc` is actually a function named `counter`. Then it can find the definition lexically. This can be accomplished by wrapping the function name with `function`, just like it can be wrapped with `quote`. Also, just like there is an abbreviation for `quote`, which is `'`, Common LISP defines an abbreviation for `function`, `#'`.

(`function` *lambda-expression*)

#' *lambda-expression*

Now, we can try it again with the function definition.

```
;;; Count the number of occurrences of the argument in a
;;; list, using mapc.

(defun count-occurrences (to-be-searched-for some-list)
  (let ((count-of-occurrences 0))
    (flet ((counter (list-element)
                    (if (equal list-element
                               to-be-searched-for)
                      (setf count-of-occurrences
                            (1+ count-of-occurrences)))))
      (mapc #'counter some-list)
      count-of-occurrences)))
 ⇒ COUNT-OCCURRENCES

;; Try the test again.
(count-occurrences 'bob *person-names*)
 ⇒ 1
```

The rule is that you should always use a `#'` in front of any symbol that is to be used as a function. This even includes the `apply` function. The next section defines `lambda` expressions, which are another way of providing a function within the same scope as the map expressions.

EXERCISES

***7.5** As stated earlier, `mapcar-alistify` terminates too early when the second argument list is shorter than the first. Write a new version that solves this problem and try to avoid the expensive solutions of doing many calls to `append` and `length`.

***7.6** Using `mapcar` define a function `count` that takes a predicate function and a list of values. `Count` returns the number of non-`nil` occurrences of the predicate applied to the values.

```
(count 'oddp '(1 2 3 4 5))
⇒ 3
```

7.3 Lambda Expressions

A `lambda` expression is an anonymous function, with all of the characteristics of a function. It allows you to define functions without inventing a lot of function names. `Lambda` expressions can be used in place of function names – as the arguments to map functions, or even as the first element of a function call. The syntax for a `lambda` expression is similar to that of a `defun` using `lambda` in the place of `defun` and there is no function name:

(lambda (*argument**) *S-expression**)

The first example demonstrates placing a `lambda` expression in place of a function invocation.

```
;; Place a lambda expression in the function name part of an
;; expression.  This is equivalent to (+ 1 2).
((lambda (a b) (+ a b)) 1 2)
⇒ 3
```

Recall that `apply` invokes the function passed as the first argument. The arguments passed to that function are the remaining arguments to `apply`. You may use a `lambda` expression in the place of the function name argument.

```
;; Lambda expressions also work with apply.
(apply '(lambda (a b) (list (list a) (list b))) '(x y))
⇒ ((X) (Y))
```

In the last example, we quoted the `lambda` expression. This is another case where we should really use the `#'` syntax. This informs LISP that the function properties rather than the list properties of the following expression are relevant. For example, it may decide to compile the body expression as LISP code, instead of as a list. If the `#'` is used, then the program will run significantly faster.

```
;; The same example as before.
```

```
(apply #'(lambda (a b) (list (list a) (list b))) '(x y))
 ⇒ ((X) (Y))

;; Try a mapcar with a lambda expression.
(mapcar #'(lambda (arg) (list arg (* arg arg)))
        '(1 3 5 7 11))
 ⇒ ((1 1) (3 9) (5 25) (7 49) (11 121))
```

When a lambda is nested within another expression it obeys standard scoping rules. Free variables in the body of the lambda expression are scoped like free variables in any other expression. A nested lambda expression has access to locals and parameters in the outside scope. This gives us the ability to write count-occurrences without the nested function counter.

```
;;; Count the number of occurrences of the argument in a
;;; list, using mapc.

(defun count-occurrences (to-be-searched-for some-list)
  (let ((count-of-occurrences 0))
    (mapc #'(lambda (list-element)
              (if (equal list-element to-be-searched-for)
                (setf count-of-occurrences
                      (1+ count-of-occurrences))))
          some-list)
    count-of-occurrences))
 ⇒ COUNT-OCCURRENCES

;; Again, we use the same test.
(count-occurrences 'bob *person-names*)
 ⇒ 1
```

This is a good example of where the #' must be used. If ' had been used, there would have been no access to the lexical variables, to-be-searched-for and count-of-occurrences, because the body of the lambda expression would have been treated as a list and not as a function body.

EXERCISES

***7.7** Define the lambda expression in count-occurrences with a ' instead of the #', invoke the function, and observe the consequences.

7.8 Write the function count that you defined in the exercises in the previous section using a lambda expression instead of an internal function.

7.9 Write a function that uses one of the mapping operators that takes a list of elements and produce a list of sequentially tagged elements.

```
(numeric-tags '(red blue green))
 ⇒ ((1 RED) (2 BLUE) (3 GREEN))
```

7.4 Other Forms of Iteration

The last two iteration constructs, `do` and `do*`, are the most general. `Do` has two required parts, the iteration clause and the test/result clause. The iteration clause introduces local variables, optionally gives them an initial value (just like in a `let` expression), and also optionally defines an expression for incrementing the local variable. The incrementing expression can be more than a simple arithmetic increment – it can be any expression evaluated at the bottom of the iteration loop and assigned to the local variable. The test/result clause, if evaluated to non-`nil`, will terminate the iteration, evaluate all of the result expressions, and return the value of the last one. The body of the iteration, which is any number of S-expressions, comes after the test/result clause. The `do` expression is like a `while` loop in other programming languages, except the test is inverted (that is, `while` *not(test)* `do` *expression*).

(do (*local-variable/initial-value/increment**) (*test result**) *S-expression**)

(do* (*local-variable/initial-value/increment**) (*test result**) *S-expression**)

In the `do` expression, the binding of the initial values to the local variables is done in parallel, as in the `let` expression. `Do*` is the same as `do`, except it binds its variables sequentially. Also, the incrementing expressions are assigned to the local variables in parallel for `do` and sequentially for `do*`. After the local variable binding, the test is evaluated to see if the iteration should terminate. If it evaluates to `nil`, then the expressions in the body are evaluated. After evaluation of the body, any local variable with an associated incrementing expression gets a new value and control goes back to the test.

As a simple test, let's write a function that computes factorial using `do`.

```
;;; Computes the length of a list iteratively.

(defun factorial (max-value)
  (do ((count 1 (1+ count))
       (result 1))
      ((> count max-value) result)
      (setf result (* count result))))
 ⇒ FACTORIAL
```

```
(factorial 6)
⇒ 720
```

To further illustrate all of the options within `do` and `do*`, the following illustrates a `do` model. Remember that the initial and incrementing expressions are optional, as in the first two local variables in this model.

```
(do ((local-var-1)
     (local-var-2 initial-expression-2)
     (local-var-3 initial-expression-3
                  increment-expression-3)
     (local-var-4 initial-expression-4
                  increment-expression-4)
     ...)
    (test result-expression-1 ...)
    (body-expression-1)
    (body-expression-2)
    ...
    (body-expression-n))
```

This achieves the same effect as the following pseudo-LISP code (this is pseudo-LISP, since labels and go-tos are not permitted in this context). Also, `psetf` assigns the incrementing expressions to the local variables. `Psetf` performs its assignment in parallel, just like the binding of initial values within a `let`:

```
(let (local-var-1
      (local-var-2 initial-expression-2)
      (local-var-3 initial-expression-3)
      (local-var-4 initial-expression-4)
      ...)
 <LoopLabel>
  (if test <go to FinishCode>)
  (body-expression-1)
  (body-expression-2)
  ...
  (body-expression-n)
  (psetf local-var-3 increment-expression-3
         local-var-4 increment-expression-4)
  ...
  <go to LoopLabel>
 <FinishCode>
  (result-expression-1)
  ...)
```

To show that these two constructs are as powerful as the previous iteration constructs, our next example is a recoding of `compute-squares`.

As a simple example, we'll recode the `compute-squares` function to use `do`.

```
;;; This is a version of compute-squares that performs the
;;; same task as the previous version that used dotimes.
;;; Compute the argument number of squares starting with
;;; zero.  Return them in an association list.

(defun compute-squares (number-of-squares)
  (do ((square-list nil)
       (each-integer 0 (1+ each-integer)))
    ((>= each-integer number-of-squares)
     (reverse square-list))
    (setf square-list
          (cons (list each-integer
                      (* each-integer each-integer))
                square-list))))
⇒ COMPUTE-SQUARES

(compute-squares 5)
⇒ ((0 0) (1 1) (2 4) (3 9) (4 16))
```

`Do` is more flexible than `dotimes`, because the iterator can start at any value, and it can increment by any value. The following does the same job as `compute-squares`, except it starts from one and only computes the squares of odd numbers.

```
;;; Compute a list of squares starting with one, except
;;; ignore the even ones.  Return them in an association
;;; list.

(defun compute-odd-squares (number-of-squares)
  (do ((squares-list nil)
       (each-integer 1 (+ each-integer 2)))
    ((>= each-integer number-of-squares)
     (reverse square-list))
    (setf square-list
          (cons (list each-integer
                      (* each-integer each-integer))
                square-list))))
⇒ COMPUTE-ODD-SQUARES

(compute-odd-squares 8)
⇒ ((1 1) (3 9) (5 25) (7 49))
```

`Do` and `do*` can also simulate the behavior of `dolist`. Notice in this version that the function must create a local variable `list-to-traverse` that then scans the list. Dolist does all of this implicitly. For a simple traverse of a list, dolist should be used over do.

```
;;; Determine the age of the oldest person in *persons*.

(defun oldest-person ()
  (do* ((list-to-traverse *persons* (cdr list-to-traverse))
        (a-person (car list-to-traverse)
                  (car list-to-traverse))
        (oldest (age a-person)))
    ((null list-to-traverse) oldest)
    (setf oldest (max oldest (age a-person)))))
⇒ OLDEST-PERSON

;; Test oldest-person.
(oldest-person)
⇒ 62
```

We can also write a function that is equivalent to mapcar. We can write mymapcar that takes only one list argument, along with the function. It calls the function on successive elements of the list and constructs a list from the results.

```
;;; Equivalent to mapcar of only one list argument.

(defun mymapcar (func list-argument)
  (do ((list-to-traverse list-argument
                         (cdr list-to-traverse))
       (new-list nil
                 (cons (apply func
                              (list (car list-to-traverse)))
                       new-list)))
    ((null list-to-traverse) (reverse new-list))))
⇒ MYMAPCAR

;; Now test mymapcar against mapcar.
(mapcar #'list '(1 2 3 4))
⇒ ((1) (2) (3) (4))

(mymapcar #'list '(1 2 3 4))
⇒ ((1) (2) (3) (4))
```

Since the incrementing expressions are evaluated after performing any assignment, the car of list-to-traverse will be the current first element. Also, notice that we are adding the new value to the front of the list, so the list is created backwards. Therefore, before returning the value, we must reverse the list. Finally, notice that there are no body expressions, since all of the work is done in the increment and test/result clauses.

It is interesting to note that `do` and `do*` constructs are about medium level in their capability. Other LISP languages provide much more powerful and general iteration constructs (for example, `for` in PSL and `loop` in ZetaLisp) that subsume the need for all of the previously defined iteration constructs. A committee is studying these constructs and may eventually propose a standard to be considered for adoption by the Common LISP community.

EXERCISES

7.10 Define a function called `mapcan` that takes a function and a list of values. `Mapcan` only returns a list of the non-`nil` results of the function applied to each value in the list.

```
(mapcan #'oddp '(1 2 3))
 ⇒ (T T)

(mapcan #'(lambda (x) (cond ((> x 5) x)(t nil))) '(1 4 6 7))
 ⇒ (6 7)
```

***7.11** As indicated in the definition of `do` and `do*`, you may define an expression with more than one iteration clause. Write a function that uses `do` or `do*`, which takes a list of elements and produces a list of sequentially tagged elements. This same problem has been done in each of the previous sections. Which one do you think is a better implementation, and why?

```
(numeric-tags '(red blue green))
 ⇒ ((1 RED) (2 BLUE) (3 GREEN))
```

7.12 Define a function called `nth-mapcar` which takes an integer, a function, and a list of values. `Nth-mapcar` applies the function to every *nth* value in the list and returns the resulting transformed list as in `mapcar`.

```
(nth-mapcar 3 #'list '(1 2 3 4 5 6))
 ⇒ ((3)(6))
```

7.5 Summary

There are many iteration constructs defined in LISP. They belong to three categories: simple iteration (`dotimes` and `dolist`); mapping iteration (`mapcar`, `maplist`, `mapc`, and `mapl`); and iteration (`do` and `do*`). Both iteration and recursion provide similar features. Selecting the appropriate one is dependent upon the particular problem that is being solved.

Chapter Exercises

Expert systems use many different techniques for representing knowledge. One common technique is known as a frame. A frame is very similar to an object. Like an object, there is a way of defining a frame template, and specifying slots for the frame. Unlike an object, most frame systems permit dynamically adding new slots to frames, allow frames to have children frames, and allow access to slots in parents automatically through inheritance. The goal of this set of exercises is to implement a simple frame system.

***1.** You are to implement `def-frame`, which is used to define the frame template, and also creates a frame instance of itself for the inheritance heirarchy. Create a `frame` object type that has at least five slots: `name`, `parent`, `children`, `instancep`, and `slots`. The `instancep` slot designates if the frame is an instance or not and the `slots` slot is an association list of slot names and values. Each slot should be initialized to the value of the variable `*unknown*` (which should be set to `'?`), if not preinitialized in the frame definition. We will see later how this feature is used. The function `def-frame` takes three arguments, the name of the frame, a list of parent frames, and a list of the slots. This should define the frame object, and link it into the heirarchy. All frame instances will be given a name. You should also keep the instances in an association list indexed by that name. Notice that the following example implies a few of the internal functions that you must correct. Do not use recursion in any of your functions; only use iteration.

```
(def-frame 'animal nil
  '(name sex type))
⇒ ANIMAL

(def-frame 'cat '(animal)
  '((type cat) fur-color weight))
⇒ CAT

*frames*
⇒ ((CAT #<Object FRAME>) (ANIMAL #<Object FRAME>))

(parent (get-frame 'cat))
⇒ (#<Object FRAME>)

(name (car (parent (get-frame 'cat))))
⇒ ANIMAL
```

***2.** Write the function `make-frame-instance`, which creates an instance of a frame. When the instance is created, the frame must be stored into `*frames*`, and it must be placed into the children list of the parent frame. The first argument to the function is the name of the frame you are making an instance. The second argument is the name of the instance frame, and the third is the list of slot initializations if any. Your function should verify that any slot initialized has been defined as a slot in any parent frame, anywhere in the heirarchy. Return the symbol `error` if a slot is to be initialized that doesn't exist in a parent.

```
(make-frame-instance 'cat 'lucky '((weight 5) (sex female)))
```

```
⇒ LUCKY

(make-frame-instance 'cat 'babs '((weight 10) (eyes blue)))
⇒ ERROR
```

***3.** Write the function **assert**, which takes three arguments. The first is the name of the frame in which to assert a value. The second is the slot name and the third is the value. Your function should search all parents to verify that the slot already exists and return **error** if it does not. Once verified, the slot value should be added to the frame argument.

```
(assert 'lucky 'fur-color 'gray)
⇒ GRAY

;; Default all animals to be female.
(assert 'animal 'sex 'female)
⇒ FEMALE

(assert 'cat 'tail-length 10)
⇒ ERROR
```

4.** Write the **ask** function which retrieves the value of the slot passed in the second argument from the frame referenced in the first argument. **Ask** should scan the hierarchy and return the first value that is not equal to ***unknown. If no value can be found or the slot doesn't exist, then simply return the value of ***unknown***. Don't forget to use iteration to find the value. (*Hint:* This actually requires a combination of iteration and recursion.)

```
(ask 'lucky 'weight)
⇒ 5

(ask 'lucky 'name)
⇒ ?

;; Now we will test the inheritance.
(make-frame-instance 'cat 'babs
                     '((weight 10) (fur-color white)))
⇒ BABS

(ask 'babs 'fur-color)
⇒ WHITE

;; See if it finds the default value in animal.
(ask 'babs 'sex)
⇒ FEMALE

;; Change the default value.
(assert 'animal 'sex 'male)
⇒ MALE

;; Verify that it changes.
(ask 'babs 'sex)
⇒ MALE
```

```
;; Set Babs sex slot to be female.
(assert 'babs 'sex 'female)
 ⇒ FEMALE

;; Verify that it is now recorded as female.
(ask 'babs 'sex)
 ⇒ FEMALE
```

5. Write the function **instances**, which returns a list of all of the frames that are instances from the argument frame. If a child is not an instance, then don't include it in the list, but do include all of its children instances. If the argument frame is already an instance frame, then return **error**.

```
(instances 'cat)
 ⇒ (#<Object FRAME> #<Object FRAME>)

(mapcar #'name (instances 'cat))
 ⇒ (LUCKY BABS)

(instances 'lucky)
 ⇒ ERROR

(mapcar #'name (instances 'animal))
 ⇒ (LUCKY BABS)
```

Function Summary

The following lists the functions and topics covered in this chapter.

- (dotimes (*symbol count return-S-expression*) *S-expression**)
- (dolist (*symbol list return-S-expression*) *S-expression**)
- (return *S-expression*)
- (mapcar *function-name list list**)
- (mapc *function-name list list**)
- (maplist *function-name list list**)
- (mapl *function-name list list**)
- (function *lambda-expression*)
- #'*lambda-expression*
- (lambda (*argument**) *S-expression**)
- (do (*local-variable/initial-value/increment**) (*test result**) *S-expression**)
- (do* (*local-variable/initial-value/increment**) (*test result**) *S-expression**)

8 MACROS

THIS CHAPTER DISCUSSES the LISP macro facility. Macros are both powerful and dangerous. They are powerful because you can tailor the programming environment, programming style, and even the LISP language to suit your needs. The danger lies in its power. You can use the full power of LISP when writing the macro and so you can create macros with bizarre side effects or different compiler and interpreter semantics. If you don't abuse the capabilities, macros are useful. To illustrate the importance of macros, our many examples will continue to be related to the data structures used in the expert system of Chapter 9.

8.1 Simple Macros

A macro translates a LISP expression into another expression. The translation occurs in the `eval` part of the LISP interpreter. When `read` gives an expression to `eval`, `eval` checks the operator to see if it is a macro. If not, each argument is evaluated and the function is called. If it's a macro, then the macro is invoked without any argument evaluation. The macro then returns a new LISP expression, which is then re-evaluated. If the macro returns an expression whose operator designates another macro, the process continues until a function is finally found.

The `defmacro` expression defines a macro and has the same syntax as `defun`. A macro produces a LISP expression that will be evaluated, so it must return a form that *can* be evaluated.

```
(defmacro macro-name(argument*) S-expression*)
```

The function `macroexpand` is a tool for debugging macros. It expands a macro and suppresses the second evaluation, returning the expanded expression. `Macroexpand` can verify that a macro is translating into the correct LISP code. `Macroexpand` takes one argument, which is the macro expression to be expanded.

```
(macroexpand S-expression)
```

Suppose that you don't like to use `car` and `cdr` to access lists – you prefer the terms `front` and `back`. You could easily implement functions with these names to perform the same operations.

```
;;; I prefer front to access the car of a list.

(defun front (some-list)
  (car some-list))
⇒ FRONT

;;; I also prefer back to access the cdr.

(defun back (some-list)
  (cdr some-list))
⇒ BACK
```

With these two function definitions, we could write code without `car` and `cdr`. For example, `oldest-person` would be written as follows:

```
;;; What is the age of the oldest person in *persons*.

(defun oldest-person ()
  (do* ((list-to-walk *persons* (back list-to-walk))
        (a-person (front list-to-walk) (front list-to-walk))
        (oldest (age a-person)))
    ((null list-to-walk) oldest)
    (setf oldest (max oldest (age a-person)))))
⇒ OLDEST-PERSON

;; Test oldest-person.
(oldest-person)
⇒ 62
```

Although the abstraction and the programming style is nice, it's not as efficient as `car` and `cdr`. There's an extra function call required to eventually get at the `car` or `cdr`. This is an excellent case for a macro. A macro will expand into the associated code, just as if the expanded code had been written there originally. So, we write `front` and `back` to translate into `car` and `cdr`.

```
;;; A macro version of front.

(defmacro front (some-list)
  (list 'car some-list))
⇒ FRONT
```

```
;;; Also, a macro version for back.

(defmacro back (some-list)
  (list 'cdr some-list))
 ⇒ BACK
```

Each of these definitions translates directly into an executable LISP expression, as demonstrated with calls to `macroexpand`.

```
;; Show the expansion of front and back.
(macroexpand '(front '(1 2 3)))
 ⇒ (CAR (QUOTE (1 2 3)))
 ⇒ T

(macroexpand '(back *persons*))
 ⇒ (CDR *PERSONS*)
 ⇒ T

;; Notice that no expansion is done on this argument.
(macroexpand '(car '(1 2 3)))
 ⇒ (CAR (QUOTE (1 2 3)))
 ⇒ NIL
```

Notice how the arguments to the macros are not evaluated. They will be evaluated in the second pass through `eval`, when it realizes that the operator (in this case `car` or `cdr`) is a function. Also, notice that `macroexpand` returned two values. The first is the expansion and the second is `T` or `nil`, which indicates whether the leading operator is a macro.

Now that we have changed `front` and `back` to be macros, `oldest-person` must be redefined. This doesn't mean that we have to modify the code, we just need to evaluate the definition again. For the macros to be properly referenced, we need to redefine the function body. This is done because the macros need to be defined before their actual use in code. If we don't redo the definition, then we might get an error.*

```
;;; What is the age of the oldest person in *persons*.

(defun oldest-person ()
  (do* ((list-to-walk *persons* (back list-to-walk))
        (a-person (front list-to-walk) (front list-to-walk))
        (oldest (age a-person)))
     ((null list-to-walk) oldest)
     (setf oldest (max oldest (age a-person)))))
 ⇒ OLDEST-PERSON
```

*Whether an error is signaled depends on the implementation. However, redefinition of the function is prudent.

```
;; Test oldest-person.
(oldest-person)
 ⇒ 62
```

A more complicated example redefines **add-person** as a macro instead of a function. The advantage of changing a function into a macro is that the arguments don't need quotes and so the calls are more natural. This is only possible when the arguments to the function are quoted symbols. The correct style defines **add-person** as a macro, which invokes **add-person-aux**, which is a function with quoted arguments.

```
;;; The add-person macro, which allows the arguments to be
;;; unquoted.

(defmacro add-person (name mother father sex age)
  (list 'add-person-aux
        (list 'quote name) (list 'quote mother)
        (list 'quote father) (list 'quote sex)
        (list 'quote age)))
 ⇒ ADD-PERSON

;;; This function does the work of adding the new person.  It
;;; is the same as the add-person function defined earlier.

(defun add-person-aux (name mother father sex age)
  (let ((new-person (make-instance 'person :name name
                                   :mother mother
                                   :father father :sex sex
                                   :age age)))
    (setf *persons* (cons new-person *persons*))
    new-person))
 ⇒ ADD-PERSON-AUX
```

First a quick test call to macroexpand to verify that the expansion is correct.

```
(macroexpand '(add-person bob joanne jim male 33))
 ⇒ (ADD-PERSON-AUX (QUOTE BOB) (QUOTE JOANNE) (QUOTE JIM)
 ⇒                 (QUOTE MALE) (QUOTE 33))
 ⇒ T

;; Expansion looks good, so invoke the macro for real.
(add-person bob joanne jim male 33)
 ⇒ #<Object PERSON>
```

The **eval** mentioned earlier is a real function that can be called when necessary. It's important in a macro where none of the arguments are evaluated.

The macro writer may need to provide explicit control of the argument evaluation or may need to evaluate a particular argument to determine the proper expansion.

```
(eval S-expression)
```

Suppose that the knowledge base has been divided into young and old people. `Add-person` must decide whether to invoke the `add-young-person` or the `add-old-person` function. The age of a person could be based on the current date and the birth date. Two new types can be defined to inherit from `person`.

```
(define-type young-person
  (:inherit-from person)
  (:var school-name)
  :all-settable
  :all-gettable
  :all-initable)
⇒ YOUNG-PERSON

(define-type old-person
  (:inherit-from person)
  (:var drivers-license-number)
  :all-settable
  :all-gettable
  :all-initable)
⇒ OLD-PERSON

;;; Compute approximate age from some birth year and the
;;; current year (assuming 1987).

(defun compute-age (birth-year)
  (- 1987 birth-year))
⇒ COMPUTE-AGE
```

The invocation of the `add-person` could appear as any of the following:

```
(add-person bob joanne jim male (compute-age 1953))
(add-person jimmy joanne jim male 32)
```

If the age is less than 16, then a `young-person` object is created, otherwise an `old-person` object is created.

```
;;; Add a young or an old person depending on their age.

(defmacro add-person (name mother father sex unevaluated-age)
  (let ((age (eval unevaluated-age)))
    (list
```

```
    (if (< age 16) 'add-young-person 'add-old-person)
    (list 'quote name) (list 'quote mother)
    (list 'quote father) (list 'quote sex) age)))
⇒ ADD-PERSON

;; Age should now be a value instead of a computation.
(macroexpand '(add-person bob joanne jim male
                          (compute-age 1953)))
⇒ (ADD-OLD-PERSON (QUOTE BOB) (QUOTE JOANNE) (QUOTE JIM)
⇒                 (QUOTE MALE) 34)
⇒ T
```

Macros can also define new control constructs. In fact, many of the constructs that we have seen so far are actually macros – `do`, `do*`, `dolist`, and `dotimes` to name just a few. `Dotimes` is of limited use since you can't specify a starting value and an increment. Therefore, we can define a new version that allows specification of more of these fields, much in the fashion of the Pascal `for`. The syntax of our `for` loop will be:

(`for` (*variable starting-value ending-value increment*) *S-expression**)

The first element after `for` is a four-element list. The syntax then allows any number of S-expressions. You can specify that the macro will take an arbitrary number of arguments by placing `&body` before the last argument.

`&body` *symbol*

The macro will translate into a `do` expression. When writing complicated macros, it's a good practice to write the invoking form and then what you expect as the result. Then you can more easily write the code for the appropriate transformation.

```
Invocation: (for (i 1 10 2) (setf result (+ i result)))
    Result: (do ((i 1 (+ i 2)))
                ((= i 10))
                (setf result (+ i result)))
```

We can write the code using this as a guide. We'll be careful to properly append all of the body expressions. Notice that local variables are used to extract each iteration specification. They aren't necessary, since all but `variable` are only used once. However, they make the expansion code much clearer.

```
;;; A for loop macro that has a variable, starting-value,
;;; ending-value and increment as the first argument list.
;;; The remaining expressions become the body of the macro.
;;; We will translate for into a "do" expression.
```

```
(defmacro for (argument-list &body body)
  (let ((variable (car argument-list))
        (starting-value (cadr argument-list))
        (ending-value (caddr argument-list))
        (increment (cadddr argument-list)))
    (append
     (list 'do
           (list (list variable starting-value
                       (list '+ variable increment)))
           (list (list '= variable ending-value)))
     body)))
⇒ FOR

;;; Compute the squares of the odd integers between 1 and the
;;; argument.

(defun compute-squares-of-odds (stop-value)
  (let ((squares nil))
    (for (i 1 stop-value 2)
         (setf squares (cons (list i (* i i)) squares)))
    (reverse squares)))
⇒ COMPUTE-SQUARES-OF-ODDS

(compute-squares-of-odds 10)
⇒ ((1 1) (3 9) (5 25) (7 49) (9 81))
```

You might also want to test if a symbol is a macro. `Macro-function` takes one argument, which must evaluate to a symbol, and returns the macro definition if it's a macro and `nil` if otherwise.

(macro-function *S-expression*)

```
(macro-function 'list)
⇒ NIL

;; The result of this evaluation is system dependent.
(macro-function 'add-person)
⇒ #<FUNCTION  Max Args= 2  Lambda Name= ADD-PERSON
⇒                Interpreted>
```

EXERCISES

***8.1** Write the functions **add-old-person** and **add-young-person** to complete the example that demonstrated **eval**.

***8.2** Modify the macro `for`, so that the increment is optional. When the increment is not specified, an increment of one is assumed.

8.3 Define a macro version of `nth`.

```
(macro-nth 1 a b c)
 ⇒ B

(macro-nth 3 a b)
 ⇒ NIL
```

8.2 Backquote

The bodies of macros often contain nested calls to `list`, `cons`, and `append`, along with various quoted expressions. Backquote makes the design of some of these expansions easier.

‘*S-expression*

On initial observation, the backquote symbol ‘ operates just like ’. The evaluation of the argument is suppressed and the result is the unevaluated argument. For example, a three-element list of three colors appears as follows:

```
'red
 ⇒ RED

`red
 ⇒ RED

'(red blue green)
 ⇒ (RED BLUE GREEN)

`(red blue green)
 ⇒ (RED BLUE GREEN)
```

Backquote appears to operate just like `quote`. The difference between the two comes from the ability to embed an unquote symbol within a backquote. The unquote symbol specifies that the following S-expression is evaluated before it's placed into the enclosing S-expression. This makes it easy to construct a list, where some parts are unevaluated and other parts are evaluated. The unquote symbol is comma "," and must precede an executable S-expression.

,*S-expression*

```
;; A number is self-evaluating, so the unquote in this
;; expression does not do anything special.
`((red 1) (blue ,2) (green ,3))
⇒ ((RED 1) (BLUE 2) (GREEN 3))

;; Define a magic number.
(setf magic 3)
⇒ 3

;; This produces values with executable S-expressions.
`((red ,(- magic 1)) (blue ,(+ magic 1))
  (green ,(* magic 2)))
⇒ ((RED 2) (BLUE 4) (GREEN 6))

;; This version doesn't have any commas, so nothing is
;; evaluated.
`((red (- magic 1)) (blue (+ magic 1)) (green (* magic 2)))
⇒ ((RED (- MAGIC 1)) (BLUE (+ MAGIC 1)) (GREEN (* MAGIC 2)))

;; An error occurs if you use a comma without a surrounding
;; backquote.
'((red ,(- magic 1)) (blue ,(+ magic 1))
  (green ,(* magic 2)))

!!!!! Error: Comma not inside a backquote.
  Condition signaled in: LISP::COMMA-MACRO.
```

The following demonstrates the `front` macro with and without backquote.

```
;;; A macro equivalent to front.

(defmacro front (arg)
  (list 'car arg))
⇒ FRONT

(macroexpand '(front '(red blue green)))
⇒ (CAR (QUOTE (RED BLUE GREEN)))
⇒ T

(front '(red blue green))
⇒ RED

;;; A macro equivalent to front, using backquote.

(defmacro front (arg)
  `(car ,arg))
⇒ FRONT
```

```
(macroexpand '(front '(red blue green)))
 ⇒ (CAR (QUOTE (RED BLUE GREEN)))
 ⇒ T

(front '(red blue green))
 ⇒ RED
```

Using the backquote and commas is a little different than using the forward quote. The forward quote expands into a call to `quote` as you have seen in many of the previous macro expansions. The backquote actually expands into the same LISP code that you would write to construct the appropriate list.

```
(macroexpand '`(car ,(list red green blue)))
 ⇒ (LIST (QUOTE CAR) (LIST RED GREEN BLUE))
 ⇒ NIL
```

The backquote facility permits another type of unquote, the splicing unquote, designated with "`,@`". The splicing unquote places the result of the argument into the S-expression with a level of parentheses removed.

`,@`*S-expression*

```
;; Define colors to contain a short list of colors.
(setf colors '(red blue green))
 ⇒ (RED BLUE GREEN)

;; Notice the result of each occurrence of colors within the
;; following.
`(colors ,colors ,@colors)
 ⇒ (COLORS (RED BLUE GREEN) RED BLUE GREEN)
```

The following demonstrates how a more complicated macro can use the backquote:

```
;;; A for loop macro that has a variable, starting-value,
;;; ending-value and increment as the first argument list.
;;; The remaining expressions become the body of the macro.
;;; We will translate for into a "do" expression.

(defmacro for (argument-list &body body)
  (let ((variable (car argument-list))
        (starting-value (cadr argument-list))
        (ending-value (caddr argument-list))
        (increment (cadddr argument-list)))
    `(do ((,variable ,starting-value
                     (+ ,variable ,increment)))
```

```
        ((= ,variable ,ending-value))
        ,@body)))
  ⇒ FOR
```

Notice how the template defined with the backquote looks just like the result that we wish to produce.

EXERCISES

8.4 Redefine the macro version of `nth` from the last section using the backquote syntax.

8.5 Given the following function from Chapter 5, recode it as a function using the backquote notation.

```
(defun make-clown-object (name shoe-size expression)
  (list (list 'name name)
        (list 'shoe-size shoe-size)
        (list 'expression expression)))
```

***8.6** Define the `while` macro that works like `while` in Pascal. The template is `(while` *test body*`)`. The macro translates into a `do` expression that evaluates the *body* while the *test* is true.

```
(setf x 0)
 ⇒ 0

(setf result nil)
 ⇒ NIL

(while (< x 10) (setf x (1+ x)) (setf result (cons x result)))
 ⇒ NIL

result
 ⇒ (10 9 8 7 6 5 4 3 2 1)
```

8.3 Destructuring with Macros

Destructuring is a way of telling the system about the syntax of the invoking macro. It saves you from breaking complicated macros into constituent parts. Destructuring is accomplished by placing a list where a macro argument is supposed to be. When a list parameter is found, the input expression is compared against the list and any symbols contained in the list parameter are bound to whatever is in the input list. For example, let's look at `add-person` again.

```
(defmacro add-person (name mother father sex unevaluated-age)
  (let ((age (eval unevaluated-age)))
    (list
     (if (< age 16) 'add-young-person 'add-old-person)
```

```
        (list 'quote name) (list 'quote mother)
        (list 'quote father) (list 'quote sex) age)))
```

In this example, there are five parameters and each will be bound to the argument in the corresponding location in the macro invocation. Suppose that for some reason we want to change the way we invoke the macro. Now, we want to invoke the macro by passing the mother and father arguments in a two-element list and likewise for the sex and age. So, the original invocation would have been:

```
(add-person bob joanne jim male (compute-age 1953))
```

While our new invocation will be:

```
(add-person bob (joanne jim) (male (compute-age 1953)))
```

Without destructuring, you would write the macro to take three arguments and use a `let` to define the symbols that represent the argument values:

```
(defmacro add-person (name second-arg third-arg)
  (let ((mother (car second-arg))
        (father (cadr second-arg))
        (sex (car third-arg))
        (age (eval (cadr third-arg))))
    (list
     (if (< age 16) 'add-young-person 'add-old-person)
     (list 'quote name) (list 'quote mother)
     (list 'quote father) (list 'quote sex) age)))
```

Destructuring restores the original definition, except for a few extra parentheses in the parameter list. The second argument is a two-element list of mother and father, so we can place this list as the second argument. We can do the same thing for the third argument. The result is a clean macro definition that specifies the syntax of the invoking macro and saves you from extracting the various arguments.

```
(defmacro add-person (name (mother father)
                           (sex unevaluated-age))
  (let ((age (eval unevaluated-age)))
    (list
     (if (< age 16) 'add-young-person 'add-old-person)
     (list 'quote name) (list 'quote mother)
     (list 'quote father) (list 'quote sex) age)))
```

The `for` macro used earlier is a perfect candidate for destructuring. The first argument is a list of the iteration specifications. Instead of breaking each apart in a `let`, we can use destructuring. Note that `&body` may be placed within the list argument to the `defmacro` to destructure an arbitrary number of expressions into one parameter.

```
;;; A for loop macro that has a variable, starting-value,
;;; ending-value and increment as the first argument list.
;;; The remaining expressions become the body of the macro.
;;; We will translate for into a "do" expression.

(defmacro for ((variable starting-value ending-value
                         increment)
               &body body)
  `(do ((,variable ,starting-value (+ ,variable ,increment)))
     ((= ,variable ,ending-value))
     ,@body))
⇒ FOR
```

Notice the difference between this and the original definition. This version uses both destructuring and backquote and makes for a nice, compact definition.

In an earlier exercise, you were given the task to change `for` so that the `increment` parameter is optional. It should use a default increment of one. This was possible, because the code that you wrote controlled the parsing of the first argument. To get this facility with destructured arguments, requires the use of `&optional`. Optional arguments may be designated by placing `&optional` before their parameters. All parameters up to the first occurrence of `&optional` are required parameters. All those mentioned after the `&optional` are optional. You may not mix required and optional parameters. Also, if you use an `&body`, it must follow all of the optional parameters. When an optional parameter is passed a value, it will be bound to that value. When it's not given a value, then it is bound to `nil`.

`&optional` *symbol*

Thus, we can now change `for` to use the `&optional`.

```
;;; A for loop macro that has a variable, starting-value,
;;; ending-value and increment as the first argument list.
;;; The remaining expressions become the body of the macro.
;;; We will translate for into a "do" expression.

(defmacro for ((variable starting-value ending-value
                         &optional increment)
               &body body)
  (if (not (numberp increment)) (setf increment 1))
  `(do ((,variable ,starting-value (+ ,variable ,increment)))
     ((= ,variable ,ending-value))
     ,@body))
```

```
 ⇒ FOR

(setf result nil)
 ⇒ NIL

(for (i 1 10) (setf result (cons i result)))
 ⇒ NIL

result
 ⇒ (9 8 7 6 5 4 3 2 1 1)
```

You can specify a default value that will be used when the optional parameter is not supplied. This is indicated by placing the optional parameter in a list with the initial value.

`&optional` (*initialization-expression*)

The use of this option further simplifies the specification of `for`. It eliminates the `if` expression and places the default value in the parameter specification.

```
;;; A for loop macro that has a variable, starting-value,
;;; ending-value and increment as the first argument list.
;;; The remaining expressions become the body of the macro.
;;; We will translate for into a "do" expression.

(defmacro for ((variable starting-value ending-value
                         &optional (increment 1))
               &body body)
  `(do ((,variable ,starting-value (+ ,variable ,increment)))
     ((= ,variable ,ending-value))
     ,@body))
 ⇒ FOR

(setf result nil)
 ⇒ NIL

(for (i 1 10) (setf result (cons i result)))
 ⇒ NIL

result
 ⇒ (9 8 7 6 5 4 3 2 1 1)
```

You can also indicate whether or not an optional parameter was actually passed a value as an argument. If you place a symbol after the initialization, it is bound to `t` when the parameter is supplied an argument value and `nil` when the value comes from the initialization specification. The specification of the supplied symbol is optional as indicated by the following syntax specification:

`&optional` (*initialization-expression symbol*)

For example, suppose that we want to force the increment to be positive when the range is increasing and negative when it is decreasing. The easiest thing to do is to check to see if the user supplied the increment argument or not. If it was not provided, then we check the range before assigning an increment value. The following version of `for` performs this operation.

```
;;; A for loop macro that has a variable, starting-value,
;;; ending-value and increment as the first argument list.
;;; The remaining expressions become the body of the macro.
;;; We will translate for into a "do" expression.  The
;;; increment defaults to one, except in the cases where the
;;; range is decreasing, where the increment is -1.

(defmacro for ((variable starting-value ending-value
                         &optional (increment 1 incrementp))
               &body body)
  (if (and (not incrementp) (> starting-value ending-value))
    (setf increment (- increment)))
  `(do ((,variable ,starting-value (+ ,variable ,increment)))
     ((= ,variable ,ending-value))
     ,@body))
 ⇒ FOR

(setf result nil)
 ⇒ NIL

(for (i 10 1) (setf result (cons i result)))
 ⇒ NIL

result
 ⇒ (2 3 4 5 6 7 8 9 10)
```

The use of optional parameters is not restricted to macros. You can also write function definitions with optional parameters. The same syntax using `&optional` may be used. One limitation is that destructuring is only permitted within macros. To specify an arbitrary number of arguments in a function you must use `&rest` instead of `&body`. They provide basically the same functionality, however, `&body` is restricted to macro definitions only. `&rest` may actually be used in macro definitions instead of `&body`. The only difference is that `&body` informs the system that the parameter will be bound to LISP code, while `&rest` doesn't have this restriction. It is similar to the difference between ' and `#'`.

`&rest` *symbol*

EXERCISES

8.7 Define your version of the **dotimes** macro. Make sure that you use destructuring and optional parameters.

***8.8** Define your version of the **dolist** macro. Make sure that you use destructuring and optional parameters.

***8.9** The solution to the last problem requires the introduction of a local variable that is used to traverse the list. What happens if the symbol that you chose is also used in the body of the **my-dolist**? What solution can you suggest?

8.4 Summary

Macros are a way of translating one LISP expression into another. They can be used to enhance the programming environment and to control the evaluation of arguments. The backquote facility helps to make writing macros easier, as it allows the expression of templates for the expansion, instead of requiring explicit construction. Finally, the use of destructuring allows you to write complicated macros which automatically extract the various parts of the macro invocation.

Chapter Exercises

***1.** Enhance the hardware maintenance configuration system in the Chapter 5 to include a set of macros for defining each hardware item and maintainers. For example, the invocation would appear as follows:

```
;; Define the upstairs laser printer, installed on 04/01/86,
;; with a 90 day PM period, Joe is the maintainer, and a 6
;; ppm speed.
(add-printer upstairs-laser (4 1 86) 90 joe (6 ppm))
;; Device dv.1, a 7945, 7/15/85 installation date, 180 day PM
;; period, Mark is the maintainer, and with 30 ms access
;; time.
(add-disk-drive dv.1 (7 15 85) 180 mark 7945 30)
;; Workstation named cons, installed 3/14/86, 180 day PM
;; period, Mark is the maintainer, a 700x1000 pixel size
;; screen, and 8 Meg of memory.
(add-workstation cons (3 14 86) 180 mark (700 1000 pixels)
                 (8 Meg))
;; The maintainer Mark, whose phone number is x8866, and
;; office address is MEB-4560.
(add-maintainer mark x8866 meb-4560)
```

***2.** There are now enough tools so that you can write a simple LISP expression evaluator. **Our-eval** must process non-lists and lists alike. If the expression to be evaluated is a symbol, then its value is returned. If it is any other non-list (like a number), then it is simply returned unevaluated. When the expression is a list, **our-eval** must check to see if the first argument is a macro or a function. In the former case, it first calls **macroexpand** and recursively invokes **our-eval** (in case the expansion returns something other than a list expression). If the operator is a function, then **apply** is called. Note that **apply** will not work on macros. The first argument must be a function name.

```
(our-eval 1)
 ⇒ 1

(our-eval '*persons*)
 ⇒ (#<Object PERSON> #<Object PERSON> #<Object PERSON>)

(our-eval '(compute-age 1953))
 ⇒ 34

(our-eval '(back '(bob jimmy patty)))
 ⇒ (JIMMY PATTY)
```

Function Summary

The following lists the functions and topics covered in this chapter.

- (defmacro *macro-name*(*argument**) *S-expression**)
- (macroexpand *S-expression*)
- (eval *S-expression*)
- &body *symbol*
- (macro-function *S-expression*)
- `
- ,
- ,@
- Destructuring
- &optional *symbol*
- &optional (*initialization-expression*)
- &optional (*initialization-expression symbol*)
- &rest *symbol*

9 CASE STUDY: EXPERT SYSTEMS

IN THIS CHAPTER, we implement an expert system programming shell, along with an expert system that solves genealogical queries. An expert system is a program that functions with some level of human expertise in a particular domain of discourse. Many different expert systems have been successfully developed. One highly successful system is Prospector [18]. Prospector's domain of discourse is geology, where the expert system "learned" how geologists find mineral deposits. Prospector searched a representation of an area in Washington for mineral deposits and found a $100,000,000 deposit of molybdenum. Successes such as this have added to the popularity of expert systems. This chapter should give you some insight into expert systems.

Expert systems generally consist of two main parts (see Figure 9.1):

1. A knowledge base – which contains facts and information about the task at hand. It also contains rules that are used to reason about the task; and
2. An inference engine – which is a program that uses the knowledge base to find matches between facts and rules. It then infers new facts and possibly even new rules.

An expert system shell is the set of functions that defines the inference engine, along with additional functions that let you define facts and rules. The knowledge engineer is the person who uses the shell to develop the knowledge base for a particular expert system.

9.1 The Genealogical Expert System

The genealogical system takes information about family trees and infers relationships. The only information provided to this system is name, father, mother, and sex. All other relationships (uncle, aunt, brother, and so on) will be inferred. The system infers these new relationships based on the particular type of inference engine being used. Many different types of inference schemes have been used. Two of the most popular are:

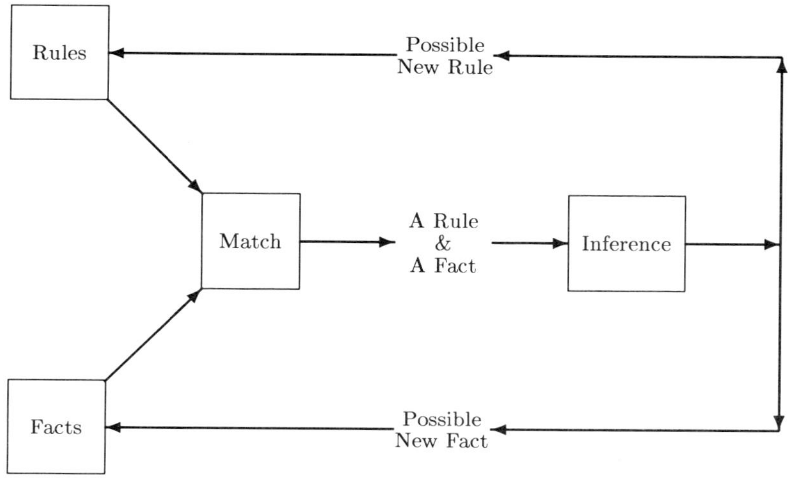

Figure 9.1 General Structure of an Expert System

1. Forward-chaining, where the rule invocations are driven by changes in the data (data-driven). The OPS [8] series of expert system shells use forward-chaining.
2. Backward-chaining, where rule invocations are driven by a goal – the inference engine tries to prove whether or not a given fact is true. EMYCIN [44] is an example of such a system.

Some systems provide both inference schemes, so the knowledge engineer can tailor the rules of inference to the scheme that best solves the problem. The genealogical system needs to answer questions like who is Jimmy's brother, is it true that Bob's sister is Patty, and so on. A backward-chaining system is good at solving these types of queries. So, we will use the backward-chaining model.

To see how this model works, let's solve a query. We must initially determine our genealogical knowledge. We will use the Kessler family, illustrated in Figure 9.2, throughout this chapter. The boxes contain siblings and the lines indicate parents. For example, Jim and Joanne are the parents of Bob, Jimmy, and Patty.

Suppose we want to know who is Bob's brother. You can see from the tree that Bob has a brother named Jimmy. How did you come to that conclusion? Remember, the only factual knowledge that you have is the mother, father, and sex of each person. You might have said to yourself, "I can prove that Bob has a brother by finding any sibling of Bob that is also male." But we don't know any siblings, because we only know about a person's parentage and sex. Therefore, we are stuck and must forget for a moment what we are trying to

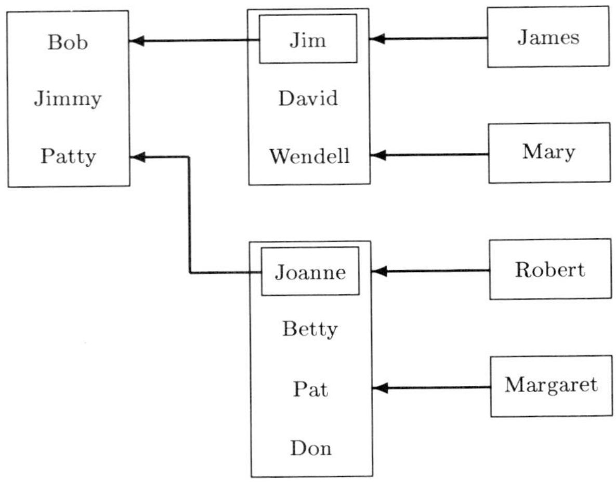

Figure 9.2 Part of the Kessler Family Tree

solve and instead establish a sub-goal to find out if Bob has any siblings. Siblings are those people who have the same parents. Are there any persons in the tree that have the same parents as Bob? In this case, both Jimmy and Patty have Jim and Joanne as their parents, just like Bob, and therefore are Bob's siblings. Now we can select any of those that are also male. In this case, Jimmy is male. Now that we have proved the sub-goal, and know a male sibling, we can go back to the original goal of finding Bob's brother. Jimmy meets the criteria and is therefore Bob's brother. A backward-chaining inference engine essentially goes through this solution process. It breaks a goal into sub-goals, trying to prove the sub-goals, and if successful has supporting evidence that the original goal is valid.

EXERCISE

***9.1** You might not have determined that Bob's brother is Jimmy using the backward-chaining approach. Instead, you might have used a technique like forward-chaining. Forward-chaining means that you work from what you know, using rules to prove new facts. These new facts may then cause other rules to be valid and then prove other new facts. Informally describe a forward-chaining solution to this query.

9.2 Knowledge Base

Expert system shells use different techniques for representing knowledge [18]. Each technique has its own peculiar set of advantages and disadvantages. One representation used in many systems is the frame. A frame is like an object that doesn't hide any slot access and doesn't have any methods except those that access the slots. Frames are also more dynamic since it is easy to add new slots to an existing frame. There are even systems that combine the features of both frames and objects [30]. The differences are not important for our expert system, so we will use objects for the knowledge representation.

The only problem with using objects for the knowledge representation is in the inference engine. For the engine to find a matching rule and fact, it must have access to all possible rules and facts. Objects, like any other data type, are very independent and can exist anywhere. For example, they can be collected into lists, stored in the slots of other objects, or simply bound to a variable. So, we need a way to collect together all objects that are a part of the expert system. We also need to classify together all objects that are the same type.

The first step defines the `person` type that represents the genealogical information. We want access to all information, so all slots must be both `:gettable` and `:settable`. The slots `name`, `mother`, `father`, and `sex` will be `:initable`, so they may be set when each person object is created. The `name` slot will be `:printable`, so we can distinguish objects when displayed. Finally, we must specify an initial value for each slot. The expert system must be able to distinguish between slots that don't have any value and those that might have a `nil` since they have no relationships. For example, the system can distinguish between not knowing if a person has an uncle and knowing that the person doesn't have an uncle. With these requirements, we can now define the `person` type.

```
;; Define the unknown value.
(defvar *unknown* '?)
 ⇒ *UNKNOWN*

;; The primary slots are name, mother, father and sex.  The
;; others will be inferred by the rule system.
(define-type person
  (:var object-name :initable)
  (:var name (:init *unknown*) :initable :printable)
  (:var mother (:init *unknown*) :initable)
  (:var father (:init *unknown*) :initable)
  (:var parent (:init *unknown*))
  (:var sex (:init *unknown*) :initable)
  (:var uncles (:init *unknown*))
  (:var aunts (:init *unknown*))
  (:var brothers (:init *unknown*))
  (:var sisters (:init *unknown*))
  (:var sibling (:init *unknown*))
  (:var cousins (:init *unknown*))
  :all-settable
  :all-gettable)
 ⇒ PERSON
```

A common operation of the inference engine is to find an object of a particular type. If all objects are simply collected into a list, then we have to scan the whole list to find each object of a designated type. If we use an association list, then we can easily find all objects of a certain type, just by using `assoc`. However, adding new objects into the middle of an association list is difficult. Consider the clown association list of previous chapters:

```
(setf clown '((name barney) (shoe-size 4)
              (expression smiling)))
 ⇒ ((NAME BARNEY) (SHOE-SIZE 4) (EXPRESSION SMILING))
```

Suppose that Barney's shoes are actually two different sizes, so you want to insert `4.5` into the association list. You can only do this with a recursive function that scans the association list and constructs a new list as it goes, searching for the matching key. If the key is found, a new association is constructed and added to the list along with the rest of the original list. The first exercise in this section asks you to implement a function that does this.

You could also do this by creating an object that holds the name of the type and a list of the children objects. The association list is then a list of objects, each specifying a type and the associated objects. This way we don't have to reconstruct the list each time we add a new object. To add a new object, we just find the type object and add the object to its internal slot. This is the scheme that we will implement.

```
;;; The information associated with a knowledge type.

(define-type knowledge-type
  (:var type-name (:init nil) :gettable :initable)
  (:var objects (:init nil) :gettable :initable))
 ⇒ KNOWLEDGE-TYPE
```

The `objects` method is automatically created and retrieves the list of objects. A new method, `add-object`, adds a new object to the list.

```
;;; Add a new object to the list of objects of a type.

(define-method (knowledge-type add-object) (new-object)
  (setf objects (cons new-object objects)))
 ⇒ ADD-OBJECT
```

Each of these `knowledge-type` objects will be stored in `*knowledge-base*`.

```
;; The global association list of knowledge types.
(defvar *knowledge-base* nil)
 ⇒ *KNOWLEDGE-BASE*
```

Now we need a function to store an object into the knowledge base. It must scan through the knowledge base and determine if a `knowledge-type` object for the specified type has already been created. If it has, then the object can be added to its `objects` slot. If not, then it is created and the object added as the first one in its `objects` slot. The function returns the argument in case any functions that call `insert-object` need to use the argument again.

```
;;; Given an object, this function inserts it into
;;; *knowledge-base*.

(defun insert-object (object)
  (labels ((find-type (type-list type)
             (cond ((null type-list) nil)
                   ((eq type (type-name (car type-list)))
                    (car type-list))
                   (t (find-type (cdr type-list) type)))))
    (let ((knowledge-type-found
           (find-type *knowledge-base*
                      (object-type object))))
      (if knowledge-type-found
        (add-object knowledge-type-found object)
        (setf *knowledge-base*
              (cons (make-instance 'knowledge-type
                                   :objects (list object)
                                   :type-name
                                   (object-type object))
                    *knowledge-base*)))
      object)))
⇒ INSERT-OBJECT
```

Now that we have a way of storing an object into the knowledge base, we also need a way of retrieving the objects associated with a particular type. The `find-objects` function scans the list, searching for a `knowledge-type` object that matches the type and returns the value in the `objects` slot. It can either recursively scan the list, comparing the argument type against the value of the `type` slot, or it can perform an iterative scan. Just for a change, we will use `dolist` instead of a recursive function.

```
;;; Search *knowledge-base* for a knowledge type object that
;;; matches the argument type.

(defun find-objects (searching-type)
  (dolist (a-type *knowledge-base*)
    (if (equal (type-name a-type) searching-type)
      (return (objects a-type)))))
⇒ FIND-OBJECTS
```

A final improvement on these functions makes it easier to add new objects into the knowledge base. The function insert-object adds the object, but requires that the object already exist. We want a facility like make-instance that creates the instance and, as a side effect, adds the created object to the knowledge base. So, we will define a new macro, add-knowledge, which has the same syntax as make-instance. It has to call make-instance and pass the result to insert-object.

```
;;; Create the object instance and insert it into the
;;; knowledge base.

(defmacro add-knowledge (&body instance-arguments)
  `(insert-object (make-instance ,@instance-arguments)))
 ⇒ ADD-KNOWLEDGE
```

We now have enough functions to define the knowledge for our expert system.

Now add-knowledge can be called to create each person. Before creating the objects, we should consider what to store in the slots referencing other person objects. We can either store the name of that person, or the person object itself. Since the knowledge associated with an object is stored in the slots of the object, we will continually need access to those slots. Storing the name then implies an extra level of indirection – whenever a name is found we must find the associated object. So, directly storing the object is the right approach. As you can see from this example, if we want to know who is Bob's father's father, we can find it more simply in the stored-object representation. All we have to do is access the name slot of the value of the father slot of the value of the father slot of the bob object. Using the stored-name representation, we have to access the slot, scan the data base to find the associated object, then access the slot, and so forth.

```
Slot        Store Name         Store Object
            #<Object BOB>      #<Object BOB>
Father        JIM                #<Object JIM>
Mother        JOANNE             #<Object JOANNE>
            #<Object JIM>      #<Object JIM>
Father        JAMES              #<Object JAMES>
Mother        MARY               #<Object MARY>
            #<Object JOANNE>   #<Object JOANNE>
Father        ROBERT             #<Object ROBERT>
Mother        MARGARET           #<Object MARGARET>
```

However, this stored object representation has a big problem. How do we create the proper family tree without infinitely creating all family relationships? In other words, how do we create the Jim object without creating both James and Mary objects. Similarly, how do we create those objects without first creating their parents. This must stop somewhere. Our solution is a cross between the two representations – we will store the name of the person into the slot when an object doesn't exist. We must also make the system robust enough to take non-object slot values. Thus, the stored objects would appear as:

```
Slot        Hybrid Store Object
            #<Object BOB>
Father        #<Object JIM>
Mother        #<Object JOANNE>
            #<Object JIM>
Father        JAMES
Mother        MARY
            #<Object JOANNE>
Father         ROBERT
Mother         MARGARET
```

With that in mind, we can now create some of the people in the Kessler family tree.

```
(setf joanne (add-knowledge 'person :name 'joanne
                            :father 'robert
                            :mother 'margaret :sex 'female))
 ⇒ #<Object PERSON NAME=JOANNE>

(setf jim (add-knowledge 'person :name 'jim :father 'james
                         :mother 'mary :sex 'male))
 ⇒ #<Object PERSON NAME=JIM>

(setf bob (add-knowledge 'person :name 'bob :father jim
                           :mother joanne :sex 'male))
 ⇒ #<Object PERSON NAME=BOB>

(setf jimmy (add-knowledge 'person :name 'jimmy :father jim
                           :mother joanne :sex 'male))
 ⇒ #<Object PERSON NAME=JIMMY>

(setf patty (add-knowledge 'person :name 'patty :father jim
                           :mother joanne :sex 'female))
 ⇒ #<Object PERSON NAME=PATTY>

;; Check to make sure that the insert functions are working
;; properly.
*knowledge-base*
 ⇒ (#<Object KNOWLEDGE-TYPE>)

(find-objects 'person)
 ⇒ (#<Object PERSON NAME=PATTY> #<Object PERSON NAME=JIMMY>
 ⇒  #<Object PERSON NAME=BOB> #<Object PERSON NAME=JIM>
 ⇒  #<Object PERSON NAME=JOANNE>)
```

EXERCISES

9.2 Write a function that takes three arguments: an association list, a key for the association list, and a value. The function is to add the key and value to the association list with the caveat that if the key already exists it must add the value to the associated list.

```
(setf clown '((name barney) (shoe-size 4)
              (expression smiling)))
⇒ ((NAME BARNEY) (SHOE-SIZE 4) (EXPRESSION SMILING))

(setf clown (add-association clown 'shoe-size 4.5))
⇒ ((NAME BARNEY) (SHOE-SIZE 4.5 4) (EXPRESSION SMILING))
```

***9.3** The list stored in `*knowledge-base*` is not directly defined to be an association list, because the key is stored in the object. Suppose that we wanted to change this representation so it is an association list. That way, we can find the objects using a call to `assoc`. Modify the functions, so that `*knowledge-base*` is an association list of type name and `knowledge-type` object. Try to change as little code as possible.

9.4 Define your own family tree and call `add-knowledge` to create each member of the family. If you don't want to use your tree, try the following Hauser family tree.

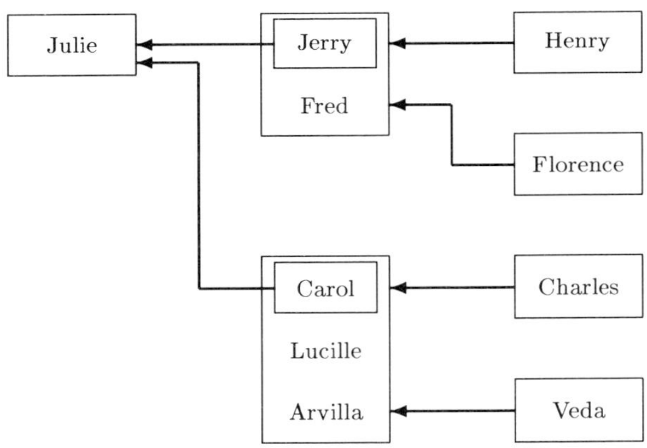

9.3 Rules

The next step for an expert system shell is to express the rules. A rule is essentially an *if-then* clause specifying that if a premise is true, then the conclusion is true. The following are pseudo-English descriptions of typical rules:

- *if* person X has a parent P and that parent P has a brother B *then* B is X's uncle
- *if* person X has a parent P and another person Y has the same parent P *then* X and Y are siblings

- *if* person X is a sibling of another person Y and Y is male *then* Y is the brother of X

These rules have much in common. Adding some structure and removing redundant English makes the commonality clearer:

- *if* (X parent-is P) and (P brother-is B) *then* (X uncle-is B)
- *if* (X parent-is P) and (Y parent-is P) *then* (X sibling-is Y)
- *if* (X sibling-is Y) and (Y sex-is male) *then* (X brother-is Y)

These three-element lists are called knowledge clauses and specify an object, slot, and value. In most of these cases, the object and the value are variables (in the last example, the value of the *sex-is* clause is a constant *male*). Use of variables makes the rules generic and capable of operating on any person. We will indicate a variable with a leading question mark. This makes it easier to recognize when a rule has generic implications. The object or value of a clause may also be a constant, in which a specific value is being specified. The slot must always specify a specific slot in an object and may not be a variable. Thus, there are four possible knowledge clauses:

1. `(object slot value)` – This indicates a specific object, with a particular slot and value.
2. `(object slot ?value)` – This indicates a specific object, with a particular slot and a variable value.
3. `(?object slot value)` – This indicates any object that has the slot and specific value.
4. `(?object slot ?value)` – This indicates any object that has the indicated slot, with any value.

This specification has a slight problem. Suppose that there exists a type that defines the characteristics of a `computer`. This might include the slot `memory` indicating how much memory is contained in a particular computer object. Also suppose there is another type that defines the characteristics of a `person` and it happens to include a `memory` slot indicating how good a memory the person has. A knowledge clause specified as

```
(?someobject memory ?somevalue)
```

could then match an object of either type. Suppose we also had a rule specifying that if someone has good memory, then that person should excel in school. The inference engine could match the premise against a computer and try to conclude that the computer will do well in school. To avoid this confusion each rule must also specify the types of all variables. Then, when the inference engine tries to find a matching object, it can be directed to look in the "right" set of types. Types can be kept in an association list of the variable and its object type. An association list is a good representation since there may be multiple variables specified in a rule. When the rule doesn't care about the type of a particular variable, a `nil` is used for its type. Thus, if the type of `?someobject` had been indicated to be `person`, then an appropriate person object could be found and the computer objects would be ignored.

So, each rule must specify the premise, the conclusion, and the variable types. Adding all of this together with a little syntactic sugar results in the following syntax for the rules given above:

```
(define-rule uncle-rule
  (type (?person person) (?person2 person) (?uncle person))
  (premise (and (?person parent ?person2)
                (?person2 brothers ?uncle)))
  (conclusion (?person uncles ?uncle)))

(define-rule sibling-rule
  (type (?person person) (?person2 person)
        (?person3 person))
  (premise (and (?person parent ?person2)
                (?person3 parent ?person2)))
  (conclusion (?person sibling ?person3)))

(define-rule brother-rule
  (type (?person person) (?person2 person))
  (premise (and (?person sibling ?person2)
                (?person2 sex male)))
  (conclusion (?person brothers ?person2)))
```

The first argument is the name of the rule, which might be used for debugging later. For example, when a rule is true, its name is printed. The type clause must enumerate every variable in the premise and conclusion clauses. Since each variable must be enumerated, the use of a leading question mark is not mandatory and is merely a convention. However, it helps when looking at a rule to see which parts are variables and which are constants. It also simplifies the implementation because the system can tell which symbol is a variable by just looking in the type list.

The premise is restricted to one knowledge clause or a conjunction of knowledge clauses using the `and` operator. The conclusion must be a single knowledge clause. Notice the careful use of different variable names. A repeated name indicates that the same object must match both the initial occurrence and any subsequent occurrences. Thus, in `uncle-rule`, `?person2` must be the parent of the person and must also have a brother.

One problem with these rules is the specification of sibling. Notice that although it specifically mentions `person` and `person3` there is no indication that they must be different. The rule system would be perfectly happy to prove that if Bob has parent Jim, and Bob has parent Jim (again), then Bob is Bob's sibling. We could design the rule system so that no two variables within a rule may be bound to the same value. On the surface, this seems reasonable, but it places an unnecessary restriction on the rule system. There may be perfectly legitimate places where two variables could be bound to the same value. For example, consider the following rule:

```
(define-rule mineral-property
  (type (?rock mineral)
        (?rock2 mineral)
        (?color spectrum)
        (?color2 spectrum))
  (premise (and (?rock color ?color)
                (?rock2 color ?color2)
                (?color is-classified bright)
                (?color2 is-classified bright))
  (conclusion (?rock is-a-kind-of ?rock2)))
```

In this case, both rocks have a color that is classified as being bright. We don't care if they are the same color or not, as long as they are a bright color. Also, notice that this rule also suffers from the problem that both `rock` and `rock2` could be bound to the same value. The proper solution permits the rule writer to specify when the variables must be different. In fact, the best solution permits the rule writer to specify any LISP expression that behaves like a predicate. The rule writer can then compare two variables and also perform any other kind of test (for example, compare a person's age with some minimum or maximum value). Since this is LISP, we can embed executable LISP code within the premise. The programmer must indicate that it is executable code and not a knowledge clause by placing some key symbol in the place of the object of the knowledge clause. We will use the symbol `test` to indicate that the following expression should be evaluated. When the rule system finds the code it can call `eval` and if non-`nil` is returned, then that part of the premise is true. The system must properly substitute the values for any variables mentioned in the expression. Using a `test` clause, `sibling-rule` would appear as follows:

```
(define-rule sibling-rule
  (type (?person person) (?person2 person) (?person3 person))
  (premise (and (?person parent ?person2)
                (?person3 parent ?person2)
                (test (not (equal (quote ?person)
                                  (quote ?person3)))))
  (conclusion (?person sibling ?person3)))
```

Notice the presence of the `quote`. This is because when the expression is evaluated, `?person` and `?person3` will be replaced with actual names as:

```
(not (equal (quote BOB) (quote JOANNE)))
```

Thus, to avoid access to an unbound variable, they must be quoted.

EXERCISES

***9.5** Write a rule using the `define-rule` syntax that defines the cousin relationship. Define rules for the following genealogical relationships: (a) aunt, (b) grandparent, and (c) grandchild.

9.6 Propose a scheme that would provide the same semantics as the `test` clause, but doesn't require quoting the variables.

***9.7** Assume that we have added `age` and `older-brother` to the `person` object. Write a rule that specifies that a person is another person's older brother.

9.4 Rule Definition Implementation

Before implementing `define-rule`, a few decisions must be made. The first decision is how to represent the rules. Since each rule has well-defined fields that must be easily accessible, an object is the perfect representation. A rule object can have name, type, premise, and conclusion slots. The next decision is where to store the rules once they are constructed. Since the inference engine must find the rules to invoke, we could represent the rules as a list of their names and then store a rule object as the value of the name symbol. A better solution maintains a list of all of the rule objects. This saves storing each object as the value of the rule-name symbol and saves time when finding another rule. The global variable `*rules*` maintains the list of rule objects.

```
;; The global variable that maintains a list of all of the
;; rules.
(defvar *rules* nil "Contains all of the rule objects")
 ⇒ *RULES*

;;; The rule object contains the four pertinent rule fields.
;;; A rule is a static structure, so once the fields are
;;; initialized there is no need to redefine them.

(define-type rule
  (:var name :printable)
  (:var type (:init nil))
  (:var premise)
  (:var conclusion)
  :all-gettable
  :all-initable)
 ⇒ RULE
```

Using these data structures, `define-rule` can be defined. The general syntax of a call to `define-rule` was shown earlier, but a typical call would appear as follows:

```
;;; Sample rule definition.

(define-rule parent-rule2
  (type (?person person) (?person2 person))
  (premise (?person mother ?person2))
  (conclusion (?person parent ?person2)))
```

By defining this as a macro, the rule name and various clauses don't need to be quoted. This is a typical use of macros and allows a more natural definition of the rules. The type clause isn't necessary if there are no variables within the various knowledge clauses. Therefore, the macro must parse the rule clauses to extract the appropriate fields. Notice that following the name of the rule is a list that is actually an association list, where the first element of each list indicates the type of clause. Thus, `assoc` can be used to extract the clauses. This has the advantage that the clauses don't need to be in any particular order. The disadvantage is that `assoc` must scan the list each time to find the appropriate clause. However, since the lists are relatively short (no more than three elements), `assoc` will not take much time. Once the fields have been extracted, `add-rule` is called to construct the object and save it in `*rules*`.

```
;;; Parse the various clauses from the rule definition and
;;; then call add-rule, which actually creates the object and
;;; saves it in the *rules* list.

(defmacro define-rule (rule-name &body rule-clauses)
  `(add-rule ',rule-name
             ',(cdr (assoc 'type rule-clauses))
             ',(cadr (assoc 'premise rule-clauses))
             ',(cadr (assoc 'conclusion rule-clauses))))
 ⇒ DEFINE-RULE
```

Notice that extracting the `type` part retrieves the `cdr` of the call to `assoc`, instead of the `cadr` as in the other cases. This is because there can be an arbitrary number of type specifications following the `type`, but the `premise` and `conclusion` may have only one clause.

```
;;; Construct a rule object and add it to the list of rules.
;;; This function returns the name of the rule as the result.

(defun add-rule (rule-name type premise conclusion)
  (setf *rules* (cons
                 (make-instance 'rule
                                :name rule-name
                                :type type
                                :premise premise
                                :conclusion conclusion)
```

```
                    *rules*))
  rule-name)
 ⇒ ADD-RULE
```

Now, we can test the system by defining a few rules and verify that `*rules*` is being properly created.

```
;;; Try each of the genealogical rules.

(define-rule uncle-rule
  (type (?person person) (?person2 person) (?uncle person))
  (premise (and (?person parent ?person2)
                (?person2 brothers ?uncle)))
  (conclusion (?person uncles ?uncle)))
 ⇒ UNCLE-RULE

(define-rule sibling-rule
  (type (?person person) (?person2 person) (?person3 person))
  (premise (and (?person parent ?person2)
                (?person3 parent ?person2)
                (test (not (equal (quote ?person)
                                  (quote ?person3))))))
  (conclusion (?person sibling ?person3)))
 ⇒ SIBLING-RULE

(define-rule brother-rule
  (type (?person person) (?person2 person))
  (premise (and (?person sibling ?person2)
                (?person2 sex male)))
  (conclusion (?person brothers ?person2)))
 ⇒ BROTHER-RULE

;; Verify that *rules* contains the appropriate objects.
*rules*
 ⇒ (#<Object RULE NAME=BROTHER-RULE>
 ⇒  #<Object RULE NAME=SIBLING-RULE>
 ⇒  #<Object RULE NAME=UNCLE-RULE>)

;; Check a field of one of the rule objects.
(premise (car *rules*))
 ⇒ (AND (?PERSON SIBLING ?PERSON2) (?PERSON2 SEX MALE))
```

Finally, to complete the definitions, we need a few more rules to define parentage.

```
(define-rule parent-rule1
  (type (?person person) (?person2 person))
  (premise (?person mother ?person2))
```

```
  (conclusion (?person parent ?person2)))
⇒ PARENT-RULE1

(define-rule parent-rule2
  (type (?person person) (?person2 person))
  (premise (?person father ?person2))
  (conclusion (?person parent ?person2)))
⇒ PARENT-RULE2
```

EXERCISES

***9.8** Write a **show** method for a rule, which returns a list describing the rule in a pseudo-English description.

```
(show (caddr *rules*))
⇒ (IN BROTHER-RULE IF ?PERSON SIBLING IS ?PERSON2 AND
⇒      ?PERSON2 SEX IS MALE THEN ?PERSON BROTHERS IS ?PERSON2
⇒      WHERE ?PERSON IS A PERSON AND ?PERSON2 IS A PERSON)
```

9.9 From the definition of the inference engine, you should notice that one of the steps requires finding a rule that can prove the assertion. Using the ***rules*** list, a **find-matching-rules** function must scan each rule until it finds one that matches or can prove the assertion. This could be very time consuming when there are a large number of rules. An optimization would be to determine a way of grouping the rules so that the function didn't have to scan all of the rules. A simple grouping would be by the type of the object in the conclusion. In our genealogical example, this wouldn't help much, since all rules reason about persons. Another technique would be to group them by the slot name specified in the conclusion. Since this cannot be a variable, it could be used to quickly isolate all rules that pertain to a particular slot. In this system, this technique would reduce the rule-scanning process so that the engine only has to look at a few rules each time. Modify the previous functions, so ***rules*** maintains the list in this order.

9.5 Backward-Chaining Inference Engine

The backward-chaining inference process is invoked by calling the `solve` function and passing it a knowledge clause called an assertion. `Solve` takes an additional argument, which is a type list of any variables that may be contained in the knowledge clause. `Solve` performs the following steps:

1. `Solve` looks into the knowledge base to determine if the assertion is already known. If it is already known, then it returns the clause, with any variables replaced with actual values. As an example, here is an invocation of `solve`.

```
(solve (list bob 'sex 'male) nil)
⇒ (#<Object PERSON NAME=BOB> SEX MALE)
```

In this example, solve must look into the Bob object and see if the sex slot has the value male. Had solve asked for female, then the result would be nil. This is because the sex slot in Bob is bound to male, which is not female. Had the slot been bound to the unknown value (the value of the global *unknown* as mentioned before), then the inference engine would access the rules and try to discover the value of the slot through inferencing techniques (step 2).

```
(solve (list bob 'sex 'female) nil)
 ⇒ NIL
```

When the value part of the knowledge clause is a variable, the engine looks into the object to see if there is a bound value and returns that value if it exists. Notice that we must provide the second argument with the list of types of the variables.

```
(solve (list Jimmy 'father '?person)
       '((?person person)))
 ⇒ (#<Object PERSON NAME=JIMMY> FATHER
 ⇒  #<Object PERSON NAME=JIM>)
```

The next example is interesting because there are two objects that could solve the query, Bob and Jimmy. The system is permitted to arbitrarily select the first one that it finds.

```
(solve (list '?person 'mother Joanne)
       '((?person person)))
 ⇒ (#<Object PERSON NAME=BOB> MOTHER
 ⇒  #<Object PERSON NAME=JOANNE>)
```

When the engine is presented with a clause with two variables, then the engine searches all of the objects to see if any have a matching slot with a known value. If it finds one, it returns it, otherwise the engine proceeds to step 2.

2. Since the assertion is not directly available in the knowledge base, the engine must try to prove it using rules. It searches the set of rules for one whose conclusion matches the assertion. In other words, it must find a rule such that if its premise were true, then the conclusion would be true, thus proving the assertion. The matching process must first check that the referenced objects are of the same type, that they have the same slot, and that the values match. For example, suppose that the following invocation of solve occurs:

```
(solve (list bob 'sibling jimmy) nil)
```

Using the rules mentioned before, the conclusion of sibling-rule would match:

```
(define-rule sibling-rule
  (type (?person person) (?person2 person)
        (?person3 person))
  (premise (and (?person parent ?person2)
                (?person3 parent ?person2)))
  (conclusion (?person sibling ?person3)))
```

This matches because `bob` is an instance of a `person`, `?person` is a `person` variable, the slot names are the same, and `jimmy` matches `?person3`. This matching causes a binding of variable names to actual values. This binding is then passed to the premise and any specified substitutions are made. So, the binding list is:

```
((?person #<Object PERSON NAME=BOB>)
 (?person3 #<Object PERSON NAME=JIMMY))
```

Using the binding the premise can be conceptually modified to be the following:

```
(premise
 (and (#<Object PERSON NAME=BOB> parent ?person2)
      (#<Object PERSON NAME=JIMMY> parent ?person2)))
```

3. The engine now tries to recursively `solve` each clause of the premise. As each premise is proved, any bindings must be passed along to any remaining premises and ultimately the conclusion. When all parts of the premise are proven to be true, then the conclusion should be returned.

   In this process we must properly maintain the list of variable bindings. As each premise is proved, any new bindings must be added to the binding list. However, if a premise can't be proved, then the system must be capable of backing up and undoing a binding. Once the binding has been undone, the engine must return to step 2 and search for another rule that might prove the assertion. Returning to the sibling example, the engine must now try to solve two assertions, the first of which can be illustrated with another call to `solve`:

```
(solve (list bob 'parent '?person2) '((?person2 person)))
```

   Once this first assertion is proven, then the second must be tried – the variable must get a new binding. Suppose that `solve`'s first result is:

```
⇒ (#<Object PERSON NAME=BOB> PARENT JOANNE)
```

   then the binding list is updated as follows:

```
((?person2 #<Object PERSON NAME=JOANNE>)
 (?person #<Object PERSON NAME=BOB>)
 (?person3 #<Object PERSON NAME=JIMMY))
```

and second assertion appears as:

```
(solve (list Jimmy 'parent Joanne) nil)
⇒ (#<Object PERSON NAME=JIMMY> PARENT
⇒  #<Object PERSON NAME=JOANNE>)
```

Since both clauses have been proved, then the original conclusion is true. The original call to `solve` produces:

```
⇒ (#<Object PERSON NAME=BOB>
⇒  SIBLING
⇒  #<Object PERSON NAME=JIMMY>)
```

EXERCISES

***9.10** Using the rules and knowledge base developed thus far, solve the following query by hand. Illustrate each step in the process.

```
(solve '(?someone brothers ?someone-else)
       '((?someone person) (?someone-else person)))
```

9.11 Describe how the steps in the inference process would be changed if an `or` operator were permitted within a premise.

9.6 Lookup

As outlined in the last section, an important part of inferencing is accessing the knowledge base and determining if a particular assertion is already true. This happens before you use any part of the rule mechanism. We will implement the `lookup` function to perform this task.

`Lookup` must take at least one argument, which is the knowledge clause that is to be found. The first step is to find the set of objects that could match the clause. When the object designator is a constant, then the set is very small, including only one element – the object. If the object designator is a variable, then all objects that are of the type designated by that variable are possible objects. This also implies that `lookup` must receive an additional argument that is the type specification for all of the variables. Once we have the set of possible objects, `lookup` scans them to find one that has a value matching the value part of the knowledge clause. If the knowledge clause has a variable value, then the function must find any object that has any legal value for that slot. A legal value is anything except for `*unknown*`.

As we saw from the calls to `solve`, once `lookup` finds a matching object, it must return some information to the caller. The information that is required is two-fold. First it must return an indication that a match was or was not found. Second, if a match is found, then it must return the bindings of any variables mentioned in the knowledge clause. The bindings will then be used by the inference engine to substitute for any variables in later premise clauses or the conclusion. You might think that we could use the bindings for double duty; if they are returned then it indicates that a match was found, while no binding list indicates that no match could be found. The problem with this is that it is possible to have a match and also not return any bindings. If the knowledge clause doesn't include any variables, then no bindings will be returned. To get around this problem, we will use the list `((T T))` to designate a match without any bindings. The list within a list must be done because a list with bindings can actually be a list of two lists of bindings.

Using this general guide, we want to design a function that performs operations as follows:

```
Invocation: (lookup (list bob 'sex 'male) nil)
   ;; See if Bob is male.
 Enter lookup:
    Assertion: (#<Object PERSON NAME=BOB> SEX MALE)
    Variables: nil
  Find all possible objects:
    (#<Object PERSON NAME=BOB>)
  Check each object for a match and return.
 Result of Lookup:
    ((T T))
Invocation: (lookup '(?person sex female)
                    '((?person person)))
   ;; Find any female.
 Enter lookup:
    Assertion: (?PERSON SEX FEMALE)
    Variables: ((?PERSON PERSON))
  Find all possible objects:
   (#<Object PERSON NAME=BOB> #<Object PERSON NAME=PATTY>
    #<Object PERSON NAME=JIMMY> #<Object PERSON NAME=JIM>
    #<Object PERSON NAME=JOANNE>)
  Check each object for a match and return.
 Result of Lookup:
   ((?PERSON #<Object PERSON NAME=PATTY>))
```

Before we write the code for `lookup`, we need to add one more feature. When we query the knowledge base as in the last example, there are actually a number of objects that match the query. We received Patty as a result, but it could have just as likely been Joanne. The inference engine needs to find a matching object and then if that object fails in some other part of the inference process, it needs to come back and find another matching object. For example, `lookup` may find Patty, but really has to find a male. Without some knowledge about the last match, `lookup` would simply return the same value each time. One technique would be to make `lookup` find all objects that match the assertion and return them as a list. This isn't good, because the routines might have to scan many objects when the first object was sufficient.

A better solution is to take advantage of the list of possibly matching objects. This is the set of all objects that could match. When a match is found, any objects remaining in the list are still possible matches. So, if the remaining object list is returned, further calls to `lookup` could use that list to find other matches. We must make `lookup` take an additional argument that is the list of objects returned from a previous call to `lookup`. If the argument is `nil` `lookup` should operate as outlined before. When it is non-`nil` `lookup` just uses the list and looks for another match. Thus, the last example would appear as follows:

```
Invocation: (lookup '(?person sex female) '((?person person))
                    nil)
   ;; Find any female.
 Enter lookup:
    Assertion: (?PERSON SEX FEMALE)
    Variables: ((?PERSON PERSON))
  Find all possible objects:
   (#<Object PERSON NAME=BOB> #<Object PERSON NAME=PATTY>
    #<Object PERSON NAME=JIMMY> #<Object PERSON NAME=JIM>
    #<Object PERSON NAME=JOANNE>)
  Check each object for a match and return.
 Result of Lookup:
   (((?PERSON #<Object PERSON NAME=PATTY>))
    (#<Object PERSON NAME=JIMMY> #<Object PERSON NAME=JIM>
     #<Object PERSON NAME=JOANNE>))
```

Thus, the `car` of the result is the bindings, while the `cdr` are any remaining possible objects. A second invocation to find another match would appear as:

```
Invocation: (lookup '(?person sex female) '((?person person))
                    '(#<Object PERSON NAME=JIMMY>
                      #<Object PERSON NAME=JIM>
                      #<Object PERSON NAME=JOANNE>))
Enter lookup:
    Assertion: (?PERSON SEX FEMALE)
    Variables: ((?PERSON PERSON))
  Old Objects: '(#<Object PERSON NAME=JIMMY>
                 #<Object PERSON NAME=JIM>
                 #<Object PERSON NAME=JOANNE>))
  Find all possible objects (just use old objects):
   (#<Object PERSON NAME=JIMMY> #<Object PERSON NAME=JIM>
    #<Object PERSON NAME=JOANNE>)
  Check each object for a match and return.
 Result of Lookup:
```

```
(((?PERSON #<Object PERSON NAME=JOANNE>))
 nil)
```

As we implement `lookup`, we must remember to use good data abstraction techniques for accessing the various parts of the knowledge clause. Retrieving each field can be accomplished with a simple macro that expands into the appropriate combination of `car` and `cdr`. Their implementation is straightforward as follows:

```
;;; Given an assertion, extracts the object part.

(defmacro object (assertion)
  `(car ,assertion))
⇒ OBJECT

;;; Given an assertion, extracts the slot part.

(defmacro slot (assertion)
  `(cadr ,assertion))
⇒ SLOT

;;; Given an assertion, extracts the value part.

(defmacro value (assertion)
  `(caddr ,assertion))
⇒ VALUE
```

Now we can implement the function `lookup`. It can be implemented in two steps. The first step is to find the list of possible objects. If the third argument is not `nil` then it is to be used as the list. Otherwise, we check to see if the object part is a variable. If it is, then `lookup` must find all objects that are of the type designated by the variable. This can be accomplished by calling the `find-objects` function defined previously. Otherwise the possible objects are just the list of the object itself. Once this list is computed, we can call an auxiliary function `find-matching-object`, which takes the list of objects and finds one that matches. It is responsible for returning the binding list, along with any possible objects that remain.

```
;;; Access the knowledge base and return a two-element list.
;;; The first is the bindings and the second is the remaining
;;; objects list.  Any bindings of the form (T T) indicate
;;; that there was a match, but no particular bindings were
;;; found.  If the name does not represent an object, then no
;;; look up is possible and lookup returns nil.

(defun lookup (assertion variables old-objects)
  (find-matching-object assertion variables
```

```
(cond (old-objects)
      ((variablep (object assertion) variables)
       (find-objects
        (variable-type (object assertion) variables)))
      ((objectp (object assertion))
       (list (object assertion)))
      (t nil))))
⇒ LOOKUP
```

You will notice that we used two auxiliary functions. One checks to see if the argument is a variable by scanning the type list to see if it is present. The other returns the type of a variable given its name.

```
;;; Checks to see if the first argument is a variable.

(defun variablep (possible-variable variable-mapping)
  (assoc possible-variable variable-mapping))
⇒ VARIABLEP

;;; Given a variable, it returns the associated type.

(defun variable-type (variable variable-mapping)
  (cadr (assoc variable variable-mapping)))
⇒ VARIABLE-TYPE
```

The implementation of `find-matching-object` requires that it scan the list of possible objects and find one that matches. To find a match, we must first get the value of the designated slot in the object. This can be done by `apply`ing the slot name to the object. This call returns the value in that slot of the object. We can then compare it against the unknown value. If it is unknown, then we need to try the next object. Otherwise we need to check to see if the slot value matches the knowledge clause value (when that clause value is not a variable). If it doesn't match, then we also need to recurse on the remaining possible objects. These two recursive calls can be combined into one with a little clever checking of values. Otherwise we have some kind of match, so the code must construct the two-element list. The first element must be the bindings and the second is the rest of the objects.

Constructing the list of bindings is a little tricky. This is because there are essentially four cases to handle – all combinations of variables and constants. We can use `append` to construct the list, utilizing the fact that if we `append` a `nil` then nothing is appended. The rest of the function can be implemented just like the other recursive list scanning functions.

```
;;; Search the list of objects to try and find one with a
;;; matching slot and value.  If the value is a variable,
;;; then the first slot without an unknown value will be
```

```
;;; returned.  This function returns a two-element list:
;;;   (((object-variable object-matched)
;;;     (value-variable slot-value)) remaining-objects)
;;;   or
;;;   (((object-variable object-matched)) remaining-objects
;;;   or
;;;   (((value-variable slot-value)) remaining-objects)
;;;   or
;;;   ((T T) remaining-objects)
;;;   or
;;;   NIL when no match.

(defun find-matching-object (assertion variables objects)
  (if objects
    (let ((slot-value (apply (slot assertion)
                             (list (car objects)))))
      (if (or (equal slot-value *unknown*)
              (and (not (variablep (value assertion)
                                   variables))
                   (not (equal slot-value
                               (value assertion)))))
        (find-matching-object assertion variables
                              (cdr objects))
        (list
         (or (append (if (variablep (value assertion)
                                    variables)
                       `((,(value assertion) ,slot-value)))
                     (if (variablep (object assertion)
                                    variables)
                       `((,(object assertion)
                          ,(car objects)))))
             '((T T)))
         (cdr objects))))
    nil))
 ⇒ FIND-MATCHING-OBJECT
```

Now that all of the support functions have been defined, we can test `lookup`. The tests try each of the four possible combinations of constants and variables.

```
;; Check for a direct lookup of object and value.
(lookup (list bob 'sex 'male) nil nil)
 ⇒ (((T T)) NIL)

;; See if Bob has a value in his mother slot.
(lookup (list bob 'mother '?x) '((?x person)) nil)
```

```
⇒ (((?X #<Object PERSON NAME=JOANNE>)) NIL)

;; See if anyone has the father slot with value Jim.
(lookup (list '?x 'father jim) '((?x person)) nil)
⇒ (((?X #<Object PERSON NAME=PATTY>) (T T))
⇒  (#<Object PERSON NAME=JIMMY> #<Object PERSON NAME=BOB>
⇒   #<Object PERSON NAME=JOANNE> #<Object PERSON NAME=JIM>))

;; This finds any object with a mother slot.
(lookup '(?x mother ?y) '((?x person) (?y person)) nil)
⇒ (((?Y #<Object PERSON NAME=JOANNE>)
⇒    (?X #<Object PERSON NAME=PATTY>))
⇒  (#<Object PERSON NAME=JIMMY> #<Object PERSON NAME=BOB>
⇒   #<Object PERSON NAME=JOANNE> #<Object PERSON NAME=JIM>))

;; Try one that should fail.
(lookup (list bob 'uncles '?y) '((?y person)) nil)
⇒ NIL
```

Now, a couple of tests to verify that lookup returns a state that can then be used again.

```
(setf state (lookup (list '?x 'father jim) '((?x person))
                    nil))
⇒ (((?X #<Object PERSON NAME=PATTY>))
⇒  (#<Object PERSON NAME=JIMMY> #<Object PERSON NAME=BOB>
⇒   #<Object PERSON NAME=JOANNE> #<Object PERSON NAME=JIM>))

(setf state (lookup (list '?x 'father jim) '((?x person))
                    (cadr state)))
⇒ (((?X #<Object PERSON NAME=JIMMY>))
⇒  (#<Object PERSON NAME=BOB> #<Object PERSON NAME=JOANNE>
⇒   #<Object PERSON NAME=JIM>))

(setf state (lookup (list '?x 'father jim) '((?x person))
                    (cadr state)))
⇒ (((?X #<Object PERSON NAME=BOB>))
⇒  (#<Object PERSON NAME=JOANNE> #<Object PERSON NAME=JIM>))

(setf state (lookup (list '?x 'father jim) '((?x person))
                    (cadr state)))
⇒ NIL
```

EXERCISE

***9.12** One problem with `lookup` is that if the type of the object variable is `nil` then no objects will be found. This is because `lookup` searches for all objects matching the type, and none are defined for `nil`. The proper solution is to specify that a `nil` type indicates that the type is unspecified and thus can be of any type. Change `lookup` so that if the type is unspecified, then any of the known objects could potentially match.

9.7 Inference Engine Design

The structure of the inference engine has been outlined in previous sections. This section discusses and demonstrates some of the fine points of its implementation. One problem for the inference engine is the possibility of backtracking. Backtracking can occur in a number of places. While the engine is trying to prove an assertion, it can suddenly determine that the assertion is unprovable. The system must undo any bindings that might have been made and try again on a different solution. This could mean trying to find another rule that will prove the assertion, or using another binding. The second case can occur when the object part of an assertion is a variable. In this case, the `lookup` function returns a list of other objects to try. For example, suppose that we are trying to find a brother of Bob. To do this, the engine must find a male sibling of Bob. It might prove that Patty is a sibling but fail to prove that Patty is male. Therefore, it must backtrack to find another sibling of Bob, like Jimmy.

The solution to the backtracking problem relates to the general philosophy of the inference engine. We'll call the two possible schemes *early* and *late* binding.

Early binding – As soon as the inference engine finds a variable, it searches the knowledge base for objects of the designated type and creates a list of them. The engine then uses an iteration control structure to try to prove the assertion with objects from the list. Since both the object and value may be variables, this means that it may try $n \times m$ combinations on each assertion (where n is the number of objects that match the object variable type and m is the number of values that match the value variable type). `Lookup` will never be called with an assertion that contains variables. This is because the engine is selecting elements from the list and substituting them into the assertion before the call.

Late binding – The engine performs a binding only with a call to `lookup`. Thus, it scans the list of applicable objects for one whose slot value matches the argument value. It will only perform one scan over all of the objects and is thus order n.

Early binding makes *blind* decisions since it looks at all possible combinations. Late binding makes more informed decisions, because it only investigates those paths that are possible based on the current knowledge. For example, suppose that the `solve` asks to find anyone with a parent:

```
(solve '(?x parent ?y) '((?x person) (?y person)))
```

Since there aren't any objects with bound parent slots, the engine must use one of the parent rules to prove the assertion. Recall that we have the following persons in our knowledge base:

Person	Father	Mother	Sex
Patty	Jim	Joanne	Female
Bob	Jim	Joanne	Male
Jimmy	Jim	Joanne	Male
Jim	James	Mary	Male
Joanne	Robert	Margaret	Female

Using early binding, the engine would find a list of all persons and create the following types of queries (this assumes a worst-case ordering):

```
;; Pseudotrace of the modified solve queries:
(solve '(PATTY PARENT BOB))
  -> (solve '(PATTY FATHER BOB)) << FAIL
  -> (solve '(PATTY MOTHER BOB)) << FAIL
  << FAIL (PATTY PARENT BOB)
(solve '(PATTY PARENT JIMMY))
  -> (solve '(PATTY FATHER JIMMY)) << FAIL
  -> (solve '(PATTY MOTHER JIMMY)) << FAIL
  << FAIL (PATTY PARENT JIMMY)
(solve '(PATTY PARENT JIM))
  -> (solve '(PATTY FATHER JIM)) >> SUCCEED
  >> Succeed (PATTY PARENT JIM)
```

Using the late binding technique, the engine would perform considerably fewer searches:

```
(solve '(?x parent ?y) '((?x person) (?y person)))
  -> (solve '(?x father ?y) '((?x person) (?y person)))
     >> SUCCEED - Lookup Finds (PATTY FATHER JIM)
  >> Succeed (PATTY PARENT JIM)
```

Since late binding seems to be a more efficient technique, it is implemented here.

The next step is to decide how to implement `solve`. Initially, you might decide to implement the code using standard recursion. As the engine finds a new rule that matches the current assertion, it recursively calls `solve` to solve each of the premises. When a call to `solve` succeeds, it returns the bound assertion, and then recurses on the remaining clauses of the premise (if any). This seems like a reasonable technique, but is flawed. This flaw can be illustrated through the following pseudotrace. For clarity all type clauses have been omitted from the trace; all variables are of type `person`.

```
(solve '(?x brother ?y))   ;; Original query
  (solve '(and (?x sibling ?y) (?y sex male)))
```

```
(solve '(?x sibling ?y))
  (solve '(and (?x parent ?z) (?y parent ?z)))
    (solve '(?x parent ?z))
      (solve '(?x father ?z))
       <-- (JIMMY FATHER JIM) ;; Arbitrarily select one
     <-- (JIMMY PARENT JIM)
    (solve '(?y parent JIM))
      (solve '(?y father JIM))
       <-- (PATTY FATHER JIM) ;; Arbitrarily select one
     <-- (PATTY PARENT JIM)
   <-- (AND (JIMMY PARENT JIM) (PATTY PARENT JIM))
 <-- (JIMMY SIBLING PATTY)
(solve '(PATTY sex male))
<-- NIL !!!!! Fail
...
```

As you can see, the failure occurs very late in the process, and the backtracking must somehow return to `(PATTY FATHER JIM)`. If no other person could be found whose father is `JIM`, then it could backtrack even farther to `(JIMMY FATHER JIM)`. Since recursion is used to maintain the state of the process, there is no way to recover and try again. In other words, once the process leaves an inner call to `solve`, it can't return. Once `solve` is deeply nested and trying to prove `(?x parent ?z)`, there are still more assertions outstanding (in this case, a `(?y sex male)` and `(?y parent ?z)`). If inner `solve`s succeed, the remaining assertions might still fail and the engine must return to the last choice and try again, *but the outstanding assertions must remain.* So, the solution is to maintain an agenda queue of impending assertions. Then if there's a failure, the recursion will return to the last choice point and can then proceed along a new path with the queue of tasks still waiting. The following trace illustrates this new technique. The second argument to this version of `solve` is the agenda list of clauses that must still be solved.

```
(solve '(?x brother ?y) nil)
| (solve '(and (?x sibling ?y) (?y sex male)) nil)
| | (solve '(?x sibling ?y) '(?y sex male))
| | | (solve '(and (?x parent ?z) (?y parent ?z))
| | |          '(?y sex male))
| | | (solve '(?x parent ?z) '((?y parent ?z)
| | | |                          (?y sex male)))
| | | | (solve '(?x father ?z) '((?y parent ?z)
| | | | |                          (?y sex male)))
| | | | | ^^^ (JIMMY FATHER JIM) ;; Arbitrarily one
| | | | | (solve '((?y parent JIM)) '((?y sex male)))
| | | | | | (solve '((?y father JIM)) '((?y sex male)))
```

```
13 | | | | | | | | ^^^ (PATTY FATHER JIM) ;; Select one
14 | | | | | | | | (solve '(PATTY sex male) nil)
15 | | | | | | | |   !!!!! Fail
16 | | | | | | | | ^^^ (BOB FATHER JIM) ;; Select another
17 | | | | | | | | (solve '(BOB sex male) nil)
18 | | | | | | | | >>> (BOB SEX MALE)
19 | | | | | | | >>> (BOB FATHER JIM)
20 | | | | | | >>> (BOB PARENT JIM)
21 | | | | | >>> (JIMMY FATHER JIM)
22 | | | | >>> (JIMMY PARENT JIM)
23 | | | >>> (AND (JIMMY PARENT JIM) (BOB PARENT JIM))
24 | | >>> (JIMMY SIBLING BOB)
25 | >>> (AND (JIMMY SIBLING BOB) (BOB SEX MALE))
26 |>> (JIMMY BROTHER BOB)
```

Notice the binding process that takes place. At line `10`, `JIM` is bound to `?z`. So, using the first element on the agenda of the clauses, `(?y parent ?z)`, the next solve substitutes the `JIM` for `?z`. Thus, the call to `solve` at lines `11` and `12` has the new assertions with bound variables replaced by their values. The replacing of variables with their new bound values can be quite intricate. The problem is that the rule designer can choose variable names within each rule, independent of the other rules. Thus, `?person` in one rule may refer to a parent, while in another rule it may refer to a sister.

In the preceding example, the variable names were carefully chosen to cause no conflicts. However, programmer-written rules can cause these difficulties. You would think that if each rule had a unique variable name, then the problem would not exist. Thus, a possible solution modifies `define-rule` and its associated functions to transform each new rule, so that it is guaranteed to have unique variable names. This seems reasonable as long as the original untransformed rule is maintained (for example, for debugging purposes). However, this won't solve the entire problem. If some rule `foo` is currently under consideration by the engine and it indirectly invokes itself, the same problem occurs. A binding to a variable within the recursively called rule could easily be taken as a binding for the original `foo` and invalidate the rule. The solution is to transform each rule as it is found by the inference engine, so a recursive rule invocation would have different variables at each recursive level.

In the previous example, notice what happens when the variables aren't unique. Just by changing the sibling clause to use `?z` instead of `?y`, the `solve` gets totally confused.

```
                    INCORRECT BINDING PROBLEM !!
Line
01 (solve '(?x brother ?y) nil)
02 | (solve '(and (?x sibling ?z) (?z sex male)) nil)
03 | | (solve '(?x sibling ?z) '(?z sex male))
```

```
| | | (solve '(and (?x parent ?z) (?y parent ?z))
| | | |        '(?z sex male))
| | | | (solve '(?x parent ?z) '((?y parent ?z)
| | | | |                        (?z sex male)))
| | | | | (solve '(?x father ?z) '((?y parent ?z)
| | | | | |                        (?z sex male)))
| | | | | | ^^^ (JIMMY FATHER JIM) ;; Select one
| | | | | | (solve '((?y parent JIM)) '((?z sex male)))
| | | | | | | (solve '((?y father JIM)) '((?z sex male)))
| | | | | | | | ^^^ (PATTY FATHER JIM) ;; Select one
| | | | | | | | (solve '(JIM sex male) nil)
| | | | | | | | >>> (JIM SEX MALE)
| | | | | | | >>> (PATTY FATHER JIM)
| | | | | | >>> (PATTY PARENT JIM)
| | | | | >>> (JIMMY FATHER JIM)
| | | | >>> (JIMMY PARENT JIM)
| | | >>> (AND (JIMMY PARENT JIM) (PATTY PARENT JIM))
| | >>> (JIMMY SIBLING PATTY)
| >>> (AND (JIMMY SIBLING PATTY) (BOB SEX MALE))
>>> (JIMMY BROTHER PATTY)
```

EXERCISES

***9.13** Much of the functionality of the `solve` algorithm comes from the state that is saved by the recursive invocations of `solve`. Propose a technique that doesn't use recursion.

***9.14** Suppose that you have the capability outlined in the previous exercise. What additional functionality does this provide?

9.8 Inference Engine Implementation

As already described, `solve` takes two arguments, the assertion and the list of variable types. The late binding technique requires that an additional argument must be provided – the agenda. Finally, `solve` should take the binding list as an argument, so any new substitutions can be made. Since we want `solve` to be the user interface and only take the first two arguments, we will make it call an auxiliary function that can perform the recursion and use the additional arguments. The `solve-aux` routine takes four arguments and will return the newly bound assertion, along with the current binding list. Also, `solve-aux` will return a two-element list, whose first element is the assertion with any variables replaced with their values. The second element is the current binding list that is used in recursive invocations to substitute the bindings in clauses. The caller of `solve` doesn't care about this binding list, so we take the `car` to return the bound assertion. With this in mind, we can write **solve** as a one-line function, remembering that the initial binding list and the initial agenda will each be **nil**.

```
;;; Interface to the user.  Actually calls solve-aux which
;;; does all of the work.  Solve-aux returns the new
;;; assertion, along with a list of bindings as the second
;;; element, which solve ignores.  The extra two arguments to
;;; solve-aux are the binding list and agenda, which are
;;; initially nil.

(defun solve (assertion variables)
  (car (solve-aux assertion variables nil nil)))
 ⇒ SOLVE
```

`Solve-aux` is the main driver function for the inference engine. It is called with an assertion to solve, the list of variables, the current binding list, and the agenda of future assertions to prove. Its implementation follows the outline given in the previous section. The function tries to prove the assertion, and if successful it checks to see if there are any other clauses on the agenda. If there are no more, then it returns the assertion, replacing all variables with their bindings. If there are more agenda items, then it recurses on the first agenda item. This is the general control flow of the function. The only remaining detail is how it tries to prove the assertion. According to our previous algorithms, we need to first look up the assertion in the knowledge base to see if it is immediately true. If it is, then we continue the control flow. If it isn't, then we must try to solve the assertion using the rules. Each of these operations is complicated enough that we can define a function for each process.

There is one more case that we must consider, which depends on how we implement the premise processing of the rules. Is it true that all assertions will be of the standard form of a knowledge clause, with object, slot, and value? The answer is no, because of the test clauses. These clauses have a **test** followed by the knowledge clause, which has different syntax than the standard knowledge clause. If we passed the test clause to `lookup`, it would fail to find the object, slot, and value. So, we either need to make sure that the assertion argument is never a test clause, or we process the test clauses specially.

The difference depends on how we implement the rule processing. We can either blindly add all of the premise clauses to the agenda, or try to perform some of the evaluation within the rule processing. Since `solve-aux` already has the mechanism for processing each premise clause, it is logical to make it handle the test clauses itself. We must also make it do that processing first, so we don't pass the different syntax clauses to the other routines.

To summarize, we will implement three separate routines to process test clauses, look up assertions in the knowledge base, and try to solve the assertion with rules as follows:

`Solve-test` – Attempt to determine if a test assertion is true or false.
`Solve-lookup` – Try to solve the assertion by accessing the knowledge base.
`Solve-with-rules` – Attempt to find a rule whose conclusion matches the assertion and then prove the rule.

The next decision is whether each of these functions should try to prove one assertion and then return the binding, or if they should prove the assertion and recursively call `solve-aux` on the remaining agenda items. The latter is a better approach because the rule processing can simply add more premise clauses to the agenda and call `solve-aux`. Otherwise a complicated mechanism would have to be implemented to handle this case. So, `solve-aux` will assume that each of these functions performs any of the tasks remaining on the agenda. This means that any result coming back is a successful completion of the entire solve task. All it has to do is install the bindings into the argument assertion and return that along with the binding list.

We must be careful with the test-clause processing. This is because of the different semantics between it and the other two operations. If the assertion is really a test clause, then the result of `solve-aux` is the result of the test clause. Otherwise, we attempt a lookup and if that fails, we then try the rules. The code for determining the binding result is a little tricky.

```
;;; This first checks to see if the assertion is a test
;;; clause and if so, it calls solve-test.  Otherwise, it
;;; tries to solve the assertion via lookup and then via
;;; rules.  If any of these succeed, the resulting binding
;;; list is used to install into the assertion and the list
;;; of bound assertion and binding list is returned.

(defun solve-aux (assertion variables binding-list agenda)
  (let ((bindings
         (if (test-clause-p assertion)
           (solve-test assertion variables binding-list
                       agenda)
           (or (solve-lookup assertion variables binding-list
                             agenda)
               (solve-with-rules assertion variables
                                 binding-list
                                 agenda)))))
    (if bindings
      (list (install-bindings assertion bindings) bindings)
      nil)))
 ⇒ SOLVE-AUX
```

The predicate `test-clause-p` determines if the assertion is a test clause, as indicated by the symbol `test` in the `car` of the assertion. Isolation of this clause into a small function makes later modification easy.

```
;;; Predicate to see if an assertion is a test clause.

(defun test-clause-p (assertion)
  (equal (car assertion) 'test))
 ⇒ TEST-CLAUSE-P
```

The processing within solve-test is the easier than solve-lookup or solve-with-rules. It simply evaluates the associated expression and if it is non-nil, it processes the rest of the agenda. If there are no remaining clauses, it returns its argument-binding list. If the test is false, then the function returns nil.

```
;;; The assertion is already known to be of the form
;;; (test evaluatable-expression). So, solve-test evaluates
;;; the assertion and then solves the remaining clauses in
;;; the agenda.

(defun solve-test (assertion variables binding-list agenda)
  (if (eval (cadr assertion))
    (if agenda
      (cadr (solve-aux (car agenda) variables
                       binding-list (cdr agenda)))
      binding-list)
    nil))
 ⇒ SOLVE-TEST
```

Solve-lookup tries to find an object in the knowledge base that proves the assertion. The trick is to decide how to use the possible objects list that is returned from the call to lookup. Remember that this list is returned by lookup so that if the solve fails on that binding, another one may be tried. The idea is to call lookup and get any matches along with the remaining possible objects. If a match is found and there are no more agenda items, then the binding created by the lookup is returned with the argument-binding list. If there are other agenda items, then solve-aux is called on the remaining items. If the solve-aux fails, then we must try to call lookup again using the remaining objects. A reasonable solution to this problem is to use iteration with do*. In the first iteration, lookup is called with nil as the possible objects argument. In successive calls, it is called with the previous possible objects list. The iteration terminates when the lookup finally returns no match, or when the call to solve-aux fails and there are no more possible objects.

The call to solve-aux is a little tricky, since it requires that we install any bindings that were created by the lookup result. These bindings must be installed on the new agenda item and any remaining items in the agenda. This is one place where it is absolutely important that variable names don't conflict across rules. We can blindly install all of the bindings specified in the list without caring if the variables came from one rule or another. They just won't conflict.

```
;;; Attempt to solve the assertion by accessing the knowledge
;;; base.

(defun solve-lookup (assertion variables binding-list agenda)
  (do* ((lookup-return (lookup assertion variables nil)
                       (lookup assertion variables
                               possibles))
        (lookup-binding (car lookup-return)
                        (car lookup-return))
        (possibles (cadr lookup-return) (cadr lookup-return))
        (solve-aux-result))
       ((null lookup-return) nil)
       (cond ((null agenda)
              (return (append lookup-binding binding-list)))
             ((setf solve-aux-result
                    (solve-aux
                     (install-bindings (car agenda)
                                       lookup-binding)
                     variables
                     (append lookup-binding binding-list)
                     (install-bindings (cdr agenda)
                                       lookup-binding)))
              (return (cadr solve-aux-result)))
             ((null possibles) (return nil)))))
⇒ SOLVE-LOOKUP
```

The `solve-with-rules` function is the most complicated of the three functions of `solve-aux`. Its basic operation is simple; it must try to find a rule that can prove the assertion, then add the premises to the agenda. It then calls `solve-aux` to work on the premise and the remaining agenda items. The problem is all of the details that `solve-with-rules` must handle. It has to be careful to change the variables in the rule so they are unique. It also has to install into the premises any bindings that may have occurred. Finally, it has a problem similar to `solve-lookup` in that it must be able to properly backtrack and try another rule when one rule fails. In the `lookup` solution, we returned a list which was used as the basis to try to find another solution. The other technique is to find all rules that match from the outset and then scan that list looking for one that can have its premise proved. Since we used the first technique in `lookup`, we will use the latter in this function.

We will call the function `find-matching-rules`. This function scans the rule base and returns all rules that could prove the assertion. The function has to return a list of two-element lists because finding a rule that matches may cause some bindings to take place. This is because the assertion may include some constant values that can be replaced in the rule or visa versa. The second part of the two-element list is the rule that matched. We can then use an iteration construct to scan the rule list searching for one that can be proven true. With all of this in mind, we can implement `solve-with-rules`, calling a number of yet-to-be-defined functions.

```
;;; Attempt to solve the assertion by finding a rule that
;;; will prove the assertion.

(defun solve-with-rules (assertion variables
                                   initial-binding
                                   agenda)
  (do* ((rule-and-bindings
          (find-matching-rules assertion variables *rules*)
          (cdr rule-and-bindings))
        (a-rule (caar rule-and-bindings)
                (caar rule-and-bindings))
        (binding-list (cadr (car rule-and-bindings))
                      (cadr (car rule-and-bindings)))
        (resulting-assertion nil))
    ((or (null rule-and-bindings) resulting-assertion)
     (cadr resulting-assertion))
    (let ((premises
            (make-list-of-premises
             (install-bindings (premise a-rule)
                               binding-list))))
      (setf resulting-assertion
            (solve-aux (car premises)
                       (append variables (type a-rule))
                       (append binding-list initial-binding)
                       (append (cdr premises) agenda))))))
⇒ SOLVE-WITH-RULES
```

Finding all of the rules that could prove the assertion is an involved process. We must scan the rule base and compare the assertion with the conclusion of each rule. We can also perform the variable renaming here, since we have to return a list of the rules and bindings. These bindings must correspond to the new variable names, so it is appropriate to do it here. This function can be implemented in the standard recursive style, scanning the rule list and constructing a new list of matched rules. It will call a function `match-assertions`, which compares two assertions to see if they match. If they do, a binding list is returned. This binding list can then be passed to `variable-renaming`, which creates a new rule definition with new, unique variables and also installs any bindings defined in the binding list. Notice that any variables mentioned in the binding list must also be replaced with their unique names.

```
;;; Find all rules that could prove the assertion argument,
;;; and returns the list of rules and the bindings returned
;;; from match-assertion.

(defun find-matching-rules (assertion variables rules)
  (cond ((null rules) nil)
        ((let ((matched-binding
                 (match-assertions assertion variables
                                   (conclusion (car rules))
                                   (type (car rules)))))
           (if matched-binding
             (cons (variable-renaming (car rules)
                                      matched-binding)
                   (find-matching-rules assertion variables
                                        (cdr rules)))
             nil)))
        (t (find-matching-rules assertion variables
                                (cdr rules)))))
⇒ FIND-MATCHING-RULES
```

`Match-assertion` takes two assertions and compares them to see if they're equal. The first argument is the assertion to be proven, and the second is a conclusion of a rule that might prove the assertion. There are two possible cases. First, if both the assertion and conclusion are non-variables, they are checked for equality. Otherwise the types of the arguments are checked for equality. For example, a `person` variable is compared against an object of type `person`. When the input assertion has a constant as an object or value and the conclusion has a variable, the mapping is immediately added to the binding list. The function returns `nil` if there's no mapping, a binding list if there is, or `((T T))` if no binding is found but the assertions match.

```
;;; Match two assertions and their variable list.  Returns a
;;; binding list if the input-assertion has any constants in
;;; positions where the rule assertions have variables.

(defun match-assertions (input-assertion
                         input-variables
                         rule-assertion
                         rule-variables)
  (let ((object-binding
          (compare-fields (object input-assertion)
                          input-variables
                          (object rule-assertion)
                          rule-variables))
        (value-binding
```

```
        (compare-fields (value input-assertion)
                        input-variables
                        (value rule-assertion)
                        rule-variables)))
    (and (equal (slot input-assertion) (slot rule-assertion))
        object-binding
        value-binding
        (list object-binding value-binding))))
⇒ MATCH-ASSERTIONS
```

Compare-fields makes sure that the two subfields of the knowledge clause match. It must check all cases of variables and constants and verify that the types match. There are a number of cases it must handle. If both fields are not variables, they can be directly compared for equality. Otherwise we have at least one variable. As stated earlier, if one of the arguments is a variable, then its type must be compared against the type of the other field. There is a difficulty here when the other field is not an object. For example, in our current knowledge base, the father slot of Jim is the symbol James instead of the object James. We could assign the type of these items to be nil and make the code assume that a nil type is generic and will match any other type. Otherwise we get the type of the variable, or the type of the object. Finally, we can just compare the types, taking care to handle a nil type.

```
;;; Compare two fields of an assertion (either an object or a
;;; value).

(defun compare-fields (field1 variables1 field2 variables2)
  (let ((field1-variablep (variablep field1 variables1))
        (field2-variablep (variablep field2 variables2)))
    (cond ((and (not field1-variablep)
                (not field2-variablep)
                (equal field1 field2))
           '(t t))
          ((let ((field1-type
                  ;; If the field1 is not a variable and not
                  ;; an object, then it will get a nil type
                  ;; here.
                  (or (and field1-variablep
                           (variable-type field1 variables1))
                      (and (objectp field1)
                           (object-type field1))))
                 (field2-type
                  ;; If the field2 is not a variable and not
                  ;; an object, then it will get a nil type
                  ;; here.
```

```
                        (or (and field2-variablep
                                 (variable-type field2 variables2))
                            (and (objectp field2)
                                 (object-type field2)))))
                (if (or (equal field1-type field2-type)
                        (null field1-type)
                        (null field2-type))
                  (list field2 field1)
                  nil)))
           (t nil))))
```

⇒ COMPARE-FIELDS

Here are some simple tests to verify that **match-assertions** produces the correct bindings.

```
(match-assertions (list bob 'sex 'male) nil
                  (list bob 'sex 'male) nil)
 ⇒ ((T T) (T T))

(match-assertions (list bob 'uncles '?x) '((?x person))
                  '(?x uncles ?y) '((?x person) (?y person)))
 ⇒ ((?X #<Object PERSON NAME=BOB>) (?Y ?X))
```

The next step is to develop **variable-renaming** and its associated functions. The **type** slot of a **rule** object specifies all of the variables that are in the rule definition. That list can be used as the basis to create a new list of mappings between the real variable name and a unique variable name. Once the mapping is created, another function can take any arbitrary LISP expression and replace all variables mentioned in the mapping with the new variable.

The function **make-mapping** creates the mapping list and **change-vars** does the replacement. **Make-mapping** uses the standard recursive style to scan the variable list and construct the new association list. It calls **get-a-variable** to return a new unique variable. An easy way to create a unique variable is to construct a new object for each new variable. The object can then contain the actual variable name for future reference. That way, we don't have to store a reverse mapping between the original variable defined in the rule and the unique variable object. Objects are a natural representation, since each call to **make-instance** creates a new object, and that object is then guaranteed to be unique.

```
;;; Given a variable list from a rule, this function creates
;;; an association list, mapping from the variable to a new
;;; unique variable.

(defun make-mapping (variables)
```

```
  (if (null variables)
    nil
    (cons (list (caar variables)
                (get-a-variable (caar variables)))
          (make-mapping (cdr variables)))))
⇒ MAKE-MAPPING

;; This type makes each variable unique, just by creating a
;; new object for each variable instance.

(define-type new-variable
  (:var var-name :initable :gettable))
⇒ NEW-VARIABLE

;;; Translate the variable into a list and tag.

(defun get-a-variable (variable)
  (make-instance 'new-variable :var-name variable))
⇒ GET-A-VARIABLE
```

With the preliminary functions in place, we can write `variable-renaming`. It must be careful with the `rule` object, because it cannot just modify all of the slot values. That would change the original rule definition and would lose the rule as specified by the user. It must create a new `rule` instance and fill in the slots with the new values.

```
;;; Create a new rule with all of the variables changed to
;;; unique names and modify the binding list in the same way.
;;; This returns a two-element list of the new rule and the
;;; modified binding.

(defun variable-renaming (rule match-binding)
  (let ((variable-mapping (make-mapping (type rule))))
    (list
     (make-instance 'rule
        :name (name rule)
        :type (install-bindings (type rule) variable-mapping)
        :premise (install-bindings (premise rule)
                                   variable-mapping)
        :conclusion (install-bindings
                     (conclusion rule) variable-mapping))
     (install-bindings match-binding variable-mapping))))
⇒ VARIABLE-RENAMING
```

`Find-matching-rules` calls `make-list-of-premises` to take the premise argument and turn it into a list of premises. If the premise has an **and** clause, then the **cdr** is returned. Otherwise it is a single premise, which is returned as a list.

```
;;; Turn the premise into a list of premises, removing the
;;; and if present or just listifying a single premise.

(defun make-list-of-premises (premise)
  (if (equal (car premise) 'and)
    (cdr premise)
    (list premise)))
 ⇒ MAKE-LIST-OF-PREMISES
```

The final function is **install-bindings**, which takes an arbitrary list and an association list, and replaces all variables mentioned in the association with their new value. This implementation is the standard recursive style where the argument is not a flat list. This requires recursing on both the **car** and **cdr**, to perform the installation.

```
;;; Given an assertion and a binding, replace all symbols
;;; mentioned in the binding list with their new value.

(defun install-bindings (assertion bindings)
  (cond ((null assertion) nil)
        ((cadr (assoc assertion bindings :test #'equal)))
        ((atom assertion) assertion)
        (t (cons (install-bindings (car assertion) bindings)
                 (install-bindings (cdr assertion)
                                   bindings)))))
 ⇒ INSTALL-BINDINGS
```

A simple test of the **install-bindings** function:

```
(install-bindings '(?x sibling ?y) '((?x bob) (?y jimmy)))
 ⇒ (BOB SIBLING JIMMY)
```

Also, **find-matching-rules** can be tested, since its primitive functions are complete.

```
(find-matching-rules (list '?x 'parent jim) '((?x person))
                     *rules*)
 ⇒ ((#<Object RULE NAME=PARENT-RULE2>
 ⇒   ((#<Object NEW-VARIABLE> ?X)
 ⇒    (#<Object NEW-VARIABLE> #<Object PERSON NAME=JIM>)))
 ⇒  (#<Object RULE NAME=PARENT-RULE1>
 ⇒   ((#<Object NEW-VARIABLE> ?X)
 ⇒    (#<Object NEW-VARIABLE> #<Object PERSON NAME=JIM>))))
```

Notice that it found two rules – there are two rules that reason about parentage – and created the bindings between the variables (now renamed) and their values.

EXERCISE

9.15 Change the functions so that they uses the rules stored in an association list of the conclusion-slot name as mentioned in previous exercises. This will make it run faster by not having to scan all of the rules, but can concentrate on only those rules that could match the slot.

9.9 Test of the Expert System

Now that the entire system has been developed, we can perform some tests. Each test will use progressively more of the system. The first one simply locates a value in the knowledge base to verify that the assertion is true, while the latter ones use many of the rules.

```
;; First a simple lookup of a value.
(solve (list bob 'sex 'male) nil)
 ⇒ (#<Object PERSON NAME=BOB> SEX MALE)

;; Another lookup with a variable value.
(solve '(?x sex ?y) '((?x person)(?y person)))
 ⇒ (#<Object PERSON NAME=PATTY> SEX FEMALE)

;; This solve requires looking into rule base to reason about
;; parents.
(solve (list patty 'parent '?x) '((?x person)))
 ⇒ (#<Object PERSON NAME=PATTY> PARENT
 ⇒  #<Object PERSON NAME=JIM>)

;; The sibling rule will invoke many other rules.
(solve (list jimmy 'sibling '?x) '((?x person)))
 ⇒ (#<Object PERSON NAME=JIMMY> SIBLING
 ⇒  #<Object PERSON NAME=PATTY>)

;; Now see if anyone has a brother.
(solve '(?x brothers ?y) '((?x person)(?y person)))
 ⇒ (#<Object PERSON NAME=PATTY> BROTHERS
 ⇒  #<Object PERSON NAME=JIMMY>)
```

Now we can try something even more complicated – checking for an uncle. The reason this is more complicated is because it exercises the code that manipulates objects with non-object `father` and `mother` slots. That is because when we define David to be the uncle, his father and mother slots are symbols instead of objects.

```
;; First check to see if there are any uncles in the
;; knowledge base.
(solve '(?x uncles ?y) '((?x person)(?y person)))
 ⇒ NIL

;; There are no uncles defined in the knowledge base, so add
;; David as Jim's brother.
(setf david (add-knowledge 'person :name 'david
                                   :father 'james
                                   :mother 'mary :sex 'male))
 ⇒ #<Object PERSON NAME=DAVID>

;; Now try the query again.
(solve '(?x uncles ?y) '((?x person)(?y person)))
 ⇒ (#<Object PERSON NAME=PATTY> UNCLES
 ⇒  #<Object PERSON NAME=DAVID>)
```

EXERCISES

***9.16** In a previous exercise, you were instructed to define some other rules for grandparent and for grandchild. Define these rules and then try to solve a grandparent and grandchild relationship. Are there any difficulties in doing this?

***9.17** In that same exercise, you were also instructed to define rules for cousin and aunt. There is not enough information in the knowledge base to make these rules work, so add some additional knowledge that could be used to find the appropriate relationships. Here are some additional facts that might be useful for the Kessler knowledge base: Bob and Julie have a son named Alex; David and Deanie have a son named Russ and a daughter named Karen; Jim has another brother named Wendell, married to Claire, with two sons – Adam and Aaron. Run `solve` to find a cousin and an aunt.

```
(solve '(?x cousins ?y) '((?x person) (?y person)))
 ⇒ (#<Object PERSON NAME=KAREN> COUSINS
 ⇒  #<Object PERSON NAME=PATTY>)

(solve '(?x aunts ?y) '((?x person) (?y person)))
 ⇒ (#<Object PERSON NAME=ALEX> AUNTS
 ⇒  #<Object PERSON NAME=PATTY>)
```

9.18 If you study the definition of uncle, and probably your definition of aunt, you might realize that we have left out the case that an aunt and uncle also gain that relationship through marriage. Define additional aunt and uncle rules to reflect this. You may not add any new slots to the original type `person`. Try to find Bob's aunt.

```
(solve `(,bob aunts ?x) '((?x person)))
 ⇒ (#<Object PERSON NAME=BOB> AUNTS DEANIE)
```

9.10 Summary

The expert system developed in this chapter uses objects for knowledge representation and a backward-chaining inference engine. The examples from this chapter solve simple genealogical queries.

Chapter Exercises

***1.** Whether or not the expert system actually asserts a fact has been carefully avoided in this example. As the system is implemented, nothing is ever asserted into the knowledge base. If one were to modify the system so that each time an assertion is proved, the information is added to the knowledge base, then the knowledge base would slowly gain more and more information. It would also allow `solve`s to find a solution faster, since previous partial solutions might not have to be proved again (for example, if it proves that Bob's parent is Jim, then it doesn't need to prove that fact again). Modify the system so that each time an assertion is proved (anywhere in the process), the value is stored in the appropriate object.

2. Enhance the assertion mechanism in the previous exercise by defining a caching flag – `*caching*`. When the flag is true, it will store all of the assertions; otherwise it will not. One argument that all assertions should always store their value is that if something is proven to be true, then it is always true. However, by allowing the flag, one could attempt a `solve` that might use erroneous information, just to see what results are given by the system. This would allow experimental calls to `solve` that don't actually affect the knowledge base.

***3.** An interesting problem with the current system is that there is no concept of multiple values within a slot. `Lookup` only knows about the presence or absence of a value. Multiple values are important for slots to indicate that there may be more than one value in a slot. For example, the `brothers` slot could contain multiple values, while `sex` should contain only one value. Frame systems usually permit the designation of each slot as to whether it is multiple or single-valued. Modify the system so that all slots are always multiple-valued. Use `nil` to indicate that a slot is undefined. Modify `lookup` and the `assert` function to store and access multiple values. Multiple values are defined to be a set, so you shouldn't add a value to a slot if it is already present in the slot.

***4.** Using our representation of knowledge, where we are using objects directly, we have a problem defining rules with constant object specifications. Notice that in the definition of `define-rule`, the various clauses are not evaluated, and thus it is impossible to place a constant object into the rule. Modify `define-rule` so this is possible. (*Hint:* Consider the use of backquote.)

```
(define-rule bogus-rule
  (type (?person person) (?person2 person) (?uncle person))
  (premise '(and (?person parent ?person2)
                 (?person2 brothers ?uncle)))
  (conclusion `(?person uncles ,jim)))
```

5. *Difficult* – One of the capabilities PROLOG has that this system lacks is the ability to find the next solution. For example, although we proved that Patty's uncle is David, we might want to find another uncle. Our current system cannot perform this task because the path to the solution is embodied in the control environment created by the recursive calls. This means that the path to the solution, along with each choice point along the way (the next set of rules to try, the next objects to peruse, and so on) must be saved in a global data structure. Modify the current system so that when `solve-next` is called (without any arguments) it returns the next possible solution.

10 I/O AND DEBUGGING

THIS CHAPTER DISCUSSES input and output (I/O) within Common LISP. It discusses formatted output, the `read` function, and streams. It then describes the primitives for portable access to files using the pathname facility. Pathnames provide you with the ability to specify file names that are system independent. The chapter concludes with a discussion of debugging in the LISP programming environment. The next three chapters develop a "role-playing" game as a case study.

10.1 Game Introduction

In a fantasy "role-playing" game, a player issues commands in order to wander around an environment without being *killed* by monsters. The player and each monster starts with "hit points," a numeric value. When that value reaches zero, the monster or player dies. The player takes points away from a monster by hitting it with a weapon. A monster takes points away from the player by hitting the player. There are also odd cases where the player can lose points by just using some weapons or the weapon mistakenly gives points to the player. All elements of the game, including the player, monsters, the rooms, and the weapons, will be modeled using objects.

We need to develop part of the game before we can introduce the various I/O functions. In order to build types, objects, and methods, we need to know a few more details of the monsters in our game:

Name – A symbol used to identify a particular monster
Type – The particular type of monster – each type of monster will have its own peculiar set of characteristics
Description – A string description that can be used to provide an interesting interaction with the player (for example, instead of using the type, the game can use a more elaborate description of the monster)
Strength – The current number of hit points remaining in the monster's life

Damage – The maximum number of hit points that the monster usually inflicts in damage
Room – The room in which the monster resides

Notice that "description" is defined as a string. A string is a sequential collection of characters, designated with leading and trailing double quote marks '"'. Strings are discussed in detail in Chapter 13.

The preceding characteristics can be used to defin the monster type.

```
;;; A monster has the following characteristics:

(define-type monster
  (:var name)
  (:var type)
  (:var description)
  (:var strength :settable)
  (:var damage :settable)
  (:var room :settable)
  :all-initable
  :all-gettable)
 ⇒ MONSTER
```

Each different monster type inherits from monster but also has its own set of unique characteristics. For example, dragon types could be defined as follows:

```
;;; A dragon is a type of monster with a few additional
;;; characteristics.

(define-type dragon
  (:inherit-from monster)
  (:var number-of-heads)
  (:var fire-breath-temperature :settable)
  :all-gettable
  :all-initable)
 ⇒ DRAGON
```

Using these types, we can now create a specific object, godzilla.

```
;; Build godzilla.
(setf godzilla
      (make-instance 'dragon
                     :name 'godzilla
                     :description
                       "Nasty fire breathing dragon"
                     :strength 10
                     :number-of-heads 1
                     :fire-breath-temperature 350
```

```
                              :damage 2))
⇒ #<Object DRAGON>
```

A function useful for making the game more interesting to **random**, which accepts a numeric argument and returns a random number between zero (inclusive) and the argument (exclusive). This can be used to randomly select different values or produce different output.

`(random` *number*`)`

A simple test of random follows:

```
(random 2)
 ⇒ 1

(random 2)
 ⇒ 0
```

EXERCISES

***10.1** Write a function `monster-enhancer` that takes no arguments, and randomly returns one of following three strings:

```
"The monster prepares to strike."
"The monster ignores your presence."
"The monster twiddles its thumbs."
```

You will have to use the function `random`.

10.2 Design a type and create an instance of the horrible monster, the evil professor. An `evil-professor` is a monster with one additional slot, the `office-number`, which is the den where the evil professor devises mysterious homework.

10.2 Formatted Printing

Common LISP defines a general purpose printing mechanism called `format`. The `format` function produces nice looking output. It takes at least two arguments – the destination of the printing and the string that is to be printed. The string is actually a template that may contain directives for printing any remaining arguments. These remaining S-expressions are printed as specified in the template. The `format` function returns `nil` except when the destination is `nil`, in which case it returns a string as defined in Chapter 13.

`(format` *destination template S-expression**`)`

If the *destination* is `t`, the result is printed on the currently selected output device (usually the terminal). So, invoking `format` with `t` and a string simply prints that string.

```
(format t "This is a test string")
 ⇒ This is a test string
 ⇒ NIL
```

The string was printed on the terminal and then `nil` was returned.

`Format`, as defined in Common LISP, specifies a complex set of directives that are close to a programming language in terms of expressive power. It can perform loops, pluralize words, translate from a number into its English word equivalent (for example, 2 into `second`), generate roman numerals, and so forth. Most programmers won't need all of these capabilities. The small set outlined here should suffice for most programming tasks. The reader is referred to [40] for details on the other directives.

A format directive is indicated with a leading ~ (tilde). The two primary directives are `~A` and `~S`. Each prints the associated S-expression, but they differ in the resulting format. An expression printed in "`read`-readable" format can be read by the LISP `read` function. The `~S` directive prints in `read`-readable format, while `~A` does not. A string produces a different result with each of these directives. A `read`-readable string must be enclosed in double quote marks, `"`, to indicate that it is a string. When the `~S` directive is used on a string, the enclosing quote marks are printed along with the string. When the `~A` directive is used these quote marks are eliminated. The `~S` directive indicates that what is being printed is in fact a string, while `~A` simply provides nice output. Note, Common LISP doesn't distinguish between an upper and lowercase directive, so you may use either `~A` or `~a`.

`~A`

`~S`

```
;; Calls to format with the various directives.
(format t "The monster ~A is bad" (name godzilla))
 ⇒ The monster GODZILLA is bad
 ⇒ NIL

(format t "~S,Description ~S"
        godzilla (description godzilla))
 ⇒ #<Object DRAGON>,Description "Nasty fire breathing dragon"
 ⇒ NIL
```

The directive ~ `%` specifies that a newline will be printed in that position.

This permits you to produce multiple lines with one call to `format`. You can also place a newline at the end of a printed line.

~%

```
(format t "Monster: ~S,~% Description ~S~%"
        godzilla (description godzilla))
⇒ Monster: #<Object DRAGON>,
⇒  Description "Nasty fire breathing dragon"
⇒ NIL
```

Suppose that when the player enters a room in our game, the code should print out the description of each monster present. The `print-presence` method will print the description of a monster along with some random text to make the game more interesting. This method is implemented with each directive so that their distinction is clear. We assume that each type of monster has its own `print-presence` method. This is so we can implement the description of each type differently (for example, we may want some monster types to be invisible under certain circumstances, or we may want to include some of the distinguishing characteristics of a particular monster type). `Print-presence` makes use of the `random` function defined in the previous section.

```
;;; Print out the fact that the monster is present, along
;;; with some fill in text to make the game more interesting.

(define-method (dragon print-presence) ()
  (format t "~S ~S is present.~%"
          (if (= (random 2) 0)
            "Danger, Danger, Danger"
            "Be careful")
          (call-method (monster description))))
⇒ PRINT-PRESENCE

;; Test it with godzilla.
(print-presence godzilla)
⇒ "Danger, Danger, Danger" "Nasty fire breathing dragon" is
⇒ present.
⇒ NIL

;; Try again to get another random value.
(print-presence godzilla)
⇒ "Be careful" "Nasty fire breathing dragon" is present.
⇒ NIL
```

Notice how the use of the `~S` directive places the quote marks in the result.

This is an example of where it would be more appropriate to use the `~A` directive.

```
;;; Print out the fact that the monster is present, along
;;; with some fill in text to make the game more interesting.

(define-method (dragon print-presence) ()
  (format t "~A ~A is present.~%"
          (if (= (random 2) 0)
            "Danger, Danger, Danger"
            "Be careful")
          (call-method (monster description))))
 ⇒ PRINT-PRESENCE

;; Test it with godzilla.
(print-presence godzilla)
 ⇒ Be careful Nasty fire breathing dragon is present.
 ⇒ NIL

;; Try again to get another random value.
(print-presence godzilla)
 ⇒ Danger, Danger, Danger Nasty fire breathing dragon is
 ⇒ present.
 ⇒ NIL
```

The formats produced by `~A` and `~S` are called `princ` and `prin1` respectively. These names come from two functions, one that prints out its argument in "nice" format (`princ`) and the other in "read-readable" format (`prin1`). These functions are simpler than `format` since they only accept one argument for printing and will send the output to the currently selected output device. They also accept a second optional stream argument designating the output location. This is discussed further in the next section. The value returned by both functions is the argument.

(princ *S-expression*)

(prin1 *S-expression*)

```
;; Illustrate the use of princ and prin1.
(princ (description godzilla))
 ⇒ Nasty fire breathing dragon
 ⇒ "Nasty fire breathing dragon"

;; Princ prints the value and returns the argument.
;; Try the same for prin1.
```

```
(prin1 (description godzilla))
 ⇒ "Nasty fire breathing dragon"
 ⇒ "Nasty fire breathing dragon"
```

Neither `princ` nor `prin1` print a newline character. Thus, multiple occurrences of either function will print on the same line. We have already seen that the ~% directive starts a new line within `format`. The `terpri` function prints a newline character that allows printing to begin at the start of the next line. There is also a function that combines `terpri` and `prin1`, which is called `print`. `Print` first performs a `terpri` and then a `prin1` of the argument – it starts a new line and then prints the argument.

(terpri)

(print *S-expression*)

```
;;; A version of the print-presence method that uses princ's.
;;; Notice the extra spaces that had to be inserted. Print
;;; out the fact that the monster is present, along with some
;;; fill in text to make the game more interesting.

(define-method (dragon print-presence) ()
  (princ
   (if (= (random 2) 0)
     "Danger, Danger, Danger "
     "Be careful "))
  (princ (call-method (monster description)))
  (princ " is present.")
  (terpri))
 ⇒ PRINT-PRESENCE

;; Test it with godzilla.
(print-presence godzilla)
 ⇒ Danger, Danger, Danger Nasty fire breathing dragon is
 ⇒ present.
 ⇒ NIL

;; Demonstrate print.  Notice the extra new line at the
;; beginning.
(print (description godzilla))
 ⇒ "Nasty fire breathing dragon"
 ⇒ "Nasty fire breathing dragon"
```

Before we leave the discussion of **format**, we need to cover a few more of the directives. The following table illustrates some of the more useful ones:

~~	Print a ~.
~D	Print as a decimal number (base 10).
~B	Print as a binary number (base 2).
~O	Print as a octal number (base 8).
~X	Print as a hexadecimal number (base 16).

```
;; Simple demonstration of these format directives.
(format t "~~D = ~D, ~~B = ~B, ~~O = ~O, and ~~X = ~X.~%"
   255 255 255 255)
⇒ ~D = 255, ~B = 11111111, ~O = 377, and ~X = FF.
⇒ NIL
```

EXERCISES

***10.3** The **describe** method prints each slot associated with an object. Define the function **my-describe** for monsters and **my-describe** for dragons. Make the dragon version invoke the monster version.

10.4 Translate the previous function definitions to use the non-**format** printing functions.

10.3 Read

The primary reading function in Common LISP is **read**. **Read** reads one S-expression from the currently selected input device and returns it as a value. Since it will read an S-expression, **read** can process any data type, including lists. The LISP system reads expressions from the programmer with the same function.

```
(read)
```

In these examples, the value to read occurs immediately following the call to **read**. The >> is the prompt from the system to provide something to read.

```
(read)
>>99
 ⇒ 99

(read)
>>dragon
 ⇒ DRAGON
```

```
(read)
>>(hello mr monster)
 ⇒ (HELLO MR MONSTER)
```

Suppose we want to implement a command parser for our game. The parser will accept commands from the player and invoke the appropriate function. We haven't implemented any of the "appropriate functions," but we can create stub functions that print a message and return. This style of development is common with LISP. We will implement the following commands:

`north`	Go in the north direction.
`south`	Go in the south direction.
`east`	Go in the east direction.
`west`	Go in the west direction.
`take thing`	Pick up something.
`drop thing`	Drop something.
`fight monster`	Fight a monster.

There are actually two classes of these commands: those that take no arguments and those that take one argument. If we used standard data-driven style, we would create an association list of the command name and the function to invoke. Some commands are similar enough to be consolidated into one – for example, there could be a single `move` command. Then `move` would be invoked by calling it with an extra argument that is the actual command. If we force all functions to take the extra argument, it simplifies their interface and may allow later consolidation of some functions into one. Although some functions will ignore this extra argument, the added flexibility is beneficial. Using bottom-up design, we first implement each of the command functions as stubs that simply print some information.

```
;;; Move in the direction specified as an argument symbol.

(defun move (direction)
  (format t "Moving ~A~%" direction))
 ⇒ MOVE

;;; Take the object specified as the argument (ignore the
;;; command).

(defun take (command thing)
  (format t "Taking ~A~%" thing))
 ⇒ TAKE

;;; Drop the specified object (ignore the command).
```

```
(defun drop (command thing)
  (format t "Dropping ~A~%" thing))
 ⇒ DROP

;;; Fight the argument monster.

(defun fight (command monster)
  (format t "Fighting ~A - Good luck.~%" monster))
 ⇒ FIGHT
```

Next we write the dispatching function `do-commands` that reads commands from the player and invokes the appropriate function. Our approach is to use data-driven style and store the commands into association lists. Thus, we must first define the mapping between the commands and their corresponding functions. They are stored in two a-lists: `*zero-arg-commands*` for commands with no arguments and `*one-arg-commands*` for those with one argument. Another global list contains the commands for terminating the read loop – the commands to quit the game. The quitting commands are stored in `*quit-commands*`.

```
;; Globals to contain the various action commands.
(defvar *zero-arg-commands*
  '((north move) (south move) (east move) (west move)))
 ⇒ *ZERO-ARG-COMMANDS*

(defvar *one-arg-commands*
  '((take take) (drop drop) (fight fight)))
 ⇒ *ONE-ARG-COMMANDS*

(defvar *quit-commands* '(quit stop halt end))
 ⇒ *QUIT-COMMANDS*
```

Notice that `*quit-commands*` is just a list of symbols and not an association list. So, we must remember to use the `member` function in `do-commands` when attempting to see if a command is a quit command. Also, notice that if we combined `take` and `drop` into a single function, then all we would have to change is the function to call as specified in `*one-arg-commands*`.

The list of commands from the user will be arbitrarily long, and therefore the function `do-commands` loops continually until it reads a quit command. An iteration construct can iteratively read a command and then dispatch on the result. We will use the `do` expression. The termination clause is triggered whenever the command is a member of `*quit-commands*`. Otherwise, we `assoc` down the two lists and `apply` the appropriate function. We must remember that those functions in `*one-arg-commands*` take an additional argument read from the player.

```
;;; Read a command from the player and execute whatever is
;;; typed. Terminate the interaction when the player types a
```

```
;;; quit command.

(defun do-commands ()
  (do ((command (read) (read))
       (command-function))
     ((member command *quit-commands*)
      (format t "Leaving the game~%"))
     (cond
      ((setf command-function
             (assoc command *zero-arg-commands*))
       (apply (cadr command-function) (list command)))
      ((setf command-function
             (assoc command *one-arg-commands*))
       (apply (cadr command-function) (list command (read))))
      (t (format t "~A is an illegal command~%" command)))))
 ⇒ DO-COMMANDS

;; A simple test of the command interaction.
(do-commands)
north
 ⇒ Moving NORTH

take wand
 ⇒ Taking WAND

run
 ⇒ RUN is an illegal command

quit
 ⇒ Leaving the game
 ⇒ NIL
```

Two other read functions, **read-char** and **read-line**, allow more control over the reading. **Read-char** reads a single character from the input device, returning that character. It will read the character directly as typed, but returns the Common LISP designation of a character with the **#** prefix. A Common LISP character can be manipulated just like any other LISP data type. It is self-quoting, so typing the character to the system produces itself as a result. Notice that the character designated with the **#** is case sensitive as illustrated in the second example.

#*character*

```
;; The character A.
#\A
```

```
 ⇒ #\A

;; The character lowercase a.
#\a
 ⇒ #\a

(equal #\a #\A)
 ⇒ NIL
```

`Read-char` reads any character, including the newline character, which is designated as `#\newline`. The `read-line` function reads an entire line up to and including the newline character and returns a string containing all of the characters within the line except for the newline character.

(read-char)

(read-line)

Suppose that while using the current version of `do-commands`, we notice that it's cumbersome to type such long command names. A possible solution would be to modify `do-commands` to read single character commands. Single character commands would permit cascading multiple commands together on a single line and could make better interaction. For example, the player could issue `nne` on one line to go north, north, and then east. We will restrict the system, so that any command argument comes after the command character and before the end of the line requiring that no other commands be present on the same line. Thus, `read-char` can extract each command and `read-line` can get any command arguments. We must first change the global lists of commands to contain character commands. Recall that we can't simply reevaluate the `defvar` expressions, but must use `setf` to change the value.

```
;; Change each of the command names.
(setf *zero-arg-commands*
  '((#\n move) (#\s move) (#\e move) (#\w move)))
 ⇒ ((#\n MOVE) (#\s MOVE) (#\e MOVE) (#\w MOVE))

(setf *one-arg-commands* '((#\t take) (#\d drop)
                           (#\f fight)))
 ⇒ ((#\t TAKE) (#\d DROP) (#\f FIGHT))

(setf *quit-commands* '(#\q #\h))
 ⇒ (#\q #\h)
```

We need to pay attention to what happens when a newline or a blank space is typed. We would like to just ignore those "white-space" characters if for some reason the player types them in. Therefore, we will make a new list of ignored commands. This will contain `#\newline` for newline characters and `#\space` for blank spaces.

`#\newline`

`#\space`

```
;; The set of characters to ignore if encountered.
(defvar *ignore-commands* '(#\newline #\space))
 ⇒ *IGNORE-COMMANDS*
```

Finally, we can define `do-single-char-commands` to process single character commands. The structure is nearly identical to `do-commands`.

```
;;; Read a single character command from the player and
;;; execute whatever is typed.  Terminate the interaction
;;; when the player types a character in the set of legal
;;; stop command characters.

(defun do-single-char-commands ()
  (do ((command (read-char) (read-char))
       (command-function))
      ((member command *quit-commands*)
       (format t "Leaving the game~%"))
      (cond
       ((member command *ignore-commands*))
       ((setf command-function
              (assoc command *zero-arg-commands*))
        (apply (cadr command-function) (list command)))
       ((setf command-function
              (assoc command *one-arg-commands*))
        (apply (cadr command-function)
               (list command (read-line))))
       (t (format t "~A is an illegal command~%" command)))))
 ⇒ DO-SINGLE-CHAR-COMMANDS
```

Now we can test the function with a few command interactions.

```
(do-single-char-commands)
nn
 ⇒ Moving n
 ⇒ Moving n
```

```
twand
 ⇒ Taking wand

q
 ⇒ Leaving the game
 ⇒ NIL
```

One problem with this is that the `read-line` doesn't do what we want. Suppose that the game player had typed `t  wand` with a few extra spaces between the `t` and the `wand`. When `read-line` performs the read after the `t`, the result will be a string with a few extra blanks in front. Also, suppose that one of the commands took a numeric argument. `Read-line` would be incorrect, because it returns a string. A `read` instead of `read-line` would solve these problems. `Read` returns the proper LISP object and ignores any superfluous blanks. However, it has the disadvantage that if the player forgets to type in a command argument, it reads the commands on the next line. A better scheme uses `read-line` to make sure that the argument is on the same line. The difficulty is how to extract the S-expression from the string. This task can be accomplished using `read-from-string`.

`(read-from-string` *string*`)`

```
;; Test read-from-string.
(read-from-string "   wand   ")
 ⇒ WAND
 ⇒ 8

;; Only reads the first one.
(read-from-string "  123  456")
 ⇒ 123
 ⇒ 6
```

Notice that `read-from-string` returns multiple values. The second value is the location within the string of the next character following the initial object that was read. As we will see later, this can be used to read multiple objects from a single string. We can now modify `do-single-char-commands` to utilize this function.

```
;;; Read a single character command from the player and
;;; perform the operation.  Terminate when a character
;;; designated as a quitting command is entered.

(defun do-single-char-commands ()
  (do ((command (read-char) (read-char))
       (command-function))
```

```
    ((member command *quit-commands*)
     (format t "Leaving the game~%"))
    (cond
     ((member command *ignore-commands*))
     ((setf command-function
            (assoc command *zero-arg-commands*))
      (apply (cadr command-function) (list command)))
     ((setf command-function
            (assoc command *one-arg-commands*))
      (apply (cadr command-function)
             (list command (read-from-string (read-line)))))
     (t (format t "~A is an illegal command~%" command)))))
 ⇒ DO-SINGLE-CHAR-COMMANDS

;; Now some simple tests.
(do-single-char-commands)
t wand
 ⇒ Taking WAND

ned     sword
 ⇒ Moving N
 ⇒ Moving E
 ⇒ Dropping SWORD

q
 ⇒ Leaving the game
 ⇒ NIL
```

EXERCISES

***10.5** Write a very simple spelling-checker function that reads words from the user and determines if the word is spelled properly. Maintain your dictionary as a list of words and check it using `member`. Initially include mother, dragon, pretty, and monster in your dictionary. When the spelling checker receives a word that isn't present in the dictionary, ask the user if it is spelled properly and add it to the dictionary if it is. When the user types `quit`, then quit the spelling process.

```
(spelling-checker)
What word do you want me to check? mother
 ⇒ MOTHER is correct.

What word do you want me to check? father
FATHER not found, is this correct (y or n)? y
 ⇒ FATHER added to dictionary.

What word do you want me to check? mnster
MNSTER not found, is this correct (y or n)? n
 ⇒ MNSTER incorrect.
```

```
What word do you want me to check? quit
 ⇒ NIL
```

10.6 Write a function that reads characters from the user and determines if the characters are a palindrome. A palindrome is a word, verse, or sentence that reads the same forward and backward. We will require that all palindromes end with a period. Also, all palindromes must match in all characters, including spaces. Thus, the famous "madam im adam" won't work because of spaces and could also fail if punctuation and capitalization had been included.

```
(palindromep)
able was i ere i saw elba.
 ⇒ T

(palindromep)
madam im adam.
 ⇒ NIL
```

***10.7** Enhance the previous definition to ignore spaces, so "madam im adam" will work.

```
(super-palindromep)
madam im adam.
 ⇒ T
```

10.4 File I/O and Streams

There are primarily two types of interactions with files. The first is the process of loading programs (either compiled or interpreted) into the LISP system. The second is the programmable interaction of reading and writing files. The process of loading files is accomplished with the `load` function. `Load` takes one argument, which is the name of the file that is to be loaded. This should be a string. We will see in the next section that the argument may also be a pathname.

(`load` *file-name*)

Suppose that we have created a file as follows and saved it as `"test.l"`. It is generally good programming style to use a standard file header.

```
;;;;;;;;;;;;;;;;;;;;;;;;;;;;;;;;;;;;;;;;;;;;;;;;;;;;;
;;;;
;;;; File:          test.l
;;;; Description:   Test of the CL load function.
;;;; Author:        Fred Hacker
;;;; Created:       27-Oct-85
;;;; Status:        Experimental
;;;;
;;;;;;;;;;;;;;;;;;;;;;;;;;;;;;;;;;;;;;;;;;;;;;;;;;;;;
```

```
; A simple top level form to indicate that we are loading the
; file.
(format t "Loading test.l~%")
;;; Define the factorial function.
(defun factorial (arg)
  (cond ((< arg 2) 1)
        (t (* arg (factorial (1- arg))))))
;;; Now a test.
(format t "The factorial of 8 is ~S~%" (factorial 8))
```

Now that we have created the file, we can load it into the LISP system.

```
;; Load in test.l.  We should see two messages from each of
;; the format expressions.
(load "test.l")
 ⇒ Loading test.l
 ⇒ The factorial of 8 is 40320
 ⇒ "test.l"
```

Anything defined in the file will now be available to you. For example, we can now use the `factorial` function within our own code.

```
(factorial 10)
 ⇒ 3628800
```

A stream in the physical sense is a fast moving small body of water. When observed from a particular location it appears that there is an infinite supply of water coming to that location. If the observer were to place leaves into the stream, they would be carried off in the order they were placed into the stream to some place else (possibly to another observer). This is analogous to streams in Common LISP. The only real difference is that the streams are not constantly moving, but are in fact controlled by the user of the stream. Reading an element from a stream prepares the stream to provide the next element. Streams may be "tied" to various devices and files, offering a uniform access to them. The system doesn't care whether an input stream is from a disk file or a keyboard.

Initial access to a stream is through the `open` function. The primary argument to `open` is the stream name, which is a string or a pathname (described later). The default is to open the stream for input. If open for output is desired, two more arguments must be supplied as described below.

(open *stream-name*)

(open *stream-name* :direction :input)

```
(open stream-name :direction :output)
```

The first two versions are identical and open the file for input.

The result of the call on `open` is a stream. A stream is a data type just like the ones that we have seen before and may be manipulated as such. A stream may be passed to functions so that their operation will apply to the particular stream. For example, the `format` function can make use of a stream. When the first argument is a stream, then output is written to the stream.

When you are finished with a stream, you close it using the function `close`. It takes one argument, the stream.

```
(close stream)
```

As a simple example, let's write some lines to a file, `test.out`. The first step is to open the file and save the stream in a variable.

```
(setf *some-stream* (open "test.out" :direction :output))
⇒ #<File Stream /u/kessler/test.out>
```

Now we can invoke `format` to the stream.

```
(format *some-stream* "This is the first line.~%")
⇒ NIL

(format *some-stream* "The factorial of 4 is ~S.~%"
        (factorial 4))
⇒ NIL
```

Finally, we close the file.

```
(close *some-stream*)
⇒ T
```

The file `test.out` contains the following:

```
This is the first line.
The factorial of 4 is 24.
```

Suppose that we want to keep a history of every command entered by the player of our game. This would permit one to replay any game.* The `play-and-record-game` function will accomplish this. `Play-and-record-game` first asks the player for the name of a history file, opens an output stream to

*This is a little contrived, because with the random operations usually present in this type of game running the same set of commands on a new game might not give the same results. However, the system could save some of its internal state in the history file to permit an actual replay of the game.

that file, performs the various commands writing them to the history file, and then closes the file when the game is over.

```
;; We will switch back to the long named commands.
(setf *zero-arg-commands*
  '((north move) (south move) (east move) (west move)))
 ⇒ ((NORTH MOVE) (SOUTH MOVE) (EAST MOVE) (WEST MOVE))

(setf *one-arg-commands* '((take take) (drop drop)
                           (fight fight)))
 ⇒ ((TAKE TAKE) (DROP DROP) (FIGHT FIGHT))

(setf *quit-commands* '(quit stop halt end))
 ⇒ (QUIT STOP HALT END)

;;; Top-level function to play the monster game.  We first
;;; ask the  player for the name of a file into which we can
;;; save the commands.

(defun play-and-record-game ()
  ;; Read and ignore the newline after the call to
  ;; (play-and-record-game)
  (read-line)
  ;; Print a prompt to ask for the file name.
  (format t "Input new history file name: ")
  (let ((history-stream
          (open (read-line) :direction :output)))
    (do-commands history-stream)
    (close history-stream)))
 ⇒ PLAY-AND-RECORD-GAME
```

Notice the initial call to `read-line`. This is required in this implementation of Common LISP, because the LISP reader only reads enough characters to parse the invocation, `(play-and-record-game)` – it reads the trailing parentheses and no more. The call to `read-line` flushes the newline character after the invocation of `(play-and-record-game)`. Then, when the prompt is printed, we get the file name as typed by the user. If we hadn't used this technique, the call to `read-line` within the `open` expression would have returned an empty string. `Do-commands` must now be redefined to save the commands into a file and also to take the history stream argument. The modification just requires writing the command to the file in a number of places.

```
;;; Read a command from the player and execute whatever is
;;; typed. Terminate the interaction when the player types a
;;; quit command.

(defun do-commands (history-stream)
```

```
  (do ((command (read) (read))
       (command-function))
    ((member command *quit-commands*)
     (format history-stream "~S~%" command)
     (format t "Leaving the game~%"))
    (format history-stream "~S~%" command)
    (cond
     ((setf command-function
            (assoc command *zero-arg-commands*))
      (apply (cadr command-function) (list command)))
     ((setf command-function
            (assoc command *one-arg-commands*))
      (let ((command-arg (read)))
           (format history-stream "~S~%" command-arg)
           (apply (cadr command-function)
                  (list command command-arg))))
     (t (format t "~A is an illegal command~%" command)))))
⇒ DO-COMMANDS
```

```
(play-and-record-game)
Input new history file name: hist.txt
north
⇒ Moving NORTH

drop wand
⇒ Dropping WAND

quit
⇒ Leaving the game
⇒ T
```

The `hist.txt` file now contains the following:

```
NORTH
DROP
WAND
QUIT
```

The second exercise of this section has you modify the function so the commands with arguments actually appear on the same line.

This definition of `do-commands` is a little cluttered with all of the calls to `format`. All commands come from the `read` function. A better solution defines an auxiliary reading function that reads the command, saves it into the file, and then returns the command that was read. This cleans up the code considerably.

```
;;; Read a command, save it into the history file, and return
;;; the command that was read.
```

```
(defun get-command (history-stream)
  (let ((command (read)))
    (format history-stream "~S~%" command)
    command))
⇒ GET-COMMAND

;;; Read a command from the player and execute whatever is
;;; typed.  Terminate the interaction when the player types a
;;; quit command.

(defun do-commands (history-stream)
  (do ((command (get-command history-stream)
                (get-command history-stream))
       (command-function))
      ((member command *quit-commands*)
       (format t "Leaving the game~%"))
      (cond
       ((setf command-function
              (assoc command *zero-arg-commands*))
        (apply (cadr command-function) (list command)))
       ((setf command-function
              (assoc command *one-arg-commands*))
        (apply (cadr command-function)
               (list command (get-command history-stream))))
       (t (format t "~A is an illegal command~%" command)))))
⇒ DO-COMMANDS
```

Now that we can create history files, we want to be able to restart from a history file. To restart means that commands are processed from the history file, instead of from the game player at the terminal. When a quit command is found in the history file, the game should shift and read from the player. We need to have some way of reading from a file. The `read` function permits an extra argument that is the input stream. A value of `t` for the input stream in the `read` function designates the terminal just like in `format`.

(`read` *optional-input-stream*)

There are three problems that we have to solve. First we have to read the commands from the history file and then switch to reading from the player. Second, when `do-commands` finds a quit command from the history file, that will signal that it is time to switch. Finally, `do-commands` cannot simply write the quit command to the history file, because it will write the intermediate quit from the original history file, which would cause premature termination of any history commands. To solve thise problems, we must first change `do-commands` to take another argument, which is the input stream. We can then change the quit processing to do something different when it gets a quit command from the history file and a quit command from the player. One important change is to insure that it doesn't print that the game is over when any quit is found. This can be solved by changing the code so that `play-game` is responsible for printing the message about leaving the game. Finally, we can change the program so it doesn't write the quit command to the history file when it is encountered.

```
;;; Read a command, save it into the history file, and return
;;; the command that was read.  If the command is a quit
;;; command, then we don't write it to the file.

(defun get-command (history-stream input-stream)
  (let ((command (read input-stream)))
    (if (not (member command *quit-commands*))
      (format history-stream "~S~%" command))
    command))
 ⇒ GET-COMMAND

;;; Read a command from the argument input-stream and execute
;;; whatever it is.  Terminate the interaction when a quit
;;; command is found.

(defun do-commands (history-stream input-stream)
  (do ((command (get-command history-stream input-stream)
                (get-command history-stream input-stream))
       (command-function))
    ((member command *quit-commands*))
    (cond
     ((setf command-function
            (assoc command *zero-arg-commands*))
      (apply (cadr command-function) (list command)))
     ((setf command-function
            (assoc command *one-arg-commands*))
      (apply (cadr command-function)
             (list command
                   (get-command history-stream
                                input-stream))))
     (t (format t "~A is an illegal command~%" command)))))
 ⇒ DO-COMMANDS
```

This new definition can now be used in `play-game`. It asks for a file to restart from and invokes `do-commands` on the file. When the restart process terminates, `do-commands` is called to continue play.

```
;;; Top level function to play the monster game.  We will
```

```
;;; ask the player for the name of a file into which we
;;; can save the commands.

(defun play-game ()
  ;; Read and ignore the newline after the call to
  ;; (play-game)
  (read-line)
  ;; Print a prompt to ask for the file name.
  (format t "Input new history file name: ")
  (let ((history-stream (open (read-line)
                              :direction :output))
        restart-file-name
        restart-stream)
    (format t
          "Restart history file name (n to not restart): ")
    (if (not (equal (setf restart-file-name (read-line))
                    "n"))
      (progn
        (do-commands history-stream
                     (setf restart-stream
                           (open restart-file-name)))
        (close restart-stream)))
    (do-commands history-stream t)
    (format t "Leaving the game~%")
    (close history-stream)))
 ⇒ PLAY-GAME

(play-game)
Input new history file name: hist2.txt
Restart history file name (n to not restart): hist.txt
 ⇒ Moving NORTH
 ⇒ Dropping WAND

south
 ⇒ Moving SOUTH

south
 ⇒ Moving SOUTH

quit
 ⇒ Leaving the game
 ⇒ T
```

The file hist2.txt contains the following:

```
NORTH
DROP
```

```
WAND
SOUTH
SOUTH
```

Notice that it doesn't include the `quit` command, because `quit` was not written to the history file. This means that the next time `do-commands` would be called on this history file, it would not properly stop the processing. In Common LISP, a **read** past the end-of-file signals an error. This is unacceptable in this case, because the function should continue the interaction with the game player. So, we want to tell the LISP system not to signal the error, but instead to return something meaningful like the `quit` symbol. This can be accomplished by calling **read** with two more arguments (after the stream argument).

(**read** *stream eof-errorp eof-value*)

The *eof-errorp* argument specifies whether or not an error should be signaled. A non-`nil` value will signal the error, while `nil` will not. The *eof-value* specifies the value to be returned when the end-of-file is recognized. In this case, `do-commands` can return whatever command is on the front of `*quit-commands*`, which will then be used to quit the command processing.

```
;;; Read a command, save it into the history file, and return
;;; the command that was read.  If the command is a quit
;;; command, then we don't write it to the file.  If we hit
;;; the end of file, we will just return a quit command.

(defun get-command (history-stream input-stream)
  (let ((command (read input-stream nil
                       (car *quit-commands*))))
    (if (not (member command *quit-commands*))
      (format history-stream "~S~%" command))
    command))
 ⇒ GET-COMMAND
```

Now we can use a file with our system without a terminating command and it will still restart with all of the commands.

```
(play-game)
Input new history file name: hist3.txt
Restart history file name (n to not restart): hist2.txt
 ⇒ Moving NORTH
 ⇒ Dropping WAND
 ⇒ Moving SOUTH
 ⇒ Moving SOUTH

quit
```

```
⇒ Leaving the game
⇒ T
```

The final stream function is `with-open-file` whose purpose is to create an environment in which LISP expressions are evaluated while a stream is open. The expression opens a stream, performs the designated operations, and when the operations are terminated, the stream is automatically closed (even if an error occurs like accessing past the end-of-file). The first argument is a list of at least two elements. The first element is a symbol will be bound to the stream. The second element is the name of the stream. Optional arguments specify how the file should be opened, like those arguments to `open`. The body expressions follow the initial list. Since the file is automatically closed upon exit from the body, this style of file access is preferable to explicit use of `open` and `close`.

(`with-open-file` (*symbol stream-name*) *S-expression**)

(`with-open-file` (*symbol stream-name*`:direction :input`) *S-expression**)

(`with-open-file` (*symbol stream-name*`:direction :output`) *S-expression**)

`Play-game` can be modified to use this function for output of the history file and reading the restart file.

```
;;; Top level function to play the monster game.  We will
;;; ask the player for the name of a file into which we
;;; can save the commands.

(defun play-game ()
  ;; Read and ignore the newline after the call to
  ;; (play-game)
  (read-line)
  ;; Print a prompt to ask for the file name.
  (format t "Input new history file name: ")
  (let ((history-file-name (read-line))
        restart-file-name)
    (format t
            "Restart history file name (n to not restart): ")
    (with-open-file
     (history-stream history-file-name :direction :output)
     (cond
      ((not (equal (setf restart-file-name (read-line)) "n"))
       (with-open-file
```

```
           (restart-stream restart-file-name)
           (do-commands history-stream restart-stream))))
        (do-commands history-stream t)
        (format t "Leaving the game~%"))))
 ⇒ PLAY-GAME

(play-game)
Input new history file name: hist4.txt
Restart history file name (n to not restart): hist2.txt
 ⇒ Moving NORTH
 ⇒ Dropping WAND
 ⇒ Moving SOUTH
 ⇒ Moving SOUTH

quit
 ⇒ Leaving the game
 ⇒ NIL
```

EXERCISES

10.8 The initial version of **play-game** had the problem that if the function were invoked with the history file name immediately following the invocation, then it would be ignored with the first call to **read-line**. Modify the function so the history file name could appear after the call and if present wouldn't bother to print a prompt message. (*Hint:* If there is no file name specified, then the value returned by the **read-line** will be the empty string designated by two double quote marks – "".)

10.9 Modify the definition of **do-commands** so the resulting history file places the arguments to commands on the same line as the command. Thus, the history file would look like:

```
NORTH
DROP WAND
QUIT
```

***10.10** Write a function that reads a file of LISP symbols and counts the number of occurrences of an argument symbol. You may assume that there are no parentheses in the file.

```
;; Count the occurrences of the second argument in the file
;; designated by the first argument.
(count-occurrences "bar.l" 'jane)
 ⇒ The file "bar.l" contains 6 occurrences of JANE.
 ⇒ 6
```

10.11 Save your **count-occurrences** function in a file and try using **load** to bring its definition into a running LISP.

10.5 Pathnames

Pathnames provide portable access to file names via a common structure that is independent of the particular operating system. A pathname consists of the following six components. Some of these may not be relevant to a particular operating system but the Common LISP implementation requires each of the following components:

host – The name of the system upon which the file is present
device – When there are multiple devices, each of which contains a file system, this component specifies that device
directory – The name of the directory of the file
name – The name of the file (this usually is the part to the left of a period in a file name)
type – The part of the file after the period in a file name (also known as the file extension on some systems) and
version – The version number of a file. When version numbers are supported in a particular file system, the number is incremented for each new version of a file. This allows users to have control over saving the old version.

The **pathname** function converts a string file name into a pathname. The pathname can then be passed to any function that expects a file name (for example, **open** and **with-open-file**). The **truename** function converts a string file name into a pathname, expanding any pseudopaths into a valid pathname. The argument to **truename** must be an existing file name. Finally, the **namestring** function converts a pathname back into the associated string file name.

(**pathname** *file-name-string*)

(**truename** *file-name-string*)

(**namestring** *pathname*)

```
;; Convert a few file names into pathnames.
(setf history-file (pathname "hist.txt"))
⇒ #.(make-pathname :host NIL :device NIL :directory NIL
⇒                  :name "hist" :type "txt" :version NIL)

(namestring history-file)
⇒ "hist.txt"

;; We use truename to get the full pathname.
```

```
(setf history-file (truename "~/hist.txt"))
⇒ #.(make-pathname :host NIL :device NIL :directory
⇒                  '("" "u" "kessler") :name "hist"
⇒                  :type "txt" :version NIL)

(namestring history-file)
⇒ "/u/kessler/hist.txt"
```

Each of the components of a pathname may be extracted by using the appropriate `pathname-*` function (where * is either `host`, `device`, `directory`, `name`, `type`, or `version`).

```
;; Extract some components of the history-file pathname.
(pathname-directory history-file)
⇒ ("" "u" "kessler")

(pathname-name history-file)
⇒ "hist"

;; Versions aren't used on this system.
(pathname-version history-file)
⇒ NIL
```

You can also merge two pathnames together using the `merge-pathnames` function.

(`merge-pathnames` *pathname pathname*)

Suppose that in our history of commands example we have a list of possible directories where the history file could be located. We can define the list such that each element in the list is a pathname with just the directory name component defined. That list might look like this:

```
;;; Create a variable that contains the list of directories.
(setf *history-directories*
      (list (pathname "~/dungeon/") (pathname "~/")
            (pathname "/usr/games/dungeon/")))
⇒ (#.(make-pathname :host NIL :device NIL
⇒                   :directory '("~" "dungeon")
⇒                   :name NIL :type NIL :version NIL)
⇒   #.(make-pathname :host NIL :device NIL :directory '("~")
⇒                   :name NIL :type NIL :version NIL)
⇒   #.(make-pathname :host NIL :device NIL :directory
⇒                   '("" "usr" "games" "dungeon") :name NIL
⇒                   :type NIL :version NIL))
```

Now suppose that we are given a history file name that doesn't have any directory information. We could then scan the list of directories, calling **merge-pathnames** to merge one directory pathname with the history file pathname to create a single pathname that includes a directory. For example:

```
(merge-pathnames (car *history-directories*)
                 (pathname "hist.txt"))
⇒ #.(make-pathname :host NIL :device NIL
⇒                  :directory '("~" "dungeon")
⇒                  :name "hist" :type "txt"
⇒                  :version NIL)
```

If we could then check to see if the file exists, we have found the history file. If the file doesn't exist, we can then check the next directory pathname and merge it with the history file name to create yet another possible file name. In order to write this function, we will need another option to **open** that lets you test to see if a file exists. The :**probe** option on :**direction** performs this operation. When **open** is called with this option, it returns T if the file exists, and **nil** otherwise.

(open *stream-name* :direction :probe)

Using these facilities, we can write **find-file**, which takes a file pathname and a list of directories as arguments. The function scans the directories searching for the location of the file. If it finds the file, the completed pathname is returned.

```
;;; Find the first argument file name in the list of
;;; directories specified in the second argument.

(defun find-file (file-pathname directory-list)
  (let (new-pathname)
    (cond
     ((null directory-list) nil)
     ((open (setf new-pathname
                  (merge-pathnames file-pathname
                                   (car directory-list)))
            :direction :probe)
      new-pathname)
     (t (find-file file-pathname (cdr directory-list))))))
⇒ FIND-FILE

;; The file is located in the second directory in
;; *history-directories*.  Neither of the other two contain
;; the file.
```

```
(find-file (pathname "hist.txt") *history-directories*)
⇒ #.(make-pathname :host NIL :device NIL :directory '("~")
⇒                  :name "hist" :type "txt" :version NIL)
```

EXERCISES

10.12 Experiment with **pathname** on your own system. Call **pathname** with the name of a couple of files, both local to your directory and other global files. Then invoke the various **pathname** accessor functions to examine how your system defines each of the component of the pathname.

***10.13** Verify that a file name and the result of calling **namestring** on the result of a call to **pathname** of the file name produce the same effective result.

```
;; On your system, how does this result compare with the
;; file name itself?
(namestring (pathname "foo.l"))
```

***10.14** Write a function that takes a list of directories and a list of files and determines if all of the files are in all of the directories. Print a list of which files are not in which directories.

```
(compare-directories
 '("/u/kessler/" "/u/muehle/" "/u/carr/")
 '("foo.l" ".login" ".cshrc"))
⇒ foo.l not in /u/muehle/, /u/carr/,
⇒ .login present in all directories
⇒ .cshrc present in all directories
⇒ NIL
```

10.6 Debugging

Every LISP system provides a different programming environment and set of debugging tools for use by programmers. Two of the most common debugging tools are `trace` and `step`. Common LISP has defined the access to these functions and the general semantics, but the individual implementation determines the information that is produced and the interaction techniques.

The most primitive debugging technique is the placement of printing functions within the body of a function. Judicious placement of calls to `format` can greatly aid in the debugging process. However, `format` has the characteristic that it generally returns `nil` so programmers must be careful where they place the expression in the code. For example, a call to `format` in the test part of a `cond` expression would result in the test failing and possibly modifying the semantics of the program. Alternatively, the `print` function returns the argument as its value. Arbitrary placement of `print` will not alter the semantics of the program. The only problem with `print` is that you can't add extra information to the printed argument without affecting the result and must settle for only printing the argument.

```
;;; Factorial function for illustration of debugging.
;;; Placement of format and print statements.
(defun factorial (arg)
  (format t "Entering factorial, arg is ~S~%" arg)
  (print
   (cond
    ((< arg 2) 1)
    (t (* arg (print (factorial (1- arg))))))))
 ⇒ FACTORIAL

;; Now call factorial, demonstrating that it is a little
;; confusing as to which print statement is printing a value.
(factorial 3)
 ⇒ Entering factorial, arg is 3
 ⇒ Entering factorial, arg is 2
 ⇒ Entering factorial, arg is 1
 ⇒ 1
 ⇒ 1
 ⇒ 2
 ⇒ 2
 ⇒ 6
 ⇒ 6
```

The `trace` macro takes an arbitrary number of function names as arguments and changes the definition of each function so that useful information is printed when the function is entered and exited. Generally, some kind of wrapping code is placed around a function that doesn't change the semantics of the function, but prints the fact that the function is being entered, prints the current bindings of the function arguments, and then executes the body. Upon exit from the body, the wrapper prints the value that will be returned and the name of the exiting function. This could also be accomplished by modifying a function to include the extra print statements, but `trace` provides a uniform mechanism. A `trace` of a function will usually illustrate the current nesting level of recursive calls on a function. The `untrace` function removes the tracing of the argument functions. If no arguments are given to `untrace`, then it removes tracing from all traced functions.

(trace *symbol**)

(untrace *symbol**)

The first demonstration is to redefine `factorial` to eliminate the debugging print statements and then `trace` its execution instead.

```
;;; Factorial function.
(defun factorial (arg)
  (if (< arg 2) 1 (* arg (factorial (1- arg)))))
 ⇒ FACTORIAL

(trace factorial)
 ⇒ (FACTORIAL)

;; Now, call factorial again.
(factorial 3)
 ⇒ FACTORIAL entry:
 ⇒ |   Arg 1: 3
 ⇒ |  FACTORIAL reentry (# 2):
 ⇒ |  |   Arg 1: 2
 ⇒ |  |  FACTORIAL reentry (# 3):
 ⇒ |  |  |   Arg 1: 1
 ⇒ |  |  FACTORIAL (# 3) return value = 1
 ⇒ |  FACTORIAL (# 2) return value = 2
 ⇒ FACTORIAL return value = 6
 ⇒ 6
```

Finally, we can trace some of the functions defined in our game example.

```
;; Trace the various functions we use to play the game.
(trace play-game do-commands move)
 ⇒ (MOVE DO-COMMANDS PLAY-GAME)

(play-game)
 ⇒ PLAY-GAME entry: (called with no arguments)

Input new history file name: hist5.txt
Restart history file name (n to not restart): hist2.txt
 ⇒ |  DO-COMMANDS entry:
 ⇒ |  |   Arg 1: #<File Stream /u/kessler/hist5.txt>
 ⇒ |  |   Arg 2: #<File Stream /u/kessler/hist2.txt>
 ⇒ |  |  MOVE entry:
 ⇒ |  |  |   Arg 1: NORTH
 ⇒ Moving NORTH
 ⇒ |  |  MOVE return value = NIL
 ⇒ Dropping WAND
 ⇒ |  |  MOVE entry:
 ⇒ |  |  |   Arg 1: SOUTH
 ⇒ Moving SOUTH
 ⇒ |  |  MOVE return value = NIL
```

```
⇒ |  |  MOVE entry:
⇒ |  |  |   Arg 1: SOUTH
⇒ Moving SOUTH
⇒ |  |  MOVE return value = NIL
⇒ |  DO-COMMANDS return value = NIL
⇒ |  DO-COMMANDS entry:
⇒ |  |   Arg 1: #<File Stream /u/kessler/hist5.txt>
⇒ |  |   Arg 2: T

east
⇒ |  |  MOVE entry:
⇒ |  |  |   Arg 1: EAST
⇒ Moving EAST
⇒ |  |  MOVE return value = NIL

halt
⇒ |  DO-COMMANDS return value = NIL
⇒ Leaving the game
⇒ PLAY-GAME return value = NIL
⇒ NIL
```

`Trace` gives the user a rough view of the execution process. `Trace` works on a function level, so functions should be kept small for it to be effective. When finer debugging is necessary, the `step` macro is useful. `Step` accepts one argument, which is an S-expression to evaluate under a control of the "stepper." This control means that as the interpreter evaluates each form and its arguments one at a time, the user is given the opportunity to observe each evaluation step in detail.

(`step` *S-expression*)

Each version of `step` is dependent upon the particular implementation. However, most versions are typically interactive, where the user controls the amount of detail of the execution that is viewed. So, if the user wants to see only the result of a particular S-expression evaluation and not the details, a command will suppress the stepping action until a result is computed. Some versions even permit retracting the evaluation of some S-expressions and changing the data. The implementation manual should be consulted for the details of the particular version of `step`.

EXERCISES

10.15 Debug the following function using `trace`:

```
;;; This function counts the number of numbers in the
;;; argument list.
```

```
;;; *** BUGGY VERSION ***

(defun count-numbers (list-of-things)
  (cond ((null list-of-things) nil)
        ((numberp (car list-of-things))
         (+ 1 (count-numbers (cdr list-of-things))))
        (t (count-numbers (cdr list-of-things)))))
 ⇒ COUNT-NUMBERS

(count-numbers '(1 4 foo 3 bar))

!!!!! Error: The argument NIL is not of type NUMBER.
  Condition signaled in: +.
```

10.16 Define the `factorial` function, and invoke your version of `step` on it. Experiment with the different options that your system may provide for you.

10.7 Summary

This chapter was directed toward input/output and some details of the debugging paradigm used in LISP. The primary output function within LISP is `format`, which has numerous options, including the ability to print in `read`-readable and `princ` format. `Format` can also construct strings or direct the output to various streams. There are a number of input forms, including `read` to read entire S-expressions, `read-line` to read an entire line, and `read-char` to read a single character. The `load` function reads entire files of S-expressions, binary code, and so on. The stream concept permits access to files, terminals, and other devices without the programmer worrying about the particular device characteristics. The pertinent operations on streams are `open`, `close`, and `with-open-file`. The latter is desired when interacting with a file. Once a stream has been opened, the stream object may be passed to the various input/output functions as the target of the operation. Pathnames provide portable access to file names. Finally, a number of techniques defined in the Common LISP standard can be used to help debug programs. Insertion of `print` statements is a primitive means, but the use of the highly system-dependent `trace` and `step` are normally used.

Chapter Exercises

***1.** Write a function to count all of the LISP symbols in a file. You may assume that there are no parentheses.

```
(count-symbols "bar.l")
 ⇒ The file "bar.l" contains 15 symbols.
 ⇒ 15
```

2. Change the above function to permit parentheses which may or may not be nested. Since **read** may return a nested list, it may be helpful to write a function to flatten a list (that is, collect all of the leaf symbols into a single list).

```
(count-symbols "bar.l")
⇒ The file "bar.l" contains 25 symbols.
⇒ 25
```

3. Enhance the function to count both the number of words and number of sentences. Print the results in a nice form for the user. As you will see in Chapter 13, LISP treats a period specially. Therefore, if you plan to use **read**, then you must place an escape character in front of it in the file. For example, the file must appear as:

```
See Dick Run \. Run Dick Run \.
```

This allows you to call **read** and compare the result against the symbol `'\.`.

***4.** Write a set of functions that accepts a file name, computes the number of occurrences of each word, and prints them out in a list, including a percentage of the total words.

```
(words "bar.l")
⇒ . present 5 times for 12.5%
⇒ JANE present 8 times for 20.0%
⇒ THERE present 1 times for 2.5%
⇒ HELLO present 2 times for 5.0%
⇒ SEE present 5 times for 12.5%
⇒ RUN present 6 times for 15.0%
⇒ DICK present 3 times for 7.5%
⇒ NOW present 1 times for 2.5%
⇒ IS present 1 times for 2.5%
⇒ THE present 1 times for 2.5%
⇒ TIME present 1 times for 2.5%
⇒ FOR present 1 times for 2.5%
⇒ ALL present 1 times for 2.5%
⇒ GOOD present 1 times for 2.5%
⇒ MEN present 1 times for 2.5%
⇒ TO present 1 times for 2.5%
⇒ COME present 1 times for 2.5%
⇒ --------
⇒ Total words: 40
⇒ NIL
```

Function Summary

The following lists the functions and topics covered in this chapter.

- `(format` *destination template S-expression** `)`
- `~A`
- `~S`

- `~%`
- `(random` *number*`)`
- `(princ` *S-expression*`)`
- `(prin1` *S-expression*`)`
- `(terpri)`
- `(print` *S-expression*`)`
- `(read)`
- `#\`*character*
- `(read-char)`
- `(read-line)`
- `#\newline`
- `#\space`
- `(read-from-string` *string*`)`
- `(load` *file-name*`)`
- Streams
- `(open` *stream-name*`)`
- `(open` *stream-name :direction :input*`)`
- `(open` *stream-name :direction :output*`)`
- `(close` *stream*`)`
- `(read` *optional-input-stream*`)`
- `(read` *stream eof-errorp eof-value*`)`
- `(with-open-file(`*symbol stream-name*`)` *S-expression**`)`
- `(with-open-file(`*symbol stream-name*`:direction :input)` *S-expression**`)`
- `(with-open-file(`*symbol stream-name*`:direction :output)` *S-expression**`)`
- `(pathname` *file-name-string*`)`
- `(truename` *file-name-string*`)`
- `(namestring` *pathname*`)`
- `(merge-pathnames` *pathname pathname*`)`
- `(open` *stream-name* `:direction :probe)`
- `(trace` *symbol**`)`
- `(untrace` *symbol**`)`
- `(step` *S-expression*`)`

11 OTHER TYPES OF DATA REPRESENTATION

OTHER TECHNIQUES for representing data are discussed in this chapter. Objects provide a method for describing and interacting with data. Defstructs are essentially the data parts of objects. They permit declaration of LISP record structures, without the associated methods. We have also seen association lists as a type of data representation scheme. They are similar to property lists which are special structures attached to symbols. Finally hash tables provide structures that function like association lists, but provide rapid access to the values. We will continue the role-playing game for examples.

11.1 Structures

Objects provide two main features:

1. The ability to create objects that have slots and values, and
2. Methods to provide access to the object.

Structures have the first feature, but lack the second. They also don't have any information-hiding capabilities, because all of the slots are accessible. `Defstruct` is the function that defines structures. Like `define-type`, `defstruct` defines the template of a structure and not an instance of one. Structures are like records in other programming languages.

The first argument to `defstruct` is the name of the structure. It may be a simple symbol or a list of the structure name and various structure options, defined later. The remaining arguments are the slot specifications. A slot specification is either the slot name, or a list with the slot name and slot options.

(`defstruct` *symbol slot**)

(`defstruct` (*symbol options*) *slot**)

When a `define-type` expression is evaluated, a number of methods are automatically defined, depending on options like `:settable`. When `defstruct` is evaluated, a number of functions are also automatically created. These functions have a default-naming convention. The following lists the default functions created for each structure. In each example, *symbol* is the name passed as the second argument to the `defstruct`.

- `make-`*symbol* – creates an instance of the structure. As with objects, each slot may be given an initial value by mentioning the slot name prefixed with a : followed by the initial value.
- *symbol*`-p` – tests to see if the argument is a structure of the defined type.
- *symbol-slot-name* – for each slot name defined in the structure, a function is created for retrieving the slot.
- `(setf (`*symbol-slot-name structure*`)` *S-expression*`)` – stores the value of the S-expression into the slot of the structure.

The following examples implement parts of the fantasy game as structures instead of objects.

```
;;; Create a monster structure.

(defstruct monster
   name
   description
   strength
   initial-strength
   initial-damage
   room)
 ⇒ MONSTER

;; Create godzilla with some of the slots initialized.
(setf godzilla (make-monster
                 :name 'godzilla
                 :initial-damage 5
                 :strength 20.0
                 :initial-strength 20.0
                 :description
                 "Nasty old fire breathing dragon"))
 ⇒ #S(MONSTER NAME GODZILLA DESCRIPTION
 ⇒            "Nasty old fire breathing dragon" STRENGTH 20.0
 ⇒            INITIAL-STRENGTH 20.0 INITIAL-DAMAGE 5
 ⇒            ROOM NIL)
```

The `#S` indicates that the following is a structure. The printed representation also lists each of the slots and their current values. Now we can try some of the accessor functions.

```
;; See if godzilla is a monster.
(monster-p godzilla)
 ⇒ T

;; Retrieve the description slot.
(monster-description godzilla)
 ⇒ "Nasty old fire breathing dragon"
```

Suppose that we want a function that decreases the strength of a monster by some specified value. The strength should never go below zero. The function gains access to `monster-strength` and also stores into that slot. The `max` function is used to verify that the strength never goes below zero. The following function performs this operation:

```
;;; Decrease the strength of the monster by the argument.

(defun decrease-strength (monster-structure
                          value-to-decrease)
  (setf (monster-strength monster-structure)
        (max 0
             (- (monster-strength monster-structure)
                value-to-decrease))))
 ⇒ DECREASE-STRENGTH

;; Test the function.
(decrease-strength godzilla 3)
 ⇒ 17.0

;; Verify that the slot value has been decreased.
(monster-strength godzilla)
 ⇒ 17.0
```

`Defstruct` lets you specify initial values for a slot, as in the `let` construct. The slot is specified as a list containing the name of the slot and the initial value expression.

```
;;; This is a new version of the monster structure with
;;; initial values.

(defstruct monster
   name
   description
   (strength 0)
   (initial-strength 0)
   (initial-damage 0)
   room)
 ⇒ MONSTER
```

```
;; Create godzilla using some initial values from the
;; defstruct.
(setf godzilla
      (make-monster :name 'godzilla :initial-strength 20.0
                    :description
                    "Nasty old fire breathing dragon"))
⇒ #S(MONSTER NAME GODZILLA DESCRIPTION
⇒            "Nasty old fire breathing dragon" STRENGTH 0
⇒            INITIAL-STRENGTH 20.0 INITIAL-DAMAGE 0
⇒            ROOM NIL)
```

You can specify a number of options that can add inheritance to the structure. You can also change the names of the automatically generated functions, or specify a function to print a structure instance. These options are specified in the list which is the first element of the `defstruct` specification. Options follow the structure name, alternating between the option name and the value. The various options are defined as follows:

- `:conc-name` – Specifies the symbol to be used on the front of all accessor functions. If the symbol is `nil`, then each accessor function is simply the name of the slot.

  (`:conc-name` *symbol*)

- `:constructor` – Specifies the name of the function that constructs the structure.

  (`:constructor` *symbol*)

- `:predicate` – Specifies the name of the predicate function that tests to see if the argument is a structure of the same type.

  (`:predicate` *symbol*)

- `:include` – This option allows specification of **one** other structure from which this structure inherits slots. When these slots are inherited, all of the access functions of the parent structure will work on both structures. This option may also include slot names with initialization specifications for any slots that will differ from the initialization in the parent structure.

  (`:include` *parent* (*slot**))

- `:print-function` – Specifies a function that prints a structure. The function takes three arguments, the structure to be printed, the destination stream, and an integer indicating the current nesting depth. Nesting depth indicates how many levels of structure have been printed. Within a parenthesized expression, each new right parenthesis indicates another nesting level. Printing a structure has a similar feature, in that it is possible to have structures within structures. The depth argument indicates how many levels deep the printing is within nested structures. Common LISP defines a global variable `*print-level*` that specifies the maximum depth that should be printed (for example, the `X` in `(A B (C (X)))` is at nesting-depth three). Thus, the print function could compare the third argument against `*print-level*` and not print anything if the argument is greater than `*print-level*`. This makes the printing of structures agree with the rest of the system when the nesting depth is controlled. A value of `nil` for `*print-level*` indicates that there is no limit on the depth.

(`:print-function` *function-name*)

`*print-level*`

A `nil` used as the `:conc-name` can cause problems when the same slot name occurs in different structures. The conflicts can make one slot name function redefine the other and then access the wrong slot. For example, suppose that a vampire and a ghost are defined as follows:

```
;;; The vampire structure.

(defstruct (vampire (:conc-name nil))
  blood-type
  strength)
 ⇒ VAMPIRE

(setf drac (make-vampire :strength 5))
 ⇒ #S(VAMPIRE BLOOD-TYPE NIL STRENGTH 5)

(strength drac)
 ⇒ 5

;;; Define the ghost structure.

(defstruct (ghost (:conc-name nil))
  strength
  flying-speed)
 ⇒ GHOST

(setf crazy (make-ghost :strength 33))
```

```
 ⇒ #S(GHOST STRENGTH 33 FLYING-SPEED NIL)

(strength crazy)
 ⇒ 33

(strength drac)
!!!!! Error: The argument #S(VAMPIRE BLOOD-TYPE NIL STRENGTH
                                                     5)
         is not of type GHOST.
  Condition signaled in: STRENGTH.
```

The following examples use these structure options. The first step is to create a dragon structure, which inherits from the monster structure.

```
;;; The dragon type, utilizing some of the previous options
;;; to change the names.

(defstruct (dragon (:include monster (initial-strength 5))
             (:conc-name drag)
             (:constructor create-dragon)
             (:predicate dragonp))
  (number-of-heads 1))
 ⇒ DRAGON

;; Create godzilla again.
(setf godzilla (create-dragon :strength 5 :description
                 "Nasty Old Fire Breathing Dragon"))
 ⇒ #S(DRAGON NAME NIL
 ⇒          DESCRIPTION "Nasty Old Fire Breathing Dragon"
 ⇒          STRENGTH 5 INITIAL-STRENGTH 5 INITIAL-DAMAGE 0
 ⇒          ROOM NIL NUMBER-OF-HEADS 1)

;; Test the predicate and access functions.
(dragonp godzilla)
 ⇒ T

(dragstrength godzilla)
 ⇒ 5
```

When we create a structure that inherits from another, all of the accessor functions of the parent also work on the child. This is only possible because multiple inheritance is not permitted.

```
;; Verify that the monster accessor also works.
(monster-strength godzilla)
 ⇒ 5
```

Finally, we can write a print function to print dragons in a different format.

```
;;; The dragon type, utilizing some of the previous options
;;; to change the names.

(defstruct (dragon (:include monster (initial-strength 5))
                   (:conc-name drag)
                   (:constructor create-dragon)
                   (:predicate dragonp)
                   (:print-function print-dragon))
  (number-of-heads 1))
 ⇒ DRAGON

;;; Now define the print function for dragons.

(defun print-dragon (struct stream level)
  (if (and *print-level* (> level *print-level*))
    nil
    (format stream "~A" (monster-description struct))))
 ⇒ PRINT-DRAGON

;; Create godzilla again.
(setf godzilla (create-dragon :strength 5 :description
                    "Nasty Old Fire Breathing Dragon"))
 ⇒ Nasty Old Fire Breathing Dragon
```

EXERCISES

***11.1** Define a structure for a player of our fantasy game. A player has the following fields: `hit-points`, `initial-strength`, `weapons`, `current-room`, `fighting`, and `name`. The `weapons` and `fighting` should be initialized to `nil`. Also, create an instance of the player structure with your name, ten hit points, and ten as the initial strength.

11.2 Enhance the player structure from the previous exercise with a print function that prints as follows:

```
(defvar *player* (make-player :name 'bob))
 ⇒ *PLAYER*

*player*
 ⇒ [Player BOB]
```

***11.3** Suppose that the `weapons` slot of the `player` structure contains a list of the weapons that the player is carrying. Write a function, `number-of-weapons`, which determines how many weapons that the player is currently carrying.

```
(setf (player-weapons *player*) '(cannon sword gun))
 ⇒ (CANNON SWORD GUN)

(number-of-weapons *player*)
 ⇒ 3
```

11.2 Property List

A property list is an extra field associated with each global symbol. So far, we have seen that a symbol may have both a value and a function definition. It may also have a property list. A property list is similar to an association list in its semantics, however its syntax is a little different. Property lists provide the same kind of key/value information except they are associated with a particular symbol. They are lists whose elements alternate between keys and values – they are not actually paired into sublists as in association lists. The `get` function scans the property list of the symbol passed as the first argument searching for a key matching the second argument.

(`get` *symbol key*)

If a match is found, then the associated value is returned, otherwise `nil` is returned. Therefore, `get` operates like `assoc`.

```
; Access a property from godzilla.
(get 'godzilla 'strength)
⇒ NIL
```

Values are stored on a symbol's property list by using `setf`. The syntax is similar to that of slot access:

(`setf` (`get` *symbol key*) *S-expression*)

This stores the value of the *S-expression* under the *key* in the property list of the *symbol*.

```
;; Store the strength value on godzilla's property list.
(setf (get 'godzilla 'strength) 10)
⇒ 10

;; Now retrieve the value to see if the store worked.
(get 'godzilla 'strength)
⇒ 10
```

When accessing property lists, the key must always be a symbol. Also, since `get` returns the value and not the list as with `assoc`, there is no way of distinguishing between a missing property (which returns `nil`) and a property with `nil` as its value. Therefore, `nil` should be used as a property's value with caution.

Properties may be removed with the `remprop` function. It takes two arguments: the symbol from which to remove the property and the key. `Remprop` returns `t` when the removal is successful and `nil` otherwise.

```
(remprop symbol key)
```

```
;; Remove the strength property from godzilla.
(get 'godzilla 'strength)
⇒ 10

(remprop 'godzilla 'strength)
⇒ T

(get 'godzilla 'strength)
⇒ NIL
```

Each of these operations deal with individual properties, not the entire property list. You may want to look at the entire list. For example, you may have forgotten the key to a particular property, or you may want to know if some operation has stored a value on the property list. The `symbol-plist` function returns the property list for its argument symbol.

```
(symbol-plist symbol)
```

The returned list is the same as an association list, except the pairing sublist structure has been removed. The keys alternate with the values and so the list is always of even length.

```
;; Place some values on the property list of godzilla and
;; then show the structure.
(setf (get 'godzilla 'name) 'godzilla)
⇒ GODZILLA

(setf (get 'godzilla 'description)
      "Nasty Fire Breathing Dragon")
⇒ "Nasty Fire Breathing Dragon"

;; Now, access the property list.
(symbol-plist 'godzilla)
⇒ (DESCRIPTION "Nasty Fire Breathing Dragon" NAME GODZILLA)
```

Other dialects of LISP have the concept of a flag within a property list. The flag is used to indicate whether or not a feature is true. These other dialects actually use the association list form for property lists. Flags are simply implemented as a single atom in the association list. Determination of whether the flag is true or not can be accomplished by invoking `member` on the association list and the flag. With the flat structure used by Common LISP, flags have to be implemented as properties, storing `T` to indicate that the flag is true. We want three operations, `flag` to set a flag, `flagp` to check a flag, and `remflag` to remove a flag. Since each of these is very simple, we can implement them as macros invoking the appropriate functions.

```
;;; Flag a key on a property list.

(defmacro flag (symbol flag-name)
  `(setf (get ,symbol ,flag-name) t))
⇒ FLAG

;;; Check to see if a flag is set.

(defmacro flagp (symbol flag-name)
  `(get ,symbol ,flag-name))
⇒ FLAGP

;;; Remove a flag from a symbol.

(defmacro remflag (symbol flag-name)
  `(remprop ,symbol ,flag-name))
⇒ REMFLAG
```

This is a useful paradigm for associating "true/false" types of values with a symbol. For example, it could be used to indicate whether or not `godzilla` is dead.

```
;; Mark godzilla as dead.
(flag 'godzilla 'dead)
⇒ T

;; Check to see if godzilla is dead.
(flagp 'godzilla 'dead)
⇒ T

;; Clear the flag on godzilla.
(remflag 'godzilla 'dead)
⇒ T

;; Verify that he is no longer dead.
(flagp 'godzilla 'dead)
⇒ NIL
```

Property lists have two notorious features that limit their usefulness. The first "feature" is that both user-defined and system programs may place values on property lists, which could result in conflicts. For example, suppose that a profiling package (one that tells how many times various functions are called) is being used to find heavily used functions. The profiling package may store the current count of function calls on the property list for a particular function. Suppose the profiling package used the key `count`, but that key was also used in a user program for some other purpose. This could result in a conflict. The second "feature" is that property lists are not bound like their associated symbols and therefore should only store global information. This is a more severe restriction and limits the usefulness of property lists. The following examples illustrate this "global" nature of property lists:

```
;;; Define a function with a local variable and access to a
;;; property list.

(defun check-property (godzilla)
  ;; Change the local godzilla.
  (setf godzilla '(Big nasty dragon))
  (format t "Godzilla's value: ~S and ~%property list ~S~%"
          godzilla (symbol-plist 'godzilla)))
 ⇒ CHECK-PROPERTY

;; First check the current value and property list of
;; godzilla as defined earlier, then call the function.
godzilla
 ⇒ Nasty Old Fire Breathing Dragon

(symbol-plist 'godzilla)
 ⇒ (DESCRIPTION "Nasty Fire Breathing Dragon" NAME GODZILLA)

(check-property godzilla)
 ⇒ Godzilla's value: (BIG NASTY DRAGON) and
 ⇒ property list (DESCRIPTION "Nasty Fire Breathing Dragon"
 ⇒                            NAME GODZILLA)
 ⇒ NIL

godzilla
 ⇒ Nasty Old Fire Breathing Dragon
```

This example illustrates that **godzilla** was rebound within the scope of the **check-property** function, but the property list was still associated with the global symbol. Therefore, one should use property lists with care.

EXERCISE

***11.4** Your goal is to design a set of macros that provide a functionality similar to **defstruct**, but use property lists instead. We will restrict the syntax so there are no options and no initial values. You specify the name of the structure and follow that by two-element lists. The first element of each two-element list is the name of the slot. The second element is the name of the function that will store into the slot. You must create function definitions for each of the functions and also install a **defsetf** for the setting function. Your macro **pl-defstruct** must translate into code that creates all of the accessor functions. Thus, given the following invocation:

```
(macroexpand '(pl-defstruct person
                            (name set-name)
                            (age set-age)
                            (sex set-sex)))
```

Your code should translate into something like:

```
⇒ (PROGN
⇒   (PROGN (DEFUN NAME (SYMBOL) (GET SYMBOL (QUOTE NAME)))
⇒          (DEFUN SET-NAME (SYMBOL VALUE)
⇒           (SETF (GET SYMBOL (QUOTE NAME)) VALUE))
⇒          (DEFSETF NAME SET-NAME))
⇒   (PROGN (DEFUN AGE (SYMBOL) (GET SYMBOL (QUOTE AGE)))
⇒          (DEFUN SET-AGE (SYMBOL VALUE)
⇒           (SETF (GET SYMBOL (QUOTE AGE)) VALUE))
⇒          (DEFSETF AGE SET-AGE))
⇒   (PROGN (DEFUN SEX (SYMBOL) (GET SYMBOL (QUOTE SEX)))
⇒          (DEFUN SET-SEX (SYMBOL VALUE)
⇒           (SETF (GET SYMBOL (QUOTE SEX)) VALUE))
⇒          (DEFSETF SEX SET-SEX))
⇒   (QUOTE PERSON))
```

In using the system as follows, notice that we don't have to actually `make` a property list structure, since it is actually stored under the symbol:

```
(pl-defstruct person (name set-name)
              (age set-age)
              (sex set-sex))
 ⇒ PERSON

(setf (age 'fred) 33)
 ⇒ 33

(age 'fred)
 ⇒ 33
```

11.3 Hash Tables

A hash table is semantically equivalent to a property list. It is a structure which, given a key, returns an associated value. The primary difference is that the hash table uses hashing to find a value and is therefore fast. Like a property list, you can store a value into a key, replacing any existing value. The following examples will perform the same operations illustrated in the previous section and use hash tables to store the information about monsters. One difference is that a hash table is a data type and therefore the actual table must be stored in some location. One option is to store the table as the value of the symbol. However, this could conflict with a symbol that already has a value. Another option is to create a hash table of hash tables (of course the hash table of hash tables must also be stored some place). The third option is to store the hash table under a key on a symbol's property list. We will use the last option to demonstrate the utility of these two paradigms.

The `make-hash-table` function creates and returns a hash table.

```
(make-hash-table)
```

To provide a functionality equivalent to property lists, we will implement each monster as a hash table. We will write our own equivalents to the property list's `get` and store operations. The store operations must check for the existence of the hash table and if not present, create one. The `gethash` function retrieves a value from a hash table. The associated `setf` form is used to store values into the hash table.

(gethash *key hash-table***)**

(setf (gethash *key hash-table***)** *S-expression***)**

Each hash table is stored under the `**hash-table**` key.

```
;;; An equivalent to get that uses hash tables instead.

(defun retrieve (symbol key)
  (gethash key
    (cond
      ((get symbol '**hash-table**))
      (t (setf (get symbol '**hash-table**)
               (make-hash-table))))))
⇒ RETRIEVE

;;; The following stores the s-expression argument in the
;;; hash table associated with the symbol argument with the
;;; key.

(defun store (symbol key s-expression)
  (setf (gethash key
          (cond
            ((get symbol '**hash-table**))
            (t (setf (get symbol '**hash-table**)
                     (make-hash-table)))))
    s-expression))
⇒ STORE

;; Access a property from godzilla.
```

```
(retrieve 'godzilla 'strength)
 ⇒ NIL
 ⇒ NIL
```

Notice that **gethash** returns two values. The second indicates whether or not a value has been found. So, returning the values `nil` and `T` indicates that the value `nil` was found.

```
;; Store the strength value on godzilla's property list.
(store 'godzilla 'strength 10)
 ⇒ 10

;; Now access the value to see if the store worked.
(retrieve 'godzilla 'strength)
 ⇒ 10
 ⇒ T

;; Try another example.
(store 'godzilla 'description "Nasty Fire Breathing Dragon")
 ⇒ "Nasty Fire Breathing Dragon"

(retrieve 'godzilla 'description)
 ⇒ "Nasty Fire Breathing Dragon"
 ⇒ T

;; Try to retrieve a value that doesn't exist.
(retrieve 'godzilla 'height)
 ⇒ NIL
 ⇒ NIL
```

In these hash tables, the key must be a symbol. If you need more general keys, such as lists, then the hash table must be constructed using the following form:

```
(make-hash-table :test #'equal)
```

This tells the hash table access functions to use the `equal` comparison when searching for a particular value. The default comparison function is `eql`, which compares symbols but not lists.*

Equivalent to the **remprop** function is **remhash** which removes a key and associated value from a hash table. Like **remprop**, `T` is returned when there is an associated key and `nil` is returned when no matching key is found.

(remhash *key hash-table***)**

*This is an over simplification; see Chapter 13 for the real truth.

```
;;; Remove an entry from our hash table based system.

(defun take-away (symbol key)
  (remhash key
    (cond
      ((get symbol '**hash-table**))
      (t (setf (get symbol '**hash-table**)
               (make-hash-table))))))
⇒ TAKE-AWAY

;; Remove the strength property from godzilla.
(retrieve 'godzilla 'strength)
⇒ 10
⇒ T

(take-away 'godzilla 'strength)
⇒ T

(retrieve 'godzilla 'strength)
⇒ NIL
⇒ NIL
```

There are a few other functions that are useful when manipulating hash tables. The first is **hash-table-p**, which tests to see if the argument is a hash table.

> (**hash-table-p** *S-expression*)

The next function is **clrhash**, which removes all elements from the hash table and returns the newly cleared table.

> (**clrhash** *hash-table*)

Finally, the **maphash** function applies a function to all elements in the hash table. The called function will be passed two arguments: the first is the key and the second is the value. This is useful for printing out all of the elements in a hash table. Note that the order in which the elements are retrieved from the hash table is completely arbitrary.

> (**maphash** *function hash-table*)

The following demonstrates the three hash table functions. First, we determine if the item stored under the ****hash-table**** key for **godzilla** is actually a hash table.

```
;; Is the item stored under **hash-table** a hash-table?
(hash-table-p (get 'godzilla '**hash-table**))
⇒ T
```

Next, we define a function that prints all of the values stored in a hash table. It takes the symbol as the argument and produces the listing. After that, the hash table is cleared and printed again to demonstrate that there are no entries remaining.

```
;;; Print out each key and value in the hash table.
(defun print-symbol (symbol)
  (maphash #'(lambda (key value)
               (format t "Key: ~S Value: ~S~%" key value))
           (get symbol '**hash-table**)))
⇒ PRINT-SYMBOL

;; Add an item, since only Description is currently present.
(store 'godzilla 'strength 10)
⇒ 10

(print-symbol 'godzilla)
⇒ Key: STRENGTH Value: 10
⇒ Key: DESCRIPTION Value: "Nasty Fire Breathing Dragon"
⇒ NIL

;; Now clear the hash table for godzilla and print the list
;; again.

;;; Clear a hash table associated with a symbol.
(defun clear-symbol (symbol)
  (clrhash (get symbol '**hash-table**)))
⇒ CLEAR-SYMBOL

(clear-symbol 'godzilla)
⇒ #<EQL Hash Table>

(print-symbol 'godzilla)
⇒ NIL
```

Since a hash table is a data object, it can be bound to variables and does not exhibit the limitations of a property list. Their access is faster than association lists, so they should generally be used when there are many elements to store in the structure.

EXERCISES

11.5 Using good coding style requires redefining `retrieve`, `store`, and `take-away` to verify initially that the item is a hash table. Modify these functions to test that the item found on the property list under `**hash-table**` is actually a hash table before it is accessed.

11.6 Instead of storing the structures associated with a monster as the value of a symbol, we could store them in a hash table. Define a hash table that contains all of the monsters, using their name as the index. Write functions to store new monsters into the hash table and to retrieve the monster structure given the monster name.

11.4 Summary

A few new methods for data representation have been described. Structures provide a subset of those facilities provided by objects, and so are useful when the full power of methods are not required. Property lists function like association lists, but are tied to symbols. The property list is good for storing global information about a particular symbol, but is not rebound like a symbol and therefore must be used with caution. The final structure is the hash table, which is also like the association and property list, since it maps between a key and a value. Hash tables generally provide the fastest method for accessing a key when the number of items is of reasonable size.

Chapter Exercises

A useful fact to know about a particular implementation is when to use hash tables instead of association lists. Develop a table that contains the times required to store and retrieve elements from association lists and hash tables that vary in the number of elements stored in the structures (place the count in the first column). The second column should contain the time required to perform the loop without doing any operations. Storing into an association list can be accomplished by `cons`ing onto the front of the list. However, retrieving a value depends on its location within the list. These two operations should be in the next two columns. Create three columns that determine the time for accessing the first element, the last element, and a middle element. The time required to retrieve an element from a hash table depends on if there is a hashing conflict. Test the hash tables on random elements and compute an average. Write the program to collect the data and then print the information similar to the following table:

Number of Elements	Empty Loop	A-list Store	Get 1st	Get Last	Get Middle	Hash Store	Get Average
1	...	...	...	...	...	...	...
...	...	...	...	...	...	...	...
n	...	...	...	...	...	...	...

Retrieving the amount of run-time an operation takes is accomplished by calling the Common LISP function `get-internal-run-time`. This returns a number that is the amount of run-time you have used in some implementation-dependent unit. The constant `internal-time-units-per-second` tells how many of these units are in each second. However, we are primarily interested in the relative performance of each category, so the actual units are not important. When doing these types of timings it is important to run the operation a large number of times and calculate an average time. Averaging is actually optional, as long as all numbers that are displayed are relative to the same number of iterations. This helps to decrease the probability of timing aberrations. If you use a loop to perform the operation many times, you should also determine the time it takes to do the loop without doing any other part of the operation. This shows how much overhead there is in the loop itself.

1. The first problem is to make sure that the set of symbols used in the association list is unique. Otherwise, there could be anomalous behavior with access to the middle or last symbol. Write a function that takes a list of words and removes any duplicates. The list of words will be taken from the words in a paragraph of this text.

```
(defvar *some-symbols*
  '(a useful fact to know about a particular
     implementation is when is it better to use hash
     tables in place of association lists develop a
     table that contains the times required to store and
     retrieve elements from association lists and hash
     tables that vary in the number of elements stored
     in the structures storing into an association list
     can be accomplished by consing onto the front of
     the list however retrieving a value depends on its
     location within the list create three columns that
     determine the time for accessing the first element
     the last element and then an average of the two
     retrieving from a hash table depends on if there is
     a hashing conflict test the hash tables on random
     elements and compute an average write the program
     to collect the data and then print the information
     similar to the following table))
⇒ *SOME-SYMBOLS*

(setf *some-symbols*
     (remove-duplicates *some-symbols* nil))
⇒ (FOLLOWING SIMILAR INFORMATION PRINT DATA COLLECT PROGRAM
⇒           WRITE COMPUTE RANDOM TEST CONFLICT HASHING
⇒           THERE IF TWO AVERAGE THEN LAST ELEMENT FIRST
⇒           ACCESSING FOR TIME DETERMINE COLUMNS THREE
⇒           CREATE WITHIN LOCATION ITS ON DEPENDS VALUE
```

```
⇒           RETRIEVING HOWEVER FRONT ONTO CONSING BY
⇒           ACCOMPLISHED BE CAN LIST AN INTO STORING
⇒           STRUCTURES STORED NUMBER VARY FROM ELEMENTS
⇒           RETRIEVE AND STORE REQUIRED TIMES THE CONTAINS
⇒           THAT TABLE DEVELOP LISTS ASSOCIATION OF PLACE
⇒           IN TABLES HASH USE BETTER IT WHEN IS
⇒           IMPLEMENTATION PARTICULAR ABOUT KNOW TO FACT
⇒           USEFUL A)
```

***2.** The next step is to write a macro which can be used to time the execution of an S-expression. It takes two arguments, the S-expression and the number of iterations, and produces an expression which will time the S-expression and return a result.

```
;; Time of a null body.
(time-form nil 10000)
 ⇒ 149

(time-form (list 'red 'blue 'green) 10000)
 ⇒ 199
```

***3.** Now write `compare-times` which takes a number of iterations to try and prints the table as defined earlier.

```
;; Part of a run.
(compare-times 500)
 ⇒ 1: [EM:8] [AS:12] [R1:10] [RL:10] [RM:10] [HS:15] [HR:10]
 ⇒ 2: [EM:6] [AS:11] [R1:10] [RL:11] [RM:11] [HS:14] [HR:11]
 ⇒ 3: [EM:8] [AS:11] [R1:10] [RL:11] [RM:11] [HS:14] [HR:11]
 ⇒ 4: [EM:7] [AS:13] [R1:10] [RL:12] [RM:11] [HS:14] [HR:11]
 ⇒ 5: [EM:8] [AS:11] [R1:11] [RL:13] [RM:11] [HS:13] [HR:10]
 ⇒ 6: [EM:8] [AS:11] [R1:10] [RL:14] [RM:12] [HS:14] [HR:11]
 ⇒ 7: [EM:8] [AS:12] [R1:10] [RL:14] [RM:12] [HS:14] [HR:11]
 ⇒ 8: [EM:8] [AS:12] [R1:9] [RL:16] [RM:12] [HS:14] [HR:11]
 ⇒ 9: [EM:7] [AS:11] [R1:10] [RL:16] [RM:13] [HS:15] [HR:10]
 ⇒ 10: [EM:7] [AS:12] [R1:10] [RL:16] [RM:13] [HS:14] [HR:10]
 ⇒ 11: [EM:8] [AS:12] [R1:10] [RL:17] [RM:14]
 ⇒ !! Break: Lisp process interrupted by user.
 ⇒   Condition signaled in: INTERPRETER::SET-VALUE.
 ⇒ Entering the debugger
```

Function Summary

The following lists the functions and topics covered in this chapter.

- `(defstruct` *symbol-with-options slot**`)`
- `(:conc-name` *symbol*`)`

- (:constructor *symbol*)
- (:predicate *symbol*)
- (:include *parent* (*slot**))
- (get *symbol key*)
- (setf (get *symbol key*) *S-expression*)
- (remprop *symbol key*)
- (symbol-plist *symbol*)
- (make-hash-table)
- (gethash *key hash-table*)
- (setf (gethash *key hash-table*) *S-expression*)
- (make-hash-table :test #'equal)
- (remhash *key hash-table*)
- (hash-table-p *S-expression*)
- (clrhash *hash-table*)
- (maphash *function hash-table*)

12 CASE STUDY: FANTASY GAME

IN THIS CASE STUDY, we continue to develop a fantasy "role-playing" game using objects to simulate the various parts of the game. These role playing games originated with the "adventure" games of the 70s, and later versions of "rogue" and "hack." In earlier chapters, objects simulated the monsters, the weapons, and the rooms that the player explores. The system has to maintain the state of the game, where the player is located, and so on. We will also develop macros to create the dungeon environment and play the game.

12.1 Object Definitions

As in many programming tasks, you should first design the data structures. If you understand the required data structures, then you understand the task itself. The first step is to design the various objects for the dungeon. Recall from Chapter 10 that each type of monster inherits characteristics from the `monster` object. We will redefine that type here and then define a couple of other monster types. We must also add another field, which is `hit-points`. The hit points indicate how close the monster or player is to losing the game. During the game, if a player's hit points become zero, then the player "dies" and the game ends. During an attack on a monster, the player and the monster take points away from each other. If the monster's hit points are reduced to zero, then the monster dies.

```
;;; This monster specification uses inheritance.  We can
;;; eliminate the type slot, since it will be implicit in the
;;; inheritance structure.

(define-type Monster
  (:var name)
  (:var description)
  (:var initial-strength (:init 0))
  (:var initial-damage (:init 0))
```

```
  (:var hit-points)
  :all-gettable
  :all-settable
  :all-initable
  )
⇒ MONSTER
```

Now we can define some monsters with interesting characteristics:

Zombie – A zombie is a soulless, mindless creature. It fights without regard for its environment or its own safety. Its accuracy is strictly random (that is, when fighting, only 50 percent of its attacks do any damage).

Dragon – A dragon is large and powerful and extremely devastating with a 100 percent accuracy.

Swarm – A swarm gets its name from the fact that it fights better when it has company – especially other swarms. Alone, its accuracy is only 40 percent, but it gains another 10 percent accuracy for each non-swarm monster in the room and 30 percent for each additional swarm.

Using these characteristics, we can define each of the monster types. We will also add a few interesting slots to each of these types.

```
;;; A dragon is a monster with a slot defining how many heads
;;; the particular dragon instance may have.

(define-type dragon
  (:inherit-from monster)
  (:var number-of-heads)
  :all-gettable
  :all-initable
  )
⇒ DRAGON

;;; This creates the swarm type.  Since, it is important to
;;; know how many other swarm and non-swarm monsters are
;;; present, this defines two slots to hold that
;;; information.

(define-type swarm
  (:inherit-from monster)
  (:var count-of-other-swarm-in-room)
  (:var count-of-non-swarm-in-room)
  :all-initable
  :all-settable
  :all-gettable
  )
```

```
⇒ SWARM

;;; The zombie type includes a slot which contains the number
;;; of years since the creature died.

(define-type zombie
  (:inherit-from monster)
  (:var years-since-death)
  :all-initable
  :all-settable
  :all-gettable
  )
⇒ ZOMBIE
```

We can save typing all of the keyword arguments and define a function which creates monsters by calling `make-instance` with the appropriate arguments.

```
;;; Create a new monster type with the monster slots
;;; initialized properly.

(defun init-monster (type name description strength damage)
  (make-instance type
                 :name name
                 :description description
                 :initial-strength strength
                 :initial-damage damage
                 :hit-points strength))
⇒ INIT-MONSTER
```

Now, we must create object definitions for the various weapons in the game. A weapon has the following characteristics:

Name – The name of the weapon
Description – A string description for interaction with the player
Damage – The number of damage points inflicted by the weapon
Lifetime – The number of uses before the weapon becomes ineffective – some weapons have an infinite lifetime, in which case this slot will have the value `nil`

This description makes the definition of the weapon type easy.

```
;;; The weapon generic type.

(define-type weapon
  (:var name)
  (:var description)
  (:var damage)
  (:var lifetime)
```

```
   :all-initable
   :all-settable
   :all-gettable)
  ⇒ WEAPON
```

As with monsters, we can now define individual types of weapons. Some of these definitions will not include any new slots – the weapon doesn't require any new distinguishing characteristics. However, we will still create an inherited type, since we need to create methods for each type of weapon. Also, if we ever decided to add a new slot to the object, we only need to change the type and not create a whole new one. In this game, we will have four weapons defined as follows:

Special – The trusty "Saturday Night Special" is very effective, but poorly made and sometimes misfires. Twenty percent of the shots will take five points away from the player. The other 80 percent are successful with a 50 percent accuracy with the same five damage points. This weapon has a lifetime of six uses.*

Wand – A magic wand, which is 100 percent accurate, produces ten hit points of damage, and has an unlimited lifetime.

Club – It's a bit brutal, but accurate (90 percent) and has an unlimited lifetime. It produces three hit points of damage.

Cannon – It isn't very accurate (75 percent), but when it hits it is guaranteed to vanquish the foe. The cannon produces one hundred hit points of damage and has a lifetime of only one.

Player Hands – When the player doesn't have any available weapons, then hands are used. They are 100 percent accurate, but only inflict one hit point of damage.

These descriptions can be used to define the types. The object system doesn't let you initialize slots defined in the parent when a type is defined. Therefore, we will have to initialize the damage, lifetime, and so on when the objects are actually created.

```
;;; The Saturday night special gun.

(define-type special
  (:inherit-from weapon)
  :all-gettable
  :all-settable
  :all-initable)
 ⇒ SPECIAL

;;; The magic wand.
```

*An interesting enhancement would be the capability of finding bullets to use to reload the gun.

```
(define-type wand
  (:inherit-from weapon)
  ;; The magic words necessary to make the wand work.
  (:var incantation)
  :all-gettable
  :all-settable
  :all-initable)
⇒ WAND

;;; Next, we define the club.

(define-type club
  (:inherit-from weapon)
  :all-gettable
  :all-settable
  :all-initable)
⇒ CLUB

;;; Finally, we define the cannon.

(define-type cannon
  (:inherit-from weapon)
  :all-settable
  :all-gettable
  :all-initable)
⇒ CANNON
```

As we did with the monsters, we will write a function to automatically create each type of weapon. Since each monster is predefined to have a damage and a lifetime, we will store those in an association list for initialization.

```
;;; This contains the initialization for the damage and
;;; lifetime for each weapon.  The first value is the damage
;;; and the second is the lifetime.

(defvar *weapon-initializations*
  '((special 5 6) (wand 10 nil) (club 3 nil) (cannon 100 1)))
⇒ *WEAPON-INITIALIZATIONS*

;;; Initialize a weapon with the weapon slot values.

(defun init-weapon (type name description)
  (let ((damage-and-lifetime
          (assoc type *weapon-initializations*)))
    (make-instance type
```

```
                         :name name
                         :description description
                         :damage (cadr damage-and-lifetime)
                         :lifetime (caddr damage-and-lifetime))))
⇒ INIT-WEAPON
```

Each room can also be implemented as an object type. The room must be able to designate its connections to other rooms (Up, Down, Left, Right), the weapons and monsters present, whether or not the player is present, a description, and the name of the room. The following type definition includes these fields. When a monster is killed, it is removed from the `monsters` slot. Also, when a weapon is taken by the player, it must be removed from the `weapons` slot.

```
(define-type room
  (:var name)
  (:var description)
  (:var connections)
  (:var weapons :settable)
  (:var monsters :settable)
  :all-initable
  :all-gettable)
⇒ ROOM
```

In order to contrast the use of objects and structures, the player is defined as a structure. It maintains the current state of the player. The following are the important fields of the player object:

Name – The name of the player, which is used in printing the various interactions
Hit Points – The number of points remaining for the player
Weapons – A list of the weapons that the player is carrying
Fighting – The monster that the player is currently fighting
Current Room – The room that the player is currently in
Initial Strength – The number of hit points that the player starts with

```
;;; The player structure.

(defstruct player
  name
  hit-points
  (weapons nil)
  current-room
  fighting
  initial-strength)
⇒ PLAYER
```

EXERCISES

12.1 Define a dagger as a weapon. The dagger has an accuracy of 50 percent and takes five hit points away from the monster. Each dagger can be characterized by its length.

***12.2** Define the following new types of monsters:

Loner – A loner wants to fight its own battles. Its accuracy is 60 percent if it is the only monster in the room. It loses 10 percent accuracy for each other monster in the room. It especially detests swarms: it loses 20 percent accuracy for each swarm in the room.

Blissterror – A Blissterror can be good or bad. Twenty-five percent of the time they give the player 50 percent of the player's remaining hit points. Twenty-five percent of the time, they take 50 percent of the player's hit points, and the rest of the time they do nothing.

Empath – Empaths are dangerous because they can tell what you are feeling. If they sense that you are strong (have more than seventy-five hit points) they hit once with perfect accuracy, taking ten points and then disappear. If you have fewer hit points, they keep attacking taking ten points each time.

12.2 Dungeon Initialization

Now that we have defined the various data structures, we will write routines to initialize the dungeon. We need the ability to create each object type and place them in the appropriate places. We can write each initialization routine as either a function or a macro. In this case, a macro works well. All of the slots that will be initialized are static objects that must be `quoted`. So, using a macro can make things easier by placing the `quotes` on the objects within the macro. The dungeon is initialized with three macros, `add-monster`, `add-room`, and `add-weapon`. In this approach there is no "global" creation of the dungeon. This means that a monster is created and placed in a room in separate commands. In fact, the monster doesn't have to be created before it's placed in a room. There is no specific check to see that all of the created objects are properly linked together, placed in rooms, and so forth. The solution to this difficulty is left as an exercise. The syntax of each macro is as follows:

```
(add-monster name type description strength damage)
(add-room name description monsters weapons connections)
(add-weapon name type description)
```

One consideration in designing this system is where to place each object. All monsters reside in a particular room and thus could be placed directly in the room object. Also, the weapons either reside in a room or are being carried by the player, and could be placed in the corresponding room or player object. Finally, the rooms could be linked by placing their objects into the connection slot. Another technique stores all of the objects in a central structure and gains access to them through a name. Storing them in a central location makes it easy to find all objects, or all monster objects, or all weapons, and so on. The dungeon is easier to define since you don't have to define circular structures. For example, you don't need to link the `ghost-room` to the left of `dragon-lair`, which is linked to the right of the `ghost-room`. A better technique is to store an association list like `((left ghost-room))` in `dragon-lair`'s list of connections, and similarly store `((right dragon-lair))` in `ghost-room`'s list of connections. This permits the use of names and does not require specific objects with circular specifications. A hash table is appropriate for this type of storage because it allows rapid access to any object given its name.

```
;;; The hash table containing all of the objects in the
;;; dungeon.

(defvar *dungeon* (make-hash-table))
 ⇒ *DUNGEON*
```

Using data abstraction, we define three functions to add, retrieve, and clear the dungeon. This localizes any changes of the data representation to these three functions. They can all be implemented as simple calls to the appropriate hashing functions.

```
;;; Add an object to the dungeon.

(defun add-object (name object)
  (setf (gethash name *dungeon*) object))
 ⇒ ADD-OBJECT

;;; Retrieve a named object from the dungeon.

(defun get-object (name)
  (gethash name *dungeon*))
 ⇒ GET-OBJECT

;;; Initialize the dungeon by removing all elements.

(defun initialize-dungeon ()
  (clrhash *dungeon*))
 ⇒ INITIALIZE-DUNGEON
```

We can now define each of the initialization macros. As mentioned before, each argument will be provided without a `quote`, so the macro must place a `quote` on any argument that is not self-evaluating, which are the symbols and lists. Using backquote notation, the quoted argument can be constructed as: `(quote ,name)` or more simply `',name`. They are equivalent, so we will use the second, shorter notation. Any value which is self-evaluating doesn't need to be quoted (like strings and numbers).

```
;;; Add a room to the dungeon.

(defmacro add-room (name description monsters weapons
                    connections)
  `(add-object ',name
               (make-instance 'room :name ',name
                              :description ,description
                              :monsters ',monsters
                              :weapons ',weapons
                              :connections ',connections)))
 ⇒ ADD-ROOM

;;; Add a monster to the dungeon.

(defmacro add-monster (name type description strength damage)
  `(add-object ',name
               (init-monster ',type
                             ',name
                             ,description
                             ,strength
                             ,damage)))
 ⇒ ADD-MONSTER

;;; Add a weapon to the dungeon.

(defmacro add-weapon (name type description)
  `(add-object ',name
               (init-weapon ',type
                            ',name
                            ,description)))
 ⇒ ADD-WEAPON
```

We still need a macro to create the player information and start the game rolling. The macro must take three arguments, the player name and initial strength, along with the name of the room in which the player begins. `Start-game` creates the player object, initializes the number of hit points, and moves the player into the first room. Moving the player into the first room is similar to moving the player around from room to room. The only difference is that movement into the first room is unconditional – during the game, the player may not leave a room before defeating all of the monsters. So, we will call a function `move-to` that unconditionally moves the player into the room. We haven't made enough decisions to implement `move-to`, so it will be left for the next section.

```
;;; The player structure.
(defvar *player* nil)
 ⇒ *PLAYER*

;;; Start the game by creating the player object and moving
;;; the player into the initial room.

(defmacro start-game (player-name strength initial-room)
  `(start-game-aux ',player-name
                   ,strength
                   ',initial-room))
 ⇒ START-GAME

;;; The auxiliary function that actually does the game
;;; starting work.

(defun start-game-aux (player-name strength initial-room)
  (setf *player* (make-player :name player-name
                              :hit-points strength
                              :initial-strength strength))
  (move-to initial-room))
 ⇒ START-GAME-AUX
```

We can now initialize the dungeon to have a few rooms, monsters, and weapons. The connections of the rooms can be completely arbitrary, which adds a challenge to maneuvering through the dungeon. Thus, moving south into a room won't necessarily mean that moving north will take you back to the original room. The following commands are placed into a file "dungeon" which can be loaded to initialize the dungeon.

```
;;; A sample dungeon, stored in the file dungeon.

(initialize-dungeon)
(add-room start "A small, uncomfortable cavern" nil (special)
          ((west terror-room)))
(add-room terror-room "A dark and musty smelling room"
          (zombie) (club)
          ((north start) (south start) (east mist-room)))
(add-room mist-room
          "It is all misty, you can't see very well"
          (swarm-1 swarm-2) (cannon)
          ((west terror-room) (east terror-room)
           (north exit)))
(add-room exit "At last!  A haven among the mists of doom"
          nil nil nil)
(add-monster zombie zombie
```

```
             "A ghastly apparition, devoid of flesh"
             5 5)
(add-monster swarm-1 swarm
            "Number one of a deadly family of unkind beastes"
             10 10)
(add-monster swarm-2 swarm
            "Number two of a deadly family of unkind beastes"
             10 10)
(add-weapon special special "Trusty Saturday Night Special")
(add-weapon cannon cannon "A cannon from the HMS Pinafore")
(add-weapon club club
            "Large club with spikes protruding from the end")
```

With the file created, the dungeon can be loaded by invoking `load` and passing it the name of the dungeon file.

```
(load "dungeon")
 ⇒ "dungeon"

;; Just to verify that the objects are in the dungeon.
(maphash #'(lambda (name object)
             (print (description object))) *dungeon*)
 ⇒ "Trusty Saturday Night Special"
 ⇒ "A small, uncomfortable cavern"
 ⇒ "Number one of a deadly family of unkind beastes"
 ⇒ "It is all misty, you can't see very well"
 ⇒ "A ghastly apparition, devoid of flesh"
 ⇒ "A dark and musty smelling room"
 ⇒ "Large club with spikes protruding from the end"
 ⇒ "A cannon from the HMS Pinafore"
 ⇒ "Number two of a deadly family of unkind beastes"
 ⇒ "At last!  A haven among the mists of doom"
 ⇒ NIL
```

EXERCISES

12.3 Write a function that checks the consistency of the dungeon. Consistency may be checked for the following cases:

1. All of the rooms must be scanned to verify that every room mentioned in a connection list has been actually created as an object.
2. The list of weapons within each room must be scanned to verify that the associated weapon object has been created.
3. Similarly, the list of monsters must be scanned to verify that all of the monsters have been created as objects.

12.4 Write a "cheat-sheet" function that prints a "map" of the dungeon to aid the player. Your output should look something like the following:

```
START -> TERROR-ROOM is to the WEST.
MIST-ROOM -> TERROR-ROOM is to the WEST.
      TERROR-ROOM is to the EAST.
      EXIT is to the NORTH.
TERROR-ROOM -> START is to the NORTH.
      START is to the SOUTH.
      MIST-ROOM is to the EAST.
EXIT ->
NIL
```

***12.5** Write `help-path`, which takes two room names and tries to find a path between the two rooms.

```
(help-path 'start 'exit)
 ⇒ ((WEST TERROR-ROOM) (EAST MIST-ROOM) (NORTH EXIT))
```

***12.6** One characteristic of the dungeon is that if you go east to get into a room, west will not necessarily take you back to the same room. Thus, the dungeon designer could easily design a dungeon layout with passages such that once you entered, you could never reach the end. Write a verification function that scans the dungeon and verifies that there are no one-way paths in the dungeon. The function that you are to write must be called with the name of the exit room.

```
(find-no-way-out-rooms 'exit)
 ⇒ NIL
```

12.3 Non-Combat Commands

In this section, we write additional commands and support code in preparation for the interaction between the monsters and player in the next section. The following defines the commands that the dungeon should support. Any that require arguments will be implemented as macros so the player doesn't have to `quote` the arguments. The others can be implemented as the following functions:

`(look)` – Describe the room and its contents.

`(walk` *direction*`)` – Move the player from the current room to the room in the *direction* indicated. The legal directions are: north, south, east, and west. If the *direction* does not lead anywhere, then a statement should be printed. Also, the player may not leave a room unless all of the monsters have been defeated.

`(weapon)` – Describe the weapons that the player is currently carrying.

`(take` *weapon*`)` – Pick up the `weapon` indicated. Any weapon object is a legal argument. A player may carry as many weapons as desired, but must drop all but one when fighting monsters. A weapon can either be carried or contained in a room object, but not both simultaneously.

`(drop` *weapon*`)` – Drop the specified *weapon* and update the player and room objects.

`(fight` *monster*`)` – This indicates which monster is selected for fighting. Any monster object is a legal argument. Once a fight is initiated, the player can then issue the first command. The monster will fight back after every command that the player issues. The battle continues until the monster's or the player's hit points goes below zero.

`(attack)` – Attack the current monster with the weapon currently being carried. Every weapon has a maximum number of uses, its lifetime. Each attack is one use of the weapon and thus decreases the total life of the weapon by one.

Notice in the description of the `fight` command that the monster has an opportunity to attack the player after every command. We have yet to develop the fighting commands, but need to allow for their addition. We can easily use a stub function, `check-for-monster-attack`. This function will initially have a null body. However, once the fighting commands have been implemented, we can redefine it to check to see if the monster should attack and, if so, initiate an attack. Stub functions aid code development but you must remember to redefine the functions once you've completed the constituent parts.

```
;;; A DUMMY VERSION until the attacking commands are defined.

(defun check-for-monster-attack ()
  nil)
 ⇒ CHECK-FOR-MONSTER-ATTACK
```

As appropriate for object-oriented programming, we should look for a common set of operations between the various objects. In this system we need to interact in a meaningful way with the player to inform about the contents of a room, the weapons, the monsters, etc. The `look` command is one in which it is important to print information about the room and its contents. Therefore, we will implement the `print-self` method for each object which prints an informative message about itself. Let's choose the room as the first object type to implement a printing method. A `look` command should print the description of the room and its contents. Just to make the game a little more fun, we will add some output expressions that are randomly printed when the room is described.

```
;;; Print out the description of the room and an arbitrary
;;; message based upon a random value.

(define-method (room print-self) ()
  (format t "The room you are in (~A) is ~A." name
          description)
  (format t (if (= (random 4) 0)
                "  You notice a strange odor.~%"
```

```
                  "~%")))
  ⇒ PRINT-SELF
```

We can do something similar for the monster and the weapon. These are generic methods, so if we wish to define a particular version of `print-self` for any particular monster or weapon we can override this definition.

```
;;; Print the presence of a monster.

(define-method (monster print-self) ()
  (format t (if (= (random 2) 0)
                "The evil ~A, ~A is present.~%"
                "The notorious ~A, ~A watches you.~%")
        name description))
 ⇒ PRINT-SELF

;;; Print a description of a weapon.

(define-method (weapon print-self) ()
  (format t
   (if (and (numberp lifetime) (= lifetime 0))
     "~A, ~A is spent and useless.~%"
     "~A, ~A awaits your use against the monsters.~%")
   name description))
 ⇒ PRINT-SELF
```

Since the player is a structure, a function `print-self` is defined instead of a method. We assume that the function's argument is the player structure. What if we had also implemented one of the other objects, like weapons, as a structure? Then we couldn't "overload" the definition of `print-self` for both functions, but would have to write `player-print-self` and `weapon-print-self`. This is one of the advantages of methods – the same method name will operate on different object types. Had we used structures we could have written generic code for a `print-self` function that checks the type of structure arguments and dispatches to the appropriate print function. In our system, there is only one structure type, so we don't need to design a dispatching system for `print-self`. Notice that when we write the body of the function we must use the qualified slot-access names. This could have been avoided had we used the `:conc-name` slot option and set it to `nil`, which would allow the slot names to be directly used. This could cause name conflicts with the slots defined for the objects so it is therefore not advisable. We might have made a bad decision to make one of the dungeon elements a structure instead of an object. We will see if the situation improves.

```
;;; Print useful information about the player.
(defun print-self (player)
```

```
  (format t "~A you have ~A hit points remaining.~%"
          (player-name player) (player-hit-points player)))
⇒ PRINT-SELF
```

We can now implement the look and weapon commands. Neither of them takes an argument, so they can be implemented as functions. They print out the pertinent information by invoking the appropriate print-self methods.

Before we can write the look command, we have to decide how to store the information on which room the player is currently in. We can store the room information in the current-room slot of the player structure, which is retrieved by player-current-room. The information that is stored in this slot should either be the actual room object, or the name of the room. If we store the name of the room, then we should write a small function to pass the room object to get-object. We will choose the first option since it saves writing yet another function, and is more efficient – we only need to access the hash table once when the player goes into a new room. With the second option, we would have to access the hash table each of the many times that we required slot information from the room. Using this information, we can write the look command. It should print the player information and then print the room object. We then invoke print-self on each weapon and monster present in the room. Finally, we call the check-for-monster-attack stub function.

```
;;; Print the status of the player and the current contents
;;; of the room.

(defun look ()
  (let ((this-room (player-current-room *player*)))
    (print-self *player*)
    (print-self this-room)
    (format t "This room contains:~%")
    (mapc #'(lambda (weapon)
              (print-self (get-object weapon)))
          (weapons this-room))
    (mapc #'(lambda (monster)
              (print-self (get-object monster)))
          (monsters this-room))
    (if (and (null (weapons this-room))
             (null (monsters this-room)))
      (format t " --- Nothing of interest~%"))
    (check-for-monster-attack)))
⇒ LOOK
```

The weapon command simply invokes print-self on each weapon.

```
;;; The weapon command prints a description of the weapon
;;; that the player is currently carrying.
```

```
(defun weapon ()
  (cond((player-weapons *player*)
        (format t "You are currently carrying:~%")
        (mapc #'(lambda (weapon)
                  (print-self (get-object weapon)))
              (player-weapons *player*)))
       (t (format t "Your pockets are empty.~%"))))
 ⇒ WEAPON
```

It would be nice to be able to test these functions now, but they can't be called until the player is placed in a room. The goal of `start-game` was to initially place the player in a room. It accomplished the feat by calling the yet-to-be-defined function, `move-to`. We might as well proceed and define `walk`, which will also require `move-to`, implement `move-to`, and then test each of the commands.

The `walk` routine must first check to see if there are any live monsters in the current room. If so, the player can't leave. If not, it must also check to see if the requested direction is a known exit from the room. If it is, then the routine moves the player to the new room and issues a `look` command. `Walk` requires an argument, so we will define it as a macro which calls the function `walk-aux` with the argument quoted.

```
;;; Walk in the direction specified in the argument.

(defmacro walk (direction)
  (list 'walk-aux (list 'quote direction)))
 ⇒ WALK
```

`Walk-aux` must determine whether the argument direction is a legal direction. We will define an auxiliary function called `legal-direction` that determines if the designated direction is legal for the given room. Notice that we must invoke `check-for-monster-attack` if there are monsters present. Otherwise, we try to walk in the direction, or print a message that we can't go in that direction.

```
;;; The actual walking is performed in this function.

(defun walk-aux (direction)
  (let ((this-room (player-current-room *player*))
        next-room)
    (cond ((monsters this-room)
           (format t
     "Sorry, you may not leave, monsters still present!!~%")
           (check-for-monster-attack))
```

```
            ((setf next-room
                   (legal-direction
                    (connections this-room) direction))
             (move-to next-room))
            (t (format t
                  "Ouch!! You just walked into a wall.~%")))))
 ⇒ WALK-AUX
```

The list of connections is an association list of direction and room name. So, legal-direction is just a call to assoc, surrounded by a call to cadr to extract the actual room name. Even though assoc may return nil, taking the cadr will still result in nil. This allows writing very short code which would otherwise require a test to see if the result is nil and then avoid taking the cadr.

```
;;; Is the direction

(defun legal-direction (connection-list direction)
  (cadr (assoc direction connection-list)))
 ⇒ LEGAL-DIRECTION
```

Finally, we can define the move-to function. Its argument is the name of the room we wish to enter. The function just stores the new room name in the current-room slot of the player (after calling get-object to get the real room object) and then calls look.

```
;;; Move the player into the room specified in the argument.

(defun move-to (room)
  (setf (player-current-room *player*) (get-object room))
  (look))
 ⇒ MOVE-TO
```

This gives enough code that we can try some simple tests.

```
;;; Start the game running.
(start-game bob 100 start)
 ⇒ BOB you have 100 hit points remaining.
 ⇒ The room you are in (START) is A small, uncomfortable
 ⇒  cavern.
 ⇒  You notice a strange odor.
 ⇒ This room contains:
 ⇒ SPECIAL, Trusty Saturday Night Special awaits your use
 ⇒   against the monsters.
 ⇒ NIL

;;; Walk in a direction.
(walk east)
```

```
⇒ Ouch!! You just walked into a wall.
⇒ NIL

;;; Go to another room.
(walk west)
⇒ BOB you have 100 hit points remaining.
⇒ The room you are in (TERROR-ROOM) is A dark and musty
⇒ smelling room.
⇒ This room contains:
⇒ CLUB, Large club with spikes protruding from the end
⇒   awaits your use against the monsters.
⇒ The notorious ZOMBIE, A ghastly apparition, devoid of
⇒   flesh watches you.
⇒ NIL

(walk north)
⇒ Sorry, you may not leave, monsters still present!!
⇒ NIL

(weapon)
⇒ Your pockets are empty.
⇒ NIL
```

The other two commands **take** and **drop** are just as easy to implement. The **take** macro must first verify that the weapon is in the room. Then it adds it to the player's list of weapons and removes it from the room contents. **Drop** first checks to see if there is a weapon to drop and, if so, performs the opposite operation to **take**. These macros require three, weapon operations for the player and room. The operations are:

has-weapon – This determines if the player or the room has the argument weapon.
give-weapon – This gives the argument weapon to the room or the player.
take-weapon – This takes a weapon from a room or the player.

Ideally these should each be implemented as methods associated with the room and player objects. However, since we decided **player** should be a structure, they must be implemented as functions for **player**. The evidence seems to be mounting against choosing a different representation like structures for **player**, since it is inconsistent with the object philosophy. The three functions and three methods follow. The only problem is removing the weapon from the list. Common LISP defines a couple of functions for removing things from lists. However, these functions are not introduced until the next chapter, so we'll write our own function to perform the task.

```
;;; An auxiliary function to remove the first argument
;;; element from second argument list.  Note, that this
;;; constructs a new list with the element removed.
```

```
(defun remove-element-from-list (element list-of-elements)
  (cond ((null list-of-elements) nil)
        ((equal element (car list-of-elements))
         (cdr list-of-elements))
        (t (cons (car list-of-elements)
                 (remove-element-from-list
                  element
                  (cdr list-of-elements))))))
⇒ REMOVE-ELEMENT-FROM-LIST

;;; Take the weapon from the player.

(defun take-weapon (player weapon)
  (setf (player-weapons player)
        (remove-element-from-list
         weapon
         (player-weapons player))))
⇒ TAKE-WEAPON

;;; Take the weapon from the room.

(define-method (room take-weapon) (weapon)
  (setf weapons (remove-element-from-list weapon weapons)))
⇒ TAKE-WEAPON

;;; Place the argument weapon into the player's weapon slot.

(defun give-weapon (player weapon)
  (setf (player-weapons player)
        (cons weapon (player-weapons player))))
⇒ GIVE-WEAPON

;;; Likewise, place the argument weapon into the room's
;;; weapon list.

(define-method (room give-weapon) (weapon)
  (setf weapons (cons weapon weapons)))
⇒ GIVE-WEAPON

;;; Finally, the has-weapon function which determines if the
;;; player is carrying the argument weapon.

(defun has-weapon (player weapon)
  (member weapon (player-weapons player)))
⇒ HAS-WEAPON

;;; This is the room version of has-weapon to see if the
```

```
;;; weapon is in the room.

(define-method (room has-weapon) (weapon-or-monster)
  (or (member weapon-or-monster weapons)
      (member weapon-or-monster monsters)))
 ⇒ HAS-WEAPON
```

Finally, we can write drop and take. They just call the appropriate primitives passing the arguments to drop or get a weapon.

```
;;; Take a weapon passed as an argument and add it to the
;;; list of weapons being carried by the player.

(defmacro take (weapon)
  `(take-aux ',weapon))
 ⇒ TAKE

;;; The actual process of taking a weapon is performed in
;;; this function.

(defun take-aux (weapon)
  (let ((this-room (player-current-room *player*)))
    (if (null (has-weapon this-room weapon))
      (format t "Sorry, that weapon is not in the room.~%")
      (progn (give-weapon *player* weapon)
             (take-weapon this-room weapon)
             (format t "~A taken.~%" weapon)))
    (check-for-monster-attack)))
 ⇒ TAKE-AUX

;;; Drop the weapon argument.
(defmacro drop (weapon)
  `(drop-aux ',weapon))
 ⇒ DROP

;;; The real work is done here.
(defun drop-aux (weapon)
  (let ((this-room (player-current-room *player*)))
    (cond ((null (has-weapon *player* weapon))
           (format
            t "Sorry, you are not carrying a ~A.~%" weapon))
          (t (take-weapon *player* weapon)
             (give-weapon this-room weapon)
             (format t "~A dropped.~%" weapon)))
    (check-for-monster-attack)))
 ⇒ DROP-AUX
```

The functions and methods to support these operations are now defined. So, we can test the calls to make sure that we can take and drop the weapons. We must verify that when we pick up the weapon it is removed from the room and also when we drop the weapon it again appears in the room.

```
(take club)
⇒ CLUB taken.
⇒ NIL

(weapon)
⇒ You are currently carrying:
⇒ CLUB, Large club with spikes protruding from the end
⇒  awaits your use against the monsters.
⇒ (CLUB)

(look)
⇒ BOB you have 100 hit points remaining.
⇒ The room you are in (TERROR-ROOM) is A dark and musty
⇒ smelling room.
⇒ This room contains:
⇒ The notorious ZOMBIE, A ghastly apparition, devoid of
⇒   flesh watches you.
⇒ NIL

(drop special)
⇒ Sorry, you are not carrying a SPECIAL.
⇒ NIL

(drop club)
⇒ CLUB dropped.
⇒ NIL

(look)
⇒ BOB you have 100 hit points remaining.
⇒ The room you are in (TERROR-ROOM) is A dark and musty
⇒ smelling room.
⇒   You notice a strange odor.
⇒ This room contains:
⇒ CLUB, Large club with spikes protruding from the end
⇒   awaits your use against the monsters.
⇒ The notorious ZOMBIE, A ghastly apparition, devoid of
⇒   flesh watches you.
⇒ NIL
```

EXERCISES

12.7 Modify the wand so that it requires the proper incantation to be said before it may be picked up.

```
;; Make a wand for testing.
(add-weapon wand wand "Magic and wonderful wand")
 ⇒ #<Object WAND>

;; Add an incantation.
(setf (incantation (get-object 'wand)) "LISP is great")
 ⇒ "LISP is great"

;; Put it in a room.
(add-room start "A small, uncomfortable cavern" nil (special wand)
          ((west terror-room)))
 ⇒ #<Object ROOM>

(start-game bob 100 start)
 ⇒ BOB you have 100 hit points remaining.
 ⇒ The room you are in (START) is A small, uncomfortable cavern.
 ⇒ This room contains:
 ⇒ SPECIAL, Trusty Saturday Night Special awaits your use against
 ⇒   the monsters.
 ⇒ WAND, Magic and wonderful wand awaits your use against the
 ⇒   monsters.
 ⇒ NIL

(take wand)
What is the incantation?
foobar
 ⇒ Wrong incantation, wand not taken.
 ⇒ NIL

(take wand)
LISP is great
 ⇒ WAND taken.
 ⇒ NIL
```

12.8 Write specialized `print-self` methods for a `dragon` and a `special`.

```
(add-monster godzilla dragon "The Tokyo Strangler" 20 20)
 ⇒ #<Object DRAGON>

(print-self (get-object 'godzilla))
 ⇒ The huge, ugly beast GODZILLA stares at you.
 ⇒ He thinks that you look like a tasty dish.
 ⇒ NIL

(print-self (get-object 'special))
 ⇒ Your trusty SPECIAL is ready for use.
 ⇒ You have 6 more bullets.
 ⇒ NIL
```

12.4 Combat Commands

This section discusses the implementation of the **fight** and **attack** commands. The **fight** command selects which monster to fight. Once the player has picked a fight with a monster, the player and monster must battle until one is defeated. After issuing the **fight** command, the player can issue one more command (usually an **attack**) before the monster starts its attack. So, **fight** should not end with a call to the **check-for-monster-attack** function. The **fight** command takes one argument, which is the monster that the player wants to battle. Once again, it will be implemented as a macro, calling an auxiliary function that does the work.

```
;;; Initiate the fight with the argument monster.

(defmacro fight (monster)
  '(fight-aux ', monster))
 ⇒ FIGHT
```

Recall that the player **defstruct** has a slot called **fighting**. This slot contains either the monster object that the player is fighting or **nil** if there is no fight in progress. Therefore, **fight-aux** must verify that the slot is **nil** before allowing the fight to begin. It must also verify that the argument monster is actually present in the room. The final check makes sure that the player is carrying only one weapon. This simplification to the game means that when the player is fighting a monster, he may only carry one weapon into battle. If a weapon's lifetime is used up, it must be dropped and another weapon selected. This gives the monster two extra commands in which to attack the player.

```
;;; The actual fight function.  It must verify that a battle
;;; is not already underway, that the monster is present and
;;; that the player is carrying at most one weapon.  The
;;; function returns the name of the monster selected for
;;; battle.

(defun fight-aux (monster)
  (cond ((player-fighting *player*)
         (format
          t "You are already engaged in a battle with ~A~%"
                 (name (player-fighting *player*))))
        ((not (monster-in-room-p
                (player-current-room *player*)
                monster))
         (format
          t "Sorry, that monster is not in the room.~%"))
        ((> (number-of-weapons *player*) 1)
```

```
            (format
             t
             "You may only wield one weapon in your battle.~%"))
           (t (setf (player-fighting *player*)
                    (get-object monster))))
  monster)
 ⇒ FIGHT-AUX
```

`Fight-Aux` requires the implementation of an additional method and function. The method determines if an argument monster is present in the room object. This is implemented with a call to `member`. Notice that the use of methods hides the representation of the monster information.

```
;;; Determine if the argument monster is in the room.

(define-method (room monster-in-room-p) (a-monster)
  (member a-monster monsters))
 ⇒ MONSTER-IN-ROOM-P
```

The additional function returns the number of weapons that the player is carrying. This is implemented with a call to `length`.

```
;;; Compute the number of weapons that the player is
;;; carrying.

(defun number-of-weapons (player)
  (length (player-weapons player)))
 ⇒ NUMBER-OF-WEAPONS
```

The last command is `attack`. If the player is fighting a monster (meaning the `fighting` slot has a value), then an attack can be issued. Once we have decided to attack, `attack` must determine the accuracy and damage of the current weapon. The accuracy and damage of each weapon was defined in its initial description. This varies between weapons, so we should write a method for each weapon that returns its accuracy and damage. We have also defined accuracy and damage for each monster and should write a method for each type of monster. Finally, to make the game more interesting, we will adjust the accuracy of a monster or weapon based upon the ratio of its current strength to its initial strength. So, we will write a set of methods for each monster and weapon that returns a list of the accuracy and damage. If a weapon exceeds its lifetime, then the player will have to either pick up another weapon or resort to using his or her hands.

Each of these methods returns a list of the accuracy and the damage. The accuracy is an integer between 0 and 100 representing the percentage of times that this weapon will inflict damage. The damage is the number of hit points that this weapon inflicts. We must handle the case where the weapon may misfire and damage the player, like in the definition of special. Damage to the opponent will always be a positive number, so a negative damage could imply that the player is injured by the use of the weapon. Using this guideline, we can write each method for the weapons. Notice that the lifetime of each weapon must be adjusted after each use. We can write one generic function for all weapons rather than individually tailored accuracy-and-damage methods.

```
;;; The accuracy and damage if we must use our hands.
(defvar *hands-accuracy-and-damage* '(100 1))
⇒ *HANDS-ACCURACY-AND-DAMAGE*

;;; The Saturday Night Special has the following
;;; characteristics:
;;; 80;;; 20;;; is 100

(define-method (special accuracy-and-damage) ()
  (if (> (lifetime self) 0)
    (if (< (random 100) 80)
      (list 50 (damage self))
      (progn
        (format t "AAAAH!! Misfire!!!~%")
        (list 100 -5)))
    (progn
      (format t "Click... Your trusty gun is empty.~%")
      *hands-accuracy-and-damage*)))
⇒ ACCURACY-AND-DAMAGE

;;; A wand is always 100

(define-method (wand accuracy-and-damage) ()
  (if (> (lifetime self) 0)
    (list 100 (damage self))
    (progn
      (format t "Your wand has lost its usefulness.~%")
      *hands-accuracy-and-damage*)))
⇒ ACCURACY-AND-DAMAGE

;;; A club is 90% effective, but does not inflict much
;;; damage.  The club has infinite lifetime, so there is no
;;; need to check the lifetime.

(define-method (club accuracy-and-damage) ()
  (list 90 (damage self)))
⇒ ACCURACY-AND-DAMAGE

;;; The cannon is 75% accurate, and always destroys the
```

```
;;; monster.

(define-method (cannon accuracy-and-damage) ()
  (if (> (lifetime self) 0)
    (list 75 (damage self))
    (progn
      (format t "The cannon is empty.~%")
      *hands-accuracy-and-damage*)))
⇒ ACCURACY-AND-DAMAGE
```

The following generic function decreases the lifetime of a weapon by one and prints an informative message if the lifetime is exhausted. The function ignores weapons that have non-numeric lifetime values, since infinite lifetime is represented as `nil`.

```
;;; Decrease the lifetime of the weapon by one.

(defun less-lifetime (weapon)
  (cond ((and (numberp (lifetime weapon))
              (> (lifetime weapon) 0))
         (setf (lifetime weapon) (1- (lifetime weapon)))
         (cond ((= (lifetime weapon) 0)
                (format t "Warning: ~A exhausted.~%"
                        (name weapon)))))))
⇒ LESS-LIFETIME
```

The accuracy of a player and a monster is adjusted downward based upon the current number of hit points versus the initial hit points. As a monster or player approaches zero hit points, their accuracy approaches zero. This is another case where using a structure for the player representation is a disadvantage. If the player had an object representation like the monster, these two functions could be combined into a single generic function. However, due to the differences, they must be defined separately.

```
;;; Adjust the accuracy of any monster based upon the current
;;; strength of the monster.

(defun adjust-monster-accuracy (object accuracy)
  (* accuracy (/ (hit-points object)
                 (initial-strength object))))
⇒ ADJUST-MONSTER-ACCURACY

;;; A similar adjustment for the player.

(defun adjust-player-accuracy (accuracy)
  (* accuracy (/ (player-hit-points *player*)
```

```
                (player-initial-strength *player*))))
  ⇒ ADJUST-PLAYER-ACCURACY
```

The following two functions adjust the points of a player and a monster by the argument number of hits points. They both print an interesting message about the effects. If the damage results in a dead monster, the function removes the monster from the list of monsters present in the current room. It also resets the `fighting` slot within `*player*`.

```
;;; Adjust the player hit points down by the argument points.

(defun adjust-points (player points)
  (setf (player-hit-points player)
        (- (player-hit-points player) points))
  (format t "You just lost ~A points for a total of ~A.~%"
          points (player-hit-points player))
  (if (<= (player-hit-points player) 0)
    (format t "You are DEAD!!!~%")))
⇒ ADJUST-POINTS

;;; Adjust the monster hit points down by the argument.

(define-method (monster adjust-points) (damage)
  (setf hit-points (- hit-points damage))
  (format t "You HIT and take ~A points.~%" damage)
  (if (<= hit-points 0)
    (progn
      (format t "You have killed ~A.~%" name)
      (remove-monster (player-current-room *player*) name)
      (setf (player-fighting *player*) nil))))
⇒ ADJUST-POINTS

;;; Remove the argument monster from the monsters slot of the
;;; current room.

(define-method (room remove-monster) (monster)
  (setf monsters (remove-element-from-list monster monsters))
  monster)
⇒ REMOVE-MONSTER
```

Now, we should have enough auxiliary functions to write the `attack` function. The `random` function will generate a number between 0 and the maximum accuracy, 100, to represent the effectiveness of the attack. If the random number is less than the accuracy, then a hit is scored. Otherwise, the player misses and no hit points are lost.

```
;;; Attack the selected monster with the weapon that the
```

```
;;; player is carrying.  Determine the accuracy and damage of
;;; the weapon and adjust the accuracy for player
;;; effectiveness.  Then reduce the lifetime of the weapon
;;; and then attack the monster.  If the random number that
;;; is generated is outside of the accuracy range, then the
;;; player misses.  Finally, give the monster a chance to
;;; attack.

(defun attack ()
  (if (null (player-fighting *player*))
    (format t "You are not fighting anyone.~%")
    ;; Let the battle begin.
    (let* ((weapon
             (get-object (car (player-weapons *player*))))
            (accuracy-and-damage
             (if weapon
                 (accuracy-and-damage weapon)
               ;; If we aren't carrying a weapon, then default
               ;; to our hands.
               *hands-accuracy-and-damage*)))
      (if weapon (less-lifetime weapon))
      (if (<= (random 100)
               (adjust-player-accuracy
                (car accuracy-and-damage)))
        (if (< (cadr accuracy-and-damage) 0)   ; Back fire.
          (adjust-points *player*
                         (- (cadr accuracy-and-damage)))
          (adjust-points
           (player-fighting *player*)
           (cadr accuracy-and-damage)))
        (format t "You MISS!!~%"))
      (check-for-monster-attack))))
⇒ ATTACK
```

The last step defines the check-for-monster-attack stub function that allows a monster to attack a player. This function is called after each command, so it must determine if a fight is in progress and if so, it attacks the player. The currently selected monster will attack in the manner specified by its type. So, we'll define a method called attack-player for each monster type. The argument to attack-player will be the attacking monster. With this information, check-for-monster-attack is trivial to define:

```
;;; Determine if currently fighting a monster and if so
;;; attack the player.
(defun check-for-monster-attack ()
```

```
    (if (player-fighting *player*)
      (attack-player (player-fighting *player*))))
  ⇒ CHECK-FOR-MONSTER-ATTACK
```

The attack-player method must perform two primary functions. The first determines the accuracy of the monster and the second attempts to hit the player. The function for determining the accuracy of each monster type was defined earlier. So, the method should print an informative message, compute the accuracy and damage, and then attack the player. Once the accuracy and damage values have been computed, each monster should attack the same way. Therefore, a generic function can be written that, given these two values, performs the attack. This function, monster-attack, adjusts the accuracy based upon the strength of the monster and then attacks. The monster attack is also done by generating a random number between 0 and 100 and determining if the value is within the accuracy range. If a hit occurs, an informative message is printed and the player's points are adjusted. Otherwise, the message indicates that the monster missed the player.

The dragon and zombie implementations of the attack-player method are straightforward.

```
;;; Dragons attack the player with 100 percent accuracy.
;;; They are very deadly and should be disposed of as
;;; rapidly as possible.

(define-method (dragon attack-player) ()
  (format t
     "The dragon attempts to smash you to smithereens.~%")
  (monster-attack 100 (initial-damage self)))
 ⇒ ATTACK-PLAYER

;;; Zombies are only 50 percent accurate.

(define-method (zombie attack-player) ()
  (format t
   "The zombie stares at you with vacant eyes... and attacks.
")
  (monster-attack 50 (initial-damage self)))
 ⇒ ATTACK-PLAYER
```

The swarm is more difficult to define, since its accuracy is dependent upon the other monsters present in the room. It has a 40-percent accuracy when alone. Each additional non-swarm monster gives it another 10 percent in accuracy, while each additional swarm gives it another 30-percent accuracy. So, the method must compute the number of swarm and non-swarm monsters present in the room. Once computed, the accuracy can be determined.

```
;;; Initially compute the accuracy of the swarm based upon
;;; the other monsters present in the room.  Note, it must be
;;; careful not to count itself when determining the number
;;; of other monsters.  Then, like the other methods it
;;; invokes monster-attack passing the derived accuracy
;;; information.

(define-method (swarm attack-player) ()
  (let ((current-room (player-current-room *player*))
        accuracy)
    (setf count-of-other-swarm-in-room
          (1- (count-swarm (monsters current-room))))
    (setf count-of-non-swarm-in-room
          (- (length (monsters current-room))
             count-of-other-swarm-in-room
             1))
    (setf accuracy
          (min (+ 40
                  (* count-of-non-swarm-in-room 10)
                  (* count-of-other-swarm-in-room 30))
               100))
    (if (> accuracy 40)
      (format t
       "The swarm senses others and attacks violently.~%")
      (format t
       "The lonely swarm weakly attempts an attack.~%"))
    (monster-attack accuracy (initial-damage self))))
⇒ ATTACK-PLAYER

;;; Given a list of monsters, determine the number that are
;;; swarms.

(defun count-swarm (monster-list)
  (apply '+
         (mapcar
          #'(lambda (monster)
              (if (equal (object-type
                          (get-object monster))
                         'swarm)
                  1
                  0))
          monster-list)))
⇒ COUNT-SWARM
```

Finally, monster-attack can be defined. It adjusts the accuracy based upon the strength of the monster, determines if there is a hit or not, and prints the appropriate messages.

```
;;; Generic function invoked by the various attack-player
;;; methods.  It adjusts the accuracy and then attacks the
;;; player.

(defun monster-attack (accuracy damage)
  (let* ((accuracy
          (adjust-monster-accuracy (player-fighting *player*)
                                   accuracy)))
    (if (< (random 100) accuracy)
      (progn
        (format t "~A HITS "
                (name (player-fighting *player*)))
        (adjust-points *player* damage))
      (format t "Whew!! The ~A Missed.~%"
              (name (player-fighting *player*))))))
 ⇒ MONSTER-ATTACK
```

This completes the definition of the functions needed to implement the game. We can now play a few commands and try to escape the dungeon alive!

```
(look)
 ⇒ BOB you have 100 hit points remaining.
 ⇒ The room you are in (TERROR-ROOM) is A dark and musty
 ⇒ smelling room.
 ⇒   You notice a strange odor.
 ⇒ This room contains:
 ⇒ CLUB, Large club with spikes protruding from the end
 ⇒   awaits your use against the monsters.
 ⇒ The notorious ZOMBIE, A ghastly apparition, devoid of
 ⇒   flesh watches you.
 ⇒ NIL

(take club)
 ⇒ CLUB taken.
 ⇒ NIL

(fight zombie)
 ⇒ ZOMBIE

(attack)
 ⇒ You HIT and take 3 points.
 ⇒ The zombie stares at you with vacant eyes... and attacks.
 ⇒ Whew!! The ZOMBIE Missed.
 ⇒ NIL
```

```
;; Notice how once we start a fight, the monster keeps on
;; fighting.
(look)
⇒ BOB you have 100 hit points remaining.
⇒ The room you are in (TERROR-ROOM) is A dark and musty
⇒ smelling room.
⇒   You notice a strange odor.
⇒ This room contains:
⇒ The notorious ZOMBIE, A ghastly apparition, devoid of
⇒   flesh watches you.
⇒ The zombie stares at you with vacant eyes... and attacks.
⇒ Whew!! The ZOMBIE Missed.
⇒ NIL

(attack)
⇒ You HIT and take 3 points.
⇒ You have killed ZOMBIE.
⇒ NIL

(look)
⇒ BOB you have 100 hit points remaining.
⇒ The room you are in (TERROR-ROOM) is A dark and musty
⇒ smelling room.
⇒ This room contains:
⇒  --- Nothing of interest
⇒ NIL

(walk north)
⇒ BOB you have 100 hit points remaining.
⇒ The room you are in (START) is A small, uncomfortable
⇒   cavern.
⇒ This room contains:
⇒ SPECIAL, Trusty Saturday Night Special awaits your use
⇒   against the monsters.
⇒ NIL

(take special)
⇒ SPECIAL taken.
⇒ NIL

(walk west)
⇒ BOB you have 100 hit points remaining.
⇒ The room you are in (TERROR-ROOM) is A dark and musty
⇒ smelling room.
⇒ This room contains:
⇒  --- Nothing of interest
```

```
⇒ NIL

(walk east)
⇒ BOB you have 100 hit points remaining.
⇒ The room you are in (MIST-ROOM) is It is all misty,
⇒   you can't see very well.
⇒ This room contains:
⇒ CANNON, A cannon from the HMS Pinafore awaits your use
⇒   against the monsters.
⇒ The evil SWARM-1, Number one of a deadly family of unkind
⇒   beastes is present.
⇒ The notorious SWARM-2, Number two of a deadly family of
⇒   unkind beastes watches you.
⇒ NIL

(fight swarm-1)
⇒ You may only wield one weapon in your battle.
⇒ SWARM-1

(drop club)
⇒ CLUB dropped.
⇒ NIL

(drop special)
⇒ SPECIAL dropped.
⇒ NIL

(take cannon)
⇒ CANNON taken.
⇒ NIL

(fight swarm-1)
⇒ SWARM-1

(attack)
⇒ Warning: CANNON exhausted.
⇒ You HIT and take 100 points.
⇒ You have killed SWARM-1.
⇒ NIL

(drop cannon)
⇒ CANNON dropped.
⇒ NIL

(take special)
⇒ SPECIAL taken.
⇒ NIL

(fight swarm-2)
```

```
⇒ SWARM-2

(attack)
⇒ You HIT and take 5 points.
⇒ The lonely swarm weakly attempts an attack.
⇒ Whew!! The SWARM-2 Missed.
⇒ NIL

(attack)
⇒ You HIT and take 5 points.
⇒ The lonely swarm weakly attempts an attack.
⇒ SWARM-2 HITS and takes 10 points, leaving 90 points.
⇒ NIL

(attack)
⇒ AAAAH!! Misfire!!!
⇒ You just lost 5 points for a total of 85.
⇒ The lonely swarm weakly attempts an attack.
⇒ Whew!! The SWARM-2 Missed.
⇒ NIL

(attack)
⇒ You MISS!!
⇒ The lonely swarm weakly attempts an attack.
⇒ Whew!! The SWARM-2 Missed.
⇒ NIL

(attack)
⇒ You MISS!!
⇒ The lonely swarm weakly attempts an attack.
⇒ SWARM-2 HITS and takes 10 points, leaving 75 points.
⇒ NIL

(attack)
⇒ Warning: SPECIAL exhausted.
⇒ You MISS!!
⇒ The lonely swarm weakly attempts an attack.
⇒ Whew!! The SWARM-2 Missed.
⇒ NIL

(attack)
⇒ Click... Your trusty gun is empty.
⇒ You HIT and take 1 points.
⇒ You have killed SWARM-2.
⇒ NIL

(drop special)
⇒ SPECIAL dropped.
```

```
⇒ NIL

(walk north)
⇒ BOB you have 75 hit points remaining.
⇒ The room you are in (EXIT) is At last!  A haven among the
⇒   mists of doom.
⇒ This room contains:
⇒  --- Nothing of interest
⇒ NIL
```

EXERCISES

***12.9** Implement the player as an object instead of using a structure. Determine the functions that must be changed to facilitate this modification.

12.10 Suppose that you could define different characteristics for the player. The player may choose to be very quick and less likely to be hit, but each hit does more damage. Otherwise, the player may be big and slow, where each hit does less damage, but the player tends to be hit more often. Define a way of specifying these characteristics, but don't permit a fast and tough player. You should also design the enhancements so that balanced speed and strength results in a game similar to the current system. The factor can be specified as a value between one and ten, inclusive.

***12.11** Implement the three new monsters defined in the previous exercises: `loner`, `blissterror`, and `empath`.

12.5 Summary

This chapter presented the design and implementation of a fantasy role-playing game. The implementation makes extensive use of objects for the various items in the dungeon and also for the representation of the dungeon itself. We represented the player as a structure, which turned out to be a bad idea. The object system provides you with automatic dispatching to the appropriate method code, and thus makes access to the various types more uniform. Structures made slot access difficult, because the structure name had to be included with each slot name. This indicates that it is better to stay with a particular representation throughout an implementation. Had we chosen structures or objects throughout, this would have been better than a mixture of the two. The chapter also used the `format` statement for the exchange between the player and the system. The game is only a beginning and could be extended in a number of ways to make it more challenging. An interesting extension is to write a rule system that helps to play the game. This task is left as one of the following chapter exercises.

Chapter Exercises

***1.** Enhance the game to define a shield. Shields are objects that may be present in a room. Once picked up, it will be automatically worn by the player. A shield has an infinite lifetime, and depending upon its type may decrease the amount of damage that the monster may be able to do. You will have to add a new slot to your `player` structure to contain the shield objects. Each shield will have a protection factor between one and five, which represents 10 to 50 percent protection. If more than one shield is being worn, the effects are multiplicative, not additive.

2. Enhance the previous exercise, so that there are different shields. Each shield has a list of the types of monsters that it will protect the player from. Modify the code so this is taken into account.

***3.** This game uses calls to LISP macros to invoke the various commands. Write a top-level looping function that reads and evaluates commands directly from the player (without the use of parentheses). Develop a language using abbreviations, (for example, `n` for `walk north`, `t` for `take`, and so on).

4. Write the `toss` command, which allows the player to throw the current weapon at the monster. The accuracy of the toss varies inversely with the monster hit points. The amount of damage is proportional to one tenth of the number of hit points that the weapon can make when conventionally used. Once a weapon is thrown, it may be picked up again with a `take` command.

5. *Difficult* – The goal of this exercise is to use the rule system developed in Chapter 9 to be an expert advisor for the dungeon player. The goal of the advisor is to help the player choose which monster to attack and which weapon to wield. The first step to implementing the rules is to change the player definition from a structure into an object. The rule system prefers to operate upon objects, and thus, this will make it much simpler. You will then have to interface the dungeon to the rule system, so that each object defined in the dungeon is accessible by the `lookup` function. Finally, you need to write some interesting rules to decide what to do. For example, a typical rule might be as follows:

```
;;; This rule says that if there is a dragon in the room and
;;; we have the cannon, then we should fight the dragon with
;;; the cannon.  It assumes that the player object is stored
;;; under the name player.

(define-rule dragon-rule
  (type (?room room) (?monster-list nil) (?weapon-list nil))
  (premise (and (player current-room ?room)
                (?room monsters ?monster-list)
                (player weapons ?weapon-list)
                (test (and (member 'dragon '?monster-list)
                           (member 'cannon '?weapon-list)))))
  (conclusion (player fight dragon)))
```

13

SEQUENCES AND SURGERY

THIS CHAPTER DISCUSSES the LISP data types which have a sequential nature, along with destructive operations on data. The string and array data types are introduced and typically the target of destructive operations. Common LISP also has destructive operations for lists. These particular operations are illustrated with a pointer representation of LISP structures which is close to the actual LISP implementation.

The case study in these chapters searches for solutions to problems using the A* heuristic-search strategy. Heuristic searching is a field of artificial intelligence where one searches to find the best solution to a difficult problem. For example, the programs that play chess use various searching algorithms to find the best move. The eight puzzle is a game that is adaptable to the A* technique. It is a three-by-three square with eight movable tiles numbered from 1 to 8. Since a three-by-three has 9 spaces for tiles, one location is free. The object of the puzzle is to take a random configuration and rearrange the tiles in some order, usually in increasing numeric order, from left to right and top to bottom. A move is made by sliding an adjacent tile into the free location, freeing the tile's original location. The location of the free space determines the number of possible moves. The following represents the board and the possible moves when the free space (designated with a blank square) is initially in the center:

1	2	3		1		3		1	2	3		1	2	3		1	2	3
4		5	=	4	2	5	or		4	5	or	4	5		or	4	8	5
6	8	7		6	8	7		6	8	7		6	8	7		6		7

The center position is the only place where there are four possible moves. From a corner position, there are only two possible moves. From a side position, there are three possible moves.

13.1 LISP Internal Representation

LISP has dynamic type-checking, so the LISP system determines the type of every LISP item at run-time. There are many different techniques for defining this run-time system. A popular technique allocates part of the machine word for the tag (indicating the type) and part for the information (either immediate data or a pointer to another LISP item). In this chapter, the tagged notation will demonstrate the internal structure of various LISP items. The visual representation is a rectangle with the tag on the left side and the information on the right side. The tag part is smaller than the information part to correspond to the actual number of bits allocated for each.* This notation is known as "box notation."

LISP Item

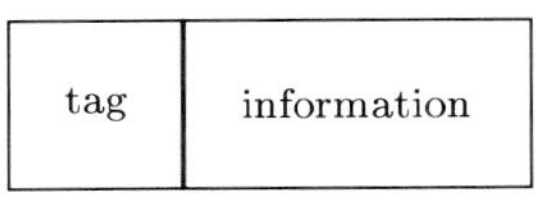

The integer data type is represented as an item with immediate data. An integer has an `int` tag and the actual numeric value in the information field. Symbols are implemented with a `sym` tag and a pointer to a symbol table location. However, to simplify our diagrams, we will place the symbol in the information part. Also, we will represent `nil` as a symbol.

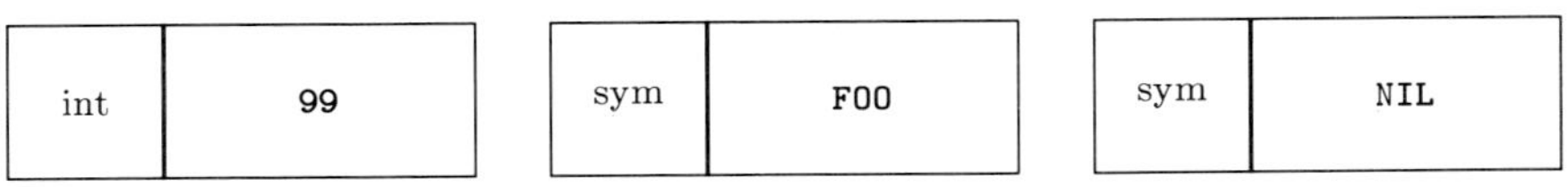

The integer 99 — The symbol FOO — NIL

Lists are constructed from `cons` cells, which contain the `car` and `cdr`. In our representation, the `car` and `cdr` are allocated sequentially with the `cons` pointing to the `car`. The box notation and the LISP system results for a `cons` of the integer 5 and `nil` and another of the integers 5 and 6 follows:

```
(cons 5 nil)
⇒ (5)
```

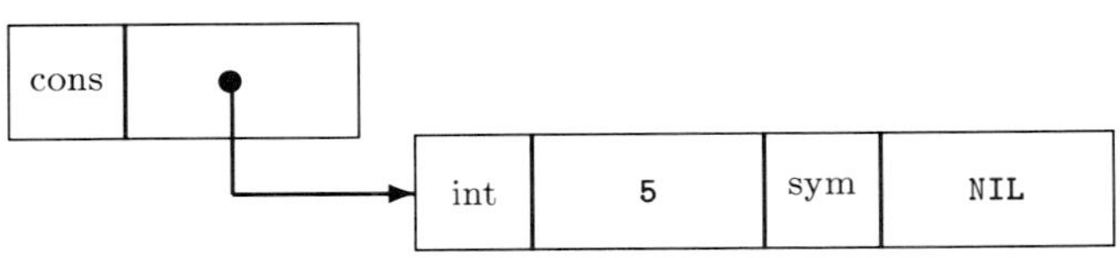

*A particular implementation may actually have other bits.

```
(cons 5 6)
⇒ (5 . 6)
```

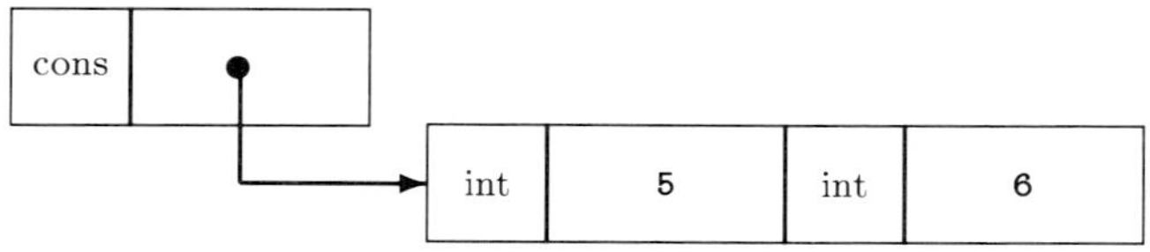

The second example with the embedded period is called "dot notation." Dot notation designates that the first part is the `car` and the second part is the `cdr`. When the `cdr` is `nil` the LISP system prints using "`list` notation" – it doesn't print the dot and the `nil`. So, if you don't see a dot, then there is an implicit `nil` in the last `cdr`. A list is constructed through repeated applications of `cons`. The appropriate terminology is to call a data type without a `nil` in the last `cdr` a `cons`, while the data type with a `null cdr` is a `list`.

```
;; This demonstrates the correspondence between list and
;; cons.
(setf foobar (list 'foo 'bar))
⇒ (FOO BAR)

(setf foobar (cons 'foo (cons 'bar nil)))
⇒ (FOO BAR)
```

Figure 13.1 is the box notation for `foobar`. We will place an arrow from the symbol `foobar` to its value. In an actual implementation, `foobar` is an index into a symbol table that contains the value.

This box notation should clarify how `car` and `cdr` operate. `Car` returns the LISP item that the `cons` directly points to. `Cdr` follows the pointer and returns the LISP item at the next location.* Figure 13.2 demonstrates access to the `car` and `cdr` of `foobar`.

If there is no trailing `nil` in a `cons`, the information requires less storage. Representing the list `(foo bar)` requires four items, while the `cons (foo . bar)` only requires two items. Also, you gain access to the second element with a `cdr` in a `cons` but with a `cadr` in a `list`. The `cdr` is more efficient, since the `cadr` performs the `cdr` and an additional `car` operation.

*The particular order of the **car** LISP item and the **cdr** LISP item is implementation dependent. Some implementations reverse the order, while others locate the pointer between the items, instead of at the beginning. Still others store the **car** and **cdr** in disjoint locations.

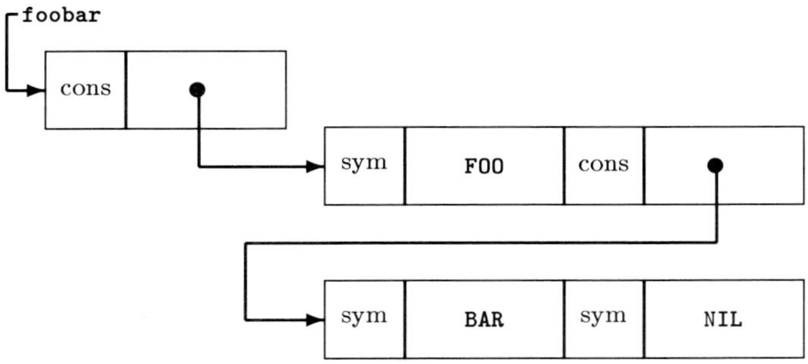

Figure 13.1 The Two-Element List

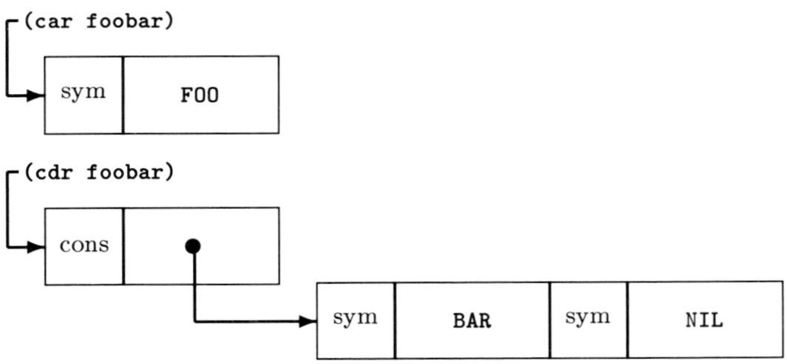

Figure 13.2 Simple **car** and **cdr** Operations on the List

```
(setf sample-cons (cons 5 6))
⇒ (5 . 6)

(cdr sample-cons)
⇒ 6

(setf sample-list (list 5 6))
⇒ (5 6)

(cadr sample-list)
⇒ 6
```

You should use `cons` when you have a small fixed number of items to group together and you want efficient storage and access. A good case is association lists and `assoc`. If you construct them with `cons` elements, you can gain access to them with `cdr` instead of `cadr`. If you write code to scan to the end of a `cons`, you should test for termination with `consp`. `Consp` is essentially the same as `listp`, except it returns `nil` when passed `nil`.

(consp *S-expression*)

```
;;; Print each element of a cons.

(defun print-element (arg)
  (if (not (consp arg))
    (print arg)
    (progn (print (car arg))
           (print-element (cdr arg)))))
⇒ PRINT-ELEMENT

(print-element (cons 'red (cons 'blue 'purple)))
⇒ RED
⇒ BLUE
⇒ PURPLE
⇒ PURPLE
```

Recall that the reason `PURPLE` is printed twice is that the first is the printed representation, while the second is the result of the function call.

```
;; Notice the final NIL with a list argument.
(print-element '(red white blue))
⇒ RED
⇒ WHITE
⇒ BLUE
⇒ NIL
⇒ NIL
```

You may construct a **cons** just by typing a dot in the appropriate place of a quoted list. You must be careful to follow the dot with only one other expression.

```
;; This demonstrates typing a dot to the LISP system.
(setf sample-cons '(5 . 6))
⇒ (5 . 6)

;; This causes an ERROR!
(setf buggy-cons '(5 . 6 7))
!!!!! Error: More than one object follows . in list.
  Condition signaled in: LISP::READ-AFTER-DOT.
```

EXERCISES

***13.1** Draw the box representation for the following lists:

```
(1 2)
(1 (2))
((1 2))
((1) 2)
```

13.2 Given the list `(setf x '((A B) C ((D)))`, draw the box representation. Then, determine the following operations by following the pointers defined in the box picture.

```
(car x)
(cdr x)
(caar x)
(cdar x)
(cadr x)
(cddr x)
(caar (cddr x))
```

13.3 Given the following box notation, write an expression that assigns to **mumble** an equivalent expression.

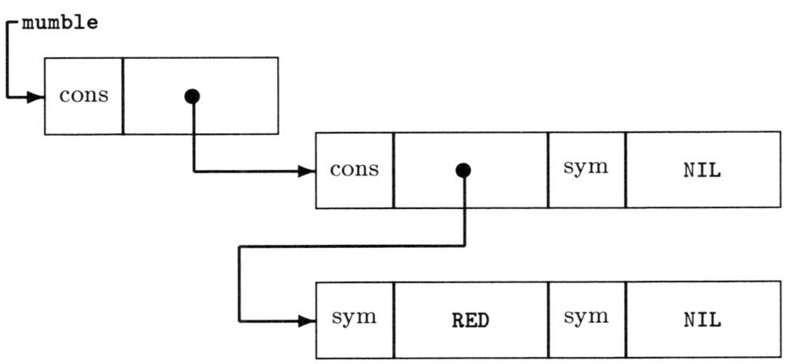

13.2 Equivalent Comparison Operators

The LISP function `equal` has been used frequently in previous chapters. `Equal` compares two LISP items to see if they are equivalent – if the items have structure, then the structures are scanned to determine if the corresponding elements are the same. `Eq` is a more primitive function that does not scan the structure. It compares the LISP items to see if they are exactly identical – no pointers are followed. The result of `eq` depends on the implementation of the LISP items. For example, if a floating point number is represented by a pointer to the bits representing the value, then two numbers with the same value may or may not be `eq` depending on the implementation. This is because they may point to different locations where the same value of the floating point number is stored. So, the Common LISP designers defined the `eql` function which is like `eq`, but if the operands are numbers of the same type, it compares their values no matter how they are implemented. So, `eql` should be used for non-structure comparisons.

(eq *S-expression S-expression*)

(eql *S-expression S-expression*)

```
;; Demonstrate comparisons using eql and equal.
(eql 3 3)
 ⇒ T

(eq 3.0 3.0)
 ⇒ NIL

(eql 3.0 3.0)
 ⇒ T

(eql '(1 (2) 3) '(1 (2) 3))
 ⇒ NIL

(equal '(1 (2) 3) '(1 (2) 3))
 ⇒ T
```

The difference between `eql` and `equal` is subtle. Be aware that the LISP system constructs completely new objects with each construction function (`cons`, `quote`, and `list`). Although they may appear to be the same, they are actually different objects. In the following example, three variables contain the same board positions. The first (`board1`) and third (`board3`) are defined with calls on `list`. This constructs two separate instances of the same structure. `Board2` is assigned the same value as `board1` and is therefore a pointer to the same structure as `board1`. `Eql` comparison returns `T` with `board1` and `board2` but `nil` with `board1` and `board3`. However, note that an `equal` comparison of `board1` and `board3` returns `T`. Notice in these comparisions, `eq` operates just line `eql`.

```
;; A particular board position.
(setf board1 (list 1 2 3 6 5 4 NIL 8 7))
⇒ (1 2 3 6 5 4 NIL 8 7)

;; Board2 has the same board position.
(setf board2 board1)
⇒ (1 2 3 6 5 4 NIL 8 7)

;; Board3 has the same board position, created as in board1.
(setf board3 (list 1 2 3 6 5 4 NIL 8 7))
⇒ (1 2 3 6 5 4 NIL 8 7)
```

Figure 13.3 illustrates the box notation for the three variables.

```
(eql board1 board2)
⇒ T

(eq board1 board2)
⇒ T

(eql board1 board3)
⇒ NIL

(eq board1 board3)
⇒ NIL

(equal board1 board3)
⇒ T
```

EXERCISES

***13.4** Using `board1` and `board2`, just defined, suppose that the following operation are performed:

```
(setf board1 (cons 99 board1))
```

What will be the result of each of these comparisons?

```
(eq (cdr board1) board2)
(eql (cdr board1) board2)
(equal (cdr board1) board2)
```

13.5 Evaluate each of these expressions without the aid of a running LISP system.

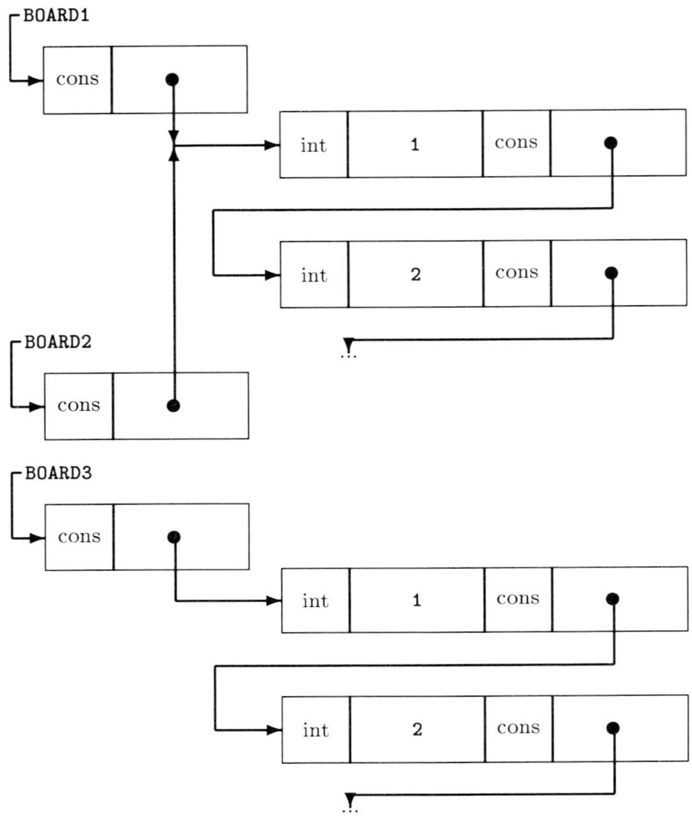

Figure 13.3 Box Notation for the Three Board Positions

Once you have determined the answers, submit each expression to a running LISP system and verify your results.

```
(setf x '(1 2 3))
(setf y '(1 2 3))
(eql (car x) (car y))
(eql (cdr x) (cdr y))
(setf z (cdr x))
(eql z (cdr x))
```

***13.6** Write `my-equal` that operates only on lists, that is equivalent to `equal`, but uses `eql` as the comparison operator.

13.3 Strings

As we have seen, strings are represented with surrounding double quote marks. A string is an ordered collection of characters. It is typically implemented with a `str` type tag and a pointer to the machines words containing the packed characters. For our purposes, we will pack four characters into each machine word.

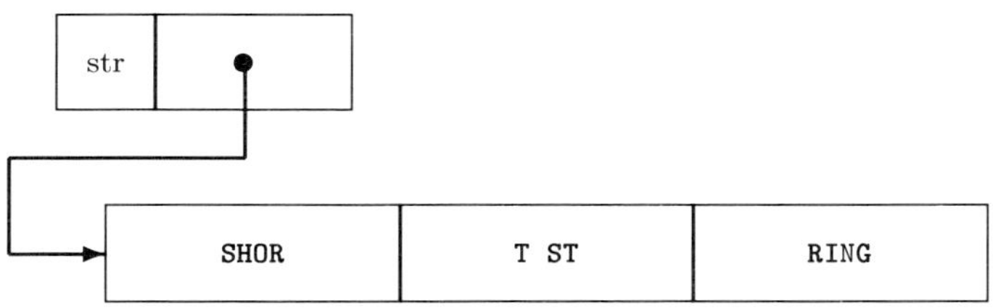

The string `"SHORT STRING"`

Since strings are represented as a sequence of machine words, you can gain access to individual characters with a technique similar to array indexing but with extra computation for the exact character. The `char` function accepts two arguments: the string and a zero-based index – the first character in a string is at index location zero. A `setf` version destructively modifies a character in a string. The `string` function accepts a character and returns a string containing that character.

(`char` *string integer*)

(`setf` (`char` *string integer*) *S-expression*)

```
(string character)
```

```
;; Experiment with char and string functions.
(setf board-row-1 "1 X 3")
 ⇒ "1 X 3"

(char board-row-1 0)
 ⇒ #\1

(char board-row-1 1)
 ⇒ #\Space

;; Replace the 1 in board-row-1 with a 2.
(setf (char board-row-1 0) #\2)
 ⇒ #\2

;; Notice that board-row-1 has been changed.
board-row-1
 ⇒ "2 X 3"

;; Convert a character back into a string.
(string (char board-row-1 0))
 ⇒ "2"

;; Restore board-row-1.
(setf board-row-1 "1 X 3")
 ⇒ "1 X 3"
```

Characters are printed with a leading `#\`. Certain special characters are printed using a symbol to make them easier to interpret, like `#\Space` for spaces and `#\Newline` for new lines.

Common LISP has functions for comparing and manipulating strings. The function `string=` compares two strings for exact equality, while `string-equal` compares strings for equality, but ignores case.

```
(string= string string)
```

```
(string-equal string string)
```

```
;; Test string= and string-equal.
(string= board-row-1 "1 X 3")
 ⇒ T

;; In the next example, the case of X is incorrect.
```

```
(string= board-row-1 "1 x 3")
⇒ NIL

(string-equal board-row-1 "1 x 3")
⇒ T
```

The standard relational operators are available for string comparison. Each takes two string arguments and returns the length of the longest matching substring. Otherwise, it returns `nil`. Strings are searched until a character differs and then it's lexically compared. A string that is a prefix of another string is defined to be < the second string.

(**string<** *string string*)

(**string>** *string string*)

(**string<=** *string string*)

(**string>=** *string string*)

(**string/=** *string string*)

```
;; Test a couple of the comparison functions.
;; The first string is a proper substring of the second.
(string< "1 X" board-row-1)
⇒ 3

(string<= "1 X 4" board-row-1)
⇒ NIL

(string> "1 X 4" board-row-1)
⇒ 4

(string>= "1 X 3" board-row-1)
⇒ 5

(string/= "1 X 3" board-row-1)
⇒ NIL

(string/= "1 X 4" board-row-1)
⇒ 4
```

There are also equivalent functions that ignore the case of the letters.

```
(string-lessp string string)
```

```
(string-greaterp string string)
```

```
(string-not-greaterp string string)
```

```
(string-not-lessp string string)
```

```
(string-not-equal string string)
```

The `make-string` function creates a string of specified size. If an initial element isn't specified, then the string is initialized in some machine-dependent way. So, the two forms for making a string are the following:

```
(make-string size)
```

```
(make-string size :initial-element character)
```

```
;; Create a string 10 characters long.
(make-string 10)
⇒ "          "

;; Notice that on this system, it initializes the string to
;; spaces.
;; Create a string of all A's.
(make-string 10 :initial-element #\A)
⇒ "AAAAAAAAAA"
```

You can also create a string using a special option to `format`. In earlier chapters, the first argument to `format` has been either `t` – which indicates the currently selected output device, or a stream – which indicates the output location. However, if you use `nil` as the first argument, the result is returned as a string. You can use this feature to convert between the various data types and a string. So, to convert from a number to a string you just use the `~S` directive.

Suppose that we wanted to create a prompt system that numbered each prompt to keep a history.

```
;;; Turns the argument history count into a prompt string.

(defun make-prompt (historycount)
  (format nil "~S cs> " historycount))
 ⇒ MAKE-PROMPT

;; Now for a test.
(make-prompt 57)
 ⇒ "57 cs> "
```

Strings are converted into symbols by calling the function `intern`. `Intern` takes a string and returns the corresponding symbol, if it exists. Otherwise, a new one is created. It also returns a second value indicating where the symbol was found. A second value of `nil` indicates that the symbol was newly created and `:internal` indicates a local symbol. If you want to `intern` strings associated with user-provided symbols, all of the characters must be in uppercase.

(intern *string*)

```
board-row-1
 ⇒ "1 X 3"

;; Turn the string into a symbol.
(intern "BOARD-ROW-1")
 ⇒ BOARD-ROW-1
 ⇒ :INTERNAL

;; Access the value of the symbol created through intern.
(eval (intern "BOARD-ROW-1"))
 ⇒ "1 X 3"
```

There are three functions for removing characters from a string. The process is called trimming. Characters to be removed are passed to the trim function as the first argument string. The second argument is the string from which you wish to remove characters. When the function sees a character in the first argument, it is removed from the string. The `string-trim` function removes all instances of the characters from the beginning and end of the string, while the `string-left-trim` only removes leading instances, and the `string-right-trim` removes trailing ones.

```
(string-trim character-string string)
```

```
(string-left-trim character-string string)
```

```
(string-right-trim character-string string)
```

Suppose that our board string may have leading and trailing brackets. They may be removed using the trim functions.

```
;; Suppose that we want to remove the surrounding spaces and
;; the leading and trailing brackets.
(setf board-level-1 "[ 1 X 3 ] ")
 ⇒ "[ 1 X 3 ] "

(setf original-board board-level-1)
 ⇒ "[ 1 X 3 ] "

(setf board-level-1
      (string-left-trim
       " ["
       (string-right-trim " ]" board-level-1)))
 ⇒ "1 X 3"

original-board
 ⇒ "[ 1 X 3 ] "

;; Or we could use string-trim to do it in one operation.
(string-trim " []" original-board)
 ⇒ "1 X 3"
```

All of these string functions create new copies of the string argument and don't destructively change the string. So, the value of `original-board` hasn't changed. Using the box notation, the link of `board-level-1` to `"[ 1 X 3 ]"` is moved to the newly constructed `"1 X 3"`. However, `original-board` still points to the original string.

The following functions convert strings into all uppercase `string-upcase`, all lowercase `string-downcase`, or capitalized `string-capitalize`. The capitalize functions capitalize the first character of all words within the string. The versions with a leading "n" destructively modify the string.

```
(string-upcase string)
```

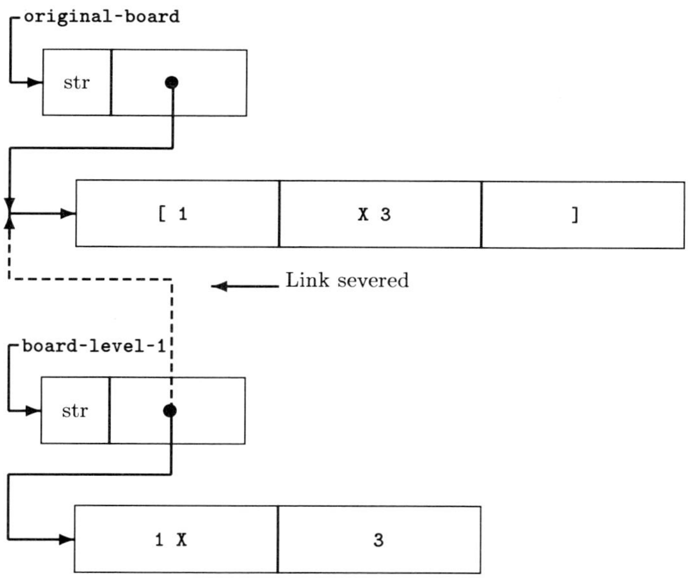


```
(string-downcase string)
```

```
(string-capitalize string)
```

```
(nstring-upcase string)
```

```
(nstring-downcase string)
```

```
(nstring-capitalize string)
```

```
;; Demonstrate the case functions.
(setf user-message "next board POSITION FOLLOWS:")
 ⇒ "next board POSITION FOLLOWS:"

;; Save user-message in another symbol.
(setf save-user-message user-message)
```

```
 ⇒ "next board POSITION FOLLOWS:"

;; Convert to uppercase.
(string-upcase user-message)
 ⇒ "NEXT BOARD POSITION FOLLOWS:"

;; Convert to lowercase.
(string-downcase user-message)
 ⇒ "next board position follows:"

;; Capitalize the string.
(string-capitalize user-message)
 ⇒ "Next Board Position Follows:"

;; Verify that both strings haven't changed.
user-message
 ⇒ "next board POSITION FOLLOWS:"

save-user-message
 ⇒ "next board POSITION FOLLOWS:"

(eq user-message save-user-message)
 ⇒ T

;; Try a destructive operation.
(nstring-capitalize user-message)
 ⇒ "Next Board Position Follows:"

;; See if save-user-message has changed.
save-user-message
 ⇒ "Next Board Position Follows:"
```

So, the call to `nstring-capitalize` destructively changes the string and both `user-message` and `save-user-message` reference the changed string.

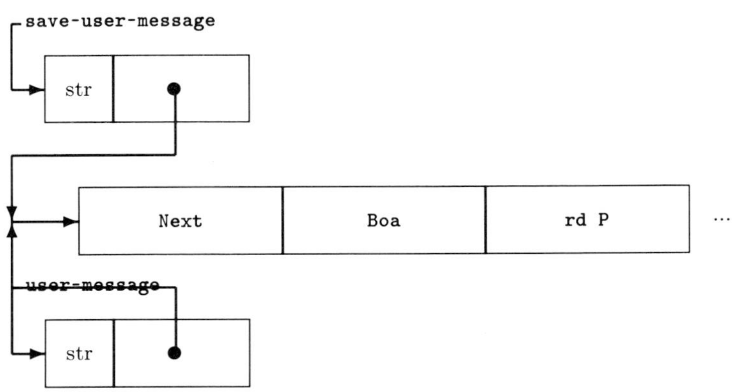

EXERCISES

13.7 Write a function `string-count` that counts the number of occurrences of the character defined in the first argument in the string in the second argument. The solution of this problem requires that you call the `length` function on the string argument to determine how many characters are in the argument. The `length` function was used in previous chapters to operate upon lists, but works equally well on strings.

```
(string-count #\A "ABBA CADABRA")
 ⇒ 5
```

13.8 Write a function that could be used in a text editor to convert the first argument (a string) as designated in the second argument. Use `u` for uppercase, `l` for lowercase, and `c` for capitalize.

```
(convert "This is a test STRING" 'l)
 ⇒ "this is a test string"
```

***13.9** Write a function to sort a list of strings in ascending or descending order, depending upon the value of the second argument. Choose your favorite sorting algorithm, but do not use `sort`.

```
(my-sort '("hi there" "hello" "gah day") 'ascending)
 ⇒ ("gah day" "hello" "hi there")

(my-sort '("hi there" "hello" "gah day") 'descending)
 ⇒ ("hi there" "hello" "gah day")
```

13.4 Arrays

Common LISP also provides a multi-dimensional `array` data type. Single dimensional arrays are called vectors. Arrays collect a fixed number of LISP items. They are often used to implement many data types, including objects and structures. Changes to any element in an `array` are always destructive. Arrays are created with the `make-array` function. The argument is an S-expression that evaluates either to an integer that represents the size of the vector, or a list of integers that are the sizes of each array dimension. The length of the list is the dimensionality of the array. You can specify a uniform initial value for each element with the `:initial-element` option. You can provide different initial values for each element using the `:initial-contents` option.

```
(make-array S-expression)
```

(make-array *S-expression* :initial-element *S-expression*)

(make-array *S-expression* :initial-contents *S-expression*)

```
;; Create a vector that represents the board of the 8-puzzle.
(setf *board* (make-array 9))
 ⇒ #(LISP::*UNDEFINED* LISP::*UNDEFINED* LISP::*UNDEFINED*
 ⇒    LISP::*UNDEFINED* LISP::*UNDEFINED* LISP::*UNDEFINED*
 ⇒    LISP::*UNDEFINED* LISP::*UNDEFINED* LISP::*UNDEFINED*)

;; Create the same vector, initialized to zero.
(setf *board* (make-array 9 :initial-element 0))
 ⇒ #(0 0 0 0 0 0 0 0 0)

;; Create the vector with initial contents specified.
(setf *board* (make-array 9 :initial-contents
                                  '(1 2 3 4 5 6 7 8 nil)))
 ⇒ #(1 2 3 4 5 6 7 8 NIL)

;; Another representation is to use a two dimensional array.
(setf *board-2d* (make-array '(3 3)))
 ⇒ #2A((LISP::*UNDEFINED* LISP::*UNDEFINED*
 ⇒                        LISP::*UNDEFINED*)
 ⇒     (LISP::*UNDEFINED* LISP::*UNDEFINED*
 ⇒                        LISP::*UNDEFINED*)
 ⇒     (LISP::*UNDEFINED* LISP::*UNDEFINED*
 ⇒                        LISP::*UNDEFINED*))

;; The same array initialized to 0.
(setf *board-2d* (make-array '(3 3) :initial-element 0))
 ⇒ #2A((0 0 0) (0 0 0) (0 0 0))

;; Finally the array with initial contents.  Notice that the
;; list provided as initial contents must be properly nested
;; according to the array dimensions.
(setf *board-2d* (make-array '(3 3) :initial-contents
                                     '((1 2 3) (4 5 6) (7 8 nil))))
 ⇒ #2A((1 2 3) (4 5 6) (7 8 NIL))
```

Notice the various printed representations for arrays. You can construct arrays using the same representation and preceding it with a quote.

```
;; A nine element vector, initialized to a particular board
;; position.
(setf *board* '#(1 2 5 7 4 NIL 3 8 6))
 ⇒ #(1 2 5 7 4 NIL 3 8 6)
```

The function `aref` is used to reference array elements. The first argument is an array, and the remaining arguments are the array indices (or index if indexing into a vector). A corresponding `setf` form stores into an array element.

(`aref` *array S-expression S-expression**)

(`setf (aref` *array S-expression S-expression**`)` *S-expression*)

In the A* algorithm you need a way to compute how far a particular board is from a solution. The better the measure, the better the chance for success. The measure that we'll use is the number of misplaced tiles. We will write a function whose first argument is the current board vector and whose second argument is the goal vector. The routine must scan the vectors, comparing the values at each index, and return a count of those that match. To write this function, we need a function that returns the number of elements in the array. The `array-dimension` function takes an array as the first argument and the dimension as the second argument. The first dimension is numbered zero.

(`array-dimension` *array S-expression*)

We can write `compare-vectors` that takes two vectors and computes the number of elements that are different. It must scan the vectors simultaneously and increment a count when they differ.

```
;;; Compute the number of values that are different between
;;; two vector arguments.  This routine is generic in that it
;;; compares the number of elements in the shortest vector
;;; (however, in reality they should be the same length).

(defun compare-vectors (current-state goal)
  (let
    ((count 0))
    (dotimes
      (vector-index
       (min (array-dimension current-state 0)
            (array-dimension goal 0))
       count)
      (if (not (equal (aref current-state vector-index)
                      (aref goal vector-index)))
        (setf count (1+ count))))))
 ⇒ COMPARE-VECTORS
```

Another useful function is **vector**, which can be used to specify all the elements of a vector when it is created, just like the function **list** for creating lists. So, you can create the various board vectors without explicitly installing each value.

```
(vector S-expression*)
```

```
;; Create the goal and current board vectors.  Nil represents
;; the position of the blank.
(setf *goal* (vector 1 2 3 4 5 6 7 8 nil))
 ⇒ #(1 2 3 4 5 6 7 8 NIL)

(setf *board* (vector 1 2 3 6 nil 4 5 8 7))
 ⇒ #(1 2 3 6 NIL 4 5 8 7)

;; Now test the compare-vectors function.
(compare-vectors *board* *goal*)
 ⇒ 5
```

Figures 13.4 and 13.5 illustrate box notation for the following expressions:

```
;; Save the current board in another symbol.
(setf *save-board* *board*)
 ⇒ #(1 2 3 6 NIL 4 5 8 7)

;; Change the positions, as if a move has been made.
(setf (aref *board* 3) NIL)
 ⇒ NIL

(setf (aref *board* 4) 6)
 ⇒ 6

;; Notice that both *board* and *save-board* have changed.
*board*
 ⇒ #(1 2 3 NIL 6 4 5 8 7)

*save-board*
 ⇒ #(1 2 3 NIL 6 4 5 8 7)
```

An important comparison function not mentioned in the earlier sections is **equalp**. The **equalp** function is the same as **equal**, except for some additional features. With **equalp**, numbers of different types can be compared. For example, a floating point and an integer representation of five would be **equalp**, but not **equal**.

```
(equalp S-expression S-expression)
```

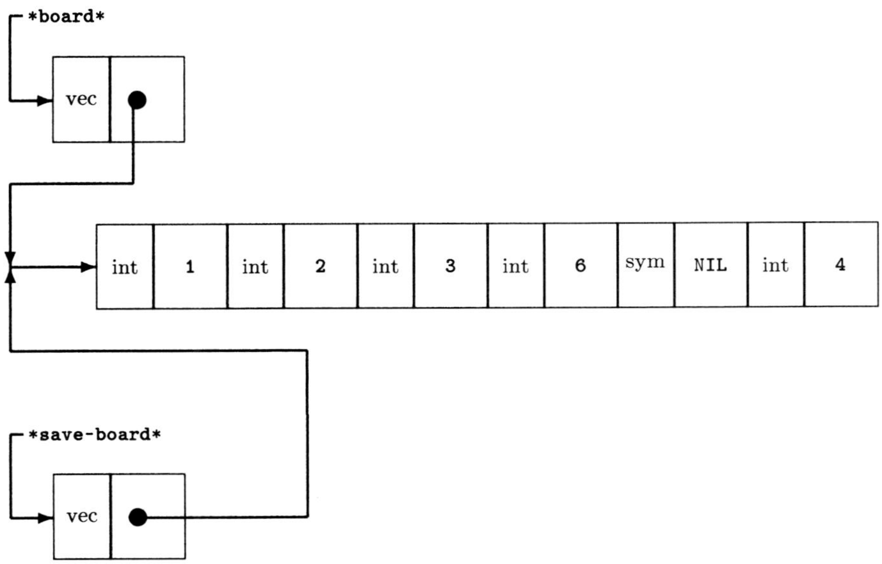

Figure 13.4 Vectors Before the **setf** Statements

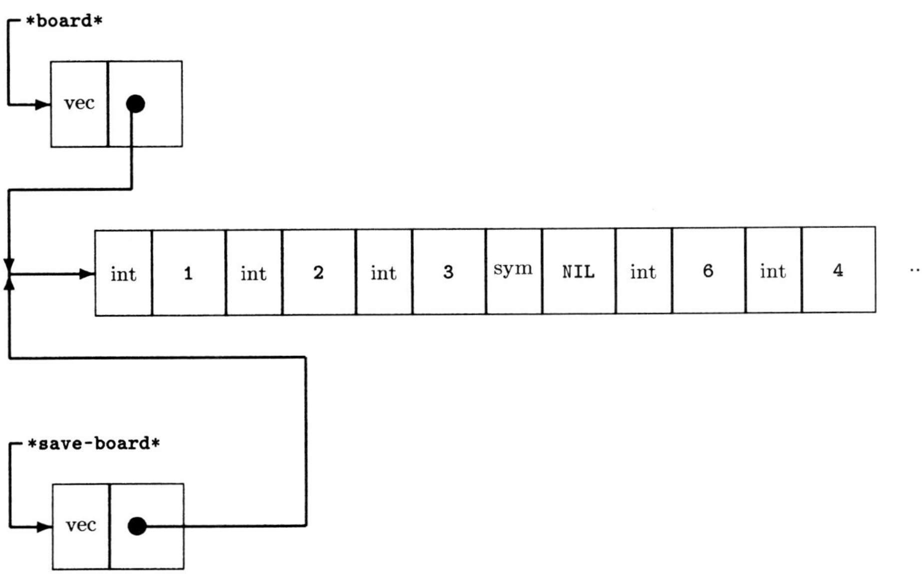

Figure 13.5 Vectors After the **setf** Statements

```
;; This shows equal and equalp of different typed numbers.
(equal 5.0 5)
 ⇒ NIL

(equalp 5.0 5)
 ⇒ T
```

The big difference between **equal** and **equalp** is that if the arguments to **equalp** have components (like an array), each component must be **equalp** for the entire result to be **equalp**. Thus, **equalp** should be used for comparing arrays.

```
;; This checks the current value of *board*.
*board*
 ⇒ #(1 2 3 NIL 6 4 5 8 7)

(equal *board* (vector 1 2 3 nil 6 4 5 8 7))
 ⇒ NIL

;; However, equalp returns T.
(equalp *board* (vector 1 2 3 nil 6 4 5 8 7))
 ⇒ T
```

EXERCISES

***13.10** Write the **move-tile** function, which given a nine-element vector representing the eight-puzzle and a direction to move, modifies the vector reflecting the move. The directions are symbols from the set **up**, **down**, **left**, or **right**. **Up** means to move the tile up into the empty square, which is represented by **nil**.

```
(setf *board* (vector 1 2 3 NIL 6 4 5 8 7))
 ⇒ #(1 2 3 NIL 6 4 5 8 7)

(move-tile *board* 'up)
 ⇒ #(1 2 3 5 6 4 NIL 8 7)
```

13.11 Enhance **move-tile** so it returns the symbol **error** if the move is illegal.

```
(move-tile *board* 'up)
 ⇒ ERROR
```

***13.12** Write the function **print-board**, which prints the nine-element board vector as three rows of elements. Also, place lines around the board as follows:

```
(print-board *board*)
 ⇒ -------------
 ⇒ | 1 | 2 | 3 |
 ⇒ -------------
 ⇒ | 5 | 6 | 4 |
 ⇒ -------------
 ⇒ |   | 8 | 7 |
 ⇒ -------------
```

13.13 Write `convert-representation`, which takes one argument representing the board. If the board is a nine-element vector it returns a three-by-three array. If the board is a three-by-three array, it returns a nine-element vector.

```
(setf *array-board* (convert-representation *board*))
⇒ #2A((1 2 3) (5 6 4) (NIL 8 7))

(convert-representation *array-board*)
⇒ #(1 2 3 5 6 4 NIL 8 7)
```

13.5 Sequences

Sequences are any of the LISP data types that have a sequential structure, namely lists, strings, and vectors. Common LISP has generic functions that operate on these types of sequences. Two sequence functions that manipulate lists are `length` and `reverse`. They operate equally well on vectors and strings.

(`length` *sequence*)

(`reverse` *sequence*)

```
;; Define the puzzle board.
(setf *board* (vector 1 2 3 6 nil 4 5 8 7))
⇒ #(1 2 3 6 NIL 4 5 8 7)

;; Reverse the board.
(reverse *board*)
⇒ #(7 8 5 4 NIL 6 3 2 1)

;; Determine the number of elements in the board.
(length *board*)
⇒ 9

;; Try them with a string.
(length "Move Left")
⇒ 9

(reverse "Move left")
⇒ "tfel evoM"
```

`Elt` returns an element within a sequence, just as `nth` operates upon lists, `aref` operates upon vectors, and `char` operates upon strings. `Elt` also has a `setf` version for destructively replacing the element of the sequence.

```
(elt sequence index)
```

```
(setf (elt sequence index) S-expression)
```

```
;; This demonstrates elt on lists, vectors and strings.
(aref *board* 5)
 ⇒ 4

(elt *board* 5)
 ⇒ 4

;; This destructively changes the first element.
(setf (elt *board* 0) 9)
 ⇒ 9

*board*
 ⇒ #(9 2 3 6 NIL 4 5 8 7)

;; Which is equivalent to the setf form for aref.
(setf (aref *board* 0) 1)
 ⇒ 1

*board*
 ⇒ #(1 2 3 6 NIL 4 5 8 7)

;; Elt operates on lists and strings.
(elt '(0 1 2 3 4 5) 3)
 ⇒ 3

(elt "Nice Move" 3)
 ⇒ #\e
```

You can create a sequence based upon a type argument using the function `make-sequence`.

```
(make-sequence type S-expression)
```

```
(make-sequence type S-expression :initial-element S-expression)
```

The type should evaluate to one of the following symbols – `vector`, `string`, and `list`. This creates a sequence of the type indicated in the first argument with length equal to the second element. You may use the `:initial-element` option to specify the initial elements. Notice the default values for each type of sequence when no initial element is specified.

```
(make-sequence 'vector 3)
 ⇒ #(LISP::*UNDEFINED* LISP::*UNDEFINED* LISP::*UNDEFINED*)

(make-sequence 'vector 3 :initial-element nil)
 ⇒ #(NIL NIL NIL)

(make-sequence 'list 5)
 ⇒ (NIL NIL NIL NIL NIL)

(make-sequence 'string 4)
 ⇒ "    "
```

You may want to apply destructive operations to a sequence without changing the original sequence. The function `copy-seq` copies the sequence before you make a destructive change. It makes a top-level copy of the argument sequence and returns the copy. Top-level means that only the sequence is copied. The various elements in the new sequence are exactly the same elements as in the original.

(copy-seq *sequence*)

In this example, we copy the vector in `*board*` into `*new-board*` and then change the first element of `*new-board*`. We then verify that only `*new-board*` is changed.

```
*board*
 ⇒ #(1 2 3 6 NIL 4 5 8 7)

(setf *new-board* (copy-seq *board*))
 ⇒ #(1 2 3 6 NIL 4 5 8 7)

(setf (elt *new-board* 0) 9)
 ⇒ 9

*new-board*
 ⇒ #(9 2 3 6 NIL 4 5 8 7)

*board*
 ⇒ #(1 2 3 6 NIL 4 5 8 7)
```

The fact that this is a top-level copy is important. New copies of nested sequences are *not* created. In this example, a destructive operation to a nested sequence occurs in both places.

```
;; *test* is a vector of vectors.
(setf *test* (vector (vector 1 2) (vector 3 4)))
 ⇒ #(#(1 2) #(3 4))
```

```
(setf *test-copy* (copy-seq *test*))
 ⇒ #(#(1 2) #(3 4))

;; Replace the first element of the first vector of
;; *test-copy*.
(setf (elt (elt *test-copy* 0) 0) 99)
 ⇒ 99

*test-copy*
 ⇒ #(#(99 2) #(3 4))

*test*
 ⇒ #(#(99 2) #(3 4))
```

The `subseq` function returns a subrange of a sequence. The first argument is the sequence and the second argument is the starting index of the subsequence. If no third argument is present, then the sequence continues through the end. If a third argument is present, then the subsequence stops before the index of the third argument.

(subseq *sequence start*)

(subseq *sequence start end*)

Suppose we want to gain access to complete rows out of the puzzle. Using the vector representation, each row is stored at location 0, 3, and 6.

```
;; Extract the first row.
(subseq *board* 0 3)
 ⇒ #(1 2 3)

;; Extract the second row.
(subseq *board* 3 6)
 ⇒ #(6 NIL 4)

;; Extract the last row.
(subseq *board* 6)
 ⇒ #(5 8 7)
```

`Concatenate` operates like `append`. It creates a new sequence that is the combined size of the arguments. The type of the new sequence is indicated by the first argument. The result type is an S-expression that must evaluate to either the symbol `string`, `vector`, or `list`. This new sequence then contains all of the elements in the remaining arguments.

```
(concatenate result-type sequence*)
```

Suppose that we want to swap the top and bottom rows of the puzzle board. Concatenate with the appropriate calls to subseq can perform the operation.

```
(concatenate 'vector (subseq *board* 6) (subseq *board* 3 6)
             (subseq *board* 0 3))
 ⇒ #(5 8 7 6 NIL 4 1 2 3)
```

The map function is like mapcar, except it operates upon strings, vectors, and lists. The only difference between them is that map's first argument specifies the result type as mentioned for concatenate.

```
(map result-type function sequence sequence*)
```

Map could be used to compute the number of tiles that are in their correct location. The following function closeness takes two arguments, the current board and the goal board. The sequences passed to map don't need to be the same type. So, we will pass the current board to closeness as a vector and the goal board as a list.

```
;;; Compute the number of tiles that are in the correct
;;; location, according to the goal board in the second
;;; argument.

(defun closeness (current-board goal-board)
  (apply #'+ (map 'list
                  #'(lambda (cb gb)
                      (if (not (equal cb gb)) 1 0))
                  current-board goal-board)))
 ⇒ CLOSENESS

;; Test closeness with *board*.
(closeness *board* '(1 2 3 4 5 6 7 8 NIL))
 ⇒ 5
```

Many of the following sequence functions do some kind of comparison or searching. They use the default eql for comparison. More complex structures require the equal comparison. This may be specified by placing :test #'equal after all of the arguments. For example, the assoc function, initially defined in Chapter 2, may also take this additional argument to allow it to find matches on more complicated objects, like nested lists. The default test is to use eql and thus won't correctly find these complicated values.

```
(assoc S-expression a-list :test #'equal)
```

```
(assoc '(1) '(((2) 99) ((1) 88) ((2) 77)))
 ⇒ NIL

;; This uses the equal test and produces the anticipated
;; answer.
(assoc '(1) '(((2) 99) ((1) 88) ((2) 77)) :test #'equal)
 ⇒ ((1) 88)
```

`Substitute` replaces occurrences of the second argument with the first argument in the sequence specified by the third argument. `Substitute` only operates on the top level, and so it doesn't substitute any nested structures. `Substitute` is not destructive.

(`substitute` *new-S-expression old-S-expression sequence*)

Substitute could replace the `nil` with an `X` to represent the empty position.

```
(substitute 'X NIL *board*)
 ⇒ #(1 2 3 6 X 4 5 8 7)

;; Notice that this is non-destructive.
*board*
 ⇒ #(1 2 3 6 NIL 4 5 8 7)
```

`Position` searches a sequence given as the second argument and finds an occurrence of the first argument. It returns the index position of the item. If an item occurs more than once in the sequence, it returns the position of the first occurrence from the left.

(`position` *item sequence*)

`Position` is ideal for finding the empty space in the 8-puzzle.

```
;; Find the empty position in *board*.
(position NIL *board*)
 ⇒ 4
```

`Count` searches a sequence, the second argument, for all occurrences of the first argument and returns the number of occurrences. If it doesn't find the item in the sequence, it returns zero.

(`count` *item sequence*)

```
(count 1 '(1 2 3 1 2 3 1 2 3))
 ⇒ 3
```

The last sequence function is `sort`. `Sort` takes two arguments, a sequence and a predicate. The predicate must take two arguments and return non-`nil` when the first argument is less than the second argument. The predicate is called during the sorting process with two elements from the sequence. Suppose that we wish to sort a list of numbers. If the predicate function is `<`, then the resulting sequence is sorted in ascending order. If the predicate function is `>` then the numbers are sorted in descending order. If the elements are more complicated structures, you must write your own predicate function to compute some kind of ordering. `Sort` performs its operation destructively and, as you can see in the example, doesn't even preserve the elements in the original list.

(sort *sequence predicate*)

The first few calls to sort demonstrate the simple sorts.

```
(setf something-to-sort '(4 22 3 1 99 5))
 ⇒ (4 22 3 1 99 5)

;; Sort in ascending numerical order.
(sort something-to-sort #'<)
 ⇒ (1 3 4 5 22 99)

;; Notice that something-to-sort changed and lost some
;; elements.
something-to-sort
 ⇒ (4 5 22 99)

;; Sort in descending order.
(sort '(4 22 3 1 99 5) #'>)
 ⇒ (99 22 5 4 3 1)
```

Alphabetical sorts of symbols are a little more difficult. We need to translate a symbol into a string so that we can use one of the string comparison functions. The function `symbol-name` translates a symbol into its corresponding print name.

(symbol-name *symbol*)

```
;; Ascending alphabetical sort.
(sort '(now is the time for all good men)
      #'(lambda (a b)
          (string< (symbol-name a) (symbol-name b))))
 ⇒ (ALL FOR GOOD IS MEN NOW THE TIME)

;; Finally, a numeric sort on the cars of lists.
```

```
(sort '((77 this) (2 that) (33 this and that))
      #'(lambda (a b) (< (car a) (car b))))
⇒ ((2 THAT) (33 THIS AND THAT) (77 THIS))
```

EXERCISES

***13.14** Define your own version of the following sequence functions: `elt`, `subseq`, `substitute`, `position`, and `count`. You may implement the functions in any order and may use your functions in the other functions. You should write a `setf` form of `elt`. Also, you may assume that the arguments will always be valid, so no error checking is required.

13.15 Write a function to convert between a string and a vector. If the argument is a string, then the result is a vector of characters and visa versa.

```
(convert "123564 87")
⇒ #(#\1 #\2 #\3 #\5 #\6 #\4 #\space #\8
⇒         #\7)
```

13.6 List Surgery

We have seen that destructive sequence operations can apply to lists. There are also destructive operations especially for lists. They should be used with caution since you can create circular lists by pointing the `cdr` to some place earlier in the list. Circular lists aren't bad if they are intentional. You can write code that knows about the circularity and doesn't try to find the end of the list.

Before viewing each of the functions, we must create some lists that can be manipulated.

```
;; Some simple lists to be used for list surgery.
(setf list-1 '(a b c))
⇒ (A B C)

(setf list-2 '(d e f))
⇒ (D E F)

(setf cdr-list-1 (cdr list-1))
⇒ (B C)

(setf cdr-list-2 (cdr list-2))
⇒ (E F)
```

Figure 13.6 illustrates the box notation for each of these lists.

We will now append the two lists together and see that nothing changes, because `append` copies the first list before appending. The boxes in Figure 13.7 demonstrate the effects.

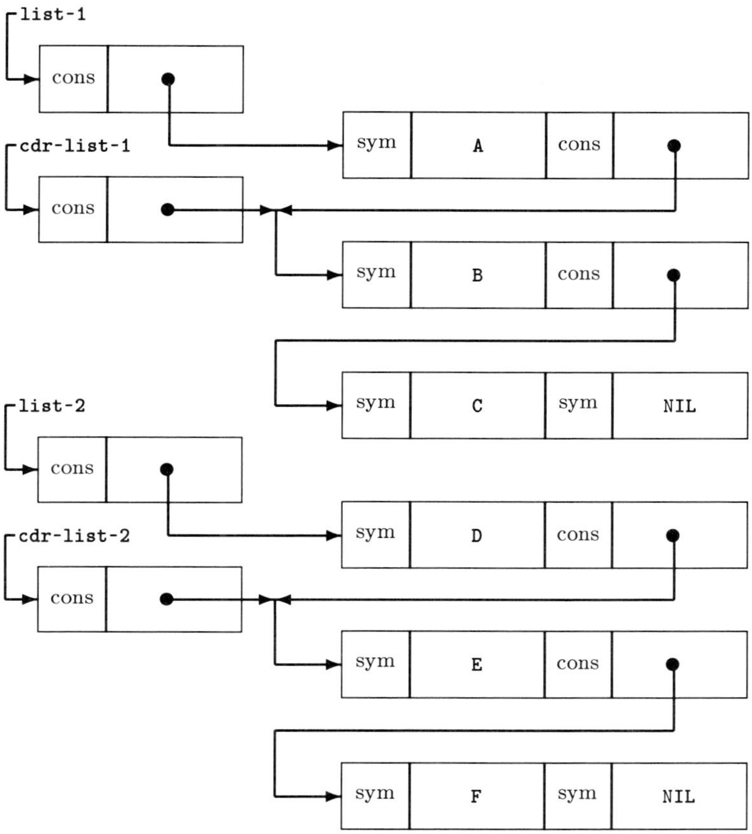

Figure 13.6 The Lists Used in the Examples

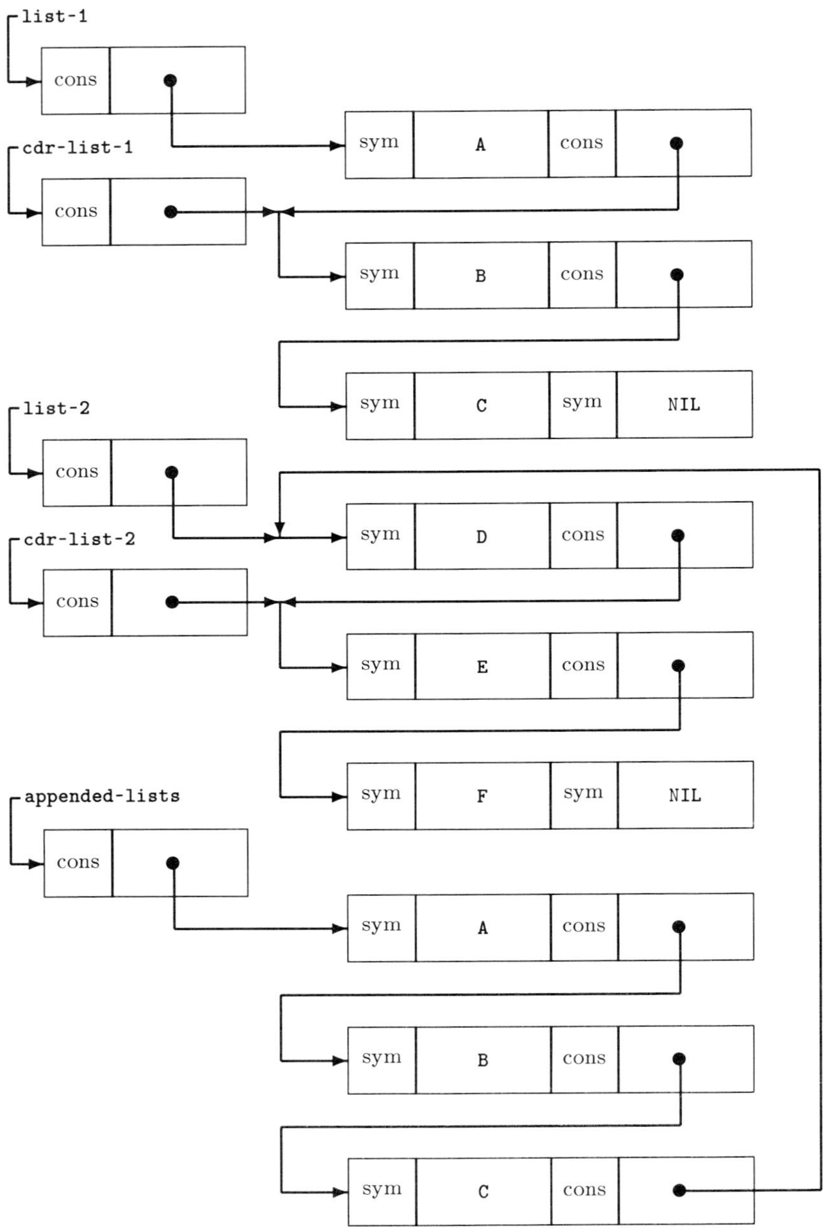

Figure 13.7 The `Append` of the Lists

```
;; Append the two lists together.
(setf appended-lists (append list-1 list-2))
 ⇒ (A B C D E F)

list-1
 ⇒ (A B C)

list-2
 ⇒ (D E F)

cdr-list-1
 ⇒ (B C)

cdr-list-2
 ⇒ (E F)
```

The `nconc` function is like `append`, except that it destructively appends the lists. The result of invoking `nconc` on these lists is demonstrated in Figure 13.8. Notice that it changes `list-1`, but `cdr-list-1` is still semantically correct – it is the `cdr` of `list-1`.

(nconc *S-expression**)

```
;; Nconc the lists.
(setf nconced-lists (nconc list-1 list-2))
 ⇒ (A B C D E F)

;; Now look at list-1 and see that it has been changed.
list-1
 ⇒ (A B C D E F)

;; No difference for list-2
list-2
 ⇒ (D E F)

;; The cdr of list-1 has also changed.
cdr-list-1
 ⇒ (B C D E F)

;; But the cdr of list-2 has not.
cdr-list-2
 ⇒ (E F)
```

The most primitive list surgery functions are `rplaca` (replace `car`) and `rplacd` (replace `cdr`). The first argument is the list that we are changing and the second argument is the new value for the `car` or the `cdr`.

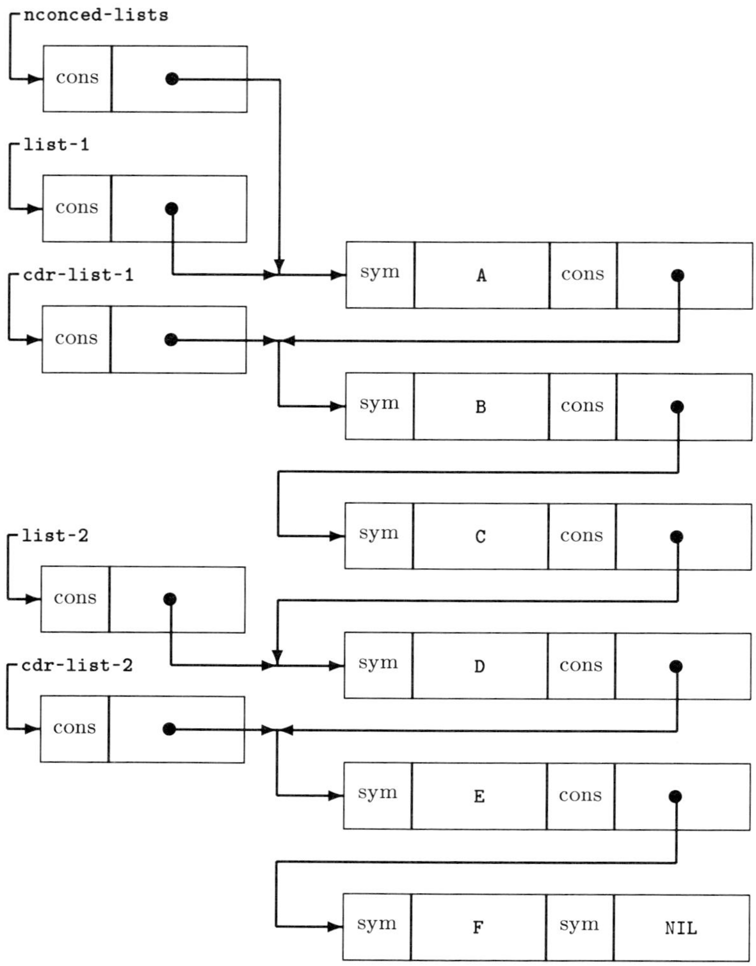

Figure 13.8 The `Nconc` of the Lists

(rplaca *S-expression S-expression*)

(rplacd *S-expression S-expression*)

There are also setf versions that correspond to rplaca and rplacd. They are indicated with a car and cdr respectively in the operator position of the setf. There is also a destructive version of nth that uses the setf syntax. This replaces the *nth* element of the list with a new value.

(setf (car *S-expression*) *S-expression*)

(setf (cdr *S-expression*) *S-expression*)

(setf (nth *index S-expression*) *S-expression*)

Figures 13.9, 13.10, and 13.11 give the box notation after each significant operation. Notice how the two LISP items with C and nil are no longer pointed to by any other LISP item. This demonstrates the creation of garbage. The system garbage collector will eventually reclaim the space used by these two items. This dynamic storage management is an important feature of LISP. You can write programs without explicitly allocating and freeing storage.

```
;; Rplaca and Rplacd replace the car and cdr's destructively.
(setf a-new-list '(a b c))
 ⇒ (A B C)

(rplaca a-new-list 34)
 ⇒ (34 B C)

a-new-list
 ⇒ (34 B C)

(rplacd (cdr a-new-list) '(new cdr))
 ⇒ (B NEW CDR)

a-new-list
 ⇒ (34 B NEW CDR)
```

The delete function destructively removes all top-level occurrences of the first argument from the second argument list. Remove is the non-destructive equivalent.

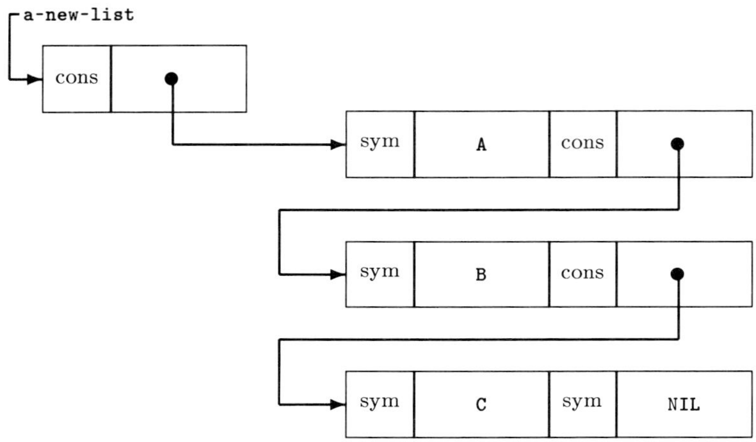

Figure 13.9 Before Calling `rplaca`

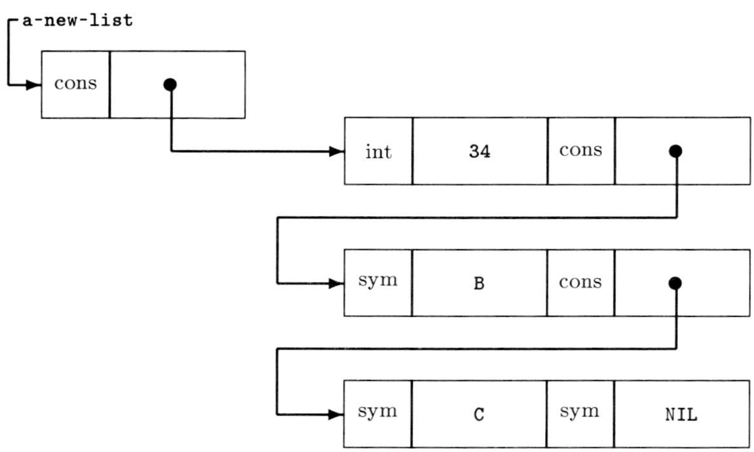

Figure 13.10 After Calling `rplaca`

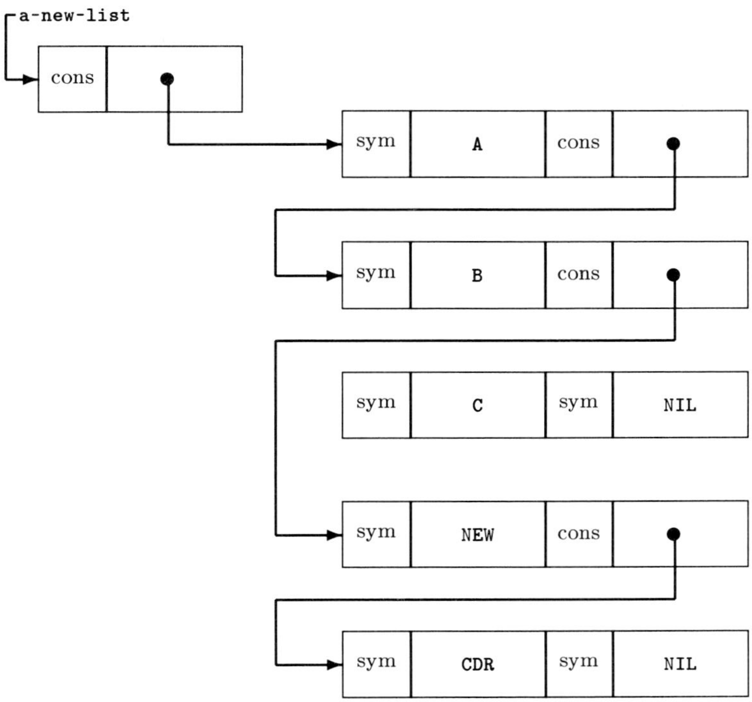

Figure 13.11 After Calling `rplacd`

(delete *S-expression S-expression*)

(remove *S-expression S-expression*)

```
;; Demonstrate the destructive and non-destructive deleting
;; functions.
(setf another-list '(a b c d e f g))
 ⇒ (A B C D E F G)

(remove 'c another-list)
 ⇒ (A B D E F G)

another-list
 ⇒ (A B C D E F G)

;; Delete is destructive.
(delete 'c another-list)
 ⇒ (A B D E F G)

another-list
 ⇒ (A B D E F G)
```

There are many more surgery functions defined in Common LISP. Please review the language description for more information [40].

EXERCISES

13.16 Write destructive and non-destructive versions of the two sequence functions, `reverse` and `remove`. Restrict the arguments to be lists.

***13.17** Write the same `move-tile` function mentioned in the arrays section, except use a list representation. In your first version, don't use any destructive operations. Don't bother with the error checking for an illegal move. In the second version, go ahead and use destructive operations and notice how much simpler the code is.

13.7 Summary

This chapter introduced an internal representation of LISP, which uses tags and pointers to define LISP items. This type of structure is needed for the run-time typing that is a characteristic of LISP. The box notation helps to explain the differences between `eql`, which compares LISP items without following any pointers and `equal`, which compares entire structures. Strings are vectors of characters and are represented in LISP with a leading and a trailing `"`. Common

LISP supports multi-dimensional arrays for creating and organizing a fixed set of data. Strings, vectors, and lists are collectively known as sequences and Common LISP has a number of functions which operate on them. Finally, Common LISP defines a number of destructive operations for lists. These operations are dangerous because they can have unexpected consequences. However, they are useful because you can simply replace parts of lists instead of reconstructing them.

Chapter Exercises

This set of exercises investigates a sub-field of artificial intelligence that was abandoned many years ago, but is now experiencing a revival. This area encompasses machine learning, where the systems do not rely on a large, precomputed knowledge base but instead derive the knowledge base during the processing. The particular task we will accomplish is an implementation of a "Predictor Using Slides and Strings" (PUSS) as proposed by John H. Andrae in "Thinking with the Teachable Machine" [4]. A PUSS is a system that makes predictions about future events based upon events it has seen before. This version will be slightly different from that of Andrae, but the results will be the same. The goal of our PUSS will be to write children's stories.

The idea of the system is to gather phrases from a "seed" story to form a knowledge base of phrases. The knowledge base is a list of the phrases along with the collection of words that follow the phrase. The system is given an initial phrase, it scans the knowledge base searching for the phrase, randomly selects a word from the associated list, and creates a new phrase to use. The system continues until a story is generated. For example, given the following story:

```
See Babs Run . Run Babs Run . See Babs Play . See Babs Run .
```

The knowledge base contains the following two-word phrases:

```
;; Phrase    Following words
((("Play" ".") "See")
 (("Babs" "Play") ".")
 (("." "See") "Babs" "Babs")
 (("Run" "Babs") "Run")
 (("." "Run") "Babs")
 (("Run" ".") "See" "Run")
 (("Babs" "Run") "." "." ".")
 (("See" "Babs") "Run" "Play" "Run"))
```

A randomly generated story might be as follows, given the initial phrase `("Run" "Babs")`:

```
Run Babs Run.
```

```
Run Babs Run.
See Babs Run.
```

1. Your first exercise is to write a function that is called with a phrase and the next word as arguments and updates the knowledge base stored in `*story-base*`. You are free to choose destructive or non-destructive operations. Note, you might want to use the `:test` option to `assoc`.

```
(defvar *story-base* nil)
 ⇒ *STORY-BASE*

(add-phrase '("See" "Babs") "Run")
 ⇒ ((("See" "Babs") "Run"))

(add-phrase '("See" "Babs") "Walk")
 ⇒ (("See" "Babs") "Walk" "Run")
```

***2.** Now write a function `learn`, which takes the name of a story file and the number of words to be used for each phrase. The function reads the words from the file and invokes `add-phrase` on each phrase and following word. You will not be able to just call `read`, because it will have difficulty with the period. You must perform the reading yourself using something like `read-char` and then construct the string. Your read routine should be robust enough to handle the spaces and newlines between words. You may assume that a period will be separated from the previous word by white space.

```
(learn "simple.story" 2)
 ⇒ NIL
```

3. Write a function that when given a phrase, returns one of the words associated with the phrase from `*story-base*`. It should scan the list, looking for the matching phrase. Once that is found, it should call `random` to select one of the associated words. That word is then returned to the caller. If the phrase is not present, then return `nil`.

```
(get-word '("See" "Babs"))
 ⇒ "Run"

(get-word '("Babs" "Run"))
 ⇒ "."
```

***4.** Write the function `build-story`, which accepts a starting phrase as an argument, along with a count of the number of sentences to generate, and prints the generated story. It should first print out the two words in the phrase in a nice format. Then it should call `get-word` to get the next word, and print that out. It then loops calling `get-word` with the new phrase constructed from the second element of the original phrase and the new word. Just for practice, use `nconc` to construct the new phrase. When the argument number of periods are printed, then stop printing.

```
(build-story '("Run" "Babs") 3)
 ⇒ Run Babs Run.
 ⇒ See Babs Run.
 ⇒ See Babs Play.
 ⇒ NIL
```

5. Write the main driver function **puss**, which takes three arguments, the name of the file to read, the size of the phrases, and the number of sentences to generate. It then invokes **learn** and **build-story**. It must randomly select a starting phrase from those in the story.

```
(puss "simple.story" 2 3)
⇒ Run Babs Run.
⇒ See Babs Play.
⇒ See Babs Run.
⇒ NIL
```

Function Summary

The following lists the functions and topics covered in this chapter.

- LISP Items with a tag and information part
- Dot Notation
- (consp *S-expression*)
- (eq *S-expression S-expression*)
- (eql *S-expression S-expression*)
- (char *string integer*)
- (string *character*)
- (string= *string string*)
- (string-equal *string string*)
- (string< *string string*)
- (string> *string string*)
- (string<= *string string*)
- (string>= *string string*)
- (string/= *string string*)
- (string-lessp *string string*)
- (string-greaterp *string string*)
- (string-not-greaterp *string string*)
- (string-not-lessp *string string*)
- (string-not-equal *string string*)
- (make-string *size*)
- (make-string *size* :initial-element *character*)
- (intern *string*)
- (string-trim *character-string string*)
- (string-left-trim *character-string string*)
- (string-right-trim *character-string string*)
- (string-upcase *string*)
- (string-downcase *string*)
- (string-capitalize *string*)
- (nstring-upcase *string*)

- (nstring-downcase *string*)
- (nstring-capitalize *string*)
- (make-array *S-expression*)
- (make-array *S-expression* :initial-element *S-expression*)
- (make-array *S-expression* :initial-contents *S-expression*)
- (aref *array S-expression S-expression**)
- (setf (aref *array S-expression S-expression**) *S-expression*)
- (array-dimension *array S-expression*)
- (vector *S-expression**)
- (equalp *S-expression S-expression*)
- (length *sequence*)
- (reverse *sequence*)
- (elt *sequence index*)
- (setf (elt *sequence index*) *S-expression*)
- (make-sequence *type S-expression*)
- (make-sequence *type S-expression* :initial-element *S-expression*)
- (copy-seq *sequence*)
- (subseq *sequence start*)
- (subseq *sequence start end*)
- (concatenate *result-type sequence**)
- (map *result-type function sequence sequence**)
- (substitute *new-S-expression old-S-expression sequence*)
- (position *item sequence*)
- (count *item sequence*)
- (sort *sequence predicate*)
- (symbol-name *symbol*)
- (nconc *S-expression**)
- (rplaca *S-expression S-expression*)
- (rplacd *S-expression S-expression*)
- (setf (car *S-expression*) *S-expression*)
- (setf (cdr *S-expression*) *S-expression*)
- (setf (nth *S-expression*) *S-expression*)
- (delete *S-expression S-expression*)
- (remove *S-expression S-expression*)

14 PROGRAMMING STYLE

CLEAR AND CONCISE LISP programs can be hard to write. Many beginning LISP programmers have preconceived ideas of style and format. Their programs look like FORTRAN, Pascal, or C programs. This chapter illustrates good LISP programming style. It shows how to modify some constructs you've already seen, and it introduces some new LISP constructs that promote better programming style.

14.1 Source File Organization

You can immediately evaluate LISP expressions by typing them to the LISP system. But, you don't usually do that with entire LISP programs. You usually prepare source files with a text editor. Large projects usually require more than one source file for the whole system. A standard format for these files makes them easier to read and maintain.

Style Rule 1: *A LISP source file should include the following ordered items: header, descriptive comments, globals, macros, and finally the functions themselves.*

Each file should have a standard header that specifies some useful information, like author, date created, last update, and so on. The following is a sample header:

```
;;;;;;;;;;;;;;;;;;;;;;;;;;;;;;;;;;;;;;;;;;;;;;;;;;;;;;;;;;;;
; File:         objects.l
; Description:  Simple Object System
; Author:       Robert R. Kessler, University of Utah
; Created:      21-May-86
; Last Change:  21-Jan-87
;
; (c) Copyright 1986, University of Utah, all rights reserved
;;;;;;;;;;;;;;;;;;;;;;;;;;;;;;;;;;;;;;;;;;;;;;;;;;;;;;;;;;;;
```

```
; Revisions:
;  21-Jan-87 (Kessler) - added :printable option to objects.
;  ...
;;;;;;;;;;;;;;;;;;;;;;;;;;;;;;;;;;;;;;;;;;;;;;;;;;;;;;;;;;;;;;
```

It's a good idea to keep a change log of program revisions as illustrated in this header. Some operating systems automatically provide this facility. If they don't, a simple recording of the change date, person responsible for the change, and description of the change is useful.

A description of the program should follow the header. It notes any interesting features, explains how the program works, and how it's organized. It's also good to note any known bugs or problems with the program. Next, list all of the variables in the file declared with `defvar`. These belong at the top of the file so they are easily seen and found. Any macro definitions used in the file should come next. This is important when you compile your file. You must define all macros used in a function before you can compile that function. So, you should place all macros at the top of the file. Finally, define the functions. If you place the *main driver* function first, your code is "top-down," and if you place it last it is "bottom-up." The choice is yours. It depends on what makes the most sense when reading the program.

Style Rule 2: *Isolate machine-dependent code in separate files to ease the burden of transporting software to new systems. Place macro and* `defvar` *definitions in separate files and create a load file to connect everything together.*

A large software project usually requires multiple files. You should group the functions into logical units. For example, the object system could be divided into the functions for object definition, method definition, and run-time support. You should also isolate those functions that are machine-dependent in a separate file. When you transport the software to a new system, the machine-dependent file will require customization, while the rest of the system should transport as is. Also, for large projects, your macro definitions and `defvars` should be in separate files. They are used throughout the code and can be loaded into those files needing their definitions. Also, you should create a "load" file, which loads all parts of the system to connect it all together.

EXERCISES

***14.1** Write a function that will add a header to a LISP source code file. Use the header outlined earlier as your guide. It should take as arguments the name of the file, the author's name, a description, and the date the file was created. The `add-header` function should then read the file and check to see if a header is already present. If it is, then nothing is done. Otherwise, it adds a header to the front of the file. Verifying that the header is present can be accomplished by looking at the second line to see if it has `; File:` at the beginning of the second line.

```
(add-header "objects.l"
            "Robert R. Kessler, University of Utah"
            "Simple Object System" "21-May-86")
 ⇒ T

(add-header "objects.l"
            "Robert R. Kessler, University of Utah"
            "Simple Object System" "21-May-86")
 ⇒ Header already on file: objects.l
 ⇒ NIL
```

Implementation of this function requires two functions which are discussed in detail in Chapter 17. In summary, **delete-file** removes its argument file from the system and **rename-file** changes the name of the first file to be the second file.

> (delete-file *file*)

> (rename-file *old-file new-file*)

14.2 Enhance the definition of the **add-header** so the created date is an optional argument. When the date is not provided, you are to use today's date. The functions for accessing date and time are described in Chapter 17, but you can use the following subroutine to return the current date as day, month, and year.

```
;;; Returns the current date as a list of day, month, and
;;; year.

(defun date ()
  (multiple-value-bind (second minute hour day month year)
    (get-decoded-time)
    (list day month year)))
 ⇒ DATE

(date)
 ⇒ (24 6 1987)
```

14.2 Function Philosophy

As you write more LISP code, you learn how to best organize your functions and how to partition the problem.

One of the first consideration is outlined in the following rule:

Style Rule 3: *Functions should generally be kept very short. A 30-line maximum is a good rule of thumb.*

A few small functions are better than a long function. They are easier to conceptualize, easier to write, and easier to maintain. You can break the problem into subproblems and write a small function for each subproblem. Most modern LISP system developers have gone to great lengths to make function calls as efficient as possible to support this style. Some LISP implementations do better than more conventional languages on tests involving only function calls (see the TAK benchmark in [15] for timings across various languages). Small functions are easier to maintain because the semantics of the interface is simpler. This decreases the chance of side effects elsewhere in the program.

Style Rule 4: *Limit the use of operations with side effects.*

Small functions are basic to functional programming [20]. Functional programming means writing functions with no side effects. You don't use any global variables and few local variables, and don't perform destructive operations. We do not advocate a pure functional programming style. However, you should avoid operations with side effects when possible.

Style Rule 5: *Use the data-driven style instead of directly coding function calls.*

Using many small functions is amenable to the data-driven style of programming. Data-driven techniques to select the function to call make it easier to modify the code and add new operations. This does not follow the functional style, since the best place to put the function selections is in a global variable. With data-driven code, you need interface functions or macros. Adding new data and their associated functions is then explicit.

Style Rule 6: *Use data-abstraction techniques.*

Data abstraction implies that access to any data item is isolated to small functions or macros. As a program evolves, new requirements invariably force changes to the data structures. Isolating data structure access results in isolating changes to the data structures. Objects provide this mechanism, which is why they are stressed in this text.

If operations are too specific, they can end up being too complicated. If you can generalize the operation, you will usually simplify the functions. For example, suppose that you want to write a program for the game of tic-tac-toe to determine if someone has won. Also, suppose that the game is represented as a list of nine elements, where any element is either `X`, `O`, or `nil`. The `nil` means the position isn't filled in with an `X` or `O` yet. The numbered elements of the list match the board as follows:

```
0 1 2
3 4 5
6 7 8
```

Thus, the following game position:

```
   X  X
O  X  O
O
```

would be represented as the following list:

```
(nil x x o x o o nil nil)
```

Your goal is to write a predicate function that is given a game represented as the above list, and an argument that is X or O, and returns T if the game has been won by the second argument, and returns nil otherwise. Recall that three of the same marks must be in a row (vertical, horizontal, or diagonal) to win. Your first implementation might appear as follows:

```
;;; Determine if the game board is a win for the second
;;; argument.
;;; WARNING -- VERY BAD VERSION.

(defun winp (board x-or-o)
  (or (and (eql (nth 0 board) x-or-o)
           (eql (nth 1 board) x-or-o)
           (eql (nth 2 board) x-or-o))
      (and (eql (nth 3 board) x-or-o)
           (eql (nth 4 board) x-or-o)
           (eql (nth 5 board) x-or-o))
    ...
  ))
```

This version has three lines for each of the 8 different combinations of a win, or 25 total lines including the defun. Notice that the and expression is identical in each instance, except the indices are different. We could extract this part as a new function and decrease the code size considerably.

```
;;; Verify if the indices as arguments are all the same as
;;; the fifth argument.

(defun check-same (board first-index second-index third-index
                   x-or-o)
  (and (eql (nth first-index board) x-or-o)
       (eql (nth second-index board) x-or-o)
       (eql (nth third-index board) x-or-o)))
⇒ CHECK-SAME

;;; Likewise, winp can be changed to reflect this new
```

```
;;; function.
;;; A BETTER VERSION - BUT STILL DIRECTLY INCLUDES THE LIST
;;; INDICES.

(defun winp (board x-or-o)
  (or (check-same board 0 1 2 x-or-o)
      (check-same board 3 4 5 x-or-o)
      (check-same board 6 7 8 x-or-o)
      (check-same board 0 3 6 x-or-o)
      (check-same board 1 4 7 x-or-o)
      (check-same board 2 5 8 x-or-o)
      (check-same board 0 4 8 x-or-o)
      (check-same board 2 4 6 x-or-o)))
⇒ WINP
```

There is still some regularity to this scanning, so it can be further improved. Horizontal scanning starts at each row and increments by one. The rows are determined by adding the number of columns to the index of the previous row. The vertical is computed similarly. The left-to-right diagonal starts at zero and is incremented by the number of columns plus one, and the other diagonal starts at the number of columns minus one and is incremented by the number of columns minus one. Using this information, we can write a generic routine that will determine if a win is present on an arbitrary-sized, square board.

```
;;; Determine if elements number of the elements of the
;;; board, starting at starting-index, incremented by
;;; increment are all equal to x-or-o.

(defun check-same (board starting-index increment elements
                         x-or-o)
  (dotimes (each-element elements t)
    (if (not (eql (nth (+ starting-index
                          (* each-element increment))
                       board)
                  x-or-o))
      (return nil))))
⇒ CHECK-SAME

;;; Check horizontal, vertical, and diagonals for any winning
;;; position.

(defun winp (board x-or-o)
  (let ((size (truncate (sqrt (length board)))))
    (or (dotimes (each-row size)
          (if (check-same board (* each-row size) 1 size
```

```
                                    x-or-o)
              (return t)))
          (dotimes (each-column size)
            (if (check-same board each-column size size x-or-o)
              (return t)))
          (check-same board 0 (1+ size) size x-or-o)
          (check-same board (1- size) (1- size) size x-or-o))))
⇒ WINP

(winp '(nil nil nil x x x o nil o) 'x)
⇒ T

(winp '(nil nil nil x x x o nil o) 'o)
⇒ NIL

(winp '(nil nil nil x o o x o x x nil o x nil o nil) 'x)
⇒ T
```

This gives us a completely general solution to the problem that is clear and easy to understand.

EXERCISES

***14.3** Rewrite the following code using good programming style outlined in this section, and especially concentrate on data-driven techniques:

```
(defun guesswhat (argument)
  (setf result 0)
  (dolist (i argument)
    (if (equal (car i) 'add)
      (setf result (+ result
                      (eval (append (list '+) (cdr i))))))
    (if (equal (car i) 'mult)
      (setf result (+ result
                      (eval (append (list '*) (cdr i))))))
    (if (equal (car i) 'minus)
      (setf result (+ result
                      (eval (append (list '-) (cdr i)))))))
  result)
```

14.4 Suppose that we changed **argument** in **guesswhat** so that it is now a vector, instead of a list. Determine what code has to be changed in your solution to make this change.

***14.5** Suppose that we change the **argument** in **guesswhat**, so it is a list of postfix operations. That means that each element contains the list of operands, followed by the operator. You should only have to change a few small functions. If not, rewrite your program so it can handle this kind of change.

14.3 Commenting

Commenting is one of the most important tools for conveying a program's meaning. Commenting begins with a good header on each file and a description of the contents of the file. The next level of commenting is for all global variables. Every global must be documented as to its use and purpose. Common LISP provides a documentation string or "doc-string" for short, which is an optional third argument to `defvar`.

(`defvar` *symbol S-expression string*)

This is nice for describing a variable. Comments describing a global are generally short, so using the doc-string keeps the declarations from becoming cluttered. Notice how the doc-string version is easier to read than the following:

```
;; Starting puzzle position.
(defvar *initial-state* nil)
;; The goal puzzle that we are to find.
(defvar *goal* nil)
```

And now the doc-string version.

```
(defvar *initial-state* nil "Starting puzzle position.")
(defvar *goal* nil "The goal puzzle that we are to find.")
```

Style Rule 7: *Use documentation strings with all calls to* `defvar`.

Doc-strings can be dynamically retrieved using the `documentation` function. `Documentation` has two arguments, the symbol whose doc-string you want to retrieve and the type of the symbol. For `defvar`, the type is the symbol `variable`.

(`documentation` *symbol type-symbol*)

This is useful if you want to find out the purpose of a variable.

```
(documentation '*initial-state* 'variable)
 ⇒ "Starting puzzle position."
```

Since `documentation` takes a type argument, you can define doc-strings for other symbols in the system. Functions and macros may be defined with a doc-string. The doc-string is optional and appears after the parameter list.

(`defun` *symbol* (*symbol**) *optional-doc-string S-expression**)

```
(defmacro macro-name (argument*) optional-doc-string S-expression*)
```

For example, the A* function might have the following description:

```
(defun A* (initial-state goal-state)
  "Searches for the set of transformations from the initial
   state into that of the goal state.  It utilizes the
   best-first algorithm, A*. For now, this is only a stub
   function."
  nil)
 ⇒ A*
```

Use the symbol function to retrieve the doc-string for functions and macros.

```
(documentation 'A* 'function)
 ⇒ "Searches for the set of transformations from the initial
 ⇒    state into that of the goal state.  It utilizes the
 ⇒    best-first algorithm, A*. For now, this is only a stub
 ⇒    function."
```

Style Rule 8: *All functions should have a comment describing what they do, what their arguments are, and what they return. List any side effects that a function performs. The comment should be placed just before the definition of the function.*

Ideally, you would like to be able to retrieve a lot of information about a function. But, trying to place too much information in a documentation string is a mistake. If you tried to place a lot of information in a documentation string, you make the function definition very hard to read. Your best bet is to place the long descriptive comment before the defun and not clutter the function definition.

Style Rule 9: *Use a documentation string to specify the argument interface.*

Some Common LISP practitioners feel that the function doc-string should describe the argument interface. This provides you with a quick way of finding the arguments to a function. However, the argument specification is then in two places. This leaves open the possibility of updating it in one place and not the other. If you decide to use style rule 9, you should always be careful to keep the doc-string current with the argument specification. In many Common LISP systems, the doc-string has been defined for all Common LISP functions. This makes it easy to find out the details of a function without going to the manual. Notice in the following example, the doc-string even includes the chapter from [40] so you can find more details on the particular function.

These rules results in the following definition for A*. Notice that if you indent the doc-string directly under the argument specification, it will remind you to change the doc-string if you change the arguments.

```
;;; Searches for the set of transformations from the initial
;;; state into that of the goal state.  It utilizes the
;;; best-first algorithm, A*. For now, this is only a stub
;;; function.

(defun A* (initial-state goal-state)
     "(A* initial-state goal-state)"
  nil)
 ⇒ A*

(documentation 'A* 'function)
 ⇒ "(A* initial-state goal-state)"

;; This shows the documentation strings stored in this CL
;; implementation.
(documentation 'reverse 'function)
 ⇒ " (reverse sequence)   [14.1]
 ⇒ The REVERSE function returns a sequence containing the
 ⇒ same elements is in the argument sequence, but in reverse
 ⇒ order.  The argument is not modified. "
```

Style Rule 10: *You should always describe the structure of your data structures and outline how you expect the data to be used.*

Comments can also describe your data structures and their anticipated manipulation. In LISP, as in other programming languages, you can write obscure code that manipulates the various data structures. For example, this convoluted piece of code returns the reverse of the flattened first three elements of `*foo*`.

```
(setf *foo* '((1) (2) (3)))
 ⇒ ((1) (2) (3))

;; Very STRANGE code -- don't write code like this.
(cons (car (elt *foo* 2)) (append (nth 1 *foo*) (car *foo*)))
 ⇒ (3 2 1)
```

A comment stating the intention of the code and the form of the data can clear up the code.

Style Rule 11: *Don't overcomment within the body, unless something very complicated is going on. Also, don't restate as a comment what the LISP code is obviously doing.*

Generally, the bodies of most functions should be clear enough that you don't need comments. Unless something very complicated is taking place, don't bother to put in a comment – don't state the obvious. As a beginning LISP programmer, you might want to use commenting as a tool to help you develop your code. In this case, you might temporarily overcomment your code to help get it working. Once you have successfully completed the code, you can remove the extraneous comments. The following function was used in the last chapter. It doesn't require comments within the body, however, we have added some to illustrate overcommenting.

```
;;; Compute the number of values that are different between
;;; two vector arguments.  This routine is generic in that it
;;; compares the number of elements in the shortest vector
;;; (however, in reality they should be the same length).
;;; THIS FUNCTION CONTAINS EXTRANEOUS COMMENTS.

(defun compare-vectors (current-state goal)
  (let ((count 0)) ; Count contains the count of the number
                   ; of values that are different between the
                   ; two argument vectors.  It is initialized
                   ; to zero.
    (dotimes
      (vector-index ; This is the variable for indexing the
                    ; vector.
       (min (array-dimension current-state 0)
            (array-dimension goal 0))
       ;; The counting stops when we exceed the minimum
       ;; length of either of the argument vectors.
       count) ; The current value of count is returned.
      (if (not (equal (aref current-state vector-index)
                      (aref goal vector-index)))
        ;; If the element of the first argument vector
        ;; indexed by vector-index is not equal to the same
        ;; element within the second argument then we
        ;; increment the count variable.
        (setf count (1+ count))))))
 ⇒ COMPARE-VECTORS
```

Not only are the comments worthless, but it is hard to pick out the LISP code from the functions. The single comment at the top of the function provides adequate detail.

Style Rule 12: *Start placing comments into your program as soon as you start writing the program.*

You should get into the habit of commenting as you code. Most beginning students write their entire programs and then place the comments into the code later. Invariably, after partially completing the program, they get involved in other tasks and forget what they have done when returning to the program. Commenting the program from the outset will always pay off in the end. Using commenting as a design aid can also provides a good study reference. As your understanding and integration of the language increases, your use of comments can diminish.

EXERCISE

***14.6** After studying the following code, rewrite it using proper commenting as defined in this section. *Hint:* Study **winp** from the preceding section.

```
(defvar *x* 'X)
(defvar *o* 'O)
(defun opposite-x-or-o (x-or-o)
  (if (eql x-or-o *x*) ; If the argument x-or-o is equal to
                       ; 'x (which is what *x* is bound to,
                       ; then
    *o* ; return the opposite value, which is 'o, which is
        ; the value of *o*
    *x* ; otherwise return the opposite of o, which is 'x.
    ))
(defun possible-win (board start increment elements x-or-o)
  (let ((opposite
         (opposite-x-or-o x-or-o))) ; compute the opposite of
                                    ; an x or an o by calling
                                    ; the opposite-x-or-o
                                    ; function and storing
                                    ; the value in the symbol
                                    ; opposite.
    (dotimes (each-element elements t)
      (if (eql (elt board (+ start (* each-element
                                      increment)))
               opposite) ; if any board position has the
                         ; opposite value, then there is no
                         ; way that this is a possible win.
                         ; Possible wins are only those board
                         ; positions that either have the
                         ; argument value or they have a nil,
                         ; which means that they don't have
                         ; an x or an o yet.
        (return nil)))))
```

14.4 Indentation and Format

Proper indentation and format doesn't affect the functioning of a LISP program. They are tools to help you and other programmers understand the program. LISP has very little syntax, so proper indentation is imperative.

Style Rule 13: *Utilize the editor you may have available.*

Utilize whatever indentation facilities you may have available. You may have a LISP-based text editor like those provided on the LISP machines, or an editor with a LISP mode like the various Emacs derivatives. Using the same tool among a whole programming staff ensures a consistent convention in all the programs.

If you don't have an editor that automatically properly indents your code, you should study the indentation used in the examples in this text. Use two spaces for each new indentation level. Place those expressions that are on the same level in the same starting column. Then you won't have to count parentheses to find out which expressions are associated with an operation. The following is the same `compare-vectors` function used earlier. Notice how difficult it is to determine the functionality when incorrect indentation is used.

```
;;; IMPROPERLY INDENTED FUNCTION

(defun compare-vectors
  (current-state goal) (let
  ((count 0)) (dotimes (vector-index
    (min (array-dimension current-state
   0) (array-dimension
   goal 0)) count) (if
  (not (equal (aref
 current-state vector-index) (aref goal
  vector-index))) (setf
  count (1+ count)))
  )))
 ⇒ COMPARE-VECTORS
```

Style Rule 14: *Indent expressions so those at the same nesting level are in the same column. One rule of thumb is to indent two spaces for each nesting level.*

Also, try to keep all of an expression on a single line. When it doesn't fit on the line, you have two options. One is to indent the first argument on the next line a few spaces to the right of the current column. The other option is to try to fit as much as possible on the first line and then indent the second line to the column of the first argument. Generally, the second option is better; however, they both can be appropriate. The advantage of the second option is that it takes fewer vertical lines. The disadvantage is that it requires everything to be indented a large number of spaces. Notice in the following examples that both forms of indentation are used. The first example illustrates the first option, and the second example shows the second option.

```
;;; INDENTATION OF EVERYTHING ON THE NEXT LINE.

(defun compare-vectors (current-state goal)
```

```
  (let ((count 0))
    (dotimes
      (vector-index
       (min
        (array-dimension current-state 0)
        (array-dimension goal 0))
       count)
      (if (not (equal
                (aref current-state vector-index)
                (aref goal vector-index)))
        (setf count (1+ count))))))
⇒ COMPARE-VECTORS

;;; INDENTATION OF EVERYTHING ON THE SAME LINE.

(defun compare-vectors (current-state goal)
  (let ((count 0))
    (dotimes (vector-index
              (min (array-dimension current-state 0)
                   (array-dimension goal 0))
              count)
      (if (not (equal (aref current-state vector-index)
                      (aref goal vector-index)))
        (setf count (1+ count))))))
⇒ COMPARE-VECTORS
```

The second version looks better. The first one is very vertical and the second is more horizontal. Generally, you should prefer the horizontal mode because it makes the functions look shorter. You should only use the vertical mode when the indentation is so large that it makes the function look ugly or overflow in width. Suppose that we replaced the `equal` with the name of some other function:

```
;;; INDENTATION IS MIXED -- BOGUS LONG FUNCTION NAME IS
;;; REPLACING THE CALL TO EQUAL.

(defun dummy-compare-vectors (current-state goal)
  (let ((count 0))
    (dotimes (vector-index
              (min (array-dimension current-state 0)
                   (array-dimension goal 0))
              count)
      (if (not (bogus-extremely-long-function-name
                (aref current-state vector-index)
                (aref goal vector-index)))
```

```
        (setf count (1+ count))))))
⇒ COMPARE-VECTORS
```

In this case you have to use vertical mode because the calls to `aref` wouldn't fit on the same line.

Style Rule 15: *Try to place all arguments to an expression on the same line as the expression operator. When this doesn't fit, try to place the first argument on the same line and indent the remaining arguments to the same column as the first argument. If this doesn't fit, place the first argument on the next line, indented a few spaces from the expression operator.*

An exception to Style Rule 15 is for expressions that introduce locals, like `let` and `let*`. In this case, it is best to provide a separate line for each local variable. This is especially important when the local variable is initialized to a complicated expression. It also makes it easy to provide a short descriptive comment about the local.

Style Rule 16: *Place local variables on their own lines.*

EXERCISES

***14.7** Rewrite the following function definition using proper indentation and commenting techniques. You should recode the function after you determine what it does.

```
(defun whatdoido (a) (let
 (result) (if (zerop
  a) 0 (apply #'+
   (dotimes (j a            result)
    (setf result (                    cons
 j result)))   ) )   )   )
```

***14.8** Rewrite the following function definition using proper indentation and commenting techniques. You may recode the function if you can determine what it does.

```
(defun
  guesswhatIdo2
  (b)
  (cond
   (b
    (if
     (>
      b
      0)
     (if
      (not
       (guesswhatIdo2
        (1- b)
       )
```

```
          )
          5
         )
        )
       )
       (t
        t)
      )
     )
```

14.5 Names and Variables

Choosing appropriate names for functions, variables, and globals is as important as writing comments. Well-designed names can make programs readable without comments.

Style Rule 17: *Use descriptive names for everything and some kind of separator character between words.*

Choose names that are descriptive, but not verbose. Some programmers will use very long names, which can actually be a hindrance. Long names can adversely affect the indentation. They can also lead to typographical errors when you have to repeatedly type them.

You should also use some kind of separator character between words in a name. Most programmers use the dash, although some prefer the underscore. In either case, a character between the words in a symbol name improves readability.

```
;; Three symbols, the first is much harder to read than the
;; other two.
'(thequickbrownfox the-quick-brown-fox the_quick_brown_fox)
 ⇒ (THEQUICKBROWNFOX THE-QUICK-BROWN-FOX THE_QUICK_BROWN_FOX)
```

Notice how Common LISP forces case conversion on names. So, mixing case, which is often done in the C programming language, is not significant.

Style Rule 18: *Avoid creating symbols that contain the special characters by using \ or the vertical bar.*

Remember that there are several special characters that can be part of a symbol name. The Common LISP designers tried not to restrict the character set, so anything that is not special (these are ( ) " # ‘ , ; ’ |) may be used to construct a symbol. Also, you can use a special character in a symbol, if you put a " \ " before that character. This is considered bad programming practice, because it can make the symbols very hard to read. For example, notice the construction of the symbol in this example:

```
(setf strange-symbol '\ (hello\ there\))
```

```
⇒ \ (HELLO\ THERE\)

(format t "~A and ~A~%" strange-symbol '(hello there))
⇒ (HELLO THERE) and (HELLO THERE)
⇒ NIL
```

It's hard to tell that the first example printed is a symbol and the second is a two-element list. You can achieve the same effect by wrapping vertical bars around the symbol. These specify that everything between the bars is the symbol exactly as specified, including case. This is also useful for creating strange symbols, but should generally be avoided.

```
(setf another-strange-symbol '|the quick brown fox|)
⇒ |the quick brown fox|
```

Style Rule 19: *Append* `-aux` *to the symbol name for auxiliary functions. They should also be defined locally to the main function using* `labels` *or* `flet`.

We have frequently written auxiliary or "helper" functions to augment a particular function. These auxiliary functions generally perform the main computation, but need additional arguments that you don't want to be visible from the outside. These functions should be named with an `-aux` added to the end of the function. This shows the reader that it is tightly coupled with the original function. You should also embed the definition of the auxiliary function within the main function using the `labels` or `flet` constructs.

Style Rule 20: *Don't chose names for symbols that are nearly identical to one another.*

The `-aux` is long enough to make a visible difference between the two function names. Don't specify symbol names that are nearly identical, because it increases the chances of typographical errors. These kinds of errors can be very difficult to find because they only appear when the program is run and produces the wrong answer.

Style Rule 21: *Use globals sparingly, declaring all uses with* `defvar` *and wrapping asterisks around their names as in* `*example*`.

You should try not to use globals. You can usually save values in local variables and then pass them around to the functions that need them. However, sometimes you need a global, for example, for maintaining an association list of operators and functions. In these cases, remember to declare the global, and wrap asterisks around the name.

Many beginning LISP programmers with experience in other languages set many undeclared global variables. These are only used to save some small state of the computation for the next expression and then are no longer used. If some value is required more than once in the function, then use a *local* variable to save that value. If the value is only used once, just embed its expression directly where it's required. Remember that every LISP expression returns a value.

We can borrow a computation that was performed in the exercises in the early chapters. Many beginning LISP programmers write solutions that look just like the first example. The second version corrects these defects.

```
;;; BAD EXAMPLE of computing the quadratic roots.

(defun roots (a b c)
  (let (result)
    (setf bsquared (* b b))
    (setf part2 (* 4 a))
    (setf part2 (* part2 c))
    (setf diff (- bsquared part2))
    (setf root-result (sqrt diff))
    (setf numerator (+ (- b) root-result))
    (setf denominator (* 2 a))
    (setf result (/ numerator denominator))
    (setf numerator (- (- b) root-result))
    (setf result
          (list result (/ numerator denominator)))
    result))
 ⇒ ROOTS

(roots 1 1 -6)
 ⇒ (2.0 -3.0)
```

In this version, locals are used to save any computation that must be done twice.

```
;;; Better version of computing the quadratic roots.

(defun roots (a b c)
  (let ((root-result (sqrt (- (* b b) (* 4 a c))))
        (denominator (* 2 a))
        (minus-b (- b)))
    (list (/ (+ minus-b root-result) denominator)
          (/ (- minus-b root-result) denominator))))
 ⇒ ROOTS

(roots 1 1 -6)
 ⇒ (2.0 -3.0)
```

The last line of the bad version of `roots` demonstrates another problem to avoid. You don't have to use a local variable to return a result of the function; all LISP functions return a value. Placing the call to `list` as the last expression will perform the same operation. This is like embedding calls to `setf` in both branches of an `if`, when one external call will suffice:

```
;;; A BAD EXAMPLE with embedded calls to setf.

(defun foo (a b)
  (let (mumble)
    (if (a < 10)
      (setf mumble (frobble a))
      (setf mumble (fumble b)))
    (list mumble (* mumble 2))))

;;; A better version that moves the embedded calls to setf
;;; outside of the call to if.

(defun foo (a b)
  (let (mumble)
    (setf mumble (if (< a 10) (frobble a) (fumble b)))
    (list mumble (* mumble 2))))

;;; The best version moves the assignment into the let
;;; initialization. Notice how short this version is as
;;; compared with the others.

(defun foo (a b)
  (let ((mumble (if (< a 10) (frobble a) (fumble b))))
    (list mumble (* mumble 2))))
```

Style Rule 22: *Limit your use of dynamically scoped variables. Write your code so that it is not affected by the type of scoping.*

Dynamic scoping can often lead to very subtle run-time errors. Common LISP has decreased the problem that was inherent in earlier LISP dialects by defaulting to lexical scoping. So, when a free variable (one that is not bound within the scope of the function) is found, it is assumed to be lexically bound. Good programming style limits the number of free variables to only the small set of globals that your program needs. Don't use any free variables at all and then your code will not depend on the scoping issues.

EXERCISES

***14.9** Modify the following procedures, so they use better names and eliminate both the gratuitous global variables and dynamic scoping. Verify that your resulting function returns the same values as demonstrated below.

```
(defvar rr '((0 . 1) (3 . 1) (6 . 1) (0 . 3) (1 . 3) (2 . 3)
            (0 . 4) (2 . 2)))
(defun compUtethetotAlnumberoFpossIBlewinsthataplaYERCAnhave
  (b i)
```

```
  (declare (special b i))
  (setf pw (mapcar #'foo rr))
  (setf r (apply #'+ pw))
  r)
(defun foo (x)
  (setf lb (length b))
  (setf sb (sqrt lb))
  (setf ele (truncate sb))
  (setf xx (possible-win b (car x) (cdr x) ele i))
  (if xx (setf r 1)
   (setf r 0))
  r)
(compUtethetotAlnumberoFpossIBlewinsthataplaYERCAnhave
  '(x nil x o nil nil o nil nil) 'x)
⇒ 4

(compUtethetotAlnumberoFpossIBlewinsthataplaYERCAnhave
  '(x nil x o nil nil o nil nil) 'o)
⇒ 3
```

14.10 The previous function uses a data base in which to determine the possible winning positions on a three-by-three tic-tac-toe board. Rewrite the function in a style similar to `winp` that can work on an arbitrary-sized square board. Remember to use proper style and call your function `count-possible-wins`.

14.6 Control Constructs

Whether to use recursion or iteration is a matter of taste. With recursion, the resulting expression occurs naturally within the function definition. Iteration requires an iteration construct, which can make your programs clearer.

Style Rule 23: *Use iteration or recursion depending on which looks better in your program.*

"Tail recursion" is exactly equivalent to iteration. Tail recursion means that there is no stack growth – the result of a function is the result of the recursive call. In other words, the last thing that a function does is perform a recursive call and immediately return that result. The function may not use the result of the recursive call in any computation. For example, the following definition of factorial is not tail recursive because the result of the recursive call is used in the computation.

```
;;; Compute the factorial of the argument using standard
;;; recursion.

(defun factorial (n)
  (if (< n 2)
```

```
    1
    (* n (factorial (1- n)))))
⇒ FACTORIAL

(trace factorial)
⇒ (FACTORIAL)

(factorial 4)
⇒ FACTORIAL entry:
⇒ |   Arg 1: 4
⇒ |  FACTORIAL reentry (# 2):
⇒ |  |   Arg 1: 3
⇒ |  |  FACTORIAL reentry (# 3):
⇒ |  |  |   Arg 1: 2
⇒ |  |  |  FACTORIAL reentry (# 4):
⇒ |  |  |  |   Arg 1: 1
⇒ |  |  |  FACTORIAL (# 4) return value = 1
⇒ |  |  FACTORIAL (# 3) return value = 2
⇒ |  FACTORIAL (# 2) return value = 6
⇒ FACTORIAL return value = 24
⇒ 24
```

The trace shows that the call is not tail recursive, because it returns different values at each level. The next example is tail recursive because the result of the innermost call returns the value of the function.

```
;;; A tail recursive definition of factorial of the first
;;; argument.

(defun factorial (n)
  (factorial-aux n 1))
⇒ FACTORIAL

(defun factorial-aux (n result)
  (if (< n 2)
    result
    (factorial-aux (1- n) (* n result))))
⇒ FACTORIAL-AUX

(trace factorial-aux)
⇒ (FACTORIAL-AUX)

(factorial 4)
⇒ FACTORIAL entry:
⇒ |   Arg 1: 4
⇒ |  FACTORIAL-AUX entry:
⇒ |  |   Arg 1: 4
```

```
⇒ |  |   Arg 2: 1
⇒ |  |  FACTORIAL-AUX reentry (# 2):
⇒ |  |  |   Arg 1: 3
⇒ |  |  |   Arg 2: 4
⇒ |  |  |  FACTORIAL-AUX reentry (# 3):
⇒ |  |  |  |   Arg 1: 2
⇒ |  |  |  |   Arg 2: 12
⇒ |  |  |  |  FACTORIAL-AUX reentry (# 4):
⇒ |  |  |  |  |   Arg 1: 1
⇒ |  |  |  |  |   Arg 2: 24
⇒ |  |  |  |  FACTORIAL-AUX (# 4) return value = 24
⇒ |  |  |  FACTORIAL-AUX (# 3) return value = 24
⇒ |  |  FACTORIAL-AUX (# 2) return value = 24
⇒ |  FACTORIAL-AUX return value = 24
⇒ FACTORIAL return value = 24
⇒ 24
```

Tail recursion is not part of the Common LISP specification, although some implementations use it. You can't count on a particular implementation supporting the concept. Languages like Scheme [34] require it as part of the language specification and encourage its use.

Style Rule 24: *Use the mapping operators when you want to transform, or access all elements of a list.*

You should use the various mapping operators when you want to do something to all elements of a list or sequence. There is no way to terminate prematurely as with recursion or the `dolist` expression.

Style Rule 25: *Use* `if` *for simple conditional expressions and* `cond` *for everything else.*

Another control issue is where to use `if` and `cond`. The `cond` expression is more powerful and is easier to use when there are a lot of conditions. The `if` expression is a primitive, allowing a single "then" and "else" clause. Consider the following when choosing between the two:

1. Is there more than one predicate required? If so, then `cond` should be used; otherwise, use the simpler `if` form.
2. Do you anticipate making future changes that require more conditions? If so, then you should use `cond`, since it's easier to add new conditions. Nested `if` expressions quickly become cluttered and hard to read.

Chapter 17 discusses three more conditional control constructs, `case`, `when`, and `unless`.

Style Rule 26: *When using a* `cond`*, always include a* `T` *clause if only to signal an error.*

You should always use a final `t` clause in a `cond`, even if all you want to do is return `nil` (the default if no predicate matches). This indicates that you want the code to return `nil` in all other cases.

Style Rule 27: *Testing the value of a variable may be accomplished by just using the variable as the predicate.*

A predicate within a control construct doesn't have to be a function call. If you want to test whether a variable `foo` is non-`nil`, write the code as follows:

```
;; INCORRECT USE OF DOUBLE NEGATIVE OPERATORS.
(if (not (null foo))
  ...
  ...)
```

Although, this is functionally correct, it is a double negative and may be eliminated. The correct sequence is:

```
;; CORRECT USE OF VARIABLE.
(if foo
  ...
  ...)
```

Style Rule 28: *It is not necessary to wrap a conditional expression around a predicate to force it to return* `t` *or* `nil`*; just use the predicate itself.*

All predicates return non-`nil` or `nil`, so it isn't necessary to place any conditional expression around a predicate to return `T` or `nil`.

```
;; INCORRECT RANGE FUNCTION THAT USES UNNECESSARY IF
;; EXPRESSION.

(defun in-range-p (value)
  (if (and (> value 65) (< value 100))
    t
    nil))

;; CORRECT USE OF THE PREDICATE BY ITSELF.

(defun in-range-p (value)
  (and (> value 65) (< value 100)))
```

Style Rule 29: `T` *and* `nil` *are not usually quoted.*

Another style issue is whether to quote `t` and `nil`. They aren't usually quoted. The only time you should quote them is when you are writing code that considers their use as the symbols `t` and `nil`. For example, you might want to store something on the property list of `nil`. In this case, you would want to quote `nil` because it is the symbol `nil` receiving a value on its property list.

```
;; Store the foo property with value 99 under the symbol nil.
(setf (get 'nil 'foo) 99)
 ⇒ 99
```

However, under most circumstances, you should not quote either `t` or `nil`.

EXERCISES

14.11 Suppose that you are given a nine-element list that represents a tic-tac-toe board containing elements which are either X, O, or `nil`. Write an iterative version using `dotimes` that sets an element of the list at an index to be X or O. You may not use destructive operations.

```
(setf board '(nil nil nil nil nil nil nil nil nil))
 ⇒ (NIL NIL NIL NIL NIL NIL NIL NIL NIL)

(setf board (place board 0 'x))
 ⇒ (X NIL NIL NIL NIL NIL NIL NIL NIL)

(setf board (place board 4 'o))
 ⇒ (X NIL NIL NIL O NIL NIL NIL NIL)
```

14.12 Define `place` as an iterative version using `mapcar`.

14.13 Define `place` recursively.

14.7 LISP Expressions

You can write LISP programs in many different ways. Many high-level operations can replace the operations of the primitive ones. In some cases, you might choose the high-level operation because you know that the types of operands may change. For instance, you might use the sequence operations instead of the type-specific ones. In other cases, you might choose the more primitive operations for efficiency. They don't need to check the types of the arguments and dispatch to the appropriate function. However, in some cases, it is more efficient and no less general. The following style rules illustrate some of these points:

Style Rule 30: *Use* `null` *or* `not` *to test if the argument is* `nil` *(see the next rule). Don't use any of the forms of* `equal` *for the comparison.*

Although each of the following are equivalent, use the `null` or `not` version.

```
(setf foo nil)
 ⇒ NIL

;; DON'T USE EQUAL TO CHECK FOR NULL VALUE.
(equal foo nil)
 ⇒ T
```

```
;; DON'T USE EQL EITHER.
(eql foo nil)
 ⇒ T

;; NULL OR NOT is the correct expression to use.
(null foo)
 ⇒ T

(not foo)
 ⇒ T
```

Style Rule 31: *Use* `null` *when examining lists and* `not` *when performing logical operations.*

Notice how the `not` version reads better than the `null` version.

```
;;; Compute the number of elements in the list argument.
;;; THIS INCORRECTLY USES NOT, INSTEAD OF NULL.

(defun my-length (some-list)
  (if (not some-list)
    0
    (+ 1 (my-length (cdr some-list)))))

;;; Compute the number of elements in the list argument.

(defun my-length (some-list)
  (if (null some-list)
    0
    (+ 1 (my-length (cdr some-list)))))
```

Style Rule 32: *If the first argument to* `append` *is a call to* `list`, *use* `cons` *instead.*

You are using `append` incorrectly if the first argument is an expression with `list` as the operator. This is equivalent to using a call to `cons`, which is less expensive. The call to `append` copies the first argument and must scan to its end.

```
(setf color 'red)
 ⇒ RED

;; INCORRECT USE OF APPEND AND LIST.
(append (list color) '(blue green))
 ⇒ (RED BLUE GREEN)

;; CORRECT VERSION USING CONS.
(cons color '(blue green))
 ⇒ (RED BLUE GREEN)
```

Style Rule 33: *If there is a possibility that your code may operate on other types of sequences, use the generic sequence function. Otherwise, use the more type-specific function.*

When you use the more type-specific functions, you must anticipate the types of data will match the functions you have chosen. If you know that you may operate on varying data structures, then choose the more general versions. Also, if you don't know if your data structures will change to other sequence types, then use the generic sequence functions just to be safe.

Style Rule 34: *Avoid direct calls to* `eval` *within your code.*

`Eval` is a very expensive LISP expression. `Eval` is the general purpose expression evaluator, so it can process any kind of LISP expression. Often, the generality of `eval` is not actually required. `Apply` may perform the same task and is simpler.

EXERCISES

***14.14** Modify the `check-same` function, defined on page 372, so it operates upon any sequence.

14.15 Here is yet another version of the `place` function from the previous section. Determine how it performs its operations and then rewrite it using good style as outlined in this section and the preceding sections.

```
(defun place (b i x)
  (setf r nil)
  (dotimes
 (ii 9)
  (cond ((= ii i)
    (setf r (append (car (list r)) (list x)))
    (setf r (append (car (list r)) (cdr b)))(return r))
        ((not (= ii i))
   (setf r (append (car (list r)) (list
   (car b))))))
  (setf b (cdr (car (list b))))
  (car (list r)))
```

14.8 Data Structures

Choosing and organizing data structures is one of the most important decisions when writing any program. The problem is compounded because LISP has so many different data structures and you can define your own data types using `defstruct` and the objects package. You often must decide how to represent a collection of data. Your two main choices are lists and arrays.

Style Rule 35: *When deciding on the representation for a collection of data, choose lists if the number of elements in the collection is arbitrary and arrays if there is a fixed set.*

If you use lists, your code rapidly becomes cluttered with calls to `car`, `cadr`, and so on. Data-abstraction functions can hide this access and make the code easier to read. However, if you have more than a few items you are better off using structures or objects. They are more efficient and imply data abstraction. Arrays once again are appropriate if you are performing "mathematical" operations, or have a fixed set of data items.

Style Rule 36: *When representing structured data, choose objects for your data type.*

This text has promoted the use of objects. They provide a nice conceptual framework for your data. They also lead to highly maintainable code. You don't have to worry about the particular data type and can just use the methods. The dungeon game in Chapter 12 showed how objects would have made writing the code much easier. It's not good practice to mix representations like we tried to do in Chapter 12.

Style Rule 37: *The preferred combinations of* c*x*r *forms are:* `car`, `cdr`, `caar`, `cadr`, `cdar`, `cddr`, `caddr`, `cadddr`, `cdddr`, *and* `cddddr`.

As you write code to manipulate lists, remember not to clutter your code with the more bizarre combinations of `car` and `cdr`. The human reader has trouble understanding which element they are trying to access. If you write code to manipulate lists past the two-combination forms (`caar`, `cadr`, `cdar`, and `cddr`) you should use a structure or object.

Some programmers do not like the names `car` and `cdr`, since their meanings are historical. So, Common LISP has defined two functions that mean the same, `first` and `rest`. These are exactly equivalent to `car` and `cdr`, respectively.

(`first` *S-expression*)

(`rest` *S-expression*)

Style Rule 38: *Use* `first` *and* `rest` *if you dislike* `car` *and* `cdr`.

Common LISP also provides functions for directly retrieving the "nth" element of the list. They can be used in place of functions like `cadr`, `caddr`, and others. Each of the functions is named the ordinal English number as illustrated in the following table:

Element Number	Function Name	c*x*r Equivalent
1	`first`	`car`
2	`second`	`cadr`
3	`third`	`caddr`
4	`fourth`	`cadddr`
5	`fifth`	`car cddddr`
6	`sixth`	`cadr cddddr`
7	`seventh`	`caddr cddddr`
8	`eighth`	`cadddr cddddr`
9	`ninth`	`car cddddr cddddr`
10	`tenth`	`cadr cddddr cddddr`

You can use these functions at your discretion, although if you are using functions much above `fifth`, then you should probably be using a structure or an object.

Style Rule 39: *Never use quoted lists, quoted arrays, or string constants in your code if there is any possibility of them being modified.*

You should be very careful when you use quoted lists, quoted arrays, or string constants in your code. If they may be destructively modified, then you should not use them. The problem arises when you try to compile your LISP code. The compiler can collapse constants that are `equal`. So, if you happened to have the same constant in two locations, a destructive modification to one could affect the other. This could be the source of very subtle bugs. If you do not use any destructive operations, then you are free to use the quoted forms as much as you like.

Destructive operations on lists can be dangerous. When the modification is done, everything that pointed to the original list sees the change. This is often not what you wanted to do. Also, destructive operations can create circular lists. Circular lists are not bad if used carefully. However, they can cause problems when trying to scan to the end, when printing them, and so forth. In the following example, we replace the `cdr` of `colors` with `colors` and create a circular structure:

```
(setf colors (list 'red 'blue 'green))
 ⇒ (RED BLUE GREEN)

;; Create a circular structure.
(rplacd colors colors)
 ⇒ (RED RED RED RED RED RED RED RED RED RED RED RED RED
 ⇒  RED RED RED RED RED RED RED RED RED RED RED RED RED
 ⇒  RED RED RED RED RED RED RED RED RED RED RED RED RED
 ⇒  RED RED RED RED RED RED RED RED RED RED RED RED RED
 ⇒  RED RED RED RED RED RED RED RED RED RED RED RED RED

 ⇒ !! Break: LISP process interrupted by user.
```

```
⇒   Condition signaled in: :NON-LISP-CODE.

⇒ Entering the debugger
```

The system tried to print the circular structure and would have continued forever, so it was interrupted. Common LISP has a mechanism for printing circular structures, which is controlled by a global variable `*print-circle*`.

`*print-circle*`

When this variable is bound to `nil` (which is the default), then no special circle printing is used. However, when it is non-`nil`, then a special printing mechanism is used that can print circular lists. The printer labels each list that is pointed to by a circular pointer with a #*n*= – where *n* is an integer. Then, in the location which points to the circular list, it places a #*n*.

```
;; Turn on circular printing capabilities.
(setf *print-circle* t)
⇒ T

;; Create the colors list again.
(setf colors (list 'red 'blue 'green))
⇒ (RED BLUE GREEN)

(rplacd colors colors)
⇒ #1=(RED . #1#)
```

Style Rule 40: *Destructive operations upon lists should be avoided. However, when they are done, you should provide full documentation as to why it is done and the effects of the operation.*

Destructive operations on lists should be used with care and should be heavily commented. The comments should indicate that a destructive operation is being performed, should describe all variables that are affected, and why the operation is being performed.

EXERCISES

14.16 Define the `place` function to use destructive operations. This is a good example where destructive operations will not hurt because it changes one element.

14.17 Suppose that you wanted to make `place` operate upon a vector. Write a version that doesn't change the argument.

***14.18** Define a data structure that includes three fields. One field is to contain a representation of the tic-tac-toe board. Another is to contain an integer value that represents the evaluation of the game board. The final field is a list of the possible next moves from the board position. Your structure should have the characteristics such that after it is created, it is easy to change the value and add to the list of next moves. This data structure is used in the Chapter Exercises.

14.9 Macros

Macros have two main uses: to enhance your programming environment and to control the evaluation of arguments to a function. In both cases, a macro returns a new expression ready for evaluation. They should not be used for any other purposes.

Style Rule 41: *Do not perform any operations that cause a side effect within a macro. The sole purpose of a macro is to return a new expression for evaluation.*

You shouldn't perform any operations with side effects in a macro. Macros can be expanded at different times depending on the particular LISP system. In some implementations of LISP, a macro is expanded into the resulting expression when a function is defined; in others it is expanded when the function is evaluated. This means that you can't count on when the side effect may actually take place.

Style Rule 42: *When using data abstraction techniques, consider the use of a macro for the operation instead of a function.*

Data abstraction should be used as much as possible. However, it can be inefficient with the extra set of function calls required. For example, if we prefer to use `head` and `tail` to represent `car` and `cdr`, then we could define them as functions. The problem is that code using calls to `head` and `tail` must actually call the functions. Had the actual `car` and `cdr` been used, a compiler might have been able to perform the operation directly and produce much better code. Thus, using macros for `head` and `tail` that expand into the appropriate code for `car` and `cdr` is the right approach.

There are problems with this approach. The first problem is that the expansion of the macro into the resulting code could be done during evaluation, depending upon the implementation. So, instead of paying for a function call that then performs the operation, you are paying for a function that expands into a LISP expression, which is then evaluated to perform the operation. This can be very expensive. The caveat is that if the code is compiled, then the macros are usually expanded during the compilation and it is therefore just as efficient as if the original operations had been included. The second difficulty is that macros make debugging a little more difficult. You cannot `trace` macros, and depending upon your implementation. You may `step` through the expansion process or the result of the expansion will already be present. These difficulties are generally minor and so macros should be used for data-abstraction operations.

When you use macros to create new programming constructs, you frequently need to use temporary variable names in the context of the macro. For example, suppose that we want to write our own version of `dolist` which expands into a `do`. Our first attempt at the macro might appear as follows. We require a local variable to contain the list that is being traversed.

```
;;; An initial version of the dolist macro.

(defmacro my-dolist ((local some-list &optional result) &body
                     body)
  `(do*
    ((the-list ,some-list (cdr the-list))
     (,local (car the-list) (car the-list)))
    ((null the-list) ,result)
    ,@body))
 ⇒ MY-DOLIST
```

```
;;; Now a test.
(my-dolist (color (list 'red 'blue 'green) 'black)
           (format t "The color: ~A~%" color))
 ⇒ The color: RED
 ⇒ The color: BLUE
 ⇒ The color: GREEN
 ⇒ BLACK
```

Now suppose that `my-dolist` had been called, except the local variable had been `the-list`. Watch what happens:

```
;;; Now another test.
(my-dolist (the-list (list 'red 'blue 'green) 'black)
           (format t "The color: ~A~%" the-list))
 ⇒ The color: RED

 ⇒ !!!!! Error: The argument RED is not a valid list.
 ⇒   Condition signaled in: CDR.

 ⇒ Entering the debugger
```

This error is the result of the two variables having the same name. The solution is to use the `gentemp` function that will generate a symbol guaranteed to be unique. It takes no arguments and returns a symbol.

```
(gentemp)
```

Thus, the corrected version of `my-dolist` appears as follows:

```
;;; A corrected version of dolist using gentemp.

(defmacro my-dolist ((local some-list &optional result) &body
                       body)
  (let ((temp-symbol (gentemp)))
    `(do*
      ((,temp-symbol ,some-list (cdr ,temp-symbol))
       (,local (car ,temp-symbol) (car ,temp-symbol)))
      ((null ,temp-symbol) ,result)
      ,@body)))
 ⇒ MY-DOLIST

;;; Now a test.
(my-dolist (the-list (list 'red 'blue 'green) 'black)
           (format t "The color: ~A~%" the-list))
 ⇒ The color: RED
 ⇒ The color: BLUE
 ⇒ The color: GREEN
 ⇒ BLACK
```

Style Rule 43: *Always* gentemp *temporaries for macro arguments that appear in the result of the macro, unless you are sure you know that the actual arguments to the macro will never have side effects.*

EXERCISES

***14.19** Redefine the following macro so it doesn't perform any side effects at macro expansion time. Also, change it to use appropriate style.

```
(defmacro ru (te &body r)
  (setf x 'do)
  (if (not te) nil
      (append (list x (list) (list te)) r)))
 ⇒ RU

(setf u 0)
 ⇒ 0

(ru (> u 5) (setf u (+ 1 u)) (format t "Next ~A~%" u))
 ⇒ Next 1
 ⇒ Next 2
 ⇒ Next 3
 ⇒ Next 4
 ⇒ Next 5
 ⇒ Next 6
 ⇒ NIL
```

***14.20** Suppose that `if` is the most primitive operation (it turns out that in Common

LISP, this is actually true). Write a macro for **cond** that translates into nested calls to **if**. Be careful of the case where there is only a predicate in the clause; your macro must not evaluate the predicate twice.

```
(macroexpand '(my-cond (x (print (+ x 1))) (y) (z nil)
                        (t (print nil))))
⇒ (LET (T1)
⇒     (IF X
⇒         (PROGN (PRINT (+ X 1)))
⇒         (IF (SETF T1 Y)
⇒             T1
⇒             (IF Z
⇒                 (PROGN NIL)
⇒                 (IF T
⇒                     (PROGN (PRINT NIL))
⇒                     NIL)))))
⇒ T
```

14.10 Summary

Good programming style is as important as the code itself. Well-commented code helps you develop and maintain software. A standard header and comment format among groups of programmers can also help improve staff productivity. Also, be careful not to overcomment a program, since that can make the code confusing. You should remember to keep functions relatively short. Data-driven style of programming, function dispatching, and data abstraction are important for decreasing maintenance time. The indentation and format of your program should be consistent to make them more readable. Always choose names that are meaningful and adopt a consistent strategy for connecting words within a symbol. You should also use globals sparingly. As you write your code, pay attention to the LISP functions and control constructs that you use – choose the most efficient and appropriate one. Finally, don't use macros for operations with side effects and make sure that they use unique temporaries.

Chapter Exercises

As you might have noticed, there have been many examples of the game tic-tac-toe within this chapter. Tic-tac-toe is a game that is well suited for searching for the best solution. It is also fairly easy to find a solution because of the limited size. However, it is not well suited to use the A* algorithm because there are two players involved. A better technique is to use minimax search strategy [31]. The essential idea of the strategy is that as each move is considered, you assume that each player is going to choose the best possible move. This implies some method for evaluating each game position to determine which is the best move. Before we get into the actual process of finding the best move, let's implement the code that evaluates a game position.

One good game evaluator is to count the number of places where a win is possible. The theory is that if you have more places than your opponent where you can still put three in a row, then you have a better chance to win. So, if you count the number of places with possible wins and subtract the number of places where your opponent can win, you will come up with a reasonable value. The larger the value, the better the board is for you. One other important fact is to be able to recognize when the game is a win or a lose for you. When this happens, the value returned should be larger (or smaller) than any of the values returned by the other count. That way, the system can recognize the difference between a good position and a winning position. In a three-by-three tic-tac-toe board, there are eight possible ways to win, so a value of 10 and -10 should be sufficient to indicate a win or a loss.

1. Write `board-value`, which given a board represented as a nine-element sequence and an `X` or `O` indicating whose move it is, returns the value of the game using the previously stated evaluation strategy. You will be able to use many of the functions developed in this chapter, like `winp`, and `count-possible-wins`.

```
(board-value '(x nil o o x nil o nil x) 'x)
 ⇒ 10

(board-value '(x nil o o x nil o nil x) 'o)
 ⇒ -10

(board-value '(x nil nil o x nil o nil nil) 'x)
 ⇒ 2
```

The idea with minimax is to generate a tree that includes all possible moves from any particular starting position. You may either generate the tree completely to all possible wins and losses, or you may generate the tree to the number of levels (also called a ply) that is provided as an argument. Once you have generated the tree, you must determine the best move. This is accomplished using minimax. The idea is fairly simple. Go to the bottom level of the tree and compute board values for each game position. The values are all with respect to whichever move is to be made at the top of the tree. These values are then propagated up the tree to the next level based upon the following criteria. If the player moving at the next level is the same as the top-level player, then the maximum of all of the board values is determined and assigned to the node in the next level. Otherwise, the minimum is computed and assigned to the node. This reflects the concept that if the player at the top node is going to select a move, he or she will select the best possible move – the one with the highest board value. If the opponent is going to make the move, then he or she will also select the best possible move, which is the one with the lowest value. This technique is performed at the next level for all nodes and then the process is

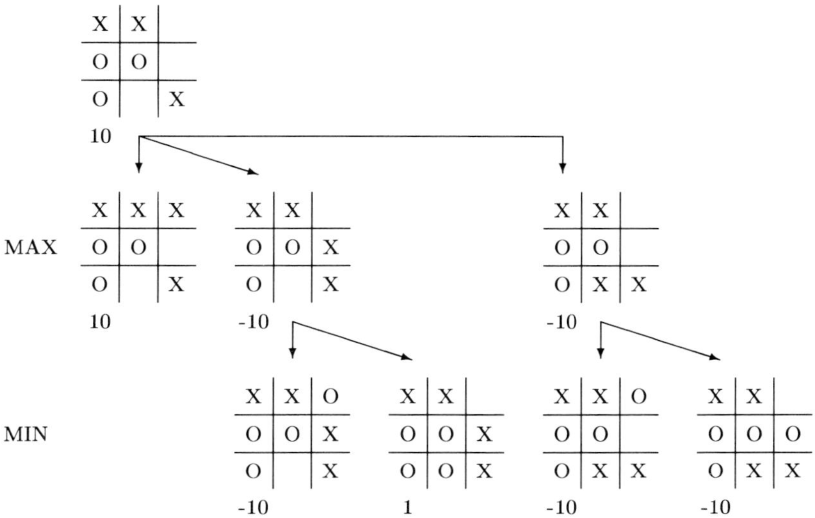

Figure 14.1 Minimax on a Small Tic-Tac-Toe Game

continued to propagate a value to the parent of the next level, and so on until all elements of the tree have values.

For example, Figure 14.1 illustrates a few levels of the tree. In the bottom layer, all of the board values are computed using `board-value`. Then, the minimum of each child is propagated to the parent. In this case, there is a winner for `X` in each child, so the `-10` is propagated. At the second level, a maximum is computed, which is `10` in the first child of the top node. Thus, the best move is to select that first child.

***2.** Write the function `generate-tree`, which takes two arguments. The first is a data structure (see previous exercises), describing the board, current value, and an empty next move list. The second argument is whose move it is. The function is to return the data structure with the propagated value and the tree of next moves defined. In this version, expand the tree as far as it will go.

```
;; This assumes that you are using objects for your data
;; structure.
(setf game
      (make-instance 'ttt-board
                     :board '(X X nil O O nil O nil X)))
 ⇒ #<Object TTT-BOARD>

(generate-tree game 'x)
 ⇒ #<Object TTT-BOARD>
```

***3.** Now that the tree is generated, we need a function to select the best move. All this function has to do is scan the list of next move nodes for the first one that matches the current board value. That move is then the one to make. Write the function `best-move`, which takes a single argument that is a board data structure. The function then returns a new board data structure that designates the one that is the best move.

```
(setf best (best-move game))
 ⇒ #<Object TTT-BOARD>

(board best)
 ⇒ (X X X O O NIL O NIL X)
```

4. As the final exercise, write a function or method that prints the board out in a nice format.

```
(print-board game)
 ⇒ X X
 ⇒ O O
 ⇒ O   X
 ⇒ NIL

(print-board best)
 ⇒ X X X
 ⇒ O O
 ⇒ O   X
 ⇒ NIL
```

Function Summary

The following lists the functions and topics covered in this chapter.

- `(defvar` *symbol S-expression string*`)`
- `(documentation` *symbol type-symbol*`)`
- `(defun` *symbol* `(`*symbol**`)` *optional-doc-string S-expression**`)`
- `(defmacro` *macro-name*`(`*argument**`)` *optional-doc-string S-expression**`)`
- `(first` *S-expression*`)`
- `(rest` *S-expression*`)`
- `*print-circle*`
- `(gentemp)`

15

CASE STUDY: A* SEARCH

SEARCHING IS SOMETIMES the most critical aspect of artificial intelligence systems. Many AI programs use search techniques to find answers. Two closely related areas that involve search are game playing and puzzle solving. Game playing usually involves two or more person games, such as chess, checkers, tic-tac-toe, for example. Puzzle-solving usually is characterized by starting with some initial state and searching solutions which can be found by generating new states and seeing if they match some goal. There are many similarities between these two problem areas, both of which are covered in this chapter. The difficultly of these problems is due to the exponential growth in the number of possible moves. Intelligent searching helps you quickly find a solution to the problem. In this chapter, we review techniques that blindly search for a solution and then cover an intelligent approach known as the A* search algorithm for solving puzzles. The exercises review a technique called minimax which is well adapted to game playing problems. This chapter makes use of object-oriented techniques for solving parts of the search problem.

15.1 Searching and the 8-Puzzle

Searching is known as a *weak method* because it lacks the power of *knowledge-based* approaches, such as expert systems. In a weak-method solution to a problem, you begin with a certain set of conditions (the initial state) and attributes of the solution (the goal state). A new set of states is then generated from the initial state using a set of legal transformations. These states are then transformed into more new states, until the goal state is reached or there are no legal transformations left. A tree best shows this process. The initial state is at the root of the tree with each succeeding level of the tree representing each legal transformation. For example, Figure 15.1 illustrates three levels of the tree for the game of tic-tac-toe. Each level is called a ply. The second ply doesn't show all of the expanded positions.

Even in this simple tic-tac-toe example, the set of legal transformations

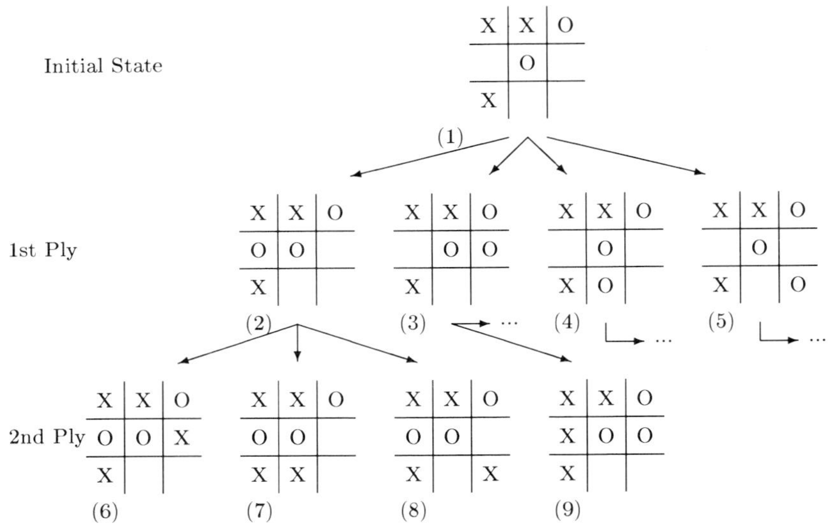

Figure 15.1 Two Levels of a Small Tic-Tac-Toe Game

for each ply is large (the second ply has twelve states). Imagine a similar tree expansion for the game of chess. Each expansion can include hundreds of different new states. Brute force expansion of the entire tree isn't possible even with today's supercomputers. Deciding which path to pursue is crucial making search strategies important.

There are many different search strategies, enumerated in any AI text book [31,9]. The most basic search strategies are categorized as *blind* search. Blind search doesn't use any domain-specific knowledge. In other words, it doesn't use any knowledge about the particular problem that it is trying to solve. Also, the new states transformed from the previous state are arbitrarily generated. The two most common blind search techniques are *depth-first* and *breadth-first*. These techniques are impractical when there are many states at each ply or there are many plies. As the name implies, depth-first means that the new states are generated down successive plies of the tree, rather than by expanding all of the states in a ply. For example, in the tic-tac-toe example states 1, then 2, and then 6 would be expanded. Then, a substate of state 6 will be expanded into the third ply. Breadth-first is just the opposite. All new states in a ply are expanded before going to the next ply. So, in the example, states are expanded in ascending, numeric order. If there is more than one solution in the tree, breadth-first will find the shortest path. However, if the depth-first search follows a lucky path, it may find a solution faster than breadth-first.

A better technique is *heuristic* search. Heuristic search uses knowledge of the particular domain to select which state to generate. Discovering a good

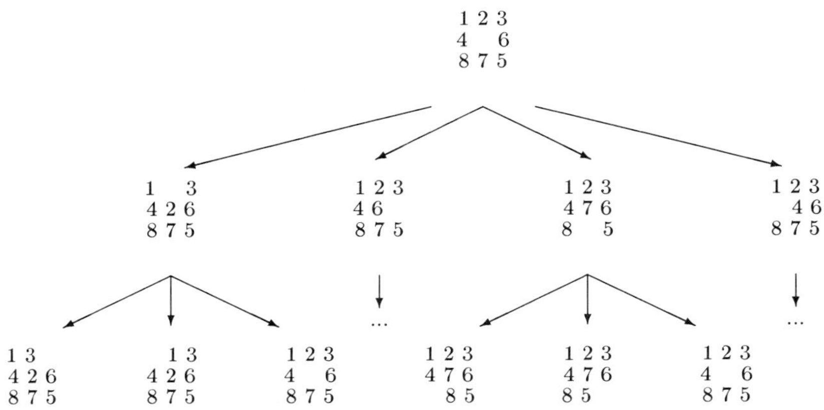

Figure 15.2 Two Levels of the 8-Puzzle

technique for evaluating each state is the key to a heuristic search. The evaluation tells how close a particular state is to the goal state. This measure of closeness depends on the problem. For example, in the tic-tac-toe example, it might indicate the number of places where the player can win, minus the number of places where the opponent can win. One interesting heuristic search is *best-first.* It expands the best state first instead of blindly expanding depth- or breadth-first states. The algorithm for a best-first search is as follows:

1. Determine if the current state is the goal state and if so, exit.
2. Generate all of the next states from the current state.
3. Select the best state from these next states and any others that you haven't already examined, make it the current state, and go back to step one.

The interesting part of this algorithm is how to select the best state. One successful technique is A* (pronounced A-star), which is described in the next section.

The 8-puzzle lends itself to weak-method solutions. You've probably seen and played with 8-puzzles or 15-puzzles before. In a square frame, 8 numbered tiles are placed, leaving one spot empty. In the initial state of the puzzle, the numbers are in a random configuration. You move the pieces until the goal state is reached. One common goal state is ascending numeric order. A move is performed by sliding a tile into the empty spot. The number of possible moves depends on the position of the empty spot. In the middle, there are four possible moves; on the side, there are three moves; and in the corner, two moves. A truncated, two-level expansion of the tree appears as follows:

Notice that each move is reversible. So, in the second ply of the tree shown in Figure 15.2, each expansion results in three new states, but one of those states is the same as the initial position. That state can be pruned from the tree. Nothing is gained by performing a move and then reversing it. Also, any board position that exists in an earlier part of the tree doesn't need to be generated. This is because there is a shorter path to the same position and therefore that shorter path should be used.

EXERCISES

15.1 Draw two-ply expansions for the game of checkers. Draw three trees – one for the starting position, one for some midpoint in the game (where there are no kings), and one for an ending position where kings are present.

15.2 Draw two-ply expansions for the game of chess. Compare the complexity with that for checkers.

***15.3** How does the presence of kings affect the expansion factor in checkers?

***15.4** Compare the similarities and differences between checkers and chess that would affect the implementation of a board evaluator for each.

15.2 The A* Algorithm

The A* Algorithm is a best-first search strategy. You determine the best state by adding the cost of getting to that state plus an estimation for the cost of reaching the goal state from this state. The cost of getting to a state is known as g. One possible value for g is the ply number. This means that it took ply number of moves to reach a particular board position. The estimation is known as h' and is determined by comparing the state against the goal state. The sum of these two values is known as f'. The state with the smallest f' is then expanded, searching for the goal. The prime ($'$) is used to designate estimated values, while the non-primed symbols designate actual values.

Figure 15.3 shows these values for some arbitrary tree. State A is expanded into B, C, and D. Each of these would have a value of 6, 7, and 11 for their f' respectively (adding the g value and the arbitrarily chosen h' value). So, A* would expand node B first into nodes E and F whose f' values would be 6 and 8. The lowest f' so far is node E, so it would be expanded into node G whose f' would be 8. At this point, the node that hasn't been examined with the least f' is C, so it would be expanded next. This process continues until a solution is found.

One implementation of the A* algorithm requires two lists, `open` and `closed`. `Open` contains the nodes that have been generated, but not yet examined. The `closed` list contains those nodes that have been examined already. A node contains information on the state, the values for g and h', and other data

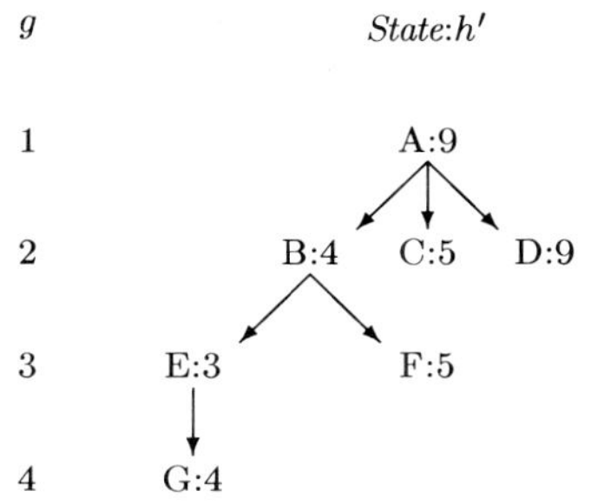

Figure 15.3 Illustration of A*

needed in the search process. Initially, `open` contains the initial state, with its g set to 0 and its h' computed as appropriate. `Closed` is initialized to `nil`. The following illustrates the steps of the algorithm:

1. Find the node on `open` with the lowest f'. Call this `best-node` and move it from `open` to `closed`.
2. If `best-node` is the goal, then exit.
3. Generate all of the new states from `best-node`. Assign them a value of g that is one greater than the g of `best-node`. For each new state, perform the following:
   a. Check to see if the state represented by `new-state` is present in the `closed` or `open` lists. Call the node found on the lists `old`. Compare g values between `new-state` and `old`. If `new-state` has a smaller value, then substitute `new-state` for `old` and make it point back to `best-node`. If `old` was on `closed`, then remove it and place it on `open`. If `new-state` has a g value that is larger than `old`, then ignore `new-state`.
   b. If `new-state` is not in either `open` or `closed`, then make it point back to `best-node` and install it in `open`.
4. Go to step 1.

Notice that the specification of A* does not depend on the particular problem to be solved. This means that with an appropriate set of interfaces, one generic implementation will work with any problem. This is a perfect application for objects. The algorithm suggests a set of characteristics that each problem must have. They can be encapsulated as a set of methods. Study the algorithm and see if you can determine the interface methods.

A node must have a g, h', and f'. It must also represent the current state. An object could be used by A* to represent each node with slots for each of these items. The representation of the current state depends on the particular problem and so must be a state object itself. In step 3a, the node object must be able to point to the parent node object. Therefore, we need another slot for the node object.

Now, let's examine the steps in the algorithm to see which methods may be required. The computation of h' depends on the state object and so must be a method associated with the object. In the first step of A* there is no new information. Each node object must be able to provide the value of f', but we already knew that from the first part. However, step 2 implies an interface between the representation of the problem state and a goal state. The system must be able to compare two states to see if they are equal. Therefore, we need a method which will compare objects. Step 3 specifies that there must be a technique for generating all new states from another state. This implies another method that operates on an object and creates a list of the transformed objects. In step 3a you again need to compare two states. Step 3b does not provide any more useful information.

Summarizing this, the implementation of A* operates upon objects of the following type:

```
;;; A node object used by the A* algorithm.

(define-type node
  (:var g (:init 0))
  (:var h-prime)
  (:var state)
  (:var parent (:init nil))
  :all-initable
  :all-settable
  :all-gettable)
 ⇒ NODE
```

The value of f' must also be provided for each node. However, it's easily computed so there's no need to maintain a slot within each slot for its value. Therefore, a simple method can return the sum of g and h'.

```
;;; The value of f' is simply the sum of g and h'.

(define-method (node f-prime) ()
  (+ g h-prime))
 ⇒ F
```

The following methods must also be provided for each problem:

`calc-h-prime` – Compute the h' of the object.
`compare-equal` – Compare whether the object invoked with the method is equal to the argument object.
`generate-transform` – Return a list of transformed objects.

A* begins with an initial state and the goal state. Therefore, the function A* accepts two arguments, an object representing the initial state, and an object representing the goal state. It returns a list of the objects representing the transformations between the initial state and the goal state. We need a function `path` that follows the parent pointers back from the goal state to the initial state, collecting the state objects into a list.

We can implement the body of A* with an iteration construct. Iteration continues until the `best-node` is equal to the goal state. `Do` or `do*` is best for this type of iteration. The body of the iteration manipulates the two lists, `open` and `closed`. The types of operations that must be performed are:

`initialize` – `Open` must be initialized to the initial state and `closed` must be initialized to `nil`.

`find-lowest-f-prime` – From step 1, this function scans `open` searching for the node with the lowest value of f'.

`move-open-to-closed` – From step 1, this function removes the node from `open` and places it on `closed`.

`find-state-in-open` – From step 3a, this function must scan the nodes in `open` to determine if any node matches the argument. It returns the matching node if present and `nil` otherwise.

`find-state-in-closed` – From step 3a, this function is the same as the function `find-state-in-open` except that it scans `closed`.

`move-closed-to-open` – From step 3a, move the argument node from `closed` to `open`.

`add-node-open` – From step 3b, this function adds the argument node to `open`.

The algorithm specifies that `open` and `closed` are lists. However, data abstraction techniques can hide the actual representation, leaving room for later optimization. This initial version will use data abstraction and a list representation. `Open` and `closed` imply that some state must be maintained. We will create a single object containing two slots and assorted methods to represent these lists. This might be considered overkill since we will only create one object and won't overload the methods. However, it supports data abstraction and isolates the functionality. `Initialize` creates the object and returns it to `A*`.

```
;;; The type that is used to maintain open and closed.

(define-type open-and-closed
  (:var open-nodes :initable)
  (:var closed-nodes (:init nil))
  :all-gettable
  :all-settable)
 ⇒ OPEN-AND-CLOSED
```

We can now implement the assorted primitive operations in either top-down or bottom-up fashion. We will use top-down and define `A*` first. As you have probably surmised, an important aspect of these types of algorithms is how quickly it finds the solution. In the case of A*, the speed it can find the solution is dependent upon the heuristic that is used. Therefore, we need a means of comparing different heuristics. One possible way to compare them is to count the number of nodes that are expanded once the final solution is found. The fewer the expanded nodes, the closer the heuristic was in getting us to our goal. We can annotate `A*` to count the number of nodes generated and print the value out just before returning a solution. As we said before, we can use `do*` to implement the algorithm. There are five variables that are introduced:

`open-closed` – This contains the object that has the `open` and `closed` lists.
`best-node` – This contains the node object of the one from the `open` list with the lowest f' value.
`new-g` – This local variable keeps track of the g values.
`old` – This is a temporary variable needed in the computations.
`nodes-expanded` – This is a count of the number of nodes expanded. It is incremented after we examine every new node.

The terminating clause is triggered when the `best-node` is the same as the `goal-node`. At that time, we print the informative message about the number of nodes expanded and then retrieve the path. The body of the `do*` is a call to `dolist`, which scans the list of generated transforms.

```
;;; A direct implementation of the A* algorithm.

(defun A* (initial-state goal-state)
  (do*
    ((open-closed
      (initialize
       (make-instance 'node :state initial-state
                      :h-prime
                      (calc-h-prime initial-state
                                    goal-state))))
     ;; Algorithm Step 1.
     (best-node (find-lowest-f-prime open-closed)
                (find-lowest-f-prime open-closed))
     (new-g 1 (1+ (g best-node)))
     old
     (nodes-expanded 0))
    ;; Algorithm Step 2.
    ((compare-equal (state best-node) goal-state)
     (format t "~A nodes were expanded~%" nodes-expanded)
     (path best-node))
    (move-open-to-closed open-closed best-node)
    ;; Algorithm Step 3.
    (dolist (new-state (generate-transform
```

```
                        (state best-node)))
        (setf nodes-expanded (1+ nodes-expanded))
        (cond ;; Algorithm Step 3a.
              ((setf old
                     (find-state-in-open open-closed
                                         new-state))
               (cond ((> (g old) new-g)
                      (setf (g old) new-g)
                      (setf (parent old) best-node))))
              ;; Algorithm Step 3a.
              ((setf old
                     (find-state-in-closed open-closed
                                           new-state))
               (cond ((> (g old) new-g)
                      (move-closed-to-open open-closed old)
                      (setf (g old) new-g)
                      (setf (parent old) best-node))))
              ;; Algorithm Step 3b.
              (t (add-node-open
                  open-closed
                  (make-instance
                   'node
                   :g new-g
                   :h-prime (calc-h-prime new-state goal-state)
                   :parent best-node
                   :state new-state))))))
⇒ A*
```

The next step is to implement the primitive operations that manipulate `open` and `closed`.

The `initialize` function has already been designed. It takes one argument, which is the initial state node, and creates an `open-and-closed` object with the state installed in `open-nodes`.

```
;;; Create the open-and-closed object and install the node.

(defun initialize (initial-node)
  (make-instance 'open-and-closed :open-nodes
                 (list initial-node)))
⇒ INITIALIZE
```

`Find-lowest-f-prime` scans the list in the `open-nodes` slot and returns the node with the lowest value for f'. The list is not sorted, so the function must look at every node in the list.

```
;;; Scan the nodes in open-nodes and return the one with the
```

```
;;; smallest value for f'.  The method assumes that there
;;; will always be at least one node on the list.

(define-method (open-and-closed find-lowest-f-prime) ()
  (let ((lowest-f-prime (f-prime (car open-nodes)))
        (node-of-lowest-f-prime (car open-nodes)))
    (dolist (each-node (cdr open-nodes))
            (cond ((< (f-prime each-node) lowest-f-prime)
                   (setf lowest-f-prime (f-prime each-node))
                   (setf node-of-lowest-f-prime each-node))))
    node-of-lowest-f-prime))
⇒ FIND-LOWEST-F-PRIME
```

We can move the nodes between the two lists with `remove` and `cons`. The node is removed from the list with `remove` and added to the new list with `cons`. The destructive version of `remove`, which is `delete`, may be used instead. This would save storage space because `remove` doesn't destroy the original list. `Move-open-to-closed` and `move-closed-to-open` invoke the appropriate `add-node-open` or `add-node-closed` methods.

```
;;; Move the argument node from open to closed.

(define-method (open-and-closed move-open-to-closed)
    (node-to-move)
  (setf open-nodes (delete node-to-move open-nodes))
  (add-node-closed self node-to-move))
⇒ MOVE-OPEN-TO-CLOSED

;;; A similar function to move the node from closed to open.

(define-method (open-and-closed move-closed-to-open)
    (node-to-move)
  (setf closed-nodes (delete node-to-move closed-nodes))
  (add-node-open self node-to-move))
⇒ MOVE-CLOSED-TO-OPEN
```

The two methods to add a node to `open` and `closed` are trivial given the list representation.

```
;;; Add the argument node to open.

(define-method (open-and-closed add-node-open) (new-node)
  (setf open-nodes (cons new-node open-nodes)))
⇒ ADD-NODE-OPEN

;;; Add the argument node to closed.
```

```
(define-method (open-and-closed add-node-closed) (new-node)
  (setf closed-nodes (cons new-node closed-nodes)))
⇒ ADD-NODE-CLOSED
```

The remaining methods search open and closed looking for a node that matches the argument. The methods then return the node if found and nil otherwise. Find-state-in-open and find-state-in-closed perform the same operation except on different lists. So, a generic auxiliary function find-state will actually find the state.

```
;;; Return a node that has a state that matches the argument
;;; state in open.

(define-method (open-and-closed find-state-in-open)
    (comparison-state)
  (find-state open-nodes comparison-state))
⇒ FIND-STATE-IN-OPEN

;;; Return a node that has a state that matches the argument
;;; state in closed.

(define-method (open-and-closed find-state-in-closed)
    (comparison-state)
  (find-state closed-nodes comparison-state))
⇒ FIND-STATE-IN-CLOSED

;;; Scan a list of nodes and return one with a matching
;;; state.

(defun find-state (node-list comparison-state)
  (cond ((null node-list) nil)
        ((compare-equal (state (car node-list))
                        comparison-state)
         (car node-list))
        (t (find-state (cdr node-list) comparison-state))))
⇒ FIND-STATE
```

The purpose of path is to retrieve the list of nodes from the goal state back to the starting state, to show the steps required to reach the goal. To accomplish this, path must scan from a node, following the parent links back to a node with a null parent. It must collect the state of each node and return them as a list. A recursive process should suffice for this problem.

```
;;; Scan the parent links, collecting into a list, the state
;;; objects of each node.  The scan proceeds backward through
;;; the tree and thus collects the states in reverse order.
;;; Thus an auxiliary function must be called to compute the
```

```
;;; list, which path must reverse before returning to the
;;; caller.

(defun path (node)
  (labels ((path-aux (node)
             (if (null (parent node))
               (list (state node))
               (cons (state node)
                     (path-aux (parent node))))))
    (reverse (path-aux node))))
 ⇒ PATH
```

This completes the definition of the A* part of the system. The next section discusses the implementation of the 8-puzzle. We first want to test `A*` on a simple example to separate the implementation of the 8-puzzle from that of `A*`. So, we need an example that's easy to implement, but provides the set of interfaces defined earlier in this section. The example must have a starting state that can be transformed into a goal state. One simple problem would use a list of numbers as the state, which can be transformed into a new list of numbers by incrementing any elements of the list. To make the test interesting, a rule will be instituted that only one element of the list may be incremented in any single transformation. Thus, the list `(1 2 3)` could produce the states `(2 2 3)`, `(1 3 3)`, and `(1 2 4)`. The goal would then be to produce a list of numbers like `(3 3 3)`. In this set of transformations, the last one will never reach the goal, so the heuristic could treat it as illegal. The calculation of h' could return a very large number so the node will never be selected as the one with the lowest value for f'. An alternative solution is to keep `generate-transform` from generating that state. To do this we would need to provide the goal state as an extra argument to `generate-transform`.

```
;;; The object that contains the list of numbers is defined
;;; as a problem type.

(define-type problem
  (:var number-list :initable :settable :gettable))
 ⇒ PROBLEM
```

The computation of h' is easy. The code must scan two lists, determine if an element of the current state is larger than the corresponding element in the goal state, and if it is, use a very large value. Otherwise the distance to the goal is the difference between the element values. These can then be summed and returned as the value for h'.

```
;;; Calc-h-prime computes the h' value for the problem.  If
;;; one element of the number list exceeds its corresponding
;;; value in the goal, then a large value is returned.  This
```

```
;;; should force this particular node to be ignored.

(define-method (problem calc-h-prime) (goal-state)
  (apply #'+ (mapcar #'(lambda (current-element goal-element)
                          (if (> current-element goal-element)
                            100000
                            (- goal-element current-element)))
                      number-list
                      (number-list goal-state))))
⇒ CALC-H-PRIME
```

Compare-equal calls equal on the two lists of numbers.

```
;;; Compare the number lists of the object and the argument
;;; object.

(define-method (problem compare-equal)
    (comparison-number-list)
  (equal number-list (number-list comparison-number-list)))
⇒ COMPARE-EQUAL
```

Generate-transform must access the list of numbers and return a list of number lists. It creates a new list by adding one to each element, so the number of lists that it must produce is equal to the length of the number list. This is an excellent application for dotimes. It can perform an iteration based upon the length of the number list, creating problem objects for each new list. An auxiliary function should actually create the new list. It should accept the list and the index count and produce a new list.

```
;;; Generate all of the transforms of the current number list
;;; and return a list of newly constructed objects.

(define-method (problem generate-transform) ()
  (let ((new-states nil))
    (dotimes (counter (length number-list))
      (setf new-states
            (cons (make-instance
                    'problem
                    :number-list
                    (new-number-list number-list counter))
                  new-states)))
    new-states))
⇒ GENERATE-TRANSFORM
```

The new transform can be generated in a number of ways. One technique scans the list and reconstructs each element until it finds the element associated with the argument index. That element is then incremented and the remaining list added to the end of the new list. Another technique would destructively replace the element with a larger value. This is acceptable, except that it would also change the original list. Therefore, it creates a copy of the original list and then replaces the appropriate element using the `setf` form of `nth`.

```
;;; Create a new list with the element corresponding to
;;; index incremented.
;;; CAUTION -- Performs a destructive operation.

(defun new-number-list (number-list index)
  (let ((new-number-list (copy-seq number-list)))
    (setf (nth index new-number-list)
          (1+ (nth index new-number-list)))
    new-number-list))
 ⇒ NEW-NUMBER-LIST
```

Now we can test the `A*`. The first step verifies that each test method works.

```
;; Create two objects, test is the initial state.
(setf *test* (make-instance 'problem :number-list '(1 1 2)))
 ⇒ #<Object PROBLEM>

;; Goal is the ultimate goal.
(setf *goal* (make-instance 'problem :number-list '(2 3 2)))
 ⇒ #<Object PROBLEM>

;; Verify the value for h'.
(calc-h-prime *test* *goal*)
 ⇒ 3

;; Test that compare-equal returns T.
(compare-equal *test* *test*)
 ⇒ T

;; Generate an initial set of transformations.
(generate-transform *test*)
 ⇒ (#<Object PROBLEM> #<Object PROBLEM> #<Object PROBLEM>)

;; Check the list of numbers in the transformation list.
(mapcar #'number-list (generate-transform *test*))
 ⇒ ((1 1 3) (1 2 2) (2 1 2))

;; Now, invoke A*.
(mapcar #'number-list (a* *test* *goal*))
 ⇒ 9 nodes were expanded
 ⇒ ((1 1 2) (2 1 2) (2 2 2) (2 3 2))
```

EXERCISES

***15.5** If the computation of h' is so bad that all states result in the same value, what kind of search does A^* eventually result in?

15.6 Define `new-number-list` without any destructive operations.

***15.7** This version of `A*` seems to solve the problem. However, it is quite slow. The process of scanning `open` and `closed` searching for matching states can be time-consuming. Implement a different representation that permits faster access. (*Hint:* Consider using a hash table.)

15.3 The 8-Puzzle

The purpose of this section is to implement the data structures, methods, and functions associated with the 8-puzzle. The operations on the 8-puzzle are completely specified by the interface to `A*`. In review, those operations are `calc-h-prime`, `compare-equal`, and `generate-transform`. We will choose a data representation of the 8-puzzle that fits in with these operations. The efficiency of the operations on a particular representation is an important consideration.

We know that the data structure for the 8-puzzle will always contain nine elements. So, the variable length nature of a list is not necessary. A vector or an array is a logical choice. Let's study how `generate-transform` determines legal moves to decide between these two. Using a vector to represent the puzzle results in a one-dimensional mapping of a two-dimensional structure. So, you move a tile in the vertical direction by subtracting or adding three from or to the index of the tile, while you move in the horizontal direction by adding or subtracting one. This is inconsistent, so we will choose a three-by-three array representation instead.

Each of the required operations must have an associated type. Therefore, we define `puzzle` which includes the current state of a puzzle position. Two additional slots will indicate the row and column of the empty position. In the previous operations, the empty location is needed for determining which tile to move. We could write code to scan the board and find that location each time a set of states is generated. A simple solution merely includes the position as explicit slot values. So, we are trading some space costs for the time required to scan the puzzle.

```
;;; The puzzle object contains the board slot which has the
;;; current state of the game.
(define-type puzzle
  (:var board)
  (:var empty-row)
  (:var empty-column)
```

```
  :all-initable
  :all-gettable
  :all-settable)
⇒ PUZZLE
```

Choosing a good heuristic is essential for finding a solution quickly. The heuristic for the 8-puzzle must give a measure of how far a puzzle is from the solution. The smaller the value, the closer the puzzle is to the solution. One simple solution counts the number of tiles that are in the wrong location. Puzzles that are close to being solved result in a number close to zero, while puzzles that are a long way from the solution result in a number close to eight. Implementation of this heuristic is a simple scan of the two arrays, incrementing a counter whenever an element does not match. We want the row and column indices to operate between zero and two inclusive, which are the sizes of the array dimensions. Instead of using a constant value, we can call `array-dimension` to determine the actual array length. Then, if the puzzle were changed to a 15-puzzle, the method wouldn't need to be changed.

```
;;; Compute the heuristic for the puzzle, which is the count
;;; of the number of tiles in incorrect locations.

(define-method (puzzle calc-h-prime) (goal-puzzle)
  (let ((counter 0))
    (dotimes (row (array-dimension board 0))
      (dotimes (column (array-dimension board 1))
        (cond ((not (equal (aref board row column)
                           (aref (board goal-puzzle) row column)))
               (setf counter (1+ counter))))))
    counter))
⇒ CALC-H-PRIME

;;; Test the heuristic: there should be 4 misplaced tiles.
(calc-h-prime (make-instance
               'puzzle :board
               (make-array '(3 3) :initial-contents
                           '((1 2 3) (6 5 4) (nil 8 7))))
              (make-instance
               'puzzle :board
               (make-array '(3 3) :initial-contents
                           '((1 2 3) (4 5 6) (7 8 nil)))))
⇒ 4
```

Using the array representation, the `compare-equal` method can just call `equalp` to tell if two arrays have the same contents.

```
;;; Determine if the argument object and the one invoked with
```

```
;;; the method have the same board positions.

(define-method (puzzle compare-equal) (other-puzzle)
  (equalp board (board other-puzzle)))
⇒ COMPARE-EQUAL

;;; Test that two newly created puzzles are identical.
(compare-equal (make-instance
                'puzzle :board
                (make-array '(3 3) :initial-contents
                            '((1 2 3) (6 5 4) (nil 8 7))))
               (make-instance
                'puzzle :board
                (make-array '(3 3) :initial-contents
                            '((1 2 3) (6 5 4) (nil 8 7)))))
⇒ T
```

The last method, `generate-transform` is the most difficult of the three. Generating each transformation from a given board position poses an interesting problem. There are three classes of positions for the empty square (center, side, and corner), but the operations for movement within one class will also vary. For example, if the empty position is in the upper-left corner, then the moves are from the tile in row 0, column 1, or the tile in row 1, column 0. A move into the empty position adds one to the column or the row of the empty position coordinates. However, if the empty position is in the lower-right corner, the moves subtract one from the column or row. You might think it's best to use a table of legal moves for all nine possible locations of the empty position.

A better solution would always generate all four possible moves and ignore those outside of the coordinate range. This leaves the correct set of legal moves. The first step in implementing this algorithm is to write a predicate that tests to see if the newly computed row and column indices are legal. In keeping with `calc-h-prime`, `array-dimension` will determine the size of the puzzle. This means that `legal-position` must take another argument, which is the board array.

```
;;; Verify if the argument row and column are within the
;;; boundaries of the third argument two-dimensional array.

(defun legal-position (row column 2d-array)
  (and (<= 0 row (1- (array-dimension 2d-array 0)))
       (<= 0 column (1- (array-dimension 2d-array 1)))))
⇒ LEGAL-POSITION

;;; A couple of small tests of this function.
(legal-position 1 2 (make-array '(3 3)))
⇒ T
```

```
(legal-position 0 3 (make-array '(3 3)))
 ⇒ NIL
```

The generate-transform method must create a new puzzle object for each new puzzle position. The easiest technique is to create a new puzzle object that has the same board position as the original board. Then when a legal move has been determined, the tile and the empty position can be switched. The method clone takes a puzzle object and returns a copy. Once again, this method doesn't assume any particular size of the board.

```
;;; Create a copy of the puzzle object.

(define-method (puzzle clone) ()
  (let ((new-puzzle
	  (make-instance 'puzzle :board
	    (make-array (list (array-dimension board 0)
			      (array-dimension board 1))))))
    (dotimes (row (array-dimension board 0))
      (dotimes (column (array-dimension board 1))
	(setf (aref (board new-puzzle) row column)
	      (aref board row column))))
    new-puzzle))
 ⇒ CLONE

;;; A simple test.
(board (clone (make-instance 'puzzle :board
		(make-array '(3 3) :initial-contents
			    '((1 2 3) (4 5 6) (7 8 nil))))))
 ⇒ #2A((1 2 3) (4 5 6) (7 8 NIL))
```

Generate-transform generates the four new positions, verifies that they are legal, clones the board, and fills in the new positions.

```
;;; Generate new puzzle transformations from the current
;;; object.
(define-method (puzzle generate-transform) ()
  (let ((new-puzzles nil)
	tile-row
	tile-column
	(empty-tile-representation
	 (aref board empty-row empty-column)))
    (dolist (new-indices '((-1 0) (0 -1) (1 0) (0 1)))
      (cond
       ((legal-position
	 (setf tile-row (+ empty-row (car new-indices)))
	 (setf tile-column (+ empty-column
```

```
                                    (cadr new-indices)))
           board)
          (setf new-puzzles (cons (clone self) new-puzzles))
          ;; Move the new tile to the empty position.
          (setf (aref (board (car new-puzzles))
                      empty-row empty-column)
                (aref (board (car new-puzzles))
                      tile-row tile-column))
          ;; Move the empty position to the old tile location.
          (setf (aref (board (car new-puzzles))
                      tile-row tile-column)
                empty-tile-representation)
          ;; Reset the empty position to point to the new
          ;; location.
          (setf (empty-row (car new-puzzles)) tile-row)
          (setf (empty-column (car new-puzzles))
                tile-column))))
    new-puzzles))
 ⇒ GENERATE-TRANSFORM

;;; Test generate-transform with a board position.
(mapcar #'board
        (generate-transform
         (make-instance 'puzzle
                        :board
                         (make-array '(3 3)
                                     :initial-contents
                                     '((1 2 3) (nil 4 5)
                                       (6 7 8)))
                        :empty-row 1 :empty-column 0)))
 ⇒ (#2A((1 2 3) (4 NIL 5) (6 7 8))
 ⇒  #2A((1 2 3) (6 4 5) (NIL 7 8))
 ⇒  #2A((NIL 2 3) (1 4 5) (6 7 8)))
```

All of the parts are now complete, so we can test `A*` on the 8-puzzle.

```
(setf *initial-state*
      (make-instance 'puzzle
                     :board
                      (make-array '(3 3)
                                  :initial-contents
                                  '((1 2 3) (nil 5 6)
                                    (4 7 8)))
                     :empty-row 1 :empty-column 0))
 ⇒ #<Object PUZZLE>
```

```
(setf *goal*
      (make-instance 'puzzle
                     :board
                      (make-array '(3 3)
                                  :initial-contents
                                  '((1 2 3) (4 5 6)
                                    (7 8 nil)))
                     :empty-row 2 :empty-column 2))
 ⇒ #<Object PUZZLE>

(mapcar #'board (a* *initial-state* *goal*))
 ⇒ 8 nodes were expanded
 ⇒ (#2A((1 2 3) (NIL 5 6) (4 7 8))
 ⇒  #2A((1 2 3) (4 5 6) (NIL 7 8))
 ⇒  #2A((1 2 3) (4 5 6) (7 NIL 8))
 ⇒  #2A((1 2 3) (4 5 6) (7 8 NIL)))
```

EXERCISES

15.8 Write a method for `puzzle` objects that prints the board in a pretty two-dimensional format. For example, `(show *goal*)` would produce:

```
1 2 3
4 5 6
7 8 X
```

***15.9** Another possible heuristic is the manhattan distance between each piece and its goal location. The manhattan distance is defined as the sum of the horizontal and vertical distance between the locations. This is more meaningful than the heuristic of counting the number of misplaced tiles, because it gives a measure of the actual distance between the tile and its desired location. Tiles that are correctly positioned receive a value of zero. Write a new version of `calc-h-prime` that uses this heuristic. Run the version on a number of tests and compare the number of nodes expanded versus the misplaced tile version.

```
;;; A different initial state, but the same final state.
;;; This is farther from the solution and thus should help to
;;; demonstrate a better heuristic.
(setf *initial-state*
      (make-instance
       'puzzle
       :board (make-array '(3 3) :initial-contents
                           '((2 6 5 ) (1 7 3 ) (4 8 nil)))
       :empty-row 2 :empty-column 2))
 ⇒ #<Object PUZZLE>

(setf *goal*
      (make-instance
```

```
        'puzzle
        :board (make-array '(3 3) :initial-contents
                           '((1 2 3) (4 5 6) (7 8 nil)))
        :empty-row 2 :empty-column 2))
 ⇒ #<Object PUZZLE>

;;; First the misplaced tile heuristic.
(mapcar #'board (a* *initial-state* *goal*))
 ⇒ 163 nodes were expanded
 ⇒ (#2A((2 6 5) (1 7 3) (4 8 NIL))
 ⇒  #2A((2 6 5) (1 7 3) (4 NIL 8))
 ⇒  #2A((2 6 5) (1 NIL 3) (4 7 8))
 ⇒  #2A((2 NIL 5) (1 6 3) (4 7 8))
 ⇒  #2A((2 5 NIL) (1 6 3) (4 7 8))
 ⇒  #2A((2 5 3) (1 6 NIL) (4 7 8))
 ⇒  #2A((2 5 3) (1 NIL 6) (4 7 8))
 ⇒  #2A((2 NIL 3) (1 5 6) (4 7 8))
 ⇒  #2A((NIL 2 3) (1 5 6) (4 7 8))
 ⇒  #2A((1 2 3) (NIL 5 6) (4 7 8))
 ⇒  #2A((1 2 3) (4 5 6) (NIL 7 8))
 ⇒  #2A((1 2 3) (4 5 6) (7 NIL 8))
 ⇒  #2A((1 2 3) (4 5 6) (7 8 NIL)))

;;; Now the new heuristic.
 ⇒ CALC-H-PRIME

 ⇒ 56 nodes were expanded
 ⇒ (#2A((2 6 5) (1 7 3) (4 8 NIL))
 ⇒  #2A((2 6 5) (1 7 3) (4 NIL 8))
 ⇒  #2A((2 6 5) (1 NIL 3) (4 7 8))
 ⇒  #2A((2 NIL 5) (1 6 3) (4 7 8))
 ⇒  #2A((2 5 NIL) (1 6 3) (4 7 8))
 ⇒  #2A((2 5 3) (1 6 NIL) (4 7 8))
 ⇒  #2A((2 5 3) (1 NIL 6) (4 7 8))
 ⇒  #2A((2 NIL 3) (1 5 6) (4 7 8))
 ⇒  #2A((NIL 2 3) (1 5 6) (4 7 8))
 ⇒  #2A((1 2 3) (NIL 5 6) (4 7 8))
 ⇒  #2A((1 2 3) (4 5 6) (NIL 7 8))
 ⇒  #2A((1 2 3) (4 5 6) (7 NIL 8))
 ⇒  #2A((1 2 3) (4 5 6) (7 8 NIL)))
```

15.4 A* Enhanced

A problem with this version of A* is that it can potentially expand nodes more than once. This happens when the algorithm scans the list of `closed` nodes and finds a match with one that has a greater g value. In this case, the algorithm states that the node is removed from `closed` and a version with the new g is placed on `open`. If a node is on `closed`, its children have already been determined and placed on one of the lists. If you move the node back to `open`, it could have its children expanded again. These children will have a lower value for g and thus will always be selected over the ones already present. Therefore, they will still lead to a shorter solution. However, this expansion could result in extra overhead through the expansion of more children than necessary.

The new path should be linked into the hierarchy, along with new values for g of all of the children. So, each node must be able to access its children. Also, when this condition arises, the tree below the node must be scanned and each g value updated to reflect the new path. Finally, there is no reason to move the node from closed to open. This will suppress the generation of extra nodes.

```
;;; A node object used by the A* algorithm, now with the
;;; children slot.

(define-type node
  (:var g (:init 0))
  (:var h-prime)
  (:var state)
  (:var parent (:init nil))
  (:var children (:init nil))
  :all-initable
  :all-settable
  :all-gettable)
 ⇒ NODE
```

Changing the definition of the `node` type requires the associated methods to be redefined. The only method currently defined is `f-prime`.

```
;;; The value of f' is simply the sum of g and h'.

(define-method (node f-prime) ()
  (+ g h-prime))
 ⇒ F
```

When updating `A*`, we need code to add the newly generated nodes to the `children` slot. It would be incorrect to put the nodes returned from the function `generate-transform` in the slot, since some of the nodes aren't needed. So, an easy solution is to write a new method that adds a child node to the list of children. Then, when each node is validated, it can be added to the list of children.

```
;;; Add a new child to the children slot of a node.

(define-method (node add-child) (new-child)
  (setf children (cons new-child children))
```

```
  new-child)
 ⇒ ADD-CHILD
```

The only additional function propagates the new g values to all children nodes. An easy implementation is to access each child node, update its g value, and then propagate the new value to its children. `Propagate` does this with `dolist` to get at each child node and a recursive call on any new children found.

```
;;; Given a node, which has a new value for g, find all
;;; children and replace their g with the new value.

(defun propagate (node)
  (let ((new-g (1+ (g node))))
    (dolist (each-child (children node))
      (setf (g each-child) new-g)
      (propagate each-child))))
 ⇒ PROPAGATE
```

Finally, `A*` can be updated to reflect this new model. The only changes are to add the children to the new `children` slot in the node, eliminate the movement from `closed` to `open`, and propagate the new g values to any children.

```
;;; A direct implementation of the A* algorithm, enhanced
;;; with code that does not generate extra states.

(defun A* (initial-state goal-state)
  (do*
    ((open-closed
      (initialize
       (make-instance 'node :state initial-state
                            :h-prime
                              (calc-h-prime
                               initial-state goal-state))))
     (best-node (find-lowest-f-prime open-closed)
                (find-lowest-f-prime open-closed))
     (new-g 1 (1+ (g best-node)))
     old
     (nodes-expanded 0))
    ((compare-equal (state best-node) goal-state)
     (format t "~A nodes were expanded~%" nodes-expanded)
     (path best-node))
    (move-open-to-closed open-closed best-node)
    (dolist (new-state (generate-transform
                          (state best-node)))
      (setf nodes-expanded (1+ nodes-expanded))
      (cond ((setf old
```

```
                (find-state-in-open open-closed
                                    new-state))
          (cond ((> (g old) new-g)
                 (setf (g old) new-g)
                 (setf (parent old) best-node)
                 (add-child best-node old)))) ; NEW
         ((setf old
                (find-state-in-closed open-closed
                                      new-state))
          (cond ((> (g old) new-g)
                 ;; NEW - Do not move it to open.
                 ;; (move-closed-to-open open-closed old)
                 (setf (g old) new-g)
                 (setf (parent old) best-node)
                 (add-child best-node old) ; NEW
                 (propagate old)))) ; NEW
         (t (add-node-open
             open-closed
             (add-child ; NEW
              best-node
              (make-instance
               'node :g new-g
               :h-prime (calc-h-prime new-state
                                      goal-state)
               :parent best-node
               :state new-state))))))))
⇒ A*
```

Now we can verify that the function still operates correctly.

```
(mapcar #'board (a* *initial-state* *goal*))
⇒ 8 nodes were expanded
⇒ (#2A((1 2 3) (NIL 5 6) (4 7 8))
⇒  #2A((1 2 3) (4 5 6) (NIL 7 8))
⇒  #2A((1 2 3) (4 5 6) (7 NIL 8))
⇒  #2A((1 2 3) (4 5 6) (7 8 NIL)))
```

EXERCISE

***15.10** Analysis of the A* algorithm should reveal that one expensive operation is the scanning of `closed` and `open`, searching for a matching node. Suppose that we eliminated this phase, generated the new nodes, and then placed them directly on `open`. What is the consequence of this action?

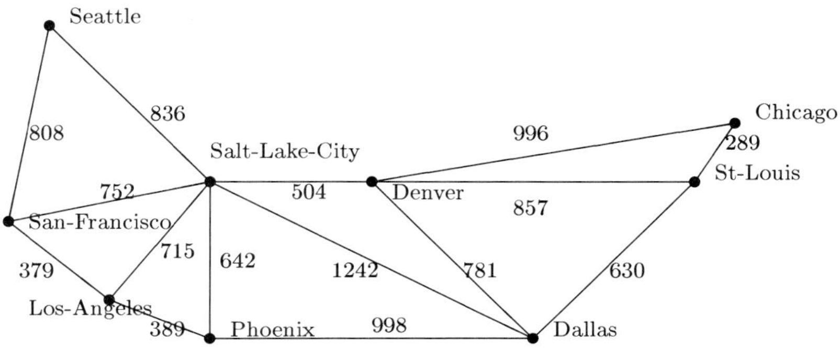

Figure 15.4 Map of Cities and Distances

15.5 Summary

Searching is an important field of artificial intelligence. The solution to many problems can be found using heuristic search strategies. One particularly good search algorithm is A*. An object-oriented implementation was presented that provides a clean interface. The 8-puzzle is particularly well adapted for this type of search. Using good programming style, the code has been designed so that a puzzle of any size may be used.

Chapter Exercises

Another problem that is amenable to the A* algorithm is that of path-finding. Suppose that you know a travel agent that wants a program to find the shortest path between various locations. Our data base consists of nine western and mid-western cities; distances between some of them, and their longitude and latitude (in degrees) are illustrated in the Figure 15.4 and the following table:

City	Longitude	Latitude
Seattle	122	47
San-Francisco	123	38
Los-Angeles	118	34
Salt-Lake-City	112	41
Phoenix	112	33
Denver	105	40
Dallas	97	33
St-Louis	90	39
Chicago	88	42

Your first step is to design a data structure suitable for representing the city information. The difficult part of this problem is figuring out how to represent the connections between the cities. If you just use one-way connections, then finding what connections that city has could be difficult. If you make the connections two-way, then you must duplicate distance information. So, it is a time and space trade-off.

1. Design the data structure for the cities, and then write the code to load in all of the pertinent information.

If we used A* as implemented in this chapter, we have a problem in the computation of the value of g. This is because we assumed that going from one level in the tree to another was the only thing necessary in computing g. In this problem, the g value is the number of miles between the cities.

2. Modify A* so it properly computes **g** to reflect the cost of moving down each level of the tree. (*Hint:* Modify the semantics of **generate-transform** to return the list of new states, along with the **g** values for each new state.)

***3.** Define each of the the A* interface methods for your city structures.

4. Write **print-route**, which prints out the route between the cities and the total mileage required to follow the route.

```
(print-route (a* (find-city 'San-Francisco)
                 (find-city 'Chicago)))
⇒ 12 nodes were expanded
⇒ Starting City: SAN-FRANCISCO
⇒     Next City: SALT-LAKE-CITY
⇒     Next City: DENVER
⇒   Destination: CHICAGO
⇒   Total miles: 2252
⇒ NIL
```

```
(print-route (a* (find-city 'San-Francisco)
                 (find-city 'Dallas)))
⇒ 8 nodes were expanded
⇒ Starting City: SAN-FRANCISCO
⇒     Next City: LOS-ANGELES
⇒     Next City: PHOENIX
⇒   Destination: DALLAS
⇒   Total miles: 1766
⇒ NIL
```

***5.** Suppose that the travel agent had a customer that refused to travel through Salt Lake City. Change your program to permit ignoring any paths through a list of cities. Also write a **route** driver function that takes a starting city, ending city, and list of forbidden cities.

```
(route 'Seattle 'Chicago nil)
⇒ 12 nodes were expanded
⇒ Starting City: SEATTLE
⇒     Next City: SALT-LAKE-CITY
⇒     Next City: DENVER
⇒   Destination: CHICAGO
```

```
⇒   Total miles: 2336
⇒ NIL

(route 'Seattle 'Chicago '(Salt-Lake-City))
⇒ 12 nodes were expanded
⇒ Starting City: SEATTLE
⇒     Next City: SAN-FRANCISCO
⇒     Next City: LOS-ANGELES
⇒     Next City: PHOENIX
⇒     Next City: DALLAS
⇒     Next City: ST-LOUIS
⇒   Destination: CHICAGO
⇒   Total miles: 3493
⇒ NIL
```

16 ERRORS, CATCH, AND THROW

IN THIS CHAPTER, we discuss how the LISP system signals errors. You can use the same technique to signal an error for users of your software. The `catch` and `throw` functions control this error facility and other structures. We also discuss how a LISP compiler would use these mechanisms.

16.1 Errors

Common LISP defines two error functions. `Error` signals errors that are not recoverable and generally places the user into the debugger. `Cerror` signals correctable errors. It also places the user into the debugger, but lets the user continue if the error is corrected. The correction process depends on the computation that signals the error.

The `error` function takes the same "n" arguments as `format` (described in Chapter 10) except for the stream argument.

(error *format-string S-expression**)

The system prints an error flag and then prints the formatted expression. What happens next is system-dependent. On some systems, you are taken into an interactive session with the debugger. Typically, you have a number of system dependent options. Some systems let the user list the functions that have been called, the current bindings of variables, and so on. This allows the user to see what caused the error and correct the code.

For example, suppose that our compiler will not compile anything that isn't a legal `lambda` expression. All `lambda` expressions must have `lambda` as the first element, and a list as the second. The compiler signals an error if it doesn't find a proper `lambda` expression. We can write `lambdap` to do this operation.

```
;;; Verify if the argument is a proper lambda expression and
;;; invoke error if it is not.  If it is proper, then return
```

```
;;; T.

(defun lambdap (lambda-expression)
  (if (and (listp lambda-expression)
           (eql (car lambda-expression) 'lambda)
           (listp (cadr lambda-expression)))
    t
    (progn
      (error "~A is not a legal lambda.~%" lambda-expression)
      (format t "This should never be printed~%"))))
 ⇒ LAMBDAP

;;; Test the lambdap with a legal lambda expression.
(lambdap '(lambda (x) (+ x x)))
 ⇒ T

;;; This test should cause an error.
(lambdap '(lambda x (+ x x)))
!!!!! Error: (LAMBDA X (+ X X)) is not a legal lambda.
  Condition signaled in: LAMBDAP.
Entering the debugger
```

At this point, we are now interacting with the debugger. Debugger commands are preceded by an exclamation point. For example, `!b` shows the execution stack. This system lets you peruse any interpreted code and look at the bindings of the variables.

```
!b
Backtrace from bottom of stack up:
i  :EVAL-FORM
i->LAMBDAP
   ERROR
```

We can then quit the debugger and return to the regular LISP system using the `!a` command.

```
!a
 ⇒ Abort to top level!
```

Notice how the underlying LISP system uses the same error mechanism. If we cause an error, then we get exactly the same results.

```
;; Define a silly function that just takes the car of its
;; argument. We use a function so when the error occurs, we
;; can see that it is on the stack.

(defun silly-function (argument)
  (car argument))
```

```
 ⇒ SILLY-FUNCTION

(silly-function 3)
!!!!! Error: The argument 3 is not a valid list.
  Condition signaled in: CAR.
Entering the debugger
!b
Backtrace from bottom of stack up:
i  :EVAL-FORM
i  SILLY-FUNCTION
 ->CAR
```

The results are essentially the same as if you wrote code that explicitly calls `error`.

`Cerror` is just like `error`, except that it takes an extra argument, which is a message that explains how to correct your error. With a continuable error, the user has the opportunity to correct the problem that caused the error.

(`cerror` *continuable-string format-string S-expression**)

The system initially performs the same operation as `error`. It then prints the continuable error message with some appropriate leading comment like "`If continued` ...". If the user wants to continue the operation, `cerror` returns control to the program. Your program must either continue with some default value, or prompt the user to supply additional information.

For example, suppose that the compiler expects a constant expression. If the argument isn't a constant, we can make the function return `nil` so that the compiler continues in a reasonable manner. The function `check-constant` performs this operation. Note, the `!c` tells the debugger to continue.

```
;;; Verify that the argument is a constant, signal an error
;;; if not. If the user continues, then return nil.

(defun check-constant (potential-constant)
  (if (or (symbolp potential-constant)
          (numberp potential-constant)
          (null potential-constant))
    potential-constant
    (progn
      (cerror "Used NIL as the default"
              "~A is an illegal constant."
              potential-constant)
     nil)))
 ⇒ CHECK-CONSTANT
```

```
(check-constant 55.6)
 ⇒ 55.6

(check-constant '(1 2 3))
!!!! Continuable error: (1 2 3) is an illegal constant.
If continued: Used NIL as the default
  Condition signaled in: CHECK-CONSTANT.
Entering the debugger
;; Now we will cause another error.
(check-constant "Is this a constant?")
!!!! Continuable error: Is this a constant? is an
  illegal constant.
If continued: Used NIL as the default
  Condition signaled in: CHECK-CONSTANT.
Entering the debugger
```

We now have caused two errors. We will continue both of them and see what happens.

```
!c
 ⇒ NIL

;; Now we can continue from the first one.
!c
 ⇒ NIL
```

Suppose we want to let the user provide another lambda expression to `lambdap` if the initial argument is not correct. `Cerror` is appropriate for this application with one slight change. That is to return the `lambda` expression if the expression is valid. `Lambdap` can recursively verify that the new expression provided by the user is valid. If the user gives another invalid expression, then another error occurs. Once a valid expression is found, then it is returned.

```
;;; Verify if the argument is a proper lambda expression and
;;; invoke error if it is not.  If it is proper, then return
;;; the lambda.

(defun lambdap (lambda-expression)
  (if (and (listp lambda-expression)
           (eql (car lambda-expression) 'lambda)
           (listp (cadr lambda-expression)))
    lambda-expression
    (progn
      (cerror "Prompts for a new lambda expression"
              "~A is not a a legal lambda.~%"
              lambda-expression)
      (format t
```

```
               "Please provide a valid lambda expression:~%")
        (lambdap (read)))))
 ⇒ LAMBDAP

;;; Test the lambdap with a legal lambda expression.
(lambdap '(lambda (x) (+ x x)))
 ⇒ (LAMBDA (X) (+ X X))

;;; This test should cause a continuable error.
(lambdap '(lambda x (+ x x)))
!!!! Continuable error: (LAMBDA X (+ X X)) is not a a legal
       lambda.
If continued: Prompts for a new lambda expression
  Condition signaled in: LAMBDAP.
Entering the debugger
```

Once again we have to issue a debugger command, `!c`, which says that we want to continue.

```
!c
Please provide a valid lambda expression:
(lambda (x) (* x x x))
 ⇒ (LAMBDA (X) (* X X X))
```

We don't have to continue from a continuable error. We are free to abort the debugger and try again.

```
(lambdap nil)
!!!! Continuable error: NIL is not a a legal lambda.
If continued: Prompts for a new lambda expression
  Condition signaled in: LAMBDAP.
Entering the debugger
!a
 ⇒ Abort to top level!
```

The Common LISP error mechanism lets you signal errors, stopping the computation and optionally continuing.

EXERCISES

***16.1** Write your own versions of **car** and **cdr** that use continuable errors. The result of the continuable error is to be the result of the function invocation – no recursion is required.

```
(c-car 1)
!!!! Continuable error: 1 is not a list.
If continued: Prompts for a value to return from c-car
  Condition signaled in: C-CAR.
```

```
Entering the debugger
!c
Input the result of (c-car 1):
99
 ⇒ 99
```

16.2 Suppose that you are writing a machine emulator. The machine takes instructions that are in a LISP-like form of (*opcode operand**). The legal opcodes are stored in an association list of the opcode name and the function to invoke. We will only implement `move` and `add` as opcodes. Each of the operands are also to be checked to see if they are valid. If an invalid opcode or operand is found, then the emulator signals an error and terminates. Write `check-valid-instructions` that takes a list of instructions and determines if all of them are legal. Choose a suitable list of opcodes and store them in an a-list `*opcodes*`. Legal operands are either integers, symbols, or two-element lists where the `car` is either `reg` or `frame` and the `cadr` is an integer.

```
(check-valid-instructions
 '((move (reg 1) (reg 2))
   (add (reg 1) (frame 3))
   (move 1 (frame 2))))
 ⇒ T

(check-valid-instructions
 '((move (reg 1) (reg 2)) (add (stack 99.3) (frame 3))))
!!!!! Error: Operand (STACK 99.3) of
          (ADD (STACK 99.3) (FRAME 3)) is invalid
  Condition signaled in: CHECK-OPERANDS.
Entering the debugger
```

16.2 Catch and Throw

The `catch` and `throw` functions transfer control across function bodies. Any dynamically bound variables are rebound to their proper values, even though functions are not properly exited. A `catch` will catch an associated result issued by a `throw`. The throw may be evaluated at any point in the execution as long as the catch is still active. Once the throw occurs, all functions between the `throw` and the `catch` are immediately exited without being evaluated, and any dynamically scoped variables are rebound. Since you can define many `catch` and `throw` points in a program, both functions take a tag argument that identifies matching `catch/throw` pairs. Generally, the tag is a symbol, but you can use anything that may be compared with the `eq` function.

(`catch` *tag S-expression**)

```
(throw tag S-expression)
```

`Catch` takes multiple S-expressions as arguments and sequentially evaluates each one until one of three things happens. If a `throw` with a matching tag is encountered during the evaluation, the evaluation is terminated and the `catch expression` returns the result of the S-expression that is thrown – the last argument in the `throw` expression. Or if a `throw` appears without a matching tag, some other previously defined `catch` would perform the catch and no more S-expressions are evaluated. Finally, if no corresponding `throw` is found while executing the S-expressions, the `catch` returns the result of the last S-expression.

A `throw` is processed by it first evaluating the last argument to get the result of the `throw`. A scan is then made of all current `catch`'s to see if any tags match. If none are found, an error is signaled. If a `catch` with a matching tag is present, the `throw` unwinds the execution stack and forces the `catch` to return the `throw` result.

The following is a simple example to illustrate the utility of these constructs.

```
;;; Defines a simple function that checks the argument and if
;;; negative it executes a throw with a 'negative' tag.
;;; Otherwise it prints the positive argument.

(defun print-positive (arg)
  (cond
   ((< arg 0)
    (throw 'negative arg)
    ;; The next line shouldn't be evaluated.
    (format t "Negative argument: ~A~%" arg))
   (t (format t "Positive argument: ~A~%" arg))))
 ⇒ PRINT-POSITIVE

;; Catch calls print-positive three times, the last of
;; which will be ignored.
(catch 'negative (print-positive 55) (print-positive -5)
  (print-positive 99))
 ⇒ Positive argument: 55
 ⇒ -5
```

Notice in this example that the positive `format` statement is printed and the negative one is never evaluated. Also, notice that the final result is from the throw, and not from one of the calls to `print-positive`. If we change the `catch` call to use another tag, we will get an error.

```
;; Catch with the wrong tag.
(catch 'positive (print-positive 55) (print-positive -5)
```

```
  (print-positive 99))
Positive argument: 55
!!!!! Error: Catch tag NEGATIVE not found in Throw
  Condition signaled in: IMPL:THROW-ERROR.
Entering the debugger
```

The `error` and `cerror` functions use a `throw` to return to the interpreter. Thus, the `eval` part of `read/eval/print` is actually enclosed within a `catch`.

As another example, suppose that we design our compiler to include a function `compile-expression`, which compiles one expression at a time. We would have to call `compile-expression` on each expression in the body of a `lambda` expression. When an expression won't compile, we have two options. One is to signal an error and stop. Another is to signal that the expression won't compile and then try to compile the next expression. The advantage to this is that you will find all error-causing expressions. Of course, the generated code won't be correct, but at least the user doesn't have to run the compiler separately for each error. Using this information and a few "stub" functions, we can write a mechanism that exhibits this behavior.

The first step is to write a stub function for `compile-expression`, which compiles the expression or performs a `throw` if there's an error. Since this is a stub function and we just want to check out the throw mechanism, we will have it randomly decide if an expression has errors. The tag that `compile-expression` uses is `comp-error`.

```
;;; STUB FUNCTION.
;;; This function is to compile a single expression.  It has
;;; two arguments, the first is the expression to compile and
;;; the second is the environment.

(defun compile-expression (exp env)
  (if (zerop (random 2))
    (progn
      (format t "Expression ~A is in error.~%" exp)
      (throw 'comp-error exp))
    (format t "Compiling ~A~%" exp)))
 ⇒ COMPILE-EXPRESSION
```

Now we can write `compile-lambda`, which compiles a single `lambda` expression. The first step is to check that the argument expression is valid by calling `lambdap`. Then it can call `compile-expression` on each of the expressions in the `lambda` body.

```
;;; Compile a lambda expression, being careful to catch any
;;; errors in the assorted expressions.  Since lambdap calls
;;; error if it is invalid, we don't need to worry about the
;;; result of the call.
```

```
(defun compile-lambda (lambda-expression)
  (lambdap lambda-expression)
  (let ((environment (cadr lambda-expression)))
    (dolist (expression (cddr lambda-expression))
      (catch 'comp-error
        (compile-expression expression environment)))))
⇒ COMPILE-LAMBDA

;; Now a test.
(compile-lambda
 '(lambda (a b) (setf a 1) (setf b (+ a b)) (print a)))
⇒ Compiling (SETF A 1)
⇒ Expression (SETF B (+ A B)) is in error.
⇒ Compiling (PRINT A)
⇒ NIL
```

This mechanism lets you compile each expression individually, searching for the valid and invalid expressions.

Another function that is similar to `catch/throw` is `unwind-protect`, which lets you evaluate a LISP expression in spite of a `throw`. If an `unwind-protected` expression is encountered during a `throw`, it will be evaluated and the `throw` will resume. This is the same mechanism that `with-open-file` uses to ensure that the file is closed even if a `throw` occurs, such as for an error.

(`unwind-protect` *S-expression S-expression**)

`Unwind-protect` takes an arbitrary number of arguments. The first is an S-expression that may or may not terminate successfully. The second and succeeding arguments are the expressions that are to be evaluated whether or not the first argument terminates successfully. `Unwind-protect` returns the result of the first S-expression if no `throw` occurs. If a `throw` has occurred, then no result is returned, since the unwinding process will continue.

We will define a simple version of the macro `with-open-file` to demonstrate `unwind-protect`. This version assumes that the file will be opened for input. It evaluates the body of the `with-open-file` as the first argument to `unwind-protect`, and then closes the stream in the rest of the expressions. We will also print a message stating that the stream is closed, so we can watch it happen. Recall that `,@` is used to splice the list value into the argument. This makes the `progn` have the correct form of arguments.

```
;;; A simplified version of with-open-file.  There are no
;;; options passed to the open expression.

(defmacro my-with-open-file ((stream filename) . forms)
  `(let
```

```
     ((,stream (open ,filename))
     (unwind-protect
       (progn ,@forms)
       (close ,stream)
       (format t "~%File: ~S closed" ,stream))))
 ⇒ MY-WITH-OPEN-FILE

;; Now look at a macro expansion of this macro.
(macroexpand '(my-with-open-file (foo "frob.txt")
                                 (print (read foo))))
 ⇒ (LET
 ⇒   ((FOO (OPEN "frob.txt")))
 ⇒   (UNWIND-PROTECT
 ⇒     (PROGN (PRINT (READ FOO)))
 ⇒     (CLOSE FOO)
 ⇒     (FORMAT T "~%File: ~S closed" FOO)))
 ⇒ T

;; Now test it out.  It should open the file and read one
;; S-expression, print it out and then close the file.
(my-with-open-file (foo "frob.txt")
                   (print (read foo)))
 ⇒ (FILE WITH ONLY ONE DUMMY S-EXPRESSION)
 ⇒ File: #<File Stream /u/kessler/frob.txt> closed
 ⇒ (FILE WITH ONLY ONE DUMMY S-EXPRESSION)

;; Now, to demonstrate that the protected file will still be
;; closed, even if we perform a throw.
(my-with-open-file (foo "frob.txt")
                   (error "Oops, we have caused an error"))
!!!!! Error: Oops, we have caused an error
  Condition signaled in: :EVAL-FORM.
Entering the debugger
;; Now, we abort the debugger and watch what happens.
!a
 ⇒ File: #<File Stream /u/kessler/frob.txt> closed
 ⇒ Abort to top level!
```

EXERCISES

16.3** Write your own version of **error**, called **my-error** that prints an error message, and then performs a **throw** with the tag **error**. Return ****error* as the error value.

```
(catch 'error (my-error "This is an error message"))
 ⇒ Error Signaled: This is an error message
 ⇒ **ERROR**
```

16.4 Write your own versions of `car` and `cdr` that call `my-error` when passed illegal arguments.

```
(catch 'error (my-car '(1 2 3)))
 ⇒ 1

(catch 'error (my-car 99))
 ⇒ Error Signaled: 99 passed to car is not a list.
 ⇒ **ERROR**
```

***16.5** Write your own LISP interpreter that calls `read`, `eval`, and `print`. However, this version traps errors using `catch` and the `error` tag. The only legal operations are calls to `my-car` and `my-cdr`. If the symbol `quit` is given to the interpreter, then it terminates.

```
(my-interpreter)
LISP> (my-car '(1 2 3))
Result: 1
LISP> (my-car 99)
Error Signaled: 99 passed to car is not a list.
LISP> (my-cdr '(a b c))
Result: (B C)
LISP> quit
 ⇒ NIL
```

16.3 Using Catch and Throw

Pattern matching is frequently performed in compilers to determine characteristics of the program they are compiling. The pattern matcher compares a pattern against a subject and returns an association list that represents the bindings between the pattern variables and what they matched. A pattern in our system is an S-expression consisting of atoms, lists, or pattern variables. A pattern variable matches any single atom or list. It is designated with a question mark preceding a symbol. Atoms within the pattern must match the same atom in the subject list. Finally, the pattern and subject list must also have exactly the same structure. The chart on page 441 illustrates the kind of matching that will be accepted by our pattern matcher.

The first step is to write an auxiliary function that determines if the argument is a pattern variable. We can call `symbol-name` and then see if the first character is a question mark.

Pattern	Subject	Match?	Binding
X	X	T	nil
X	Y	nil	nil
?X	X	T	(?X X)
?X	(A B C)	T	(?X (A B C))
(A B)	(A B)	T	nil
(A ?X)	(A (B C))	T	(?X (B C))
(?X ?Y)	(A (B C))	T	(?X A) (?Y (B C))
(?X . ?Y)	(A B C D)	T	(?X A) (?Y (B C D))

```
;;; Is the argument a symbol and does it start with a ?.

(defun variablep (pattern-variable)
  (and (symbolp pattern-variable)
       (equal (char (symbol-name pattern-variable) 0) #\?)))
⇒ VARIABLEP

;; Test the function.
(variablep 'foo)
⇒ NIL

(variablep '?X)
⇒ T
```

The match function looks very much like the code for equal. It compares the various elements of the pattern and subject and returns any bindings. If we don't find a match, we will throw out of the function. This makes it very easy to terminate. We don't need to check for a failure in every recursive result. This function checks each of the cases, recursively scanning the two lists.

```
;;; Match a pattern against a subject list and return an
;;; a-list of the pattern variable/subject part bindings.  If
;;; the match fails, perform a throw with tag 'nomatch.

(defun match (pattern subject)
  (cond ((and (null subject) (null pattern)) nil)
        ((variablep pattern) (list (list pattern subject)))
        ((eql pattern subject) nil)
        ((and (listp pattern) (listp subject))
         (append (match (car pattern) (car subject))
                 (match (cdr pattern) (cdr subject))))
        (t (throw 'nomatch 'nomatch))))
```

```
⇒ MATCH

;; Now some tests.
(catch 'nomatch (match 'x 'x))
⇒ NIL

(catch 'nomatch (match 'x 'y))
⇒ NOMATCH

(catch 'nomatch (match '?x 'x))
⇒ ((?X X))

(catch 'nomatch (match '?x '(a b)))
⇒ ((?X (A B)))

(catch 'nomatch (match '(a b) '(a b)))
⇒ NIL

(catch 'nomatch (match '(a ?x) '(a (b c))))
⇒ ((?X (B C)))

(catch 'nomatch (match '(?x . ?y) '(a b c d e)))
⇒ ((?X A) (?Y (B C D E)))
```

Our pattern matching system also needs rules. A rule is a pattern and body. The body is an S-expression that is evaluated when the pattern succeeds in matching. The S-expression is evaluated in a context where each of the pattern variables is bound to whatever they matched. So, when a match is found, then some LISP code is executed.

These rules can be collected into a list called a rule block. They should be ordered from most specific to most general. Then a rule interpreter scans the rules searching for one that matches. If the most specific rules are first, they'll be matched if a subject has more specific elements. When the rule interpreter finds a matching pattern in a rule, it can then evaluate the body and return the result of that evaluation. We will see later how you can recursively invoke the rule interpreter for a very powerful transformation system.

We must create the environment for the S-expression with all of the bindings. Each pattern variable is also a LISP variable, so we could place them in a `let`.

```
(eval `(let
         ,(match '(?x ?y) '(a b))
         (list 'result ?x ?y)))
!!!!! Error: The symbol A has no value.
  Condition signaled in: SYMBOL-VALUE.
Entering the debugger
```

The problem with this is evident if we call `macroexpand` instead of doing the evaluation.

```
(macroexpand `(let
                 ,(match '(?x ?y) '(a b))
               (list 'result ?x ?y)))
⇒ (LET ((?X A) (?Y B)) (LIST (QUOTE RESULT) ?X ?Y))
⇒ NIL
```

The problem is that the bindings must be quoted. We have to change `match` so it wraps a `quote` around the binding as follows:

```
;;; Match a pattern against a subject list and return an
;;; a-list of the pattern variable/subject part bindings.  If
;;; the match fails, perform a throw with tag 'nomatch.  The
;;; binding includes a quote, so we can just place it into a
;;; let in the rule interpreter.

(defun match (pattern subject)
  (cond ((and (null subject) (null pattern)) nil)
        ((variablep pattern) `((,pattern ',subject)))
        ((eql pattern subject) nil)
        ((and (listp pattern) (listp subject))
         (append (match (car pattern) (car subject))
                 (match (cdr pattern) (cdr subject))))
        (t (throw 'nomatch 'nomatch))))
⇒ MATCH

;; A few more tests to make sure that the quote is present.
(catch 'nomatch (match '?x 'x))
⇒ ((?X (QUOTE X)))

(catch 'nomatch (match '?x '(a b)))
⇒ ((?X (QUOTE (A B))))
```

The rule interpreter takes two arguments, a rule block and the subject. It scans the rules until it finds a match. Then a `let` is created with the bindings and the S-expression is evaluated. This adapts itself well to either recursive or iterative implementation. We'll choose the recursive version.

```
;;; A rule interpreter takes a rule block and a subject list
;;; and finds a pattern which matches and returns the
;;; evaluation  of the rule body.

(defun rule-interpreter (rule-block subject)
  (let
    (bindings)
    (cond
     ((null rule-block) nil)
     ((listp (setf bindings
```

```
                  (catch 'nomatch (match (caar rule-block)
                                          subject))))
        (eval `(let ,bindings
                    ,@(cdr (car rule-block)))))
       (t (rule-interpreter (cdr rule-block) subject)))))
   ⇒ RULE-INTERPRETER
```

An operation performed by many compilers is algebraic simplification. For example, if an expression includes the addition of a zero, then the addition isn't necessary. So, we can create a rule block that does simplification for addition and multiplication as follows:

```
;; Create a simple set of rules to perform simplification of
;; algebraic expressions.
(setf algebra-rule-block '(
   ((+ 0 ?X) ?X)
   ((+ ?X 0) ?X)
   ((* ?X 1) ?X)
   ((* 1 ?X) ?X)
   ((* ?X 0) 0)
   ((* 0 ?X) 0)
   (?X ?X)))
⇒ (((+ 0 ?X) ?X) ((+ ?X 0) ?X) ((* ?X 1) ?X)
⇒  ((* 1 ?X) ?X) ((* ?X 0) 0) ((* 0 ?X) 0)
⇒  (?X ?X))
```

Using these rules, we can now test out the rule interpreter.

```
(rule-interpreter algebra-rule-block '(+ X 0))
⇒ X

(rule-interpreter algebra-rule-block '(* 0 Y))
⇒ 0

(rule-interpreter algebra-rule-block '(* Y 7))
⇒ (* Y 7)
```

This is acceptable, but it needs one further enhancement. It doesn't find all of the simplifications if an element is more than a simple symbol.

```
(rule-interpreter algebra-rule-block '(+ (* X 1) 0))
⇒ (* X 1)
```

We can easily change the rules to recursively invoke the simplification process before returning a value.

```
;; Create a simple set of rules to perform simplification of
```

```
;; algebraic expressions.
(setf algebra-rule-block '(
   ((+ 0 ?X) (rule-interpreter algebra-rule-block ?X))
   ((+ ?X 0) (rule-interpreter algebra-rule-block ?X))
   ((+ ?X ?Y) (list '+
                    (rule-interpreter algebra-rule-block ?X)
                    (rule-interpreter algebra-rule-block
                                      ?Y)))
   ((* ?X 1) (rule-interpreter algebra-rule-block ?X))
   ((* 1 ?X) (rule-interpreter algebra-rule-block ?X))
   ((* ?X 0) 0)
   ((* 0 ?X) 0)
   ((* ?X ?Y) (list '*
                    (rule-interpreter algebra-rule-block ?X)
                    (rule-interpreter algebra-rule-block
                                      ?Y)))
   (?X ?X)))
⇒ (((+ 0 ?X) (RULE-INTERPRETER ALGEBRA-RULE-BLOCK ?X))
⇒  ((+ ?X 0) (RULE-INTERPRETER ALGEBRA-RULE-BLOCK ?X))
⇒  ((+ ?X ?Y)
⇒   (LIST (QUOTE +)
⇒         (RULE-INTERPRETER ALGEBRA-RULE-BLOCK ?X)
⇒         (RULE-INTERPRETER ALGEBRA-RULE-BLOCK ?Y)))
⇒  ((* ?X 1) (RULE-INTERPRETER ALGEBRA-RULE-BLOCK ?X))
⇒  ((* 1 ?X) (RULE-INTERPRETER ALGEBRA-RULE-BLOCK ?X))
⇒  ((* ?X 0) 0)
⇒  ((* 0 ?X) 0)
⇒  ((* ?X ?Y)
⇒   (LIST (QUOTE *)
⇒         (RULE-INTERPRETER ALGEBRA-RULE-BLOCK ?X)
⇒         (RULE-INTERPRETER ALGEBRA-RULE-BLOCK ?Y)))
⇒  (?X ?X))

;; See if it still works for the single-level ones.
(rule-interpreter algebra-rule-block '(+ X 0))
⇒ X

;; Now a more complicated version.
(rule-interpreter algebra-rule-block '(+ (* X 1) 0))
⇒ X

(rule-interpreter algebra-rule-block '(* (+ X 0) (* X 1)))
⇒ (* X X)
```

EXERCISES

16.6 Write `match` without using `throw` to escape from the match process. Notice the additional complexity that this causes over the simpler `throw` version.

***16.7** Explain why the pattern `(?X . ?Y)` matches any list with at least one element. (*Hint:* You might want to trace `match` to see what is happening.)

16.4 Summary

The error mechanism provided is simple, yet elegant. The two error functions, `error` and `cerror` permit the specification of non-continuable and continuable errors. Non-continuable errors are fatal errors that require that you start over again. The continuable errors allow you to continue the execution as dictated by the code that follows the call to `cerror`. The functions `catch` and `throw` are used for their non-local exit capabilities. They should be used with caution because their coding can lead to obscure errors. However, they can make some programs much simpler as demonstrated with the `match` function in the last section. Also, `catch` and `throw` are natural for implementing operations like `error` and `cerror`.

Chapter Exercises

This set of exercises will be used to implement some of the functions of Common LISP using `catch` and `throw`. We have already seen that it can be used to implement the two error functions. We will use it to implement the `return-from` and `block` expressions.

The expressions `block` and `return-from` have not been previously discussed, but they are Common LISP primitives that are used to implement many of the other Common LISP control structures. `Block` takes an arbitrary number of arguments, the first of which is the symbol that names the block.

`(block` *symbol S-expression** `)`

The remaining S-expressions are to be evaluated within the block. The result of the `block` is the result of the evaluation of the last expression unless a `return-from` is executed. `Return-from` specifies a block name and a value. The result of the block is then the value of the `return-from`.

`(return-from` *symbol S-expression*`)`

The symbols are used with the `blocks` and `return-froms` because they may be arbitrarily nested. Note that Common LISP specifies that each function definition creates a block whose name is the name of the function. That means you can place a `return-from` with the name of the function within any function to rapidly escape from the function.

```
;;; A simple example of a block and return-from.
(block foo
  (let ((a 1) (b 2))
    (format t "Inside of let.~%")
    (return-from foo (+ a b))
    (format t "Shouldn't be printed.~%")))
 ⇒ Inside of let.
 ⇒ 3
```

Typically `block` and `return-from` are not implemented using `catch` and `throw`. This is because the `return-from` must be lexically scoped within the `block`. The `catch` and `throw` are more powerful than necessary since they can operate outside of the lexical scope. However, for our purposes, we can implement these two functions using the capabilities of `catch` and `throw`.

***1.** Implement your own version of `block` called `xblock`.

***2.** Implement your own version of `return-from` called `xreturn-from`. Test this with `xblock` as follows:

```
;;; A simple example of a block and return-from.
(xblock foo
  (let ((a 1) (b 2))
    (format t "Inside of let.~%")
    (xreturn-from foo (+ a b))
    (format t "Shouldn't be printed.~%")))
 ⇒ Inside of let.
 ⇒ 3
```

3. Implement `just-return` which returns from the current block without using a name. It takes only one argument, which is the value to return from the block. You might have to change `xblock`.

```
(xblock foo
  (+ (xblock bar
       (format t "Inside bar.~%")
       (just-return 99)
       (format t "Should be ignored.~%"))
     1))
 ⇒ Inside bar.
 ⇒ 100
```

4. *Difficult* – Your goal is to implement `super-xreturn`, which returns its argument value out of all nested `xblocks`. It only takes one argument, which is the value to return. (*Hint:* You may find that using dynamic variables helps. Be careful to make sure that you don't change your environment such that running the code a second time won't work.)

```
;;; A simple example of a block and return-from.
(xblock foo
  (let ((a 1) (b 2))
    (xblock bar
      (format t "Inside of second block.~%")
      (super-xreturn (+ a b))
      (format t "Shouldn't be printed.~%"))
    (format t "This also shouldn't be printed.~%"))
  (format t "Neither should this.~%"))
⇒ Inside of second block.
⇒ 3
```

Function Summary

The following lists the functions and topics covered in this chapter.

- `(error` *format-string S-expression*`*)`
- `(cerror` *continuable-string format-string S-expression*`*)`
- `(catch` *tag S-expression*`*)`
- `(throw` *tag S-expression*`)`
- `(unwind-protect` *S-expression S-expression*`*)`
- `(block` *symbol S-expression*`*)`
- `(return-from` *symbol S-expression*`)`

17 LISPUCOPIA

THIS CHAPTER IS a mixture of LISP constructs that weren't covered by the case studies in the previous chapters. The first topic is the package system, which solves the problem of conflicting symbol names. We then discuss some additional control constructs. We also cover a few operations that make LISP code a little easier to write. The next topic is how to return multiple values. We've seen that system functions can return multiple values. This section describes how to return and capture multiple values in your own code. We then discuss read macros. These are the macros like ' that save typing and expand macros during the reading process. We then cover LISP compilation and how to make your programs run faster. The last section discusses closures, which are data structures that couple some LISP code and the environment in which to run the code. Closures are useful paradigms for constructs like objects.

17.1 Packages

The package system addresses a shortcoming of many earlier LISP systems, in which all LISP symbols reside in a single, symbol table. LISP lets you change the value of any global symbol, modify property lists associated with a symbol, or even redefine any LISP function. So, you could easily define a function with the same name as some very important internal function used by the LISP system. The LISP system has a documented user interface with a known set of functions, but there are also internal functions needed by the LISP system. The added flexibility comes at the cost of being able to destroy an execution.

Common LISP includes the package system to try to fix this problem. The package system makes it harder to totally ruin your system and provides a level of data abstraction as a side benefit.

We will review how symbols are constructed to learn how packages work. The function `intern` takes a string as an argument and returns the associated symbol. In older LISP systems, `intern` would scan a hash table or an association list (known historically as the *obarray* or *oblist*) that would map the string name

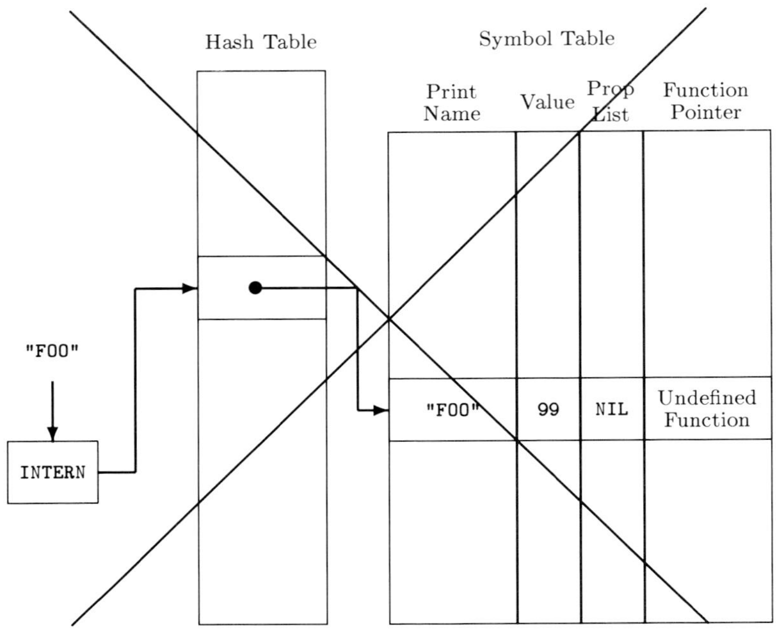

Figure 17.1 OUTDATED Intern Process

of the symbol into a location in a symbol table. If a symbol is found with that string name, also known as print name, then the symbol itself is returned. The symbol is a pointer into the symbol table where the string name, value, property list, and function pointer can be found. If it doesn't find a matching symbol, then it creates a new entry and provides default values for each field of the symbol. Some implementations don't use a fixed, symbol table, but instead store the fields associated with a symbol in the heap.* Figure 17.1 shows the *interning* process. Any symbol that is read will go through this process. Note that strings are not stored in the print name slot of the table. They are actually stored in the heap. We have placed them directly in the symbol table to simplify the figure.

The package system uses many hash tables, each associated with a particular package. There is still only one symbol table, so a symbol is defined to have a *home* package. The function `intern` takes an optional extra argument, which is the package in which to `intern` the symbol. If no package is given, then the symbol is interned into the current package, which is bound to `*package*`. Figure 17.2 illustrates this configuration.

The package system lets you have *internal* and *external* symbols. The only symbols accessible from a package are the externals. You can override this

*The heap is a large data area where most values reside. To help with the clarity of the figures, the heap is not shown.

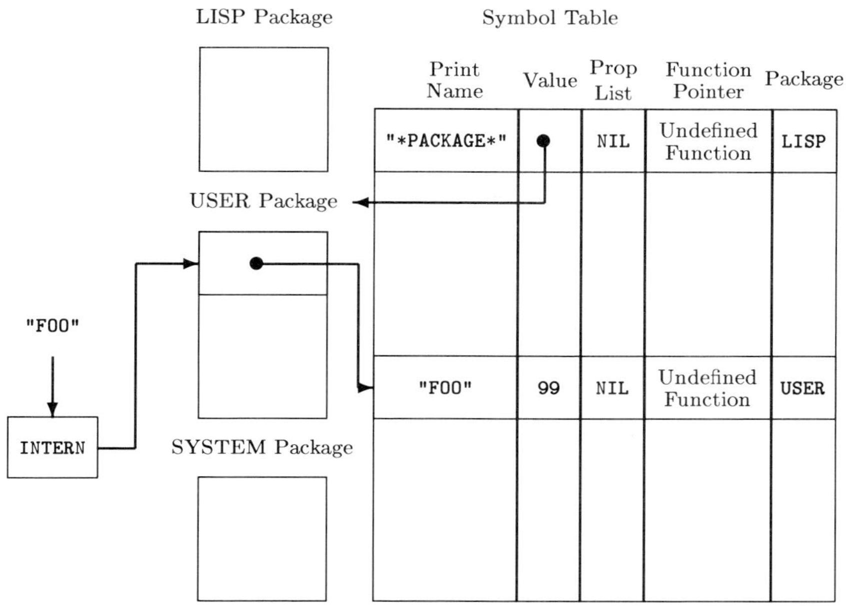

Figure 17.2 Intern Process in Common LISP

mechanism and access the internal symbols, but you have to explicitly indicate your intention. A symbol accessible from a package is always internal or external, never both.

By default, there are a minimum of four packages that exist in every implementation of Common LISP :

`lisp` – This package contains all of Common LISP primitives. The external symbols are the symbols that we have seen throughout this text, like `car`, `+`, and `*package*`. There may be internal symbols that are used to implement these primitives, but you should ignore them.

`user` – This is the default initial package. As you define new symbols, they are placed in this package.

`system` – This is a place where a LISP implementation may place other symbols that it uses. Typically, it includes some external symbols that you may call. For example in HP Common LISP, it includes the `exit` function which is used to terminate the LISP session. You should consult your Common LISP implementation guide for a list of the useful symbols.

`keyword` – This package contains all of the keywords defined in the system. We have seen many keywords in previous chapters – they are indicated with a leading colon. For example, when we initialize a slot in an object, we specify the slot name with a keyword. All keywords evaluate to themselves so they don't need to be explicitly quoted.

You get to an external symbol in another package by placing the package name and a colon just before the symbol name. Internal symbols can be accessed by placing two colons between the package name and the symbol. For example, the initial package is `user` and all of the LISP primitives are defined in `lisp`. Let's use packages to access some of the symbols. First, we'll see what the current package is by looking at the value of `*package*`.

`*package*`

```
*package*
 ⇒ #<Package USER>
```

This indicates that we are currently in the `user` package. To access the external symbol `car` in the `lisp` package, we have to prefix the name with `lisp:`.

```
;; Invoke the lisp car on a list.
(lisp:car '(1 2 3))
 ⇒ 1
```

This seems to work just fine. However, you might be wondering how we were able to define any functions, or do any operations without prefixing all of those symbols with `lisp:`. We would have to write something like the following just to define a simple function:

```
;;; Computes the sum of the squares of the two arguments.
(lisp:defun sum-of-squares (a b)
  (lisp:+ (lisp:expt a 2) (lisp:expt b 2)))
 ⇒ SUM-OF-SQUARES

(sum-of-squares 3 4)
 ⇒ 25
```

The package system lets you create packages that inherit all of the external symbols of another package. When an external symbol is inherited, it's as if the symbol were defined in the current package. Thus, `car` is defined as an external symbol in the `lisp` package, but `user` inherits all of those symbols, so it is as if those symbols are really internal to the `user` package. This inheritance process only goes to one level. So, if `lisp` inherited some symbols from another package, they wouldn't be passed along to the `user` package, unless they were explicitly made into external symbols in the `lisp` package. As you create or access packages, most of them inherit (the proper term is *use*) the `lisp` package.

One of the useful features of the package system is the ability to *shadow* other symbols. This is a process by which you effectively undo the use of a symbol from another package. This is useful if you want to change the definition of some LISP function, but don't want to destroy the original definition. After you shadow a symbol, the original definition is available by prefixing it with the package. Accesses without the prefix will use the new local definition. The `shadow` function shadows a symbol. It takes either a single symbol as an argument, or a list of symbols.

(shadow *symbol*)

(shadow (*symbol**))

For example, in Chapter 3, we defined our own version of `length` which we called `my-length`, which computed the length of a list. As we learned in Chapter 13, `length` operates upon any sequence, not just lists. So, our definition of `length` was semantically different from that of the Common LISP standard. Suppose that we want to restrict `length` to only operate on lists. Then we could write the following code:

```
;; We will define our own version.
(shadow 'length)
;;; Compute the length of the argument list.

(defun length (some-list)
  (if (null some-list)
    0
    (1+ (length (cdr some-list)))))
 ⇒ LENGTH

;; Now a test.
(length '(red blue green))
 ⇒ 3

(lisp:length '(red blue green))
 ⇒ 3

;; Notice that there is a difference.
(length (vector 1 2 3))
!!!!! Error: The argument #(1 2 3) is not a valid list.
  Condition signaled in: CDR.
Entering the debugger
;; Now the real version is passed a vector.
(lisp:length (vector 1 2 3))
 ⇒ 3
```

So, by shadowing the original definition, all calls to `length` see the newly defined version.

The function `in-package` switches between packages. Its first argument is the name of the package as either a symbol or a string. If the package doesn't exist, one is automatically created for you. The main effect of this function is to change `*package*` to be the new package.

```
(in-package package-name)
```

For example, we can switch to the `lisp` package as follows:

```
*package*
 ⇒ #<Package USER>
(in-package 'lisp)
 ⇒ #<Package LISP>
*package*
 ⇒ #<Package LISP>
```

`In-package` takes two optional arguments, indicated with the `:nicknames` and `:use` keywords. The first indicates any nicknames that you would like to add to the package. A nickname is another way of naming the package. For example, the `system` package has the nickname `sys`, which can be used anywhere the name `system` is used. Remember that all keywords are optional and they may be provided in any order.

```
(in-package :nicknames S-expression :use S-expression)
```

```
(in-package 'sys)
 ⇒ #<Package SYSTEM>
```

The `:use` keyword specifies any additional packages that are to be used by the package. These are especially important if the package doesn't exist. If no `:use` is specified, then the `lisp` package is automatically inherited. If you don't want to use `lisp`, then you must supply a `nil` as the value.

```
;; Create and switch to a package that doesn't use anything.
(in-package 'foobar :use nil)
 ⇒ #<Package FOOBAR>
;; Now, if we try anything, then it will fail because we
;; don't have access to the lisp package.
(car '(1 2 3))
!!!! Continuable error: Undefined function 'CAR' applied or
       called.
If continued: will reapply 'CAR' to the argument
```

```
        list ((1 2 3)).
    Condition signaled in: :EVAL-FORM.
  Entering the debugger
```

Now that no symbols are directly available, we can't even switch back to the `user` package, without qualifying the `in-package` with a package name.

```
(in-package 'user)
!!!! Continuable error: Undefined function 'IN-PACKAGE'
      applied  or called.
If continued: will reapply 'IN-PACKAGE' to the argument list
      (USER).
  Condition signaled in: :EVAL-FORM.
Entering the debugger
;; Remember to prefix with lisp: to get back to the user
;; package.
(lisp:in-package 'user)
⇒ #<Package USER>
```

You may sometime want to create a package that doesn't use the `lisp` package, but you must remember that you have to explicitly place the `lisp` package on the front of each LISP symbol while in that package.

If you want to use another package from the current package, you need not call `in-package` on the current package. You can use `use-package`, which adds the external symbols defined in the argument list of packages into the current package. `Use-package` takes either a single package or package-name argument, or a list of packages and/or package names.

(`use-package` *package-or-package-name*)

(`use-package` (*package-or-package-name**))

```
;; Add foobar to the list of currently used packages.
(use-package '(foobar))
⇒ T
```

Some functions require that you pass them an actual package instead of just the package name. The function `find-package` can be used to search for a package matching the argument name and return that package.

(`find-package` *package-name*)

For example, `intern` may take an optional package as a second argument. This interns the string in the package designated by the optional argument.

`(intern` *string package*`)`

```
(find-package 'lisp)
 ⇒ #<Package LISP>

;;; Intern mumble in the lisp package
(setf mumble-symbol (intern "MUMBLE" (find-package 'lisp)))
 ⇒ LISP::MUMBLE
```

Notice that it prints `mumble` as an internal symbol within the `lisp` package. Now, by calling `set`, we can give it a value for later examination. Recall that unlike `setf`, `set` evaluates its first argument.

```
(set mumble-symbol 55)
 ⇒ 55

lisp::mumble
 ⇒ 55

;; It is not an internal symbol.
lisp:mumble
!!!!! Error: The symbol "MUMBLE" is not external in the
        package #<Package LISP>.
  Condition signaled in: LISP::READ-TOKEN.
Entering the debugger
;; It is also not in the user package.
mumble
!!!!! Error: The symbol MUMBLE has no value.
  Condition signaled in: SYMBOL-VALUE.
Entering the debugger
```

The function `find-symbol` is identical to `intern` except it doesn't create the symbol if it can't find it. Both `intern` and `find-symbol` return a second value, which indicates the type of the argument symbol. It returns `:internal`, `:external`, or `:inherited`, the latter indicating that the symbol was inherited from another package and that it is also internal.

`(find-symbol` *string-or-symbol*`)`

`(find-symbol` *string-or-symbol package*`)`

```
(find-symbol "CAR")
 ⇒ CAR
 ⇒ :INHERITED

(find-symbol "CAR" (find-package 'lisp))
 ⇒ CAR
 ⇒ :EXTERNAL
```

As you construct your own packages, you will want to define which symbols are to be external. To accomplish this, you must call the **export** function, passing it the list of symbols that you wish to be external.

(export *symbol*)

(export (*symbol**))

Generally, you should place this statement at the top of the file that contains your application. That way, it is clear to a reader what symbols they should be using for access into your code.

```
(in-package 'yet-another-package :nicknames '(yap))
 ⇒ #<Package YET-ANOTHER-PACKAGE>

(export '(colors red blue green))
 ⇒ T

(setf colors '(red blue green))
 ⇒ (RED BLUE GREEN)

(setf red 24)
 ⇒ 24

(setf purple 44)
 ⇒ 44
```

Now we can switch to another package that will use this one and access the external symbols.

```
(in-package 'another-one :use '(yap lisp))
 ⇒ #<Package ANOTHER-ONE>

colors
 ⇒ (RED BLUE GREEN)

red
 ⇒ 24

;; This symbol wasn't exported, so it should generate an
```

```
;; error.
purple
!!!!! Error: The symbol PURPLE has no value.
  Condition signaled in: SYMBOL-VALUE.
Entering the debugger
;; Switch back to the normal user package.
(in-package 'user)
 ⇒ #<Package USER>
```

The `do-symbols` expression is an iteration construct that allows access to the symbols in a package. It has the same syntax as `dolist` and binds the local variable to successive symbols within a package.

`(do-symbols` (*symbol package S-expression*) *S-expression**`)`

Both the *package* and the result *S-expression* are optional.

For example, we can determine the number of symbols in the `lisp` package.

```
(defun count-symbols ()
  (let ((count 0))
    (do-symbols (symbol (find-package 'lisp))
      (setf count (1+ count)))
    (format t "~A total symbols in the lisp package.~%"
            count)))
 ⇒ COUNT-SYMBOLS
```

```
(count-symbols)
 ⇒ 3452 total symbols in the lisp package.
 ⇒ NIL
```

You can also remove symbols from a package by using `unintern`. This removes the symbol reference from the package. If the symbol is removed from its home package, then a `nil` is placed in its package field of the symbol table. Symbols without a home package are printed with a sharp sign as the package name.

`(unintern` *symbol*`)`

`(unintern` *symbol package*`)`

```
(in-package 'yap)
 ⇒ #<Package YET-ANOTHER-PACKAGE>
```

```
(unintern 'red)
 ⇒ T

red
!!!!! Error: The symbol RED has no value.
  Condition signaled in: SYMBOL-VALUE.
Entering the debugger
colors
 ⇒ (#:RED BLUE GREEN)
```

This means that the symbol has been removed from the package. So, when we evaluate `red`, it has no value. The symbol still exists as in the `colors` list. Also, it still has a value, except we can't type any expression that directly gets the value.

```
#:red
!!!!! Error: The symbol #:RED has no value.
  Condition signaled in: SYMBOL-VALUE.
Entering the debugger
```

The only way to get at the value is to use the symbol as it was stored in `colors`.

```
(car colors)
 ⇒ #:RED

(symbol-value (car colors))
 ⇒ 24
```

You remove access to an uninterned symbol from any code by evaluating it after the symbol is uninterned. This is because `intern` can't find the symbol. However, any code that used the symbol before the call to `unintern` will still function properly. This is because a symbol is actually an index into the symbol table and uninterning the symbol doesn't affect any symbol table fields except for the home package field. You can use this technique to make sure that no user can get at the values of your symbols. Also, if all references to the symbol have been eliminated, then the space allocated in the symbol table may be reused. It is also useful in conjunction with the function `gensym`. This is just like `gentemp`, except it generates an uninterned symbol. This is especially useful within a macro expansion, since there is no way for the user to type in an expression that will interfere with an uninterned symbol.

(gensym)

Notice how a symbol created with `gentemp` is interned, which means that we can define code which uses it.

```
(gensym)
```

```
 ⇒ #:G15

(gentemp)
 ⇒ T1

(setf tempsymbol (gentemp))
 ⇒ T2

(setf t2 100)
 ⇒ 100

(symbol-value tempsymbol)
 ⇒ 100
```

In Chapter 14, we used **gentemp** to create a temporary symbol when we expanded **my-dolist** into a **do***. A **gensym** would work just as well:

```
(shadow 'dolist)
 ⇒ T

;;; This is our version of dolist, which uses gensym for the
;;; temporary variable.

(defmacro dolist ((local some-list &optional result)
                  &body body)
  (let ((temp-symbol (gensym)))
    `(do*
      ((,temp-symbol ,some-list (cdr ,temp-symbol))
       (,local (car ,temp-symbol) (car ,temp-symbol)))
      ((null ,temp-symbol) ,result)
      ,@body)))
 ⇒ DOLIST

;;; Now a test.
(dolist (the-list (list 'red 'blue 'green) 'black)
  (format t "The color: ~A~%" the-list))
 ⇒ The color: RED
 ⇒ The color: BLUE
 ⇒ The color: GREEN
 ⇒ BLACK
```

In [40, Chapter 11], the minute details of the package system are discussed, along with a number of other package related functions. You should study it carefully if you plan to do anything more complicated than the operations outlined here. Pay close attention to the example [40, Section 11.9, pp 189-192] that discusses the proper style for constructing files with packages.

EXERCISES

***17.1** In Chapter 15, we defined a program that would do A* searching. Suppose that we wished to place this set of functions within a package. Describe how you would organize the code so a user could just use the **astar** package and interface functions.

17.2 Very old dialects of LISP actually returned the property list of a symbol when a symbol was passed to **cdr** [2, page 266]. This was related to the list implementation of each symbol and its associated fields. Write a new version of **cdr** which does the same operation.

```
(cdr '(red blue green))
 ⇒ (BLUE GREEN)

(setf (get 'red 'color-value) 44)
 ⇒ 44

(cdr 'red)
 ⇒ (COLOR-VALUE 44)
```

***17.3** *Difficult* – Joe Hacker wants to write a macro **shadow-wrapper**, which allows the redefinition of a function in a package that inherits from another package without changing the original version of the function.

```
(in-package 'foobar)
 ⇒ #<Package FOOBAR>

(export '(bar shadow-wrapper))
 ⇒ T

(defun bar (a b) (+ (- a) b))
 ⇒ BAR

(bar 2 3)
 ⇒ 1

(in-package 'mumble :use '(lisp foobar))
 ⇒ #<Package MUMBLE>

(bar 2 3)
 ⇒ 1

(shadow-wrapper bar (defun bar (a b) (* a b)))
 ⇒ BAR

(bar 2 3)
 ⇒ 6

(foobar:bar 2 3)
 ⇒ 1
```

The purpose is to compose the shadow and function definition into a single macro. Why doesn't Joe's first attempt work?

```
;;; BUGGY VERSION????
```

```
(defmacro shadow-wrapper (fun definition)
  `(progn
     (shadow ',fun)
     ,definition))
 ⇒ SHADOW-WRAPPER

(shadow-wrapper bar (defun bar (a b) (* a b)))
 ⇒ FOOBAR:BAR

(bar 2 3)
!!!! Continuable error: Undefined function 'BAR' applied or
       called.
If continued: will reapply 'BAR' to the argument list (2 3).
  Condition signaled in: :EVAL-FORM.
Entering the debugger
;; The old bar in foobar should still return 1.
(foobar:bar 2 3)
 ⇒ 6
```

So, there isn't a new `bar` and the old definition changed. Why?

***17.4** *Difficult* – Help Joe Hacker out and write a definition for `shadow-wrapper` that behaves properly.

17.2 Additional Control Constructs

Common LISP provides some additional control constructs that can make your programming task easier. Common LISP uses some of these to implement other control expressions that we have seen. Other control constructs are macros that expand into some familiar expressions.

The first set of constructs are the Common LISP primitive control expressions. These are `block`, `return-from`, `tagbody`, and `go`. The `block` expression specifies a name for the block, along with a set of S-expressions. These S-expressions are evaluated in sequence, and the `block` returns the result of the last expression.

> `(block` *symbol S-expression** `)`

The `return-from` expression interrupts the sequential evaluation of the `block` body with an early exit. It has two arguments, the name of the block to exit and the value to return from the block.

> `(return-from` *symbol S-expression*`)`

When a `return-from` is evaluated, the symbol argument is compared against all outer blocks to find the matching block name. Then the matching block returns the value of the second argument. If no matching block name is found, then an error is generated. The block names have full lexical characteristics, so it is possible to shadow block names. All functions have an implicit `block` defined around their bodies where the name of the `block` is the name of the function. This means that you can do a `return-from` anywhere in the body of the function to exit immediately from the function.

Common LISP also defines the `return` expression, which is the same as a `return-from` with a `nil` as the symbol. Some expressions place a `block` with a `nil` name within their code. This makes the `return` exit from the code. The four iteration constructs `dolist`, `dotimes`, `do`, and `do*` all provide this feature.

(`return` *S-expression*)

The last control primitive, `tagbody`, provides an environment in which you can transfer control via a `go` expression.

(`tagbody` *tag-or-list-expression**)

tag-or-list-expression ← symbol

tag-or-list-expression ← (*S-expression*)

(`go` *tag*)

The `tagbody` consists of an arbitrary number of *tag*s or list expressions. A tag is either a symbol or an integer and is the label that is the target of a `go`. When the evaluator is processing a `tagbody` expression, it ignores any tags and just evaluates the list expressions. When it finds a `go`, it transfers control to the expression immediately following the matching tag. If no matching tag is found, then an error is signaled. `Tagbody` always returns `nil`.

```
;;; Small example of tagbody and go which computes
;;; factorial. The return-from isn't really necessary, since
;;; we can just return the value of result out of the let,
;;; but it helps to demonstrate its functionality.

(defun factorial (n)
  (let ((result 1)
        (counter 1))
    (tagbody
```

```
      top-of-loop
      (setf result (* result counter))
      (setf counter (1+ counter))
      (if (<= counter n)
        (go top-of-loop)
        (return-from factorial result)))))
 ⇒ FACTORIAL
```

```
(factorial 5)
 ⇒ 120
```

As a further example, we can use all of these control primitives to implement some of the complex control expressions. For example, we will implement `dotimes` as a macro that expands into these primitives. We must remember to use a `block` with a `nil` name, so the user may place a `return` within the code. Also, the label can't conflict with any other labels, so we must call `gensym` to get a temporary symbol.

```
(shadow 'dotimes)
 ⇒ T

;;; A version of dotimes that expands into the LISP control
;;; primitives

(defmacro dotimes ((variable max &optional result)
                   &body body)
  (let ((local-label (gensym)))
    `(block nil
       (let ((,variable 0))
         (tagbody
           ,local-label
           (if (>= ,variable ,max) (return ,result))
           (tagbody ,@body)
           (setf ,variable (1+ ,variable))
           (go ,local-label))))))
 ⇒ DOTIMES

(macroexpand '(dotimes (i 5) (print i)))
 ⇒ (BLOCK NIL (LET ((I 0)) (TAGBODY #:G25 (IF (>= I 5)
 ⇒  (RETURN NIL)) (TAGBODY (PRINT I)) (SETF I (\1+ I))
 ⇒  (GO #:G25))))
 ⇒ T
```

Notice that the expansion of `my-dotimes` is very difficult to read. The LISP system prints the results without any formatting. Common LISP defines `pprint` which *pretty prints* its argument. This makes the output readable.

```
(pprint S-expression)
```

```
;; Try again, this time using pprint so we can read the code.
(pprint (macroexpand '(dotimes (i 5) (print i))))
⇒ (BLOCK NIL
⇒         (LET ((I 0))
⇒           (TAGBODY
⇒            #:G27
⇒              (IF (>= I 5) (RETURN NIL))
⇒              (TAGBODY (PRINT I))
⇒              (SETF I (\1+ I))
⇒              (GO #:G27))))
```

You can also change the default of the system so that it prints all expressions in pretty form. This is controlled by `*print-pretty*`. When its value is non-`nil`, then all printing is in the pretty format.

```
*print-pretty*
```

Early LISP implementations included what was called the *program* feature using the `prog` expression. `Prog` introduces local variables and lets you transfer control through the use of `go` and `return`. The early versions of `prog` didn't let you specify initial values for any local variables as with the `let` construct. Common LISP also includes the `prog` construct to maintain compatibility with these early LISP systems. `Prog*` uses sequential binding similar to `let*`.

```
(prog local tag-or-list-expression)
```

```
(prog* local tag-or-list-expression)
```

The *local* is defined in Chapter 3 as the specification of local variables to `let` and `let*`. It is generally not good style to use these constructs.

Two other control structures are related to `progn`. `Prog1` and `prog2` operate like `progn` except that the value returned by the expressions is not the value of the last expression, but is the value of the first expression for `prog1` and the second expression for `prog2`.

```
(prog1 S-expression S-expression*)
```

(prog2 *S-expression S-expression S-expression**)

These expressions will save a value, perform some operation, and then return the value. All of this mechanism is handled with the `prog1` and `prog2` macros. Both `prog1` and `prog2` only return a single value, even if the appropriate S-expression attempts to return multiple values.

Suppose that you have a list of elements and you wish to remove and return the first element. `Prog1` is perfect for that operation.

```
(defvar *clowns* '(bozo clarabell happy))
 ⇒ *CLOWNS*

(prog1
  (car *clowns*)
  (setf *clowns* (cdr *clowns*)))
 ⇒ BOZO
```

Without the benefits of `prog1`, you would have to write something like the following:

```
(setf *clowns* (cons 'bozo *clowns*))
 ⇒ (BOZO CLARABELL HAPPY)

(let ((result (car *clowns*)))
  (setf *clowns* (cdr *clowns*))
  result)
 ⇒ BOZO
```

The `if` expression is the Common LISP primitive conditional expression. All others are defined in terms of `if`. Two additional conditional expressions are `when` and `unless`. They are essentially the *then-expression* and *else-expression* of an `if` expression. If the *test* is true in `when`, then the associated S-expressions are evaluated. Likewise, if the *test* is false in `unless`, then the S-expressions are evaluated.

(when *test-expression S-expression**)

(unless *test-expression S-expression**)

The advantage of using `when` over an `if` is that it provides an implicit `progn` of the S-expressions, which makes the code slightly shorter. The `unless` saves either placing a `nil` in the *then* expression, or wrapping a `not` around the test. It also provides an implicit `progn`.

```
(when (= (length *clowns*) 2)
```

```
  (print (car *clowns*))
  (print (cadr *clowns*)))
⇒ CLARABELL
⇒ HAPPY
⇒ HAPPY

;; The else clause will be false and nil returned.
(unless (= (length *clowns*) 2)
  (print (car *clowns*))
  (print (cadr *clowns*)))
⇒ NIL
```

Their implementation as macros is fairly simple. They expand into `if` expressions with an explicit `progn` placed in the code.

```
(shadow 'when)
⇒ T

(defmacro when (test &body body)
  `(if ,test (progn ,@body)))
⇒ WHEN

(when (= (length *clowns*) 2)
  (print (car *clowns*))
  (print (cadr *clowns*)))
⇒ CLARABELL
⇒ HAPPY
⇒ HAPPY
```

Another important control construct is `case`. Like the `case` statements in other programming languages, it allows selection of expressions based upon the value of a key expression.

(`case` *S-expression keys-and-expressions**)

keys-and-expressions ← (*keylist S-expression**)

keylist ← (*key**)

keylist ← *key*

keylist ← `otherwise`

keylist ← `t`

The first S-expression in a `case` is evaluated to produce a *key*. A key is any LISP data type that can be compared with the `eql` function. Typical keys are symbols, integers, or characters. Each keylist is scanned to see if the key is a member of the list. The keylists are not evaluated. If there is only one key in a keylist, that key doesn't need to be parenthesized. If one matches, the associated S-expressions are evaluated as if enclosed in a `progn`. The value of the `case` is then the value of the last S-expression in the implicit `progn` of the matching keylist. Either `otherwise` or `t` may be used for a default case. This must be the last *keys-and-expressions* and always succeeds.

```
(case (car *clowns*)
  (bozo (format t "Has floppy shoes.~%"))
  ((clarabell happy) (format t "Is wild and crazy.~%"))
  (otherwise (format t "An unknown clown.~%")))
⇒ Is wild and crazy.
⇒ NIL
```

We can now implement the `case` macro. It operates like a `cond` with a little extra processing. The macro has to evaluate the expression to determine the key, and then expand into calls to `member` or `eql` to see if a key matches. We must also be careful to transform an `otherwise` into a `t` for use in the `cond`. A non-`list` keylist can be either `t`, `otherwise`, or an atom for `eql` testing. This is an example of where `case` could be used. But, how can we write a `case` expression to see if its key is `otherwise` or `t` when they are already considered to be special keys within `case`? If we place the symbol within a keylist, the underlying `case` macro will work properly. However, we must be careful to use the real `case` expression in the lisp package.

```
;; Test to see if we can use case on otherwise and t.
(case 'otherwise
  ((otherwise t) (format t "Matched Otherwise or T~%"))
  (otherwise (format t "Didn't match~%")))
⇒ Matched Otherwise or T
⇒ NIL
```

This seems to work, so we can now write the `case` macro. The first step is to allocate a symbol that will hold the value of the key. This can be placed within a `let`, which will evaluate the first S-expression and produce the key value. Then each clause is to be placed within the body of a `cond`. When the keylist is actually a list, we must add a `member` as the test for the clause. Otherwise we need to check for the terminating `otherwise` or `t` and generate a final `t` clause. If we just have a key, then we simply generate an `eql` test. This is fairly tricky code with all of the backquotes, unquotes, and quotes, so you should study it carefully.

```
(shadow 'case)
⇒ T
```

```
;;; Our own version of the case macro.  It doesn't check that
```

```
;;; the otherwise or t clause is the last one.

(defmacro case (key-generator &body clauses)
  (let ((key (gensym)))
  `(let ((,key ,key-generator))
     (cond ,@(mapcar
              #'(lambda (each-clause)
                  (if (listp (car each-clause))
                    `((member ,key ',(car each-clause))
                      ,@(cdr each-clause))
                    (lisp:case (car each-clause)
                      ((otherwise t)
                       (cons t (cdr each-clause)))
                      (otherwise
                       `((eql ,key ',(car each-clause))
                         ,@(cdr each-clause))))))
              clauses)))))
⇒ CASE

(pprint (macroexpand
         '(case (car *clowns*)
            ((bozo happy) (format t "Very Nice~%"))
            (clarabell (format t "Very Old~%"))
            (otherwise (format t "Unknown Clown~%")))))
⇒ (LET ((#:G17 (CAR *CLOWNS*)))
⇒   (COND ((MEMBER #:G17 (QUOTE (BOZO HAPPY)))
⇒          (FORMAT T "Very Nice~%"))
⇒         ((EQL #:G17 (QUOTE CLARABELL))
⇒          (FORMAT T "Very Old~%"))
⇒         (T (FORMAT T "Unknown Clown~%"))))

(case (car *clowns*)
  ((bozo happy) (format t "Very Nice~%"))
  (clarabell (format t "Very Old~%"))
  (otherwise (format t "Unknown Clown~%")))
⇒ Very Old
⇒ NIL
```

All of the iteration constructs were defined in Chapter 7 except `loop`. `Loop` is the simplest form of iteration – it evaluates its expressions indefinitely. It only terminates through explicit action, like the evaluation of a `return`, `return-from`, or even a `throw`. `Loop` does not have an explicit facility for introducing local variables, `go`'s, and so forth. It evaluates all of its expressions forever.

(`loop` *S-expression**)

This example of `loop` acts just like a `while` loop from other programming languages.

```
;;; Loop through the argument list and print out the
;;; elements.

(defun print-list (lst)
  (loop
    (if (null lst) (return nil))
    (print (car lst))
    (setf lst (cdr lst))))
 ⇒ PRINT-LIST

(print-list *clowns*)
 ⇒ CLARABELL
 ⇒ HAPPY
 ⇒ NIL
```

The generation of the `loop` macro is a straightforward expansion into a `tagbody` as follows. As with the other constructs, it expands into a `block` with a `nil` label.

```
(shadow 'loop)
 ⇒ T

(defmacro loop (&body body)
  (let ((loop-label (gensym)))
   `(block nil
      (tagbody
       ,loop-label
        ,@body
        (go ,loop-label)))))
 ⇒ LOOP

(pprint (macroexpand '(loop
                         (setf x (1+ x))
                         (if (> x 5) (return x))
                         (print x))))
 ⇒ (BLOCK NIL
 ⇒        (TAGBODY
 ⇒         #:G33
 ⇒           (SETF X (\1+ X))
 ⇒           (IF (> X 5) (RETURN X))
 ⇒           (PRINT X)
 ⇒           (GO #:G33)))

(let ((x 2))
```

```
(loop
  (setf x (1+ x))
  (if (> x 5) (return x))
  (format t "~A " x)))
⇒ 3 4 5
⇒ 6
```

The last control operation introduced in this section is `funcall`. It is like `apply` since it evaluates its first argument to decide which function to call. However, the arguments to the function appear directly following the expression for the function. No extra list construction is required.

(`funcall` *S-expression S-expression**)

`Apply` should be used when the arguments are already constructed into a list, since it extracts the arguments from the list. All `funcall` does is invoke the function passing it all the remaining arguments. In most LISP implementations, `funcall` is more efficient than `apply`. It can also look less cluttered, since there aren't any calls to `list`.

To illustrate these features, we will return to our sample LISP compiler. It must compile many different kinds of expressions. Some are simple function invocations, while others are more complicated because they are *special forms.* A special form is an expression that isn't a macro and doesn't have the standard argument evaluation strategy that regular expressions have. For example, `if` and `setq` are two special forms that must be compiled differently than a simple function call. Not all of their arguments are evaluated in the same way. Using standard data-driven techniques, we might develop an association list of the functions that compile each of these special forms. Using stub functions, this would appear as follows:

```
;;; Compile the if special form.
;;; STUB function.

(defun compile-if (if-expression)
  (format t "Compiling if.~%"))
⇒ COMPILE-IF

;;; Compile the setq special form.

(defun compile-setq (setq-expression)
  (format t "Compiling setq.~%"))
⇒ COMPILE-SETQ

(defvar *special-forms* '((if . compile-if)
                          (setq . compile-setq))
```

```
  "A-list of special form compile functions.")
 ⇒ *SPECIAL-FORMS*

;;; Predicate to see if the argument is one of the special
;;; forms that we can compile.

(defun compile-special-form-p (symbol)
  (assoc symbol *special-forms*))
 ⇒ COMPILE-SPECIAL-FORM-P
```

We can now write a dummy function that compiles each expression. This function includes only the bare minimum to demonstrate the use of `funcall`.

```
;;; Compile an expression.
;;; ONLY PARTIALLY COMPLETE.

(defun compile-expression (expression)
  (cond ((compile-special-form-p (car expression))
         (funcall (cdr (assoc (car expression)
                              *special-forms*))
                  expression))
        (t (error "Can't compile ~A~%" expression))))
 ⇒ COMPILE-EXPRESSION

(compile-expression '(if a b c))
 ⇒ Compiling if.
 ⇒ NIL

(compile-expression '(setq x 1))
 ⇒ Compiling setq.
 ⇒ NIL

(compile-expression '(bar 1 2))
!!!!! Error: Can't compile (BAR 1 2)
  Condition signaled in: COMPILE-EXPRESSION.
Entering the debugger
```

EXERCISES

17.5 Write your own version of `dolist`.

```
(dolist (element '(red blue green))
  (format t "~A " element))
 ⇒ RED BLUE GREEN
 ⇒ NIL
```

***17.6** Write your own version of `prog`.

17.7 Write your own macro version of `prog1`.

17.8 Write your own macro version of `prog2`.

17.3 Miscellaneous Operations

This section includes those constructs that really didn't fit into any of the other categories. Some are list operations, while others are file access operations. We also discuss how to define functions that take keyword arguments.

Common LISP defines many more list operations than were needed in this text. You are encouraged to examine [40] for a description of the various operations. Two operations that are quite useful are `push` and `pop`.

(`push` *S-expression S-expression*)

(`pop` *S-expression*)

You probably have noticed patterns of S-expressions that you use a lot. One frequent operation is to `cons` a new element onto the front of a list maintained in some variable. `Push` is a macro that performs just that operation. The Common LISP designers realized that it was worthwhile to standardize with a common name and functionality. `Pop` removes the first element of a list and stores the result into the same variable.

For example, our compiler must be able to generate code for the target machine. Each target machine instruction is in LAP (LISP Assembly Program) format as (*operator operand**). As each instruction is generated, we must place it on a list of all of the instructions. The use of `push` is perfect for this application.

```
(defvar *object-code* nil "List of generated instructions.")
 ⇒ *OBJECT-CODE*

;;; Define the emit function, which adds the argument LAP
;;; instruction to list of generated code.
(defun emit (instruction)
  (push instruction *object-code*)
  instruction)
 ⇒ EMIT

(emit '(move (reg 1) (reg 2)))
 ⇒ (MOVE (REG 1) (REG 2))

(emit '(jump foo))
 ⇒ (JUMP FOO)

*object-code*
```

```
 ⇒ ((JUMP FOO) (MOVE (REG 1) (REG 2)))
```

Likewise, pop removes an element from a list.

```
(pop *object-code*)
 ⇒ (JUMP FOO)

*object-code*
 ⇒ ((MOVE (REG 1) (REG 2)))
```

Another useful function is `last`, which returns the last `cons` of its argument. This is a quick way to retrieve the last element of a list, which is the `car` of the result of `last`.

```
(last '(red blue green))
 ⇒ (GREEN)

(last '(red blue . green))
 ⇒ (BLUE . GREEN)
```

Common LISP defines a number of operations that are useful when processing files, `rename-file`, `delete-file`, and `probe-file`. These are enumerated below. In each of the descriptions, *file* can be either a pathname, string, or stream.

(`rename-file` *file new-name*)

(`delete-file` *file*)

(`probe-file` *file*)

`rename-file` – This changes the name of the file represented in the first argument to be that of the second argument. It returns three values, the pathname of the new-name, the truename of the file before it was renamed, and the truename of the file after it is renamed.

```
;; Notice the use of UNIX file names here.
(rename-file "~/bookl/dungeon" "~/bookl/old-dungeon")
 ⇒ #.(make-pathname :host NIL :device NIL
 ⇒                  :directory '("~" "bookl")
 ⇒                  :name "old-dungeon" :type NIL
 ⇒                  :version NIL)
 ⇒ #.(make-pathname :host NIL :device NIL
 ⇒                  :directory
```

```
⇒                          '("" "u" "kessler" "bookl")
⇒                        :name "dungeon" :type NIL
⇒                        :version NIL)
⇒ #.(make-pathname :host NIL :device NIL
⇒                        :directory
⇒                          '("" "u" "kessler" "bookl")
⇒                        :name "old-dungeon" :type NIL
⇒                        :version NIL)
```

`delete-file` – This deletes the file named in the argument. It returns a non-`nil` value when successful. Common LISP doesn't specify what is to be returned if the deletion is unsuccessful and is therefore implementation-dependent.

```
(delete-file "~/bookl/dummy")
⇒ T

;; See what this implementation does if the file
;; doesn't exist.
(delete-file "~/bookl/dummy")
⇒ T
```

`probe-file` – This determines if the argument file exists. If it does, the truename pathname is returned; otherwise, `nil` is returned.

```
(probe-file "~/bookl/old-dungeon")
⇒ #.(make-pathname :host NIL :device NIL
⇒                        :directory
⇒                          '("" "u" "kessler" "bookl")
⇒                        :name "old-dungeon" :type NIL
⇒                        :version NIL)

(probe-file "~/bookl/dummy")
⇒ NIL
```

In Chapter 8, the various lambda-list keywords were discussed, including `&optional`, `&rest`, and `&body`. There are two more keywords that we must describe to complete the set: `&key` and `&allow-other-keys`.

The lambda-list keyword `&key` allows you to define keyword arguments. A keyword argument must follow an `&rest` keyword if present. When you call a function defined to have keyword arguments, all of them are optional and they may be supplied in any order. The syntax of a keyword argument is similar to `&optional` with a few other features.

`&key` *key-parameter**

key-parameter ← *symbol*

key-parameter ← (*symbol initialization-expression symbol*)

key-parameter ← ((*keyword symbol*) *initialization-expression symbol*)

When a *symbol* is used for the key parameter, then a keyword of the same name is created. That can be overridden by specifying a keyword directly, as the syntax indicates. Also, if a keyword is not provided in the call, the parameter will be bound to the value of the initialization expression, if it's specified, and `nil` otherwise. The final *symbol* is a variable that will be bound to `t` when the parameter is supplied an argument value and `nil` when the value comes from the initialization expression. Both the *initialization-expression* and final *symbol* are optional.

We have been calling system functions with keywords throughout this text. For example, recall that many of the sequence functions from Chapter 13 take a `:test` argument that lets you specify the test to use. If we wanted to find the first element in a sequence that was greater than the argument, we would write:

```
(find 8 '(2 4 6 8 9 10 11 13 15) :test #'<)
 ⇒ 9
```

Suppose that we want a similar function, except restricted to lists. It must also return a list of all elements that match the test. If no `:test` argument is supplied, then we will use `eql` as the test. The function would appear as follows:

```
;;; Find and return a list of all matching elements.

(defun find-all (matcher some-list &key (test #'eql))
  (cond ((null some-list) nil)
        ((funcall test matcher (car some-list))
         (cons (car some-list)
               (find-all matcher (cdr some-list)
                         :test test)))
        (t (find-all matcher (cdr some-list) :test test))))
 ⇒ FIND-ALL

;; First using the default case of not specifying a test.
(find-all 8 '(1 3 8 4 8 9 8))
 ⇒ (8 8 8)

;; Now a test is specified.
(find-all 8 '(2 4 6 8 9 10 11 13 15) :test #'<)
 ⇒ (9 10 11 13 15)
```

The next keyword, `&allow-other-keys` must follow `&key` and indicates that the system should generate an error only when this function is called with those keywords specified in the `&key` parameters. The other keys could be extracted if an `&rest` is provided, since it will include all keywords passed to the function.

```
;;; Dummy function to demonstrate &allow-other-keys.

(defun foo (&rest all-args &key size &allow-other-keys)
  (list all-args size))
 ⇒ FOO

;; Notice how the all-args parameter has the complete
;; parameter list and size is properly bound to the keyword
;; provided value.
(foo :length 5 :size 10 :width 4)
 ⇒ ((:LENGTH 5 :SIZE 10 :WIDTH 4) 10)
```

EXERCISES

***17.9** Define your own `simple-push` and `simple-pop` macros that only operate upon a symbol for the second argument. Be sure to put in a check that it is in fact a symbol and signal an error if it is not.

```
(defvar *colors* nil)
 ⇒ *COLORS*

(simple-push 'red *colors*)
 ⇒ (RED)

(simple-push 'blue *colors*)
 ⇒ (BLUE RED)

(simple-push 'green '(blue red purple))
!!!!! Error: (QUOTE (BLUE RED PURPLE)) must be a symbol in
        simple-push
  Condition signaled in: SIMPLE-PUSH.
Entering the debugger
(simple-pop *colors*)
 ⇒ BLUE

*colors*
 ⇒ (RED)
```

***17.10** Suppose that we extend `simple-push` and `simple-pop` so they properly handle the case where location argument could perform a side effect. Rewrite their definitions so they don't evaluate their expression argument twice.

```
(simple-push 'black (print '*colors*))
 ⇒ *COLORS*
 ⇒ (BLACK RED)

(simple-pop (print '*colors*))
```

```
⇒ *COLORS*
⇒ BLACK
```

17.11 Write your own version of the `last` function. Take care to properly handle both `lists` and `conses`.

```
(last '(red blue green))
 ⇒ (GREEN)

(last '(red blue . green))
 ⇒ (BLUE . GREEN)
```

17.12 Suppose that you dislike the fact that the division operation `/` produces a rational number when dividing two integer numbers. You would prefer that it truncate the value. Write your own version of `/` that by default truncates the value. You must also allow the specification of a `:operation` keyword to change the operation to be something else like `floor`. Due to the restrictions of `&key` and `&rest`, you may not specify both a keyword argument and an arbitrary number of arguments like is present in the real version of `/`. Therefore, restrict the new function so it takes one or two values.

```
(/ 4 3)
 ⇒ 1
 ⇒ 1

(/ 8)
 ⇒ 0
 ⇒ 1

(/ 8 5 :operation #'floor)
 ⇒ 1
 ⇒ 3

(/ 8 2.0)
 ⇒ 4.0
```

17.4 Multiple Values

As we have seen throughout this text, if we want to return more than one value, we usually construct a list of the values and then return that list. When we need the individual values, we extract them from the list. This isn't very efficient, since is requires many conses. It is also cumbersome to extract the values from the list.

The `values` function supports the Common LISP multiple value functionality. `Values` takes an arbitrary number of S-expression arguments and returns all of them separately.

(`values` *S-expression**)

The LISP interpreter prints out each value as it is returned. In a simple example, the following returns three values.

```
(values 1 (car '(red blue green)) "hello there")
 ⇒ 1
 ⇒ RED
 ⇒ "hello there"
```

Multiple values must be passed along in a computation as long as an operation doesn't explicitly use the values. Thus, in the following example, the function `foo` returns the result of the function `bar`, which returns multiple values. Thus, `foo` must also return multiple values.

```
;;; Simple function that calls bar to demonstrate that
;;; multiple values can be passed along from function to
;;; function.

(defun foo (some-list)
  (bar some-list))
 ⇒ FOO

;;; This function generates multiple values.

(defun bar (some-list)
  (values (car some-list) (cadr some-list)))
 ⇒ BAR

(foo '(red blue green))
 ⇒ RED
 ⇒ BLUE
```

If only one of the multiple values is used, the rest are ignored. For example, the `floor` function returns two values; one is the result of the division, and the other is the remainder. If `floor` is part of a computation, then the remainder is ignored.

```
;; Notice that floor returns two values.
(floor 10 3)
 ⇒ 3
 ⇒ 1

;; However, if we use floor in a computation, the extra value
;; is ignored.
(+ (floor 10 3) 2)
 ⇒ 5
```

It's easy to use just the first of the multiple values. If you want to use any of the other values, you must use one of the many multiple-value access functions. Two of the more useful functions are `multiple-value-bind` and `multiple-value-list`. The first function operates just like a `let`, except the local variables are initialized by multiple values.

(multiple-value-bind (*symbol**) *S-expression S-expression**)

As you may recall from Chapter 10, the `read-from-string` function returns two values; one is the S-expression read, and the other is the ending location of the S-expression within the string. We can use `multiple-value-bind` and `subseq` to extract the S-expression and return a new string with that S-expression removed. We will return these as multiple values using `values`.

```
;;; Read the S-expression from the string, return it, along
;;; with the string with the S-expression removed.
(defun read-and-update (string)
  (multiple-value-bind
    (s-expression end-position)
    (read-from-string string)
    (values s-expression (subseq string end-position))))
 ⇒ READ-AND-UPDATE

(read-and-update "hello there")
 ⇒ HELLO
 ⇒ "there"
```

If the number of locals and the number of values returned are not the same, the following rules apply:

1. If there are more locals than multiple values, then the extra locals are initialized to `nil`.
2. If there are more values than there are locals, then all of the extra values are ignored. This is effectively like the `floor` example above. Since only one value was required, the other was thrown away.

We can use `multiple-value-bind` to write a `remainder` function using `floor`.

```
;;; Returns the floor version of a remainder on the two
;;; arguments.

(defun remainder (dividend divisor)
  (multiple-value-bind (result remainder)
    (floor dividend divisor)
    remainder))
 ⇒ REMAINDER
```

```
(remainder 10 3)
⇒ 1
```

As the name implies, `multiple-value-list` constructs a list of the multiple values returned from evaluating its single argument.

```
(multiple-value-list S-expression)
```

These two examples show different ways to turn the two values returned from `floor` into a list.

```
;;; Return a list of the floor results.

(defun listify-floor (dividend divisor)
  (multiple-value-bind (result remainder)
    (floor dividend divisor)
    (list result remainder)))
⇒ LISTIFY-FLOOR

(listify-floor 10 3)
⇒ (3 1)

;;; Another version that uses multiple-value-list.

(defun listify-floor (dividend divisor)
  (multiple-value-list (floor dividend divisor)))
⇒ LISTIFY-FLOOR

(listify-floor 10 3)
⇒ (3 1)
```

Another function that returns multiple values is `get-decoded-time`. It returns nine values relating to the current date and time: second, minute, hour, day, month, year, an integer indicating the day of the week (0 is Monday up to 6 which is Sunday), a flag indicating whether daylight savings time is currently in effect, and the current time zone, which is the integer number of time zones west of Greenwich Mean Time.

```
(get-decoded-time)
```

Just calling the function to print out all of the values results in the following:

```
(get-decoded-time)
⇒ 23
⇒ 27
```

```
⇒ 11
⇒ 9
⇒ 8
⇒ 1987
⇒ 6
⇒ T
⇒ 7
```

If we wanted a function that just returned the current year, we could call `multiple-value-bind` to obtain the first six values and return only the sixth one. The others can be safely ignored.

```
;;; Returns the current year.

(defun this-year ()
  (multiple-value-bind (second minute hour day month year)
    (get-decoded-time)
    year))
⇒ THIS-YEAR

(this-year)
⇒ 1987
```

Multiple values can also be handy in functions which find variables for compilation. One of the more difficult parts of a compiler is the code which processes variables. The compiler in the next chapter only handles static, lexical variables; no specials are allowed. They are introduced either as function parameters, or variables within nested `lambda`s. Since a function is actually a `lambda` expression, then the compiler must process nested lambda expressions. Each of the variables will be allocated to some place on the stack, which is divided into what are called *frames*. Each `lambda` expression introduces a set of variables as illustrated below:

```
;;; This nonsensical function has 3 frames of variables.

(defun foo (a b)
  ((lambda (x y)
     (setf y (+ a b))
     ((lambda (z b)
        (setf x (+ x b)))
      a 8))
   b 3))
```

At the inner `setf` to `x`, the stack might look like the following:

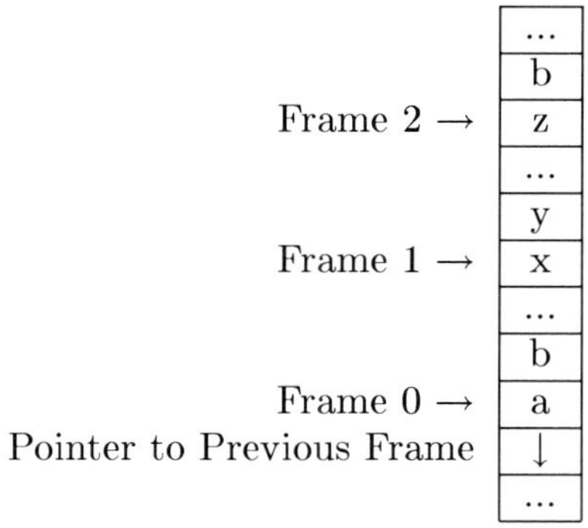

Each variable is characterized by its frame number and its offset within the frame. The following code are examples of a set of functions which model this behavior. We can create a list of frame objects, which contain the stack location and the list of local variables. Remember that the variables will always have the same offset from the beginning of the frame, but not always the same stack index since a function can be called in different contexts. When we need to find a variable, we will return the appropriate frame number, and the offset within the frame. Note that we have to keep this list in reverse order, because variables can shadow the definition of other variables, like the `b` variable in the previous example.

```
(defvar *frames* nil "The list of frame objects.")
 ⇒ *FRAMES*

;;; The frame object, includes the frame number, the list of
;;; local variables, and the stack location of the base of
;;; the frame.

(define-type frame
  (:var frame-number)
  (:var variables)
  (:var stack-location)
  :all-initable
  :all-gettable)
 ⇒ FRAME

;;; Add a new frame to the frame stack.

(defun add-frame (variables current-stack-top)
  (push (make-instance 'frame
```

```
                              :frame-number
                                (if (null *frames*)
                                  0
                                  (1+ (frame-number
                                        (car *frames*))))
                              :variables variables
                              :stack-location current-stack-top)
         *frames*)
  (frame-number (car *frames*)))
⇒ ADD-FRAME

;;; Remove the top frame from the list.

(defun remove-frame ()
  (pop *frames*))
⇒ REMOVE-FRAME

;;; Scan for the variable and return the frame number and
;;; offset.

(defun find-variable (variable)
  (dolist (each-frame *frames*)
    (let ((index (position variable
                           (variables each-frame))))
      (if index
        (return (values (frame-number each-frame) index))))))
⇒ FIND-VARIABLE

;; Now some simple tests of the functions, creating a set of
;; variables as defined in the foo example.
(add-frame '(a b) 10)
⇒ 0

(find-variable 'b)
⇒ 0
⇒ 1

(add-frame '(x y) 15)
⇒ 1

(add-frame '(z b) 25)
⇒ 2

(find-variable 'b)
⇒ 2
⇒ 1
```

The compiler in the next chapter uses a different model. Instead of computing frames and offsets, it assumes that variables are all static and thus can be stored with the exact stack location. It keeps track of the stack top and then computes the offset from the current top to find the variable.

EXERCISES

17.13 Change the / expression from the last exercise in the previous sections so that it only returns one value.

```
(/ 4 3)
 ⇒ 1

(/ 8)
 ⇒ 0

(/ 8 5 :operation #'floor)
 ⇒ 1

(/ 8 2.0)
 ⇒ 4.0
```

***17.14** Write a function that counts the number of internal and external symbols in a package and prints the counts. (*Hint:* Use the result of `find-symbol` to determine the type of each symbol.)

```
(count-internal-and-external (find-package 'lisp))
 ⇒ Count is 2362 internal and 1093 external.
 ⇒ NIL
```

***17.15** Write a function that returns the current date as a string of the form "hh:mm mm/dd/yy Dayoftheweek."

```
(string-date)
 ⇒ "8:48 8/10/87 Monday"
```

17.16 Some people prefer that their date strings are printed with leading zeros, so they always are the same length. Modify the previous `string-date` function so it prints two digit values for hours, minutes, day, month, and year. Try using `~2,'0D` instead of `~A` for the `format` directive. This syntax says to print the argument in two columns, with zeros used as a pad character instead of blanks, and in decimal notation. Many directives of a similar nature are defined in Steele [40], and which should be consulted for these complex operations.

```
(string-date)
 ⇒ "08:56 08/10/87 Monday"
```

***17.17** Write a function that returns the exact stack location of a variable using the model developed in this chapter. You must call `find-variable` in your solution. The function is passed the actual stack location of frame zero.

```
(location 'b 40)
 ⇒ 56
```

17.5 Read Macros

read A read macro is expanded when read, rather than when it is evaluated. They are generally used to save typing. For example, ' is a read macro that expands into `quote`. It saves the overhead of typing `quote`. `#'` expands into `function` for the same reason. Common LISP provides a number of these read macros.

`#.` evaluates the S-expression that follows it when the expression is read. This allows computation at read-time, instead of during evaluation.

```
'(1 2 #.(plus 1 2 3) 5)
 ⇒ (1 2 6 5)
```

Read macros also define numbers in different bases. The syntax is a sharp sign, followed by a decimal number indicating the base, then an `r` and finally the number in the designated base.

`#`*base*`r`*number*

```
;; The hexadecimal number FF.
#16rff
 ⇒ 255

;; An octal 123.
#8r123
 ⇒ 83

;; Finally, a binary number.
#2r1011
 ⇒ 11
```

The popular bases have their own read macro versions. These are `#x` for hexadecimal, `#o` for octal, and `#b` for binary.

`#x`*number*
`#o`*number*
`#b`*number*

```
;; The various bases representing decimal 15.
(+ #xf #o17 #b1111 15)
 ⇒ 60
```

The base in which numbers are printed is defined in the global variable `*print-base*`. The initial default is `10`, but can be changed to any decimal value representing the base.

```
*print-base*
```

```
;; Change the printing base to 16.
(setf *print-base* 16)
 ⇒ 10

255
 ⇒ FF

#xf90f
 ⇒ F90F

;; Restore the printing base back to 10.
(setf *print-base* 10)
 ⇒ 10
```

Single-character, user-defined macros can be created with the function **set-macro-character**.* This function takes the macro character being defined and the name of the function that is to be invoked when that macro character is found. When the macro character is read, the function named in the **set-dispatch-macro-character** is called. This function must return an S-expression that is then used in further processing by the **read**. For example, suppose that we want to translate all **$** characters into the symbol DOLLARS. The function then returns the symbol DOLLARS which is used in the **read** process. You must define the translation function to take two arguments. The first is the stream from which the macro character was read, and the second is the character that invoked the function. The second argument lets you define the same function on multiple characters, and the function can decipher the invoking character.

(set-macro-character *character function*)

Using the **$** example, the function **return-dollar** can be defined to take the two arguments mentioned above and then return the symbol DOLLARS. After we define the function, we can call **set-macro-character**. It is important that we define the function before we call **set-macro-character**; otherwise an error occurs.

```
;;; Make all $'s into a DOLLARS.
```

*See Chapter 22, page 364, of reference [40], for a discussion of the techniques which are used for two character macros using the **set-dispatch-macro-character** function.

```
(defun return-dollar (stream char)
  '(quote dollars))
 ⇒ RETURN-DOLLAR

;; Define the macro character.
(set-macro-character #\$ #'return-dollar)
 ⇒ #<FUNCTION  Max Args= 2  Lambda Name= RETURN-DOLLAR
 ⇒                Interpreted>

;; Test the macro
(list $100 $150)
 ⇒ (DOLLARS 100 DOLLARS 150)
```

This is not very useful because it cannot be used at the top level. Watch what happens when $99 is evaluated at the top level.

```
$99
 ⇒ DOLLARS
 ⇒ 99
```

The reader processes the $, resulting in DOLLARS and then the 99. The function should read the following number and return a list with DOLLARS in the car and the number in the cadr.

```
;;; Process a $ and the following number.

(defun return-dollar (stream char)
  `(quote (dollars ,(read stream))))
 ⇒ PROCESS-DOLLAR
```

We must redefine the character after changing the definition.

```
;; Define the macro character.
(set-macro-character #\$ #'return-dollar)
 ⇒ #<FUNCTION  Max Args= 2  Lambda Name= RETURN-DOLLAR
 ⇒                Interpreted>

$99
 ⇒ (DOLLARS 99)
```

EXERCISES

***17.18** Suppose that you frequently write code that increments or decrements a symbol and then assigns the resulting value to the same symbol. Write two read macros, ^ and @, that translate into the appropriate statement. If an argument is given, then it adds or subtracts that amount, instead of one.

```
(defun count-symbols (package)
  (let ((count 0))
```

```
    (do-symbols (symbol package count)
      ^count)))))
 ⇒ COUNT-SYMBOLS

(count-symbols *package*)
 ⇒ 786
```

17.19 As you know, objects print out in the following syntax:

```
⇒ #<Object FOO>
```

It might be nice to be able to just access an object by using a similar syntax:

```
(setf my-auto [great-model-t])
```

The problem is that the `FOO` in printed representation is the name of the type, and doesn't reflect the particular object. You could have five objects of type `FOO` and their printed representation would be exactly the same. This is pretty difficult to handle. However, in many cases, each object does actually have a unique name, sometimes even placed in a `name` slot. So, if `great-model-t` is the name of an instance, instead of an object, maybe we could use that to get the object.

Let's assume that any object with a `name` slot that is initialized when the object is created with `make-instance` is one that we will be able to access using the read macro syntax. Propose a technique for retrieving an object once your program has the value of its name slot.

17.20 Implement your solution to the previous problem – the mechanism to retrieve an object given its name. In the next exercise, you will implement the read macro. (*Hint:* If you want to make a new function that does everything a previous function does, but you don't have the source code, then you can use `symbol-function` to copy the definition into another function.) For example:

```
(setf (symbol-function 'same-as-+) (symbol-function '+))
 ⇒ #<FUNCTION  Max Args= *  Lambda Name= +  Compiled #x100C38>

(same-as-+ 1 2 3)
 ⇒ 6
```

***17.21** Implement the read macro that will find an object given its name as follows:

```
;; A simple auto type.
(define-type auto
  (:var name :printable)
  (:var size)
  (:var cylinders)
  :all-initable
  :all-gettable
  :all-settable)
 ⇒ AUTO

;; Create an instance of the auto type.
(setf y (make-instance 'auto :name 'great-model-t
                       :size 'small :cylinders 4))
```

```
  ⇒ #<Object AUTO NAME=GREAT-MODEL-T>

;; Find the instance using the read macro syntax.
(setf bobs-car [great-model-t])
  ⇒ #<Object AUTO NAME=GREAT-MODEL-T>
```

17.6 Making Your Code Run Faster

The techniques used in this section can be ignored by the beginning LISP programmer. Once you have gained more experience, you can return to this section to develop ways of making your programs run faster.

As you develop more LISP-based applications, you will undoubtedly want to make your code run faster. In a LISP system, this is usually accomplished by compiling your code. Some LISP systems automatically compile all functions, so they will already run as fast as possible. If they don't, you will want to compile the code yourself. There are two main compiler functions, `compile` and `compile-file`.

(`compile` *symbol optional-definition*)

(`compile-file` *pathname*)

The `compile` expression compiles a single function, while `compile-file` will compile the contents of an entire file into a loadable binary file.

For example, we can create a simple function and then compile it using `compile`.

```
;;; A simple function to demonstrate compilation.

(defun foo (a b)
  (+ a b))
 ⇒ FOO

(foo 3 4)
 ⇒ 7

;; Notice that it says foo is interpreted
(symbol-function 'foo)
 ⇒ #<FUNCTION  Max Args= 2  Lambda Name= FOO  Interpreted>

;; Now compile it.
(compile 'foo)
 ⇒ FOO
```

```
;; Verify that it still operates properly
(foo 3 4)
⇒ 7

;; Now look at the result of symbol-function to see how it
;; has changed.
(symbol-function 'foo)
⇒ #<FUNCTION  Max Args= 2  Lambda Name= FOO
⇒              Compiled #x250FE0>
```

How functions are printed is system-dependent. Under HP Common LISP, a compiled function includes the address of where the code is stored.

Compiling a whole file is easy using `compile-file`. For example, the following compiles the object system which is defined in Chapter 5 and listed in Appendix A.

```
(compile-file "~/bookl/objects.l")
⇒ compiling to output file: ~/bookl/objects.b
⇒ compiling file: ~/bookl/objects.l
⇒ COPY-GENERIC-TYPE MAKE-GENERIC-TYPE SETF-PARENTS PARENTS
⇒ SETF-OBJECT-TYPE OBJECT-TYPE GENERIC-TYPE-P !!! Warning:
⇒ local variable PRINTLEVEL is unnecessary OBJECT-PRINTER
⇒ PRINT-PRINTABLES DEFINE-TYPE EXTRACT-SLOTS
⇒ EXTRACT-TYPE-OPTIONS DETERMINE-INHERITOR FIND-ALL
⇒ LIST-SYMBOL-OBJECTP PROCESS-SLOTS PROCESS-SLOTS-AUX
⇒ ...
⇒ end of file: ~/bookl/objects.l
⇒ T
```

Notice that it gives some informative messages and then lists each function as it is compiled. Since the messages printed are all system-dependent, you will have to try it on your system to see how it works. After you compile a file, you can load it into the current environment using `load`.

(load *pathname*)

```
(load "~/bookl/objects")
⇒ "/u/kessler/bookl/objects.b"
```

On this system, the load returns the name of the file that it loaded. This version of Common LISP will always load the most recent version of a file, whether it be source code or compiled binary code. So, if you change the source code without recompiling it, it will load in the the changed source file when you evaluate the same `load` expression.

If your need for speed is critical, you can optimize your code. First you must disassemble the code. This lets you see the compiled code that is generated for your LISP code. The function **disassemble** is used for this purpose. These examples are run under HPCL on an HP 9000/350, so the assembly code is for the Motorola 68020 processor.

```
(disassemble symbol)
```

```
;; Disassemble the code for the foo function defined earlier.
(disassemble 'foo)
D0250FE6 5547           (subq.w #2 d7)
D0250FE8 6706           (beq.b D0250FF0)
D0250FEA 4EB9 9001 B206 (jsr (function PRIM:WRONG-ARG-COUNT))
D0250FF0 7E02           (moveq #2 d7)
D0250FF2 4EF9 9004 36F2 (jmp (function +))
D0250FF8 9024 BB08      (fullword (quote FOO))
 ⇒ NIL
```

You should follow these guidelines when optimizing your programs. It's a good idea to get your program working correctly before you start optimizing because if the program breaks, you know that it was caused by an improperly applied optimization.

- Only optimize your program where you will get the most gain. If you optimize your program in a place that is executed only 1 percent of the time, then the best possible speed improvement is only 1 percent [22]. Generally you want to:
  1. Leave initialization parts of your program alone unless they are very complicated. This code is usually only executed once and therefore is a small part of the execution of the program as a whole.
  2. Study your program to find the inner loops. This is where most of the execution happens. Try to find a more efficient way to accomplish the task inside the loop.
  3. Do measurements of your working program. This can help to isolate the "hot spots." Some systems provide profiling tools that can analyze an entire program, and tell you things like the number of function calls, the amount of time spent in each function, and so on. You can also write a simple version of a profiling tool with **get-internal-run-time**. This function returns the amount of cpu time that you have currently used and can be used to compute the time you spend in each function.

```
(get-internal-run-time)
```

The primary profiling tools provided by Common LISP are `time` and `room`. `Time` takes an S-expression as an argument, evaluates it, returns the result, and, as a side effect, prints the time it took to evaluate the expression.

(time *S-expression*)

`Room` prints information on the amount of pertinent LISP data spaces available. This can point to areas of code that are using significant amounts of storage.

(room)

```
;; Time a non-compiled and compiled function.
(defun count-adds (number)
  (dotimes (count number)
    (+ count number)))
⇒ COUNT-ADDS

;; Check the result of room.
(room)
⇒ Dynamic Heap: 5,818,172 bytes total
⇒               3,447,728 bytes used
⇒               2,370,444 bytes free  41% free
⇒ Static Heap:    1,721,740 bytes free

(time (count-adds 10000))
⇒ Real time:    4.20 s
⇒ Run time:     3.92 s
⇒ NIL

(room)
⇒ Dynamic Heap: 5,818,172 bytes total
⇒               3,700,408 bytes used
⇒               2,117,764 bytes free  36% free
⇒ Static Heap:    1,721,740 bytes free

;; Notice that the evaluation of the count-adds
;; used about 5% of the dynamic heap space.
(compile 'count-adds)
⇒ COUNT-ADDS

(room)
⇒ Dynamic Heap: 5,818,172 bytes total
⇒               3,713,592 bytes used
```

```
⇒                   2,104,580 bytes free  36% free
⇒ Static Heap:        1,721,652 bytes free

(time (count-adds 10000))
⇒ Real time:      1.18 s
⇒ Run time:       0.92 s
⇒ NIL

;; Now see if the compiled code took less space.
(room)
⇒ Dynamic Heap: 5,818,172 bytes total
⇒                   3,965,848 bytes used
⇒                   1,852,324 bytes free  32% free
⇒ Static Heap:        1,721,652 bytes free
```

- Avoid calling functions that dynamically allocate storage by creating lists, vectors, or strings, or those functions with `&rest` arguments. If you reuse your data structures, you can achieve the kind of efficiencies that are typical with C and assembly language. For example, destructive operations can eliminate list construction and improve efficiency. Of course these have all of the caveats that we have discussed previously.
- Add declarations to your functions. Since LISP performs type analysis at run-time, the more type checking you can move to compile time, the more efficient your code should become. The syntax for declaring types of variables is similar to that of dynamic variables. Simply give the name and a list of the variables.

  `(declare (`*type-name symbol**`)*)`

  Typical *type-names* are `fixnum`, `integer`, `float`, `vector`, `array`, `string`, and so on. Consult your Common LISP implementation guide for a list of the supported types. The next example illustrates how you can also provide a range of values for a particular type. You must include the name `type` to use this range declaration.

```
;;; Modify foo, so it includes type definitions.  A is
;;; guaranteed to be a fixnum -- an integer that fits
;;; into a machine word.  While b is a very small
;;; fixnum in the range of zero to seven.

(defun foo (a b)
  (declare (fixnum a) (type (fixnum 0 7) b))
  (+ a b))
 ⇒ FOO
```

- You should also turn on optimizations by using the `optimize` option on declare and proclaim. Proclaim has the same syntax as declare, except it is a global declaration that is made at the top level and the arguments are evaluated.

```
(proclaim S-expression*)
```

There are three optimization parameters that may be controlled: speed, space, and safety. They each take a value between zero and three. The higher the value, the more important that particular optimization is defined to be. Generally, in fully debugged code, you want to make speed a three, safety a zero, and ignore space. Let's see what this declaration does to the definition of foo.

```
(compile 'foo)
 ⇒ FOO

(disassemble 'foo)
D0253EC6 5547           (subq.w #2 d7)
D0253EC8 6706           (beq.b D0253ED0)
D0253ECA 4EB9 9001 B206 (jsr
                         (function
                          PRIM:WRONG-ARG-COUNT))
D0253ED0 7E02           (moveq #2 d7)
D0253ED2 4EF9 9004 36F2 (jmp (function +))
D0253ED8 9024 BB08      (fullword (quote FOO))
 ⇒ NIL

;; Now, we turn on the optimizations.
(proclaim '(optimize (speed 3) (safety 0)))
 ⇒ NIL

(defun foo (a b)
  (declare (fixnum a) (type (fixnum 0 7) b))
  (+ a b))
 ⇒ FOO

(disassemble 'foo)
D0253EE6 7E02           (moveq #2 d7)
D0253EE8 4EF9 9004 36F2 (jmp (function +))
D0253EEE 9024 BB08      (fullword (quote FOO))
 ⇒ NIL
```

As you can see, HP Common LISP doesn't optimize the call to +, but other LISP implementations might do so.* However, it did eliminate the call to

*There is a way to do this in HP Common LISP that is mentioned later using the global variable in the extn: package – extn:system-lisp.

check the number of arguments.

- As mentioned earlier, look at generated code and be aware of what the compiler does with various operations.
  1. Avoid the use of special variables. They are generally expensive at runtime, because of their dynamic nature.
  2. Use **defconstant** to declare constants. These are better than using **defvar**, because the compiler can substitute the value for the variable constant. You may not, however, change the value of a declared constant.

(**defconstant** *symbol S-expression string-comment*)

```
(defconstant *a-one-constant* 1)
 ⇒ *A-ONE-CONSTANT*

(defvar *a-one-variable* 1)
 ⇒ *A-ONE-VARIABLE*

(defun foo (a) (+ a *a-one-variable*))
 ⇒ FOO

(compile 'foo)
 ⇒ FOO

(disassemble 'foo)
D0253EFE 2239 9024 EAC0 (move.l
                          (special *A-ONE-VARIABLE*)
                          d1)
D0253F04 7E02           (moveq #2 d7)
D0253F06 4EF9 9004 36F2 (jmp (function +))
D0253F0C 9024 BB08      (fullword (quote FOO))
 ⇒ NIL

;; This will compile the value of the constant
;; directly into the function body.
(defun foo (a) (+ a *a-one-constant*))
 ⇒ FOO

(compile 'foo)
 ⇒ FOO

(disassemble 'foo)
D0253F16 7201           (moveq #1 d1)
D0253F18 7E02           (moveq #2 d7)
D0253F1A 4EF9 9004 36F2 (jmp (function +))
D0253F20 9024 BB08      (fullword (quote FOO))
```

```
⇒ NIL
```

3. The concept of tail recursion was mentioned in Chapter 14. We transformed some recursive function calls into the equivalent iteration constructs. If you want to rely on this transformation, you should carefully study the disassembled code to make sure that it is actually performing the optimization. If not, you might get surprising results, like stack overflow.

```
;;; Dummy function to see if tail recursion is
;;; happening.
;;; WARNING -- THE EXECUTION OF THIS CODE WOULD
;;; CAUSE AN INFINITE LOOP, IT IS ONLY TO BE USED
;;; FOR COMPILATION DEMONSTRATION PURPOSES.
(defun test-tail-recursion (arg)
  (test-tail-recursion arg))
 ⇒ TEST-TAIL-RECURSION

(compile 'test-tail-recursion)
 ⇒ TEST-TAIL-RECURSION

(disassemble 'test-tail-recursion)
D0253C6E 5347           (subq.w #1 d7)
D0253C70 6706           (beq.b D0253C78)
D0253C72 4EB9 9001 B206 (jsr
                         (function
                          PRIM:WRONG-ARG-COUNT))
D0253C78 7E01           (moveq #1 d7)
D0253C7A 4EF9 9024 ED92 (jmp
                         (function
                          TEST-TAIL-RECURSION))
D0253C80 9024 ED90      (fullword
                         (quote
                          TEST-TAIL-RECURSION))
 ⇒ NIL
```

Notice that the last instruction is a `jmp`, which implies that it is doing a tail recursive call. If this optimization was not being performed, you would see a `jsr` instruction (subroutine call) followed by an `rts` (exit).

- Avoid evaluating quoted expressions. This means that you have to call `eval`, which is what you are trying to avoid by compiling your code. On some systems, the compiled code is 10 to 100 times more efficient than interpreted code. It is acceptable to use `apply` or `funcall`, since they don't imply the use of `eval`.
- Study the implementation guide for your particular Common LISP. It usu-

ally gives hints and techniques for producing optimal code under that implementation. For example, HPCL includes an interesting optimization. It says that when the optimization is on, all arithmetic operations are declared to be on fixnum operands, and it can use direct machine instructions. There is absolutely no checking performed, so you must be careful.

```
;; WARNING - THIS ONLY WORKS ON HP COMMON LISP!!!
(proclaim '(extn:system-lisp t))
 ⇒ NIL

;;; Arguments MUST be fixnums and their sum must
;;; not exceed the fixnum range.
(defun foo (a b) (+ a b))
 ⇒ FOO

(compile 'foo)
 ⇒ FOO

(disassemble 'foo)
D0253F2E 2640          (movea.l d0 a3)
D0253F30 2801          (move.l d1 d4)
D0253F32 200B          (move.l a3 d0)
D0253F34 D084          (add.l d4 d0)
D0253F36 4E75          (rts)
D0253F38 9024 BB08     (fullword (quote FOO))
 ⇒ NIL

(proclaim '(extn:system-lisp nil))
 ⇒ NIL
```

EXERCISES

17.22 Given the following two functions, one which uses a special variable and one which doesn't, compile them and compare their codes to see which is more efficient.

```
(defun uses-special (a)
  (declare (special a))
  (setf a (+ a a))
  a)
 ⇒ USES-SPECIAL

(defun no-special (a)
  (setf a (+ a a))
  a)
 ⇒ NO-SPECIAL
```

17.23 Compare the execution time of the previous two functions and see which one takes the longest. Attempt to determine exactly how long it takes to execute each function. Generally, the timing resolution on your machine isn't sufficient to just call the function once and expect to get reliable results. You have to call it many times and compute an average.

17.7 Closures

The concept of a *closure* has been hinted at in earlier chapters, but not explicitly stated. A closure is a coupling of some LISP code and the environment in which to execute the code. Common LISP has lexical closures, which are created with the `function` operation. Whenever you use `function` or its read macro `#'`, then you are potentially creating a closure. The LISP system may not actually create a closure if there is no environment to save with the code. This will be shown in more detail later. We have used `function` when we wanted an anonymous function, like with `mapcar` in Chapter 7. In these cases, the closure usually has access to the code defined in the `lambda` expression and a set of variables, which is its environment. All of these instances of closures have been localized within a function and therefore can be optimized by the LISP system. Suppose that we define a function that returns a `lambda` expression instead of using it locally.

```
(defun return-lambda ()
  #'(lambda (arg1 arg2) (+ arg1 arg2)))
⇒ RETURN-LAMBDA

(setf a-lambda (return-lambda))
⇒ #<FUNCTION  Max Args= 2  Lambda Name= :UNNAMED
⇒              Interpreted>

(funcall a-lambda 3 4)
⇒ 7
```

This is similar to data-driven programming except it uses an anonymous lambda. The key feature of this `lambda` expression is that there are no free variables within its body. So, it doesn't require any external environment to execute its code. All it needs are two arguments. However, suppose that we change this function a bit as follows:

```
(defun return-lambda ()
  (let ((extra-add 4))
    #'(lambda (arg1 arg2) (+ arg1 arg2 extra-add))))
⇒ RETURN-LAMBDA

(setf a-lambda (return-lambda))
⇒ #<CLOSURE  Max Args= 2  Lambda Name= :UNNAMED
⇒             Interpreted>

(funcall a-lambda 3 4)
⇒ 11
```

The LISP system claims that it has returned a closure, not just a function. The `lambda` expression references a free variable and therefore requires an environment along with its executable code. If we replaced the `extra-add` in the expression with the constant 4, it would produce the same result. Let's make it more interesting with one more modification. Instead of simply returning the value, we will assign the result of the addition to the local variable.

```
(defun return-lambda ()
  (let ((extra-add 4))
    #'(lambda (arg1 arg2) (setf extra-add
                               (+ arg1 arg2 extra-add)))))
⇒ RETURN-LAMBDA

(setf a-lambda (return-lambda))
⇒ #<CLOSURE  Max Args= 2  Lambda Name= :UNNAMED
⇒              Interpreted>

(funcall a-lambda 3 4)
⇒ 11

(funcall a-lambda 3 4)
⇒ 18
```

Notice that the second call to the closure produced a different result than the first. The closure's local environment can be updated and changed by the code within the closure. Environments can even be shared.

```
(defun return-two-lambdas ()
  (let ((extra-add 4))
    (values #'(lambda (arg1 arg2) (+ arg1 arg2 extra-add))
            #'(lambda (new-extra-add)
                (setf extra-add new-extra-add)))))
⇒ RETURN-TWO-LAMBDAS

(multiple-value-bind (add-lambda set-lambda)
  (return-two-lambdas)
  (format t "Result 1 ~A~%" (funcall add-lambda 3 4))
  (format t "Result 2 ~A~%" (funcall set-lambda 0))
  (format t "Result 3 ~A~%" (funcall add-lambda 3 4)))
⇒ Result 1 11
⇒ Result 2 0
⇒ Result 3 7
⇒ NIL
```

Each of the two closures returned from `return-two-lambdas` had separate executable code, but they shared the same environment, in this case the local variable `extra-add`. Notice that the closures save state between calls, just like objects. You can actually implement objects as closures. The exercises at the end of this section explore this possibility further.

Closures are conceptually a nice, clean mechanism. However, implementing them efficiently can be difficult [32]. A system that implements closures well must do a lot of analysis to determine how a closure will be used and the status of its free variables. If this analysis is done properly, the system can optimize closures so that the environment isn't required making their use more efficient [42,25]. The first example in this section illustrated this, as the `lambda` expression that was returned was a function and not a closure. The implementation is part of the "funarg" problem [29]. Funarg is an acronym for functional argument, which refers to passing functions as arguments. This is exactly what we are doing with closures.

There are two kinds of funargs, upward and downward. An upward funarg is what we have seen in this section. A closure is passed back from a function call. The main implication of this is that the environment must be allocated in the heap. This is the most general case and means that the code needs to update variables stored in the environment. It also means that the environment must exist for as long as a LISP item points to it.

The only real optimization for the upward case is being able to determine that no environment is needed, so it can be treated like a regular function. The downward funarg case is ripe for possible optimizations. As the name implies, a downward funarg is only passed deeper into the execution of the program. All of the free variables that it can reach are still available on the stack. The `lambda` expressions in the calls to the mapping functions are downward funargs. They never existed outside of their execution context, so they can be implemented more efficiently.

To demonstrate the costs of each type of funarg, we now implement the same code using an upward and then a downward funarg. In particular we'll implement a loop similar to the one in the `count-adds` example.

```
;;; Return a closure.

(defun return-lambda ()
  (let ((extra-add 0))
    #'(lambda (arg) (setf extra-add (+ extra-add arg)))))
⇒ RETURN-LAMBDA

;;; Loop argument number of times calling the closure.

(defun time-upward (number closure)
  (dotimes (count number)
    (funcall closure count)))
⇒ TIME-UPWARD

;;; Loop argument number of times, calling a downward funarg.
```

```
(defun time-downward (number)
  (let* ((extra-add 0)
         (downward #'(lambda (arg)
                       (setf extra-add (+ extra-add arg)))))
    (dotimes (count number)
      (funcall downward count))))
⇒ TIME-DOWNWARD

(compile 'return-lambda)
⇒ RETURN-LAMBDA

(compile 'time-upward)
⇒ TIME-UPWARD

(compile 'time-downward)
⇒ TIME-DOWNWARD

(time (time-upward 10000 (return-lambda)))
⇒ Real time:    2.72 s
⇒ Run time:     1.30 s
⇒ NIL

(time (time-downward 10000))
⇒ Real time:    2.46 s
⇒ Run time:     1.28 s
⇒ NIL
```

This indicates that the times are actually very close. So, this particular implementation of Common LISP doesn't do any optimizations for downward closures. Actually, you can force the HPCL system to do this optimization at the expense of not allowing upward closures. The following performs this declaration, but is HP *system-dependent.*

```
;;; Loop argument number of times, calling a downward funarg.

(defun time-downward (number)
  (declare (extn:upward-closures nil))
  (let* ((extra-add 0)
         (downward #'(lambda (arg)
                       (setf extra-add (+ extra-add arg)))))
    (dotimes (count number)
      (funcall downward count))))
⇒ TIME-DOWNWARD

(compile 'time-downward)
⇒ TIME-DOWNWARD

(time (time-downward 10000))
```

```
⇒ Real time:    2.18 s
⇒ Run time:     1.22 s
⇒ NIL
```

This made it run a little faster but not much.

EXERCISES

***17.24** Propose a technique for implementing objects using closures. Don't worry about syntax, just a functional technique for doing the implementation.

***17.25** Using the scheme outlined in the previous exercise, write the appropriate functions to create a clown object with three slots: `nose-color`, `shoe-size`, and `smile`. Write methods to allow access to each slot, and demonstrate that you can change a clown's smile to be a `grin` and then verify that it is set by retrieving the value.

17.26 Run the same timing experiment that was done at the end of this chapter on your system. Try to determine if your downward closures are more efficient than the upward ones.

17.8 Summary

This chapter covered a wide array of topics. We saw that the package system solves the problem of symbol conflicts. Packages also help to add some data abstraction by placing all of the symbols for a particular application within one package with a well-defined interface. The LISP primitive control constructs `block`, `return-from`, `tagbody`, and `go` are a good set of primitives. Although you would rarely program directly with these expressions, they are available for writing more interesting and more complex control expressions. Multiple values is a relatively new concept to LISP. It's quite useful when you wish to return more than one value. It is more efficient to use this mechanism than to construct a list of the results for a single value system. Read macros allow you to write macros that are expanded when an expression is read. The `compile` and `compile-file` expressions are used to compile functions and files to make your programs run faster. Other techniques to improve execution speed were outlined in that section. Finally, closures are an important concept in Common LISP. They capture some LISP code and the environment to run it into one data structure. The closure may be used just like any other function and opens the way for interesting applications, like an object-oriented programming package.

Chapter Exercises

In this set of exercises you will design an emulator for the machine that is the target of the compiler developed in the next chapter. The machine is relatively straightforward and consists of the following characteristics:

- A register bank of eight general-purpose registers. They are numbered from zero to seven.
- A data stack, which can be considered to be infinite (therefore, a list implementation might be the best), which is where all data operations occur.
- A program stack, which contains return addresses.
- Memory, which is to contain the data memory. The address mapping is a simple numeric index for storing and retrieving memory elements.
- Instructions are maintained in a separate list of LAP (LISP Assembly Program).
- The possible addressing modes are:

  `(reg` *integer*`)` – This refers to the register indexed by the integer.

  `(stack` *integer*`)` - This references elements from the stack, indexed from the current top of the stack. The operand `(stack 0)` is the top of the stack; `(stack 1)` is the second element; and so forth.

  `(memory` *integer*`)` - This returns the data stored in the memory indexed by the argument.

  integer - Simple integer constants are allowed as source operands.

- The machine includes the following operational instructions.

  `(move source destination)` – This copies a single word from the location designated by `source` to the location of `destination`.

  `(push source)` – This pushes the contents of `source` onto the data stack.

  `(pop number)` – This pops the given number of stack entries from the stack. Use `move` to get things from the stack.

  `(add source destination)` – This is a two-address 32-bit addition.

  `(sub source destination)` – This is a two-address 32-bit subtraction.

- Finally, our machine includes the following control instructions:

  `(jump label)` – This transfers control to the given label.

  `label` – This can be any sort of atom.

  `(call label)` – This pushes the next program address onto the program stack, and transfers control to the given label.

  `(return)` – Return from a subroutine call. If a `return` is done outside of a subroutine, then it will return to the system, effectively halting a program.

  `(halt)` – This stops the execution.

***1.** Design the data structures to model the machine. Plan on having 100 memory elements, an arbitrarily long stack, and eight registers. Also write your interface primitives for access to the machine resources.

2. Write two primitive functions, `retrieve` and `store`. `Retrieve` takes an operand as specified above and retrieves the value stored in that operand location. If the operand is not a list, then `retrieve` should just return it as a legal value. The `store` function stores the second argument in the operand location as specified by the first operand. In both cases, if an illegal operand is found, then an `error` should be signaled.

***3.** Write the functions that emulate the operational instructions.

All of the control instructions use a symbol as the label designating the target of the operation. Their implementation can be accomplished with one of two methods. You can either scan the entire list of instructions every time a control operation is done, searching for the location of the label, or you can construct a symbol table that points to the label locations. This second alternative is the better choice.

***4.** Write the function that scans the instructions and constructs a symbol table of all of the locations of the symbols. If you store your instructions as a list, then the symbol table entries should point to the place in the list with the label. If you store the instructions as a vector, then you should store an index into the vector.

5. Write the functions for the control instructions that include `jump`, `call`, and `return`. Once again, don't forget to `shadow` the `return` symbol.

6. Write the function `load`, which takes a list of instructions as an argument, constructs the symbol, performs any initialization required, and prepares the machine for execution.

```
(load '((push 99) (move 14 (reg 0))
        (add (stack 0) (reg 0)) (halt)))
 ⇒ #<Object MACHINE>
```

***7.** Finally, write the function `run`, which starts the emulation going. When it is finished, it should dump the contents of register zero, since that is the location of all functions. The function assumes that the instructions are executed starting with the first one. Test the execution of the code that you have generated or use the compiler from the next chapter.

```
(run)
 ⇒ Register 0 contains: 113
 ⇒ NIL
```

8. Now that you have written and debugged the emulator, you can place it within its own package, `machine-emulator` with a nickname of `me`. Determine which symbols should be external to the package, and write the initial code to provide the interface.

Function Summary

The following lists the functions and topics covered in this chapter.

- `*package*`
- `(shadow` *symbol*`)`
- `(shadow (`*symbol**`))`
- `(in-package` *package-name*`)`
- `(in-package :nicknames` *S-expression* `:use` *S-expression*`)`
- `(use-package (`*package-or-package-name**`)`
- `(find-package` *package-name*`)`
- `(intern` *string package*`)`
- `(find-symbol` *string-or-symbol*`)`
- `(find-symbol` *string-or-symbol package*`)`
- `(export` *symbol*`)`
- `(export (`*symbol**`))`
- `(do-symbols (`*symbol package S-expression*`)` *S-expression**`)`
- `(unintern` *symbol*`)`
- `(unintern` *symbol package*`)`
- `(gensym)`
- `(block` *symbol S-expression**`)`
- `(return-from` *symbol S-expression*`)`
- `(return` *S-expression*`)`
- `(tagbody` *tag-or-list-expression**`)`
- `(go` *tag*`)`
- `(pprint` *S-expression*`)`
- `*print-pretty*`
- `(prog` *local tag-or-list-expression*`)`
- `(prog*` *local tag-or-list-expression*`)`
- `(prog1` *S-expression S-expression**`)`
- `(prog2` *S-expression S-expression S-expression**`)`
- `(when` *test-expression S-expression**`)`
- `(unless` *test-expression S-expression**`)`
- `(case` *S-expression keys-and-expressions**`)`
- `(loop` *S-expression**`)`
- `(funcall` *S-expression S-expression**`)`
- `(push` *S-expression S-expression*`)`
- `(pop` *S-expression*`)`
- `(rename-file` *file new-name*`)`
- `(delete-file` *file*`)`
- `(probe-file` *file*`)`
- `&key` *key-parameter**
- `(values` *S-expression**`)`
- `(multiple-value-bind (`*symbol**`)` *S-expression S-expression**`)`
- `(multiple-value-list` *S-expression*`)`

- (get-decoded-time)
- #*base*r*number*
- #x*number*
- #o*number*
- #b*number*
- *print-base*
- (set-macro-character *character function*)
- (set-dispatch-macro-character *dispatch-char char function*)
- (make-dispatch-macro-character *character*)
- (compile *symbol optional-definition*)
- (compile-file *pathname*)
- (load *pathname*)
- (disassemble *symbol*)
- (get-internal-run-time)
- (time *S-expression*)
- (room)
- (declare (*type-name symbol**)*)
- (proclaim *S-expression**)
- (defconstant *symbol S-expression string-comment*)

18 CASE STUDY: A MICRO LISP SYSTEM

LISP TEXTBOOKS traditionally define a LISP processor using the processor itself. Self-definition can be done in any language – C and Pascal compilers are typically done this way. However, it's particularly easy with LISP, so much so that we can do much of it in one chapter. To make things more interesting, we shall skip over the interpreter and concentrate on a compiler. The target of our compiler is an extremely simple abstract machine. It has some registers, a stack, a memory, and about a dozen instructions –just enough to write programs. The exercises in the previous chapter developed the code for the abstract machine.

18.1 Source Language

The full Common LISP language is somewhat complex to compile because of multiple values, complicated control constructs, full upward funargs, and so forth. Therefore we will define a subset that includes only the following features:

- *Constant numbers and symbols (no lists).* This restriction means that we don't need a run-time system. We can compile simple LISP expressions and then directly execute them on our abstract machine emulator.
- *Local lexical variables (no specials).* Once again, dynamic variables require the support of a run-time system. If we restrict the compiler to only use lexical variables, we can compute their values at compile time.
- *Functions with only required parameters (no optional parameters).* Some Common LISP systems can successfully compile away the use of nearly all of the lambda-list keywords [38]. However, some keywords do need run-time support, so we will restrict our system to required arguments and avoid the problems of optionals, keywords, and so on.
- *Macros.* A macro transforms some LISP code into more LISP code. Therefore, as long as the resulting code is in our subset, we can use as many macros as we need.
- *Special forms* `quote`, `if`, `progn`, *and* `setq`. These few special forms are enough to write simple functions.

- *Function calls.* The compiler will compile everything else as a function call. Functions must be defined before they're called from a program, or they won't run on the emulator.
  The primitive arithmetic operations that we will define are all word-based. For example, `word-+` performs a full 32-bit word arithmetic addition on its arguments. The following operations will be defined:

  `word--` – This is a 32-bit subtraction.

  `word-*` – This is a 32-bit multiplication.

  `word-=` – This is a 32-bit equal comparison of the arguments. The result will be either `T` or `nil`.

  `word-<` – This is a 32-bit comparison that returns `T` if the first argument is less than the second and `nil` otherwise.

  `word->` – This is a 32-bit comparison that returns `T` if the first argument is greater than the second and `nil` otherwise.

Everything else will be eliminated from the subset.

EXERCISES

***18.1** The only way to introduce local variables is with `lambda`. Write `let` and `let*` as macros that expand into the appropriate set of `lambda` expressions.

```
(macroexpand '(let ((a 1) (b 2)) (+ a b)))
⇒ ((LAMBDA (A B) (+ A B)) 1 2)
⇒ T

(let ((a 1) (b 2)) (+ a b))
⇒ 3
```

18.2 Try to write `factorial` in this tiny subset of LISP. What will happen if you give the function an argument of 50?

18.2 Target Machine

The target machine is a simple but common architecture. We don't want to use an assembler, so the machine will consist of distinct data and program areas. The data areas include a register bank, memory, and data stack, all 32-bits wide, while the program area consists of the program and a program stack, both of which are S-expressions.

The set of registers is general purpose, indexed from 0 to 7. The data stack is infinite, starting with position 0 as the top of the stack. Memory is an unspecified number of 32-bit words.

The addressing modes are as follows. All of them may be used as sources. *Integer* is the only one that may not be used as a destination.

`(reg` *integer*`)` – This refers to the register indexed by the integer.

`(stack` *integer*`)` – This references elements from the stack, indexed from the current top of the stack. The operand `(stack 0)` is the top of the stack; `(stack 1)` is the second element; and so forth.

`(memory` *integer*`)` – This returns the data stored in the memory indexed by the argument.

integer – Simple integer constants are allowed as source operands.

This is an enumeration of the various instructions.

`(move` *source destination*`)` – This copies a single word from the location designated by the addressing mode *source* to the location of *destination.*

`(push` *source*`)` – This pushes the contents of *source* onto the data stack.

`(pop` *integer*`)` – This pops the given number of stack entries from the stack. Use `move` to get things from the stack.

`(add` *source destination*`)` – This is a two-address 32-bit addition.

`(sub` *source destination*`)` – This is a two-address 32-bit subtraction of destination minus source.

`(mul` *source destination*`)` – This is a two-address 32-bit multiplication.

label - This can be any sort of atom.

`(jump` *label*`)` - This transfers control to the given label.

`(jumpif` *test source source label*`)` - This transfers control to the given label if the test on the two *source* operands is true. The *test* may be either `eq`, `gt`, or `lt`.

`(call` *label*`)` - This pushes the next program address onto the program stack, and transfers control to the given label.

`(return)` – Return from a subroutine call. If a `return` is done outside of a subroutine, then it will return to the system, effectively halting a program.

`(halt)` – This stops the execution.

EXERCISES

18.3 Write the target machine code for the function `word-=`. The function must return the symbol `T` or `nil` as a result in register zero. You may move `'t` or `nil` into `(reg 0)` to produce these results. The arguments are on the stack and must be removed before returning a value.

***18.4** Write code for the target machine that computes factorial. You may assume the integer for which you are to compute the factorial is in `(reg 0)` and that the result should be placed back into the same register.

18.3 LISP Compilers

LISP compilers are fundamentally like the compilers for any other programming language [1]. They typically have many passes or phases that transform a source program into an equivalent target program. However, the usual lexical analysis and parsing phases are part of the LISP *reader* instead, so the compiler doesn't need to do that work itself. Note that this doesn't mean that LISP systems don't do lexical analysis or parsing. The work has just been split into a separate `read` function that can be used in other places as well.

On the other hand, the reader parses LISP code only into S-expressions. This form is easy to manipulate, but it's not particularly flexible. For instance, suppose we want to store the type of each function subexpression during optimization or definition. We could then use the information for data-flow analysis [1]. But, there is no place to store this information directly with the `cons` cells of a program. So, many LISP compilers have a first phase that transforms S-expressions into a set of cross-linked structures or objects. This phase can also check syntax. For example, it can verify that `setq` only sets the values of variables and not numbers. Macros are usually expanded at this time, since they are transformations of the source code.

The next phase usually generates code. It can either generate machine-independent intermediate code, or produce a particular machine's instructions directly. The first has the advantage of simplifying compiler retargeting, which is a worthy goal given the current variety of machines. However, the second often produces better code for the machine in question. Subsequent phases translate the code into more specific forms, then either use a LISP-coded assembler or else a system's assembler to produce object files. Many compilers have additional phases dedicated to optimization [7,24,25,42]. Our compiler, however, won't use any of these fancy techniques. It will be a single phase compiler that doesn't optimize and that generates the target machine code directly from the source. The compiled code won't perform well – the exercises at the end of the chapter describe some optimizations you can try.

EXERCISES

***18.5** Syntax checking of LISP expressions could be performed by writing little functions that test the various elements of the expression to see if they meet the syntax. Another way would be to write patterns and then use a pattern matcher to check each expression. Choose one of these methods and write a syntax checker for the special forms and `defun` of our limited subset of LISP that we are to compile. Signal an error whenever invalid syntax is found.

```
(syntax-checker '(if bar))
 ⇒ (IF BAR) invalid syntax for IF
 ⇒ NIL

(syntax-checker '(defun foo fee (+ fee 3)))
 ⇒ (DEFUN FOO FEE (+ FEE 3)) invalid syntax for DEFUN
 ⇒ NIL
```

18.6 *Difficult* – Our target machine is simple and highly orthogonal. The orthogonality means that all of the registers are completely general purpose, and all operations may use any particular addressing mode. There are few actual machines that provide this amount of flexibility. This means that our target machine could be considered to be an intermediate machine, which could then be retargetted to a real machine. Select a machine that you are familiar with and write a translator from the instructions of our target machine into your machine.

18.4 Compiler Implementation

The compilation process is like the Lisp evaluation process. For simple function calls, each argument is evaluated and then the function is invoked. In the compiler, each argument is compiled and then code is generated to call the function. For macros, we simply invoke `macroexpand` and then either evaluate or compile the result depending on the process. The compilation and evaluation processes are so similar that `compile-expression` could compile the various expressions by mimicking the Lisp evaluator. Recursive invocations of the function could compile the different parts of an expression, such as the arguments to functions.

An important role of the compiler is to properly compile variables. The function being compiled may introduce a set of variables and each `lambda` application defines a set of variables as well. The variables will *live* on the stack, but we must remember their exact location. So, we must construct a structure similar to the environments described in Chapter 6 that will enable us to keep track of the variables. The environment structure must permit shadowing of variable names with new variables when an internal `lambda` expression hides the definition of another variable. A properly maintained list of variable specifications should suit our purposes. Therefore, the function `compile-expression` will take two arguments, the expression to compile and an environment list. It should check the type of the expression and dispatch to an appropriate compilation function. The following definition meets these goals.

```
;;; Compile an expression from our limited subset of Lisp.
;;; This function may be invoked recursively to compile the
;;; various subparts of an expression.

(defun compile-expression (exp env)
  (cond ((integerp exp) (compile-integer exp))
        ((symbolp exp) (compile-variable exp env))
        ((atom exp) (cant-compile exp))
        ((listp (car exp))
         (compile-call (car exp) (cdr exp) env))
        ((macro-function (car exp))
         (compile-expression (macroexpand exp) env))
        ((compiler-special-form-p (car exp))
         (funcall (special-form-compiler (car exp)) exp env))
```

```
        (t (compile-call (car exp) (cdr exp) env))))
⇒ COMPILE-EXPRESSION
```

We must define `compiler-special-form-p` as a stub function that returns `nil`, since we are going to do the special forms in the next section.

```
;;; STUB VERSION, SIMPLY RETURNS NIL.

(defun compiler-special-form-p (expression)
  nil)
⇒ COMPILER-SPECIAL-FORM-P
```

This top-down approach to the design of the compiler leaves many undefined functions, but it suggests an approach to the compilation process. Notice the clever ordering of the tests. After checking for integers and symbols, we immediately check for any other kind of atom, in which case we have an error condition and will call `cant-compile` to signal the error. Otherwise we know that it must be a list and can start checking the list elements. We first check the `car` of the expression to see if it is itself a list. If it is, then we probably have a `lambda` application and can compile it just like we compile a function call. Otherwise we check for macros and special forms. Finally, if none of those cases are valid, all that can be left is a regular function call, which will be compiled by `compile-call`.

We will assume that register 0 is an "accumulator" – all results of expressions will end up in register 0. This detail is handled by the function `result-register`.

```
;;; Returns the register target of all expressions.

(defun result-register ()
  '(reg 0))
⇒ RESULT-REGISTER
```

Compiling an integer constant produces an instruction that loads that constant into register 0. We have to concern ourselves with the size of the integer. Since our target machine is designed with a 32-bit word, the integer representation can't exceed 32-bits. Also, we need a way to distinguish between integers and symbols, and later on `cons`s. Three different types can be distinguished with two-bit values. Each type will be assigned a value between 0 and 3, which will then be placed in the tag of the value. The run-time system will then be able to distinguish the type of something by looking at the tag. This scheme is similar to that which was discussed in Chapter 13.

We can now define `compile-integer` to move the integer argument into the result register. For this and succeeding functions, we will call a function that generates the appropriate code. This data abstraction hides the details of the instructions from the compiler functions.

```
(defconstant smallest-integer (- (expt 2 32))
  "The smallest legal integer.")
 ⇒ SMALLEST-INTEGER

(defconstant largest-integer (1- (expt 2 32))
  "The largest legal integer.")
 ⇒ LARGEST-INTEGER

;;; Verify that the argument integer is legal and then
;;; generate the appropriate move.  If it isn't, then signal
;;; an error.

(defun compile-integer (integer)
  (if (<= smallest-integer integer largest-integer)
    (emit-move integer (result-register))
    (cant-compile integer)))
 ⇒ COMPILE-INTEGER
```

Let's consider the compilation of a global function call such as `cons`. We know that the result must end up in register 0, since `(cons 1 2)` is an expression. What about the arguments? LISP systems are divided on the best method of passing arguments, whether pushed on the stack or distributed among registers. Rather than fuel the debate, we will adopt the simpler stack protocol, and push the first argument on the stack first, then the second, and so forth. The function performing the call will do this, so it must also arrange to adjust the stack when the call returns. Here is an example of compiling `(cons 45 92)`:

```
(move 45 (reg 0))
(push (reg 0))
(move 92 (reg 0))
(push (reg 0))
(call cons)
(pop 2)
```

Note that we could have pushed 45 and 92 directly, but we already decided to put the results of all expressions into register 0. So, `compile-integer` simply places its result into register 0. As the function compiles the arguments, each result must be pushed onto the stack. Notice how this works fine even for more complex arguments. Suppose that we are compiling `(foo (bar 1) (baz 2))`. Then the code would look like the following:

```
(move 1 (reg 0))
(push (reg 0))
(call bar)
(pop 1)
(push (reg 0))  ;; Push the result of the call to bar
(move 2 (reg 0))
```

```
(push (reg 0))
(call baz)
(pop 1)
(push (reg 0))  ;; Push the result of the call to baz
(call foo)
(pop 2)
```

Here is the function that calls `compile-expression` to compile the arguments into register 0. It then pushes register 0.

```
;;; Given a list of the argument expressions, this function
;;; compiles the expressions and then pushes the results in
;;; preparation of a function call.

(defun compile-arguments (args env)
  (when args
    (compile-expression (car args) env)
    (emit-push (result-register))
    (compile-arguments (cdr args) env)))
⇒ COMPILE-ARGUMENTS
```

We can now write `compile-call`. It has to compile the arguments, generate a `call`, and then pop off the arguments to clean up the stack.

```
;;; Compile a call to a function.
;;; LIMITED VERSION -- LOOK FOR LATER ENHANCEMENTS.

(defun compile-call (function-name arguments env)
  (compile-arguments arguments env)
  (emit-call function-name)
  (emit-pop (length arguments)))
⇒ COMPILE-CALL
```

If we define the four emit functions, we can test out this code. Since we will want to run the compiled code, our emit functions will add the new instructions to a list of compiled object code. The top-level compilation function must remember to reset the list to `nil` at the beginning of each function compilation.

We must be able to find the top of the stack at any time for locating variables. Therefore, we must define another global variable `*top*`, which is updated with each `push` and `pop`.

```
(defvar *object-code* nil "Compiled object code.")
⇒ *OBJECT-CODE*

(defvar *top* 0 "Counter to maintain top of the stack.")
⇒ *TOP*

;;; Add a move instruction to the object code.
```

```
(defun emit-move (from to)
  (push '(move ,from ,to) *object-code*))
 ⇒ EMIT-MOVE

;;; Add a push instruction onto the object code list.  This
;;; also maintains the correct count of the top of the stack
;;; in *top*.

(defun emit-push (place)
  (setf *top* (1+ *top*))
  (push '(push ,place) *object-code*))
 ⇒ EMIT-PUSH

;;; Add a pop instruction onto the object code list.

(defun emit-pop (place)
  (setf *top* (- *top* place))
  (push '(pop ,place) *object-code*))
 ⇒ EMIT-POP

;;; Add a call instruction onto the object code list.

(defun emit-call (name)
  (push '(call ,name) *object-code*))
 ⇒ EMIT-CALL
```

Now we can try the functions and see if the correct object code is generated.

```
(compile-expression '(cons 45 92) nil)
 ⇒ ((POP 2) (CALL CONS) (PUSH (REG 0)) (MOVE 92 (REG 0))
 ⇒  (PUSH (REG 0)) (MOVE 45 (REG 0)))

(pprint (reverse *object-code*))
 ⇒ ((MOVE 45 (REG 0))
 ⇒  (PUSH (REG 0))
 ⇒  (MOVE 92 (REG 0))
 ⇒  (PUSH (REG 0))
 ⇒  (CALL CONS)
 ⇒  (POP 2))

;;; To make things easier as we debug the system.

(defun compile-and-print (expression)
  (setf *object-code* nil)
  (compile-expression expression nil)
  (pprint (reverse *object-code*)))
 ⇒ COMPILE-AND-PRINT
```

```
(compile-and-print '(foo (bar 1) (baz 2)))
⇒ ((MOVE 1 (REG 0))
⇒  (PUSH (REG 0))
⇒  (CALL BAR)
⇒  (POP 1)
⇒  (PUSH (REG 0))
⇒  (MOVE 2 (REG 0))
⇒  (PUSH (REG 0))
⇒  (CALL BAZ)
⇒  (POP 1)
⇒  (PUSH (REG 0))
⇒  (CALL FOO)
⇒  (POP 2))
```

`Compile-expression` also calls the function `compile-call` when we are applying an anonymous `lambda`. So, we must enhance the definition to handle `lambdas`. Also, we need to add a way to compile functions whose code is substituted in line. This in-line substitution process is called *opencoding.* Opencoding provides two advantages: performance improvement and a way to define primitive operations. For example, if we want to generate the `add` machine instruction, we need a way to specify that `word-+` translates into that instruction. We must also specify how to do that translation. In this simple compiler, opencoded functions look like functions except we don't generate a `call` instruction. Instead, we patch in the appropriate instructions. For example, suppose that we wish to compile `(word-+ 2 3)`. Using our model, the compiler would generate the following as it would for a normal function:

```
((MOVE 2 (REG 0))
 (PUSH (REG 0))
 (MOVE 3 (REG 0))
 (PUSH (REG 0))
 (CALL WORD-+)
 (POP 2))
```

We haven't told the system that `word-+` is special, so the code appears as a normal function call. However, we would prefer if the following code were generated:

```
((MOVE 2 (REG 0))
 (PUSH (REG 0))
 (MOVE 3 (REG 0))
 (PUSH (REG 0))
 (MOVE (STACK 0) (REG 0))
 (ADD (STACK 1) (REG 0))
 (POP 2))
```

With this information, we can now write the complete compile-call.

```
;;; Generate the code to call the function named in the first
;;; argument, with the arguments in the second, and the
;;; environment in the third.

(defun compile-call (fun arguments env)
  (compile-arguments arguments env)
  (cond ((opencodep fun (length arguments))
         (expand-open-code fun))
        ((symbolp fun)
         (emit-call fun))
        ((and (listp fun) (equal (car fun) 'lambda))
         (compile-lambda fun env))
        (t (cant-compile (cons fun arguments))))
  (emit-pop (length arguments)))
 ⇒ COMPILE-CALL
```

Compiling a lambda application is the same as compiling a progn with some local variables on the data stack. We'll need to locate the local variables later when we compile the variables in the body of the lambda. This operation is interesting because the variables will already be allocated on the stack. Notice in the previous definition of compile-call, that the first operation compiles the arguments. So, each argument will have a fixed location on the stack, relative to the start of the lambda. We just need to save the location of the variables for later reference. Since we have been maintaining the top of the stack in relation to the beginning of the function, the computed stack location can be recorded. The information on the variable should be stored in the environment argument. We need to know the name of the variable and its current position on the stack.

```
;;; The object representing a variable binding.

(define-type binding
  (:var name)
  (:var stack-position)
  :all-initable
  :all-gettable)
 ⇒ BINDING
```

Now we can write compile-lambda. It first adds the pertinent information to the environment argument, and then compiles the body of the lambda as if it were embedded in a progn.

```
;;; Compile a lambda application.  We enhance the environment
;;; to include the new variables, using the current value of
;;; *top* to point to the last variable.
```

```
(defun compile-lambda (lambda-expression env)
  (let ((newenv env)
        (current-top *top*))
    (dolist (var (reverse (cadr lambda-expression)))
      (push (make-instance 'binding
                           :name var
                           :stack-position current-top)
            newenv)
      (setf current-top (1- current-top)))
    (compile-expression `(progn ,@(cddr lambda-expression))
                        newenv)))
⇒ COMPILE-LAMBDA
```

Finally, we can define the opencoded functions. We need to store the function that will be expanded into instructions and also the code into which it will expand. We also store the number of arguments expected by the function for error-checking purposes. An object is again a natural way to represent this information.

```
;;; The object specifying the opencode information for each
;;; opencoded function.

(define-type opencode
  (:var name)
  (:var argument-count)
  (:var instructions)
  :all-initable
  :all-gettable)
⇒ OPENCODE

(defvar *opencodings* nil
  "Table of opencode objects for the various functions.")
⇒ *OPENCODINGS*
```

Now we can write **opencodep** to access the data base of opencoded functions and determine if the argument is an opencoded function. It must also signal an error if the wrong number of arguments were passed.

```
;;; Search through *opencodings* for the object with the
;;; matching function name.

(defun find-opencode (function-name)
  (find function-name *opencodings*
        :test #'(lambda (function-name object)
                  (eq (name object) function-name))))
⇒ FIND-OPENCODE
```

```
;;; See if the first argument function name is an open coded
;;; routine and check the argument count.

(defun opencodep (function-name number-of-arguments)
  (let ((opencode-object (find-opencode function-name)))
    (if opencode-object
      (if (= number-of-arguments
             (argument-count opencode-object))
        t
        nil)
      nil)))
⇒ OPENCODEP
```

The expand-open-code function just has to insert the instructions into the object code.

```
;;; Given the function name, add all of the instructions
;;; defined for the opencode to the object code.

(defun expand-open-code (function-name)
  (mapc #'emit-instruction
        (instructions (find-opencode function-name))))
⇒ EXPAND-OPEN-CODE

;;; The emit-instruction just adds the argument instruction
;;; to the object code.

(defun emit-instruction (instruction)
  (push instruction *object-code*))
⇒ EMIT-INSTRUCTION
```

We still need to define a few opencoded routines. Using data-driven techniques, we write a macro that defines an opencoded routine. It creates the object and adds it to the list of opencode objects.

```
;;; This macro permits the definition of an opencoded
;;; routine.

(defmacro defopen (function-name number-of-args &rest code)
  `(progn
     (push (make-instance 'opencode
                          :name ',function-name
                          :argument-count ,number-of-args
                          :instructions ',code)
           *opencodings*)
     ',function-name))
```

```
 ⇒ DEFOPEN

;;; Defines word addition.

(defopen word-+ 2
  (move (stack 1) (reg 0))
  (add (stack 0) (reg 0)))
 ⇒ WORD-+

;;; Word subtraction.

(defopen word-- 2
  (move (stack 1) (reg 0))
  (sub (stack 0) (reg 0)))
 ⇒ WORD--

;;; And finally, word multiplication.

(defopen word-* 2
  (move (stack 1) (reg 0))
  (mul (stack 0) (reg 0)))
 ⇒ WORD-*
```

We can test on the same example that we hand-generated for `word-+`.

```
(compile-and-print '(word-+ 2 3))
 ⇒ ((MOVE 2 (REG 0))
 ⇒  (PUSH (REG 0))
 ⇒  (MOVE 3 (REG 0))
 ⇒  (PUSH (REG 0))
 ⇒  (MOVE (STACK 1) (REG 0))
 ⇒  (ADD (STACK 0) (REG 0))
 ⇒  (POP 2))
```

We still aren't ready to test the code for the `lambda` application. We must still define the special form `progn`, which is done in the next section. The other remaining problem is that any local variables within the body of the `lambda` must be properly handled. We know the location of all variables with respect to the beginning of the function definition. This won't help when the function has been called by another function, because the actual stack offset is determined at run time. For example, during compilation of `foo`, we may know that the variables `a` and `b` are at stack locations 3 and 4. However, the function is actually called by two other functions, like `bar` and `baz`, and they won't be at the same locations as illustrated by Figure 18.1.

There are a couple of solutions to this problem. The first is to keep a pointer to the base of each function and index relative to that pointer. The second is to be able to compute the distance between the current stack top and

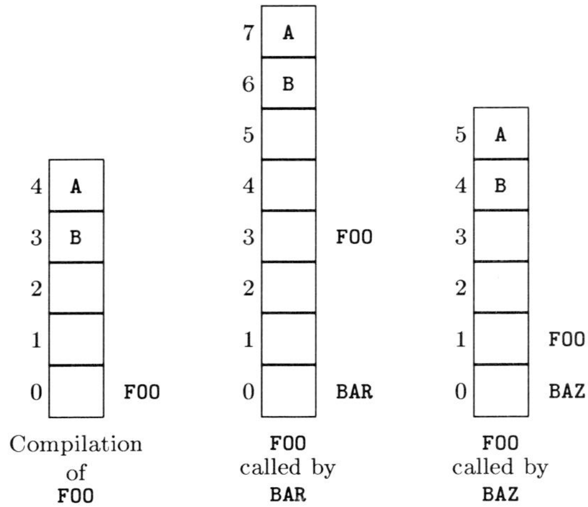

Figure 18.1 Various Variable Locations

the function. The first solution requires that we maintain a separate pointer that is pushed onto the stack at each function call. The second solution is simpler if we can always determine the current size of the stack. Since the only items placed on the stack use push and pop, we always know where the stack top is. So, when we compile a variable access, we generate code to move the stack location into the result register. The stack location is the difference between the current value of *top* and the stack-position in the binding object.

```
;;; Move the appropriate stack location into the result
;;; register.

(defun compile-variable (variable-name env)
  (emit-move (variable-location variable-name env)
             (result-register)))
⇒ COMPILE-VARIABLE

;;; Compute the location of the argument variable.

(defun variable-location (variable-name env)
  (let ((binding-object
          (find variable-name env
                :test #'(lambda (variable-name binding-object)
                          (eq (name binding-object)
                              variable-name)))))
    (if (not binding-object)
      (unknown-variable variable-name))
```

```
    (relative-stack-reference
     (stack-position binding-object))))
⇒ VARIABLE-LOCATION

(defun relative-stack-reference (position)
  '(stack ,(- *top* position)))
⇒ RELATIVE-STACK-REFERENCE
```

If we compile a `lambda` expression, it will incorrectly process the `progn` as a function call. Otherwise it should properly handle variable accesses.

```
;; THIS RESULT WILL INCORRECTLY CALL THE FUNCTION PROGN
;; BECAUSE NO SPECIAL FORM COMPILER HAS YET BEEN DESIGNED.
(compile-and-print '((lambda (a b) (word-- a b)) 3 4))
⇒ ((MOVE 3 (REG 0))
⇒  (PUSH (REG 0))
⇒  (MOVE 4 (REG 0))
⇒  (PUSH (REG 0))
⇒  (MOVE (STACK 1) (REG 0))
⇒  (PUSH (REG 0))
⇒  (MOVE (STACK 1) (REG 0))
⇒  (PUSH (REG 0))
⇒  (MOVE (STACK 1) (REG 0))
⇒  (SUB (STACK 0) (REG 0))
⇒  (POP 2)
⇒  (PUSH (REG 0))
⇒  (CALL PROGN)
⇒  (POP 1)
⇒  (POP 2))
```

EXERCISES

18.7 *Difficult* – What are the advantages and disadvantages of using a stack for function arguments instead of general-purpose registers? Consider the location of the stack and the relative differences in speed between registers and memory.

***18.8** Suppose that we changed the protocol so we didn't use an accumulator register but pushed the result of all operations onto the stack. How would this change the generated code? What is the difficulty of this "optimization?"

18.5 Special Forms

Recall that *special forms* are LISP expressions that aren't macros and don't follow the rule of evaluating the arguments and then calling the function. Special forms in Common LISP vary. The forms that this compiler will handle are different enough to rule out combining their functionality. We will build a long `case` expression, one case per special form.

```
(case (car form)
  (quote ...)
  (setq ...)
  ...)
```

This doesn't fit with data-driven programming, which is particularly appropriate for this case. We don't want to have to change some `case` expression for each new special form. Thus, we will define a macro that defines the code generation for a special form as follows:

```
(define-special-form name . code)
```

This macro adds the name and code into an a-list of special form code generators. The compiler can then `funcall` the associated code of a particular special form.

```
(defvar *sp-compilers* nil
  "A-list of special form names and code.")
⇒ *SP-COMPILERS*

;;; Is the argument name a special form in the a-list?

(defun compiler-special-form-p (name)
  (assoc name *sp-compilers*))
⇒ COMPILER-SPECIAL-FORM-P

;;; Retrieve the code associated with a particular special
;;; form name.

(defun special-form-compiler (name)
  (cadr (assoc name *sp-compilers*)))
⇒ SPECIAL-FORM-COMPILER

;;; Define the special form compilation code.

(defmacro define-compile (name args &rest code)
  `(progn
     (push (list ',name #'(lambda ,args ,@code))
           *sp-compilers*)
     ',name))
⇒ DEFINE-COMPILE
```

Now we can write the expressions which compile the code for each of the special forms. Perhaps the simplest case to compile is `progn`. We just have to generate the code by sequentially calling `compile-expression` on each expression.

```
;;; Compile progn's as a sequence of expressions.

(define-compile progn (progn-expression env)
  (mapc #'(lambda (expression)
            (compile-expression expression env))
        (cdr progn-expression)))
⇒ PROGN
```

We can now try compiling that `lambda` expression from the last section and make sure that it doesn't incorrectly call `progn` as a function.

```
(compile-and-print '((lambda (a b) (word-- a b)) 3 4))
⇒ ((MOVE 3 (REG 0))
⇒  (PUSH (REG 0))
⇒  (MOVE 4 (REG 0))
⇒  (PUSH (REG 0))
⇒  (MOVE (STACK 1) (REG 0))
⇒  (PUSH (REG 0))
⇒  (MOVE (STACK 1) (REG 0))
⇒  (PUSH (REG 0))
⇒  (MOVE (STACK 1) (REG 0))
⇒  (SUB (STACK 0) (REG 0))
⇒  (POP 2)
⇒  (POP 2))
```

The code for `setq` is simple to generate, but its syntax in Common LISP is more complicated. A compiler must be very strict on syntax checking. We first check the syntax in the `setq` expression and then compile the expression. The expression will leave its result in the result register. Then we generate a `move` instruction to place the contents of the result register into the appropriate variable location. The code that computed the variable location for retrieval can also be used for storing. Finally, we can let `setq` take multiple sets of arguments by recursively calling `compile-expression`. This is a relatively easy enhancement, which provides a more correct implementation of `setq`.

```
;;; Compile the setq special form.  This performs some syntax
;;; checking and then generates the code to compile the
;;; value, and move the result to the variable location.

(define-compile setq (expression env)
  (cond ((null (cdr expression)))
        ((null (cddr expression)) (bad-syntax expression))
        ((not (symbolp (cadr expression)))
         (bad-syntax expression))
```

```
          (t (compile-expression (caddr expression) env)
             (emit-move (result-register)
                        (variable-location
                         (cadr expression) env))
             (if (cdddr expression)
               (compile-expression
                `(setq ,@(cdddr expression)) env)))))
⇒ SETQ
```

This is another test to make sure that the correct code is generated.

```
(compile-and-print
 '((lambda (a b) (setq a 3) (setq b 5) (word-+ a b)) 1 1))
⇒ ((MOVE 1 (REG 0))
⇒  (PUSH (REG 0))
⇒  (MOVE 1 (REG 0))
⇒  (PUSH (REG 0))                ;; Location 1
⇒  (MOVE 3 (REG 0))
⇒  (MOVE (REG 0) (STACK 1))
⇒  (MOVE 5 (REG 0))
⇒  (MOVE (REG 0) (STACK 0))      ;; Location 2
⇒  (MOVE (STACK 1) (REG 0))
⇒  (PUSH (REG 0))
⇒  (MOVE (STACK 1) (REG 0))
⇒  (PUSH (REG 0))
⇒  (MOVE (STACK 1) (REG 0))      ;; Location 3
⇒  (ADD (STACK 0) (REG 0))
⇒  (POP 2)
⇒  (POP 2))                      ;; Location 4
```

In the first exercise of this section, you will draw a picture of the stack at the locations marked in this result.

The next special form is the conditional `if`. Compilation of `if` requires that we compile the predicate and then test to see if the result is `nil` or not. If it is `nil`, then we branch to the code in the *else* clause; otherwise we branch to the code in the *then* clause. The test that determines if the value of the predicate is `nil` or not is a little tricky. We haven't built any mechanism for representing symbols as tagged items. So, for now, we will just use a random value to represent nil and fix it up later. `Gentemp` can generate some temporary labels that we need for branching. The behavior is the same whether or not there is an *else* clause, but we need to be able to compile a `nil` when there is no *else* clause. Once again, we need to check the syntax of the expression. In this case, we must have at least a *then* clause.

```
;;; THIS USES A DUMMY REPRESENTATION OF NIL.
(defvar *representation-nil* 99
```

```
  "The tagged representation of nil.")
 ⇒ *REPRESENTATION-NIL*

;;; Compile the if special form.

(define-compile if (expression env)
  (if (null (cddr expression)) (bad-syntax expression))
  (let ((else-label (gentemp))
        (final-label (gentemp)))
    (compile-expression (car (cdr expression)) env)
    (emit-jumpif 'eq '(reg 0) *representation-nil*
                 else-label)
    (compile-expression (caddr expression) env)
    (emit-jump final-label)
    (emit-label else-label)
    (if (null (cadddr expression))
      (compile-expression *representation-nil* nil)
      (compile-expression (cadddr expression) env))
    (emit-label final-label)))
 ⇒ IF
```

We need to define the various emit functions to generate the code for each of these new conditions.

```
;;; Generate a jumpif instruction.

(defun emit-jumpif (test operand1 operand2 label)
  (push `(jumpif ,test ,operand1 ,operand2 ,label)
        *object-code*))
 ⇒ EMIT-TEST

;;; Generate a jump instruction.

(defun emit-jump (label)
  (push `(jump ,label) *object-code*))
 ⇒ EMIT-JUMP

;;; Generate a label.

(defun emit-label (label)
  (push label *object-code*))
 ⇒ EMIT-LABEL
```

Here is a simple example:

```
(compile-and-print `((lambda (x) (if x 3 4))
                     ,*representation-nil*))
```

```
⇒ ((MOVE 99 (REG 0))
⇒  (PUSH (REG 0))
⇒  (MOVE (STACK 0) (REG 0))
⇒  (JUMPIF EQ (REG 0) 99 T3)
⇒  (MOVE 3 (REG 0))
⇒  (JUMP T4)
⇒  T3
⇒  (MOVE 4 (REG 0))
⇒  T4
⇒  (POP 1))
```

The last special form, `quote`, is potentially more difficult to compile. The difficulty is deciding how compiled code can directly represent LISP data types. Constants such as numbers are easy, since they can be treated like their unquoted counterparts. We can also process symbols, as long as we have an appropriate run-time tagging scheme. We will only deal with these two types of `quoted` data types and leave others as an exercise. The process of converting a symbol into its numeric representation is just like the `intern` LISP process, so we will define a similar function of the same name.

We need to develop a symbol table of all symbols and their corresponding word representation. Whenever we find a familiar symbol, we can return the word representation. Otherwise we derive a new one and save it in the table. The first step is to `shadow` the symbols `intern` and `find-symbol`. We will use both of them in the process.

```
(shadow '(intern find-symbol))
 ⇒ T
```

Now we can create the symbol table. We will use an association list of symbol name and symbol value.

```
(defvar *next-symbol* 0 "Counter for each new symbol.")
 ⇒ *NEXT-SYMBOL*

(defvar *symbol-table* nil
  "The symbol table association list.")
 ⇒ *SYMBOL-TABLE*
```

The `intern` function either returns the symbol that it found in the table, or creates a new symbol and returns the new symbol value.

```
;;; Return the word representation for the argument symbol.

(defun intern (symbol)
  (or (find-symbol symbol) (add-symbol symbol)))
 ⇒ INTERN

;;; Scan the association list for the symbol and return the
```

```
;;; associated word representation if the symbol is present,
;;; nil otherwise.

(defun find-symbol (symbol)
  (cdr (assoc symbol *symbol-table*)))
 ⇒ FIND-SYMBOL
```

Adding a symbol to the association list is easy, but we need to be able to add a tag to the value stored in `*next-symbol*`. We are using two tag bits in the top bits of a 32-bit word. As previously mentioned, these tag bits are used to distinguish between the various items to differentiate their type at run-time. So, we need a technique for assigning the appropriate tag bits to each symbol object. An easy technique is to add the representation of these bits to the symbol value. Once completed, the 32-bit representation of the symbol will have the binary `01` in the top two bits and the symbol index in the lower 30 bits.

```
(defconstant *symbol-tag* #x40000000 "Tag value for symbol.")
 ⇒ *SYMBOL-TAG*

;;; Make a new symbol table entry for the argument symbol and
;;; store the word representation of the new symbol.  We also
;;; need to return that word representation.

(defun add-symbol (symbol)
  (let ((word-symbol
          (add-symbol-tag
           (setf *next-symbol* (1+ *next-symbol*)))))
    (push (cons symbol word-symbol) *symbol-table*)
    word-symbol))
 ⇒ ADD-SYMBOL

;;; Put a symbol tag on the argument.

(defun add-symbol-tag (n)
  (+ *symbol-tag* n))
 ⇒ ADD-SYMBOL-TAG
```

Now we can test this out with a few symbols.

```
(intern nil)
 ⇒ 1073741825

;; It is hard to tell if this value is correct, so we can
;; change the output base to be 16.
(setf *print-base* 16)
 ⇒ 10

;; Now try it again
```

```
(intern nil)
 ⇒ 40000001

;; See if we get a new value.
(intern 'foo)
 ⇒ 40000002

;; Check that nil is still the first symbol.
(intern nil)
 ⇒ 40000001

;; Restore the printout base.
(setf *print-base* 10)
 ⇒ 10
```

Now that we have a true representation for `nil`, we have to set up the variable so future compilations will be correct.

```
(setf *representation-nil* (intern nil))
 ⇒ 1073741825
```

Finally, we can get back to compiling quoted constants. We first need a function that moves a quoted symbol into the result register. This function calls `intern` on its symbol argument. Then the `quote` special form compiler can invoke the appropriate function based on the type of the quoted argument.

```
;;; Compile a quoted symbol by placing the numeric equivalent
;;; into the result register.

(defun compile-quoted-symbol (symbol)
  (emit-move (intern symbol) (result-register)))
 ⇒ COMPILE-QUOTED-SYMBOL

(defvar *quoted-expressions*
  '((integerp . compile-integer)
    (symbolp . compile-quoted-symbol)
    (consp . cant-compile))
  "A-list of quoted expression types and their functions.")
 ⇒ *QUOTED-EXPRESSIONS*

;;; Compile quote as a special form.  This only knows how to
;;; compile integers and symbols.  All others cause an error.

(define-compile quote (expression env)
  (let ((value (cadr expression)))
    (dolist (each-quote-fun *quoted-expressions*
                            (cant-compile expression))
      (if (funcall (car each-quote-fun) value)
```

```
          (return (funcall (cdr each-quote-fun) value)))))
 ⇒ QUOTE
```

Finally, another test of some quoted items.

```
(compile-and-print
 '((lambda (x) (setq x 'foo) (list x '3)) 9))
 ⇒ ((MOVE 9 (REG 0))
 ⇒  (PUSH (REG 0))
 ⇒  (MOVE 1073741826 (REG 0))
 ⇒  (MOVE (REG 0) (STACK 0))
 ⇒  (MOVE (STACK 0) (REG 0))
 ⇒  (PUSH (REG 0))
 ⇒  (MOVE 3 (REG 0))
 ⇒  (PUSH (REG 0))
 ⇒  (CALL LIST)
 ⇒  (POP 2)
 ⇒  (POP 1))
```

EXERCISES

18.9 Using the code that was generated with the calls to `setq`, draw a picture of what the stack looks like after executing the instruction in each labeled location.

***18.10** How could the compilation of `if` be improved?

18.11 What changes are necessary to handle specialized predicate functions efficiently? If you recall from the definition of `eq`, it must compare the two arguments and then return a `T` or `nil` as appropriate. The `if` special form then tests the result of the call to `eq` and branches to the appropriate code. Determine a way to avoid this overhead of calling the `eq` function and the unnecessary returning of `T` and `nil` just to determine which branch of the `if` to take.

```
(compile-and-print '((lambda (a b) (if (eq a b) 3 4)) 1 2))
 ⇒ ((MOVE 1 (REG 0))
 ⇒  (PUSH (REG 0))
 ⇒  (MOVE 2 (REG 0))
 ⇒  (PUSH (REG 0))
 ⇒  (MOVE (STACK 1) (REG 0))
 ⇒  (PUSH (REG 0))
 ⇒  (MOVE (STACK 1) (REG 0))
 ⇒  (PUSH (REG 0))
 ⇒  (CALL EQ)
 ⇒  (POP 2)
 ⇒  (JUMPIF EQ (REG 0) 99 T5)
 ⇒  (MOVE 3 (REG 0))
 ⇒  (JUMP T6)
 ⇒  T5
```

```
⇒  (MOVE 4 (REG 0))
⇒  T6
⇒  (POP 2))
```

***18.12** Add the ability to compile code for quoted lists.

18.13 Does your answer to the previous exercise work in the presence of destructive operations?

18.6 Completing the Compiler

In the previous sections, we have used a number of low-level routines that require some initialization. We have been calling `compile-and-print`, but it doesn't do everything necessary such as smooth error handling. Therefore, we will define a new function, `compile`, which takes care of these details.

First, we must `shadow` the definition of `compile`. We can then use the same interface to our compiler as we do with the LISP system. This makes it easy for the user to remember the name of the compilation function; it is the same as the LISP compilation function. The only problem caused by this is that we must remember to call `lisp:compile` if we want to compile a function with the LISP compiler.

```
(shadow '(compile))
⇒ T
```

The `compile` function should initialize all of the appropriate globals and then establish a `catch` for compiler errors. This way, if we get an error during compilation, we can gracefully terminate the compilation. The compiler should also be able to compile individual expressions as well as function definitions. One problem with compiling an expression is executing that code on the target machine. Normally, when a compiled program is loaded, nothing is actually executed until one of the defined functions is called. The trick we will use is to mark the beginning and end of each expression with a label that would tell the machine to immediately execute the code up to the ending magic label.

```
(defconstant *executable-code-start* '**START**
  "Label which indicates the beginning of executable code.")
⇒ *EXECUTABLE-CODE-START*

(defconstant *executable-code-end* '**END**
  "Label which indicates the end of executable code.")
⇒ *EXECUTABLE-CODE-END*

;;; Compile the argument expression and return the generated
;;; object code.  A defun is compiled as a labelled lambda
;;; expression, while other expressions are compiled directly
;;; with labels to delineate the boundaries of the code.
```

```
(defun compile (expression)
  (init-object-code)
  (setf *top* 0)
  (catch 'compile-error
    (if (and (listp expression) (eq (car expression) 'defun))
        (compile-defun expression)
        (progn
          (emit-label *executable-code-start*)
          (compile-expression expression nil)
          (emit-label *executable-code-end*)))
    (reverse *object-code*)))
⇒ COMPILE

;;; Set the object code list to empty.

(defun init-object-code ()
  (setf *object-code* nil))
⇒ INIT-OBJECT-CODE
```

A defun is simply a lambda expression with a label. So, we will first check the defun's syntax. Then we can generate a label and invoke compile-lambda on the body.

```
;;; Generate code for a function definition.  Produce a
;;; label for output and then call compile-lambda on the
;;; body.

(defun compile-defun (expression)
  (cond ((and (symbolp (cadr expression))
              (listp (caddr expression)))
         (emit-label (cadr expression))
         (compile-lambda `(lambda ,@(cddr expression)) nil)
         (emit-return))
        (t (bad-syntax expression))))
⇒ COMPILE-DEFUN

;;; Emit a return instruction.

(defun emit-return ()
  (push '(return) *object-code*))
⇒ EMIT-RETURN
```

We can now test compile on a function definition.

```
(pprint (compile '(defun foo (a b) (word-* a b))))
⇒ (FOO
⇒  (MOVE (STACK 1) (REG 0))
```

```
⇒  (PUSH (REG 0))
⇒  (MOVE (STACK 1) (REG 0))
⇒  (PUSH (REG 0))
⇒  (MOVE (STACK 1) (REG 0))
⇒  (MUL (STACK 0) (REG 0))
⇒  (POP 2)
⇒  (RETURN))

(pprint (compile '(word-* 3 4)))
⇒ (**START**
⇒  (MOVE 3 (REG 0))
⇒  (PUSH (REG 0))
⇒  (MOVE 4 (REG 0))
⇒  (PUSH (REG 0))
⇒  (MOVE (STACK 1) (REG 0))
⇒  (MUL (STACK 0) (REG 0))
⇒  (POP 2)
⇒  **END**)
```

Finally, we need the routines that perform some error-signaling. Each routine clears the currently compiled object code, so the result of the call to `compile` will be empty. It is important that each error message provide as much information about the error as possible. This helps the user track down the bugs.

```
;;; For some reason, we can't compile the argument
;;; expression.

(defun cant-compile (expression)
  (format t "Error: Cannot compile expression ~S~%"
          expression)
  (init-object-code)
  (throw 'compile-error nil))
⇒ CANT-COMPILE

;;; The argument expression doesn't have valid LISP syntax.

(defun bad-syntax (expression)
  (format t "Error: ~S has incorrect syntax~%" expression)
  (init-object-code)
  (throw 'compile-error nil))
⇒ BAD-SYNTAX

;;; The argument variable is unknown.

(defun unknown-variable (variable)
  (format t "Error: Undefined free variable ~S~%" variable)
```

```
  (init-object-code)
  (throw 'compile-error nil))
⇒ UNKNOWN-VARIABLE
```

Now a couple tests that should cause some errors.

```
(compile '(defun (a) (+ a 3)))
⇒ Error: (DEFUN (A) (+ A 3)) has incorrect syntax
⇒ NIL

(compile '(defun foo (a) (+ a b)))
⇒ Error: Undefined free variable B
⇒ NIL
```

EXERCISES

***18.14** Compile your definition of `factorial` and verify that it will produce the correct result.

18.15 Write a `compile-file` that works like the standard Common LISP one. It should be sufficient to write the object code as S-expressions into a text file. Don't forget to `shadow`! If the file `foo.l` contains the following S-expressions:

```
(defun foo (a b)
  (word-+ a b))
(foo 3 4)
```

Then the result is:

```
(compile-file "foo.l")
 ⇒ NIL
```

The contents of `"foo.b"` is:

```
(FOO
 (MOVE (STACK 1) (REG 0))
 (PUSH (REG 0))
 (MOVE (STACK 1) (REG 0))
 (PUSH (REG 0))
 (MOVE (STACK 1) (REG 0))
 (ADD (STACK 0) (REG 0))
 (POP 2)
 (RETURN))
(**START**
 (MOVE 3 (REG 0))
 (PUSH (REG 0))
 (MOVE 4 (REG 0))
 (PUSH (REG 0))
 (CALL FOO)
 (POP 2)
 **END**)
```

18.16 One problem with this definition of `compile` is that once an error occurs, there is no way to continue the compilation of that expression. So, if you have a function with more than one error you will have to compile it twice to track down both problems. Study the various LISP expressions that can generate errors and propose a scheme that tries to find as many errors as possible. Your solution should be able to produce something like the following:

```
(compile '(defun foo (a b) (+ a b c) bar '(3 4)))
⇒ SCOMP Error: Undefined free variable C
⇒ SCOMP Error: Undefined free variable BAR
⇒ SCOMP Error: Cannot compile expression (3 4)
⇒ NIL
```

18.7 Summary

A simple LISP compiler has been introduced. It has many of the features of compilers in use today, including open-codes, special-form compilation, and a powerful target machine. It was a good idea to follow the LISP evaluator for the design of the main compilation routine `compile-expression`, because we could get something running very quickly. Computing the location of local variables is a little tricky, but referring to the top of the stack works very well. A tagging scheme was used to represent the three data types of the language: positive integers, negative integers, and symbols. Although the resulting compiler generates very inefficient code, the code is still legal and would work on a machine emulator.

Chapter Exercises

This set of exercises enhance the compiler with new functionality and the ability to generate better code.

***1.** Peephole optimization is the process of searching for small sequences of instructions that can be combined into a single more efficient instruction. It is generally added as a final pass in a compiler and is used to provide some optimizations that are too difficult to accomplish in earlier phases of the compiler. There has been a lot of research into automatically generating peephole optimizers from machine descriptions [12,23]. We will take a simpler approach here. If you study the code that has been generated by this compiler, you will see a pattern of `move` instructions followed by `push` instructions. Write a peephole optimizer that performs this optimization.

```
(pprint (compile '(defun foo (a b) (word-+ a b))))
⇒ (FOO
⇒  (MOVE (STACK 1) (REG 0))
⇒  (PUSH (REG 0))
⇒  (MOVE (STACK 1) (REG 0))
```

```
⇒   (PUSH (REG 0))
⇒   (MOVE (STACK 1) (REG 0))
⇒   (ADD (STACK 0) (REG 0))
⇒   (POP 2)
⇒   (RETURN))
```

```
(pprint (peephole (compile '(defun foo (a b) (word-+ a b)))))
⇒ (FOO
⇒   (PUSH (STACK 1))
⇒   (PUSH (STACK 1))
⇒   (MOVE (STACK 1) (REG 0))
⇒   (ADD (STACK 0) (REG 0))
⇒   (POP 2)
⇒   (RETURN))
```

2. Having top-level expressions within compiled LISP code is nice, but we can't have any expressions that use a variable value, since it won't exist. Add the capability of having global variable by allocating memory space for them. We will define the restriction that any global variable used in a computation must first be defined using `defvar`.

```
(pprint (compile '(defvar *size* 10)))
⇒ (**START** (MOVE 10 (REG 0))
⇒            (MOVE (REG 0) (MEMORY 0))
⇒            **END**)
```

```
(pprint (compile '(setf *size* (+ *size* 1))))
⇒ (**START**
⇒   (MOVE (MEMORY 0) (REG 0))
⇒   (PUSH (REG 0))
⇒   (MOVE 1 (REG 0))
⇒   (PUSH (REG 0))
⇒   (CALL +)
⇒   (POP 2)
⇒   (MOVE (REG 0) (MEMORY 0))
⇒   **END**)
```

```
(pprint (compile '(defun foo (x) (* *size* x))))
⇒ (FOO
⇒   (MOVE (MEMORY 0) (REG 0))
⇒   (PUSH (REG 0))
⇒   (MOVE (STACK 1) (REG 0))
⇒   (PUSH (REG 0))
⇒   (CALL *)
⇒   (POP 2)
⇒   (RETURN))
```

***3.** *Difficult* – Write the run-time support for **cons**, **car**, and **cdr**. You might want to study Chapter 13 again to understand the ramifications of working with pointers and tags. These must be described in such a way that they can be compiled by the compiler and then used by other code. (*Hint:* The use of `defvar` from the previous exercise will help.)

4. *Difficult* – The last exercise illustrated the techniques of writing a LISP run-time system in a context that can be compiled by our LISP compiler. One point that was glossed over was the problem of running out of space. In the previous answer, we allocated space for 100 items, which could quickly be used up. In the answer, we called the function `reclaim`, which is the "garbage collector." Investigate the various garbage collection schemes proposed in the literature and implement one for this system.

5. *Difficult* – Look at the object code and see if there are obvious sections of bad code. Write functions that remove the bad code, then compare before and after performance of the code. Consider trying some of the optimizations outlined in [1]. For example, constant folding, where you evaluate constant computations at compile time, or constant propagation, where after you discover a variable with a constant value you propagate that value to further computations instead of using the variable.

A
Object System

THE COMMON LISP code of the simple object system used in this textbook follows. The system uses defstructs as a means to implement the objects. The primary reason for using defstructs is that it automatically produces the various accessor functions and also provides a print method.

```
;;;;;;;;;;;;;;;;;;;;;;;;;;;;;;;;;;;;;;;;;;;;;;;;;;;;;;;;;;;;
;;;;
;;;; File:          objects.l
;;;; Description:   Simple objects system.
;;;; Author:        Robert R. Kessler, University of Utah
;;;; Created:       21-May-86
;;;; Modified:
;;;; Language:      Lisp
;;;; Package:       USER
;;;;
;;;;;;;;;;;;;;;;;;;;;;;;;;;;;;;;;;;;;;;;;;;;;;;;;;;;;;;;;;;;

(provide "bobjects")

;;; A bug in this code is that if we define a generic
;;; function, then it will not be called on the object, if
;;; the method still exists.

;;; All types will inherit-from the following generic-type.
;;; This  permits definition of generic slots and also typep
;;; checks to see if an object is one of our objects.

(defstruct (generic-type (:conc-name nil)
                         (:print-function object-printer))
           object-type
           parents
           )
```

```
;;; Generic print routine for an object.

(defun object-printer (object stream printlevel)
  (let
    ((type-name (object-type object)))
    (format stream "#<Object ~S" type-name)
    (print-printables type-name stream object
                      (printables type-name))))

;;; Print out all of the printable slots.

(defun print-printables (type-name stream object slots)
  (if (null slots)
    (format stream ">")
    (progn
      (format stream " ~S=~S" (car slots)
              (apply (get-actual-name (car slots) type-name)
                     (list object)))
      (print-printables type-name stream object
                        (cdr slots)))))

;;; Special variable of the code being collected for
;;; inclusion in the result of define-type.

(defvar *code-to-be-evaluated* nil)


;;;;;;;;;;;;;;;;;;;;;;;;;;;;;;;;;;;;;;;;;;;;;;;;;;;;;;;;;;;
;;;;;;;;;;;;;;;;;;;;;;;;;;;;;;;;;;;;;;;;;;;;;;;;;;;;;;;;;;;

;;; Define an object type, consisting of a name and slot
;;; descriptors. One of the big problems with the idea of
;;; using a defstruct to represent an object is that all of
;;; the slot accessors are always defined.  There is no way
;;; to suppress their definition and thus one can't use
;;; information hiding.  One technique is to add a bizzare
;;; conc-name to the slot name, so one wouldn't normally use
;;; it as the name of a slot.

(defmacro define-type (type-name &rest slots)
  (let
    ((*code-to-be-evaluated* nil)
     (options (extract-type-options slots)))
    (initialize-type type-name)
```

```
      (determine-inheritor type-name options)
      (eval '(defstruct
               (,type-name
                (:print-function object-printer)
                (:include generic-type
                  (object-type (quote ,type-name))))
               ,@(process-slots type-name
                  (extract-slots slots) options)))
      (store-typep type-name)
      '(let (slots
             (type-name ',type-name))
         (initialize-type ',type-name)
         (determine-inheritor ',type-name ',options)
         (setf slots (process-slots ',type-name
                       (extract-slots ',slots)
                       ',options))
         (eval
          '(defstruct (,type-name
                       (:print-function object-printer)
                       (:include generic-type
                          (object-type (quote ,type-name))))
            ,@slots))
         (store-typep (quote ,type-name))
         ,@*code-to-be-evaluated*
         (quote ,type-name))))

;;;;;;;;;;;;;;;;;;;;;;;;;;;;;;;;;;;;;;;;;;;;;;;;;;;;;;;;;;;;;;;;

;;; Extracts the slots from a list of slots and slot options.

(defun extract-slots (slots)
  (cond
   ((null slots) nil)
   ((type-optionp (car slots))
    (extract-slots (cdr slots)))
   (t (cons (car slots)
            (extract-slots (cdr slots))))))

;;; Extract the type options and return as a list.

(defun extract-type-options (slots)
  (cond
   ((null slots) nil)
   ((type-optionp (car slots))
```

```
     (cons (car slots)
           (extract-type-options (cdr slots))))
    (t (extract-type-options (cdr slots)))))

;;;;;;;;;;;;;;;;;;;;;;;;;;;;;;;;;;;;;;;;;;;;;;;;;;;;;;;;;;;;;;;;

;;; Determine the parent types of this type.  They will be
;;; stored as a list of slots in the defstruct.

(defun determine-inheritor (type-name options)
  (let
    ;; Get a list of all of the parents of this type.
    ((inherits (find-all :inherit-from options)))
    ;; Make sure that each is a legal type.
    (list-symbol-objectp inherits)
    ;; Save the names of the parent.
    (store-parent type-name inherits)
    inherits))

;;; Searches the pseudo a-list for all occurrences of the car
;;; of a list matching the a-list elements.  It ignores those
;;; elements that are not lists.

(defun find-all (search pseudo-a-list)
  (cond ((null pseudo-a-list) nil)
        ((and (consp (car pseudo-a-list))
              (equal search (caar pseudo-a-list)))
         (append (cdar pseudo-a-list)
                 (find-all search (cdr pseudo-a-list))))
        (t (find-all search (cdr pseudo-a-list)))))

;;; Verify that each argument is a legal type.

(defun list-symbol-objectp (list-of-types)
  (cond ((null list-of-types) nil)
        ((not (symbol-objectp (car list-of-types)))
         (error "~S is not a known type to inherit"
                (car list-of-types)))
        (t (list-symbol-objectp (cdr list-of-types)))))

;;; Process the slots.

(defun process-slots (type-name slots options)
  (if (null slots)
```

```
    nil
    (cons (process-slots-aux type-name (car slots) options)
          (process-slots type-name (cdr slots) options))))

(defun process-slots-aux (type-name slot options)
  (let*
    ((slot-struct (parse-slot-description slot options
                                          type-name))
     (slot-name (slot-slot-name slot-struct))
     (method-access-name
      (build-separated-name type-name slot-name "-"))
     (method-set-name
      (build-separated-name 'set slot-name "-"))
     (method-set-function-name
      (build-separated-name type-name method-set-name "$"))
     )
    (store-slot-name type-name slot-name method-access-name)
    (if (slot-gettable slot-struct)
      (progn
        (store-method-name type-name slot-name
                           method-access-name)
        (define-generic slot-name nil)))
    (if (slot-settable slot-struct)
      (progn
        (store-method-name type-name method-set-name
                           method-set-function-name)
        (define-generic method-set-name '(value-to-set))
        (push `(defsetf ,slot-name ,method-set-name)
              *code-to-be-evaluated*)
        (push `(setf (symbol-function
                      (quote ,method-set-function-name))
                     (function
                      (lambda (object value)
                        (setf (,method-access-name object)
                              value))))
              *code-to-be-evaluated*)))
    (if (slot-initable slot-struct)
      (store-initable type-name slot-name))
    (if (slot-printable slot-struct)
      (store-printable type-name slot-name))
    (if (slot-initial-value slot-struct)
      `(,slot-name ,(slot-initial-value slot-struct))
      slot-name)))
;;;;;;;;;;;;;;;;;;;;;;;;;;;;;;;;;;;;;;;;;;;;;;;;;;;;;;;;;;;;;
```

```
;;; Process a single slot using generic type option
;;; information.
;;; A slot has the following syntax:
;;;   (:var slotname) or
;;;   (:var slotname slot-options)
;;; A slot option may be any or all of the following:
;;;   (:init initial-value-s-expression) or
;;;   :initable or
;;;   :settable or
;;;   :gettable or
;;;   :printable
;;; Since the type options may also specify define the
;;; characteristics of a slot, we need a technique for
;;; determining the status of every slot.  We define a
;;; defstruct the status of each accessor for a slot.

(defstruct slot
    slot-name
    (initial-value nil)
    initable
    settable
    gettable
    printable)

;;; Parse a slot description and return a slot structure that
;;; contains all of the pertinent information.

(defun parse-slot-description (slot type-options type-name)
  (let
    ((slot-struct
      (make-slot :initable (member :all-initable
                                   type-options)
                 :settable (member :all-settable
                                   type-options)
                 :gettable (member :all-gettable
                                   type-options)
                 :printable (member :all-printable
                                    type-options))))
    (parse-slot-description-aux slot-struct slot type-options
                                type-name)
    slot-struct))

;;; Auxiliary function that looks at each slot element and
;;; fills in the appropriate part of the slot structure.
```

```
(defun parse-slot-description-aux (slot-struct slot
                                                 type-options
                                                 type-name)
  (cond ((null slot) nil)
        ((consp (car slot))
         (cond ((equal (caar slot) :init)
                (setf (slot-initial-value slot-struct)
                      (cadr (car slot)))
                (parse-slot-description-aux slot-struct
                                            (cdr slot)
                                            type-options
                                            type-name))
               (t (error "Unknown slot option ~S"
                         (car slot)))))
        (t (case (car slot)
             (:initable (setf (slot-initable slot-struct) t))
             (:gettable (setf (slot-gettable slot-struct) t))
             (:settable (setf (slot-settable slot-struct) t))
             (:printable (setf (slot-printable slot-struct)
                               t))
             (:var (setf (slot-slot-name slot-struct)
                         (cadr slot))
                   (setf slot (cdr slot)))
             (t (error "Unknown slot option ~S" (car slot))))
           (parse-slot-description-aux slot-struct (cdr slot)
                                       type-options
                                       type-name))))
;;;;;;;;;;;;;;;;;;;;;;;;;;;;;;;;;;;;;;;;;;;;;;;;;;;;;;;;;;;;

;;; Create a name from the two arguments separated by the
;;; third.  This could be as defstruct accessor functions,
;;; among others.

(defun build-separated-name (type-name slot separator)
  (intern (concatenate 'string (symbol-name type-name)
                       separator (symbol-name slot))))

;;; Is the argument a legal type option.

(defun type-optionp (type-option)
  (or (member type-option '(:all-gettable :all-settable
                                          :all-initable))
      (and (consp type-option)
           (member (car type-option) '(:inherit-from)))))
```

```
;;;;;;;;;;;;;;;;;;;;;;;;;;;;;;;;;;;;;;;;;;;;;;;;;;;;;;;;;;;
;;;;;;;;;;;;;;;;; Access to Type Info ;;;;;;;;;;;;;;;;;;;;;;
;;;;;;;;;;;;;;;;;;;;;;;;;;;;;;;;;;;;;;;;;;;;;;;;;;;;;;;;;;;;

;;; Reset all of the information associated with the type.

(defun initialize-type (type-name)
  (setf (get type-name 'slots) nil)
  (setf (get type-name 'initable) nil)
  (setf (get type-name 'typep) nil)
  (setf (get type-name 'parent) nil)
  (setf (get type-name 'methods) nil)
  (setf (get type-name 'printable) nil))

;;;;;;;;;;;;;;;;;;;;;; Method Access ;;;;;;;;;;;;;;;;;;;;;;

;;; Retrieve the names of the methods and their function
;;; names.

(defun get-method-names (type-name)
  (get type-name 'methods))

;;; Extract the actual function name given the method name.

(defun get-actual-name (method-name type-name)
  (cdr (assoc method-name (get-method-names type-name))))

;;; Store a new method and its associated function name.

(defun store-method-name (type-name method-name access-name)
  (setf (get type-name 'methods)
        (cons (cons method-name access-name)
              (get type-name 'methods))))

;;; Merge the method names from the first argument into the
;;; method names of the second argument.

(defun merge-method-names (add-methods addee-methods)
  (dolist
    (each-method (get-method-names add-methods))
    (store-method-name addee-methods (car each-method)
                       (cdr each-method))))

;;;;;;;;;;;;;;;;;;;;;;;; Slot Access ;;;;;;;;;;;;;;;;;;;;;;
```

```
;;; Retrieve the slots associated with a frame.

(defun get-slot-names (type-name)
  (get type-name 'slots))

;;; Store a new slot name into the slot list.

(defun store-slot-name (type-name slot-name slot-access-name)
  (setf (get type-name 'slots)
        (cons (cons slot-name slot-access-name)
              (get type-name 'slots))))

;;; Merge the method names from the first argument into the
;;; method names of the second argument.

(defun merge-slot-names (add-slots addee-slots)
  (dolist
    (each-slot (get-slot-names add-slots))
    (store-slot-name addee-slots (car each-slot)
                     (cdr each-slot))))

;;;;;;;;;;;;;;;;;;;;; Initable Access ;;;;;;;;;;;;;;;;;;;;;;

;;; Get the list of initable keywords.

(defun get-initable (type-name)
  (get type-name 'initable))

;;; Store a new initable slot name.

(defun store-initable (type-name slot)
  (setf (get type-name 'initable)
        (cons (make-keyword slot)
              (get type-name 'initable))))

;;; Merge the initable slot names from the first argument
;;; into the initable slot names of the second argument.

(defun merge-initable-names (add-initable addee-initable)
  (dolist
    (each-initable (get-initable add-initable))
    (store-initable addee-initable each-initable)))

;;;;;;;;;;;;;;;;;;;;;;;;;; Type Access ;;;;;;;;;;;;;;;;;;;;;;
```

```
;;; Check to see if the symbol names a type.

(defun symbol-objectp (symbol)
  (get symbol 'typep))

;;; Mark this symbol as being a type.

(defun store-typep (type)
  (setf (get type 'typep) t))

;;;;;;;;;;;;;;;;;;;;;; Parent Access ;;;;;;;;;;;;;;;;;;;;;;

;;; Store the parent of the type

(defun store-parent (type-name parent)
  (setf (get type-name 'parent) parent))

;;; Get the list of parents of this type.

(defun get-parent (type-name)
  (get type-name 'parent))

;;;;;;;;;;;;;;;;; Access Generic Function ;;;;;;;;;;;;;;;;;

;;; Mark the argument function as existing.

(defun store-user-function (function-name user-function)
  (setf (get function-name 'user-function) user-function))

;;; See if a function of the same name as the method exists.

(defun user-function (function-name)
  (get function-name 'user-function))

;;;;;;;;;;;;;;;;;;;; Printable slots ;;;;;;;;;;;;;;;;;;;;;;

;;; Store the names of any printable slots.

(defun store-printable (type-name slot-name)
  (setf (get type-name 'printable)
        (adjoin slot-name (printables type-name))))

;;; Return the list of printable slots.
```

```
(defun printables (type-name)
  (get type-name 'printable))

;;;;;;;;;;;;;;;;;;;; Is it an object ;;;;;;;;;;;;;;;;;;;;;

;;; Test to see if the argument is an object (an instance of
;;; a type).

(defun objectp (object)
  (typep object 'generic-type))

;;;;;;;;;;;;;;;;;;;;;;;; Utilities ;;;;;;;;;;;;;;;;;;;;;;;;

;;; Make the argument into a keyword, by adding a : to the
;;; front.

(defun make-keyword (symbol)
  (intern (symbol-name symbol) (find-package 'keyword)))

;;;;;;;;;;;;;;;;;;;;;;;;;;;;;;;;;;;;;;;;;;;;;;;;;;;;;;;;;;;;

;;; Is the argument already a generic slot function.
;;; This code uses property lists for no real reason.  We
;;; could easily use a global variable, hash table, or any
;;; number of techniques.  As long as these two functions are
;;; compatible, then it doesn't
;;; really matter.

(defun genericp (slot-function)
  (get slot-function 'generic-function))
;;; Mark the argument as being generic slot function.

(defun add-generic (slot-function)
  (setf (get slot-function 'generic-function) t))

;;;;;;;;;;;;;;;;;;;;;;;;;;;;;;;;;;;;;;;;;;;;;;;;;;;;;;;;;;;;
;;; Define the generic method dispatching function.  We only
;;; need to do this once for each new generic method name.

(defun define-generic (method-name extra-args)
  ;; Only define a generic function if a generic function
  ;; hasn't already been defined.
  (cond
   ((not (genericp method-name))
```

```
    (create-generic-function method-name extra-args)
    (add-generic method-name))))

;;; Defines the generic method dispatching function.  It
;;; verifies that the argument is an object, picks up the
;;; actual function name and then invokes it.

(defun create-generic-function (method-name extra-args)
  (let
    ((user-function
      (build-separated-name 'USER method-name "$$")))
    ;; If there is already a generic function of the same
    ;; name as the method that we are about to define, then
    ;; save it away as a user function.
    (cond ((and (fboundp method-name)
                (not (fboundp user-function)))
           (store-user-function method-name user-function)
           (setf (symbol-function user-function)
                 (symbol-function method-name))))
    (setf (symbol-function method-name)
          `(lambda (self ,@extra-args)
             (let
               ((user-fn (user-function
                           (quote ,method-name))))
               (cond
                ((objectp self)
                 (let*
                   ((type-name (object-type self))
                    (actual-name-and-self
                     (get-a-method (quote ,method-name)
                                   type-name self))
                    (target-object
                     (cdr actual-name-and-self))
                    (actual-name
                     (car actual-name-and-self)))
                   (cond ((and user-fn (not actual-name))
                          (setf actual-name user-fn)
                          (setf target-object self))
                         ((not actual-name)
                          (error
                           "~S is not a known method for ~S"
                           (quote ,method-name)
                           type-name)))
                   (apply actual-name
```

```
                        (list target-object
                              ,@extra-args))))
              (user-fn
               (apply user-fn
                      (list self ,@extra-args)))
              (t (error
                  "~S is not an object, invoked with ~S"
                  self (quote ,method-name))))))))

(defun get-a-method (method-name type-name self)
  (let
    ((actual-name (get-actual-name method-name type-name)))
    (cond ((not actual-name)
           (find-parent-method method-name (parents self)))
          (t (cons actual-name self)))))

(defun find-parent-method (method-name parent-list)
  (cond ((null parent-list) nil)
        ((get-a-method method-name (caar parent-list)
                       (cdar parent-list)))
        (t (find-parent-method method-name
                               (cdr parent-list)))))

;;;;;;;;;;;;;;;;;;;;;;;;;;;;;;;;;;;;;;;;;;;;;;;;;;;;;;;;;;;;

;;;;;;;;;;;;;;;;;;;;;;;;;;;;;;;;;;;;;;;;;;;;;;;;;;;;;;;;;;;;

;;; Make an object of a specified type.  General syntax is:
;;; (make-instance type-name initializationoptions).
;;; An initialization option is a keyword and value.  Only
;;; those slots that have been defined to be initable are
;;; permitted to be initialized.

(defun make-instance (type-name &rest initial-options)
  (cond ((not (symbol-objectp type-name))
         (error "~S is not a known type" type-name))
        (t (verify-legal-options initial-options
                                 (find-initables type-name))
           (make-instance-aux type-name initial-options))))

(defun make-instance-aux (type-name initial-options)
  (let
      (instance
       (options-for-parents
```

```
        (parent-options initial-options type-name)))
    (setf instance
          (apply (build-separated-name 'make type-name "-")
                 (current-options initial-options
                                  type-name)))
    ;; For each parent, we need to make the object and load
    ;; it into the parents slot of the defstruct.
    (dolist (each-parent (get-parent type-name))
      (setf (parents instance)
            (cons (cons each-parent
                        (make-instance-aux
                         each-parent options-for-parents))
                  (parents instance))))
    instance))

;;; Constructs a list of the initial options for this type.

(defun current-options (options type-name)
  (cond ((null options) nil)
        ((member (car options) (get-initable type-name))
         (cons (car options)
               (cons (cadr options)
                     (current-options (cddr options)
                                      type-name))))
        (t (current-options (cddr options) type-name))))

;;; Constructs the list of the initial options that are NOT
;;; for this type.  These are passed on to the parents.

(defun parent-options (options type-name)
  (cond ((null options) nil)
        ((member (car options) (get-initable type-name))
         (parent-options (cddr options) type-name))
        (t (cons (car options)
                 (cons (cadr options)
                       (parent-options (cddr options)
                                       type-name))))))

;;; From the argument type to all of the parents, find the
;;; list of initable slots.  Return that list.

(defun find-initables (type-name)
  (append (get-initable type-name)
          (find-initables-aux (get-parent type-name))))
```

```
;;; Auxiliary function to  scan the parent list and find all
;;; of the initable slots.

(defun find-initables-aux (parents)
  (cond ((null parents) nil)
        (t (append (find-initables (car parents))
                   (find-initables-aux (cdr parents))))))

;;; Verify that the option list of the first argument is
;;; allowed to be inited.  If it is not allowed, then signal
;;; an error.

(defun verify-legal-options (option-list legal-options)
  (cond ((null option-list) nil)
        ((member (car option-list) legal-options)
         (verify-legal-options (cddr option-list)
                               legal-options))
        (t (error "~S is not an initable option"
                  (car option-list)))))

;;;;;;;;;;;;;;;;;;;;;;;;;;;;;;;;;;;;;;;;;;;;;;;;;;;;;;;;;;;;
;;;;;;;;;;;;;;;;;;;;;;;;;;;;;;;;;;;;;;;;;;;;;;;;;;;;;;;;;;;;

;;; Define a method for a specific type.  General syntax is:
;;; (define-method (type-name method-name) (arg-list) body)
;;; Within the body of the method, any of the slots of the
;;; type may be accessed directly.  Thus, we need to
;;; transform the body so that every occurrence of a slot
;;; name symbol is transformed into the appropriate defstruct
;;; access function.  For now, we will use a simple tree
;;; traversal routine that just searches for a slot name and
;;; replaces it with the correct defstruct access method.

(defmacro define-method ((type-name method-name) arg-list
                         &rest body)
  (let
    ((method-function-name
      (build-separated-name type-name method-name "$")))
    (cond ((not (symbol-objectp type-name))
           (error "~S is not a known type" type-name)))
    (define-generic method-name arg-list)
    (store-method-name type-name method-name
                       method-function-name)
```

```
    `(progn
       ;; We need to define a generic function associated
       ;; with the method name.  Then we store under the
       ;; method descriptions, the method name and the actual
       ;; function name.  The actual function name will be a
       ;; composition of the type name and the method name.
       (define-generic ',method-name ',arg-list)
       ;; Store the method access name.
       (store-method-name ',type-name ',method-name
                          ',method-function-name)
       ;; Define the function.
       (defun ,method-function-name (self ,@arg-list)
         ,@(transform (copy-tree body)
                      (get-slot-names type-name)))
       (quote ,method-name))))

;;; Simple transformation system.  The only special form that
;;; this function cares to process is quote.

(defun transform (code slot-list)
  (transform-sexprs code slot-list)
  code)

;;; Transform each s-expression in the body of the function.

(defun transform-sexprs (code slot-list)
  (let
    (slot-found)
    (cond ((null code) nil)
          ;; If an s-expr is a simple atom, then must
          ;; transform it by itself.
          ((and (atom (car code))
                (setf slot-found
                      (assoc (car code) slot-list)))
           (rplaca code `(,(cdr slot-found) self))
           (transform-sexprs (cdr code) slot-list))
          (t (transform-aux (car code) slot-list)
             (transform-sexprs (cdr code) slot-list)))))

;;; The actual transformation process (destructive).

(defun transform-aux (code slot-list)
  (cond ((null code) nil)
        ((atom code) code)
```

```
        ((equal (car code) 'quote)
         nil)
        ((equal (car code) 'call-method)
         (rplacd code (cons 'self (cdr code)))
         (transform-operands (cdddr code) slot-list))
        ((listp (car code))
         (transform-aux (car code) slot-list)
         (transform-aux (cdr code) slot-list))
        (t (transform-operands (cdr code) slot-list))))
(defun transform-operands (code slot-list)
  (let
    (slot-found)
    (cond ((null code) nil)
          ((atom code) nil)
          ((listp (car code))
           (transform-aux (car code) slot-list)
           (transform-operands (cdr code) slot-list))
          ((setf slot-found (assoc (car code) slot-list))
           (rplaca code `(,(cdr slot-found) self))
           (transform-operands (cdr code) slot-list))
          (t (transform-operands (car code) slot-list)
             (transform-operands (cdr code) slot-list)))))

;;;;;;;;;;;;;;;;;;;;;;;;;;;;;;;;;;;;;;;;;;;;;;;;;;;;;;;;;;;;
;;;;;;;;;;;;;;;;;;;;;;;;;;;;;;;;;;;;;;;;;;;;;;;;;;;;;;;;;;;;

;;; To be able to do multiple inheritance, we need to have a
;;; new slot in every object that is a list of all of the
;;; parent objects.  That way, to invoke a parent method, it
;;; has to extract the correct object from the list and then
;;; call the method.  This would correct the problem with
;;; single inheritance of being able to have slots that
;;; conflict with slot names of parents.  It seems like a
;;; simple system could be implemented as follows:
;;;    object: ( ... parent ....)
;;;    parent: ((typename . object) (typename2 . object2)
;;;             ...)
;;; Need to add a transformation to transform so that
;;; call-method is given an additional argument (first) which
;;; is self.

;;; The only way to access a parent method is to use the
;;; call-method form.  The transformation system must change
```

```
;;; all call-method invocations to include an extra argument
;;; (the first one), which is the object itself.

(defmacro call-method (object (typename methodname)
                              &rest args)
  `(call-method-internal ,object (quote ,typename)
                         (quote ,methodname)
                         ,@args))

;;; Internal function that does the actual method invocation.

(defun call-method-internal (object typename methodname
                                    &rest args)
  (let*
    ((parent-object (cdr (assoc typename (parents object)))))
    (cond ((not parent-object)
           (error "~S does not have parent ~S"
                  (object-type object)
                  typename)))
    (apply methodname parent-object args)))

;;;;;;;;;;;;;;;;;;;;;;;;;;;;;;;;;;;;;;;;;;;;;;;;;;;;;;;;;;;;
;;; List all of the slots in an object and their current
;;; values.

(defun describe (obj)
  (dolist (each-slot (get-slot-names (object-type obj)))
    (format t " ~A: ~A~%" (car each-slot)
            (funcall (cdr each-slot) obj)))
  (dolist (each-parent (parents obj))
    (describe (cdr each-parent))))

;;;;;;;;;;;;;;;;;;;;;;;;;;;;;;;;;;;;;;;;;;;;;;;;;;;;;;;;;;;;
;;;;;;;;;;;;;;;;;;;;;;;;;;;;;;;;;;;;;;;;;;;;;;;;;;;;;;;;;;;;

;;; Some major modification of the system to allow a
;;; function with the same name as a method.
;;; WARNING CHANGES THE DEFINITION OF DEFUN.

(eval-when (load compile eval)
  (cond
   ((not (macro-function 'old-defun))
    (format t "Defining old-defun~%")
```

```
        (setf (macro-function 'old-defun)
              (macro-function 'defun)))))

(defmacro defun (function-name arg-list &rest body)
  (cond
   ((or (not (fboundp 'genericp))
        (not (genericp function-name)))
    `(old-defun ,function-name ,arg-list ,@body))
   (t (let
        ((user-name
          (build-separated-name 'USER function-name "$$")))
        `(progn
           (old-defun ,user-name ,arg-list ,@body)
           (store-user-function (quote ,function-name)
                                (quote ,user-name))
           (quote ,function-name))))))
```

B

Answers to Selected Exercises

Chapter 2

2.1 Every LISP expression returns a value.

2.5 All except `smallest-degree` are lists.

2.7 A `nil` argument to `append` is ignored, while a `nil` given to `list` produces a `nil` in that place in the list.

2.8 There is no difference.

2.10 They are the same, both evaluating to `3`.

2.11 The value for `x` is 3, the fourth element.

2.13 `Add-alist` returns a new association list with the key and value added as associations.

```
(defun add-alist (key value alist)
  (cons (list key value) alist))
```

2.14 The middle term of the polynomial is computed as the cross product of the other terms.

```
(defun multiply-first-degree-polynomial (poly1 poly2)
  (list (* (car poly1) (car poly2))
        (+ (* (car poly1) (cadr poly2))
           (* (cadr poly1) (car poly2)))
        (* (cadr poly1) (cadr poly2))))
```

Chapter Exercises

1. The definition of the function `quadratic` is:

```
(defun quadratic (a b c)
```

```
(/ (+ (- b)
      (sqrt (- (*  b b)
               (* 4 a c))))
   (* 2 a)))
```

2. The definition of `extract` is a simple invocation of `nth`:

```
(defun extract (polynomial n)
  (nth n polynomial))
```

3. `One-root` calls the functions defined in the previous two exercises to compute a root of a polynomial:

```
(defun one-root (polynomial)
  (quadratic (extract polynomial 2)
             (extract polynomial 1)
             (extract polynomial 0)))
```

Chapter 3

3.1 `Atom-and-list` determines if its argument is both an atom and a list:

```
(defun atom-and-list (object)
  (null object))
```

3.4 New version of `coefficient-from-term`:

```
(defun coefficient-from-term (term)
  (if (numberp term)
    term
    (if (equal (car term) '*)
      (cadr term)
      1)))
```

3.5 Yet another version of `coefficient-from-term`:

```
(defun coefficient-from-term (term)
  (if (numberp term)
    term
    (if (symbolp term)
      1
      (if (equal (car term) '*)
        (cadr term)
        1))))
```

3.6 Modified version of `quadratic` to perform error checking:

```
(defun quad-aux (a b c)
  (- (* b b)
     (* 4 a c)))
```

```
(defun quadratic (a b c)
  (cond ((< (quad-aux a b c ) 0) 'error)
        (T (/ (+ (- b)
                 (sqrt (quad-aux a b c)))
              (* 2 a)))))
```

3.8 Extract the constant term from a polynomial in prefix notation:

```
(defun const-term (poly)
  (cond ((numberp poly) poly)
        ((atom poly) 0)
        ((equal '+ (car poly)) ; at least two terms
         (cond ((numberp (cadr poly)) (cadr poly))
               ((numberp (caddr poly)) (caddr poly))
               ((numberp (cadddr poly)) (cadddr poly))
               (T 0)))))
```

3.10 The equivalent of `(or a b c)` is:

```
(cond (a)
      (b)
      (c)
      (T nil))
```

3.11 Further enhancement to error checking in `quadratic`:

```
(defun quadratic (a b c)
  (cond ((and (numberp a)
              (numberp b)
              (numberp c)
              (>= (quad-aux a b c) 0))
         (/ (+ (- b)
               (sqrt (quad-aux a b c)))
            (* 2 a)))
        (T 'error)))
```

3.12 The definitions of `my-assoc` and `my-reverse`.

```
(defun my-assoc (key data)
  (cond ((null data) nil)
        ((equal (caar data) key) (car data))
        (T (my-assoc key (cdr data)))))

(defun my-reverse (object)
  (if (null object)
    nil
    (append (my-reverse (cdr object))
            (list (car object)))))
```

3.13 The definition of `super-reverse` is:

```
(defun super-reverse (object)
  (cond ((null object) nil)
        ((atom object) object)
        (t (append (super-reverse (cdr object))
                   (list (super-reverse
                           (car object)))))))
```

3.16 Our version of the `nth` function:

```
(defun my-nth (n alist)
  (cond ((null alist) nil)
        ((< n 0) 'error-on-n)
        ((= n 0) (car alist))
        (T (my-nth (1- n) (cdr alist)))))
```

3.19 Compute the slope of two points:

```
(defun slope (p1 p2)
  (let ((denominator (- (car p2) (car p1))))
    (if (= denominator 0)
      'infinity
      (/ (- (cadr p2) (cadr p1)) denominator))))
```

3.20 Determine if three points are on the same line:

```
(defun collinearp (p1 p2 p3)
  (= (slope p1 p2)
     (slope p2 p3)))
```

3.21 Determine if the third point is on the line between the first two points:

```
(defun between (p1 p2 between-point)
  (and (collinearp p1 p2 between-point)
       (or (<= (car p1) (car between-point) (car p2))
           (<= (car p2) (car between-point) (car p1))
           (or (<= (cadr p1) (cadr between-point)
                   (cadr p2))
               (<= (cadr p2) (cadr between-point)
                   (cadr p1))))))
```

3.22 A version of `internal-to-external-aux` which uses a variable that contains the polynomial variable:

```
(defvar *poly-variable* 'x)

(defun internal-to-external-aux (coefficients
                                  current-exponent)
  (cond ((null coefficients) nil)
        ((= (car coefficients) 0)
         (internal-to-external-aux
```

```
                (cdr coefficients)
                (1+ current-exponent)))
              (t (cons
                  (list '*
                        (car coefficients)
                        (list '** *poly-variable*
                              current-exponent))
                  (internal-to-external-aux
                   (cdr coefficients)
                   (1+ current-exponent))))))
```

3.23 My-map applies a predicate to each element of a list:

```
(defun my-map (predicate values)
  (if (null values)
    nil
    (cons (apply predicate (list (car values)))
          (my-map predicate (cdr values)))))
```

Chapter Exercises

1. This is another version of quadratic that computes both roots:

```
(defun quadratic (a b c)
  (let (inner)
    (cond ((and (numberp a)
                (numberp b)
                (numberp c)
                (< (setf inner (quad-aux a b c)) 0))
           'error)
          (t (setf inner (sqrt inner))
             (list (/ (+ (- b) inner) (* 2 a))
                   (/ (- (- b) inner) (* 2 a)))))))
```

2. Roots returns the first-degree polynomial roots of the argument polynomial:

```
(defun roots (polynomial)
  (let ((both-roots
         (quadratic (caddr polynomial)
                    (cadr polynomial)
                    (car polynomial))))
    (list (list (car both-roots) 1)
          (list (cadr both-roots) 1))))
```

Chapter 4

4.1 The following functions translate an infix version of a polynomial into a prefix version. Later exercises perform the full translation into the internal form.

```
;;; Transform the polynomial into a list of infix terms.
;;; Notice that when a - is encountered, the sign of the
;;; next constant is changed, or a -1 * the next element
;;; is inserted.
(defun list-of-terms (polynomial)
  (cond ((null polynomial) (list nil))
        ((equal (car polynomial) '+)
         (cons nil (list-of-terms (cdr polynomial))))
        ((equal (car polynomial) '-)
         (if (numberp (cadr polynomial))
           (cons nil (list-of-terms
                      (cons (- (cadr polynomial))
                            (cddr polynomial))))
           (cons nil
                 (list-of-terms
                  (cons -1
                        (cons '*
                              (cdr polynomial))))))))
        (t (let ((term-and-poly
                  (list-of-terms (cdr polynomial))))
             (cons (cons (car polynomial)
                         (car term-and-poly))
                   (cdr term-and-poly))))))
⇒ LIST-OF-TERMS

(list-of-terms '(33))
⇒ ((33))

(list-of-terms '(x + 33))
⇒ ((X) (33))

(list-of-terms '(33 * x))
⇒ ((33 * X))

(list-of-terms '(33 * x ** 3 - x))
⇒ ((33 * X ** 3) (-1 * X))

(list-of-terms '(4 * x ** 2 - 3 * x + 99))
⇒ ((4 * X ** 2) (-3 * X) (99))

;;; Convert a single term from infix to prefix.  This is
;;; easy, since the second element of the list is the
;;; operator (if present).
(defun convert-term (term)
  (if (null (cadr term))
```

```
      (car term)
      (list (cadr term) (car term) (convert-term
                                      (cddr term)))))
 ⇒ CONVERT-TERM

(convert-term '(99))
 ⇒ 99

(convert-term '(x))
 ⇒ X

(convert-term '(3 * x))
 ⇒ (* 3 X)

(convert-term '(x ** 2))
 ⇒ (** X 2)

(convert-term '(-3 * x ** 3))
 ⇒ (* -3 (** X 3))

;;; Convert the polynomial into a prefix representation.
;;; There will be a leading +, if there is more than one
;;; term.
(defun infix-to-prefix (polynomial)
  (let ((terms (list-of-terms polynomial)))
    (if (cdr terms)
      (cons '+ (infix-to-prefix-aux terms))
      (car (infix-to-prefix-aux terms)))))
 ⇒ INFIX-TO-PREFIX

;;; Convert each term into prefix notation.
(defun infix-to-prefix-aux (terms)
  (if (null terms)
    nil
    (cons (convert-term (car terms))
          (infix-to-prefix-aux (cdr terms)))))
 ⇒ INFIX-TO-PREFIX-AUX
```

4.3 You can either implement your own sorting algorithm, or try using `sort` described in Chapter 13 or [40, Chapter 14]. This version uses `sort`.

```
;;; Sort the terms from smallest to largest exponent.
;;; Then invoke build-internal-form-aux to extract the
;;; coefficients.
(defun build-internal-form (terms)
  (build-internal-form-aux
   (sort terms '< :key 'exponent-of-term) 0))

;;; Extract the coefficients from the terms, placing a
```

```
;;; zero where there is no term with the correct
;;; exponent.
(defun build-internal-form-aux (terms exponent)
  (if (null terms)
    nil
    (if (= (exponent-of-term (car terms)) exponent)
      (cons (coefficient-of-term (car terms))
            (build-internal-form-aux (cdr terms)
                                     (1+ exponent)))
      (cons 0 (build-internal-form-aux terms
                                       (1+ exponent))))))

;;; New definition of external-to-internal that calls the
;;; simpler version of build-internal-form.
(defun external-to-internal (polynomial)
  (build-internal-form
   (if (and (listp polynomial)
            (equal (car polynomial) '+))
     (cdr polynomial)
     (list polynomial))))
```

4.6 A version of `build-list-of-terms` that constructs the list in the proper order:

```
(defun build-list-of-terms (list-of-coefficients
                            exponent)
  (if (null list-of-coefficients)
    nil
    (let ((tmp (convert-term (car list-of-coefficients)
                             exponent)))
      (if tmp
          (cons tmp
                (build-list-of-terms
                 (cdr list-of-coefficients)
                 (1+ exponent)))
        (build-list-of-terms
         (cdr list-of-coefficients)
         (1+ exponent))))))
```

4.9 `Zero-degreep` is true as long as a `nil` or zeros are found after the first element.

```
(defun zero-degreep (coefficients)
  (zero-degreep-aux (cdr coefficients)))

(defun zero-degreep-aux (coefficients)
  (cond ((null coefficients) t)
```

```
            ((= (car coefficients) 0)
             (zero-degreep-aux (cdr coefficients)))
            (t nil)))

(defun poly-derivative (polynomial)
  (if (zero-degreep polynomial)
    '(0)
    (poly-derivative-aux (cdr polynomial) 1)))
```

4.10 Since it is not possible to determine if a zero is significant or not, the best solution is to truncate the trailing zeros after constructing the result. An easy solution is to reverse the list, scan until a non-zero is found and return the reverse remaining list.

```
(defun zero-truncate (polynomial)
  (reverse (zero-truncate-aux (reverse polynomial))))

(defun zero-truncate-aux (polynomial)
  (cond ((null polynomial)
         (list 0)) ;; If all zeros, then return (0).
        ((= (car polynomial) 0)
         (zero-truncate-aux (cdr polynomial)))
        (t polynomial)))
```

4.11 `Unaryp` determines if the operator is a unary operator. This code assumes that there are only binary and unary operators.

```
(defun operator (expression)
  (car expression))

(defun first-operand (expression)
  (cadr expression))

(defun second-operand (expression)
  (caddr expression))

(defun manipulate (operation-and-polynomials)
  (let* ((operation (operator operation-and-polynomials))
         (operand-1
          (external-to-internal
           (first-operand operation-and-polynomials)))
         (operand-2
          (if (not (equal operation 'df))
            (external-to-internal
             (second-operand operation-and-polynomials))
            nil)))
    (internal-to-external
     (cond ((equal operation '+)
            (poly-add operand-1 operand-2))
```

```
((equal operation '-)
 (poly-subtract operand-1 operand-2))
(t (poly-derivative operand-1))))))
```

4.14 Observing the table, the solution is to be able to multiply each element of one polynomial by the other polynomial. Thus, the primitive is the function `constant-times-poly`. `Poly-multiply-aux` recursively adds the polynomials adding the appropriate number of zeros to the front of each polynomial.

```
(defun constant-times-poly (constant polynomial)
  (if (null polynomial)
    nil
    (cons (* constant (car polynomial))
          (constant-times-poly constant
                               (cdr polynomial)))))

(defun poly-multiply-aux (poly-1 poly-2 zeros)
  (let ((one-multiplication
         (constant-times-poly (car poly-2)
                              (append zeros poly-1))))
    (if (null (cdr poly-2))
      one-multiplication
      (poly-add
       one-multiplication
       (poly-multiply-aux poly-1 (cdr poly-2)
                          (cons 0 zeros))))))

(defun poly-multiply (poly-1 poly-2)
  (poly-multiply-aux poly-1 poly-2 nil))

(add-operator '* 'poly-multiply)
```

Chapter Exercises

1. These functions pass an exponent value, dividing each element by the current exponent. The main function `poly-integral` adds the constant zero term to the polynomial.

```
(defun poly-integral (polynomial)
  (cons 0 (poly-integral-aux polynomial 1)))

(defun poly-integral-aux (polynomial exponent)
  (if (null polynomial)
    nil
    (cons (/ (car polynomial) exponent)
          (poly-integral-aux (cdr polynomial)
                             (1+ exponent)))))

(add-operator 'int 'poly-integral)
```

2. Division is accomplished by computing the exact value that eliminates the leading coefficient. It is then used to compute the remainder and the factor is saved. These are collected into a list whose leading element is the remainder and rest is the factor.

```
(defun poly-division-aux (poly-1 poly-2)
  (if (null (cddr poly-1))
    (compute-remainder-and-factor poly-1 poly-2)
    (let ((previous-term
           (poly-division-aux (cdr poly-1) poly-2)))
      (append
       (compute-remainder-and-factor
        (list (car poly-1) (car previous-term))
        poly-2)
       (cdr previous-term)))))

(defun compute-remainder-and-factor (poly-1 poly-2)
  (let ((new-term (/ (cadr poly-1) (cadr poly-2))))
    (list (- (car poly-1) (* new-term (car poly-2)))
          new-term)))

(defun poly-division (poly-1 poly-2)
  (cdr (poly-division-aux poly-1 poly-2)))

(poly-division '(-10 -11 6) '(2 3))

(add-operator '/ 'poly-division)
```

Chapter 5

5.2 This method returns a new clown object when the new shoe size is different.

```
(defun new-shoes (clown new-shoe-size)
  (if (= (shoe-size clown) new-shoe-size)
    clown
    (cons (list 'shoe-size new-shoe-size) clown)))
```

5.3 One technique would be to store all objects in another association list. An object would then be a unique reference into the association list to retrieve the actual object data. Updating a field in an object would then require changing the global association list.

5.4 You can choose as many slots as you think are necessary; these are simply representative.

```
(define-type cat
  (:var color)
  (:var breed)
  (:var age)
```

```
  (:var favorite-cat-food)
  (:var sound (:init 'meow))
  (:var volume-of-purr))

(define-type dog
  (:var color)
  (:var breed)
  (:var age)
  (:var favorite-dog-food)
  (:var sound (:init 'bark))
  (:var tricks))
```

5.5 The technique is to store the result of a call to `make-instance` in the slot.

5.7 Nothing. They are all the same.

5.8 The definition of the methods for dog tricks:

```
(define-method (dog train) (new-trick)
  (cond ((not (member new-trick tricks))
         (setf tricks (cons new-trick tricks)))))

(define-method (dog trickp) (trick-to-check)
  (member trick-to-check tricks))

(define-method (dog showtime) ()
  (let ((list-parts
         (randomly-sort-list tricks
                             (random (length tricks)))))
    (append (cadr list-parts) (car list-parts))))

(defun randomly-sort-list (list-to-sort index)
  (cond ((= index 0) (list nil list-to-sort))
        (t (let ((remaining-list
                  (randomly-sort-list (cdr list-to-sort)
                                      (1- index))))
             (list
              (cons (car list-to-sort)
                    (car remaining-list))
              (cadr remaining-list))))))
```

5.10 The first solution is the obvious one using a cond statement. The second uses the fact that `append`ing a nil is ignored.

```
(define-method (person parent) ()
  (cond ((and father mother) (list father mother))
        ((father (list father)))
        ((mother (list mother)))
        (t nil)))
```

```
(define-method (person parent) ()
  (append (and father (list father))
          (and mother (list mother))))
```

5.11 First we redefine the person type. Next are the definitions of `set-brother` and `set-sister`.

```
(define-type person
  (:var name :initable)
  (:var mother :initable)
  (:var father :initable)
  (:var sex :initable)
  (:var sibling (:init *unknown*) :settable)
  (:var sister (:init *unknown*) :settable)
  (:var brother (:init *unknown*) :settable)
  :all-gettable
  )

(define-method (person set-brother) (new-brother)
  (cond ((not (equal brother new-brother))
         (setf brother new-brother)
         (let (brother-object)
           (cond ((and (boundp new-brother)
                       (objectp
                        (setf brother-object
                              (symbol-value
                               new-brother))))
                  (if (equal sex 'male)
                    (set-brother brother-object name)
                    (set-sister brother-object name)))))
           new-brother))))

(define-method (person set-sister) (new-sister)
  (cond ((not (equal sister new-sister))
         (setf sister new-sister)
         (let (sister-object)
           (cond ((and (boundp new-sister)
                       (objectp
                        (setf sister-object
                              (symbol-value
                               new-sister))))
                  (if (equal sex 'male)
                    (set-brother sister-object name)
                    (set-sister sister-object name))))
           new-sister))))
```

5.13 The implementation of **gene-mapping** requires the services of an auxiliary function to construct the list of ones and zeros. Otherwise, the implementation is straight forward.

```
(define-type person
  (:var name :initable)
  (:var mother :initable)
  (:var father :initable)
  (:var sex :initable)
  (:var sibling (:init *unknown*) :settable)
  (:var genes :initable :settable)
  :all-gettable
  )

(define-method (person gene-mapping) ()
  (gene-mapping-aux genes))

(defun gene-mapping-aux (gene-alist)
  (if (null gene-alist)
    nil
    (cons (if (equal (cadr (car gene-alist)) 'dominant)
              1
              0)
          (gene-mapping-aux (cdr gene-alist)))))

(define-method (person gene-summary) ()
  (if (>= (apply '+ (gene-mapping self)) 2)
    'dominant
    'recessive))
```

5.16 This is a new version of the Titanian type with fields for genes. **Add-gene** and **gene-summary** are now generic functions that will operate upon either Titanians or Earthlings.

```
(define-type Titanian
  (:var name :initable)
  (:var parent :initable :settable)
  (:var siblings (:init nil) :settable)
  (:var children (:init nil) :settable)
  (:var chemical-nutrient (:init 'gredzlit) :settable)
  (:var upper-brain-size (:init *unknown*) :settable)
  (:var lower-brain-size (:init *unknown*) :settable)
  (:var dominant-genes :initable :settable)
  (:var recessive-genes :initable :settable)
  :all-gettable
  )
```

```
(defun add-gene (object gene-type gene-name)
  (if (equal gene-type 'dominant)
    (setf (dominant-genes object)
          (cons gene-name (dominant-genes object)))
    (setf (recessive-genes object)
          (cons gene-name (recessive-genes object)))))

(defun gene-summary (object)
  (if (> (length (dominant-genes object))
         (length (recessive-genes object)))
    'dominant
    'recessive))
```

5.19 Notice how `cat` and `dog` override the definition of `pet`'s `sound` slot with a new initial value.

```
(define-type pet
  (:var breed)
  (:var name)
  (:var color)
  (:var age)
  (:var owner)
  (:var sound)
  :all-initable)

(define-type cat
  (:inherit-from pet)
  (:var favorite-cat-food)
  (:var sound (:init 'meow))
  (:var volume-of-purr)
  :all-initable)

(define-type dog
  (:inherit-from pet)
  (:var favorite-dog-food)
  (:var sound (:init 'bark))
  (:var tricks)
  :all-initable)
```

5.20 `Gets-a-pet` is straightforward, except that it must use `self` to store the person object in the pet object. `Owners-name` just asks for the name of the object stored in the owner slot. Notice the use of `name` and that the object system correctly determines where to get the `name` out of each object.

```
(define-method (person gets-a-pet) (name breed color)
  (make-instance 'cat :owner self :name name :breed breed
                 :color color))
⇒ GETS-A-PET
```

```
(define-method (pet owners-name) ()
  (name owner))
⇒ OWNERS-NAME

(setf bob (make-instance 'person :name 'bob))
⇒ #<Object PERSON>

(setf lucky (gets-a-pet bob 'lucky 'mixed 'gray))
⇒ #<Object CAT>

(owners-name lucky)
⇒ BOB
```

5.22 This structure forces cat and dog to have multiple parents.

```
(define-type pet
  (:var breed)
  (:var name)
  (:var age)
  (:var owner)
  (:var sound)
  :all-initable)

(define-type mammal
  (:var hair-color)
  :all-initable)

(define-type cat
  (:inherit-from pet mammal)
  (:var favorite-cat-food)
  (:var sound (:init 'meow))
  (:var volume-of-purr)
  :all-initable)

(define-type dog
  (:inherit-from pet mammal)
  (:var favorite-dog-food)
  (:var sound (:init 'bark))
  (:var tricks)
  :all-initable)
```

Chapter Exercises

1. Using this information, we can create the following objects.

```
(define-type hardware
  (:inherit-from name)
```

```
    (:var date-installed)
    (:var pm-period)
    (:var date-last-pm)
    (:var maintainer)
    :all-gettable
    :all-settable
    :all-initable)

  (define-type maintainer
    (:inherit-from name)
    (:var phone-number)
    (:var office-address)
    :all-gettable
    :all-settable
    :all-initable)
```

2. The following definitions describe each of the three types of hardware:

```
(define-type printer
  (:inherit-from hardware)
  (:var speed)
  :all-gettable
  :all-settable
  :all-initable)

(define-type disk-drive
  (:inherit-from hardware)
  (:var type)
  (:var access-time)
  :all-gettable
  :all-settable
  :all-initable)

(define-type workstation
  (:inherit-from hardware)
  (:var screen-size)
  (:var amount-of-memory)
  :all-gettable
  :all-settable
  :all-initable)
```

3. Since `not-working` is generic to all hardware, we can define it on the `hardware` type. We also need a `dump-information` method to return useful information such as who to call.

```
(define-method (maintainer dump-information) ()
  (list (call-method name name)
        'at phone
```

```
            'in office-address))

(define-method (hardware not-working) ()
  (append (list 'device (call-method name name)
                'lastpm date-last-pm)
          (dump-information maintainer)))
```

Chapter 6

6.2 The result happens to be the same as the previous answer. The inner `let*` is still ignored, but the initial value of `b` bound in the `let*` is different. In the first example, it is bound to the parameter `c`, while in the second it is bound to `b`, because `c` is bound to `b`. However, `b` is immediately assigned the value 5 and that is its result.

```
(1 5 2)
```

6.4 This time, the result is completely different because the computation of `b` in the first `let*` is dependent upon the previous `c` which is not then changed. Also, `a` depends on this current binding of `b` and therefore it has a different value as follows:

```
(25 10 5)
```

6.5 This contour diagram includes four levels because of the nested `let` expressions.

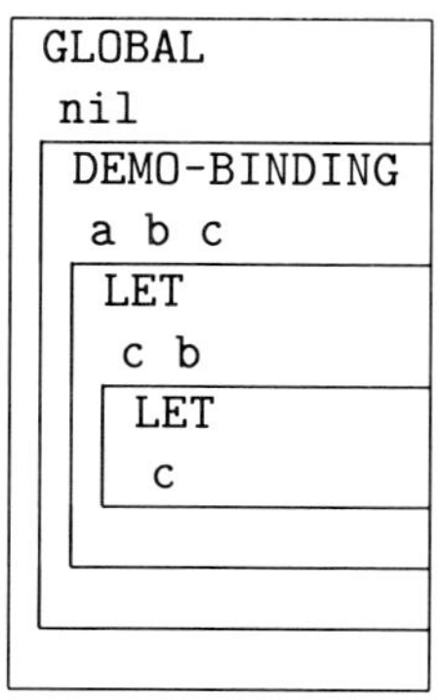

6.6 Since the first `let*` has two local variables, this requires the equivalent of two `let` contours, one for each variable. This is because of the access to `c` with the `let*` must be the `c` in the `let*` and not the parameter.

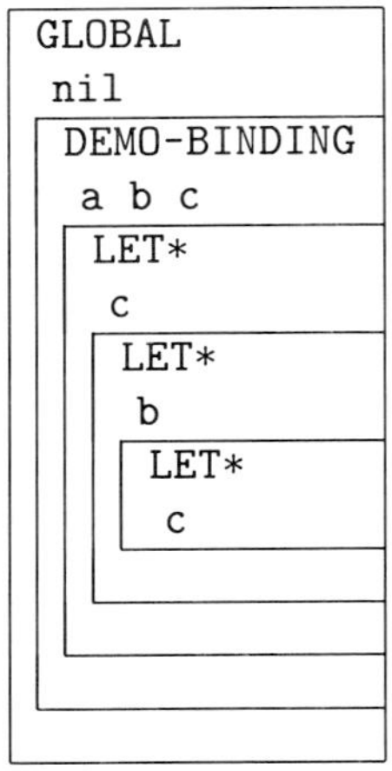

6.8 The transformation follows:

```
(defun make-a-person (parameters)
  (let ((env (add-environment
               (alistify '(name father mother sex)
                         parameters)
               nil)))
    (store '*person-names*
           (cons (lookup 'name env)
                 (lookup '*person-names* env))
           env)
    (make-instance 'person
                   :name (lookup 'name env)
                   (lookup 'mother env)
                   (lookup 'father env)
                   (lookup 'sex env))))
```

6.11 There is no difference between a free variable in a recursive and a non-recursive function.

6.13 There is no way that one arbitrary function can directly determine what other function called it. Therefore, the only way to communicate this information is through a variable only known to the caller and callee. The caller can first set the variable to some value. The callee can then check that the variable has been set before performing its processing and it must remember to reset the variable value in case the callee is invoked again. As long as no other function knows about the variable, this solution will work.

Chapter Exercises

1. These functions each take the arguments as specified and produce the new code as defined in the templates.

```
(defun translate-defun (definition)
  (let ((name (cadr definition))
        (arguments (caddr definition))
        (body (cdddr definition)))
    (list
     'defun name '(parameter)
     (cons 'let
           (cons
            (list (list 'env
                        (list 'add-environment
                              (list 'alistify
                                    (list 'quote
                                          arguments)
                                    'parameter)
                              nil)))
            (translate body))))))

(defun get-local-names (locals)
  (cond ((null locals) nil)
        ((listp (car locals))
         (cons (caar locals)
               (get-local-names (cdr locals))))
        (t (cons (car locals)
                 (get-local-names (cdr locals))))))

(defun get-local-values (locals)
  (cond ((null locals) nil)
        ((listp (car locals))
         (cons (cadr (car locals))
               (get-local-values (cdr locals))))
        (t (cons nil
                 (get-local-values (cdr locals))))))

(defun translate-let (let-expression)
  (let ((locals (cadr let-expression))
        (body (cddr let-expression)))
    (list 'let '(return-value)
          (list 'setf 'env
                (list 'add-environment
                      (list 'alistify
                            (list 'quote
                                  (get-local-names
```

```
                                     locals))
                              (list 'quote
                                    (get-local-values
                                     locals)))
                        'env))
            (list 'setf 'return-value
                  (cons 'progn (translate body)))
            '(setf env (remove-environment))
            'return-value)))

(defun translate-variable (variable)
  (list 'lookup (list 'quote variable) 'env))

(defun translate-set (set-expression)
  (let ((variable (cadr set-expression))
        (value (caddr set-expression)))
    (list 'store (list 'quote variable)
          (translate value) 'env)))
```

2. We store the symbol and its associated translation function in an association list. Translate then scans the argument, invoking the translation function when appropriate. The difficult part of this is how do we translate the symbols which are variables, but don't translate the function names. The solution requires another function which scans the argument list and calls `translate` on each element. Thus, if a variable is encountered, it is translated by itself in `translate`.

```
(defvar *translations*
  '((defun translate-defun) (let translate-let)
    (setf translate-set)))

(defun translate (s-expression)
  (cond ((null s-expression) nil)
        ((symbolp s-expression)
         (translate-variable s-expression))
        ((not (listp s-expression))
         s-expression)
        ((equal (car s-expression) 'quote)
         s-expression)
        ((let ((found-expression
                (cadr (assoc (car s-expression)
                             *translations*))))
           (if found-expression
             (apply found-expression (list s-expression))
             nil)))
        ((symbolp (car s-expression))
         (cons (car s-expression)
               (translate-function-args
```

```
                (cdr s-expression))))
          (t (cons (translate (car s-expression))
                   (translate (cdr s-expression))))))

(defun translate-function-args (arguments)
  (if (null arguments)
    nil
    (cons (translate (car arguments))
          (translate-function-args (cdr arguments)))))
```

Chapter 7

7.1 The recursive versions follow:

```
(defun oldest-person ()
    (labels ((oldest-person-aux (person-list oldest)
               (if (null person-list)
                 oldest
                 (oldest-person-aux (cdr person-list)
                    (max oldest (car person-list))))))
      (oldest-person-aux (cdr *persons*)
                         (car *persons*))))

(defun find-person-over-age (age-for-comparison)
  (labels ((find-person-over-age-aux (person-list)
             (cond ((null person-list) nil)
                   ((> (age (car person-list))
                       age-for-comparison)
                    (car person-list))
                   (t (find-person-over-age-aux
                       (cdr person-list))))))
    (find-person-over-age-aux *persons*)))
```

7.4 This is an interesting problem that demonstrates the use of `return` to terminate the iteration prematurely. Notice that we don't bother to allocate a temporary variable to hold `list-2` as it is scanned. Since `list-2` is only required during the comparison, we can just use it in the code.

```
(defun first-difference (list-1 list-2)
  (dolist (first-element list-1 nil)
    (if (not (equal first-element (car list-2)))
      (return (list first-element (car list-2))))
    (setf list-2 (cdr list-2))))
```

7.5 There are a number of solutions, but most are expensive. For example, you could append a list of `nil`'s to the shorter list. This is expensive because you have to compute the lengths of the two lists and then perform an append operation. The best solution is to use the original version of `alistify` which did the construction correctly.

7.6 A tricky solution is to force the designated function to produce a zero or a one depending on whether the result is true or `nil`. Then `+` can be applied to the resulting list producing a value. Try another technique, like writing a `lambda` expression which increments a variable and returns that value.

```
(defun count (funct some-list)
  (flet
    ((count-aux (element)
        (if (apply funct (list element)) 1 0)))
    (apply #'+ (mapcar #'count-aux some-list))))
```

7.7 This version incorrectly uses `'` instead of `#'`.

```
;;; Count the number of occurrences of the argument in a
;;; list, using mapc.
(defun count-occurrences (to-be-searched-for some-list)
  (let ((count-of-occurrences 0))
    (mapc '(lambda (list-element)
             (if (equal list-element to-be-searched-for)
               (setf count-of-occurrences
                     (1+ count-of-occurrences))))
          some-list)
    count-of-occurrences))
 ⇒ COUNT-OCCURRENCES

;; Again, we use the same test.
(count-occurrences 'bob *person-names*)
!!!!! Error: The symbol TO-BE-SEARCHED-FOR has no value.
```

7.11 Notice that in this solution, we don't need to have anybody, as all of the iteration clauses provide the required information. The solution is a little tricky, because of the ordering of the iteration clauses. The `result` must be initially `nil` to handle the case when the argument is `nil`. On the second iteration through, the first list is added to the result, although both `counter` and `element` were determined in the first iteration. The `mapcar` solution from the previous section seems to be cleaner because its goal is to construct a list which is required in this problem.

```
(defun numeric-tags (some-list)
  (do* ((result nil (cons (list counter element) result))
        (the-list some-list (cdr the-list))
        (element (car the-list) (car the-list))
        (counter 1 (1+ counter)))
       ((null the-list) (reverse result))))
```

Chapter Exercises

1. We must create the frame object, the globals which contain the unknown value, and the association list of frames. Then `make-slots-into-alist` transforms a slot list possibly with initial values into a assocition list with the slots initialized to the value of `*unknown*`. Finally, we can define `def-frame` as specified in the exercise:

```
(define-type frame
  (:var parent (:init nil))
  (:var children (:init nil))
  (:var instancep (:init nil))
  (:var slots (:init nil))
  (:var name)
  :all-settable
  :all-gettable
  :all-initable)

(defvar *frames* nil)

(defun get-frame (name)
  (cadr (assoc name *frames*)))

(defvar *unknown* '?)

(defun make-slots-into-alist (slots)
  (mapcar #'(lambda (slot)
              (cond ((symbolp slot)
                     (list slot *unknown*))
                    ((null (cdr slot))
                     (list slot *unknown*))
                    (t slot)))
          slots))

(defun create-frame (frame-name parent slots instancep)
  (let ((new-frame
          (make-instance 'frame :instancep instancep
                         :name frame-name
                         :parent parent
                         :slots slots)))
    (setf *frames* (cons (list frame-name new-frame)
                         *frames*))
    (dolist (each-parent parent)
      (setf (children each-parent)
            (cons new-frame (children each-parent))))
    new-frame))

(defun def-frame (frame-name parents slots)
  (create-frame frame-name
```

```
                    (mapcar #'get-frame parents)
                    (make-slots-into-alist slots)
                    nil)
      frame-name)
```

2. The only difficult part of this function is the verification that all of the slots exist in some parent. Thus, we had to write a function which scans the parents and their parents, and so forth, looking for a slot.

```
(defun slotp (slot-name frame)
  (if (assoc slot-name (slots frame))
    t
    (dolist (each-parent (parent frame) nil)
      (if (slotp slot-name each-parent)
        (return t)))))

(defun make-frame-instance (parent frame-name
                                   initial-slots)
  (if (dolist (each-slot initial-slots t)
        (if (not (slotp (if (atom each-slot)
                             each-slot
                             (car each-slot))
                         (get-frame parent)))
          (return nil)))
    (create-frame frame-name
                  (list (get-frame parent))
                  (make-slots-into-alist initial-slots)
                  t)
    'error))
```

3. This is straightforward, once you realize that all you have to do to assign a new value to a slot in the association list is to add the name and value to the front of the list. Nothing more complicated is required.

```
(defun assert (frame slot value)
  (let ((the-frame (get-frame frame)))
    (if (slotp slot the-frame)
      (progn
        (setf (slots the-frame)
              (cons (list slot value)
                    (slots the-frame)))
        value)
      'error)))
```

4. This requires the implementation of a function that works just like `slotp`, except that it returns the value of the slot.

```
(defun ask-with-frame (frame slot-name)
```

```
  (let ((slot-value (assoc slot-name (slots frame))))
    (if slot-value
      (cadr slot-value)
      (dolist (each-parent (parent frame) *unknown*)
        (let ((ask-result
                (ask-with-frame each-parent slot-name)))
          (if (not (equal ask-result *unknown*))
            (return ask-result)))))))

(defun ask (frame slot-name)
  (ask-with-frame (get-frame frame) slot-name))
```

Chapter 8

8.1 These functions are trivial and just invoke the appropriate `make-instance`.

```
(defun add-old-person (name mother father sex age)
  (add-a-person 'old-person name mother father sex age))

(defun add-a-person (person-type name mother father sex
                                  age)
  (let ((new-person
         (make-instance person-type
                        :name name :mother mother
                        :father father :sex sex
                        :age age)))
    (setf *persons* (cons new-person *persons*))
    new-person))

(defun add-young-person (name mother father sex age)
  (add-a-person 'young-person name mother father
               sex age))
```

8.2 This is an easy change. All the code has to do is check to see if `increment` is `nil` and if so, replace it with a one.

```
(defmacro for (argument-list &body body)
  (let ((variable (car argument-list))
        (starting-value (cadr argument-list))
        (ending-value (caddr argument-list))
        (increment (or (cadddr argument-list) 1)))
    (append
     (list
      'do
      (list (list variable starting-value
                  (list '+ variable increment)))
      (list (list '= variable ending-value)))
     body)))
```

8.6 The translation is pretty simple. There is only a test clause and the body.

```
(defmacro while (test &body body)
  `(do ()
     ((not ,test))
     ,@body))
```

8.8 The `dolist` macro translates into a call on `do`.

```
(defmacro my-dolist ((variable some-list &optional
                                return-expression)
                      &body body)
  `(do* ((list-to-walk ,some-list (cdr list-to-walk))
         (,variable (car list-to-walk)
                    (car list-to-walk)))
     ((null list-to-walk) ,return-expression)
     ,@body))
```

8.9 This is a subtle problem with macros that will be addressed in later chapters. In this case, if the body includes the same symbol then some conflict will occur and the function will not execute properly. One solution is to choose a name which no one would likely use in their program. For example, `***moosefish***` has been popular. Another solution is to scan the code in the body to see if the symbol is present and warn the user of the fact. The ultimate solution is to use system-generated symbols, which are discussed in later chapters.

Chapter Exercises

1. Each macro is fairly simple, translating into the appropriate invocation of `make-instance`:

```
(defmacro add-printer (name installed-date pm-period
                            maintainer speed)
  `(make-instance 'printer :name ',name
                  :date-installed ',installed-date
                  :pm-period ',pm-period
                  :maintainer ',maintainer
                  :speed ',speed))

(defmacro add-disk-drive (name installed-date pm-period
                               maintainer type
                               access-time)
  `(make-instance 'printer :name ',name
                  :date-installed ',installed-date
                  :pm-period ',pm-period
                  :maintainer ',maintainer
                  :type ',type
                  :access-time ',access-time))
```

```
(defmacro add-workstation (name installed-date pm-period
                                maintainer screen-size
                                amount-of-memory)
  `(make-instance 'printer :name ',name
                  :date-installed ',installed-date
                  :pm-period ',pm-period
                  :maintainer ',maintainer
                  :screen-size ',screen-size
                  :amount-of-memory ',amount-of-memory))

(defmacro add-maintainer (name phone-number
                               office-address)
  `(make-instance 'printer :name ',name
                  :phone-number ',phone-number
                  :office-address ',office-address))
```

2. The code for `our-eval` follows. You might want to consider experimenting with the code yourself.

```
;; A simple LISP evaluator.
(defun our-eval (expression)
  (cond ((symbolp expression) (symbol-value expression))
        ((not (listp expression)) expression)
        ((equal (car expression) 'quote)
         (cadr expression))
        ((macro-function (car expression))
         (our-eval (macroexpand expression)))
        (t (apply (car expression)
                  (mapcar #'our-eval
                          (cdr expression))))))
```

Chapter 9

9.1 The first step would be to find out if anyone has the same parents as Bob, Joanne, and Jim. All people with the same parents are siblings. So, Bob has two siblings Jimmy and Patty. The next step is to determine which, if any, of the siblings are male. A male sibling is a brother; thus Jimmy is Bob's only brother.

9.3 We can leave the object type the same and just not use the `type-name` slot. Thus, we don't have to change `add-knowledge`, but do have to modify `insert-object` and `find-objects`. However, notice that both of them are much simpler than the previous versions.

```
(defun insert-object (object)
  (let ((knowledge-type-found
         (assoc (object-type object) *knowledge-base*)))
    (if knowledge-type-found
```

```
          (add-object (cadr knowledge-type-found) object)
          (setf *knowledge-base*
                (cons
                 (list (object-type object)
                       (make-instance 'knowledge-type
                                      :objects
                                      (list object)
                                      :type-name
                                      (object-type
                                       object)))
                 *knowledge-base*)))
        object))

(defun find-objects (searching-type)
  (let ((type (assoc searching-type *knowledge-base*)))
    (if type (objects (cadr type)) nil)))
```

9.5 Two people are cousins if they have a parents which are siblings. The aunt rule is the same as the uncle version except a sister is used and we have to define the sister rule. Grandparents and grandchildren are rules that go through an intermediate parent. *Note*: we would have to modify the definition of the `person` object to include these slots. Also notice that the premises for the grandparent and grandchild rules are the same as you would expect.

```
(define-rule cousin-rule
  (type (?person person) (?person2 person)
        (?person3 person) (?person4 person))
  (premise (and (?person parent ?person2)
                (?person3 parent ?person4)
                (?person2 sibling ?person4)))
  (conclusion (?person cousins ?person3)))

(define-rule aunt-rule
  (type (?person person) (?person2 person)
        (?aunt person))
  (premise (and (?person parent ?person2)
                (?person2 sisters ?aunt)))
  (conclusion (?person aunts ?aunt)))

(define-rule sister-rule
  (type (?person person) (?person2 person))
  (premise (and (?person sibling ?person2)
                (?person2 sex female)))
  (conclusion (?person sisters ?person2)))

(define-rule grandparent-rule
  (type (?person person) (?person2 person)
        (?person3 person))
```

```
  (premise (and (?person parent ?person2)
                (?person2 parent ?person3)))
  (conclusion (?person grandparents ?person3)))

(define-rule grandchild-rule
  (type (?person person) (?person2 person)
        (?person3 person))
  (premise (and (?person parent ?person2)
                (?person2 parent ?person3)))
  (conclusion (?person3 grandchilds ?person)))
```

9.7 This requires the use of the test clause on ages.

```
(define-rule older-brother
  (type (?person person) (?person2 person)
        (?age-person nil) (?age-person2 nil))
  (premise (and (?person brother ?person2)
                (?person age ?age-person)
                (?person2 age ?age-person2)
                (test (> ?age-person2 ?age-person))))
  (conclusion (?person older-brother ?person2)))
```

9.8 This function takes the information in the object apart and returns a appropriate list. We need one auxiliary function which takes a list and returns the list with embedded ands and places the is in the appropriate place.

```
(defun andify-and-process (some-list clause-or-type)
  (flet ((process (clause)
           (if clause-or-type
             `(,(car clause) ,(cadr clause)
               is ,(caddr clause))
             `(,(car clause) is a ,(cadr clause)))))
    (cond ((null (cdr some-list)) (process
                                    (car some-list)))
          (t (append (process (car some-list))
                     (cons 'and (andify-and-process
                                  (cdr some-list)
                                  clause-or-type)))))))

(define-method (rule show) ()
  `(in ,name if ,@(andify-and-process
                    (if (eq (car premise) 'and)
                      (cdr premise)
                      (list premise))
                    t)
      then ,@(andify-and-process (list conclusion) t)
      where ,@(andify-and-process type nil)))
```

9.10 The process would proceed as follows:

1. See if there is a `person` object with a `brothers` slot that is bound to a value. If there is, return it; otherwise go to the next step.
2. See if there is any rule which can assert a value for the `brothers` slot. The `brother-rule` will perform that task.
3. Next see if there is anyone that has a `sibling` slot bound to a value. This causes the `sibling-rule` to be used if no person object includes a bound slot value.
4. This process continues with the `parent-rule` which we can prove for various persons in the data base.
5. As each parent is proven, it is checked to see if there is another person that has the same parents. When that condition is met, the sibling rule is proven.
6. Now that we have two siblings, we have to check the `sex` slot of the second to see if it is `male`. If it is, then we can prove the brother rule and succeed. If not, we have to scan for other siblings.

9.12 This requires that we implement a new function similar to `find-objects`, except that it finds all objects. `Find-all-objects` does just that. Once that is implemented, the modification to `lookup` is straightforward.

```
(defun find-all-objects ()
  (let ((result nil))
    (dolist (a-type *knowledge-base* result)
      (setf result (append result (objects a-type))))))

(defun lookup (assertion variables old-objects)
  (find-matching-object assertion variables
      (cond (old-objects)
            ((variablep (object assertion) variables)
             (let ((type (variable-type
                          (object assertion)
                          variables)))
               (if type
                 (find-objects type)
                 (find-all-objects))))
            ((objectp (object assertion))
             (list (object assertion)))
            (t nil))))
```

9.13 Each level requires saving the state of anything that may be continued. This includes the list of possible objects from `lookup` and the list of rules that have not been tried. Also, any bindings that must be rolled back must be saved.

9.14 If the state is saved in a global variable, then it could be resumed at the place where the engine succeeded. At that point, an artificial failure could be generated and the next solution found. Thus, instead of finding the first solution, this could be used to find all solutions.

9.16 Grandparent and grandchild are not slots defined in the person object and thus the system will fail when it tries to look up the value of the grandparent or grandchild slot. The solution is to add these slots to the `person` type and then redefine all of the elements in the knowledge base. Once that is accomplished, you can run these queries.

9.17 Alex's aunt is Patty, while Russ and Karen are cousins of Bob, Jimmy, and Patty. So, defining these people should allow the relationships to be solved. There are others mentioned in the list that could apply, but these will suffice.

```
(setf alex (add-knowledge 'person :name 'alex :father bob
                          :mother 'julie :sex 'male))

(setf russ (add-knowledge 'person :name 'russ
                          :father david
                          :mother 'deanie :sex 'male))

(setf karen (add-knowledge 'person :name 'karen
                           :father david
                           :mother 'deanie :sex 'female))
```

Chapter Exercises

1. Since nothing is actually proven until the whole query is proved, the best place for the `assert` is within `solve-aux`. At the point when it gets a legal set of bindings, the assertion is true and the data can be added to the object. So, this solution performs the assert at the bottom of `solve-aux`. We can perform a trick by making `assert` return its argument. Then we don't need to save the call to `install-bindings` in a local variable, since it needs to be used in two places (as a part of the `assert` and as the result of the function). The difficult part of `assert` is that we have to somehow store the value in the slot. A very inefficient way is to call `eval` on the `setf` expression. We will see in later chapters how to do this more efficiently.

```
(defun solve-aux (assertion variables binding-list
                            agenda)
  (let ((bindings
         (if (test-clause-p assertion)
           (solve-test assertion variables binding-list
                       agenda)
           (or (solve-lookup assertion variables
                             binding-list agenda)
               (solve-with-rules assertion variables
                                 binding-list agenda)))))
    (if bindings
```

```
          (list (assert (install-bindings assertion
                                          bindings))
                bindings)
          nil)))

(defun assert (clause)
  (if (and (= (length clause) 3)
           (objectp (object clause)))
    (eval `(setf (,(slot clause) ',(object clause))
                 ',(value clause))))
  clause)
```

3. The change to `assert` is pretty easy. We just have to check that the value is not already present before we add it to the list. The more difficult part is how to change `lookup` and its associated functions to handle the list argument. It's easy to handle the case where we are just seeing if a particular value is present in the current slot list. However, the difficulty appears when we have a variable value. This means that we must return each element of the list as a possible match, before going on to the next possible object. For example, if we have a slot with `jim`, `bob`, and `patty` as values, a variable query should return `jim` first, then `bob`, then `patty`, and finally go on to the next object. So, we have to modify the semantics of the possible objects to also return any remaining values first, and the possible objects second. The function `lookup` can be modified to return the extra values when the function is called again, until there are no more values and then it calls `find-matching-object` to get the next object. We must be careful to make sure that a `nil` is returned once there are no more possible values and no more objects. Since we seem to have to return so many values, we are better off creating an object which can then be returned and the slots accessed accordingly. The object has to include the old-objects list, the remaining values, and the last binding list. This is so `lookup` can return the new binding list as appropriate. `Lookup` assumes that the first element of the binding list is the binding between the slot variable and its value.

```
(defun assert (clause)
  (if (and (= (length clause) 3)
           (objectp (object clause))
           *caching*)
    (let ((old-value (apply (slot-clause)
                            (list (object clause)))))
      (if (not (member (value clause) old-value))
        (eval `(setf (,(slot clause) ',(object clause))
                     (cons ',(value clause)
                           ',old-value))))))
  clause)
```

```
;; Change the definition of the unbound slot to be nil.
(setf *unknown* nil)

(define-type possible
  (:var old-binding)
  (:var remaining-values (:init nil))
  (:var remaining-objects (:init nil))
  :all-initable
  :all-gettable
  :all-settable)

(defun lookup (assertion variables possible-object)
  (if (and possible-object
           (remaining-values possible-object))
    (let ((new-binding
           (cons (list (caar (old-binding
                               possible-object))
                       (car
                        (remaining-values
                         possible-object)))
                 (cdr (old-binding possible-object)))))
      (setf (old-binding possible-object) new-binding)
      (setf (remaining-values possible-object)
            (cdr (remaining-values possible-object)))
      (list new-binding possible-object))
    (find-matching-object assertion variables
      (cond (possible-object
             (remaining-objects possible-object))
            ((variablep (object assertion) variables)
             (find-objects
              (variable-type (object assertion)
                             variables)))
            ((objectp (object assertion))
             (list (object assertion)))
            (t nil)))))

(defun find-matching-object (assertion variables objects)
  (if objects
    (let ((slot-value (apply (slot assertion)
                             (list (car objects)))))
      (if (or (equal slot-value *unknown*)
              (and (not (variablep (value assertion)
                                   variables))
                   (not (member (value assertion)
                                slot-value))))
        (find-matching-object assertion variables
```

```
                              (cdr objects))
        (let ((new-possible
                (make-instance 'possible
                              :remaining-objects
                              (cdr objects))))
          (if (variablep (value assertion) variables)
            (setf (remaining-values new-possible)
                  (cdr slot-value)))
          (setf (old-binding new-possible)
                (or
                 (append (if (variablep (value assertion)
                                        variables)
                             '(( ,(value assertion)
                                 ,(car slot-value))))
                         (if (variablep
                              (object assertion)
                              variables)
                             '(( ,(object assertion)
                                 ,(car objects)))))
                 '((T T))))
          (list (old-binding new-possible)
                (if (and (null
                          (remaining-values
                           new-possible))
                         (null
                          (remaining-objects
                           new-possible)))
                  nil
                  new-possible)))))
    nil))
```

4. This is easy because we force the user to quote or backquote the premise and the conclusion. And therefore, all we have to do is remove the quotes from the definition of `define-rule` as follows.

```
(defmacro define-rule (rule-name &body rule-clauses)
  '(add-rule ',rule-name
             ',(cdr (assoc 'type rule-clauses))
             ,(cadr (assoc 'premise rule-clauses))
             ,(cadr (assoc 'conclusion rule-clauses))))
```

This solution isn't very clean because we force the user to place quotes on the premise and conclusions even when there are no constant objects. A better solution is to use a read macro `#.`, defined in Chapter 17. By placing it in front of an expression, it will evaluate the expression at *read* time and place the definition in the list as follows. Notice the result of calling **macroexpand** on a rule using this read macro.

```
(macroexpand
 '(define-rule bogus-rule
   (type (?person person) (?person2 person) (?uncle person))
   (premise (and (?person parent ?person2)
                 (?person2 brothers ?uncle)))
   (conclusion (?person uncles #.jim))))
⇒ (ADD-RULE (QUOTE BOGUS-RULE)
⇒           (QUOTE ((?PERSON PERSON) (?PERSON2 PERSON)
⇒                   (?UNCLE PERSON)))
⇒           (QUOTE
⇒             (AND (?PERSON PARENT ?PERSON2)
⇒                  (?PERSON2 BROTHERS ?UNCLE)))
⇒           (QUOTE (?PERSON UNCLES
⇒                           #<Object PERSON NAME=JIM>)))
```

Chapter 10

10.1 We simply invoke random and select one of the strings.

```
(defun monster-enhancer ()
  (let ((selector (random 3)))
    (cond ((= selector 0)
           "The monster <prepares to strike.")
          ((= selector 1)
           "The monster ignores your presence.")
          (t "The monster twiddles its thumbs.")))))
```

10.3 Each my-describe method knows how to print the slots associated with the object and invokes the parent when appropriate. We have generalized this with a generic slot printing function, which prints all of the slots associated with a particular type.

```
(defun print-slots (slot-names object)
  (dolist (each-slot slot-names)
    (format t " ~A: ~S~%" each-slot
            (apply each-slot (list object)))))

(define-method (monster my-describe) ()
  (print-slots '(name type description strength damage)
               self))

(define-method (dragon my-describe) ()
  (print-slots '(fire-breath-temperature number-of-heads)
               self)
  (call-method (monster my-describe)))
```

10.5 A `do` loop is appropriate for this function which gets words until the user types a command to stop the spelling process.

```
(defvar *stop-spelling* '(quit))
(defvar *dictionary* '(monster dragon pretty mother))
(defun get-word ()
  (format t "What word do you want me to check? ")
  (read))
(defun spelling-checker ()
  (do ((next-word (get-word) (get-word)))
   ((member next-word *stop-spelling*))
   (if (member next-word *dictionary*)
     (format t "~S is correct.~%" next-word)
     (progn
       (format t
          "~S not found, is this correct (y or n)? "
          next-word)
       (if (equal (read) 'y)
         (progn
           (format t
             "~S added to dictionary.~%" next-word)
           (setf *dictionary*
                 (cons next-word *dictionary*)))
         (format t "~S incorrect.~%" next-word))))))
```

10.7 We simply don't add spaces to the list of characters.

```
(defun super-palindromep ()
  (labels
      ((super-palindromep-aux ()
           (let ((next-character (read-char)))
             (cond ((equal next-character #)
                    nil)
                   ((equal next-character # )
                    (super-palindromep-aux))
                   (t (cons next-character
                            (super-palindromep-aux)))))))
    ;; Strip any characters after the invocation.
    (read-line)
    (let ((character-list (super-palindromep-aux)))
      (equal character-list (reverse character-list)))))
```

10.10 This function opens the file, reads each symbol, counting the matching ones, and then closes the file when the end is found. The only difficult part is choosing something to return that indicates end of file, which won't be confused with a symbol that is already present in the file.

```
(defun count-occurrences (file-name symbol)
  (with-open-file (read-stream file-name
                               :direction :input)
    (do ((symbol-read
           (read read-stream nil '**finished**)
           (read read-stream nil '**finished**))
          (occurrences 0))
        ((equal symbol-read '**finished**)
         (format t
           "The file ~S contains ~A occurrences of ~A.~%"
           file-name occurrences symbol)
         occurrences)
        (if (equal symbol symbol-read)
          (setf occurrences (1+ occurrences))))))
```

10.13 All we have to do is call `namestring` on `pathname` and look at the results for different file names.

```
(equal (namestring (pathname "/u/kessler/foo.l"))
       "/u/kessler/foo.l")
⇒ T

(equal (namestring (pathname "foo.l"))
       "foo.l")
⇒ T
```

10.14 This requires two nested loops to scan all of the files and then check the directories by merging the file and directory.

```
(defun compare-directories (directories files)
  (labels ((check-directories (file directories)
             (if (null directories)
               nil
               (if (open (merge-pathnames
                           (pathname (car directories))
                           (pathname file))
                          :direction :probe)
                 (check-directories
                  file (cdr directories))
                 (cons (car directories)
                       (check-directories
                        file (cdr directories)))))))
    (dolist (each-file files)
      (let ((not-present
              (check-directories each-file directories)))
        (if not-present
          (progn
```

```
          (format t "~A not in " each-file)
          (dolist (each-directory not-present)
            (format t "~A, " each-directory))
          (terpri))
        (format t "~A present in all directories~%"
                each-file))))))
```

Chapter Exercises

1. This is a simpler version of `count-occurrences` in an earlier exercise.

```
(defun count-symbols (file-name)
  (with-open-file (read-stream file-name
                               :direction :input)
    (do ((symbol-read
           (read read-stream nil '**finished**)
           (read read-stream nil '**finished**))
          (symbols 0))
         ((equal symbol-read '**finished**)
          (format t
            "The file ~S contains ~A symbols.~%"
            file-name symbols)
          symbols)
         (if (symbolp symbol-read)
           (setf symbols (1+ symbols))))))
```

4. One solution is to translate the words in the file into a list. Then, we write a function which scans the list, counting the number of occurrences of each element. This solution is expensive in time, because it must make `n` passes over the list, where `n` is the number of works in the list.

```
(defun words-in-list (some-list)
  (cond ((null some-list) nil)
        ((symbolp some-list) (list some-list))
        ((not (listp some-list)) nil)
        (t (append (words-in-list (car some-list))
                   (words-in-list (cdr some-list))))))

(defun listify-file (file-name)
  (with-open-file (read-stream file-name
                               :direction :input)
    (do ((symbol-read
           (read read-stream nil '**finished**)
           (read read-stream nil '**finished**))
          (words nil))
         ((equal symbol-read '**finished**)
          words)
```

```
        (cond ((symbolp symbol-read)
               (setf words (cons symbol-read words)))
              ((listp symbol-read)
               (setf words
                     (append (words-in-list symbol-read)
                             words))))))

(defun count-matches (word word-list)
  (cond ((null word-list) 0)
        ((equal word (car word-list))
         (1+ (count-matches word (cdr word-list))))
        (t (count-matches word (cdr word-list)))))

(defun words (file-name)
  (do* ((word-list (listify-file file-name)
                   (cdr word-list))
        (total-words (length word-list))
        (words-done nil)
        (each-word (car word-list) (car word-list)))
       ((null word-list)
        (format t "--------~%Total words: ~A~%"
                total-words))
       (if (not (member each-word words-done))
         (let ((count
                (count-matches each-word word-list)))
           (format t "~A present ~A times for ~A%~%"
                   each-word count
                   (* (/ count total-words) 100.0))
           (setf words-done (cons each-word
                                  words-done))))))
```

Chapter 11

11.1 The player structure is simple, as follows:

```
(defstruct player
  name
  hit-points
  (weapons nil)
  current-room
  (fighting nil)
  initial-strength)

(make-player :name 'bob :hit-points 10
             :initial-strength 10)
```

11.3 All the function must do is compute the length of the weapons list.

```
(defun number-of-weapons (player)
  (length (player-weapons *player*)))
```

11.4 We must make use of `&rest` to get all of the slot names and `mapcar` to scan all of the slots.

```
(defmacro pl-defstruct (name &rest slots)
  `(progn
     ,@(mapcar #'build-accessor slots)
     ',name))

(defun build-accessor (slot-and-set-slot-name)
  `(progn
     (defun ,(car slot-and-set-slot-name) (symbol)
       (get symbol ',(car slot-and-set-slot-name)))
     (defun ,(cadr slot-and-set-slot-name) (symbol value)
       (setf (get symbol ',(car slot-and-set-slot-name))
             value))
     (defsetf ,(car slot-and-set-slot-name)
       ,(cadr slot-and-set-slot-name))))
```

Chapter Exercises

2. The macro translates into a `let` and `dotimes`. The `dotimes` performs the S-expression as many times as specified and then returns the difference in times.

```
(defmacro time-form (form iterations)
  `(let ((the-time (get-internal-run-time)))
     (dotimes (i ,iterations)
       ,form)
     (- (get-internal-run-time) the-time)))
```

3. The `compare-times` function uses a huge `do` expression to define all of the required variables for access to the places in the association list and the hash table. One very tricky part is how it determines the number of times to `cons` a new element on the front of the association list. It times the iteration number of calls to `cons` on a dummy association list, which adds all those elements to the list. Then it adds the one new association before doing the other timing. The results indicate that hash tables are better after only a very few elements have been added.

```
(defun time-nil (iterations)
  (format t "[EM:~A] "
          (time-form nil iterations)))

(defun time-add-alist (iterations symbol counter)
  (let (test-dummy-alist)
    (format t "[AS:~A] "
            (time-form
```

```
              (setf test-dummy-alist
                    (cons (list symbol counter)
                          test-dummy-alist))
              iterations))))

(defun time-access-alist (iterations symbol alist type)
  (format t "[R~A:~A] " type
          (time-form (assoc symbol alist)
                     iterations)))

(defun time-hash-store (iterations symbol table value)
  (format t "[HS:~A] "
          (time-form
           (setf (gethash symbol table) value)
           iterations)))

(defun time-get-hash (iterations symbol table)
  (format t "[HR:~A]~%"
          (time-form (gethash symbol table)
                     iterations)))

(defun compare-times (iterations)
  (do* ((element-counter 1 (+ 1 element-counter))
        (all-symbols *some-symbols* (cdr all-symbols))
        (half-walk *some-symbols*
                   (if (oddp element-counter)
                     (cdr half-walk)
                     half-walk))
        (first-symbol (car all-symbols)
                      (car all-symbols))
        (last-symbol (car all-symbols))
        (used-symbols (list first-symbol)
                      (cons (car all-symbols)
                            used-symbols))
        (random-symbol first-symbol
                       (nth (random element-counter)
                            used-symbols))
        (test-alist
         (list (list first-symbol element-counter))
         (cons (list first-symbol element-counter)
               test-alist))
        (test-hash-table (make-hash-table)))
       ((null all-symbols))
       (format t "~A: " element-counter)
       (time-nil iterations)
       (time-add-alist iterations first-symbol
```

```
                  element-counter)
(time-access-alist iterations first-symbol
                   test-alist "1")
(time-access-alist iterations last-symbol
                   test-alist "L")
;; Middle symbol
(time-access-alist iterations (car half-walk)
                   test-alist "M")
(time-hash-store iterations first-symbol
                 test-hash-table
                 element-counter)
(time-get-hash iterations random-symbol
               test-hash-table)))
```

Chapter 12

12.2 Each of these monsters inherit from the `monster` type and have additional slots.

```
(define-type loner
  (:inherit-from monster)
  (:var swarms-in-room)
  (:var others-in-room)
  :all-gettable
  :all-settable
  :all-initable)

(define-type blissterror
  (:inherit-from monster)
  (:var current-mood)
  :all-gettable
  :all-settable
  :all-initable)

(define-type empath
  (:inherit-from monster)
  (:var players-state)
  :all-gettable
  :all-settable
  :all-initable)
```

12.5 The solution is to begin from the first room, and search the connections for the second room. It must maintain a list of the rooms found on the path and if it ever comes to the same room twice, that path has to be ignored. The path list is kept as an association list of the room name and direction so an `assoc` can be used to get the room.

```
(defun help-path (room-1 room-2)
  (let (path)
    (labels
        ((find-room (room-name path)
           (cond ((null path) nil)
                 ((equal (cadr (car path)) room-name))
                 (t (find-room room-name (cdr path)))))
         (help-path-aux (current-room path)
           (dolist (each-room
                     (connections
                      (get-object current-room)))
             (cond ((equal (cadr each-room) room-2)
                    (return (cons each-room path)))
                   ((not (find-room (cadr each-room) path))
                    (let ((new-path
                           (help-path-aux
                            (cadr each-room)
                            (cons each-room path))))
                      (if new-path (return new-path))))))))
      (cond ((equal room-1 room-2) t)
            ((setf path (help-path-aux room-1 nil))
             (reverse path))
            (t nil)))))
```

12.6 The idea of this solution is to use the previous `help-path` function to find paths between all of the rooms and the exit room. As a small optimization, we will maintain a list of the rooms found in the paths to the exit and not bother to check any rooms that are included in the paths of previous paths to the exit.

```
(defun find-no-way-out-rooms (exit-room)
  (let (ok-rooms
        (no-way-out-rooms nil))
    (labels ((convert-path (path)
               (if (null path)
                 nil
                 (progn
                   (setf ok-rooms (cons (cadr (car path))
                                        ok-rooms))
                   (convert-path (cdr path)))))
             (check-room (name object)
               (if (and (equal (object-type object) 'room)
                        (not (member name ok-rooms)))
                 (let ((path (help-path name exit-room)))
```

```
                  (if path
                    (progn
                      (if (listp path)
                        (convert-path path))
                      (setf ok-rooms (cons name ok-rooms)))
                    (setf no-way-out-rooms
                          (cons name no-way-out-rooms))))))
    (maphash #'check-room *dungeon*)
    no-way-out-rooms)))
```

12.9 Implementing the player as an object instead of as a structure results in changes to nearly all of the code. Since the structure definition required placing `player-` on the front of every slot access, all functions and methods which have these embedded in them would have to be changed. Also, the functions that were written to provide an interface to the player structure that is similar to the method interface (like `print-self`) must be changed to be methods. Finally, some functions can be removed. For example, `adjust-monster-accuracy` and `adjust-player-accuracy` can be combined into a single `adjust-accuracy` function. So, the change is quite massive. The player object is implemented as follows:

```
(define-type player
  (:var name :initable)
  (:var hit-points :initable :settable)
  (:var weapons (:init nil) :settable)
  (:var current-room :initable :settable)
  (:var fighting :settable)
  (:var initial-strength :initable)
  :all-gettable)
```

12.11 Each of these `attack-player` methods is derived from the description in the exercises of section 12.1.

```
(define-method (loner attack-player) ()
  (let ((current-room (player-current-room *player))
        accuracy)
    (setf swarms-in-room
          (count-swarm (monsters current-room)))
    (setf others-in-room (- (length (monsters current-room))
                            swarms-in-room
                            1))
    (setf accuracy (min (- 60
                           (* swarms-in-room 20)
                           (* others-in-room 10))
                        0))
    (if (< accuracy 60)
```

```
        (format t
          "The loner sees others and weakly attacks.~%")
        (format t
          "The loner is alone and attacks viciously.~%"))
      (monster-attack accuracy (initial-damage self))))

(define-method (blissterror attack-player) ()
  (monster-attack 50 (* (if (< (random 2) 1) 1 -1)
                        (player-hit-points *player*))))

(define-method (empath attack-player) ()
  (let ((disappear (>= (player-hit-points *player*) 75)))
    (monster-attack 100 10)
    (if disappear
      (progn
        (format t "The empath ~A disappears.~%"
                (call-method (monster name)))
        (remove-monster (player-current-room *player*)
                        (call-method (monster name)))
        (setf (player-fighting *player*) nil)))))
```

Chapter Exercises

1. We first add a new slot to the player structure, define the `shield` object, and modify the `room` object. We have not shown the code, but `add-room` must be modified to take an additional argument, a new macro `add-shield` must be written, and the functions `take-aux` and `drop-aux` must be modified to accept either a shield or a weapon. Finally, we modify the `monster-attack` function to provide the appropriate protection for the player.

```
(defstruct player
  name
  hit-points
  (weapons nil)
  current-room
  fighting
  initial-strength
  (shields nil))

(define-type shield
  (:var name)
  (:var description)
  (:var protection)
  :all-initable
  :all-gettable)

(define-type room
  (:var name)
```

```
  (:var description)
  (:var connections)
  (:var weapons :settable)
  (:var monsters :settable)
  (:var shields :settable)
  :all-initable
  :all-gettable)

(defun adjust-damage (damage shields)
  (if (null shields)
    damage
    (adjust-damage (* damage (protection (car shields)))
                   (cdr shields))))

(defun monster-attack (accuracy damage)
  (let* ((accuracy
           (adjust-monster-accuracy (player-fighting *player*)
                                    accuracy))
          (damage (adjust-damage damage
                                 (player-shields *player*))))
    (if (< (random 100) accuracy)
      (progn
        (format t "~A HITS "
                (name (player-fighting *player*)))
        (adjust-points *player* damage))
      (format t "Whew!! The ~A Missed.~%"
              (name (player-fighting *player*))))))
```

3. Since we have defined macros for some of the interface operations, those must be avoided since Common LISP doesn't permit calling apply on a macro. The trick is to call the auxiliary function passing it the appropriate arguments.

```
(defvar *zero-arg-commands*
  '((#\l look) (#\a attack) (#\c weapon)))

(defvar *movement-command* #'walk-aux)

(defvar *one-arg-commands*
  '((#\t take-aux) (#\d drop-aux) (#\f fight-aux)))

(defvar *direction-transformations*
  '((#\n north) (#\e east) (#\s south) (#\w west)))

(defvar *quit-commands* '(#\q))

(defvar *ignore-commands* '(#\space #\newline))

(defun start-game-aux (player-name strength initial-room)
  (setf *player* (make-player :name player-name
                              :hit-points strength
```

```
                                   :initial-strength strength))
  (read-line)
  (move-to initial-room)
  (do ((next-command (read-char) (read-char))
       lookup)
      ((member next-command *quit-commands*))
      (cond ((setf lookup
                   (assoc next-command
                          *direction-transformations*))
             (apply *movement-command* (cdr lookup)))
            ((setf lookup
                   (assoc next-command
                          *zero-arg-commands*))
             (apply (cadr lookup) nil))
            ((setf lookup
                   (assoc next-command
                          *one-arg-commands*))
             (apply (cadr lookup) (list (read))))
            ((member next-command *ignore-commands*))
            (t (format t "~A Illegal command.~%"
                       next-command)))))
```

Chapter 13

13.1 All but the first list requires three sets of cons pairs.

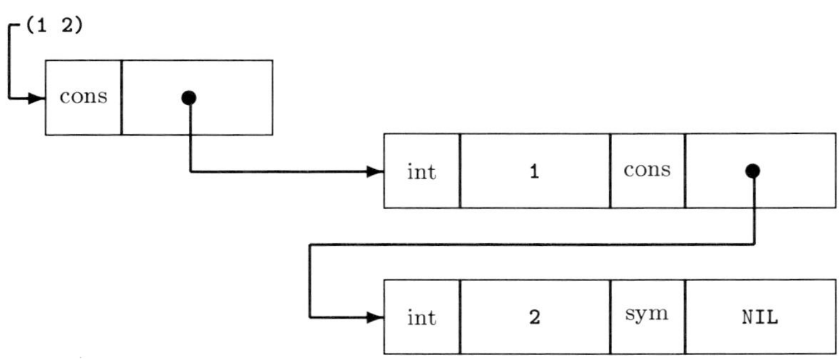

See the other diagrams on page 606.

13.4 Each of these returns T because the cdr of board1 and board2 point to exactly the same structure. If you don't believe this, then draw a diagram of the operations and see what happens.

13.6 A standard recursive procedure is all that is required. It is a good idea to

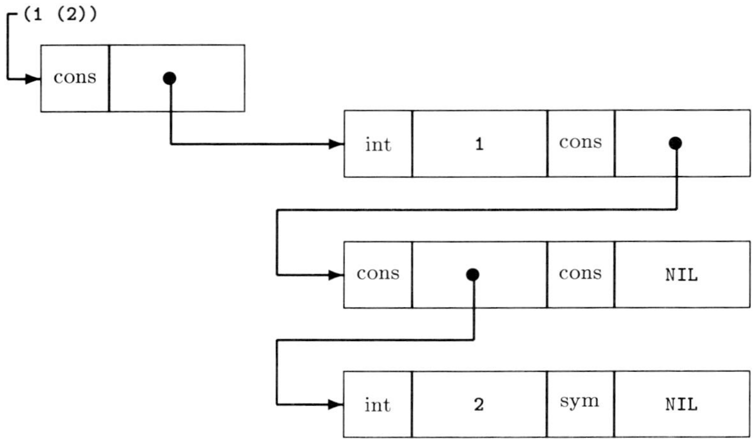
(1 (2))
cons
int
1
cons
cons
cons
NIL
int
2
sym
NIL

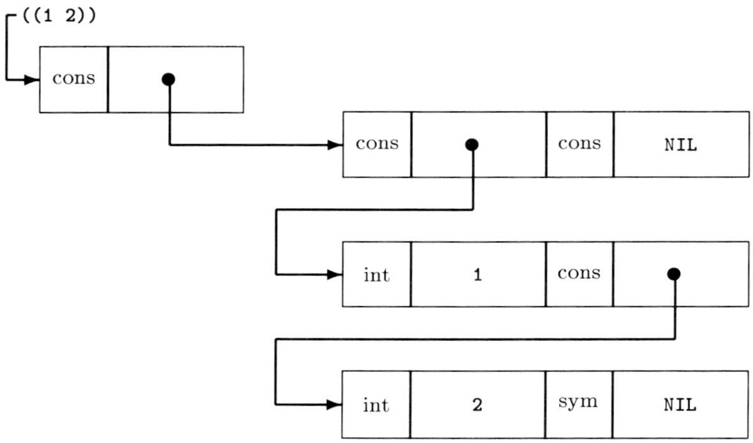
((1 2))
cons
cons
cons
NIL
int
1
cons
int
2
sym
NIL

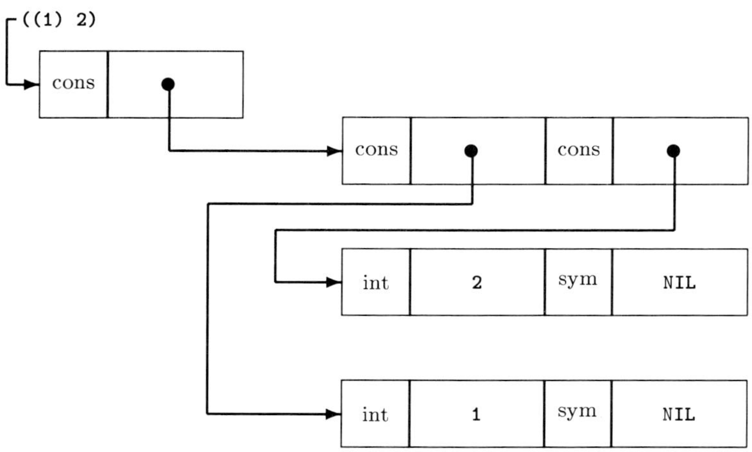
((1) 2)
cons
cons
cons
int
2
sym
NIL
int
1
sym
NIL

first check that the arguments are eql before scanning the list. That way you can save the scan if they happen to be the same.

```
;;; Compare two lists using recursion and eql.
(defun my-equal (list-a list-b)
  (cond ((eql list-a list-b) t)
        ((not (and (listp list-a) (listp list-b)))
         (eql list-a list-b))
        (t (and (my-equal (car list-a)
                          (car list-b))
                (my-equal (cdr list-a)
                          (cdr list-b))))))
```

13.9 A bubble sort is relatively easy to implement. This is expensive in both time and space.

```
;; The order in which to sort specifies the comparison
;; operation.
(defvar *order*
  '((ascending string>) (descending string<)))
;;; Sort the strings using a bubble sort.  The second
;;; argument specifies either ascending or descending
;;; order.  The sort is finished whenever no changes are
;;; made to the list.
(defun my-sort (strings order)
  (let ((changed nil)
        (operation (cadr (assoc order *order*)))
        (new-list nil))
    (labels ((sort-strings (string-list)
               (cond ((null (cdr string-list))
                      string-list)
                     ((apply operation
                             (list (car string-list)
                                   (cadr string-list)))
                      (setf changed t)
                      (cons (cadr string-list)
                            (sort-strings
                             (cons (car string-list)
                                   (cddr string-list)))))
                     (t (cons (car string-list)
                              (sort-strings
                               (cdr string-list)))))))
      (setf new-list (sort-strings strings))
      (if changed (my-sort new-list order) new-list))))
```

13.10 Each movement can be computed by adding or subtracting the appropriate amount from the index of the empty position. The amount to add or subtract is defined in the variable *move-amount*.

```
;; Amount to move a tile for a particular command.
(defvar *move-amount* '((up 3) (down -3) (left -1)
                        (right 1)))
;;; Move the tile into the empty square based upon the
;;; direction.
(defun move-tile (board direction)
  (let* ((empty-position
          (dotimes (index 9)
            (if (null (aref board index))
              (return index))))
         (other-index
          (+ empty-position
             (cadr (assoc direction *move-amount*)))))
    (setf (aref board empty-position)
          (aref board other-index))
    (setf (aref board other-index) nil)
    board))
```

13.12 Two nested dotimes loops suffice for this particular operation.

```
(defun print-board (board)
  (format t "-------------~%")
  (dotimes (row 3)
    (format t "| ")
    (dotimes (column 3)
      (format t "~A | "
              (cond ((aref board (+ (* row 3) column)))
                    (t " "))))
    (format t "~%-------------~%")))
```

13.14 The first function to implement is my-elt and the associated setf version. These can then be used in later functions.

```
;;; Access an element of the sequence.
(defun my-elt (sequence element)
  (cond ((stringp sequence) (char sequence element))
        ((vectorp sequence) (aref sequence element))
        ((listp sequence) (nth element sequence))))

;;; Store into an element of the sequence.
(defun my-setf-elt (sequence element new-value)
  (cond ((stringp sequence)
         (setf (char sequence element) new-value))
        ((vectorp sequence)
```

```
          (setf (aref sequence element) new-value))
         ((listp sequence)
          (setf (nth element sequence) new-value))))

;;; Make the setf form using my-elt.
(defsetf my-elt my-setf-elt)

;;; Extract the subsequence from the argument.
(defun my-subseq (sequence start &optional
                                 (end (length sequence)))
  (let* ((seq-length (- end start))
         (new-sequence
          (make-sequence
           (cond ((stringp sequence) 'string)
                 ((listp sequence) 'list)
                 (t 'vector))
           seq-length)))
    (dotimes (seq-index seq-length)
      (setf (my-elt new-sequence seq-index)
            (my-elt sequence (+ seq-index start))))
    new-sequence)))

;;; Replace all occurrences of the second argument with
;;; the first argument in the third argument.  This
;;; performs destructive operations to a copy of the
;;; argument sequence.
(defun my-substitute (new-value old-value sequence)
  (let ((new-seq (copy-seq sequence)))
    (dotimes (index (length new-seq))
      (if (eql old-value (my-elt new-seq index))
        (setf (my-elt new-seq index) new-value)))
    new-seq))

;;; Search the sequence for the location of the first
;;; argument.
(defun my-position (element sequence)
  (dotimes (index (length sequence) nil)
    (if (eql element (my-elt sequence index))
      (return index))))

;;; Scan the sequence and return a count of all matches
;;; to the first argument.
(defun my-count (element sequence)
  (let ((count 0))
    (dotimes (index (length sequence) count)
      (if (eql (my-elt sequence index) element)
        (setf count (1+ count))))))
```

13.17 The first version is complicated by reconstructing the list. The second version is just like the original array version except `nth` is used in the assignments.

```
;; Amount to move a tile for a particular command.
(defvar *move-amount* '((up 3) (down -3) (left -1)
                        (right 1)))
;;; Move the tile into the empty square based upon the
;;; direction.
(defun move-tile (board direction)
  (let* ((empty-position
           (dotimes (index 9)
             (if (null (nth index board))
               (return index))))
         (other-index
          (+ empty-position
             (cadr (assoc direction *move-amount*))))
         (other-value (nth other-index board)))
    (labels ((move-tile-aux (board index)
               (cond ((null board) nil)
                     (t (cons
                          (cond ((= index empty-position)
                                 other-value)
                                ((= index other-index)
                                 nil)
                                (t (car board)))
                          (move-tile-aux (cdr board)
                                         (1+ index)))))))
      (move-tile-aux board 0))))

;;; Move the tile into the empty square based upon the
;;; direction.
(defun move-tile (board direction)
  (let* ((empty-position
           (dotimes (index 9)
             (if (null (nth index board))
               (return index))))
         (other-index
          (+ empty-position
             (cadr (assoc direction *move-amount*)))))
    (setf (nth empty-position board)
          (nth other-index board))
    (setf (nth other-index board) nil)
    board))
```

Chapter Exercises

2. The first step is to write `read-word` which will read one word from the argument stream. It requires a few auxiliary functions. Then `learn` can be defined to build the story base.

```
;;; Is the argument a white space character
(defun white-space-p (character)
  (member character '(#\space #\newline #\tab)))
(defvar *eof* 'eof "Indicate an end of file.")
;;; Convert the argument from a list into a string.
(defun list-to-string (characters)
  (let ((new-string (make-string (length characters))))
    (dotimes (index (length characters) new-string)
      (setf (elt new-string index)
            (elt characters index)))))
;;; Read a word from the stream.  This routine first
;;; skips over all white space until it finds a regular
;;; character.  It then reads the characters until it
;;; finds another white space character.  The preceding
;;; characters and then converted into a string and
;;; returned.  If end of file is found while scanning for
;;; white space, then nil is returned.
(defun read-word (stream)
  (flet ((get-char ()
             (read-char stream nil *eof*))
         (eofp (character)
             (eql character *eof*)))
    (let ((word-chars
             (do ((next-char (get-char) (get-char)))
               ((or (not (white-space-p next-char))
                    (eofp next-char))
                next-char))))
      (if (eofp word-chars)
        nil
        (do* ((chars (list word-chars)
                     (cons next-char chars))
              (next-char (get-char) (get-char)))
             ((or (white-space-p next-char)
                  (eofp next-char))
              (list-to-string (reverse chars))))))))
;;; Given a story and size of phrases, this function
;;; reads the story and stores adds the phrases to the
;;; knowledge base.  This function assumes that there are
;;; at least phrase size words in the story.
```

```
(defun learn (story-name phrase-size)
  (let ((story (open story-name :direction :input))
        (seed nil))
    (setf *story-base* nil)
    (dotimes (each-word phrase-size)
      (setf seed (cons (read-word story) seed)))
    (setf seed (reverse seed))
    (do ((next-word (read-word story) (read-word story)))
        ((null next-word))
        (add-phrase seed next-word)
        (setf seed (append (cdr seed)
                           (list next-word))))))
```

4. This isn't too difficult. It just has to work on building each sentence and then print it out. The tricky part is to print the story in a nice format, placing spaces and newlines in the right places.

```
;;; Generate a story from the seed phrase.  It will have
;;; at least the number of sentences as designated in the
;;; second argument.  As each word is generated, it is
;;; printed and added to the phrase list.
;;; WARNING - THIS LOCALLY PERFORMS DESTRUCTIVE
;;; OPERATIONS.
(defun build-story (seed-phrase sentence-count)
  (let ((phrase (copy-seq seed-phrase)))
    (format t "~A" (car seed-phrase))
    (dolist (word (cdr seed-phrase))
      (format t " ~A" word))
    (do ((sentences 0)
         (next-word (get-word phrase) (get-word phrase))
         (new-sentence nil))
        ((or (null next-word)
             (= sentences sentence-count)))
        (if (string= next-word ".")
          (progn
            (setf sentences (1+ sentences))
            (format t ".~%")
            (setf new-sentence t))
          (if new-sentence
            (progn (format t "~A" next-word)
                   (setf new-sentence nil))
            (format t " ~A" next-word)))
        (setf phrase (cdr phrase))
        (nconc phrase (list next-word)))))
```

Chapter 14

14.1 As stated in the exercise description, there are two phases. The first determines if there is a header, and the second adds the new lines to the file.

```
;;; Add a file header to the first argument.  If the file
;;; already has a header, then print a message.  Since we
;;; effectively need two files, this routine deletes any
;;; backup file that may be present, renames the argument
;;; file to be a backup file, then creates a new version
;;; with a header.
(defun add-header (file-name author description date)
  (labels ((header-present ()
             (with-open-file
              (file file-name :direction :input)
              (read-line file nil nil)
              (let ((line (read-line file nil nil)))
                (if (and line
                         (string-equal (subseq line 0 7)
                                       "; File:"))
                  t
                  nil)))))
    (if (header-present)
      (format t "Header already on file: ~a~%" file-name)
      (let ((new-file-backup
             (concatenate 'string file-name ".bak")))
        (delete-file new-file-backup)
        (rename-file file-name new-file-backup)
        (with-open-file (new-file file-name :direction
                                  :output)
          (format new-file
           ";;;;;;;;;;;;;;;;;;;;;;;;;;;;;;;;;;;;;;;;;;;;;;
; File:          ~A
; Description:   ~A
; Author:        ~A
; Created:       ~A
; Last Change:   ~A
;;;;;;;;;;;;;;;;;;;;;;;;;;;;;;;;;;;;;;;;;;;;;;~%"
           file-name
           description
           author
           date
           date)
          (with-open-file
           (old-file new-file-backup :direction :input)
```

```
            (do ((new-line (read-line old-file nil nil)
                           (read-line old-file nil nil)))
                ((not new-line))
                (format new-file "~A~%" new-line)))))))
```

14.3 The change is to make this data-driven and remove the unnecessary calls to eval.

```
(defvar *operators* '((add . +) (mult . *) (minus . -))
  "A-list of operators and their actual LISP names.")
(defun guesswhat (list-of-expressions)
  (apply #'+
         (mapcar #'(lambda (element)
                     (apply (cdr (assoc (car element)
                                        *operators*))
                            (cdr element)))
                 list-of-expressions)))
```

14.5 We need to change the way the operator and elements are accessed. In the previous version, they were simple `car` and `cdr`. We need to be able to get the `last` element and everything but the last element. A very simple method is to count the length of the sequence and access the last element, while everything but the last can be determined by retrieving a subsequence.

```
;;; Retrieve the appropriate operator based upon postfix
;;; notation.
(defun operator (expression)
  (cdr (assoc (elt expression (1- (length expression)))
              *operators*)))
;;; Retrieve the operands, which are the first n-1
;;; elements.
(defun operands (expression)
  (subseq expression 0 (1- (length expression))))
;;; This version operates upon any sequence of
;;; expressions and postfix expressions.
(defun guesswhat (expressions)
  (apply #'+
         (map 'list
              #'(lambda (element)
                  (apply (operator element)
                         (operands element)))
              expressions)))
```

14.6 Notice that in this solution, none of the internal comments are really necessary.

```
(defvar *x* 'X "Indicates an X mark in the board.")
```

```
(defvar *o* 'O "Indicates an O mark in the board.")

;;; Convert the x-or-o
(defun opposite-x-or-o (x-or-o)
  (if (eql x-or-o *x*) *o* *x*))

;;; Determine if the board at the start and increment is
;;; a possible winning position.  This means that there
;;; are no marks of the other player blocking any of the
;;; positions.
(defun possible-win (board start increment elements
                           x-or-o)
  (let ((opposite (opposite-x-or-o x-or-o)))
    (dotimes (each-element elements t)
      (if (eql (elt board (+ start (* each-element
                                      increment)))
               opposite)
          (return nil)))))
```

14.7 In this function, the `zerop` test is unnecessary, because if the argument is zero or less, then the `dotimes` returns a zero.

```
;;; This function computes the sum of the integers
;;; between zero and the argument (exclusive).

(defun integer-sum (exclusive-max-value)
  (let ((result 0))
    (dotimes (each-integer exclusive-max-value result)
      (setf result (+ each-integer result)))))
```

14.8 This function actually returns 5 when the argument is odd and positive, `T` when the argument is `nil`, and `nil` otherwise.

```
;;; This purpose of this function is very obscure.

(defun guesswhatIdo2 (argument)
  (cond ((and (integerp argument) (oddp argument)) 5)
        ((null argument) t)
        (t nil)))
```

14.9 The whole set of messy functions can be collapsed into a single clean function, `possible-wins`.

```
(defvar *rows* '((0 . 1) (3 . 1) (6 . 1) (0 . 3) (1 . 3)
                 (2 . 3) (0 . 4) (2 . 2))
  "Starting index and increment to find 3 in a row.")

;;; The number of possible wins for the argument player.
;;; It is computed by summing the number possible wins
;;; for the player.
(defun count-possible-wins (board x-or-o)
```

```
  (let ((size (truncate (sqrt (length board)))))
    (apply #'+
           (mapcar #'(lambda (each-row)
                       (if (possible-win board
                                         (car each-row)
                                         (cdr each-row)
                                         size
                                         x-or-o)
                           1
                           0))
                   *rows*))))
```

```
(count-possible-wins '(x nil x o nil nil o nil nil) 'x)
⇒ 4
```

```
(count-possible-wins '(x nil x o nil nil o nil nil) 'o)
⇒ 3
```

14.14 The change is simple: just replace the call to `nth` with a call to `elt`.

```
(defun check-same (board starting-index increment
                         elements x-or-o)
  (dotimes (each-element elements t)
    (if (not (eql (elt (+ starting-index
                          (* each-element increment))
                       board)
                  x-or-o))
      (return nil))))
```

14.18 An object will work quite well for this structure.

```
;;; The board object, which has fields for the board,
;;; the current board value and the list of children
;;; objects.
(define-type ttt-board
  (:var board)
  (:var value :settable)
  (:var children :settable (:init nil))
  :all-initable
  :all-gettable)
```

14.19 If you study the macro carefully, you will realize that it is a repeat-until loop. It repeats the body expressions until the test is true.

```
;;; Repeat the body expressions until the test is true.
(defmacro repeat-until (test &body body)
  `(do () (,test) ,@body))
```

14.20 A recursive solution works well in this case, so using a local function is an obvious solution. Notice how the function doesn't bother to generate the outer `let` expression if there are no locals required.

```
(defmacro my-cond (&body body)
  (let ((locals nil)
        (result nil))
    (labels ((expand-clauses (clauses)
               (cond ((null clauses) nil)
                     ((null (cdar clauses))
                      (setf locals
                            (cons (gentemp) locals))
                      `(if (setf ,(car locals)
                                 ,(caar clauses))
                           ,(car locals)
                           ,(expand-clauses
                             (cdr clauses))))
                     (t `(if ,(caar clauses)
                             (progn ,@(cdar clauses))
                             ,(expand-clauses
                               (cdr clauses)))))))
      (setf result (expand-clauses body))
      (if (null locals)
        result
        `(let ,locals ,result)))))
```

Chapter Exercises

2. This version is a little wasteful in that it initially computes the board value of every node even though it will be overridden in the propagation phase. However, it makes it easy to determine when a winning or losing position is found, so it doesn't have to expand those tree nodes any further.

```
;;; Generate the children in a breadth-first manner.
;;; When we reach a leaf node, this function bubbles the
;;; min and max values backward.

(defun generate-tree (board original-x-or-o)
  (labels
      ((generate-tree-aux (board x-or-o)
         (setf (children board) nil)
         (dotimes (board-index 9)
           (if (null (elt (board board) board-index))
             (let ((new-board
                     (make-instance
```

```
                         'ttt-board
                         :board (copy-seq (board board)))))
                  (setf (elt (board new-board) board-index)
                         x-or-o)
                  (setf (value new-board)
                         (board-value (board new-board)
                                      original-x-or-o))
                  (setf (children board)
                         (cons new-board
                               (children board))))))
           (dolist (each-child (children board))
             (if (< *losing-value* (value each-child)
                    *winning-value*)
               (generate-tree-aux
                each-child
                (opposite-x-or-o x-or-o))))
           (if (children board)
             (setf (value board)
                   (apply (if (eql x-or-o original-x-or-o)
                              #'max
                              #'min)
                          (mapcar #'value
                                  (children board)))))
           board))
      (generate-tree-aux board original-x-or-o)))
```

3. This is a simple function that scans the list of children looking for the matching `board` object.

```
;;; Given a board tree, find the best move from the
;;; children.

(defun best-move (board)
  (dolist (each-child (children board))
    (if (= (value board) (value each-child))
      (return each-child))))
```

Chapter 15

15.3 A king can move in any direction, therefore it can at most double the number of moves at each tree level.

15.4 Some similarities include the following, but you may be able to think of more:

1. Both games are on a finite board, and actually use the same board.
2. Only one piece may move per turn.

3. Pawns in chess and checkers may be promoted to more powerful pieces when they reach the last row.

Some of the differences include:

1. In checkers, a side can be forced into taking a particular jump if one is available. While in chess, the only place this happens is when a king is in check.
2. In checkers, it is possible to make multiple jumps, which is not allowed in chess.
3. In checkers, because a side must take a jump, it is possible to create situations where the other side must take a move that you create by offering a jump. This means that the board evaluator can know exactly the next move and decrease the search space.

15.5 It deteriorates into a breadth-first search. If h' can be ignored, then only g is used in the computation. Thus, all nodes at a level will be expanded and evaluated before going down a new level.

15.7 Changing the representation to be a hash table requires changing all of the methods associated with `open-and-closed`. However, this localizes the changes, requiring no further changes to `A*`.

```
(define-type open-and-closed
  (:var open-nodes (:init (make-hash-table :test #'equal)))
  (:var closed-nodes
        (:init (make-hash-table :test #'equal)))
  :all-gettable
  :all-settable)

;;; Create the open-and-closed object and install the
;;; node.

(defun initialize (initial-node)
  (let ((new-oc (make-instance 'open-and-closed)))
    (add-node-open new-oc initial-node)
    new-oc))

;;; Scan the nodes in open-nodes and return the one with
;;; the smallest value for f'.  The method assumes that
;;; there will always be at least one node on the list.

(define-method (open-and-closed find-lowest-f-prime) ()
  (let ((lowest-f-prime 1000000000000)
        (node-of-lowest-f-prime nil))
    (maphash #'(lambda (state-of-node each-node)
                 (if (< (f-prime each-node) lowest-f-prime)
                   (progn
                     (setf lowest-f-prime
```

```
                             (f-prime each-node))
                          (setf node-of-lowest-f-prime
                             each-node))))
                  open-nodes)
    node-of-lowest-f-prime))

;;; Move the argument node from open to closed.

(define-method (open-and-closed move-open-to-closed)
    (node-to-move)
  (remhash (state node-to-move) open-nodes)
  (add-node-closed self node-to-move))

;;; A similar function to move the node from closed to
;;; open.

(define-method (open-and-closed move-closed-to-open)
    (node-to-move)
  (remhash (state node-to-move) closed-nodes)
  (add-node-open self node-to-move))

;;; Add the argument node to open.

(define-method (open-and-closed add-node-open) (new-node)
  (setf (gethash (state new-node) open-nodes) new-node))

;;; Add the argument node to closed.

(define-method (open-and-closed add-node-closed)
    (new-node)
  (setf (gethash (state new-node) closed-nodes)
        new-node))

;;; Return a node that has a state that matches the
;;; argument state in open.

(define-method (open-and-closed find-state-in-open)
    (comparison-state)
  (gethash comparison-state open-nodes))

;;; Return a node that has a state that matches the
;;; argument state in closed.

(define-method (open-and-closed find-state-in-closed)
    (comparison-state)
  (gethash comparison-state closed-nodes))
```

15.9 This solution requires scanning the current board in sequence and then searching the goal board for the actual position of the tile. Once it is found, the computation of the manhattan distance is easy.

```
;;; The heuristic is computed as the sum of the manhattan
;;; distances between each tile and its goal location.
```

```
(define-method (puzzle calc-h-prime) (goal-puzzle)
  (labels ((find-tile (tile-value)
             (dotimes (row (array-dimension
                             (board goal-puzzle) 0))
               (let ((result
                       (dotimes
                           (column (array-dimension
                                     (board goal-puzzle)
                                     0) nil)
                         (if (equal
                              tile-value
                              (aref (board goal-puzzle)
                                    row
                                    column))
                           (return (cons row column))))))
                 (if result (return result))))))
    (let ((manhattan-sum 0)
          found-row-and-column)
      (dotimes (row (array-dimension board 0))
        (dotimes (column (array-dimension board 1))
          (setf found-row-and-column
                (find-tile (aref board row column)))
          (setf manhattan-sum
                (+ manhattan-sum
                   (abs
                    (- (car found-row-and-column) row))
                   (abs
                    (- (cdr found-row-and-column)
                       column))))))
      manhattan-sum)))
```

15.10 This means that we will never take advantage of old knowledge of paths that have already been explored. Thus, we may explore a node more than once. This means that we will place more nodes on `open` than necessary. Determining if the time savings of not bothering to scan the two lists outweighs the cost of exploring the same node more than once requires empirical data based upon measurement of the two options on some set of tests. Intuitively, using faster access to `open` and `closed` seems like a better compromise.

Chapter Exercises

3. The modification to `A*` permits `generate-transform` to return the value in the `connections` slot. The heuristic value can be estimated as the straight-line distance using the longitude and latitude and converting them to degrees.

```
;;; Return an a-list of the next states and g value for
;;; getting to that state from the current state.  In
;;; this case, the miles stored in the connections list
;;; is perfect.

(define-method (city generate-transform) ()
  connections)

;;; A reasonable heuristic is the distance between the
;;; city and the goal city.  Convert the degrees to miles
;;; by multiplying the degrees by 67 (24,000 mile
;;; circumference divided by 360 degrees).

(define-method (city calc-h-prime) (goal-city)
  (* 67 (sqrt (+ (expt (- longitude (longitude
                                      goal-city)) 2)
                 (expt (- latitude
                          (latitude goal-city))
                       2)))))

;;; They cities are equal if their objects are equal.

(define-method (city compare-equal) (other-city)
  (equalp self other-city))
```

5. There are a number of ways to solve this. The easiest technique is to change `generate-transform` so it never generates a city in a list of forbidden cities. Since we don't want to change `A*` to pass an additional argument, the idea is to place the list of cities in a global variable.

```
(defvar *forbidden-cities* nil
  "List of forbidden cities.")

;;; New version of generate-transform which doesn't
;;; include any cities in the forbidden list.  This
;;; includes a simple optimization that if
;;; *forbidden-cities* is null, then it just returns the
;;; list of connections, otherwise it returns the
;;; modified connections list.

(define-method (city generate-transform) ()
  (labels ((generate-transform-aux (cities)
             (cond ((null cities) nil)
                   ((member (caar cities)
                            *forbidden-cities*)
                    (generate-transform-aux
                     (cdr cities)))
                   (t (cons (car cities)
                            (generate-transform-aux
                             (cdr cities)))))))
```

```
    (if (null *forbidden-cities*)
      connections
      (generate-transform-aux connections))))
```

```
;;; The driver function which invokes A* and the
;;; print-route functions.

(defun route (starting-city ending-city forbidden)
  (setf *forbidden-cities*
        (mapcar #'find-city forbidden))
  (print-route (a* (find-city starting-city)
                   (find-city ending-city))))
```

Chapter 16

16.1 Both of these functions call `cerror` and if continued, return whatever is provided by the user.

```
;;; A continuable version of car.

(defun c-car (argument)
  (if (listp argument)
    (car argument)
    (progn
      (cerror "Prompts for a value to return from c-car"
              "~A is not a list." argument)
      (format t
        "Input the result of (c-car ~a):~%" argument)
      (read))))

;;; Likewise a similar version for cdr.

(defun c-cdr (argument)
  (if (listp argument)
    (cdr argument)
    (progn
      (cerror "Prompts for a value to return from c-cdr"
              "~A is not a list." argument)
      (format t
        "Input the result of (c-cdr ~a):~%" argument)
      (read))))
```

16.3 The solution of this requires the use of `&rest` to get all of the arguments which are passed to `format`. Then a `throw` is performed.

```
(defvar error-result '**error**
  "Result of an error from my-error")

;;; Our own version of error which doesn't go into the
;;; debugger, it just performs a throw.
```

```
(defun my-error (&rest format-args)
  (format t "Error Signaled: ")
  (apply #'format (cons t format-args))
  (throw 'error error-result))
```

16.5 This interpreter prints a prompting string allowing user input, evaluates the expression, prints the result, and tries again. It wraps a `catch` around the `eval` to catch any evaluation errors.

```
;;; A simple interpreter.

(defun my-interpreter ()
  (flet ((prompt-and-read ()
           (format t "LISP> ")
           (read)))
    (do ((expression (prompt-and-read) (prompt-and-read))
         (result))
        ((eq expression 'quit))
        (if (not (eq (setf result
                           (catch 'error
                             (eval expression)))
                     error-result))
          (format t "~%Result: ~A~%" result)
          (terpri)))))
```

16.7 The dot in the pattern indicates that `?Y` is the whole `cdr`. Since it is a variable, it will match any `cdr` and thus the subject list must have one element to match the `?X` and anything else (including `nil`) will match the `?Y`. This clever mechanism allows matching arbitrary length patterns and didn't require any additional mechanism.

Chapter Exercises

1. This is a natural for a macro that expands into a call to `catch`. We can even use the arbitrary number of arguments to `catch` to get the same functionality for `block`.

```
;;; The first argument is the block name and the rest are
;;; the S-expressions.

(defmacro xblock (name &body s-expressions)
  `(catch ',name ,@s-expressions))
```

2. This macro just turns into a `throw`.

```
;;; Return-from the value from the named block.
(defmacro xreturn-from (name value)
  `(throw ',name ,value))
```

Chapter 17

17.1 The only interface to the caller is through the A* function, and the three interface methods. Thus, the file would appear as follows:

```
(in-package 'astar :nicknames '(a*))
(export '(a* calc-h-prime compare-equal
          generate-transform))
...
Various functions
...
```

17.3 The solution lies in careful study of the buggy transcript. Notice that the result of the call to `shadow-wrapper` is not `bar`, but is `foobar:bar`. This means that when the `defun` is evaluated, the result is a change to the original definition, and not the one in `mumble`. If we look at a macro expansion, there is still no hint as to what is happening.

```
(macroexpand
 '(shadow-wrapper bar (defun bar (a b) (* a b))))
⇒ (PROGN (SHADOW (QUOTE BAR))
⇒        (DEFUN BAR (A B) (* A B)))
⇒ T
```

This looks just fine. The problem is a relationship between the LISP reader and the package system. The first step in the interpreter is to read in the expression. Even before the macro starts the processing, the `bar` in the function name and the one in the `defun` have been turned into symbols and reference the inherited symbol `foobar:bar`. Thus, when the `progn` is evaluated, the `shadow` properly removes the definition of `bar`, *but* the `defun` now redefines the `foobar` version. Thus, before the evaluation of the `progn`, the expression appears as follows:

```
(PROGN (SHADOW (QUOTE FOOBAR:BAR))
       (DEFUN FOOBAR:BAR (A B) (* A B)))
```

17.4 The answer is very tricky. You have to save the previous function definition using `symbol-function` and then switch them back after the function is defined.

```
(defmacro shadow-wrapper (fun definition)
  `(let ((old-fun (symbol-function ',fun))
         (shadowed-name nil))
     ,definition
     (shadow ',fun)
     (setf shadowed-name
           (find-symbol (symbol-name ',fun)))
     (setf (symbol-function shadowed-name)
           (symbol-function ',fun))
```

```
        (setf (symbol-function ',fun) old-fun)
        shadowed-name))
```

17.6 The prog expression expands into a combination of the primitives let, block, and tagbody.

```
(shadow 'prog)

(defmacro prog (locals &body body)
  (let ((local-label (gensym)))
    `(block nil
       (let ,locals
         (tagbody
           ,@body)))))
```

17.9 Using backquote makes these macros easy to define. Simple-pop can take advantage of prog1 to return the valued popped off the list.

```
(defmacro simple-push (value symbol)
  (if (not (symbolp symbol))
    (error "~A must be a symbol in simple-push" symbol)
    `(setf ,symbol (cons ,value ,symbol))))

(defmacro simple-pop (symbol)
  (if (not (symbolp symbol))
    (error "~A must be a symbol in simple-pop" symbol)
    `(prog1
        (car ,symbol)
       (setf ,symbol (cdr ,symbol)))))
```

17.10 This requires evaluating the location argument and storing it into a variable for use in the assignment. Use of a generated variable guarantees that there are no conflicts with variables that might be used in the value or location.

```
(defmacro simple-push (value location)
  (let ((local-variable (gensym)))
    `(let ((,local-variable ,location))
       (set ,local-variable
            (cons ,value
                  (symbol-value ,local-variable))))))

(defmacro simple-pop (location)
  (let ((local-variable (gensym)))
    `(let ((,local-variable ,location))
       (prog1
         (car (symbol-value ,local-variable))
         (set ,local-variable
              (cdr (symbol-value ,local-variable)))))))
```

17.14 If we use find-symbol on each symbol that is returned from do-symbols, we can look at the second value to see what its type is.

```
(defun count-internal-and-external (package)
  (let ((internal 0)
        (external 0))
    (do-symbols (symbol package)
      (multiple-value-bind (ignore type)
        (find-symbol (symbol-name symbol) package)
        (if (eq type :internal)
          (setf internal (1+ internal))
          (setf external (1+ external)))))
    (format t "Count is ~A internal and ~A external.~%"
            internal external)))
```

17.15 The only difficult part of this function is to turn the numeric day of the week into an actual name. Since the integer is a number from zero to six, a vector is a logical representation.

```
(defvar *day-of-week*
  (make-array 7 :initial-contents
              '("Monday" "Tuesday" "Wednesday" "Thursday"
                "Friday" "Saturday" "Sunday")))

(defun string-date ()
  (multiple-value-bind (ignore minute hour day month year
                        dow)
    (get-decoded-time)
    (format nil "~A:~A ~A/~A/~A ~A" hour minute month day
            (- year 1900) (aref *day-of-week* dow))))
```

17.17 This function retrieves the values by calling `find-variable`, then scans `*frames*` to find the stack location, and returns the sum.

```
(defun location (variable frame-zero-offset)
  (multiple-value-bind (frame offset)
    (find-variable variable)
    (+ (- (dolist (each-frame *frames*)
            (if (= (frame-number each-frame) frame)
              (return (stack-location each-frame))))
          (stack-location (car (last *frames*))))
       offset
       frame-zero-offset)))
```

17.18 All we have to do is read the next symbol and then generate the appropriate S-expression.

```
(defun generate-inc-or-dec (stream character)
  (let ((symbol (read stream)))
    `(setf ,symbol
```

```
            (,(if (eql character #\^ ) '+ '-) ,symbol 1))))
(set-macro-character #\^  #'generate-inc-or-dec)
(set-macro-character #\@ #'generate-inc-or-dec)
```

17.21 We use `set-macro-character` to establish the macro. We can call `read` to extract the name of the automobile, but that might include the `]` in the symbol. However, if there is a space following the name and then the `]`, we will have to `read` the extra `]`. This is an easier solution than reading a character at a time to try and extract the symbol. So, this solution uses `read` with some extra processing to eliminate the `]`.

```
(defun read-object (stream character)
  (let* ((object-name (read stream))
         (object-string (symbol-name object-name)))
    (if (eql (elt object-string
                  (1- (length object-string)))
             #\])
      (setf object-name
            (intern (string-right-trim
                     "]" object-string)))
      (if (not (eql (read stream) ']))
        (error "Illegal syntax for reading object")))
    (list 'quote (lookup-object object-name))))
(set-macro-character #\[ #'read-object)
```

17.24 The way to do this is to define a function like `make-clown`, which is responsible for returning a closure representing the object. Included in the closure are all of the methods associated with the object and all of the slots. The expressions that are evaluated when the closure is called are dispatching code which selects which method to call. Once the method is called, an internal function is then called and the appropriate action is taken. The first argument to the closure is the method name and the remaining are the arguments for the method.

17.25 The previous answer outlined the technique for developing the following code. The only tricky part is that the method name comes in as a symbol, which you can't just `apply` within the `lambda` expression. This is because lexically, it is not the same as the local function names. Therefore, we have to do a `case` to get the function.

```
(defun make-clown ()
  (let (nose-color shoe-size smile)
    #'(lambda (method-name &rest args)
        (flet ((nose-color () nose-color)
               (shoe-size () shoe-size)
               (smile () smile)
               (set-nose-color (new-value)
```

```
                (setf nose-color new-value))
              (set-shoe-size (new-value)
                (setf shoe-size new-value))
              (set-smile (new-value)
                (setf smile new-value)))
         (apply (case method-name
                  (nose-color #'nose-color)
                  (shoe-size #'shoe-size)
                  (smile #'smile)
                  (set-nose-color #'set-nose-color)
                  (set-shoe-size #'set-shoe-size)
                  (set-smile #'set-smile)
                  (otherwise
                   (error "~A is an unknown method"
                          method-name)))
                args)))))
```

```
(setf bozo (make-clown))
⇒ #<CLOSURE  Max Args= *  Lambda Name= :UNNAMED
⇒             Interpreted>
```

```
(funcall bozo 'set-smile 'grin)
⇒ GRIN
```

```
(funcall bozo 'smile)
⇒ GRIN
```

Chapter Exercises

1. If we define a machine object that contains each of the data structures, then it makes it easy to write methods to retrieve and store values into the data structures.

```
(defconstant *max-registers* 8
  "Total registers in the machine.")
```

```
(defconstant *max-memory* 100 "Maximum size of memory.")
```

```
;;; A machine object has the four necessary fields.  The
;;; register is a vector of the registers, the stack is a
;;; list, memory is a vector, and the instructions are as
;;; a list in the program slot.  The symbol-table slot
;;; contains the list of symbols and their location
;;; within the instruction list, and the pc (program
;;; counter) points to the next instruction to execute.
(define-type machine
  (:var register
       (:init (make-array *max-registers*
```

```
                              :initial-element 0)))
  (:var stack (:init nil))
  (:var program-stack (:init nil))
  (:var memory
        (:init (make-array *max-memory*
                              :initial-element 0)))
  (:var program)
  (:var symbol-table (:init nil))
  (:var pc)
  :all-initable
  :all-settable
  :all-gettable)

;;; Return the value in the register register-number.
(define-method (machine get-reg) (register-number)
  (aref register register-number))

;;; Set the value in the register register-number.
(define-method (machine set-reg) (register-number value)
  (setf (aref register register-number) value))

;;; Push a value onto the stack.
(define-method (machine push-data-stack) (value)
  (setf stack (cons value stack)))

;;; Pop a value off the stack.
(define-method (machine pop-data-stack) ()
  (lisp:pop stack))

;;; Retrieve a value in the stack, indexed by the
;;; argument.
(define-method (machine get-data-stack) (index)
  (nth index stack))

;;; Store a value into the stack, indexed by the first
;;; argument.
;;; WARNING -- PERFORMS A DESTRUCTIVE LIST OPERATION.
(define-method (machine set-data-stack) (index value)
  (setf (nth index stack) value))

;;; Retrieve a value from the memory at the index location.
(define-method (machine get-mem) (index)
  (aref memory index))

;;; Store the value into the memory at the index
;;; location.
(define-method (machine set-mem) (index value)
  (setf (aref memory index) value))

(defvar *machine* nil "The machine object.")
```

3. These functions aren't too difficult given the primitives defined in the last two exercises.

```
;;; Get the value in the source and store it into the
;;; destination. All operands are valid for source and
;;; destination except for integer constants which may
;;; not be a destination.
(defun move-instruction (source destination)
  (store destination (retrieve source)))
;;; Push the value onto the stack.
(defun push-value (source)
  (push-data-stack *machine* (retrieve source)))
;;; Pop the argument number of elements off the stack.
(defun pop-value (number)
  (dotimes (counter number)
    (pop-data-stack *machine*)))
;;; Add the source to the destination.
(defun add-instruction (source destination)
  (store destination (+ (retrieve source)
                        (retrieve destination))))
;;; Subtract the value of the source from the
;;; destination.
(defun sub-instruction (source destination)
  (store destination (- (retrieve destination)
                        (retrieve source))))
```

4. A list representation for the instructions is just fine.

```
(defun make-symbol-table (instructions)
  (cond ((null instructions) nil)
        ((symbolp (car instructions))
         (cons (cons (car instructions) instructions)
               (make-symbol-table (cdr instructions))))
        (t (make-symbol-table (cdr instructions)))))
```

7. Everything should be ready, so all run has to do is execute each instruction until it finds a `halt`. Once that is found, it exits and prints the contents of register zero.

```
(define-method (machine next-instruction) ()
  (lisp:pop pc))

(defvar *machine-instructions*
  '((move . move-instruction) (push . push-value)
    (pop . pop-value) (add . add-instruction)
    (sub . sub-instruction) (jump . jump-instruction)
```

```
    (call . call-instruction)
    (return . return-instruction)))

(defun run ()
  (do ((inst (next-instruction *machine*)
             (next-instruction *machine*)))
      ((equal inst '(halt)))
      (if (listp inst)
        (apply (cdr (assoc (car inst)
                           *machine-instructions*))
               (cdr inst))))
  (format t "Register 0 contains: ~A~%"
          (retrieve '(reg 0))))
```

Chapter 18

18.1 `Let` expands into a single `lambda`, while `let*` has to expand into nested `lambdas`. We require an auxiliary function which parses the local list. In this case, `parse-locals` returns two values, the list of variables and the list of initial values.

```
(shadow '(let let*))

(defun parse-locals (local-list)
  (if (null local-list)
    (values nil nil)
    (let ((local (if (symbolp (car local-list))
                     (list (car local-list))
                     (car local-list))))
      (multiple-value-bind (variables initial-values)
        (parse-locals (cdr local-list))
        (values (cons (car local) variables)
                (cons (cadr local) initial-values))))))

(defmacro let (locals &body body)
  (multiple-value-bind (variables initial-values)
    (parse-locals locals)
    `((lambda ,variables ,@body)
      ,@initial-values)))

(defmacro let* (locals &body body)
  (multiple-value-bind (variables initial-values)
    (parse-locals locals)
    (labels ((make-lambdas (locals initial-values)
               (if (null locals)
                 body
                 `(((lambda ,(list (car locals))
```

```
                      ,@(make-lambdas
                          (cdr locals)
                          (cdr initial-values)))
                    ,(car initial-values))))))
      (car (make-lambdas variables initial-values)))))
```

18.4 The target machine code performs the looping required by factorial, and computes the appropriate result. It doesn't check for overflow, since there are no instructions to determine when overflow occurs. Register 1 contains the counter from the starting value down to one.

```
 (jumpif lt (reg 0) 1 return-one) ;; Check that the
                                 ;; argument is at least a one
                                 ;; and if not just return a
                                 ;; one.
 (move (reg 0) (reg 1))          ;; Save counter value
top
 (jumpif lt (reg 1) 1 done) ;; See if finished
 (sub 1 (reg 1))                 ;; Decrease counter
 (mul (reg 1) (reg 0))           ;; Multiply next value
 (jump top)                      ;; Cycle again
return-one
 (move 1 (reg 0))                ;; Return the value one
done
 (halt)                          ;; Result is in (reg 0).
```

18.5 Each special form gets its own syntax checking routine, which recursively calls `syntax-checker` on each subelement.

```
(defvar *syntax-table* nil)

(defmacro add-syntax (name S-expression)
  `(progn
     (push (cons ',name ,S-expression) *syntax-table*)
     ',name))

(add-syntax defun #'(lambda (exp)
                      (and (symbolp (cadr exp))
                           (listp (caddr exp))
                           (syntax-checker
                            (cons 'progn (cdddr exp))))))

(add-syntax setq #'(lambda (exp)
                     (and (symbolp (cadr exp))
                          (cddr exp)
                          (syntax-checker (cddr exp)))))

(add-syntax quote #'(lambda (exp)
                      (or (integerp (cadr exp))
```

```
                          (symbolp (cadr exp))
                          (null (cddr exp)))))

(add-syntax if #'(lambda (exp)
                   (and (cddr exp)
                        (not (cddddr exp))
                        (syntax-checker (cadr exp))
                        (syntax-checker (caddr exp))
                        (syntax-checker (cadddr exp)))))

(add-syntax progn #'(lambda (exp)
                      (dolist (each-exp exp t)
                        (if (not (listp each-exp))
                          (return nil)
                          (syntax-checker each-exp)))))

(add-syntax lambda #'(lambda (exp)
                       (and (listp (cadr exp))
                            (syntax-checker
                             (cons 'progn (cddr exp))))))

(defun syntax-checker (expression)
  (cond ((null expression) t)
        ((atom expression) t)
        ((let ((syntax
                (cdr (assoc (car expression)
                            *syntax-table*))))
           (if syntax
             (cond ((funcall syntax expression))
                   (t (format t
                        "~A invalid syntax for ~A~%"
                        expression (car expression))
                      nil))
             (dolist (each-operand (cdr expression) t)
               (if (not (syntax-checker each-operand))
                 (return nil))))))
        (t nil)))
```

18.10 You should store `nil` in a register, and jumps should be short-circuited when possible.

18.12 One way to accomplish this is to translate the quoted list into an expression of calls to `cons`. This allows the mechanism and representation of a list to be embedded within the run-time system and not compiled directly into the code. The following functions perform this operation. We must also change the `quote` special form to call `transform-quoted-expression` and then `compile-expression` on the result.

```
(defun transform-quoted-expression (expression)
  (cond ((integerp expression) expression)
        ((symbolp expression) `(quote ,expression))
        ((not (consp expression))
         (bad-syntax expression))
        (t `(cons ,(transform-quoted-expression
                    (car expression))
                  ,(transform-quoted-expression
                    (cdr expression))))))

(push '(consp . transform-quoted-expression)
      *quoted-expressions*)
```

18.14 The result of compiling `factorial` is:

```
(pprint (compile
         '(defun factorial (n)
            (if (word-< n 1)
              1
              (word-* n (factorial (word-- n 1)))))))
⇒ (FACTORIAL
⇒  (MOVE (STACK 0) (REG 0))
⇒  (PUSH (REG 0))
⇒  (MOVE 1 (REG 0))
⇒  (PUSH (REG 0))
⇒  (CALL WORD-<)
⇒  (POP 2)
⇒  (JUMPIF EQ (REG 0) 1073741825 T13)
⇒  (MOVE 1 (REG 0))
⇒  (JUMP T14)
⇒  T13
⇒  (MOVE (STACK 0) (REG 0))
⇒  (PUSH (REG 0))
⇒  (MOVE (STACK 1) (REG 0))
⇒  (PUSH (REG 0))
⇒  (MOVE 1 (REG 0))
⇒  (PUSH (REG 0))
⇒  (MOVE (STACK 1) (REG 0))
⇒  (SUB (STACK 0) (REG 0))
⇒  (POP 2)
⇒  (PUSH (REG 0))
⇒  (CALL FACTORIAL)
⇒  (POP 1)
⇒  (PUSH (REG 0))
⇒  (MOVE (STACK 1) (REG 0))
⇒  (MUL (STACK 0) (REG 0))
```

```
⇒   (POP 2)
⇒   T14
⇒   (RETURN))
```

Chapter Exercises

1. This version just optimizes `move`, `push` pairs. It scans the instructions looking for ones that match and generates the new instruction. When the new one is found, the optimizer is recursively called with the new instruction on the front of the rest of the instruction list. If there were more optimization patterns available, this might allow another one to be done with the new initial instruction.

```
(defmacro destination (instruction)
  `(caddr ,instruction))

(defmacro source (instruction)
  `(cadr ,instruction))

(defmacro operator (instruction)
  `(car ,instruction))

(defun optimize-pair (instruction1 instruction2)
  (if (and (listp instruction1)
           (listp instruction2)
           (eq (operator instruction1) 'move)
           (eq (operator instruction2) 'push)
           (equal (destination instruction1)
                  (source instruction2)))
    `(push ,(source instruction1))
    nil))

(defun peephole (instructions)
  (if (null (cdr instructions))
    instructions
    (let ((new-inst (optimize-pair (car instructions)
                                   (cadr instructions))))
      (if new-inst
        (peephole (cons new-inst (cddr instructions)))
        (cons (car instructions)
              (peephole (cdr instructions)))))))
```

3. The first problem is how to allocate some memory so that no other programs will touch it. In the previous exercise, global symbols were allocated to memory based upon the global *next-memory*. All we have to do is increment this counter by the size of the `cons` space and therefore no other program will disturb it. We must also save the current starting location for the `cons` cells and a pointer to the last available location. We can easily allocate these as globals using `defvar` from the previous exercise. Then we define each of the functions to access the appropriate memory locations. You might notice the use of `reclaim`, which is discussed in the exercise 4, page 538.

```
(defconstant *heap-size* 100
  "The size of the heap, which is used for cons cells.")
(pprint (compile `(defvar *heap-bottom* ,*next-memory*)))
(setf *next-memory* (+ *next-memory* *heap-size*))
(pprint (compile '(defvar *heap-next* *heap-bottom*)))
(pprint (compile `(defvar *heap-last* ,*next-memory*)))
(pprint
 (compile '(defun cons (item1 item2)
            (if (word-> (word-+ *heap-next* 2)
                        *heap-last*)
              (reclaim))
            ((lambda (result)
               (putmem (word-+ *heap-next* 1) item1)
               (putmem (word-+ *heap-next* 2) item2)
               (setf *heap-next*
                     (word-+ *heap-next* 2))
              result)
             (word-+ #xc0000000 *heap-next*)))))
;;; Warning, these both do not do any type checking.
;;; They both assume that their argument will always be a
;;; cons.
(pprint (compile '(defun car (item)
                    (setf item (word-- item #xc0000000))
                    (getmem item))))
(pprint (compile '(defun cdr (item)
                    (setf item (word-- item #xc0000000))
                    (getmem (word-+ item 1)))))
;; Definition of getmem and putmem, the primitives for
;; accessing memory.
(GETMEM
 (MOVE (MEMORY (STACK 0)) (REG 0))
 PUTMEM
 (MOVE (STACK 0) (MEMORY (STACK 1)))
 (MOVE (STACK 0) (REG 0)))
```

Bibliography

1. A. V. Aho, R. Sethi, and J. D. Ullman. *Compilers: Principles, Techniques, and Tools.* Addison-Wesley, Reading, Mass., 1986.
2. J. R. Allen. *The Anatomy of LISP.* McGraw-Hill, 1979.
3. J. W. Anderson, W. F. Galway, R. R. Kessler, H. Melenk, and W. Neun. Implementing and Optimizing Lisp for the Cray. *IEEE Software*, 74–83, July 1987.
4. J. H. Andrae. *Thinking with the Teachable Machine.* Academic Press, 1977.
5. H. G. Baker. List Processing in Real Time on a Serial Computer. *Communications of the ACM*, 21(4):280–294, April 1978.
6. D. Bobrow. CommonLoops Merging Lisp and Object-Oriented Programming. In *OOPSLA 86 Conference Proceedings*, pages 17–29, Xerox Palo Alto Research Center, 1986.
7. R. A. Brooks, D. B. Posner, J. L. McDonald, J. L. White, E. Benson, and R. P. Gabriel. Design of an Optimizing, Dynamically Retargetable Compiler for Common Lisp. In *Proc. 1986 ACM Conference on Lisp and Functional Programming*, pages 67–85, ACM SIGPLAN/SIGACT/SIGART, Cambridge, Mass., August 1986.
8. L. Brownston, E. Farrell, E. Kant, and N. Martin. *Programming Expert Systems in OPS5.* Addison Wesley, Reading, Mass., 1985.
9. E. Charniak and D. McDermott. *Introduction to Artificial Intelligence.* Addison Wesley, Reading, Mass., 1988.
10. A. Church. *The Calculi of Lambda-Conversion.* Princeton University Press, Princeton, N.J., 1941.
11. W. F. Clocksin and C. S. Mellish. *Programming in Prolog.* Springer-Verlag, Berlin, Heidelberg, New York, 1981.
12. J. W. Davidson and C. W. Fraser. Register Allocation and Exhaustive Peephole Optimization. *Software – Practice and Experience*, 14(9):857–865, September 1984.
13. L. P. Deutsch and D. G. Bobrow. An Efficient, Incremental, Automatic Garbage Collector. *Communications of the ACM*, 19(10):522–526, October 1976.
14. J. K. Foderaro and K. L. Sklower. *The Franz Lisp Manual.* Technical Report, University of California, Berkeley, Calif., September 1981.
15. R. P. Gabriel. *Performance and Evaluation of Lisp Systems.* MIT Press, Cambridge, Mass., 1985.

16. A. Goldberg and D. Robson. *SMALLTALK-80 The Language And Its Implementation.* Addison-Wesley, Reading, Mass., 1983.

17. M. L. Griss, E. Benson, and G. Q. Maguire Jr. PSL: A Portable LISP System. In *Proc. 1982 ACM Symposium on LISP and Functional Programming*, pages 88–97, 1982.

18. F. Hayes-Roth, D. A. Waterman, and D. B. Lenat. *Building Expert Systems.* Addison-Wesley, Reading, Mass., 1983.

19. A. C. Hearn. *REDUCE User's Manual Version 3.3.* Technical Report CP78, The Rand Corporation, Santa Monica, Calif., 1987.

20. P. Henderson. *Functional Programming Application and Implementation.* Prentice-Hall International, 1980.

21. A. Kay. Computer Software. *Scientific American*, 53–59, September 1984.

22. B. W. Kernighan and P. J. Plauger. *Software Tools.* Addison-Wesley, Reading, Mass., 1976.

23. R. R. Kessler. Peep – An Architectural Description Driven Peephole Optimizer. In *Proceedings of the SIGPLAN 84 Symposium on Compiler Construction*, 1984.

24. R. R. Kessler, J. C. Peterson, H. Carr, G. P. Duggan, J. Knell, and J. J. Krohnfeldt. EPIC – A Retargetable, Highly Optimizing Lisp Compiler. In *Proceedings of the SIGPLAN 86 Symposium on Compiler Construction*, pages 118–130, 1986.

25. D. Kranz, R. Kelsey, J. Rees, P. Hudak, J. Philbin, and N. Adams. ORBIT: An Optimizing Compiler for Scheme. In *Proceedings of the SIGPLAN 86 Symposium on Compiler Construction*, pages 219–233, 1986.

26. Mathlab Group Project MAC. *MACSYMA Reference Manual.* MIT, Cambridge, Mass., 1975.

27. J. McCarthy. LISP – Notes on its Past and Future. In *Proc. 1980 LISP Conference*, pages v–viii, 1980.

28. J. McCarthy, P. W. Abrahams, D. J. Edwards, T. P. Hunt, and M. I. Levin. *LISP 1.5 Programmer's Manual.* MIT Press, Cambridge, Mass., 1965.

29. J. Moses. The Function of Function in Lisp. *SIGSAM Bulletin*, 21(12):13–27, July 1970.

30. E. G. Muehle. *FROBS: A Merger of Two Knowledge Representation Paradigms.* Master's thesis, Dept. Computer Science, University of Utah, August 1987.

31. N. J. Nilsson. *Principles of Artificial Intelligence.* Morgan Kaufmann, 1980.

32. J. A. Padget and J. Fitch. Closurize and Concentrate. In *Conf. Rec. of the 12th POPL*, 1985.

33. K. M. Pitman. *The Revised MACLISP Manual.* Technical Report MIT/LCS/TR-295, MIT, May 1983.

34. J. Rees and W. Clinger. Revised^3 Report on the Algorithmic Language Scheme. *SIGPLAN Notices*, 21(12):37–79, December 1986.

35. J. A. Rees, N. I. Adams, and J. R. Meehan. *The T Manual.* Technical Report, Yale University, New Haven, Conn., May 1983.

36. A. D. Rich and D. R. Stoutemyer. Capabilities of the muMATH-78 Computer Algebra System for the Intel-8080 Microprocessor. In *Proceedings of SYMSAC-79, Marseille*, pages 242–248, SIGSAM, Springer-Verlag, 1979.

37. Martin Rudalics. Distributed Copying Garbage Collection. In *Proc. 1986 ACM Conference on Lisp and Functional Programming*, pages 364–372, ACM SIGPLAN/SIGACT/SIGART, Cambridge, Mass., August 1986.

38. S. T. Shebs and S. J. Loosemore. *Portable Common Lisp Subset User's Guide.* PASS Project Opnote 86-04, Dept. Computer Science, University of Utah, May 1986.

39. A. Snyder. *CommonObjects: An Overview.* Technical Report, Hewlett-Packard, 1986.

40. G. L. Steele. *Common Lisp: The Language.* Digital Press, 1984.

41. G. L. Steele. Multiprocessing Compactifying Garbage Collection. *Communications of the ACM*, 18(9):495–508, September 1975.

42. G. L. Steele. *RABBIT: A Compiler for SCHEME.* AI Memo 474, MIT AI Lab, Cambridge, Mass., May 1978.

43. W. Teitelman et al. *Interlisp Reference Manual, (3d Revision).* Technical Report, Xerox Palo Alto Research Center, 1978.

44. W. vanMelle, A. C. Scott, J. S. Bennett, and M. Peairs. *The EMYCIN Manual.* HPP Memo HPP-81-16, Stanford University Computer Science Department, Palo Alto, Calif, October 1981.

45. D. Weinreb and D. Moon. *LISP Machine Manual, 4th ed.* MIT Press, Cambridge, Mass., July 1981.

INDEX

T

U

V

W